ISBN 978-0-265-90792-4
PIBN 10908003

LONGWELL & CUMMINGS'

Indiana

ogansport Directory

1897-98

VOL. IV

BEING A COMPLETE INDEX TO THE RESIDENTS OF THE CITY
ALSO, A CLASSIFIED

BUSINESS DIRECTORY

GAZETTEER OF CASS COUNTY

AND

THER USEFUL INFORMATION CONCERNING CITY, COUNTY, STATE
AND MISCELLANEOUS MATTER

FRANK J. MURPHY
COMPILER AND MANAGER

SUBSCRIPTION PRICE, THREE DOLLARS
AFTER PUBLICATION, FOUR DOLLARS

GENERAL INDEX.

1426011

INDEX TO ADVERTISEMENTS.

INTRODUCTION.

The fourth volume of our Logansport and Cass County Directory is here presented with the belief that it is complete and accurate. Careful and competent assistants have aided in its compilation, and every effort has been made and expense incurred to insure correctness and perfection in all respects.

An impression seems to exist that in order to issue a directory all that is necessary is to send out men, get some names, arrange and print them, write a preface and deliver the books to the subscribers. As a matter of fact, such is not the case; names are taken in duplicate and the facts are proven as are accounts in a double entry system of bookkeeping. The hardest labor, most careful workmanship, and heaviest expense are required in perfecting discrepancies and omissions which are discovered by the duplicate system. A complete directory is never the result of a single canvass, and is only arrived at by a liberal expenditure of both time and money, utilizing every year the information obtained in previous issues. Directory publishing is a vocation peculiar to itself, and can be carried on properly only by those educated in and thoroughly conversant with its numerous details, which require years of training.

Notwithstanding the general business depression throughout the country, Logansport continues to show a healthy increase in population and business interests, which is gratifying to every citizen. In respect to healthfulness, comfortable or even luxurious living, business opportunities, educational advantages and social and religious associations it is not excelled, and the citizens have reason to be proud of the city that has grown up, as may be truthfully claimed, without booming.

POPULATION.

As a basis on which to figure population we desire to say that some directory publishers use the multiple 3 to each name. This we have always contended is too high, and consequently we use, and have always used, the multiple 2½. This volume contains **9525** names; deducting 10 per cent (**952**) for duplicate names of business firms, we have **8573** names (above the age of 15 years and not including wives), and by using the multiple 2½ we show a population for Logansport and suburbs of **21,433**.

In conclusion, we desire to thank our many patrons for the support they have given us, and trust that the result of our efforts will meet with their approval and appreciation.

Very respectfully,

LONGWELL & CUMMINGS.

DON'T LEND YOUR DIRECTORY

An Appeal to our Subscribers:

We would offer a suggestion to those who, from business neces-
sities, or actuated simply by a public spirit, have favored us with an
order for a book:

DON'T LEND YOUR DIRECTORY.

We receive many complaints from our patrons to the effect that
they are bothered so much by borrowers. Borrowers, generally, are
chronically such. The man who borrows a Directory never buys one,
never subscribes for it (or for anything else). These same individuals, when asked to subscribe, "don't need it," "never have any
use for it," "know everybody." Yet the virgin freshness of its leaves
has hardly been sullied by human touch before this *nuisance* wants
to borrow your Directory. Again we ask,

DON'T LEND YOUR DIRECTORY.

You may not get it back. A man who is not honest with himself
cannot be honest with others. The business man who asks to borrow
your Directory told our solicitor he "didn't need one." Take him
at his word.

LONGWELL & CUMMINGS,

Publishers.

The Wabash Line

· · TO ·

✦ Toledo, New York, Boston, ✦

AND ALL EASTERN POINTS.

· · TO · ·

ST. LOUIS

KANSAS CITY

QUINCY

AND

ALL

WESTERN

POINTS

· SUPERB EQUIPMENT,

Consisting of Vestibule Trains, Free Chair Cars, Fast Freight, Fruit Express Trains, and all the last approved appliances.

RATES AS LOW

As the Lowest on both Freight and Passenger business.

IT IS ACKNOWLEDGED

By all that no road MAKES FASTER TIME than the Wabash.

·M. KNIGHT,
FREIGHT TRAFFIC MANAGER,
ST. LOUIS.

· C. S. CRANE,
GENERAL PASSENGER AND TICKET AGENT,
ST. LOUIS.

C. G. NEWELL, AGENT, LOGANSPORT, IND.

...The New...
MASONIC TEMPLE,

NORTHEAST CORNER FOURTH AND NORTH STREETS,

LOGANSPORT, IND.

CORNER STONE LAID FEBRUARY 15, 1896.
DEDICATED MAY 19, 1897.

DIRECTORY 1896.

JEHU T. ELLIOTT	JOSEPH L. LINVILL	ISAAC SHIDELER
NEVANCE R. DONALDSON	MAX J. FISHER WM. D. PRATT	ALLEN RICHARDSON
OLIVER B. SARGENT	SIDNEY A. VAUGHN	WM. BEDWARDS

MASONIC ORGANIZATIONS.

Tipton Lodge, No. 33, F. & A. M., Charter issued November 26, 1828.

* * *

Orient Lodge, No. 272, F. & A. M., Charter issued May 28, 1891.

* * *

Logan Chapter, No. 2, R. A. M., Charter issued from General Grand Chapter United States, September 17, 1841; from Grand Chapter Indiana, May 21, 1858.

Logansport Council, No. 11, R. & S. M., Charter issued May 15, 1858.

* * *

St. John Commandry, No. 24, K. T., Charter issued April 2, 1873.

* * *

Fidelity Chapter, No. 58, O. E. S., Charter issued April 8, 1885.

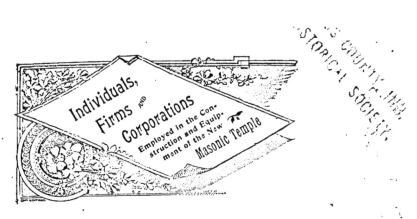

Individuals, Firms and Corporations Employed in the Construction and Equipment of the New Masonic Temple

ARCHITECT:
JOSEPH E. CRAIN, Masonic Temple

GENERAL CONTRACTOR:
ALLEN LEWIS, 210 Burlington Ave.

SUPERINTENDENT:
ALLEN RICHARDSON, 315 Fifth St.

BRICK AND STONE WORK:
JOHN MEDLAND & SONS,
98 Eel River Ave.

STRUCTURAL IRON:
LOGANSPORT CONSTRUCTION CO.
Office 322 Third Street.

LUMBER AND PLANING MILL WORK:
STEVENS BROS.,
N. W. Corner First and Canal.

PLUMBING, STEAM HEATING, ELECTRIC AND GAS FIXTURES:
STEVENS & BEDWARDS, 424 Market St.

CORNICE, GALVINIZED IRON WORK AND SLATE ROOFING:
MAX JENNINGS, 316-318 Fifth St.

BOILERS FOR STEAM HEATING PLANT:
ATLAS ENGINE WORKS,
Indianapolis, Ind.

ENGINES FOR MOTIVE POWER:
LAMBERT GAS & GASOLINE ENGINE CO.
Anderson, Ind.
W. B. Place, Gen'l Agt., Logansport.

DRAPERIES, CARPETS, WALL PAPER AND WINDOW SHADES:
H. WILER & CO., Fourth and Broadway

PAINTING AND DECORATING:
JOHN C. BEATTY, 628 Linden Ave.

ELECTRICAL CONTRACTOR:
J. W. BLACKFORD, 314 Pearl Street.

LODGE AND CLUB ROOM FURNITURE, AND UPHOLSTERING:
J. W. HENDERSON & SONS, Mfrs. of Furniture and Mantels, 320 Fourth St.

TO THE INTELLIGENT PURCHASER OF PRINT- ED MATTER, UPON WHOM MAY FORTUNE SMILE, THESE:

WOULDST thou, O, gentle read- er, make thine effort succeed, whether it be to advertise thy wares, to pub- lish an an- nouncement, or to get the uttermost benefit in any branch of the erstwhile mystery of imprinting? Then hark ye! here is a word for thine ear upon which it behooveth thee to ponder well in the secret places of thine understanding. *Listen:*

· When thou hast printing to be done get good printing.

When books first began to multiply with mysterious frequency, the peo- ple ascribed the new writing, which we now know as imprinting, to the handiwork of the devil; and even in this day and generation there are some printers who must be agents of His Satanic Majesty, for how otherwise are they enabled to glut the market with printing, even of the cheap-and-nasty-kind, at less than the cost of production, unless they steal the paper, and produce the types from the hell box of their more scrupulous fellows?

Opposed to this interpretation of the printer's art (alas! too often to be better described as blacksmith's botch work) is that of the master printer who tries; who provides himself with the latest implements of his craft; who studies the works of the old masters of the art; and who charges accordingly.

Avail thyself of this; for even if his charge be many ducats in ad- vance of that of his fellow-crafts- man, it will put broad pieces of gold in thy pouch by attracting the read- er's attention to thy statement and insensibly forming his opinion that thy house is perforce as good as thy printed matter.

Let not the cost deter thee; for should the good printer's charge be double that of the cheaper crafts- man, the wage of the postman re- mains the same; the other fixed charges are still fixed; and what seemeth to be an increase of an hundred fold in cost is found to be but a tithe.

For instance, let us suppose thou desirest to sow the good grain of thy advertisement broadcast through- out the land. To accomplish thy fell purpose thou must perforce be at these costs for each thousand disseminated, be they broadsides, or bulls, or indulgences, to-wit:

Envelopes, say two ducats; in- scribing same, one ducat; carriage (in fees to the courier with the gray livery) twenty ducats; folding, in- serting and sealing, one ducat; total fixed charge, twenty-four golden du- cats. This total must be expended whether or no, and to it must be added the fee for imprinting, which it be but two ducats, the price desir- ed by many short-sighted wights who pose as patrons of the liberal arts, will fix the grand total at six- and-twenty ducats. Now, if perad- venture the printer persuadeth thee to expend double the amount allot- ted for his product, the actual cost is not doubled, but is increased less than eight per centum, while the ele- ment of effect is doubled or trebled.

Avail thyself of all that lyeth in the art; and let us be thy servants in the matter.

LONGWELL & CUMMINGS, to be found in the new Masonic Temple, in the Fourth and North streets, in the city of Logansport, Indiana.

LONGWELL & CUMMINGS'

BIENNIAL

DIRECTORY

OF

LOGANSPORT AND CASS COUNTY

1897-98.

MISCELLANEOUS INFORMATION.

City Government.

City Building, containing all the city offices, council chamber and police court, n. w. cor 3d and Broadway

CITY OFFICERS

Mayor—George P McKee
City Clerk—John B Winters
City Treasurer—George E Barnett
City Attorney— George C Taber
City Civil Engineer—W B Ray
Street Commissioner—George E Jamison
Chief Fire Department—Charles D Sellers
City Health Officer—Dr N W Cady
Supt of Water Works—Henry H Montfort
City Electician—Walter Scribner
Clerk Electric Light Department—F P Rogers
Clerk Water Works—David A Middleton

CITY COMMISSIONERS

First Ward—Dennis Uhl
Second Ward—Francis M Harwood
Third Ward—Wm Burgman
Fourth Ward—Lemuel G Patterson
Fifth Ward—Nevance R Donaldson

BOARD OF PUBLIC IMPROVEMENTS

Hiram D Hattery, pres; Joshua C Hadley, secy; George W Haigh, member

Meetings—The Board meets on call of the president or secretary, at the Council Chamber

BOARD OF HEALTH

Dr Arthur J Hermann, pres, Dr Nelson W Cady, secy; Dr John H Shultz and Dyer B McConnell; George H Houton, Sanitary Inspector

COMMON COUNCIL

Meets first and third Wednesdays of each month
President—George P McKee
Clerk—John B Winters

COUNCILMEN

Term expires 1898	*Term expires 1900*
First Ward.....Charles Ringleben......Hiram D Hattery
Second Ward...George W Haigh.......Frederick A Dykeman
Third Ward....Wm H Keiser..........Adam Graf
Fourth Ward...Joshua C Hadley........Stephen B Boyer
Fifth Ward....Joseph Kenney.........Charles L Woll

STANDING COMMITTEES

1897-98

Finance—Messrs Hadley, Ringleben, Woll
Claims—Messrs Graf, Ringleben, Boyer
Ordinance—Messrs Hattery, Hadley, Kenney
Streets—Messrs Haigh Ringleben, Keiser
Sewers—Messrs Woll, Keiser, Boyer
Electric Light—Messrs Boyer, Haigh, Keiser
Water Works—Messrs Ringleben Hadley, Graf
Fire—Messrs Haigh, Kenney, Dykeman
Cemetery—Messrs Dykeman, Boyer, Kenney
Printing—Messrs Kenney, Keiser, Hadley
Park—Messrs Keiser, Kenney, Ringleben
Pratt Fund—The Mayor, Messrs Hadley, Woll

POLICE DEPARTMENT

Headquarters, City Building

Board of Metropolitan Police Commissioners—Dyer B McConnell pres, Theodore R Sewell and John J Sheerin

Secretary—Thomas Norris

The regular meeting of the Board of Metropolitan Police Commissioners is on the third Monday of each month 7:30 p. m., at 210 4th

Police Judge—George P McKee
Captain of Police—James Foley
Sergeant—Thomas Norris
Patrolmen—James T Kleckner, Benjamin Deane, George H

Houghton, Andrew Wirwahn, Wm Nading, Barnard Z Birch, Vincent A Skelton, Richard N Costello, Charles N Webster, Wm Schreyer, J Edmund Liming, Thomas Miller, George Graham

FIRE DEPARTMENT

Headquarters, n s North 1 e Sixth

Council Committee— Messrs Haigh, Kenney and Dykeman
Chief Engineer—Charles D Sellers
Hook and Ladder Company No 2, s e cor 6th and Broadway— Captain, James Viney; ladderman, Charles McCloskey
Hose Company No 3, w s 15th bet Market and Spear—Captain, David Bowman; pipeman, Jacob Westeweller
Hose Company No 4, n s North 1 e 6th—Captain, O Clinton Whitesell; driver, Julius Kloenne
Hose Company No 5, w s Front bet Broadway and Pawnee—Captain, Charles Livingston; pipeman, Elmer Wagner

FIRE ALARM BOXES

12—cor Berkley and Duret	33—No 3 Engine House
13—cor 13th and Wright	34—cor 5th and High
14—cor 17th and Market	35—cor 3d and Market
15—cor 13th and Broadway	36—cor 1st and Market
16—cor 9th and North	41—cor n 6th and Hanna
17—cor 8th and Market	42—cor Colfax and Burlington av
18—cor Creek and Michigan av	43—cor 19th and Broadway
19—cor Sycamore and Columbia	44—No 4 Engine House
21—cor 3d and North	45—cor 16th and High
22—No 2 Engine House	51—cor 12th and Spear
23—cor Miami and Sycamore	52—cor 12th and High
24—cor Bates and Heth	53—cor 23d and Broadway
25—cor Cicott and Market	54—cor 17th and Smead
26—cor Brown and Linden av	55—No 5 Engine House
27—cor Helm and Wilkinson	56—cor 15th and Toledo
28—Ash & Hadley's factory	61- Panhandle Shops
31—cor 5th and Market	62—cor Illinois and Indiana
32—cor 4th and Broadway	

Asylums, Hospitals, Etc.

Cass County Orphans' Home—s e cor Pleasant Hill and McCarty; Elizabeth Craighead, matron
Cass County Poor Asylum—3½ m n e city; Frederick Homburg, supt
Home for the Friendless—630 Race; Margaret A Smith, matron
Northern Indiana Hospital for Insane, 2 m west city; Dr Joseph G Rogers, medical supt .
St Joseph's Hospital—south side Logansport and Western road, 1 east Anthony, conducted by Sisters of St Francis

Banks and Bankers

City National Bank—Incorporated June, 1897; capital stock $200,-000; John Gray, pres; Isaac N Crawford, vice-pres; Frank R Fowler, cash; s w cor 4th and Broadway

First National Bank—Incorporated 1883; capital stock $250,000; surplus $18,000; Andrew J Murdock, pres; Wm T Wilson vice-pres; Wm W Ross, cash; John F Brookmeyer, assistant cashier; 314 4th

Logansport State Bank—Organized May 22, 1893; capital stock, $50,000; surplus and undivided profits, $17,582; George W Seybold, pres; Victor E Seiter, vice-pres; Wm C Thomas, cashier; s e cor 4th and Market

Building, Loan and Savings Associations

Cass County Building & Loan Association—Incorporated 1889; capital stock, $1,000,000.00; John Gray, pres; Edith Matt, secy; J C Hadley treas; 406 Broadway

National Loan and Savings Association of Indiana—Incorporated 1890; capital stock $1,000,000.00; Alexander Hardy, pres; John B Winters, vice-pres; Charles G Dodge, secy; Charles B Stevenson, treas; 323 Broadway

Northwestern Loan and Investment Co—Incorporated 1896; capital stock, $100,000.00; Charles L Woll, pres; Joseph L Linvill, vice-pres; James T Cockburn, secy; Wm H Porter, treas

Cemeteries

Hebrew Cemetery—Between Pleasant Hill and Clifton av, north of Hanna; Solomon Wise, pres; Matthias J Herz, secy; Jacob Herz, treas

Mt Hope Cemetery—Between Pleasant Hill and Clifton av, north of Hanna; Henry Voss, sexton

Old Cemetery—9th and Spencer

St Vincent de Paul Cemetery—Between Pleasant Hill and Clifton av, north of Hanna; Lawrence Redmond, sexton

Churches and Sunday Schools

BAPTIST

Second Baptist Church—n e cor 7th and Broadway; Rev Francis M Huckleberry, pastor   Services, Sunday 11 a m and 7:30 p m; Sunday school 9:45 a m; prayer meeting Thursdays, 7:30 p m

CATHOLIC

St Bridget's Catholic Church—n e cor Wheatland and Wilkinson; Rev Bernard Kroeger, rector   Services, Sunday, mass 8 and 10 a m, vespers and benediction 3 p m; Sunday school 2 p m; week day mass 8 a m

St Joseph's Catholic Church—n w cor 2d and Market; Rev Henry

Koehne rector Services, Sunday, mass 8 and 10 a m, vespers and benediction 3 p m; Sunday school 2:30 p m; week day mass 8 a m

St Vincent de Paul Catholic Church—s w cor 9th and Spencer; Very Rev Matthew E Campion rector Services, Sunday, mass 8 and 10 a m, vespers and benediction 3 p m; Sunday school 2:30 p m; week day mass 7:45 a m

CHRISTIAN

Ninth Street Christian Church—s w cor 9th and Spear; ————, pastor Services, Sunday 11 a m and 7:30 p m; Sunday school 9:30 a m; prayer meeting Thursdays, 7:30 p m

EPISCOPAL

Trinity Episcopal Church—n w cor 7th and Market; Rev Frank C Coolbaugh, rector Services, Sunday 7 and 11 a m and 7:30 p m; Sunday school 9:45 a m; prayer meeting Fridays 7:30 p m

EVANGELICAL

Evangelical Church, n e cor Wheatland and Brown; Rev Wm E Snyder, pastor Services, Sunday 10:30 a m and 7:30 p m; prayer meeting Wednesdays 7:30 p m, Thursdays 8 p m

LUTHERAN

St Jacob's German Lutheran Church—n e cor 9th and Spear; Rev Martin Tiremenstein, pastor Services, Sunday, 10 a m; Sunday school 2:30 p m; prayer meeting Wednesdays 7:30 p m

St Luke's English Lutheran Church—s w cor First and Market; Rev E B Shaner, pastor Services, Sunday 11 a m and 7:30 p m; Sunday school 9:30 a m; prayer meeting Thursdays 7:30 p m

MENNONITE BRETHREN IN CHRIST

Rescue Mission—124 6th; Herman D Herrod, leader Services, Sunday 10:30 a m and 8 p m; prayer meeting daily 8 p m

METHODIST EPISCOPAL

African M E Church (Colored)—s e cor Market and Cicott; Rev Louis Pettiford, pastor Services, Sunday 10:30 a m and 7:30 p m; Sunday school 3 p m; prayer meeting Thursdays 7:30 p m

Broadway M E Church—n e cor 8th and Broadway; Rev Ephraim L Semans, pastor Services, Sunday 11 a m and 7:30 p m; Sunday school 9:45 a m; Prayer meeting Thursdays 7:30 p m

Market Street M E Church—s s Market bet 14th and 15th; Rev Wm S Stewart, pastor Services Sunday 10:45 a m and 7:30 p m; Sunday school 9:30 a m; prayer meeting Thursdays 7:30 p m

Wheatland Street M E Church—n e cor Wheatland and Barron; Rev Jacob K Walts, pastor Services, Sunday 10:45 a m and 7:30 p m; Sunday school 9:30 a m; prayer meeting Thursdays 7:30 p m

PRESBYTERIAN

Broadway Presbyterian Church—s w cor 9th and Broadway; ————, pastor Services, Sunday 11 a m and 7:30 p m; Sunday school 9:30 a m; prayer meeting Thursdays 7:30 p m

Cumberland Presbyterian Church—north side w Broadway, 2 east Brown; Rev James W McDonald, pastor   Services, Sunday 11 a m and 7:45 p m; Sunday school 9:45 a m; prayer meeting Thursdays 7:45 p m

First Presbyterian Church—s e cor 7th and Spencer; Rev Douglas P Putnam, pastor   Services, Sunday 11 a m and 7:30 p m; Sunday school 9:30 a m; prayer meeting Thursdays 7:30 p m

SCIENTISTS

First Church of Christ, Scientists—south side Broadway bet 8th and 9th; services Sunday 11 a m

SEVENTH DAY ADVENTISTS

Seventh Day Adventist Church—510 Sycamore; Rev Oren S Hadley, pastor Services Saturday 3 p m; Sabbath school 2:30 p m; Preaching Sunday 7:30 p m; prayer meeting Wednesdays 7:30 p m

UNITED BRETHREN

North Logan U B Church—n e cor Sugar and Oak; Rev George W Lambert, pastor   Services, Sunday, 7:30 p m; Sunday school 10:30 a m; prayer meeting Thursdays 7:30 p m

South Side U B Church—n w cor Washington and Lincoln (S T); Rev George W Lambert, pastor Services every alternate Sunday 7:30 p m; Sunday school every Sunday 10 a m; prayer meeting Wednesdays 7:30 p m

UNIVERSALIST

First Universalist Church—south side Broadway bet 8th and 9th; ————, pastor; Services, Sunday 8 p m; Sunday school 10 a m

VOLUNTEERS

American Volunteers—315 3d; Captain Maurice Murphy, post commander Services, Sunday 10:30 a m, 3 p m and 8 p m; prayer meeting daily 8 p m

YOUNG MENS' CHRISTIAN ASSOCIATION

Railroad Branch Y M C A—410 Canal; A Clinton Davisson, genl secy; Services, Sunday 3 p m

MISSION SUNDAY SCHOOL

Mission Sunday School First Presbyterian Church—1627 George; A M Rankin, supt; Miss Helen E Noon, secy Services every Sunday 2:45 p m

Clubs

Baldwin Club, The—H Atwood Percival, pres; Willard C Fitzer, vice-pres and secy; Robert Humphreys, treas

Logansport Driving Club, The—J A Brooks, pres; Fred A Dykeman, vice-pres; Charles A Spry, treas; J T Tomlinson, secy

Masonic Club—Masonic Temple, n e cor 4th and North; Henry C Cushman, pres; Charles E Dykeman, first vice-pres; Victor E Seiter, second vice-pres; David A Middleton, secy; Joseph L Linvill, treas

Our Club—s e cor 4th and North; Edward W Kelley, pres; Edward Grace, vice-pres; Harry M Shideler, treas; Walter W Chandler, secy

Pottawattamie Club—s w cor Broadway and Pearl, John C Nelson, pres; Zachary Taylor, vice-pres; John F Brookmeyer, treas; Charles B Stevenson, secy

Vandalia Club—115½ Sycamore; Frank E Gross, pres; Frederick Ross, vice-pres; Albert Campbell, secy and treas

Woman's Club—Mrs Ella J Arthur, pres; Mrs Emma Barnes, vice-pres; Mrs Mae Barnfield, secy; Mrs Clara Funk, treas

Courts

CASS CIRCUIT COURT

Judge—Dudley H Chase
Clerk—Andrew P Flynn
Terms of Circuit Court—First Monday in January, April, September and November

COMMISSIONERS' COURT

Abraham Shideler, Joseph E Crain and Daniel Woodhouse, commissioners
Terms of Commissioners' Court—First Monday in March, June, September and December

Federal Officers

Postmaster—Valentine C Hanawalt; post office 216 Market
United States Commissioner—George W Funk 406½ Broadway
United States Board of Pension Examiners—Dr J S Smith pres, Galveston; Dr Charles P Duchess secy, Walton; Dr Charles L Thomas treas, Logansport Meets every Wednesday, room 1 Masonic Temple

Labor Organizations

(All Unions, except the Railroad Organizations, meet at Trades Assembly Hall, n e cor 4th and Market)

Bricklayers and Stonemasons Union No 15—Meets second and fourth Tuesday evenings of each month, John Guss, pres; James Pierce, vice-pres; Lewis Sheets, secy; Joseph Yager, treas

Cigar Makers International Union of America, Local Union No 215—Meets first Tuesday evening of each month, C P Collet, pres; Charles Brown, vice-pres; Charles Euphrat, fin and cor secy; Isaac Johnston, treas

Logansport Typographical Union No 196—Meets third Sunday of each month, H W Peters, pres; H L Irons, vice-pres; Archelaus Duncan, secy-treas; Thomas L Davis rec secy

Logansport Association No 14, Stationary Engineers—Meets every alternate Sunday in office of City Electric Light Plant, C C Custer, pres; F A Updegraff, Vice-pres; Adam Snider, secy; Andrew J Baltzell, treas

Plumbers, Steam and Gas Fitters Union No 148—Meets on call of secretary, Henry Roach, pres; Harry Rodefer, vice-pres; John Holland, secy, Harry Wickwire, treas

Trades and Labor Assembly—Meets second and fourth Tuesday evening of each month, Milo Gibson, pres; Mack Langton, vice-pres; James Sparrow, secy; Julius Wertheim, treas

United Brewery Workmen—Union No 78; meets third Tuesday of each month Carl Bauer, pres; Herman Meier, vice-pres; Fred Bopp, finan secy; Chris Benning, rec secy; Fred Popowski, treas

RAILROAD ORGANIZATIONS

Brotherhood of Locomotive Engineers, Logan Division No 20—Meets first and third Sundays of each month at 2 p m, n e cor 6th and Broadway Charles Laing, C E; J Harvey Williams, F A E; Jeremiah S Clewell, treas

Brotherhood of Locomotive Firemen, Good Will Lodge No 52—Meets first and third Mondays of each month s e cor 4th and Market Marion E Green, master; Dennis P Graney, secy

Brotherhood of Locomotive Firemen, Wm D Robinson Lodge No 53 Meets first and third Sundays of each month at 2:30 p m, s e cor 4th and Market Robert D Collins, master; Edwin B Booth, secy; Harry Chapman, chairman grievance com

Brotherhood of Railway Trainmen, Fidelity Lodge, No 109—Meets every Sunday at 9:30 a m, s e cor 4th and Market Virgil L De Bolt, master; Matthew F Roles, secy

Order Railway Conductors, Logan Division No. 119—Meets first and third Sundays of each month at 2 p m, s e cor 4th and Market Thomos F Murphy, C C; Hyman S Coats, secy

LADIES AUXILIARIES

The Grand International Auxiliary to the Brotherhood of Locomotive Engineers

The Grand International Auxiliary to the Brotherhood of Locomotive Engineers was organized at Chicago, Illinois, October 2, 1887 The present grand officers of this Association are as follows: Mrs W A Murdock, grand president, Chicago, Illinois; Mary E Cassell, grand vice-president, Columbus, Ohio; Mrs Harry St Clair, grand secretary, Logansport, Indiana; Mrs M L Robertson, grand treasurer, Toledo, Ohio; Mrs F S Bowley, grand chaplain, San Francisco, California; Mrs Byron Baker, grand guide, Ottawa, Ontario, Canada; Mrs R B Adams, grand sentinel, Roanoke, Va; Mrs C Durnell, president of insurance, Fort Wayne, Indiana; Mrs M C Orr, secretary and treasurer of insurance, Peoria, Illinois. The sub-divisions of this

order now number 228, and extend to almost all railroad centers in the United States and Canada. All supplies for organizing and carrying on this work are furnished by the Grand Secretary, Mrs Harry St Clair, of this city, who also receives all moneys paid into the grand division by the sub-divisions. To elevate the social standing of the families of the members of the B of L E, to assist them in time of sickness or trouble, and to insure them against want in case of death, were the paramount objects of the founders of this society. The principles that are inculcated as the basis of its fundamental character are Fidelity, Love, Charity, Harmony and Protection.

Local Lodge Charity Division No 4, G I A to the B of L E— Meets second and fourth Thursdays of each month, n e cor 6th and Broadway Mrs John Truman, pres; Mrs Pierce Richardson, vice-pres; Mrs Harry St Clair, secy; Mrs M E Cooper, treas; Mrs B V Pitman, ins agt

Myzpha Lodge No 26, L A to B of R T— Meets every Thursday s e cor 4th and Market Kate Sullivan, M; Ella Crawshaw, V M; Belle Smith, secy; Augusta Stevens, treas

Bridge City Division, No 42, L A to the O R C— Meets first and third Wednesdays of each month, s e cor 4th and Market Mrs Hyman S Coats, pres; Mrs Charles A Neal, vice-pres; Mrs John Hunter, secy and treas

---

Libraries

Cass County Law Library—Court House

Eel Township Library—basement Masonic Temple Robert F Johnston librarian Open from 8 a m to 4 p m Sunday excepted

Logansport Public Library—616 Broadway S Elizabeth McCullough, librarian Circulating and reference department open from 9 a m to 9 p m, Sundays and legal holidays excepted

---

Musical Societies, Bands and Orchestras

Germania Singing Society—George Weigand, pres; Henry Kruck, vice-pres; John Guss, secy; John G Keip, treas Meets in Trades Assembly Hall on call of secretary

Elks' Band—Kreuzberger Bldg s w cor 3d and Market Robert Cramer, leader; Milo C Harley, secy; Charles A Smith, mgr

Elite Mandolin Orchestra—505 Broadway Edgar E Powell, director and manager

Fornoff's Orchestra—416 4th Michael L Fornoff, leader

Steinhart's Orchestra—315½ 3d Wm Steinhart, leader

Newspapers

DAILY

Logansport Journal (morning)—established 1875 The Logansport Journal Co, publishers, 217-219 4th

Logansport Pharos (evening)—established 1874 Louthain and Barnes, publishers, 216 4th

Logansport Reporter (evening)—established 1889 J Edmund Sutton, publisher, 218 6th

SEMI-WEEKLY

Logansport Journal—established 1849 The Logansport Journal Co, publishers, 217-219 4th

Logansport Pharos—established 1844 Louthain & Barnes, publishers, 216 4th

Logansport Reporter—established January 1, 1897 J Edmund Sutton, publisher, 218 6th

WEEKLY

Logansport Advance—established 1892 J Edmund Sutton, publisher, 218 6th

Logansport Chronicle—established 1876 H James McSheehy, publisher, 324½ Broadway

Logansport Times—established 1886 Charles O Fenton, publisher, 222 4th

Sternenbanner (German)—established 1882 Peter Wallrath, publisher, 205 Market

MONTHLY

Home Music Journal—established 1892 The Home Music Co, publishers, 200 4th

---

Post Office

216 Market

Office Hours--General delivery, 7 a m to 7 p m Money order and registry dept, 7 a m to 7 p m Sunday general delivery and carriers' window, 9 to 10 a m'

Postmaster—Valentine C Hanawalt

Assistant Postmaster }
Money Order Clerk } Ethel Lynas

General Delivery Clerk—Robert Manders

Distributing Clerk—Thomas E Wilder

Mailing Clerks—Thomas S Shaffrey, Austin O'Connell

Special Delivery Messenger—Joseph J Shaffrey

Letter Carriers--Dist No 1, Joseph Herman; dist No 2, John W Parker; dist No 3, Wm A Graffis; dist No 4, John D Turley; dist No 5, Alvin Denbo; dist No 6, Dennis McCarty; dist No 7, Charles A Enyart; dist No 8, Henry Horst; dist No 9, John W Bussard Substitute Carriers: No 1, James D Murphy; No 2, Wm R Floyd

---

Public Buildings, Blocks, Halls, Etc.

Baldwin-Thornton Building--208-210 4th

Barnett Hotel--n e cor 2d and Market

Barnes Block—s e cor 5th and Market

Broadway Rink—s s Broadway 2 e 6th

City Building—n w cor 3d and Broadway
County Jail—321 North
Court House—s w cor 4th and North
Crawford Block—n w cor 5th and Broadway
Dolan & McHale Hall—408-410 Broadway
G A R Hall—324-326 Market
Haney Block—409-411 Broadway
High School Building—n w cor 7th and Broadway
I O O F Hall—s w cor Pearl and Broadway
Keystone Block—n w cor 6th and Broadway
Kreuzberger's Hall—s w cor 3d and Market
K of P Castle Hall—s e cor 5th and Market
Magee Block—317-325 4th
Masonic Temple—n e cor 4th and North
McCaffrey Block—n e cor 6th and Broadway
Opera House Block—s w cor 3d and Broadway
Post Office—216 Market
Progress Hall—n w cor 4th and Market
Public Library Building—616 Broadway
St Bridget's Hall—s e cor Wilkinson and Linden av
St Joseph's Hall—u w cor 2d and Market
St Vincent's Hall—s e cor 8th and Spencer
Smith Block—310-314 Broadway
State National Bank Building—s w cor 4th and Broadway
Spry Block—s e cor Pearl and Broadway
Trades Assembly Hall—n e cor 4th and Market

Public Parks

Ball Park—n s George, east of 26th
Court Park—north to Court, east of 3d
Driving Park—n s George, east of 26th
Riverside Park—from 10th to 15th north of High
Spencer Park—east of 26th

Railroads

Pittsburg, Cincinnati, Chicago and St Louis Railway Co—Passenger station cor 4th and Canal; John A McCullough, ticket agt Freight depot s s Duret between Scott and Taylor; N R Donaldson, frt agt

Terre Haute and Indianapolis Railroad Co (Vandalia Line)—Passenger station and freight depot, s e cor Sycamore and Godfrey; John C Edgeworth, local agt

Wabash Railroad Co—Passenger station cor 9th and Lytle; freight depot cor Ewing and Lytle; Charles G Newell, local agent; Eel River branch passenger station and freight depot e s Vine north Marydyke James L Steele agent

Gc
97
L8
18
14

Schools

PUBLIC SCHOOLS

Board of School Trustees

Office, 214 4th

President—James D McNitt
Secretary—Quincy A Myers
Treasurer—Jehu T Elliott
Superintendent—Albert H Douglass

Supervisors and Teachers Special Branches

Music—Louis D Eichhorn

Location School Buildings

High School—cor 7th and Broadway, David C Arthur prin
Central School—cor 13th and Broadway, Albert J Martin prin
Eighth Street School—cor 8th and High, Ida Covault prin
North Side School—cor Horney and Norcross, G N Berry prin
Sixteenth Street School—cor 16th and Wright, Ellen Comingore prin
South Side School—w s Tanguy between Clay and Tipton, P B Shinn prin

West Side Schools

Bates Street Building—cor Plum and Bates, George R Fish prin
Cicott Street Building—cor Wabash av and Cicott
Plum Street Building—cor Plum and Miami

MISCELLANEOUS SCHOOLS AND COLLEGES

Free Kintergarten—616 Broadway, Geneva M Nichols prin
Hall's Business College—n w cor 6th and Broadway, Charles F Moore pres and gen mgr
Holy Angels Academy (for girls)—s e cor 9th and Broadway under auspices Sisters of the Holy Cross
Michael's Business College—310-314 Broadway, G W Michael pres; Wm H Atha secy; L H Boyd treas
St Bridget's Parochial School—n e cor Wheatland and Wilkinson under auspices Sisters of St Joseph
St Jacob's Lutheran School—n w cor 6th and Market
St Joseph's Parochial School—n w cor 2d and Market under auspices Sisters of Notre Dame
St Vincent De Paul Parochial School(for boys)—s e cor 8th and Spencer under auspices Sisters of the Holy Cross

SECRET AND BENEVOLENT SOCIETIES

Masonic

All orders meet at Masonic Temple n e cor 4th and North

(*See also page 14*)

Tipton Lodge No 35 F & A M—Meets first and third Fridays of

each month, Edward E Emrich, W M; Wm W Whitmore, S W; George S Kistler, J W; Victor E Seiter, treas; Eli Greensfelder, secy

Orient Lodge No 272 F & A M—Meets second and fourth Fridays of each month, James Walklin W M; Wm W Hilton, S W; Harry A Jameson, J W; Joseph L Linvill, treas; John Y Wood, secy

Logan Chapter No 2 R A M—Meets from September to March, on second Monday of each month at 7 p m, from March to September 7:30 p m, Joseph L Linvill H P; Cott Barnett, K; Isaac Shideler, scribe; Henry Tucker, treas; Samuel B Richardson, secy

Logansport Council No 11 R & S M—Meets the Wednesday following the second Monday of each month, Cott Barnett, Ill M; Joseph Linvill, Dep Ill M; Thomas Austin, treas; Samuel B Richardson, sec

St John Commandery, No 24, K T—Meets first Monday of each month at 7 p m Isaac Shideler, E C; Oliver B Sargent, G; Dudley H Chase, C G; Thomas Austin, treas; Samuel B Richardson, recorder

Fidelity Chapter, No 58, O E S—Meets first Tuesday of each month at 7:30 p m Susan Robinson, W M; Henry H Montfort, W P; Ida Custer, A M; Sarah Horn, secy; Lydia Eldridge, treas

Masonic Temple Association—Meets first and third Thursdays of each month Jehu T Elliott, pres; Joseph L Linvill, secy; Isaac Shideler, treas

Masonic Club—Henry C Cushman, pres; Charles E Dykeman, first vice-pres; Victor E Seiter, second vice-pres; David A Middleton, secy; Joseph L Linvill, treas

Independent Order of Odd Fellows

All orders, except the Canton, meet at Odd Fellows' Hall, s w cor Pearl and Broadway

Eel River Lodge, No 417—Meets every Tuesday evening W C Scott, N G; Clark Gray, V G; J D Allison, secy; E E March, treas

Logan Lodge, No 40—Meets every Monday evening Frank Henke, N G; W C Goldsberry, V G; L G Hanna, secy; John Hawkins, treas

St Gotthardt Lodge, No 574—Meets every Wednesday evening John Heitzmann, N G; John Meyer, V G; Herman Warner, secy; Ferdinand Burgman, treas

Cass Encampment, No 119—Meets first and third Thursdays of each month W O B Thompson, C P; W C Goldsberry, S W; Frank Berndt, scribe; J D Allison, treas

Canton Logansport, No 15, P M—Meets first Wednesday of each month, 412½ Broadway Drill meeting every Wednesday J D Allison, capt; John Livengood, lieut; Carey D Herrick, clerk; Rudolph Berndt, treas

Jewel Lodge No 541 D of R—Meets first and third Fridays of each month Jennie DeLong, N G; Katherine Dear, V G; Emma Briggs, secy; Emma Harley treas

Purity Lodge No 127 D of R—Meets second and fourth Fridays of each month Jennie Goldsberry, N G; Mary B Herrick V G; Laura E Ramsey, secy; Sarah McCormick, treas

Knights of Pythias

All Lodges meet at Pythian Castle s e cor 5th and Market

Bridge City Lodge No 305— Meets every Tuesday evening Henry Baughman, C C; Edward Kelly, K R and S; Thomas Manders, N of F; Emmett Mulholland M of E

Apollo Lodge No 62— Meets every Friday evening George Gonser, C C; S P Anderson, K of R and S; Wm H Porter, M of F; Fred Davis M of E

Logan Co No 26 U R— Meets second Thursday of each Month W S Neff capt; S P Anderson, secy; Wm H Porter, treas

Logansport Pythian Castle Association—Meets every Tuesday evening Harry K Orr, pres; George B Barron, vice-pres; S P Anderson, secy; Wm H Porter, treas

Diana Temple No 30 Rathbone Sisters—Meets every Monday evening Mrs Florence Bowman, M E C; Mrs Ella B Swadener, M of R and C; Mrs Nellie Truman M of F

Improved Order of Red Men

All orders meet 314½ 4th

Wea Tribe, No 170— Meets every Thursday Walter L Closson, P; John Youngker, S; Alvin Denbo, C of R; George Scharff, C of W; John B Shaver, K of W; Scott B Price, agt and fin secy ins dept

Wea Hayloft, No 170½— Meets every Friday evening Francis A McCarter, C H; Wm B De Motte, A C H; Scott E Price, C of S; John F Gangloff, K of B

Logan Council, No 89, D of P— Meets every Thursday evening Alice Warner, Prophetess; Alice Grubbs, Pocahontas; Mary Updegraff, C of R; Lewis E Grubbs, C of W; Scott E Price, special agt and col ins dept

Minisee Council, No 66, D of P— Meets every Wednesday evening Kate Dalrymple Prophetess; Lucinda Pierson, Pocahontas; Alice Jackson, C of R; Gottlieb Schott, K of W; Mrs Myra Kirk C of W

Independent Order of Foresters

High Court of Indiana—High Court sessions are held annually The next meeting will be held at Terre Haute, Indiana, in February, 1898 C H Roehrig, H C R, Evansville, Ind; G W Goff, H V C R, Rensselaer, Ind; Wm W Wilson, H Secy, 1209 Market, Logansport, Ind; J K E Risk, H Treas, Lafayette, Ind

Court Noble, No 975— Meets every Thursday, n e cor 6th and Broadway Charles D Sellers, C R; Thomas McKeever, V C R; Wm P McGrew, fin secy; Lucian B Barron, secy; Charles B Longwell, treas

Grand Army of the Republic

Hall 324-326 Market

Post No 14— Meets second and fourth Tuesdays of each month John B Winters, C; Charles H Barron, S V C; John Ensfield, Jr V C; Rodney Strain, adj; Joseph E Crain, Q M

Lincoln Circle No 1 Ladies of the G A R— Meets first and third

Tuesdays of each month Mrs Earl Stewart, pres; Mrs Charlotte Burns, vice-pres; Mrs Jessie N Beatty, secy; Mrs E N Howard, treas

Women's Relief Corps No 30— Meets second and fourth Tuesdays of each month Maria L Schlater, pres; Nina Higbee, secy

Benevolent and Protective Order of Elks

Logansport Lodge No 66—Meets first and third Thursdays of each month s w cor 3d and Market H J McSheehy, E R; J G Powell, E Leading K; John Flanegin, E Loyal K; T S Freeman, E Lecturing K; O A Means, Secy; V E Seiter, treas

Order of the Continental Fraternal Union

Logansport Lodges—Meet the second and fourth Wednesdays of each month Progress Hall C W SeLegue, pres; George Scharff vice-pres; Clinton L Dilley sr, accountant

Woodmen of the World

Maple Camp No 2— Meets first and third Mondays of each month 327½ Market Thomas Porter, C C; N A Irvine, secy; Eginhard Schmitt treas

Modern Woodmen of America

Logansport Camp No 4389—Meets second and fourth Wednesdays of each month n e cor 6th and Broadway George E Jamison, V C; Eugene E Davis, W A; C E Trickle, Clerk; Archelaus Duncan, E B

Royal Arcanum

Noble Council, No 369—Meets first and third Mondays of each month, 327½ Market. Robert Manders, R; E M Walden V R; S D Brandt, secy; J McC Johnston, treas

Tribe of Ben Hur

Tirzah Court, No 11—Meets every Wednesday, n e cor 6th and Broadway W S Rosier, C; W S Wirick, J; Eva Wilson, scribe

Knights of the Maccabees

Alpha Tent, No 7— Meets fourth Monday of each month, 327½ Market Allen Lewis Sir K C; Wm H Legg, L C; Wm Grace, R K; T W Purkey, F R .

Chosen Friends

Logan Council, No 21—Meets first and Third Tuesdays of each month, Progress Hall Mrs Joseph Hanke, C; Mrs Kate Dalrymple, secy; Alvin Denbo, treas

Knights and Ladies of Security

Eureka Council, No 499—Meets second and fourth Wednesdays of each month, Progress Hall James Gilmore, pres; Florene E Grable, vice-pres; John F Kelly, secy; Benjamin F Sharts, treas

Court of Honor

Alpha Court, No 201—Meets first and third Fridays of each
month, 327½ Market A C Davisson, C; Perry Wilson, V C; James
C Murphy, R; N A Irvine, treas

Knights of Honor

Wabash Lodge, No 1831—Meets every Monday, Progress Hall
Louis Epstine, dict; B M Murray, vice-dict; James S Bolt, R; C L
Alford, F R; Michael Fornoff, treas

Logan Lodge, No 1246—Meets every Wednesday evening, 327½
Market John Klinck, D; B Fulerick, V D; Nelson A Irvine, rep;
Peter S Linquist, treas

Knights and Ladies of Honor

Western Star Lodge No 1601—Meets every Friday night n e cor
6th and Broadway Anna Cohee, P; Mary Humphrey, V P; Adam
Snider, secy; Frank E Wilkinson, treas

Independent Order Good Templars

GRAND LODGE OF INDIANA

The Grand Lodge meets annually the Second Wednesday in
October s e cor 4th and Market I S Wade, G C T, Lafayette; Alice
Collins, G V T, Logansport; Thomas J Legg, G Secy, Logansport;
Bart A Harding, G Treas, Shelbyville

LOCAL LODGES

South Logan Lodge No 429—Meets every Monday evening s e
cor Shultz and Kloenne (S T) Fred Buckleman, C T; Nelson
Webb, secy; L G Smith, treas

Knights of St John

St George Commandery No 279—Meets second and fourth Fridays of each month at St Joseph's Hall Charles Ruhl, commander;
George Baker, cor secy; Henry Peters, fin secy; George Snider,
treas

St Matthews Commandery No 256—Meets second and fourth Fridays of each month at St Vincent's Hall John R Fox, commander;
Wm Whitehead, fin secy; John E Irwin, treas

Ladies Auxiliary to St Matthews Commandery No 256—Meets
second and fourth Thursdays of each month at designated residence
of members Mrs John E Irwin, pres; Mrs C W ScLegue secy and treas

Ancient Order of Hibernians

Division No 1—Meets second Tuesday of each month n e cor 6th
and Broadway Michael C Wade, county pres; Edward Gormerly, pres;
Frank E Hanley, vice pres; Patrick Mahoney, secy; David Loftus, treas

Travelers Protective Association

Post F—Meets fourth Saturday of each month s e cor 4th and Market Joseph H Reitemeier, pres; Henry C Willey, vice pres; Wm C Fisher secy and treas

Miscellaneous Societies

National Association of Letter Carriers, No 323—Meet on call of secretary Alvin Denbo, pres; Dennis McCarthy secy

Cass County Medical Society—Meets the Fourth Thursday of each month at 313 Pearl Nelson W Cady, pres; E P Gould, vice-pres; J Z Powell, secy and treas

North Central Indiana Poultry and Pet Stock Association Richard Twells, pres; Horatio Thornton, vice-pres; Sol D Brandt, secy; Cott Barnett, treas

Logansport Theosophical Society—Meets every Sunday, 2 p m, 416½ Market Melvina McQuinston, pres; James Gilbert, vice-pres; D E Delzell, secy; Charles Buhrmester, treas

St Joseph's Mutual Benevolent Society—Meets first Sunday of each month, St Joseph's Hall John Hartz, pres; John Gross, secy

Catholic Benevolent Legion, Council No 190—Meets first and third Wednesdays of each month, St Bridget's Hall Peter Mahoney, pres; Peter Schrader, secy; Thomas McKeever, treas

St Vincent's Total Abstinence Cadets—Meets third Sunday of each month, St Vincent's Hall Thomas Sheerin, pres, John Follen, fin secy; Clarence Shaffrey, cor secy

Young People's Total Abstinence Society of St Vincent de Paul Church Meets third Sunday of each month, St Vincent's Hall Owen Follen, jr, pres; Mary Walsh, secy

Young People's Temperance Society of St Bridget's Church— Meets first Tuesday of each month, St Bridget's Hall John Regan, pres; Ella Regan treas; James Conway, jr, secy

The Genus Council, No 1—Meets on call G C Alex B Boyer, pres and L H G

Logansport Humane Society— Meets on call of secretary at 206 4th Elihu S Rice, pres; Joshua C Hadley, vice-pres; George W Walters, secy; John J Hildebrandt, treas

Logansport Woman's Christian Temperance Union— Meets every alternate Wednesday at Home for the Friendless Esther L Grable, pres; Mary J Washburn, secy; Elizabeth A Troutman, treas

STREET AND AVENUE GUIDE

THE NOTATION OF LOCATIONS

Logansport is numbered on the Philadelphia plan, which is the most approved of modern conveniences for the notation of locations Each block, by this system, constitutes a hundred numbers; even numbers will be found on the north and east side of the streets, odd numbers on the south and west side: thus the s e cor 4th and Market would be numbered 401 and the doors going east 403, 405, etc, until

the intersection of 5th street be reached, then in like manner from the east side of 5th street, the numbers would be 501, 503, 505, etc; to 6th street   By this means, with any given number, we can tell just how many blocks that number can be found from the initial of enumeration

First street is the basis of numbering from west to east between the rivers High street is the basis of numbering from north to south between the rivers Eel river is the basis of numbering from south to north on the North Side   North Sixth, the continuation of Sixth north of Eel River, is the basis of numbering on the North Side, east to corporation line and west to Brown

Brown is basis of numbering on the West Side

Front is the basis of numbering from south to north on the West Side until Brown is reached, when the numbers begin at Wabash River

The Wabash River is the basis of numbering from north to south on the South side

---

A—from Market south to Helm 1 w Wilkinson

Anthony—from Wabash River south to Burlington road 1 w Burlington av

Ash—from Water north 1 w Sycamore

Aster—from Water south to Eel River R R 1 e Garden

B—from Wabash River north to Market 2 w Wilkinson

Balsam—from Water south to Daisy 3 e Holland

Barron—from Wabash River north to Pratt 1 w Brown

Bartlett—from Anthony west to Standley 2 s Wabash R R

Bates—from junction Ottawa and Plum w to city limits 5 n Market

Bell—from Clifton av e to Michigan av 1 n Hanna

Berkley—from Wabash River north to Spencer 3 e 5th

Biddle—from Standley west 2 s Wabash R R (S T)

Biddle Av—continuation of 3d crossing Biddle Island

Bluff—from Heber to Mill 1 n Midland av

Bringhurst—from 7th to 8th 1 n Race

Broadway—from Eel River av east to city limits 1 n Market

Broadway (West)—from Eel river west to city limits 1 n w Market

Brown—from Pratt south to Melbourne av 1 w Eel River

Burlington Av—from Wabash River south to city limits continuation 3d

C—from Market south to Helm 3 w Wilkinson

Calla—from Garden west 1 n Bates

Canal—from Eel River east to Berkley 1 n Wabash River

Canty—from Daisy to Pink 1 e Holland

Cecil—from Michigan av to Vandalia R R 2 n Eel River

Center—from Sycamore west to city limits 1 n Columbia

Charles—from Standley west 1 s Wabash R R (S T)

Charles—from Wabash River to Wabash R R 2 w Anthony

Chicago—from Water north to Pollard 2 w Sycamore

Chestnut—from Ottawa north to Tecumseh 1 west n 6th

Cicott—from Wabash River north to Pratt 2 w Brown

Claude--from Michigan av to Vandalia R R 4 n Eel River
Clay—from Anthony east to city limits 5 s Wabash River
Clifton Av—from Hanna north to city limits 3 w Michigan av
Coles--from Hamilton Race south to Clay 3 e Burlington av
Colfax—from Burlington av east to Coles 1 s Wabash River
College--from Water north to Pollard 1 e Sycamore
Columbia--from n 6th west to city limits 1 n Water
Conrad--from Michigan av west 1 n junction Michigan av and Horney
Cottage--from Midland av north to Vandalia R R 1 e Michigan av
Court—from 3d to 4th 1 n Broadway
Creek--from Quincy north to city limits 1 w Michigan av
Culbertson—from Standley east to Anthony 4 s Wabash R R (S T)
Cummings—from Cecil north to Maple 1 e Michigan av
D- from Market to Wabash River 4 w Wilkinson
Daisy—from Holland east to Aster 2 n Bates
Dakota—from Bates north 2 w Vandalia R R (Dunkirk)
Day—from Tipton to Clay 3 w Burlington av
Delaware—from Bates north 1 w Vandalia R R (Dunkirk)
Dizardie--from Reynolds to Peters 1 s Wabash River (Biddle Island)
Douglas--from 15th to 16th 2 s Eel River
Duret—from Berkley east to 9th continuation of Canal
Dykeman--from 17th to 23d 3 north Wabash River
Eel River Av—from confluence of Eel and Wabash River north east to junction 4th and High 1 e Eel River
Eighteenth—from High south to Usher 18 e Eel River av
Eighth—from Eel River south to Spencer 8 e Eel River av
Elam—from Powell north 1 e Clifton av
Eleventh—from RiversidePark south to Erie av 11 e Eel River av
Elm—from junction 7th and Spencer south to Wabash River 2 e 5th
Elm—from Eel River north to Eel River R R 1 w Sycamore
Erie Av—from junction 5th and Market south east to city limits 3 n Wabash River
Ewing—from Erie av south to Lytle 1 e 9th
Fifteenth—from Eel River south to Erie av thence southwest to Wabash River
Fifth—from Canal north to Eel River 5 e Eel River av
Findley—from Michigan av east to Cummings 3 n Eel River
First—from Wabash River north to Eel River av 2 e Eel River
Fitch—from Spear south to George 1 e 11th
Fourteenth—from Riverside Park south to Erie av thence southwest to Wabash R R
Fourth—from Wabash River north to Eel River 4 e Eel River av
Frank—from Howard south to Culbertson 3 e Wabash R R (S T)
Franklin—from Horney west 5 n Eel River
Front—from junction w Wabash av and Helm northeast to Sycamore 1 w Eel River
Fulton—from Michigan av west to Clifton av 4 n Eel River
Garden—from Bates north to Daisy 1 e Holland

Gate—from Biddle av west to Reynolds 1 s Wabash River (Biddle's Island)

George—from 11th east to city limits 2 s Market

Godfrey—from Sycamore east to Willow 4 n Eel River

Grove—from Tipton south to Clay 2 w Burlington av

Hamilton—from Hamilton Race south to Clay 4 e Burlington av

Hanna—from Clifton av southwest 4 n Eel River

Hargrave—from Stanley north 2 e Clifton av

Hazel—from 19th east to city limits 8 s Market

Heath—from Bates south to State 3 w Brown

Heber—from Midland av north to Vandalia R R 3 e Michigan av

Helm—from Wabash River west to Park av 2 s w Market

Henry—from n 6th east to Clifton av 5 n Eel River

High—from 4th east to city limits 3 n Market

Hillside—from Sycamore e 1 s junction Sycamore and Pleasant Hill

Holland—from Wheatland north to city limits 6 w Brown

Horney—from Michigan av n to city limits 2 e Clifton av

Howard—from Anthony west 1 s Wabash R R (S T)

Huber—north and south across Biddle Island 3 w Biddle av

Humphrey—from Hamilton Race south to Clay 2 e Burlington av

Illinois—from Wabash River north to P C C & St L Ry 2 e 12th

Indiana—from 12th east to P C C & St L Ry shops 2 n Wabash River

Jackson—from Clifton av east 6 n Hanna

James—from John south to Wabash R R 1 w Anthony

Jefferson—from Clifton av east 7 n Hanna

Jefferson—from 17th east to city limits 1 n Erie av

John—from Michigan av west to Creek 2 n junction Horney and Michigan av

John—from Anthony west to Charles 1 s Logansport and Western road

Johnson—from Fulton north to city limits 1 e Clifton av

Kloenne—from Wabash R R south to Culbertson 1 e Standley (S T)

Knowlton—from 17th to Wabash River 2 s Wabash R R

La Rose—from Columbia north 1 e Sycamore

Liberty—from Water north to Pollard 3 w Sycamore

Lincoln—from Standley west 3 s Wabash R R (S T)

Linden Av—from n 6th west to city limits 3 n w Market

Lisbon—from Springer south 1 w Horney

Lobelia—from Daisy north to Water 2 e Holland

Lockwood—from Wabash River north to Melbourne av 2 e Vandalia R R

Logan—from Wright south to Erie av 1 e 13th

Logansport and Western Road—from Burlington av west along south shore Wabash River

Lynas—continuation Standley from Washington tp road south 1 w Burlington road

Lytle—from 9th to Ewing 1 s Erie av

McCarty—from Pleasant Hill north 1 e Pleasant Grove

ison Av—from Wheatland north to Bates 5 w Brown
nolia--from old W & E Canal n to Richardville 1 e Sycamore
n—from Anthony east 2 s Wabash River
le—from Michigan av east to Cummings 5 n Eel River
ion--from Sycamore east to Pleasant Grove 1 n Pleasant Hill
ket—from Eel river east to city limits 2 n Wabash River
ket (West)—from Eel River west to city limits 4 n Wabash

ydyke--from Elm west to Uhl 1 n Ottawa
sachusetts—from Delaware west 1 n Bates (Dunkirk)
'ock Av—from Biddle south 3 w Standley (S T)
bourne Av—from Eel River west to city limits 1 s w Market
mt—from Brown east to Michigan av 3 n Eel River
hael--from Logansport and Western road south to Wabash
Cicott street bridge
tigan Av—from n 6th and Eel River northeast to city limits
s—from 15th to 16th 1 s Eel River
—from Midland av north to Vandalia R R 4 e Michigan av
ley—from Clifton av west 3 n Mt Hope Cemetery
roe—from Clifton av east 6 n Hanna
tgomery—from Hamilton Race south to Clay 1 e Burlington av
gan—from Smith south to Vandalia R R 1 e Michigan av
rell—from Clifton av east to Michigan av 1 s Hanna
ada—from Bates north 4 w Vandalia R R (Dunkirk)
teenth—from Wabash River north to High 19 e Eel River av
h—from Eel River south to Lytle 9 e Eel River av
ross—from Michigan av west to Pleasant Grove 5 n Eel

h—from Eel River av east to city limits 2 n Market
—from Wabash River north to Erie av 1 e 5th
—from Sugar north 1 e Michigan av
—from Illinois north to 17th 1 n Wabash River
va—from Plum east 2 n Linden av
—from 15th east 6 s Market
e—from Eel River west to Brown 1 s Linden av
y—from Pink north to Water 1 e Holland
Av—from Wabash River north to Wheatland 3 e Van R R
nec—from w Broadway to Plum 1 n Front
l—from Market north to Broadway 1 e 4th
l (North)—from Linden av north to Ottawa 1 e Sycamore
s—north and south across Biddle's Island 3 w Biddle av
—from Balsam west to Holland 3 n Bates
ant Grove—from Pleasant Hill north to city limits 2 e Syc-

ant Hill—from Ottawa north-west to Sycamore 1 w Clifton
—from Front north to Ottowa 3 w Sycamore
rd—from College w 2 n Columbia
ll—from Clifton av east to Horney 9 n Hanna
—from Brown west to city limits 4 n w Market
y—from Michigan av to Creek 2 n junction Michigan av
ey

Race—from 6th to 10th 4 n Market

Railroad—Wilkinson north-west to Market along south side P & St L Ry 1 north Melbourne av

Reynolds—north and south across Biddle Island 1 w Biddle av

Richardville—east and west from Sycamore 1 s Columbia

Rose—from Pleasant Hill north 1 w Pleasant Grove

Russell—from Reynolds west to Peters 1 s Wabash River (Bid- s Island)

Scott—from Wabash River to P C C & St L Ry 1 w 12th

Second—from Wabash River north to Eel River av 2 e Eel River

Seventeenth—from Wabash to Eel River 17 e Eel River av

Seventh—from Spencer north to Eel River 7 e Eel River av

Shaw—from Clifton av w 1 n Mt Hope Cemetery

Sherman—from Biddle south 1 w Standley (S T)

Short—from 14th west to Logan 1 s Wright

Shultz—Anthony west to Standley 3 s Wabash R R (S T)

Silver—from Fulton south 1 e Clifton av

Sixteenth—from Wabash R R north to Eel River 16 e Eel River av

Sixth—from Erie av north to Eel River 6 e Eel River av

Sixth (North)—continuation of 6th from Eel River n to Pleas- Hill

Skelton—Pleasant Grove west to Rose 1 n Pleasant Hill

Smead—from 12th east to city limits 3 s Market

Smith—from Michigan av east 6 n Eel River

Spear—from 8th east to city limits 1 s Market

Spencer—from 7th to 9th 1 s Market

Spring—9th to 10 1 s Spear

Spring—Sycamore east 1 s Hillside

Springer—Horney west to Johnson 1 n Franklin

Sonora—from Bates north

Standley—from Logansport and Western road south 1 w Cicott et bridge (S T)

Stanley—Clifton av east to Horney 6 n Franklin

Star—from Fulton to Wayne 2 e Clifton av

State—Heath west to D 2 n Wabash River

Stevens—17th to 19th 1 n Wabash River

Stevenson—Sycamore east to Pleasant Grove 2 n Pleasant Hill

Sugar—Michigan av east to Oak 2 n junction Horney and Mich- av

Sycamore—continuation of 3d from Eel River north to city limits

Tanguy—Tipton south to Clay 1 w Burlington av

Taylor—Wabash River north to P C C & St L Ry 1 e Berkley

Tecumseh—Willow east to Chestnut 1 n Ottawa

Tenth—from Toledo north to Eel River 10 e Eel River av

Third—from Canal north to Eel River 3 e Eel River av

Thirteenth—from Wabash R R north to high 13 e Eel River av

Thompson—from Stanley north 1 e Clifton av

Tipton—from Coles west to Wabash R R 3 s Wabash River

Toledo—from 10th south-east to 21st 1 s Erie av

Treen—from Fulton north 1 w Horney

Twelfth—from Wabash River north to High 12 e Eel River av

Twentieth—from Wabash River north to High 20 e Eel River av
Twenty-fifth—George north to High 25 e Eel River av
Twenty-first—from North south to Otto from Wabash R R south
·to Knowlton 21 e Eel River av
Twenty-fourth—from George north to High 24 e Eel River av
Twenty-second—High south to Usher from·Wabash R R s to
Wabash River 22 e Eel River av
· *Twenty-third*—George north to North, from Wabash River north
to Wabash R R 23 e Eel river av
Uhl—from Plum west 2 n Bates
Usher—from 14th east 5 s Market
Vernon—Bates north 5 w Vandalia R R [Dunkirk]
Vine—from Eel River north 2 w Sycamore
Wabash Av (East)—from 4th east to 17th along north bank Wa-
bash River
Wabash Av (West)—from junction Front and Helm west along
north bank Wabash River to city limits
. *Wall*—4th to Pearl 1 n Market
Wall (North)—Linden av north to Ottawa 1 w n 6th
Washington—Plum west to Garden 6 n w Market
Washington—from Biddle south 2 w Standley (S T)
Water—from Sycamore northwest along north bank old W & E
Canal to city limits
Wayne—Clifton av east to Michigan av 2 n Hanna
Webster—Clifton av east to Johnson 1 n Franklin
Western Av—Wabash River north to w Market 1 e Vandalia R R
Wheatland—Brown west to city limits 2 n w Market
Wilkinson—Wabash River north to Bates 4 w Brown
Williams—Midland av north to Vandalia R R 2 e Michigan av
· *Willow*—Ottawa north 2 e Sycamore
Woodland—Bates north 1 w Plum
Wright—from 12th east to city limits 4 s Market

..Das Sternenbanner

Office, 205 Market Street LOGANSPORT, IND.

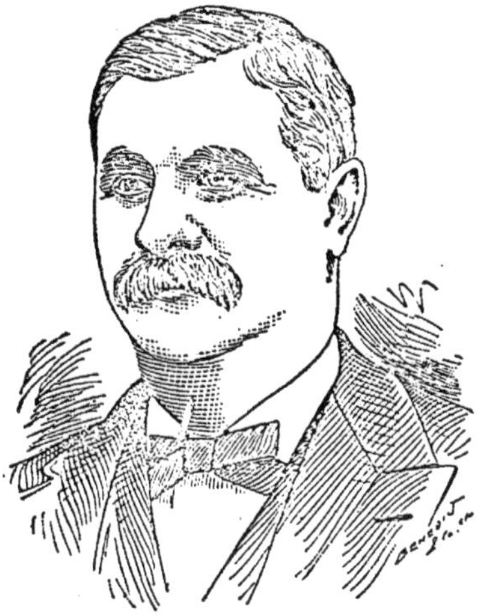

PETER WALLRATH, Editor and Proprietor

❧ ❧ ❧

A Live Newspaper, Publishing All the News
A First-rate Advertising Medium

❧ ❧ ❧

A complete and thoroughly equipped
❧ ❧ JOB PRINTING OFFICE ❧ ❧
in connection ❧ ❧ Samples and Prices
promptly furnished ❧ ❧ ❧ ❧ ❧ ❧ ❧

❧ ❧ ❧

Peter Wallrath, Agent for All Ocean Steamers

❧ Parties desiring further information
please address or call on ❧ ❧ ❧ ❧ ❧

PETER WALLRATH, Logansport, Ind.

DON'T — These items suggest something that you need ?

Abstract Legal Cap
Advertising Novelties
Announcements, Wedding
Badges
Baggage Tags
Bags for Coin
Bank Pass Books
Bill Books
Bill Heads
Binders for Magazines
Binding. all classes
Blank Books, stock
Blank Books, to order
Blank Notes, Receipts, etc
Blotters
Board Clips
Bond Papers
Boxes, Wedding Cake
Bread and Milk Checks
Briefs
Building & Loan Assn Books
Business Cards
By-Laws and Constitutions
Cabinet Letter Files
Calendars
Carbon Papers
Cardboards
Cards, Engraved and Printed
Cards, Invitation
Cards, Visiting
Cash Books
Catalogue Printing
Certificates, Corporation, etc
Circulars, Letter and Note
Coin Wrappers
Collection Registers
Commencement Programs
Copying Books
Copying Pads
Copying Presses
Coupon Books
Day Books
Debit and Credit Slips
Depositors' Ledgers
Diaries
Directories, City and County
Discount Registers
Dividend Registers
Dodgers
Draft Registers

Drafts, Notes and Receipts
Electrotyping
Embossing
Engraving, Steel and Copper
Envelopes, Catalogue
Envelopes, Clasp
Envelopes, Commercial
Envelopes, Congress Tie
Envelopes, Official
Envelopes, Wedding
Erasers, Knife
Erasers, Rubber
Eyelets
Fancy Stationery
Files, Letter, etc
Flat Opening Blank Books
For Rent and Sale Cards
Fountain Pens
Glue in bottles
Grocers' Books
Gummed Labels
Hand Bills
Head and Tail Statements
Hotel Registers
Hotel Stationery
Indelible Ink
Indexed Memo Books
Indexes, Ledger
Initial Seals
Ink Stands
Inks, standard grades
Invitation Cards & Cabinets
Invoice Books
Japanese Napkins
Journals, stock and to order
Justice Dockets
Kalamazoo Book Holders
Knives, Erasing
Labels
Lead Pencils
Ledgers, stock and to order
Legal Blanks
Legal Cap
Legal Wrappers
Letter Heads
Lithographing
Magazine Binding
Mailing Tubes
Manila Paper

Menu Cards
Milk Books
Miniature Blank Books
Mucilage
Notarial Seals
Note Heads
Notes, Drafts and Receipts
Order Books
Pamphlet Printing
Pass Books
Paper, of every description
Paper Fasteners
Pencils
Penholders
Pens, best grades
Perfumed Sealing Wax
Placards
Posters
Prepared Paste
Price Tickets, Assorted
Printing in all lines
Programs
Rent Receipts
Restaurant Coupon Books
Roll Manila Wrapping
Roll Paper Cutters
Rubber Bands
Rubber Stamps
Rulers
Ruling, to order
Sealing Wax
Seals, Corporation & Notary
Shipping Tags
Society Address Cards
Statements
Tablets, Writing
Time Books
Toilet Paper and Fixtures
Trial Balance Books
Typewriter Paper
Typewriter Ribbons
Vest Pocket Memo Books
Visiting Cards, Engraved
Visiting Cards, Printed
Waterman's Fountain Pens
Wedding Cake Boxes
Wedding Invitations
Wrapping Paper
Writing Paper

OUR NEW LOCATION

LONGWELL & CUMMINGS PRINTERS BINDERS
BLANK BOOKS

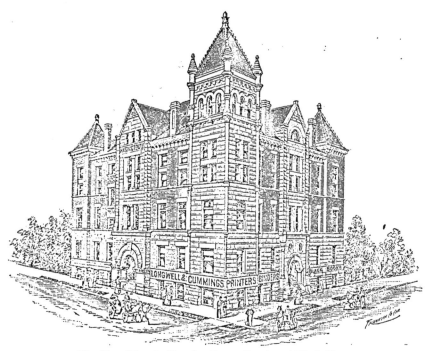

The New Masonic Temple—Corner Fourth and North Streets.

LONGWELL & CUMMINGS

Printers . .
Binders . .
Stationers .

IT is with no small degree of pride—properly seasoned with a becoming sense of modesty—that the undersigned submit this circular to the public, calling attention to our removal to new and stately quarters. ❧ An exterior cut, herewith shown, of the new Masonic Temple, will convey to those personally unacquainted with this noble structure, an excellent idea of the location of our new office. ❧ A brief description of the arrangement of the quarters we occupy therein need not be deemed amiss. ❧ We have the entire basement floor, with the exception of a small room occupied as the office of the township trustee, possessing in all a floor space of more than 4,000 square feet. In comparison with our late inadequate and greatly cramped quarters, this is an enormous advantage, and one which we dare to believe will be appreciated by the public whose interests in the printing way we desire to constantly serve. This new location gives us the finest counting room, the neatest private office, the best lighted and airiest composing room, the solidest floor for presses and engine, a large fireproof vault, well-arranged binding facilities, and the most convenient stock-room of any printing house in the state. The entire basement has been remodeled and constructed especially for us, from plans securing the largest measure of convenience in every department, and we boast, modestly, the possession of a printing establishment which will prove in full keeping with the metropolitan advancement of the city whose people boast so prideful a building as the one to which we point you in this circular. ❧ By this change, and by the addition of facilities which we were utterly unable to employ in our formerly restricted location, we are now in a position to do a class of work heretofore unsolicited, and to furnish supplies which we were before unable to handle or to display. ❧ In this connection we will make a specialty of blank book work, all kinds of county and bank supplies, book printing, and a variety of work which has heretofore been done only at a disadvantage. ❧ In society and commercial printing we will now be better equipped than ever to maintain the gratifying supremacy which we have enjoyed in that line. ❧ All the advantages which we now possess will be equally shared by our customers, and it is with a great deal of pleasure that we invite you to call and inspect our facilities for insuring satisfactory service in any branch of the art preservative in which you may happen to be interested either immediately or prospectively. ❧ We confidently trust to prove our ability to interest you. With a concluding assurance of our most sincere thanks for the countless favors extended by a liberal public in the past, and acknowledging our recognition of the deep and lasting obligations under which we rest in relation to that public, we beg to remain, as ever,

Your Most Humble Printermen,

THE
STANDARD
OF
EXCELLENCE
IN
FOUNTAIN PENS
IS THE
WATERMAN IDEAL

A RELIABLE fountain pen is now regarded everywhere by progressive people as the most practical and convenient writing instrument—a grateful relief from the drudgery of "dip" pens and untidy inkstands. **The very best fountain pen is "Waterman's Ideal."**

It consists of:

A gold pen, the best that can be made.

A hard rubber holder of the best shape and the finest finish, containing an ink reservoir; and

A Feed that conducts the ink from the reservoir to the pen point with absolute uniformity and certainty.

The best writing tool known, the common pen, has, as its distinctive feature, **"the split"** between the nibs, without which it will not write.

The special feature of the feeding device in the "Ideal" is its splits, which draw the ink from the reservoir to the pen with the same reliability that the split of the pen draws the ink to the paper, and both respond to the act of writing with automatic regularity.

LONGWELL &
CUMMINGS.....

Sole

Agents

Masonic Temple
Logansport, Ind.

PRICE LIST						
GOLD PEN AND HOLDER COMPLETE					GOLD PEN	
Nos *	Plain, Chased or Mottled	Gold Mounted and Chased	Nos *	Plain, Threaded or Mottled	Gold Pen Only	Nos.
2	$2.50	$3.50	12	$2.50	$1.25	2
3	3.50	4.50	13	3.50	1.50	3
4	4.00	5.50	14	4.00	1.75	4
5	5.00	6.00	15	5.00	2.25	5
6	6.00	7.00	16	6.00	2.75	6

*Old Style, Nos. 2 to 6; New Style, Nos. 12 to 16.

44

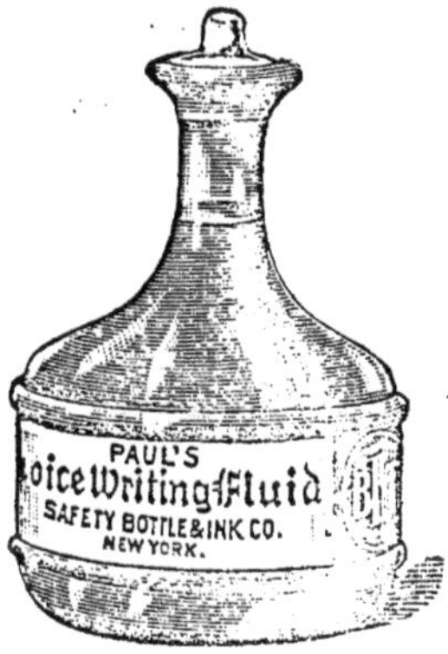
PAUL'S
SAFETY BOTTLE & INK CO.
NEW YORK.

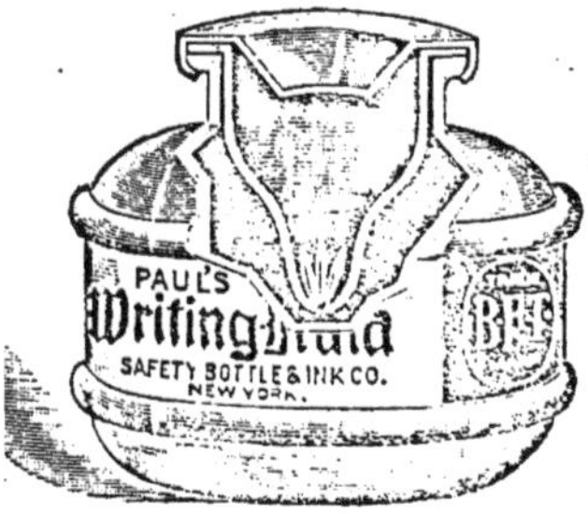
PAUL'S
SAFETY BOTTLE & INK CO.

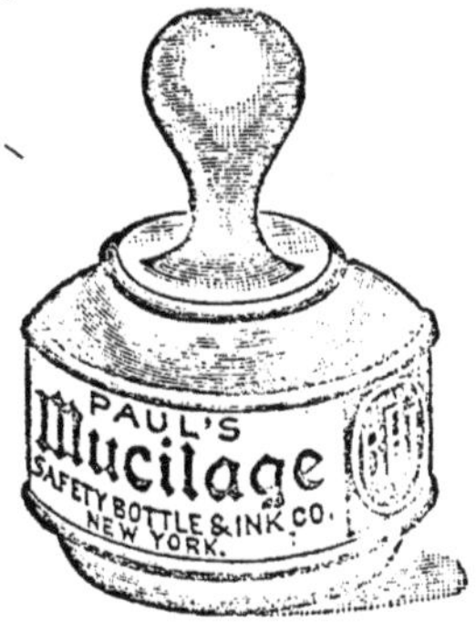
PAUL'S
Mucilage
SAFETY BOTTLE & INK CO.
NEW YORK.

ADDITIONS, CORRECTIONS, REMOVALS, ETC.

Alber John [Betty D], (Snyder & Alber), h1210 Broadway
Ayers Joseph [Harriet], lab, h 210 Heath
Baker Charles L [Lilley], carp, h 511 12th
Bower Wm A, wks Clover Leaf Dairy b same
Bricker H C & Co (Harry C Bricker, Walter F Wilson), fruits, confections, etc, 509 Broadway
Cahl Henry F [Laura], watchman Panhandle shops, h 811 Ottawa
Carmell Wm [Nettie], saloon, 411 Market h same
City National Bank, John Gray pres, Isaac N Crawford vice-pres, Frank R Fowler cashier, s w cor 4th and Broadway (*See adv back cover*)
Clark James, lab, b 602 Ottawa
Craig Joseph S [Minerva], notions 42S Broadway, h 816 North
Fowler Frank R [Cora F], cashier City National Bank, b The Barnett
Goodman Bros (Harry & Solomon), clothiers, 313 4th
Goodman Harry (Goodman Bros), h Philadelphia, Pa
Goodman Solomon (Goodman Bros), h Philadelphia, Pa
Hayes Ida J, lieut American Volunteers, b 315½ 3d
Henderson Wm S [Alice], saloon, 425 12th, h same
Hogan Rev Wm, asst rector St Vincent de Paul Catholic church, h s w cor 9th and Spencer
Hurd Leona, b 1614 Broadway
Hurd Otho P, student, b 1614 Broadway
Hurd Willard E [Fannie E], grain dealer, 114 5th, h 1614 Broadway
McDonald Rev James W, pastor Cumberland Presbyterian church, b 1001 Wilkinson
Murphy Maurice F [Minnie], capt American Volunteers, h 315½ 3d
Nordyke Lillian, student **Hall's Business College,** b 1514 High
Ray Bros (Lewis and Andrew), grocers, 402 Market
Reder Schuyler C [Clara], laundry, 504 12th, h s w cor 12th and Erie av
Stapleton John J, grocer, 431 Broadway
Uhl Dennis & Co (Dennis and C Harry Uhl), successors D & C H Uhl, cor Front and Melbourne av
Watts Wm H [Lillie Z], clk D N Watts, h 1206 Linden av
Western Introduction Co, novelty mnfrs, factory 407½ 4th, office 401 Broadway

LONGWELL & CUMMINGS'

LOGANSPORT CITY DIRECTORY.

1897-98.

ABBREVIATIONS.

agt	agent	mkr	maker	s	south
b	boards	mnfg	manufacturing	s e	southeast
bet	between	mnfr	manufacturer	s s	south side
bkkpr	bookkeeper	n	north	s w	southwest
bldg	building	n e	northeast	secy	secretary
blk	block	n s	north side	ship	shipping
carp	carpenter	n w	northwest	S T	Shultztown
clk	clerk	opp	opposite	stenogr	stenographer
condr	conductor	pk	park	supt	superintendent
cor	corner	P O	post office	tel opr	telegraph operator
del	delivery	pres	president	tmstr	teamster
dpty	deputy	prin	principal	tp	township
e	east	propr	proprietor	treas	treasurer
e s	east side	pub	publisher	w	west
h	house	r	rooms	w s	west side
insp	inspector	rd	road	Wab	Wabash
lab	laborer	rep	repairer	wks	works
Logan	Logansport	Rev	Reverend	wid	widow

Where numbers appear before the second street in the location place of business or residence, it has reference to the number of doors from the corner. Thus: s s Market, 2 w 3d, means south side of Market 2 doors west of 3d.

Where a woman's name appears after a man's, in brackets, it means she is the man's wife.

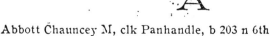

A

Abbott Chauncey M, clk Panhandle, b 203 n 6th
Abbott Frank H H, painter, b 406 Pleasant Hill
Abbott Mary E, [wid Abner], b 203 n 6th
Abbott Minnie B, b 203 n 6th
Abrams Wm B [Minnie], steam fitter Linton & Graf, b 416 2d
Ackerman A Marie [wid Thomas], b 2 Melbourne av
Adams Cornelius [Sophia M], clk, h 809 North
Adams Elmira [wid Robert] h n s Culbertson 2 w Frank (S T)
Adams Express Co, Herbert A Brown agt, 318 4th
Adams S Frances, clk sheriff's office, b 321 North
Adams George, fireman Panhandle, r 1069 Toledo
Adams Isiah A [Susanna], county sheriff, h 321 North
Adams T Jefferson [Emma], barber, h 429½ 5th
Adams Jessie, h 403 Canal
Adams John S, student, b 432 Sycamore
Adams Nellie A, teacher, b 809 North
Adams Robert W, lab, b n s Culbertson 2 w Frank (S T)
Adamsky Herman [Minnie], foreman, h 53 Washington
African Methodist Episcopal Church, Rev Louis Pettiford pastor, s e cor Market and Cicott

gr Panhandle, r 1224 Wright
\Margaret], grocer, 1201 Smead; saloon, 633 12th; h

Winifred], mach Panhandle, h 1205 Smead
:lk, F Wm Klein, b 4 Sycamore
D, domestic, 703 High
ir, h s s Wabash River rd, 4 e Coles
Rose] mach hd Panhandle, h 16 Helm
, mach hd Panhandle, b 16 Helm
b 16 Helm
ipper Julius Wagner, b 16 Helm
ressmkr, b r 12, 313½ 4th
), b 624 North
vid Jacob], h 518 Fitch
ty D], trav agt, h 1210 Broadway
ary C], carp, h 722 Michigan av
del clk, b 914 Lytle
Barbara], clk Wiler & Wise, h 923 Linden av
Ella] car rep, h 113 Ash
la], brakeman Panhandle, h 707 Ottawa
), domestic, 615 Market
a, domestic, 1215 Broadway
Rose], mach Panhandle, h 1724 Smead
d, clk Henry A. Stoll, b 1724 Smead
l [Mary], lab, h 1419 Indiana
seamstress, b 1724 Smead
, John B. Skinner, mgr, 321 Broadway
, lab, b 229 Osage
h 725 Broadway
w H [Eliza], cabinet mkr, h 1012 Spear
ina, domestic, 829 Market
d W [Elizabeth], condr Panhandle, h 1120 North
ce S, student, b 1120 North
ı L [Ellen A], (L A Alford & Son,) h 425 5th
l (Corrington L Alford), cigar mfrs, 425 5th
[innie B], janitor Panhandle sta, h 726 Miami
Anna], stone mason, h 188 w Wabash av
atchman, h 6 Melbourne av
r, b 1013 High
ry M] porter Wiler & Wise, h 123 Cicott
iiter, r 188 w Wabash av
ysician, 314½ 4th, b Johnston Hotel
, b 500 Melbourne av
na R] car insp Panhandle, h 500 Melbourne av
lbert A], b 2206 Broadway
tic, 1230 North
', peddler, h 123 Cicott

Ask the Clerk
at the Hotel for
the . . . . . .

Work Done in 5 Hours
WITHOUT EXTRA CHARGE.

☆ LAUNDRY LISTS.

GEO. OTT, Propr.

405 Market Street.

Allen Pink, student, b 188 w Wabash av
Allen Ross W, lab, b 500 Melbourne av
Allen Samuel, engr, b 603 12th
Allhands Wm, painter, b 220 Findley
Allison Blanche M, student, b 602 Helm
Allison Charles R, depot clk Adams Ex Co, b 602 Helm
Allison O Everett [Olive], brakeman, h 1427 North
Allison James D [Mary E] tel opr, h 602 Helm
Alspaugh Hattie S, b 314 Michigan av
Alspaugh James, carp, r 315½ 4th
Aman Anna, seamstress Insane hospital, b same
Aman Anthony J [Alice E], blksmith, h n w cor Clay and Montgomery
Aman Joseph A [Lusetta] carriage mfr, 101 Burlington av, h 219 Burlington av
American Express Co., Herbert A Brown, agt, 318 4th
Ammons Albert, harness mkr, Kreis Bros Mfg Co, b 102 9th
Ammons Claude, b 102 9th
Ammons Lillie, b 102 9th
Ammons Minnie E, b 102 9th
Ammons Pearl O, b 102 9th
Ammons Thomas W [Jennie], foreman Kreis Bros Mfg Co, h 102 9th
Amos Alpha, domestic, 406 High
Amos Walter R, clk Panhandle, b 730 North
Anderson Albert W [Mame T], barber, h 710 Miami
Anderson Alfred L [Jewel], propr The Corner Sample Room, s e cor 3rd and Broadway, h 322½ Broadway
Anderson David, lab, b 821 19th
Anderson Edward W [Johanna] clk Panhandle, h 1801 North
Anderson Ethel J, b 223 Findley
Anderson Frederick, blksmith, b 2227 High
Anderson Harry W, comp, b 1801 North
Anderson Harvey, clerk Panhandle, r 613½ Broadway
Anderson Hattie, domestic, 224 w Broadway
Anderson James, buggy-washer James O'Donnell, r 322½ Broadway
Anderson John A [Josephine], lab, h 821 19th
Anderson John D [Mary], real est agt, h e s Sycamore, 4 s Pleasant Hill
Anderson John D [Tina], h 200 Hanna
Anderson Joseph B [Elizabeth], (Anderson & Harrington), h 223 Findley
Anderson Josie E, student, b 223 Findley
Anderson E Laurence, del clk Campbell's Laundry, b 1801 North
Anderson T Le Roy [Louise] blksmith George Harrison, h 415 19th
Anderson Lulu, b 821 19th
Anderson Roland W [Elizabeth], blksmith, n w cor 18th and Stevens, h 2227 High

Go
97
L8
18
14

Anderson Samuel P [Kate], tel opr, Panhandle, h 128 Plum
Anderson Sarah J [wid David B], h 524 North
Anderson & Harrington (Joseph B. Anderson, Ormus L. Harring-
 ton), photographers, 421 5th., (See adv class photographers).
Andrew, Floyd W, student Hall's Business College, b 315 Coles
Anheier Arthur J [Dorothea], (Baker & Anheier), h 321 w Broadway
Anheier Jacob A [Mattie], barber, 418 3d, h 424 3d
Anheier John, brakeman Panhandle, b 1415 Indiana
Annis Eliza [wid Herbert], h 616 Sycamore
Annis George W, b 1418 High
Appel Alexander [Barbara], agt J O Cole's Peru Brewery, 1100
 Toledo, h same
Apple Wm M [Harriet], farmer, h e s Clifton, 1 n Stanley
Apt Jesse E [Sarah J], lab, h 1420 Water
Apt Samuel, b 418½ 3rd
Archer Mary A [wid Thomas W], b s w cor 22nd and Broadway
Armstrong Emma [wid John W], h 1914 Smead
Armstrong Lawrence M, tel opr, b 206 State
Armstrong Martha [wid Wm], b 1705 Spear
Armstrong Thomas E, clk Panhandle, r 1120 North
Armstrong Wm [Emma], sect foreman, h 206 State
Arnold Charles F. [Albertina], lab, h 211 Burlington av
Arnold Charles W, supt creamery, b 100 Bates
Arnold Harry, cabinet mkr b w s Standley, 1 s Biddle (S T)
Arnold Mary, b 211 Burlington av
Arnold Mary [wid Wm] b 211 Burlington av
Arrick John E [Rellie], brakeman, h 415 2d
Arthur Abraham [Mary], lab, h 1613 Douglass
Arthur David C [Ella J], prin high school, h 816 North
Arthur Elizabeth [wid Wm], h 1430 Market
Arthur Jennie E, b 1119 Toledo
Arthur John, lineman W U Tel Co, b 611 North
Arthurhults Anna, domestic, b 2 Spring
Artis Eva A, domestic, 729 Market
Artrip Benjamin, lab, b s s Wabash River rd, 7 w 18th
Ash George [Matilda], (Ash & Hadley), h 524 w Broadway
Ash & Hadley (George Ash, Joshua C Hadley), furniture, 425-427
 Market, also props Logansport Furniture Co, 303-307 Linden av
Ashby John M [E Alice], teacher, h 735 Spencer
Ashworth Thomas [Laura J], porter, h 25 Elm
Asire George, student, b 1331 North
Asire George H [Alice], steam fitter A W Stevens, h 1331 North
Asmus Gustave [Wilhelmina], blksmth, h 828 Linden av
Asmus Gustave F, tailor H G Tucker, b 828 Linden av
Atha Wm H, sec'y Michael's Business College, b 700 Bringhurst
Atkinson Tiburtius M [Mary E], clk, h 723 Wilkinson
Atlee Elizabeth [wid Edward], boarding, 418½ 3d

Go
97
L8
18
14

H. J. CRISMOND, 312 Market Street,
Gasoline Stoves, Screen Doors and Windows.

| ATZ | 55 | BAI |

Atzner Caroline, domestic, 228 w Broadway
Aughe June, b 1620 Broadway
Aughe Wm D [Catharine M], h 1620 Broadway
Aughinbaugh George C [Catharine], candymkr T M Quigley & Co, 1808 Broadway
Aults Hattie, domestic, 1400 North
Austin Joseph C [Hallie J], bkkpr, h 306 Helm
Austin Thomas [Mary], gen'l foreman Panhandle shops, h 1606 High
Austin Thomas, jr [Mary], mach Panhandle, h 1708 Knowlton
Ayers George W [Jennie], engr Panhandle, h 1614 Market
Ayers James J [Amanda A], engr city water works, h 803 Race
Ayres James Wm, lab, b 803 Race
Ayres John M [Nellie], switchman Panhandle, h 724 Race
Ayres Mary E, b 803 Race
Ayres Richard [Charity], lab, h 706 e Wabash av

B

Baade John, teamster Ash & Hadley, b 308 Linden av
Babb Catharine [wid Wm], h 117 5th
Bachrach Belle, student **Hall's Business College,** b 525 Market
Bacon Isaac T [Pauline], condr Panhandle, h 1829 Spear
Bacon Willard, carp, b 1829 Spear
Baer (*see also Baire*)
Baer Albert [Emma], lab, h w s Michigan av, 2 w John
Baer Asa F, student **Hall's Business College,** b 223 Montgomery
Baer Benjamin, lab, h 223 Montgomery
Baer Bessie, b 223 Montgomery
Baer Isaac, clk Wiler & Wise, b 610 Market
Baer John W, b 422 9th
Baggs Carrie, stenogr George Harrison, b 715 North
Bailey Alvin, porter Hotel Johnston, b same
Bailey Anna, domestic, 1006 Broadway
Bailey Asa, mason, b 1504 Water
Bailey John [Lydia], plasterer, h e s Washington, 2 s Lincoln (S T)
Bailey Lulu M, b 824 12th
Bailey Mary E, domestic, 808 North
Bailey Monroe, w end Bates (Dunkirk)
Bailey Ranaldo A, chiropodist, 414 North, r same
Bailey Wm L [Prudence], plasterer, h n s Shultz, 1 w Kloenne (S T)
Baird John K [May], fireman, h 1803 Spear
Baire (*see also Baer*)
Baire J Edward, lab, b e s Creek, 2 n John
Baire John [Almeda], lab, h e s Creek, 2 n John

aire Minnie, student, b e s Creek, 2 n John
!aker Amelia [wid Henry], h 507 w Broadway
!aker Arthur N [Lillie L], optician, 310 4th, h 622 North
!aker Bessie A, student, b 613 Pratt
!aker Catharine, b 1600 High
!aker Charles, tinner, b 1621 Smead
!aker Charles A [Nora], fireman, h 1312 Smead
!aker Charles D, brakeman Panhandle, b 1243 Toledo
!aker Charles E, paper-hanger, Logansport Wall Paper Co, b 127 Cicott
!aker Charles L [Lillie], carp, h 111 Melbourne av
!aker Clarence L, bkkpr J J Hildebrandt, b 613 Pratt
!aker Edward P [Elizabeth], carp Panhandle, h 2014 Smead
!aker's European Hotel, Baker & Anheier, proprs, 318–320 Canal
!aker Frank W, bartender, r 116 6th
!aker Frederick, b 1600 High
!aker George H [Katie E], mason, h 401 w Market
!aker George N [Lida A], clk, h 127 Cicott
aker George W, h s s Logan & Western rd, 2 w Burlington av
aker Gertrude B, b 1528 Toledo
aker Harvey E, boilermaker, 1243 Toledo
aker Henry P [Josephine M], clk J T Flanegin, h 507 w Broadway
aker Ira J [Eliza A], rectal and rupture specialist, 415½ Broadway, h 613 Pratt   (See adv front cover)
aker Isaac, b 720 e Wabash av
aker Jacob, carp, b s s Logan & Western rd, 2 w Burlington av
aker Jacob W [Sarah], carp, h 1243 Toledo
aker Jesse W [Minerva A], painter, 820 Sycamore, h same
aker John, b 2014 Smead
aker John, brakeman Panhandle, r 1 State Nat'l Bank Bldg
aker John [Catherine] h 1621 Smead
aker John M [Amanda C], (Baker & Anheier), h 108 Canal
aker John S [Helen M], tmstr, h 127 Cicott
ker John W, engr Panhandle, r 417½ Market
ker Joseph [Cora], lab, h w s Washington, 1 s Biddle (S T)
ker Katie M, student, b 127 Cicott
ker, Lena, b 1600 High
ker Peter, h 219 3d
ıker Theresa [wid John], ice, 1600 High, h same
ıker Wm A, engr, b 324 3d
ıker Wm E [Mary E], tinner, J T Flanegin, h 531 Helm
ıker Wm H, mach, b 1621 Smead
ıker & Anheier (John M Baker, Arthur J Anheier), proprs Baker's European Hotel, 318–320 Canal
ldwin Daniel P [India], capitalist, 15-16 Baldwin-Thornton Bldg, h n e cor 7th and Market
ldwin Deborah [wid Sidney] h 318 First

HERZ, The Tailor
409 MARKET STREET.

Our Reputation for Good Work AND Artistic Styles Is Well Established.

BAL · 57 BAR

Baldwin Jennie S, bkkpr, b 318 First
Baldwin Lizzie [wid Charles L], dressmkr, 117 Melbourne av, h same
Baldwin Minnie, laundress, b 219 13th
Baldwin Wm, h n s Wash tp rd, 2 w Sherman
Balinger John [Sarah], lab, h 718 12th
Ball Albert A [Nellie], electric light trimmer, h 1102 Toledo
Ball Angeline, domestic, 1426 High
Ball Angeline M, student, b 911 Race
Ball Anna E [wid Robert M], h 911 Race
Ball Ferdinand [Mary] h 1531 Spear
Ball Margaret, domestic, s w cor 22d and Broadway
Ball Mary [wid John], h n e cor 17th and Stevens
Ball Wm, mach b n e cor 17th and Stevens
Ball J Wm, pressman, Longwell & Cummings, b 911 Race
Ballard John W [Ellen M], physician, 400½ Market, h 100 Market
Ballard Milroy, student, b 100 Market
Baller John C [Eva], bartender, h 120 Pawnee
Ballinger John [Sadie], lab, 718 12th
Ballou (see also Beaullieu)
Ballou Emma, b 1828 Spear
Ballou Frank M [Catharine], lab, h 1816 Broadway
Ballou C Foney, del clk, b 515 Fitch
Ballou Hattie, clk, b 1816 Broadway
Ballou John M [Martha] car rep Panhandle, h 515 Fitch
Ballou Joseph, truckman Wabash, b 1828 Spear
Ballou Ozro Wm, mach Panhandle, b 515 Fitch
Ballou Sarah [wid Robert], h 1828 Spear
Baltzell Andrew J [Margaret], engr electric light wks, h 1314 George
Baltzell Joseph, lab, b 306 Pratt
Baltzell Noah [Emma], lab, h 306 Pratt
Banes George L, lab, r 207½ 6th
Banks Anna [wid Joseph], b 126 Helm
Banta Henry J [Margaret], physician, 131 Wheatland, h same
Banta John [Eliza A], farmer, h 125 Wheatland
Banta Vefaffa, student, b 131 Wheatland
Bantz Louis M [Margaret], brakeman Panhandle, h 6 Cicott
Bantz Walter, brakeman Panhandle, r 9 State National Bank Bldg
Barcus Richard H [Emma], h 1620 North
Barker Ephraim E, b 126 Wheatland
Barker Grace A, b 1122 High
Barker Iva L, dressmkr, b 419 Helm
Barker Joseph [Fannie], mach Panhandle, h 1122 High
Barker Milo E [S Ella], mail mess p o, h 2 Spring
Barker Susan N, domestic, 136 Eel River av
Barnard Frances E, b 1422 High
Barnard Moses [Sarah], junk, n w cor 6th and High, h 117 9th

Barnard Robert C, civil engr Panhandle, r 314 North

Barnes Alfred H, student, b 1016 Linden av

Barnes Benjamin, mason, b 228 Front

Barnes Charles, carp, b 324 Sycamore

Barnes Charles H, mason, b 228 Front

Barnes Charles R [Emma], trav agt J C Bridge, b 521 High

Barnes Charles W, stone mason, b 1016 Linden ave

Barnes W Curry, mason, b 228 Front

Barnes Elizabeth [wid Thomas] h 217 Wheatland

Barnes Emma, b 225 w Market

Barnes George [Mary L], cement contractor, 219 Plumb, h same (See adv class cement contrs)

Barnes George W, b 228 Front

Barnes Grace, ironer, Insane Hospital, b same

Barnes Harry A [Lavinia], mason, 1016 Linden av, h same

Barnes James I, mason, b 228 Front

Barnes John E [Elizabeth J], contractor, 228 Front, h same

Barnes John H mason, b 225 w Market

Barnes John W [Emma], (Louthain & Barnes), h 506 10th

Barnes Joseph, b 219 Plum

Barnes Sarah [wid John], h 225 w Market

Barnes Walter E, student, b 219 Plum

Barnett Amelia K, student Hall's Business College, b 527 Broadway

Barnett Atwater C [Johanna], saloon, 309 Broadway, h 306 North

Barnett Benjamin F [Anna L], agr impls, 507 Broadway, h 1422 High

Barnett Clarence H, student Hall's Business College, b 123 7th

Barnett George E [Roxie E], city treas, h 74 Michigan av

Barnett Marie, 1506 Broadway

Barnett News and Cigar Stand, Walsh & Tyner, proprs, n e cor 2d and Market

Barnett Susan M, boarding, 527 Broadway

Barnett The, Emil F Keller, mgr, n e cor 2d and Market

Barney Simeon J [Hattie], boilermkr Panhandle, h 1412 Wright

Barnfield John H [Mae S], physician and surgeon, 311½ 4th, h 918 Broadway

Barnhart Harriett [wid John], b 119 Broadway

Barnhart Henry P, student, b 119 Broadway

Barnhart John H [Caroline], (John Barnhart & Son), h 119 Broadway

Barnhart John McC, student, b 119 Broadway

Barnhart John & Son, (John H Barnhart), stoves, 422 Broadway

Barr Alexander E [Rachel A], carp, h 212 Bates

Barnett Rose [wid Edward], b s w cor Clay and Humphrey

Barrett Thomas [Dora], lab, h 718 Ottawa

Barron Burgess, helper A W Stevens, b 429 5th

Barron Dyer B, plumber, b 429 5th

Barron Elizabeth L, b 416 Montgomery

Barron George B, bkkpr A W Stevens, b 804 Race

G(
9'
L&
1!
1·

Barron Jacob M, carpet weaver, 429 5th, h same
Barron Jesse M, plumber, b 429 5th
Barron John C, mach, b 206 6th
Barron Lucian B, mach hd, b 324 3d
Barron Mary J [wid Napoleon B], h 804 Race
Barron Nettie, b 804 Race
Barry (see also Berry)
Barry James, lab, h 1902 Spear
Barry Katharine, b 1113 Toledo
Barry Margaret, dressmkr, 1113 Toledo, h same
Barry Patrick, lab, h 1113 Toledo
Barschab Clara, b 207 Colfax
Barschab John, butcher, b 719 Ottawa
Barschab Martin Wm [Rosa], car rep Panhandle, b 719 Ottawa
Bartlett Wm W [Lulu], engr, h 2111 Broadway
Barton Albert, finisher, b 1302 Spear
Barton Dora, domestic, 730 North
Basket Jacob, lab, h 418 w Market
Bassler Anna, student, b 2116 Market
Batchelor Jay, student, b 1503 Spear
Bates Peter, agent, r 207½ 6th
Bates Samuel E, harnessmkr Kreis Bros Mfg Co, b n e cor Canal and
     Oak
Bates Uriah K [Jemima], tmstr, h e s Burlington rd, 4s Wash tp rd
Bates Willard A, lab, b e s Burlington rd, 4 s Wash tp rd
Batzell Andrew J [Louise], engr, h 1314 George
Bauer (see also Bower)
Bauer Albert [Daisy], painter, h 61 Bates
Bauer Andrew A, del clk, b 914 Lytle
Bauer Anton A, section hd, b 914 Lytle
Bauer Carl [Catharine], cellerman Columbia Brew Co, h 204 n Pearl
Bauer Clara, b 603 Melbourne av
Bauer David J lab, b 2010 George
Bauer Felix B [Barbara], lab, h 618 Helm
Bauer Frank [Carrie], baker, 10 Front, h same
Bauer Jacob [Ann], section hd, h 914 Lytle
Bauer John J [A Mary], wine, beer, liquors and cigars, 223 4th, h
     603 Melbourne av
Bauer Lena J, b 603 Melbourne av
Bauer Lucetta [wid George], h 2010 George
Bauer Lucy, clk, b 2010 George
Bauer Mary, clk Wiler & Wise, b 603 Melbourne av
Bauer Michael [Louise T], baker, h 127 Woodland
Bauer Minnie F, domestic, 510 Melbourne av
Bauer Nicholas A, bartender J J Bauer, b 603 Melbourne av
Bauer Susanna [wid Felix] h 603 Melbourne av
Bauer Valentine [Catharine] bartender John Eckert, h 410 Grove

)lished 1867.   Still in the Lead.

DRY GOODS, CLOAKS, FURS,
l1 Broadway.   WILER & WISE,   306 Fourth Street.

60   BEA

hman Frank E, wood wkr I N Cool, h Morgan Hill rd, 2½ m
  e city
1ann (*see also Bowman and Baughman*)
1ann Alois [Catharine], mach hd Panhandle, h 814 20th
1ann Charles J, blksmith, b 1309 George
1ann Frederick H [Dora], mach hd, h 1725 Smead
1ann, John [Christiana], cellerman R Kreuzberger, h 230 Montgomery
1ann Louis [Margaret], h 1309 George
Anthony, bartender, b 701 Melbourne av
1 Josiah [Matilda], watchman Panhandle, h 1523 North
1 Mary, dressmkr, 1523 North, b same
er Abraham G, student **Hall's Business College**, b 324 Sycamore
h Charles H [Dora], agt, h 1220 Smead
h Dora, dressmkr, 1220 Smead, h same
h Martin J [Mary], trav agt, h 1521 Broadway
hler Jesse, lab Stevens Bros, b 427½ 5th
hler Margaret, wks Campbell's laundry, h 427½ 5th
(*see also Beale, Beall and Beel*)
George, brakeman Panhandle, r 111 4th
Joseph A, engr Panhandle, r 414 First
e Jason W, student, b 123 7th
e Katherine E, clk G W Seybold & Bros, b 511 w Market
e, Thomas L [Belle], h 123 7th
l Albert A, newsdealer, 510½ Broadway, b 1408 Ohio
l Dora M, student, b 1408 Ohio
l Edward A [Rose F], newsdealer, h 1408 Ohio
l E Munson, tinner, b 1408 Ohio
1 Charles F [Aurelia], engr Panhandle, h 1917 North
1 Charles J, boilermaker Panhandle, b 1919 North
1 Frank J, teamster, b w s Water, 1 e Holland
1 Frank P [Mary A], mach, h n s Water, 1 e Holland
1 Genevieve M, bkkpr, b n s Water, 1 e Holland
1 Mame, b n s Water, 1 e Holland
1 May E, milliner, b 1917 North
1er, Andrew M, candy mkr Bridge City Candy Co, b 410 w Market
1er Charles, teamster, b 410 w Market
1er Edward J, driver Indianapolis Brewing Co, b 410 w Market
1er Frank [Minnie], h 320½ Broadway
1er Jacob H [Adda], mach hd, h 15 Columbia
1er John [Mary], carp Panhandle, h 410 w Market
1er Wm, teamster, b 410 w Market
  Louis B, drugs, 409 12th, r same
Charles, carp Philip Voorhees, b 434 Sycamore
1 Mary [wid Lowry], h 514 Linden av
ey Emma, domestic, s s Wash tp rd, 2 w Burlington rd
ie John H, mach Panhandle, b 603 12th

DeWitt C [Ella T], commission merchant, 417 5th, h 10 Osage
Emma S, dressmkr, 1314 Linden av, h same
John C [Jessie M], house and sign painter, paper hanger
  decorator, 628 Linden av, h same (See adv class painters)
John H, brakeman panhandle, r 417½ Market
Wm H, grocer, e s Heath, 1 n Wheatland, h 1314 Linden av
u Ida B [wid Silvio H], real estate, 1902 North, h same
Hattie M, stripper John Mulcahy, b e s Horney, 2 n Franklin
Henry S [Florence D], lab, h w s Liberty, 1 n Water
Orra H, lab, h e s Horney, 2 n Franklin
Frank W [Cora M], brakeman, h 107 Melbourne av
ee also Beebe).
laude R, insp C U Tel Co, b 113 4th
Ida F [wid George L], real estate, 113 4th, h same
Melnotte N [Alta M] asst city engr, h 23 Bates
Philander [Sarah J], lab, h 312 Eel River av
Alois [Helena S], eng insp Panhandle, h 1806 Knowlton
lam [Margaret A], mill wright, h 329 Cummings
arles A, tmstr, b s e cor 21st and Wright
Frank, del clk, Wm J. Parker, b 329 Cummings
orge [Viola], lab, h 500 Chicago
arry J, student, b 329 Cummings
argaret [wid Wm], b 700 21st
aude, student, b 329 Cummings
orman A [Ella], broker, h 1508 High
alter, student, b s e cor 21st and Wright
m W [Margaret], comp, h s e cor 21st and Wright
Carl F, harnessmkr Kreis Bros Mfg Co, b 1307 Wright
Charles J, clk Logansport Wall Paper Co, b 100 Canal
Harmon V [Johnson, Becker & Co], h Clyde O
Henry S [Mary M], carp, h 1307 Wright
Margaret [wid John], b 620 12th
Mary, b 100 Canal
Mary [wid Martin], laundress, h 122 Pratt
Nellie M, b 100 Canal
Otto M, student, b 1307 Wright
Theophilus M [Mary E], drayman, h 411 Melbourne av
Alice, student, r 112 Market
h Stanley C, engr Panhandle, b 1921 Broadway
ee also Beebe)
drian [Rose], plasterer, h 202 Burlington av
harles A [Anna], lawyer, h 1318 Smead
Dry Goods Store, Wiler & Wise, props, 409-411 Broadway
  306 4th (See adv left top lines)
e Beal, Beale and Beall)
nes A, lab, b 817 17th
an D [Catharine], h 817 17th

G
9

eel John H [Mary E], car rep, Panhandle, h 1618 Smead
eel Wm V [Effie], clk, h 306 Montgomery
eeler Samuel S [Missouri], hostler E F Stewart, h 600½ Broadway
eeson Ella, waiter, b 5½ Sycamore
eezley Elmer E [Alice D], crater I N Cool, h 414 16th
ehmer Joseph [Dorothea], harnessmkr, h 901 Linden av
ehmer Lennie, b 901 Linden av
ehmer Walter J, (Twells & Behmer), b 901 Linden av
ehmer Wilma, student, b 901 Linden av
ehrens Frederick, h 524 Linden av
ehrens Mary, stenogr, b 524 Linden av
ell Alfred [Harriet], lab, h s s Wash tp rd, 4 w Burlington rd
ell Anna E, teacher, b 1516 High
ell Charles [Emma J], brakeman Panhandle, h 414½ 4th
ell Charles T [Emma R], h 22 Claude
ell Daisy, teacher Free Kindergarten, b 919 Spear
ell Elisha V [Martha A], carp, h 1518 High
ell George, student, b 1210 Spear
ell Jessie A, student, b 1518 High
ell Jethro, clk, b 1210 Spear
ell John [Emma], section hand, h 203 w Wabash ave
ell Joseph, agt, r 407½ Market
ell Mahlon [Martha J], lumber, h 919 Spear
ell Mark I [Sarah], cigarmkr Julius Wagner, h 23 Pleasant Grove
ell Nancy E, student, b 22 Claude
ell Wm H [Elmira], h 1516 High
ell Wm H [Lydia A], physician and surgeon, 313 Pearl, h 1220
    Market
ell Wm H W [Nancy E], flour and feed, 415 12th, h 1210 Spear
ender Alvis, lab, b cor 21st and Usher
ender Anthony, lab, b 1425 George
ender Bernard, lab, b 1425 George
ender David S [Helen A], railway mail clk, h 702 Vine
ender Egidius [Caroline], lab, h 1425 George
ender Frances, domestic, 1210 Broadway
ender John [Louise], eng insp Panhandle, h 1710 Knowlton
ender Martha [wid Andrew], b s w cor Anthony and Bartlett (S T)
ender Mary, b 1425 George
ender Wm, painter, b s w cor Anthony and Bartlett (S T)
enefield Bertha, b 217 13th
enefield John L [Bertha], granite polisher Schuyler Powell, h s s
    Wab River rd, 1 w 18th
enefield Martha [wid John W], b 217 13th
enica Catharine, teacher, b 1625 High
enica Dorothy, teacher, b 1625 High
enica Louis C, candymkr, b 1625 High
enica Henry H, lumber buyer, h 1625 High

G
9
L

Benjamin Addie [wid B Ennis], b 2227 High
Benjamin Frank, student, b 501 Melbourne av
Benner George W [Sarah A], tmstr, h 219 Melbourne av
Benner Harley, student **Hall's Business College**, b Kokomo rd, 3 m s city
Benner James [Jennie], timber buyer, h 229 Main
Benner John [Lulu], timber buyer, h 411 Humphrey
Benner, John W, clk, b 219 Melbourne av
Bennett Arthur, b 730 Miami
Bennett Charles E, tmstr h 730 Miami
Bennett Edgar J, tailor H G Tucker, r 630 North
Bennett Frederick [Louise M], lab, 12 Uhl
Bennett George H [Lydia J], lab, b 12 Uhl
Bennett George W [Catharine C], saw mill, 1308 Toledo, h 623 12th
Bennett Lottie [wid Isaac], h 730 Miami
Bennett Minnie E, b 730 Miami
Bennett Noah [Minnie], lab, h 1706 Knowlton
Bennett D Roland, elevator man G W Seybold & Bros, b w s Clifton av, 3 n city limits
Bennett Rosa A, b w s Holland 1 n Pink
Bennett Wm F [Susan E], blksmith, h 1234 High
Benning Christopher [Elizabeth], hostler Columbia Brew Co, h n s Culbertson, 3 w Anthony (S T)
Benning Julius, condr Panhandle, b 211 Burlington av
Benning Mary [wid Christian], b 211 Burlington av
Benton Allen G [Mary], ins agt, h 19 McCarty
Benson John [May], contractor, carpenter and builder, 2200 Broadway, h same
Benson John A, b 2123 High
Berg Carl H, clk, b 516 e Wabash av
Berg Christian F [Lena], blksmth Panhandle, h 515 e Wabash av
Berg Christopher [Louise], blksmith Panhandle, h 430 e Wabash av
Berg J Henry [Christina], lab, h 109 Colfax
Berghager Louis, cigarmkr John Mulcahy, b 114 7th
Bergin Josephine, attendant Insane Hospital, b same
Bergin Winifred, laundress Insane Hospital, b same
Bergmann, (*see also Burgman*)
Bergmann Carl, student, b 529 Sycamore
Bergmann Emma L, b 116 Front
Bergmann Frank J, cigarmkr Julius Wagner, b 125 Front
Bergmann Henry F [Caroline L], tel opr Panhandle, h 228 w Broadway
Bergmann Mary wid Frank, h 125 Front
Bergmann Mary G, cashier G W Seybold & Bros, b 125 Front
Bergmann Wm F [Geneta], clk, h 116 Front
Berndt Albert, b 629 17th
Berndt Frank, lab, b n s Charles, 3 w Standley (S T)
Berndt Frank J [Catherine], cigarmkr Julius Wagner, h 315 15th

G
9
L

Berndt Herman [Mary], mach Panhandle, h 1812 Smead
Berndt Rudolph [Caroline], foreman Panhandle, h 629 17th
Berndt Rudolph H, boilermkr, b 629 17th
Bernfield Wm J, clk Schmitt & Heinly, b 1127 Market
Bernheisle Maude, attendant Insane Hospital, b same
Beroth Carrie, b 824 12th
Beroth Frank O [Emma], clk Panhandle, h 1619 North
Beroth George D, clk Aaron Greensfelder, b 824 12th
Beroth, Harriet I, bindery girl, b 824 12th
Beroth Jacob J [Theresa], blksmth, h 824 12th
Berry (see also Barry)
Berry Charles W, mach hd Panhandle, b 314 Linden av
Berry Corey L [Lizzie], condr Panhandle, h 805 North
Berry Graham N [Ella W], teacher, h 2331 Broadway
Berry John, fireman Panhandle, b 805 North
Berry Martha T wid Henry, h 314 Linden av
Berry Murillo, carp, b 828 Sycamore
Berry Percy, student, b 828 Sycamore
Berry Samuel H, shoemkr, 331 Sycamore, b 3 Columbia
Berry Wm A, mach hd Panhandle, b 314 Linden av
Berry Wils [Emma], artist, 828 Sycamore, h same
Berryman Horace C [Mary H], brakeman. h 521 Melbourne av
Berryman Bertha W, student, 801 Melbourne av
Berryman Jerome [Sarah E], truckman, h 801 Melbourne av
Berwanger Bros & Co (Louis and Henry Berwanger and Joseph
     Frankenthal), proprs The Hub Clothing Co, 313 4th
Berwanger Henry (Berwanger Bros & Co), r 403 High
Berwanger Joseph L, student, b 210 8th
Berwanger Louis [Hanna], (Berwanger Bros & Co), h 210 8th
Beshoar James [Lucy A], fresh and salt meats, fish and poultry,
     204 w Market, h 509 Wilkinson
Best John B, secy and treas Hall's Business College, h Chase. Ind
Best Wm, fireman Panhandle, r 415½ 3d
Bettcher Clara E, student, b 2000 Spear
Bettcher Frederick [Mary], coppersmith Panhandle, h 2116 Spear
Bettcher Martin [Mary], gardener, h 2000 Spear
Bethage Wm, fireman, b 426 12th
Bethke Henry, cook Insane Hospital, b same
Bethke Elizabeth [wid Henry], h 522 w Market
Bevan Carrie D, books, 406 Broadway, b 901 Spear
Bevan Charles W, clk, b 423 North
Bevan Earl U, plumber, b 423 North
Bevan Ethel H, student, b 423 North
Bevan Glenora J, b 901 Spear
Bevan Malvina H [wid George], h 901 Spear
Bevan May B, b 423 North
Bevan Wm H, feed yard, 508 North, h 423 North

G
9
L
l

Bevan Winifred L, teacher, b 901 Spear
Beyer (see also Bryer and Byers)
Beyer Jacob A, clk G W Seybold & Bros, b 1430 Usher
Beyer Theodore [Madaline], lab, h 1430 Usher
Bible Wm E [Hettie], (Glassbrenner & Bible), h 322½ Pearl
Biddle Anna M M, h 109 Market
Biddle Frank E [Ora], brakeman, h 616 Chicago
Biddle Horace P, lawyer, h 1 Biddle av
Bieg Louis J [Ella], grocer, 1830 Broadway, h 1801 Broadway
Bigger Martha A, h 222 Findley
Biggs John [Emma], tmstr, h 15 McCarty
Biggs Wm, b 15 McCarty
Biggs Wm E, lab, b 54 Washington
Bigley Louis H [H Jennie], clk, h 416 Helm
Billman Charles D [Marie E], trav sales Schuyler Powell, h 118
    Washington
Bimesdarfer J Braiden [Jennie], porter, h 117 Melbourne av
Bimesdarfer Elizabeth [wid John], h 1826 Market
Bimesdarfer Sadie, domestic, b 1826 Market
Bingaman Abraham, lab, h w s Berkley, 1 s Spencer
Bingaman Jacob J [Elisa], h 310 ½ Market
Bingaman John, lab, h w s Berkley, 1 s Spencer
Binney Eva [wid George W], carpet weaver, 10 Columbia, h same
Binney B Frank [Sarah], confectioner, 121 6th, h same
Binney Harry, lab, b 509 14th
Binney Levi [Elizabeth], constable, h 509 14th
Birch Margaret, domestic, 111 11th
Birkenruth Carrie, stenogr, b 718 Broadway
Birkenruth Isaac, hostler I N Cash, b 718 Broadway
Birkenruth Jennie, student, b 718 Broadway
Birkenruth Sarah, b 718 Broadway
Birkenruth Simon [Mollie], h 718 Broadway
Birkenruth Solomon, clk Sol H Cohn, b 718 Broadway
Bischoff Emma A, dressmkr, 809 Race, h same
Bischoff Jacob R [Emma A], comp, h 809 Race
Bischoff Wm H [Eva I], comp, h 809 Race
Biscomb Samuel [Mary M], foreman, h 208 Washington
Biscomb Walter, bookbinder, b 208 Washington
Bishop Willis M [Virgie], b 527 Miami
Bismarck Magnolia [wid G Frederick], b 409 North
Bizzell J Edward [Cora], barber H B Turner's, h 51 Bates
Black Harry E, mach hd Panhandle, b 211 Montgomery
Black Jacob F [Amanda C], h 211 Montgomery
Black John, cook Island View Hotel, b same
Black John A, blksmth, b 211 Montgomery
Black Joseph F, tinner C A Eberlein, b 211 Montgomery
Black Mary [wid James], h 1615 High

G
9
L
1

186,000,000 of Life Insurance

WAS WRITTEN BY THE

:TROPOLITAN LIFE, of New York, in 1896

W. O. WASHBURN,
Superintendent
Logansport District,

Crawford Block.

,A 66 BOA

ick Nollie, b 1615 High

ick Oliver H [Dorothy E], carp, h 12 Balsom

ickburn Henry, agt, b 418½ 3d

icketor Norman, cook, b 79 Washington

icketor Wm, b 1317 Wright

ackford John W [Emma], electrician, 314 Pearl, h s w cor Findley and Cummings

ackstone Harry B [Bertha], trav agt, h 1208 North

ake George C [Rose], fireman Vandalia, h 115 Sycamore

ake James [Kate], h 1306 Indiana

aker Harvey Alice, carp, h s s Pleasant Hill, 1 e Sycamore

aker Lydia, student, b s s Pleasant Hill, 1 e Sycamore

akeslee, Wm, student **Hall's Business College,** b Kokomo rd, 2½ m s city

anchard Charles [Henrietta], editor, h 206 Michigan av

anche Gertrude, b 1243 Toledo

ankenship Alice F, h 928 Toledo

aser Edward J, clk Wiler & Wise, b 1424 Usher

aser Emma, student, b 1424 Usher

aser Jacob [Rosa], painter, h 1424 Usher

aser Rosa, dressmkr, b 1424 Usher

asingham Frank N Emma, trav agt, h 1419 High

asingham Gertrude, stenogr and notary Nelson & Myers, b 1419 High

asingham John [Isabelle], lumber mnfr, h 2012 Broadway

asingham Maud, student, b 1419 High

asingham Mary, b 2012 Broadway

asingham Otto, civ engr, b 1419 High

asingham Susan, student, b 1419 High

·ick Frederick Rosa, coppersmith, h 1113 20th

·ick Julius H, lab, b 1113 20th

gh (*see also Blygh*)

gh Agnes, bkkpr N J Bligh, b 309½ Market

gh Catharine [wid Bernard], h 1428 Smead

gh Martin J [Catharine A], wholesale and retail wines and liquors, 408 3d and 305 Market, h 309½ Market

ss Edward B, yd clk Vandalia, b 303 Sycamore

ss June, b 916 Market

dget Allen, lab, b 1300 e Wabash av

menthaler Bertha, student, b 315 Sycamore

menthaler Caroline [wid Frederick], boarding, 315 Sycamore

menthaler Louis [Mary], foreman Jas O'Donnell, h 322 Linden av

gh (*see also Bligh*)

gh Edward [Florence L], carp, h 90 Washington

ird of Metropolitan Police Commissioners, Dyer B McConnell, pres, Theodore R Sewell, John J Sheerin, Thomas Norris, secy, city bldg

We use Steam—others work by hand. By doing so we can do you Better Work and Save you Money. TRY US. ♨ ♨ ♨ ♨

Schuyler Powell
1031-1035 Toledo St.

BOD 67 BOP

Blumenthaler Helen, clk Wiler & Wise, b 315 Sycamore

Bodle Lewis [Catharine], lab, h s s Wab River rd, 2 w 18th

Boeckelman Catharine A, wks Campbell's laundry, b s s Howard, 3 w Frank (S T)

Boeckelman Frederick F [Sophia], mason, h s s Howard, 3 w Frank (S T)

Boeckelman Frederick H, mason, b s s Howard, 3 w Frank (S T)

Boerger (*see also Burger*)

Boerger Bros (Wm H and George W), grocers, 419 Broadway

Boerger Charles H, miller D & C H Uhl, b 203 Helm

Boerger Frederick [Minnie], wagonmkr, s s Burlington and Western pike, 1 w Burlington av, h 300 Helm

Boerger George W (Boerger Bros), b 203 Helm

Boerger John S [Carrie L], wagonmkr, h 319 Helm

Boerger Margaret [wid Frederick], h 203 Helm

Boerger Minnie, b 203 Helm

Boerger Wm H [Mary], (Boerger Bros), h 125 w Market

Boggs Curtis, fireman Panhandle, r 1069 Toledo

Bogue Owen [Mary E], porter M J Bligh, h 305½ Market

Bolen George W [Rosa B], lab, h e s Sherman, 2 s Biddle (S T)

Bolen Lilly M, student, b e s Sherman, 2 s Biddle (S T)

Bolley Bernard [Hulda], mach h n w cor Anthony and Shultz (S T)

Bolley Catharine [wid John], h n w cor Anthony and Culbertson (S T)

Bolley John, b n w cor Anthony and Culbertson (S T)

Bolt James S [Elizabeth], carp, h 418 Montgomery

Botlon Elizabeth, b e s Burlington rd, 10 s Wash tp rd

Bolton John [Jennie], butcher, h 207 Colfax

Bond Luther L, fireman Panhandle, r 1412 Wright

Bond Thomas C, student, b 730 Broadway

Boner Charles, head painter Insane Hospital, b same

Booker Callie E [wid Claiborne], dressmkr, 309½ 4th, h same

Booker Joseph, third cook The Barnett, b 522 Linden av

Boone Charles, waiter, r 306½ Market

Boost Charles O [Susan], car rep Panhandle, h 621 17th

Booth Alice E, music teacher, 1107 Broadway, b same

Booth Burrell W [Elizabeth], merch tailor, 313½ 4th, h 1107 Broadway

Booth Edwin B, fireman Vandalia, b 1107 Broadway

Booth Elijah P [Louise], farmer, h s e cor Columbia and Chicago

Booth Jasper N [Martha M], trav agt, h 415 North

Booth Nancy [wid DeHart], b 1004 North

Bopp Barbara [wid Wm], b 400 Melbourne av

Bopp Charles F [Christina], lab, h s e cor Horney and Franklin

Bopp Charles W, student, b s e cor Horney and Franklin

Bopp Emma, b 620 Race

Bopp Etta, wks Maiben's laundry, b 620 Race

The Best in the Business.
DRY GOODS,
CLOAKS.   FURS.

Wiler & Wise,
409-411 BROADWAY.
306 FOURTH STREET.

BOP   68   BOY

Bopp Frederick C [Anna A], cellarman Columbia Brew Co, h 116 Melbourne av

Bopp Laura, domestic, n e cor 6th and Henry

Bopp Olia E, cashier Wm J Parker, b 620 Race

Bopp F Tillie, wks Campbell's laundry, b 620 Race

Bopp Wm F [Christina], saloon, 13 6th, h 620 Race

Bordner Ella, domestic, 321 Sycamore

Borges Dorothy A [wid Ernest], h 18 Columbia

Borges Ernest S [Jessie], fireman Panhandle, h 814 17th

Borkbort Albert, student **Hall's Business College,** b Asylum rd, 2½ m w city

Boroughs Orin T, prin West Side schools. b 717 Wilkinson

Bosh Rosa, domestic, b 7½ Sycamore

Bosher Mary, domestic, 216 3d

Bossert James, driver Adams Ex Co, b 318 Eel River av

Boussum Mary [wid Samuel], h s e cor Standley and L & W rd

Bowen A W & Co (Alvin W and B Frank Bowen), publishers, n w cor Erie av and Elm

Bowen Alvin W [Henrietta], (A W Bowen & Co), h 310 North

Bowen B Frank (A W Bowen & Co), h La Grange, Ind

Bowen John [Charlotte], rd supervisor Vandalia, h 713 Miami

Bowen Lydia A [wid John W], h 127 State

Bowen Wm A, lab, b 127 State

Bower (*see also Bauer*)

Bower Charles O [Dora L], engr, h 2018 George

Bower David J, mach, b 2010 George

Bowers Lillie, domestic, h 410 Railroad

Bowers Nora E, seamstress, h 410 Railroad

Bowles Susan M, dressmkr, 1302 Broadway, b same

Bowley Milton, teamster, b c s Balsam 1 n Daisy

Bowman (*see also Bauman and Baughman*)

Bowman Charles W [Margaret], car rep Panhandle, h 630 Linden av

Bowman Cora M, student, b 630 Linden av

Bowman David P [Florence], driver hose co no 3, h 1418 Spear

Bowman Elizabeth [wid John], b 1418 Spear

Bowman Francis S, clk, b 630 Linden av

Bowman Frank M, attendant Insane Hospital, b same

Bowman Ira, lab Insane Hospital, b same

Bowman John [Josephine], tmstr Parker & Johnston, h 219 Grove

Bowman Louis E, clk, r Baker's European Hotel

Bowman Malinda A [wid Hezekiah], h 634 Linden av

Bowman Wilbur S, engr Vandalia, b 634 Linden av

Bowman Wm E [Emma J], fireman Panhandle, h 1326 George

Bowyer Frank D [Mollie], motorman, h 1819 Broadway

Boyd Charles, condr Vandalia, r 315 Sycamore

Boyd Luther H [Cornelia], treas Michael's Business College, h 432 Sycamore

Boyer Alexander B, artist, b 729 North
Boyer Armell, b 1815 George
Boyer Arthur S [Sadie], carp, h 1916 George
Boyer Atlanta A, finisher, b 601 Michigan av
Boyer A Belle, seamstress, b 601 Michigan av
Boyer George W [Mary], carp, h 1815 George
Boyer Helen P, student, b 729 North
Boyer John W [Nettie], brakeman Panhandle, h 2017 Market
Boyer John W [Rose], brakeman Vandalia, h 214½ 6th
Boyer Mary J, student, b 729 North
Boyer Sarah C, domestic, 322 w Broadway
Boyer Stephen B [M Josephine], secy and treas Logan Milling Co
   and The Logansport Journal Co, h 729 North
Boyes Norton [Lulu], fireman Panhandle, h 814 16th
Boyland Edward S [MaryE], asst foreman The Reporter, h 1224 North
Boyle Catharine, b 1916 Smead
Boyle Hugh [Margaret], h 109 4th
Boyle Katharine, domestic, 200 Eel River av
Boyle Rosa, domestic, 2102 Broadway
Bozarth Cyrus, barber, b 4 Uhl
Bozer Francis M [Jennie A], dentist, State National Bank Blk, s
   w cor 4th and Broadway, h 114 Pawnee
Bradfield Benjamin D [Marietta], physician and surgeon, 318 3d, h
   816 Market
Bradfield Constance, domestic, 1013 North
Bradfield John E, student, b 816 Market
Bradley Catharine [wid Patrick], h n s Miami, 1 e 6th
Bradley John, porter Wide Awake Grocery, r 1108 North
Bradley Lena, domestic, 805 Market
Bradley Sarah E [wid Japheth W], b 218 w Broadway
Bragg Augustus J [Elizabeth], fireman Panhandle, h 1612 Market
Braithwaite Peggy [wid James], h 721 Race
Brandt Solomon D [Clara], bkkpr, h 2230 High
Brannon Wm, fireman Vandalia, b 321 Sycamore
Brant Henry H, agt, b 322½ Pearl
Brauer Edmund, lab Insane Hospital, b same
Breckenridge Charles [Belle], carp, h 1105 Market
Breckenridge Charles McV, stenogr J T McNary, b 1105 Market
Breckenridge Charlotte, dressmkr, 1105 Market, b same
Breckenridge Estelle, b 1105 Market
Breckenridge Mary B, clk T A Spry, b 1105 Market
Breitenfeld Hattie, student, b 430 Humphrey
Brennan Wm, fireman, r 315 Sycamore
Brenneke August [Magdalen], lab, h 220 Burlington av
Brenneke Lucy, student, b 220 Burlington av
Brenneke Mary, cook Insane Hospital, b same
Brenner Andrew [Anna], car insp Panhandle, h 1821 Toledo

Brentlinger Frederick, barber, b 601 Chicago
Brentlinger Albert F [H Josephine], clk Wm J Parker, h 601 Chicago
Brewer Wm [Mary], weighmaster Panhandle, h 1628 North
Breymer Frank [Anna], lab, h w s Wilkinson, 1 n Melbourne av
Brice Ellen [wid John], h 10 Illinois
Brice Frank W, lab, b 10 Illinois
Bricker Harry C, paper hanger, b 1714 Smead
Bricker Samuel [Lana I], engr Panhandle, h 1714 Smead
Bridge Arthur, student, b 1114 Broadway
Bridge City Candy Co, Joseph H Reitemeier pres, Charles H Schafer secy and treas, mnfg and wholesale confectioners, 303, 305, 307 3d (See adv class confectioners)
Bridge City Construction Co, Maurice J Winfield pres, Charles J Reynolds secy and treas, Biddle Island (See adv back fly leaf)
Bridge Helen, student, b 1114 Broadway
Bridge James C, pianos and organs, 410 Broadway, h 1114 Broadway
Bridge Newton [Allie M], carp, h 114 w Wabash av
Briggs Charles E, painter, b 1905 Market
Briggs Claude C, bkkpr Elliott & Co, b 928 Linden av
Briggs Ethel V, student, b 2014 Broadway
Briggs Frederick J [Emma L], lawyer and insurance, 218½ 4th, h 108 Pawnee
Briggs Harry F [Emma], trav agt Elliott & Co, h 928 Linden av
Briggs Harry M, student, b 2014 Broadway
Briggs James J [Anna], trav agt, h 1905 Market
Briggs Lorena, student, b 108 Pawnee
Briggs Otto, painter, b 1905 Market
Briggs Wm W [Luella], del clk, h 2014 Broadway
Bright Wm, mach, b 60 Front
Briner Andrew [Edith], lab, h 419 13th
Bringhurst Alfred T, pharmacist W H Bringhurst, b 728 Market
Bringhurst Josephine T, b 728 Market
Bringhurst Thomas H [Elizabeth], h 730 Broadway
Bringhurst W H [Anna], druggist 308 Market, h 728 Market
Brinkerhoff Alice, b 1613 Broadway
Brinknell Mary E, agt, b 228 State
Briscoe John, messenger Adams Express Co, r same
Britton Anna C, b 60 Washington
Britton Cora A, clk Wiler & Wise, b 311 Melbourne av
Britton Effie M, dressmkr, b 311 Melbourne av
Britton Lawrence, lab, b 60 Washington
Britton Margaret, domestic, 704 North
Britton Mary, b 60 Washington
Britton Montraville [Eliza], painter, h 311 Melbourne av
Britton Richard F [Kate S], carp, h 43 Washington
Britton Walter, clk Wiler & Wise, b 311 Melbourne av
Britton Wm, fireman, b 60 Washington

G
9
L

Brixius Estella, dressmkr, b 806 High

Brixius Wm P [Elizabeth M], blksmith Panhandle, h 806 High

Brixius Wm P, jr, clk J W Henderson & Sons, b 806 High

Broadway M E Church, Rev Ephraim L Semans pastor, n e cor 8th and Broadway

Broadway Presbyterian Church, Rev H Atwood Percival pastor, s w cor 9th and Broadway

Brockman Austin, engr The Barnett, b same

Brockman Catharine [wid Peter], h 618 Canal

Brockman Harry, bartender, r 207 3rd

Brockman Peter [Catharine], clk, b 618 Canal

Brockman Tandy S, r 207 3rd

Brogan Patrick [Ann], lab, h 227 College

Brogan Susan, dressmkr, 227 College, b same

Brokaw Elizabeth [wid Abraham], b 1406 Market

Broker Effie, domestic, 321 North

Bromisch George [Anna], mach hd, h 12 Michigan av

Bronson Effie, clk Wiler & Wise, b 228 Front

Brookmeyer John F, asst cashier First National Bank, b 1301 High

Brookmeyer Henry [Elizabeth], h 1301 High

Brooks Alexander [Anna E], h 713 Linden av

Brooks Anna E [wid James], h 219 w Broadway

Brooks Charles R [Letitia O], lab, h 47 Washington

Brooks Edward O, lab, b 713 Linden av

Brooks Frank E, lab, b 713 Linden av

Brooks Frank J, barber, b 219 w Broadway

Brooks Harry, barber, b 219 w Broadway

Brooks James A [Helen T], poultry, s e cor Canal and Elm, h 2300 Broadway

Brooks John F, student, b 2300 Broadway

Brooks Lindsey G [Margaret L], barber, 302 5th, h 219 w Broadway

Brosier Charles E [Capitola], brakeman Panhandle, h 1402 Spear

Brosier James [Sarah], h 525 Fitch

Brothers Roland L [Georgia], clk, h rear 1816 Market

Broun (*see also Brown*)

Broun George F, barber, h 623 Miami

Brower Aaron [Caroline], lab, h 67 Washington

Brower Jesse C, teacher, b 67 Washington

Brower Myrtle G, b 67 Washington

Brower Pearl M, teacher, b 67 Washington

Brown (*see also Broun*)

Brown S Adelia, clk, b 616 North

Brown Charles M, comp, b 407 High

Brown Charles M [Hettie B], engr Panhandle, h 925 High

Brown G Charles, cigarmkr, b 25 Bates

Brown Daniel [Mary], saloon, 314 3d, h same

Brown Delbert C, gas fitter, b 25 Bates

G
9

Brown Edward J, student, b 26 Market
Brown Elisha, brakeman Panhandle, b 415½ 3d
Brown Eliza E [wid John], h 25 Bates
Brown Elizabeth P [wid Wm], r 613½ Broadway
Brown Ella, laundress, b 12 n Elm
Brown Ellen [wid John], h 927 Market
Brown Ellen [wid Wm], laundress, h 12 n Elm
Brown Harry W, student, b 1112 Market
Brown Harvey A [Mercilia], h 429 Sycamore
Brown Henry O [Laura], car rep Panhandle, h 817 19th
Brown Herbert A [Lizzie W], agt Adams Ex Co, h 26 Market
Brown James C [Mary E], molder, h 8 Bates
Brown James H [Margaret], h 1915 North
Brown James P, hostler James O'Donnell, r Biddle Island
Brown John H, cigarmkr, b 12 Elm
Brown John W [Louisa], painter, h 312 Linden av
Brown Levi H [Mary J], h 217 Eel River av
Brown Mabel, b 25 Bates
Brown Matilda M, h 117 Melbourne av
Brown Nellie, teacher physical culture and oratory Hall's Business
    College, b 1114 Broadway
Brown Oliver E, lab, b 25 Bates
Brown Rosa, r 207½ 6th
Brown Sarah [wid George] domestic, 406 Pleasant Hill
Brown Sarah A [wid John T], h w s Michigan av, 1 n Vandalia R R
Brown Susan [wid Samuel K], b 724 11th
Brown Wilbur C [Lucy], brakeman Panhandle, h 724 11th
Brown Walter, lab, b 1919 High
Brown Wiley S, embalmer C L Woll, r 417 Market
Brown Wm, lab, h 12 n Elm
Brown Wm H [Otie], h 1112 Market
Brown Wm I, baggageman Panhandle, r 613½ Broadway
Brownewell Della E, dressmkr, 403½ Broadway, h same
Brownewell George W [Della E], trav agt Schuyler Powell, h 403½
    Broadway
Brubaker Albert [Anna], lab, h 717 13th
Bruce Charles O, student, **Hall's Business College**, b 123 7th
Bruce Robert J [Sarah], supt bridges Panhandle, h 131 Helm
Bruggeman H Otto, student **Hall's Business College**, b 313 7th
Bruggeman Rose A [wid Wm A], milliner 416 Market, h 313 7th
Bruggeman Wm C, clk, b 313 7th
Brumbaugh Theodore E [Minnie J], agt Arbuckle Bros, 310½
    Market, h 800 Melbourne av
Bryan M Luther [Retta], blksmith Panhandle, h 1622 Spear
Bryant Anna B, dressmkr 514 Canal, h same
Bryant Ethel, student, b 355 Sycamore
Bryant R Frank [Milda], restaurant, 355 Sycamore, h same

Ǎ, The Tailor | Our Motto:
MARKET STREET.
FAIR TREATMENT TO ALL.

73 BUN

die, b 355 Sycamore
ılso Beyer and Byers)
d E [Anna], clk Logansport & W V Gas Co, h 830 Race
ıbeth, teacher, b 830 Race
ie, dressmkr 830 Race, h same
·ge [Eva], mach Panhandle, h 1329 Smead
b [Catharine], mach hd Panhandle, h 1329 Smead
Ѵm [Sarah A], tmstr, h e s Balsam, 1 n Daisy
Alexander Ν [Mary A], physician, h 1631 Spear
Claude W, brakeman Panhandle, h 419½ Ѵarket
James Ν [Florence], clk Walker & Ranch, h s e cor 7th
:inghurst
Martha, h 1105 Linden av
Mary A S [wid John], nurse, h 319½ Pearl
Ѵollie J, h 419½ Ѵarket
Ray, clk W H Porter, b 415½ 3d
Wm, student Hall's Business College, b 455 Ѵichigan av
a M E [wid Edmund G], h 114 4th
,ouise, b 201 Ѵain
ophia, b 201 Ѵain
ophia [wid Henry], h 201 Ѵain
Ѵm, lab, b 201 Ѵain
ıniel, lab, b 52 Uhl
mes [Josephine]. cornicemkr, b 415½ 3d·
hn miner, b 52 Uhl
ıry [wid Ѵichael], h 52 Uhl
·chael, lab, b 52 Uhl
trick, lab, b 52 Uhl
mothy, cupola tender Bridge City Construction Co, b 52 Uhl
ın, wks Bridge City Construction Co, b 52 Uhl
m F, porter H B Turner, b 522 Linden av
hn [Margaret], gardener, h 116 Washington
e L [Lorena], mach Panhandle, h 808 17th
. [Mary C], condr Panhandle, h 1416 Smead
Bertha, milliner, b 2114 Market
Charles [Anna], cigarmkr, h 2114 Market
Henry C [Caroline], foreman, h e s Burlington rd, 1 s
p rd
Tillie, student, b 2114 Ѵarket
:orge, del clk Burgman & Bro, b 1920 George
er A [Mary C], (Bundy & Rea), h 222 Michigan av
ea (Jasper A Bundy, Terrence Rea), meat market, 222
ın av
·red H, h 201 State
man [Elizabeth], contractor 101 Pratt, h same
ie M, b 612 Chicago
·is C [Nannie], hostler, h 612 Chicago

.rnard Z [Maria], patrolman, h 112 Bates
1eodore [Sarah], painter, h 1313 George
1omas W [Rosa B], carp, h 217 Washington
d Angeline, student, b 1509 George
d James [Julia], lab, h 1509 George
harles, student, b 3½ m n e city
usan, asst matron Cass County Poor Asylum, b same
1arles, brakeman Panhandle, r 111 4th
:ee also Boerger)
'rank [Johanna], lab, h 806 19th
Abner E [Lillie], car rep Panhandle, h 1627 George
Fannie M [wid Isaac], h 526 w Market
Ida M, teacher, b 514 15th
Willard, packer D & C H Uhl, b 526 w Market
Caroline, b 216 Tanguy
Edward, lab, b 216 Tanguy
Wm [Ellen], teamster, h 216 Tanguy
i (see also Bergmann)
ı Charles P [Nellie A], mach Panhandle, h 1615 Smead
1 Cycle Co, C Wm Burgman, Mgr, s e cor 5th and Market
. Edward, student, b 720 15th
ı Emma, clk Logansport Wall Paper Co, b 1504 Smead
1 Ferdinand [Mary], Burgman & Bro) h 1504 Smead
Flora, b n s Logan & Western pike, 1 w Burlington av
1 Gustav [Catharine], (Burgman & Bro), h 720 15th
Harry C, meat market, 618 15th, b 1504 Smead
Hattie M, clk Wiler & Wise, b n s Logan & Western pike,
Burlington av
John, baker Insane Hospital, b same
Leopold [Mary A], clk Burgman & Bro, h 1617 Spear
Mary F, b 1400 Market
Minnie, student, b n s Logan & Western pike, 1 w Bur-
ɔn av
Otto, student, b 720 15th
ı Wm [Henrietta], saloon and confectionery 1-3 Burlington
n s Logan & Western pike, 1 w Burlington av
C Wm, mgr Burgman Cycle Co, b 720 15th
& Bro (Gustav and Ferdinand), grocers, wines, liquors
gts Finlay Brewing Co, n e cor 15th and Smead
:les W [Katharine], cornicemkr, h 417 Ottawa
:lotte, dressmkr, b 417 Ottawa
:rt, cigarmkr, b 417 Ottawa
.nna A, domestic, b 518 w Broadway
ı [Bridget], lab, h 518 w Broadway
E, trainmaster Vandalia, b The Barnett
on T [Etta], cooper, h 417 Ottawa
xander [Sarah E], lumber dealer, h 627 Ottawa

Burke Esther A [wid Madison R], b 314 12th
Burke James P [Kate A], h 320 Melbourne av
Burke Lulu S, b 627 Ottawa
Burke Wm H, tmstr, b 627 Ottawa
Burket Lillian C, b 1206 Linden av
Burket James [Margaret], carp, h 1206 Linden av
Burkhardt Albert, cook Insane Hospital, b same
Burkit H Frank, clk Excelsior Mfg Co, r 308½ 4th
Burkit Robert, janitor Masonic Temple, r 308½ 4th
Burlingame Lillian E, teacher, b 812 North
Burnett John [Abigail L], shoemkr 104 Sycamore, h 627 Chicago
Burnham Bertha, ironer Insane Hospital, b same
Burns Anna, b 831 Race
Burns Bros (Patrick and James), saloon 514 Broadway
Burns Charles, b 1122 Market
Burns H Edward [Lillie M], foreman Marshall's Steam Laundry, h 522 Chicago
Burns Elizabeth B, wks T M Quigley & Co, b 7 Horney
Burns Ellen, b 831 Race
Burns George D, lab, b 1201½ Market
Burns Grace, b 821 Race
Burns Harry E [May], foreman, h 520 Chicago
Burns James, billiards 203 6th, (Burns Bros), b 831 Race
Burns John, clk J H Foley, b 200 Colfax
Burns Leonidas H [Lottie], painter 7 Horney, h same
Burns Mary B, wks T M Quigley & Co, b 7 Horney
Burns Mary E, dressmkr, 310½ Market, h same
Burns Matilda, laundress, h 1201½ Market
Burns Michael, stone mason, b 312 Melbourne av
Burns Michael [Catharine], h 821 Race
Burns Ola, b 1201½ Market
Burns Patrick (Burns Bros), b 831 Race
Burns Theresa, b 831 Race
Burns Wm, engr Panhandle, r 111 4th
Burns Wm, brakeman Panhandle, b 624 North
Burns Wm, artist, b 821 Race
Burns Wm H, brakeman, b 7 Horney
Burrow John F, vice pres King Drill Co, h 310½ 4th
Burrows George B [Mattie], plasterer, h 202½ 6th
Burrows George W, lather, b 202½ 6th
Burrows Minnie, b 202½ 6th
Burtis Henry, mach hd, b 1827 High
Burtis James, teamster, b 27 n 6th
Burtis Lafayette [Mary E], lab Columbia Brew Co, h 1827 North
Burtis Mildred, domestic, b 27 n 6th
Burtis Wm [Sarah E], lab, h 27 n 6th
Burwell John M, baker Insane Hospital, b same

The Busy Bee Hive, 409-411 Broadway.
306 Fourth Street.
Dry Goods, Cloaks, Furs.

BUS | 76 | BYE

Busard (*see also Bussard and Bossert*)
Busard Maria G [wid Daniel], h 524 North
Bush David L [Nancy V D], contr, 117 7th, h same
Bush Frances M, student, b w s Johnson, 1 s Franklin
Bush George, engr Panhandle, r 1069 Toledo
Bush George W, lab, b 316 6th
Bush Lillian J, b 117 7th
Bush Rachael, h 18 Main
Bush Wade II, billiards, 307 Broadway, b 117 7th
Bushing Clara, h 215 5th
Bushing John E [Orpha A], agt, h 214½ 6th
Bushing Mary [wid Wm], b 214½ 6th
Bushing Wm, property man, b 214½ 6th
Busjahn Frederick, tailor, b 212 Osage
Busjahn Frederick A [Josephine], physician 407 4th, also county
    coroner, h 1500 Broadway
Busjahn John J (Busjahn & Schneider), r 308 4th
Busjahn Margaret, h 212 Osage
Busjahn & Schneider (John J Busjahn, John W Schneider), drugs,
    paints, oils, varnishes, etc, 308 4th   (See adv front cover)
Buss August, floor man James O'Donnell, r 408½ 3d
Bussard (*see also Busard and Bossert*)
Bussard John W [Edith L], letter carrier, h 427 Burlington av
Busy Bee Hive Dry Goods Store, Wiler & Wise, proprs, 409-411
    Broadway and 306 4th   (See adv left top lines)
Butler Catharine E [wid Abraham C], b 602 Canal
Butler Charles A [Sarah], clk Panhandle, h 1722 Broadway
Butler John J, cigarmkr, b 602 Canal
Butterworth J Albert, clk, b 1327 High
Butterworth Amelia, clk John Gray, b 1327 High
Butterworth Anna, b 1327 High
Butterworth John, engr Panhandle, r 508 e Wabash av
Butterworth Margaret, b 1817 Spear
Butterworth May, bkkpr S N Closson, b 1327 High
Butterworth Thomas [Ellen], street contr 1327 High, h same
Butterworth Thomas J [Rebecca A], truckman Panhandle, h 1817
    Spear
Butterworth C Wm, bkkpr Thompson Lumber Co, b 1327 High
Button George, baggageman Panhandle, r 408½ 3rd
Button James II, trav agt, b Baker's European Hotel
Button Jessie M, b 419½ Market
Butz Andrew [Polly], carp, h 209 Colfax
Butz Norman [Edna], lab, h 127 Cole
Butz Wm [Fannie], clk, h 209 Colfax
Byers (*see also Beyer and Bryer*)
Byers Edmund A, mach opr The Journal, b 523½ Broadway
Byers Caroline M [wid John M], h 817 Market

yers Mary E, b 817 Market
yers Maxwell, student, b 817 Market
yers Morton L, engr M of W Panhandle, b 817 Market
yersdaugh Henry, engr Vandalia, b 321 Sycamore

C

adwallader Horace F [Etta B], engr, h 610 Chicago
ady Nelson W [Jennie M], physician and surgeon 600½ Broadway, h 1108 Market
ahill (*see also Cahl*)
ahill Anna [wid Michael], h 400 w Broadway
ahill Daniel C [Julia A], lab, h 717 Linden av
ahill James [Catharine], lab, h 417 Grove
ahill James B, student **Hall's Business College,** b 417 Grove
ahill John [Katharine], del clk Vincent Kardes, h 1406 Smead
ahill Katharine [wid Wm], h 417½ Market
ahill Matthew F, lab, b 417½ Market
ahill Michael, h 602 Canal
ahl (*see also Cahill*)
ahl Anna, domestic, 525 Chicago
ahl Henry F [Laura], watchman Panhandle shops, h 1423 Erie av
ain (*see also Kane*)
ain Samuel [Anna M], car rep Panhandle, h 207 Bates
aldwell John W [Laura], fireman, h 1700 Spear
allahan John [Theresa], lab, h 717 Ottawa
allahan Josie E, dressmkr, b 717 Ottawa
allahan Michael [Bridget], baggage agt, h 116 Wheatland
allahan Theresa F, mach opr W D Craig, b 717 Ottawa
allin John F [Jessie L], mach hd Hillock & Pitman, 1408 Broadway
alloway Frank B, attendant Insane Hospital, b same
alvert Harry S [Lucy M], fireman Panhandle, h 1614 Spear
ambish C & Co (Chas and Lawrence Cambish), fruits, 509 Broadway
ambish Charles (C Cambish & Co), h 509 Broadway
ambish (C Cambish & Co), h 509 Broadway
amp David E, condr Panhandle, r 6 Canal
ampbell Albert, del clk Maiben's Laundry, b 118 State
ampbell Arthur, comp, b 310½ Broadway
ampbell Benjamin F [Mary E], h 1702 High
ampbell Blanche, student, b 1702 High
ampbell Clements F [Louisiana], h 112 Hanna
ampbell Edward, bartender, b 515 11th
ampbell Edward F, clk, b 704 Ottawa
ampbell Edward F [Bessie], brakeman Vandalia, h n w cor Columbia and Liberty

Campbell Elizabeth, mach opr W D Craig, b 515 11th
Campbell Elizabeth, clk T A Spry, b 704 Ottawa
Campbell Frank P, lab, b 515 11th
Campbell George W [Louise M], second hand goods, 518 Broadway, h 717 High
Campbell George W [Nancy J], engr Vandalia, h 1323 Market
Campbell Jane [wid Wm H], h 213 Cole
Campbell Jessie C, mach opr W D Craig, b 607 12th
Campbell John J [Jennie M], propr Campbell's Steam Laundry, h 2026 Broadway
Campbell Julia, wks laundry, b 515 11th
Campbell Malinda [wid Robert B], b n w cor Columbia and Liberty
Campbell Margaret [wid Patrick], h 704 Ottawa
Campbell Matilda P [wid Thomas J], h 118 State
Campbell Morris [Mary], lab, h 515 11th
Campbell Samuel G, book binder, b 717 High
Campbell Samuel P [Elizabeth], lab, h e s Dakota 1 n Bates (Dunkirk)
Campbell Steam Laundry, John J Campbell, propr, 429 Market
Campbell Wm D [Mary], h 219 Linden av
Campbell Wm H, condr Panhandle, b Island View Hotel
Campion (see also Champion)
Campion John [Sarah], boilermkr, h 615 18th
Campion Julia [wid Matthew], h 808 e Wabash av
Campion Mary E, opr Logansport M Tel Co, b s w cor 9th and Spencer
Campion Matthew, lab, b 808 e Wabash av
Campion Very Rev Matthew E, rector St Vincent De Paul Catholic Church, h s w cor 9th and Spencer
Canedy (see also Kennedy)
Canedy Everett H, lab, r 1219 Toledo
Canfield Asel O [Sarah A], boarding, n e cor Canal and Oak
Canfield Sarah A, oculist n e cor Canal and Oak, h same
Cann George W [Fannie B], clk Panhandle, h 222 Osage
Cannon Dennis, turner Ash & Hadley, h 113 Helm
Cannon Margaret, b 113 Helm
Cannon Mary, b 113 Helm
Cantley John M [America], fruit grower, h e s Burlington rd, 11 s Wash tp rd
Cantley Walter G, student, b e s Burlington rd 11 s Wash tp rd
Cantner Joseph, lab, h 517 Linden av
Cantner Mary, laundress, h n s Miami 1 e 6th
Cantner Ollie, b 517 Linden av
Cantner Wm, lab, b n s Miami 1 e 6th
Capron Wells D [Anna], piano tuner 219 Sycamore, h same
Carew Amanda U [wid John C], h 1423 High
Carew Charles C, fireman Panhandle, b 1503 Broadway
Carew Harry L, waiter, r 302 North
Carew John C, b 1503 Broadway

H. J. GRISMOND, 312 Market Street,
All Kinds of Metal Roofing.

| CAR | 79 | CAR |

Carew Leo K, student, b 817 Linden av
Carew Mary E [wid John H], h 1503 Broadway
Carew Wm G [Frances], engr Vandalia, h 817 Linden av
Carey George W, b 621 Chicago
Carl Martin C [Elizabeth], wks C L Dilley & Co, h 410 Day
Carle Margaret [wid Frederick], h 310 w Market
Carle Maude L, stripper Julius Wagner, b 310 w Market
Carl May, bindery girl, b 310 w Market
Carmell Jesse S [Catharine C], condr Panhandle, h 1214 Spear
Carmell Wm [Nettie] b 520 Canal
Carney (see also Kearney)
Carney Allie, bkkpr C L Dilley & Co, b Royal Center rd, 4 m n city
Carney Frank [Mary], fireman Panhandle, h 226 State
Carney Iva D, b 629 Linden av
Carney James H [Sarah], blksmth, h 426 Burlington av
Carney James M [Josephine], lab, h 1909 Broadway
Carney Maude L, attendant Insane Hospital, b same
Carney N Rebecca [wid Wm], h 629 Linden av
Carney Thomas F, fireman Panhandle, b 1828 Spear
Carpenter Anna [wid Wm T], h 121 Osage
Carpenter Richard [Jane], lab, h 419 Day
Carr Beecher S, clk, b 304 Linden av
Carr Charles, lab, b 202 Hanna
Carr Samuel [Sarah], carp, h 304 Linden av
Carr Thos, fireman Panhandle, r 1069 Toledo
Carr Wm, b e s Washington, 3 s Biddle (S T)
Carriger George H [Mary A], mach hd Panhandle, h 603 12th
Carriger Mary A, boarding, 603 12th
Carriger Viola, b 603 12th
Carriger G Wm [Mamie], stage manager, b 603 12th
Carroll Anna, waiter Hotel Johnston, b same
Carroll Anthony, wks Wm Heppe & Sons, b s s L & W rd, 3 w Anthony
Carroll Catharine [wid Patrick], h s s L & W rd, 3 w Anthony
Carroll Cecelia [wid Peter], laundress, h 213 Wheatland
Carroll Eli J [Theresa], engr Panhandle, h 1224 High
Carroll Charles L, student, b 1229 North
Carroll Ella, domestic, 115 9th
Carroll Gertrude A, b 1229 North
Carroll John, b 1229 North
Carroll John F, merchant tailor, 1222 Broadway, b 1229 North (See adv p 6)
Carroll Mary, domestic, 1002 Broadway
Carroll Patrick, tmstr, b 324 Sycamore
Carroll Robert [Margaret], trav agt, h 1229 North
Carroll Robert J, plumber A W Stevens, b 1229 North
Carroll Simon [Bridget], brakeman Panhandle, h 1216 Wright
Carroll Thomas E, student, b 1229 North

Carroll Wm J, student, b 1229 North
Carson Blanche I, wks Bridge City Candy Co, b 212½ 6th
Carson Charles E, bootblack Aaron Greensfelder, b e s Royal Center
  pike, 3 n city limits
Carson Everet A, marble cutter Schuyler Powell, b 212½ 6th
Carson Hattie, domestic, 2328 Broadway
Carson John [Charlotte], lab, h 212½ 6th
Carson Sadie, student Hall's Business College, b s e cor Sycamore
  and Pleasant Hill
Cart George [Emma], lab, h 1726 Toledo
Carter Charles E [Fannie M], cigar mnfr 416 w Market, h same
Carter Earl B, clk, b s e cor State and Wilkinson
Carter Frank J [Nellie M], barber, 312 3d, h 126 Helm
Carter Harry E, clk, b s e cor State and Wilkinson
Carter James A [Ora], barber 1 w Market, h 703 Melbourne av
Carter Jane [wid Daniel], b s e cor State and Wilkinson
Carter Joseph, lab, h 126 Helm
Carter Madison C, barber, b 126 Helm
Carter Orpha, lab Cass County Poor Asylum, b same
Carter Wm H H, meats 220 Market, b s e cor State and Wilkinson
Cary Adelaide K [wid Wm H], b 1111 George
Case George A, clk Island View Hotel, b same
Case Harry D [Carrie M], propr Island View Hotel, h same
Case Mattie J [wid Charles B], h 218½ Market
Case W Roy, finisher, b 521 High
Case Wallace L, finisher, b 521 High
Cash (see also Kasch)
Cash Isaac N [Sarah A], county treasurer, also livery and sale stable
  209 Market, h 1130 Market
Cashdollar Albert J [Marcella], condr Panhandle, h 615 13th
Cass Circuit Court, Dudley H Chase judge, Andrew P Flynn clerk
Cass County Building & Loan Association, John Gray pres, Edith M
  Matt secy, Joshua C Hadley, treas, 406 Broadway
Cass County Court House, s w cor 4th and North
Cass County Jail, 321 North
Cass County Officials, see County Officials
Cass County Orphans' Home, Elizabeth Craighead matron, s e cor
  Pleasant Hill and McCarty
Cass County Poor Asylum, Frederick Homburg supt, 3½ m n e city
Cassel Adaline [wid Andrew], b 1820 Smead
Cassel James L [Adria], motorman, h 1820 Smead
Cassidy Elizabeth [wid James A], h 1069 Toledo
Cassidy John M [Margaret E], b 1069 Toledo
Cassidy Samuel C [Mary A], condr Panhandle, h 1811 George
Cassidy Wm S [Emma D W], foreman Panhandle, h 1916 North
Cassube Albert, student, b 723 Linden av
Cassube Barbara E, mach opr W D Craig, b 700 Melbourne av

Cassube Wm [Barbara], tailor W D Craig, h 700 Melbourne av
Cassube Wm C [Martha A], carp Panhandle, h 723 Linden av
Castle Bert M, clk Melvin Castle, b 112 Sycamore
Castle Mary [wid Thomas], b 416 Miami
Castle Maude, stenogr J T Elliott & Son, b 416 Miami
Castle Melvin [Susan A], grocer 101–103 Sycamore, h 112 Sycamore
Castle Melvin J, painter, h 808 Sycamore
Castle Myrtle, student, b 416 Miami
Castle Peter [Elizabeth], saloon 311 Pearl, h 416 Miami
Catterlin Cecil F, cook 123 Melbourne av
Catterlin Lizzie A, domestic 123 Melbourne av
Cavin Julia, b 2023 Spear
Cavin Maurice [Amanda], eng hostler Panhandle, h 2023 Spear
Cavin Maurice L. student, b 2023 Spear
Cavin Thomas [Emma], contractor 1628 Toledo, h same
Caw Samuel T [Mariba], painter, h 200 Bates
Cecchinni Peter (Cecchinni & Riebling) r 18 Front
Cecchinni & Riebling (Peter Cecchinni, Herman Riebling), statue
    mnfrs 18 Front
Central Union Telephone Co, John B Skinner mgr, 315½ 4th
Chalk Bertha, dressmkr, b 16 n 6th
Chamberlain Ida, domestic, b 221 Montgomery
Chambers Fannie, domestic Insane Hospital
Chambers Leon O, student, b 101 Hanna
Chambers Oliver [Mary A] (Enyart & Chambers), h 101 Hanna
Champe George E [A Luella], tel opr Wabash, h 314 12th
Champion (see also Campion)
Champion Gustavus G, clk, b 1511 Market
Champion Hugh P [Gretta], brakeman, h 1511 Market
Champion Wm J [Nora], caller Panhandle, h n e cor Brown and w
    Broadway
Chandler A Anna [wid Edward E], h 416 North
Chandler Walter W, clk, b 416 North
Chapin Amy, b 1906 Spear
Chapman Charles D, tmstr, b 217 Broadway
Chapman Charles E, painter, b 519 Canal
Chapman George [Malinda], feed yd 507 and 512 North and 217
    Broadway, h 217 Broadway
Chapman Harry, fireman Vandalia, b 115 7th
Chapman Julia, h 115 7th
Chapman [Milton J], clk, b 217 Broadway
Chapman Minnie, student, b 217 Broadway
Chapman Walter S [Mary S], mach, h 708 Linden av
Chappel Elizabeth, domestic, 217 6th
Chappelear Harry B [Martha], clk, h 1825 Broadway
Chappelear Jessie, student Hall's Business College, b 1915 Broadway
Chappelow B Earl, asst city editor The Reporter, b 1007 North

SUPRPLUS of the METROPOLITAN LIFE
——————— at the end of 1896, over ☞ $5,000,000
Number of Claims Paid During Year, 63,909

CHA   82   CLA

Chappelow Fay E, electrician, b 1007 North
Chappelow John A [Adelia C], lawyer 222½ 4th, h 1007 North
Chapple Thomas W [Elizabeth], engr Columbia Brew Co, h 1426 Wright
Charboneau Wm, painter Insane Hospital, b same
Charles Abraham [Katharine], vice pres and genl foreman A B Keeport & Co, h Keeport, Ind, 4 m e city
Chase Abel S, b 619 Michigan av
Chase **Dudley** H [Grace M], Judge Cass Circuit Court, h 829 North
Chase Charles D, student, b 829 North
Chase George P, lawyer 220 4th, b 829 North
Chase Mary H, b 829 North
Chase Phillip, engr, r 608 e Wabash av
Chase Thomas I, b 829 North
Chase Wm, foreman Panhandle, r 303½ Pearl
Chatman George, porter, b 313 Miami
Chatman Maria [wid Orlando], b 313 Miami
Chester Hannah M [wid Joseph], b 115 9th
Chetwood L Albert, b n s Bates 1 w Vandalia R R (Dunkirk)
Chetwood Samuel P, engr, b w s Holland 1 n Pink
Chidester James C [Josephine], h 86 Michigan av
Chidester Minnie P, student, b 86 Michigan av
Chilcott Benjamin B [Alida], carp, h 29 Pleasant Grove
Chilcott Garfield, lab, b 29 Pleasant Grove
Childers James, broom mkr, b 416 e Wabash av
Chilver Charles B [Emma], book binder, h 1106 Spear
Choen Charles D, b s w cor 18th and Wright
Choen Harry H, stripper, b s w cor 18th and Wright
Choen Sarah [wid John], h s w cor 18th and Wright
Chrispen Frank T [Josie], lab, h n s Bates 8 w Vandalia R R (Dunkirk)
Christa Charles, lineman Wabash, r 302 North
Christian Church, Rev Thaddeus L Freeman pastor, s w cor 9th and Spear
Church Carl H [Louise], jeweler 519 Broadway, h 520½ Broadway
Church of Christ Scientists, s s Broadway bet 8th and 9th
Churchman Carrie, student, b 3 Eel River av
Churchman Mary E, laundress, h 3 Eel River av
Churchman O Victoria, student, b 3 Eel River av
Cilley Edward M, tel opr W U Telegraph Co, b 1721 North
Cilley George W, clk Panhandle, b 1721 North
Cilley Harry E [Julia A], tel opr Panhandle, h 1721 North
City Building, containing all the city offices and police court, n w cor 3d and Broadway
Clark (*see also Clarke*)
Clark Charles, tinner, b 603 12th
Clark Charles [Ella], lab, h 119 Washington

UP-TO-DATE IN DESIGNS OF MONUMENT
We Operate the Only Steam Granite Works in the State.
SCHUYLER POWELL,   1031-1035 TOLEDO STREE·

CLA   83   CL

Clark Edith, r 322½ Market
Clark George W [Anna], hostler E F Stewart, h 16 Biddle av
Clark Henry L, carp Panhandle, h 1629 Market
Clark James, lab, b 209 Wheatland
Clark John B [Emma], watchman Logan Milling Co, h 526 Chicag
Clark Joseph [Daisy], yd clk Panhandle, h 1222 Wright
Clark Levi M [Cora M], painter, h 315½ Market
Clark Olive, student, b 16 Biddle av
Clark Wm E [Margaret], farmer, h n s Wash tp rd 3 w Sherman
Clarke (see also Clark)
Clarke Edward F, cashr McCaffrey Bros, b 1109 Market
Clarke James A [Alice], gardener, h 1109 Market
Clarke Leo J, student, b 1109 Market
Clarke Stella F, student, b 1109 Market
Clarke Wm L, clk, b 1109 Market
Clary Bert W [Sarah], car insp, h 1927 Market
Clary J Frank [Etta M], clk J D Ferguson & Jenks, h 14 Helm
Clary George E [Elizabeth A], carp O J Stouffer, h 511 Michigan a
Clary Hattie F, milliner, b 417 High
Clary John C [Narcissa], h 6 Columbia
Clary John T [Ella], car rep Panhandle, h 6 Columbia
Clary Lillian C, milliner, b 417 High
Clary Mollie E, clk Schmitt & Heinly, b 417 High
Clary Wm D [Elizabeth J], h 417 High
Clary Wm I, student, b 511 Michigan av
Clem Emanuel A, livery stable 315 8th, r 725 Broadway
Clevenger Bros (Lafayette R and George W), real estate and loans
   7 Masonic Temple
Clevenger George W [Mary B] (Clevenger Bros), h 1526 Broadwa
Clevenger Lafayette R [Minnie B] (Clevenger Bros), h 2214 Broadwa
Clevenger Mahala A [wid Basil S], h 719 Michigan av
Clewell Jeremiah S [Alida], mach Panhandle, h 1921 Broadway
Clewell Lillian W, student, b 1921 Broadway
Clewell Ruth S, student, b 1921 Broadway
Clifford Bridget, attendant Insane Hospital, b same
Clifford Dennis, lab, b 1310 Indiana
Clifford Ellen [wid Michael], h 721 Chicago
Clifford John [Mary], h 1310 Indiana
Clifford Margaret, b 1310 Indiana
Cline (see also Klein and Kline)
Cline Bros (Otto L and Rene), tinners, 500 Broadway
Cline Otto L [Belle R] (Cline Bros), h 630 North
Cline Rene [Lillie] (Cline Bros), h 114 7th
Clinger George E [Mary F], foreman, h 17 Melbourne av
Clipp Augustus, pressman, b 100 Helm
Close Carrie M, clk, b 1132 High
Close Daniel [Margaret], engr Panhandle, h 1132 High

Closson. Amasa, b 2125 Broadway
Closson Daniel D, clk, r 523½ Broadway
Closson Edgar D [Margaret M], insurance and loans, 222 4th, saw mill s e cor 15 and Toledo, h 2125 Broadway
Closson Edna R, student, b 216 8th
Closson Homer C (Homer Closson & Co), b 216 8th
Closson Homer & Co (Homer C and Seymour N Closson), drugs, paints and oils, 506 Broadway
Closson Seymour M [Ella], insurance, real estate and loans, 319½ Pearl (Homer Closson & Co) (W L Closson & Co), h 216 8th
Closson Walter L [Helen] (W L Closson & Co), h 124 Sycamore
Closson W L & Co (Walter L and Seymour N Closson), cigar mnfrs 402½ Broadway, billiard room 316 Broadway
Cloud Gouldsmith [Lydia A], lab, h n w cor Johnson and Fulton
Cloud Jas F, lab, b n w cor Johnson and Fulton
Clover Leaf Dairy, Jacob G Minneman prop, Asylum rd, ½ m w Cicott st bridge (See adv class dairies)
Clugston Calvin E [May], lineman Log M Tel Co, h 620 Chicago
Clymer David C [Ella], clk Hub Clothing Co, h 512 w Wabash av
Clymer David H, b 512 w Wabash ave
Coale (*see also Cole and Kohl*)
Coale Vincent N [Hannah G], foreman car rep Wabash, h 1401 North
Coats (*see also Kohts*)
Coats Esther H [wid Joseph], b 2013 Spear
Coats Hyman S [Ida], condr Panhandle, h 2013 Spear
Coats Joseph, b 2013 Spear
Cochley Abram M [Jessie], carp Panhandle, h 209 Bates
Cochran Anderson [Margaret], carp, h n s Shultz 4 w Frank (S T)
Cochran Roy E, student, b 529 Sycamore
Cockburn Bros (James T, Joseph C and George W), real estate, loans and insurance, 8 Masonic Temple   (See adv p 8)
Cockburn Eliza W [wid George F], h 1316 North
Cockburn George W (Cockburn Bros), mgr fire ins dept, b 1316 North
Cockburn James T [Katie T], (Cockburn Bros), mgr real estate and loan dept, h 1717 High
Cockburn Joseph C (Cockburn Bros), mgr life ins dept, b 1316 North
Cockburn Maria, music teacher, 1316 North, b same
Cockburn Mary J, stenogr Cockburn Bros, b 1316 High
Cody Edward F [Josephine], car insp Panhandle, h 1835 Toledo
Coffman (*see also Kaufman*)
Coffman Hillary, poultry man Insane Hospital, b same
Cogley George W [Eva M], fireman, h 1220 Toledo
Cogley W Robert [Minnie], fireman Panhandle, h 1809 George
Cohee Daniel [Catharine], lab, h s w cor Clay and Burlington av
Cohee Emanuel [Mary A], h 415½ 3d
Cohee Etta, attendant Insane Hospital, b same
Cohee George L, carp Panhandle, r 604 12th

Ask the Clerk at the Hotel for the ......

Work Done In 6 Hours WITHOUT EXTRA CHARGE.

☆ LAUNDRY LISTS.

GEO. OTT, Propr.

405 Market Street.

COH 85 COL

Cohee George M [Minnie], mach Panhandle, h 604 12th
Cohee Grace, attendant Insane Hospital, b same
Cohee Jason, attendant Insane Hospital, b same
Cohee Morris [Anna], lab, h s s Wab R R 2 w Tanguy
Cohee Vincent D [Marilla], farm foreman Insane Hospital, b same
Cohee Wm, bartender, b 415½ 3d
Cohee Wm J, student, b 415½ 3d
Cohn Sol H [Bessie], cut rate tickets, cigars, tobacco, books, stationery, newspapers and periodicals, 326 Market, h 1117 North
Coil (*see also Coyle*)
Coil Edith, student, b 202 Burlington av
Coil Susan, Laundress, h 202 Burlington av
Coil Walter, cooper, b 213 Berkley
Cole (*see also Coale and Kohl*)
Cole Albert A, hostler, b 610 Linden av
Cole Alice, b 530 Ottawa
Cole Eleanor, domestic, 1125 Market
Coleman (*see also Kollman*)
Coleman Artha L [wid Jonathan C], h 125 Melbourne av
Coleman Asa, physician 322 3d, h 404 7th
Coleman Bertha, dressmkr, b 125 Melbourne av
Coleman C Denby, student, b 404 7th
Coleman Harriet, b 404 7th
Coleman Henry F [Mary F], civ engr and mgr Logansport Construction Co, 322 3d, h 2226 Broadway
Coleman Manford M, student, b 125 Melbourne ave
Coleman Smiley, dressmkr, b 125 Melbourne ave
Coleman Texanna, milliner, b 125 Melbourne ave
Collett Blanche Z, teacher, b 1010 North
Collett Charles P [Amanda], cigarmkr, h 628 Sycamore
Collett Wm S [Bertha], fireman Panhandle, b 1631 Spear
Collins Charles [Mary], h 1328 George
Collins Edith, student, b 1931 Jefferson
Collins Elizabeth J, h 619 Miami
Collins Ella, dressmkr, b 69 Washington
Collins Gertrude M, bkkpr, b 1924 Market
Collins Jeremiah, plasterer, b 77 Washington
Collins John [Eva], driver Adams Ex Co, h 631 11th
Collins Louis D, fireman Vandalia, b 619 Miami
Collins Minnie, seamstress, b 69 Washington
Collins Nellie, dressmkr, b 69 Washington
Collins Priscilla, domestic 2530 Broadway
Collins Raleigh [Lillie], carriage trimmer, h 705 Race
Collins Robert D [Alice G], fireman Vandalia, h 19 Elm
Collins Robert H, book binder, b 206 6th
Collins Thomas [Mary], yd master Panhandle, h 1931 Jefferson
Collins Timothy [Mary], lab, h 69 Washington

Colstau Charles, teamster, b 1609 Douglass
Colter Charles, student, b 432 Sycamore
Columbia Brewing Co, John G Keip secy and genl mgr, n w cor 5th and High
Comer Cora, b 523 Fitch
Comer Lucy E [wid Wm C], dressmkr, b 523 Fitch
Comingore Catharine, b 1205 Market
Comingore Ellen, teacher, h 1205 Market
Comingore J Frank, comp, b 1205 Market
Conaughton Catharine, clk, b 1402 Broadway
Condon Mary D [wid John W], h 709 High
Condon Wm [Mary], h 620 North
Coney Sarah, domestic 7 Biddle Island
Congdon John E, driver, b 1914 George
Conklin Thomas R [Clara], teamster, h 511 Sycamore
Conley James, brakeman Vandalia, b 324 Sycamore
Conlin Mary, attendant Insane Hospital, b same
Conn Eliza E [wid Edward], h 208 Canal
Conn Eunice, dressmkr, b 5 Biddle's Island
Conn Jane, 5 Biddle's Island
Conn Robert M, mach Bridge City Construction Co, b 5 Biddle's Island
Conn Wm P [Mary], lab, h 1108 Spear
Connery James, granite cutter Schuyler Powell, b s w cor 12th and George
Connolly Thomas, b 706 Duret
Connors Ella, student, b 1209 Toledo
Connors Margaret [wid John], h 320 Melbourne av
Connors Martin [Margaret], clk Panhandle, h 1020 Toledo
Connors Michael [Sarah], caller Panhandle, h 1209 Toledo
Connors Nellie, domestic 916 Market
Connors Nellie, student **Hall's Business College,** b 6 Uhl
Connors Patrick, caller Panhandle, b 1209 Toledo
Connors Patrick, finisher Ash & Hadley, h 6 Uhl
Connors Sarah, boarding, 1209 Toledo
Conover Mahlon [E Josephine], h 107 5th
Conrad Elsie J [wid Samuel A], b 1910 Market
Conrad Henry [Maud M], painter, h 18 Main
Conrad John [Theresa], lab, h 1529 Niles
Conrad Nicholas J, clk, b 226 Market
Conrad Olive, domestic, 74 Michigan av
Conrad Virgil [Belle], grocer 427 5th, h 700 Michigan av
Conrad Wm H, clk, h 427 5th
Conrad Wm T [Margaret J], mnfr wire fence, h 3 Horney
Conroy James, marble cutter, b 603 12th
Conroy Martin [Margaret], h 426 Pratt
Conroy Thomas M [Ella J], lab, h 52 Washington
Conway James [Honora E], plasterer, h 77 Washington

H. J. CRISMOND, 312 Market Street,
Gasoline Stoves, Screen Doors and Windows.

| CON | 87 | COR |

Conway James J, plasterer, b 77 Washington
Conway Mary J, student, b 77 Washington
Cook (*see also Cooke*)
Cook Albert, engr Vandalia, r 315 Sycamore
Cook Anthony [Jennie], boilermkr Panhandle, h 906 14th
Cook Corydon W [Elizabeth] mach hd, h 225 College
Cook Daniel A, candymkr Bridge City Candy Co, b 225 College
Cook Elizabeth [wid Casper], h 1712 George
Cook Frank, attendant Insane Hospital, b same
Cook George W [Anna T], sect foreman, h 706 e Wabash av
Cook James A [Sarah], carp 609 Chicago, h same
Cook Jacob, clk Schmitt & Heinley, b 1712 George
Cook Robert, student, b 1503 Spear
Cooke (*see also Cook*)
Cooke Alden S [Nancy], h 16 n 6th
Cooke Clemmie, dressmkr 16 n 6th, b same
Cooke Nellie, teacher, r 914 Broadway
Cookson Joseph R [Rosa], lab, h 523 Pratt
Cool Frank C, student, b 2001 North
Cool Isaac N [Alice A], carriage mnfr s e cor 14th and Toledo, h
   2001 North
Cool Sidney M, bkkpr I N Cool, b 2001 North
Cool Vina F, student, b 2001 North
Coolbaugh Rev Frank C [Ella S], pastor Trinity Episcopal Church,
   h 319 7th
Coolbaugh Frank E, clk Panhandle, b 319 7th
Coolbaugh Marion, student, b 319 7th
Coon (*see also Koon, Koons, Kuhn and Kuns*)
Coon E Frank [Christina], lab, h 1330 Smead
Cooper John [Mary E], clk, h 1914 George
Cooper Mary E, grocer 1701 George, h 1914 George
Cooper Oliver W [Harriet], ins agt, h 1506 Spear
Cooper U Stacy [Juniette], brakeman, h 1320 George
Copeland (*see also Coupland*)
Copeland Alexander [Elizabeth], clk, h n s Barkley, 2 e Clifton av
Copeland Burtis [Nella], truckman, h s s Barkley, 1 e Clifton av
Copeland Claudius, student, b n s Barkley, 2 e Clifton av
Coplen Simeon R [Sarah], lab, h n s Wab River pike, 1 e 18th
Coppock Elwood, agt, b 1211 Toledo
Coppock Laban G [Emma], lab, h n s Culbertson, 3 w Frank (S T)
Coppock Lembert W, clk The Barnett, b same
Corbett Wm C [Ella], vet surgeon 116 Canal, h same
Corbit Martin [Margaret], lab, h 223 Washington
Corcoran Agnes C, mach opr W D Craig, b 1221 Toledo
Corcoran Bridget [wid Michael], h 1221 Toledo
Corcoran Elizabeth, dressmkr, b 1221 Toledo
Corcoran Mollie M, mach opr W D Craig, b 1221 Toledo

LOGANSPORT WALL PAPER CO.
Furnishes the Best Wall Paper Hangers and Decorators,
407 MARKET STREET.

| COR | 88 | COT |

Corcoran Sylvester, b 1221 Toledo
Corcoran Thomas, tmstr, b 1221 Toledo
Cordell Charles M [Anna E], real estate 15 State National Bank Bld'g h 1423 High
Corden Daniel [Johanna], street contr 900 17th, h same
Corden John [Elizabeth], lab, h 507 Fitch
Corden Julia M, b 900 17th
Corden Mamie M, dressmkr, 900 17th, b same
Corden Mary, student, b 507 Fitch
Corden Michael B [Catharine], mach Panhandle, h 801 17th
Corden Michael E, lab, b 900 17th
Corden Nellie, student, b 900 17th
Corden Wm G, tel opr, b 900 17th
Cornell Amy [wid Joseph], b 1413 George
Cornell A Frank, county supt of schools, h Galveston, Ind
Cornell Ruby L, music teacher 611 Race, h same
Cornell Wm [Annetta], second hand goods 12 6th, h 611 Race
Corner Sample Room, The, Alfred L Anderson, propr, 300 3d
Cornwell Emma D, stenogr Lairy & Mahoney, b 1430 North
Cornwell James L, clk, b 1430 North
Cornwell Jane E [wid Jesse], h 1430 North
Cornwell Lewis J, clk G W Seybold & Bros, b 1430 North
Cory J Bert, comp, b 207 Bates
Cory Harry, clk, b 12 Biddle av
Cory Isaac N [Elizabeth], commission merchant 311 5th, h 12 Biddle av
Cosgriff John J, attendant Insane Hospital, b same
Coss Lewis C [Mary E], blksmth, h 419 Pleasant Hill
Costello Minnie E, domestic, b 722 Michigan av
Costello Richard C, student, b 722 Michigan av
Costello Richard M [Sarah E], patrolman, h 605 High
Costello Wm K, del clk McCaffrey Bros, r 117 5th
Costenborder Nathan [Margaret], electrician J J Hildebrandt, h 820 Race
Costenborder Walter E, marble polisher Schuyler Powell, b 820 Race
Cotner Andrew [Susan], lab, h 607 Linden av
Cotner Daniel M [Jane], well driller, h 7 Columbia
Cotner George [Anna], farmer, h 1013 High
Cotner Harry, bartender, r 509 Canal
Cotner Isabelle, h 728 Linden av
Cotner James A, lawyer 222½ 4th, b 1013 High
Cotner John, plasterer, b s s Clay 2 w Humphrey
Cotner John A [Emma], fireman Panhandle, h 2005 George
Cotner Minnie, domestic, b s s Clay 2 w Humphrey
Cotner Samuel, tmstr, b s s Clay 2 w Humphrey
Cotner Wm [Nancy], plasterer, h s s Clay 2 w Humphrey
Cotner Wm [Rose], plasterer, h n e cor Culbertson and Standley (S T)
Cotner Wm E [Emma, mat mkr, h 424 Day

Cotton George [Alice E], condr Panhandle, h 1714 Broadway
Coughlan John F [Jennie], foreman, h 514 13th
Coughlin Katherine A, b 423½ 4th
Coughlin Timothy, condr Panhandle, b Island View Hotel
Coulson John F, drugs 304 Market, h 720 North
County Assessor's Office, John Hynes assessor, court house
County Auditor's Office, Josiah G Powell auditor; court house
County Clerk's Office, Andrew P Flynn clerk, court house
County Commissioner's Office, Abraham Shideler pres, Joseph E Crain, Daniel Woodhouse, commissioners, court house
County Coroner's Office, Frederick A Busjahn coroner, 407 4th
County Jail 321 North
County Recorder's Office, Jacob W Wright recorder, court house
County Sheriff's Office, Isaiah A Adams sheriff, Charles W Homburg sheriff elect, court house
County Superintendent's Office, A Frank Cornell supt, court house
County Surveyor's Office, Harry W Troutman surveyor, court house
County Treasurer's Office, Isaac N Cash treasurer, court house
Coupland (*see also Copeland*)
Coupland Susan L, agt, b 1230 Broadway
Court House, s e cor 4th and North
Courtney Catharine, mach opr W D Craig, b 616 Ottawa
Courtney Edward, tel opr Panhandle, b 616 Ottawa
Courtney Emma, student, b 616 Ottawa
Courtney John, cigarmkr, b 616 Ottawa
Courtney John, cigarmkr, b 408 Railroad
Courtney Julia, comp The Chronicle, b 408 Railroad
Courtney Michael [Anna], lab, h 616 Ottawa
Courtney Michael E [Susannah], tel opr Panhandle, h 729 Linden av
Courtney Orlea, h 408 Railroad
Courtney Owen, lab, b 611 North
Courtney Simon, h 408 Railroad
Courtney Thomas, h 408 Railroad
Courtney Thomas [Catharine], condr Panhandle, h 804 Linden av
Covault Anna, teacher, b 812 North
Covault Ida, teacher, b 812 North
Covault Joseph E, b 812 North
Cowan Harry A [Ada M], pharmacist B F Keesling, h 613 Linden av
Cowgill Charles [Laura E], buggy washer E F Stewart, h 16 Melbourne av
Cowgill Nathan C, physician 203 Sycamore, h same
Cowgill Ora, clk D W Powlen, h 203 Sycamore
Cox Jacob J, bill poster, b 202½ 6th
Cox John N [Nettie], barber, h 123 State
Cox Nellie [wid James E], h 315½ 3rd
Cox Ora E, teacher, r 806 North
Cox Sherman, hostler, b 1813 North

Cox Wm R, hoop coiler, b 1209 Toledo

Coyle (*see also Coil*)

Coyle Frank P [Minnie] (Coyle & Landry), h 317½ 3rd

Coyle James [Gertrude], asst sexton Mt Hope cemetery, h n w cor Pleasant Hill and McCarty

Coyle & Landry (Frank P Coyle, Otto B Landry), saloon 417 3rd

Cozatt Usul A, student, b 626 Linden av

Cragan Anna, student, b 1919 Market

Cragan Caleb J [Margaret], carp, h 1919 Market

Cragan Harry [Minnie], car rep, h w s Burlington rd, 4 s Wash tp rd

Cragan Homer J, student Hall's Business College, b Kokomo rd, 3 m s city

Cragan Isadora, teacher, b 1919 Market

Cragan Paul, student, b 1919 Market

Cragun Sylvester S, horse breeder rear 518 North, h Marion pike, 5 m s e city

Craig Harry, student, b 2029 Broadway

Craig Isaac N [Catharine], engr Panhandle, h 2029 Broadway

Craig John, fireman, b 2029 Broadway

Craig Joseph [Minerva], h 816 North

Craig Wm D [Fannie M], merchant tailor, clothing and overall mnfr 416 Broadway, h 2306 Broadway (See adv back cover)

Craighead Ada, domestic Orphans' Home

Craighead Elizabeth [wid James A], matron Orphans' Home, h same

Crain (*see also Crane*)

Crain Barton R, plumber A W Stevens, b 2202 North

Crain Charlotte B, b 2202 North

Crain Harriet A, clk T A Spry, b 2202 North

Crain Horace E, student **Hall's Business College**, b 2202 North

Crain Joseph E [Sarah], architect and superintendent 4-5 Masonic Temple, also county commissioner, h 2202 North (See adv class architects

Crain Rodney J [Evelyn], blksmith, b 2202 North

Crain Schuyler C, draughtsman J E Crain, b 2202 North

Cramer Burrell J, student, b 1910 Market

Cramer Elburt E, student, b 1910 Market

Cramer Frederick R, cabinet mkr, b 825 Race

Cramer Louis M, painter I N Cool, b 825 Race

Cramer John W [Ellen], brakeman Panhandle, h 716 11th

Cramer Robert W [Amanda], cabinet mkr, h 825 Race

Cramer Walter H, student, b 1910 Market

Cramer Wm H [Effie], carp, h 1910 Market

Crane (*see also Crain*)

Crane Charles A [Nellie], brakeman Panhandle, h 1229 Toledo

Crawford Nettie S, stenogr Metropolitan Life Ins'Co, b 1427 North
Crawford Wm, lab, b w s Michigan av 1 n Vandalia R R
Crawford Wilson [Ella], lab, h 23 Ottawa
Crawshaw George [Ella], condr Panhandle, h 1123 Erie av
Creery (see also-McCrary)
Creery Conrad E, lab, b 423½ Market
Creery Leland S, painter I N Cool, b 423½ Market
Creery Louise, h 423½ Market
Creery Roy V, trimmer I N Cool, b 423½ Market
Creery Silenus S, plumber J J Hildebrandt, b 423½ Market
Crim James, lab, b 930 Toledo
Crim Martha J [wid Lewis], h 930 Toledo
Crismond Horace J [Lillie A], hardware, mantels, grates, stoves, tinware, bicycles and sole agent for Stransky steel ware 312 Market, also secy and treas Excelsior Mfg Co, h 1613 Broadway (See adv right top lines)
Crismond John W [Mary E], physician 528 Broadway, h 320 Pearl
Crispen Willis [Leota], lab, h 606 w Broadway
Crist Barbara [wid Wm], h 214 N Pearl
Crist Frank, agt, b 1327 George
Crites Franklin [Elizabeth], brakeman Panhandle, h 316 12th
Crockett Lee O, b 221 w Broadway
Crockett Moses M [Lucinda J], h 221 w Broadway
Croll John [Susan], trav agt, h 8 Melbourne av
Cromer Albert, brakeman Panhandle, r 403 High
Cromer Charles O, b 208 Canal
Cromer Elizabeth J [wid David P], nurse 208 Canal, h same
Cromer Minnie M, clk, b 208 Canal
Cromer Col Robert [Mary A], propr Logansport Cement Works, h 412 Melbourne av (See adv p 5)
Cromer Robert H, bkkpr Logansport Cement Works, b 412 Melbourne av
Cronin Bessie, teacher, b 130 Osage
Cronin David, wks broom factory, b 416 e Wabash av
Cronin David, lab, b 225 Washington
Cronin Honora [wid David], h 225 Washington
Cronin James [Mary], h 416 e Wabash av
Cronin Margaret, b 225 Washington
Cronin Mary A, domestic, r 225 Washington
Cronin Thomas, lab, b 416 e Wabash av
Crook Mary E [wid Charles S], h 214 Barron
Crooks Josiah S [Nora], poultry fancier, h w s Royal Center pike, 2 n Pleasant Hill
Crookshank Frank W [Viola B], engr Vandalia, h 118 Osage
Crosby Mary J [wid James], h 14 Biddle av
Crosby Ruby, waiter Hotel Johnston, b 14 Biddle av
Crowe Daniel V [Margaret], engr Vandalia, h 800 Linden av

Croxford Anna E [wid Joshua], h 1405 Wright
Croxford Wm, lab, b 521 High
Cuff Wm, butcher McCaffrey Bros, r 430 North
Cullen Mirble A, packer, b 355 Sycamore
Cullen Sadie, b 4 Canal
Culler Harry L, comp, b Logan House
Culp Harvey H, bkkpr, b n e cor Hanna and Pleasant Hill
Culp Joseph M [Minerva B], barber and dancing teacher 219 6th, h
    n e cor Hanna and Pleasant Hill
Culver Harvey J, b cor 7th and Bringhurst
Cumberland Presbyterian Church, ——————— pastor, n s Broad-
    way, 2 e Brown
Cumming (*see also Cummings and Cummins*)
Cumming John [Mattie], paper hanger Logansport Wall Paper Co, h
    1818 Broadway
Cummings Daisy J, student, b 2007 Market
Cummings Edward E, clk, b e s Treen, 2 s Norcross
Cummings Emily [wid John G], h 405 w Broadway
Cummings George M [Mary E], agt Metropolitan Life Ins Co, h 2007
    Market
Cummings Harvey, carp, b n s Bates,, 2 w Vandalia R R (Dunkirk)
Cummings Harvey R [Phebe J] (Cummings & Morgan) h 414
    w Market
Cummings Horace W [Clara E], bkkpr, h e s Liberty, 3 s Columbia
Cummings James M, waiter, b e s Treen 2 s Norcross
Cummings Jessie F, millinery and fancy goods 405 Broadway, b 405
    w Broadway
Cummings John G, lather, b e s Treen 2 s Norcross
Cummings Mame R, b e s Treen 2 s Norcross
Cummings Nellie, b 405 w Broadway
Cummings Thomas J [Celestia], foreman, h e s Treen 2 s Norcross
Cummings H Wm [Clara E], bkkpr, h 525 Liberty
Cummings Wm G (Longwell & Cummings), b 405 w Broadway
Cummings & Morgan (Harvey R Cummings, Felix S Morgan), up-
    bolsterers and furniture mnfrs 229 3d (See adv p 7)
Cummins (*see also Cumming and Cummings*)
Cummins Ollie A [May], bkkpr, h 1810 North
Cummins Susan A [wid Robert], b 1810 North
Cunningham Carrie, domestic 907 North
Cunningham Edward [Julia], clk J H Foley, h 1829 Market
Cunningham Mary [wid Terrence], h 414 19th
Cunningham Margaret, b 414 19th
Cunningham Marguerite, stenogr, b 531 Helm
Cunningham Patrick F [Fannie B], restaurant 401 Canal, b same
Cunningham Wm G [Fannie P], brakeman Panhandle, h 1920 Spear·
Cupp Allen J, del clk W I Shearer, b 1224 Wright
Cuppy (*see also Koppe*)

Cuppy David [Eliza], watchman, h 1530 Toledo
Cuppy Hattie, b 1530 Toledo
Current Lemuel [Thankful], lab, h e s Mich av 1 n Sugar
Curtis Albert, b 200 Montgomery
Curtis Jessie, b 513 North
Curtis Sarah A [wid Samuel C], h 200 Montgomery
Curtis Ward S, engr Vandalia, b 200 Montgomery
Curtis Wm N [Lillian], lab, h 7 Osage
Cushman Adah R, teacher, b 112 8th
Cushman Henry C [Ruth E], dentist 418½ Broadway, h 112 8th
Cushman Mame A, teacher, b 112 8th
Cushman Marie O, student, b 112 8th
Custer Anna N [wid John L], b 2016 Broadway
Custer Clarence C [Millie], asst city electrician, h 212 Michigan av
Custer Daisy M, clk, b 227 North
Custer Frank C [Rosa B], motorman, h 2015 Broadway
Custer Geo A, lawyer 7–8 Baldwin-Thornton Bldg, b 1197 Broadway
Custer Grace A, teacher, b 610 Broadway
Custer Ivy S, laundress, b 1216 Spear
Custer Louise S [wid Wm], laundress, h 1216 Spear
Custer M Maude, clk G W Seybold & Bros, b 456 Michigan av
Custer Samuel A [Anna J], h 456 Michigan av
Custer Willis C [Lou F], painter, h 227 North

D

Dabney Lady I, student, b 413½ Broadway
Dacy Ellen [wid Jeremiah], h 205 Wheatland
Dacy Mary, dressmkr, b 205 Wheatland
Daggett Andrew [Sarah], lab, h 1606 Toledo

Daily Dennis, jr, student, b 1324 Spear
Daily Levi [Mary], lab, h s e cor Michigan av and Smith
Dale Barbara [wid Joseph A], b 700 High
Dale Henry B [Ellen], mason, h s s Shultz, 2 e Frank (S T)
Dale Lillie, nurse 216 Broadway, h same
Dale Martha [wid Eli], b 108 Hanna
Dale Matilda A [wid James], h 216 Broadway
Dale Wm H [Agnes], monument setter Schuyler Powell h 1324 Smead
Dalrymple Lillie M, clk, b 506½ Broadway
Dalrymple Samuel H [Kate], engr, h 506½ Broadway
Dalrymple Stella E, mach opr The Journal, b 506½ Broadway
Dalzell (see also Delzell)
Dalzell J Henry, brakeman Panhandle, b 1217 Market
Damm Samuel M [Rhoda], carp, h 430 Tanguy
Darlington John R, carp, h 1511 Wright
Darlington Olive, b 1511 Wright
Darlington Sarah, b 1511 Wright
Darrah Frank M [M Margaret], painter Holbruner & Uhl, h 223
    Wheatland
Darrah Thomas W [Mary J], harnessmkr, h 223 Wheatland
Darter Frank [Jennie], fireman Panhandle, h 1026 Toledo
Davenport S Catharine [wid Clark S], h 319½ 3rd
Davenport Harry, clk J T Elliott & Son, b 624 North
Davidson (see also Davisson)
Davidson Guy R [Minnie], carp, b 815 Race
Davidson Jacob [Elizabeth A], janitor High School Bldg, h 815 Race
Davis Albin [Minnie], carp, h 613 Chicago
Davis Charles, brickmason, b 500 Canal
Davis Daniel, b n s Bartlett 4 w Anthony (S T)
Davis Edgar W [Elizabeth], baggageman Panhandle, h s s Tipton 2
    w Day
Davis Edward E, attendant Insane hospital, b same
Davis Eugene E [Mary E], comp, h 1501 High
Davis Fannie [wid John], agt, h 315½ 4th
Davis B Frank [Mattie], brakeman Panhandle, h 1331 George
Davis Frederick [Minnie], clk J D Ferguson & Jenks, h 217 w Market
Davis George W [Henrietta], bridge carp, h w s Holland 1 s State
Davis Jacob P, painter, b w s Holland 1 s State
Davis Jennie, seamstress Insane Hospital, b same
Davis John, b 1612 Broadway
Davis John H, b 1229 North
Davis John M [Jennie M], lab, h 603 Liberty
Davis Josephus [Mary J], lab, h n s Bartlett 4 w Anthony (S T)
Davis Matilda H [wid John D], h 316½ Market
Davis Theodore [Rose B], car rep Panhandle, h 106 State
Davis Thomas L, comp Longwell & Cummings, r 414 North
Davisson (see also Davidson)

H. J. GRISMOND, 312 Market Street,
Hardware, Stoves and Tinware.

DAV | 95 | DEH

Davisson A Clinton [Nellie B], gen secy Y M C A, h 919 Spear
Davisson James G [Flora], painter, h 58 Front
Dawes Jennie C, h 627 Miami
Day Bessie L, student, b 927 Spear
Day Edward M, bottler Columbia Brew Co, b 316 Burlington av
Day Harry, student, b 506 12th
Day James A [Emily J], tinner C A Eberlein, h 927 Spear
Day John [Mary], h 316 Burlington av
Day John jr, b 316 Burlington av
Day Nicholas [Catharine], barber 504 12th, h 506 12th
Dean Anna B, student, b 1101 Spear
Dean Mary L, teacher, b 1101 Spear
Dean Sarah, h 419½ 4th
Dean Sidney, student, b 419½ 4th
Dean Timothy [Julia], mach Panhandle, h 1101 Spear
Deane Benjamin [Elizabeth], patrolman, h s w cor 13th and High
Deane Charles J, clk Panhandle, b s w cor 13th and High
Deane Ellen, domestic 2226 Broadway
Deauer Allen J, lab, b 220 Burlington av
Deauer Eliza A [wid John F] h 220 Burlington av
Dear Charles K [Mary C], paper ruler, h 1429 North
DeArmand Sarah [wid Joseph], boarding 511 Canal
Debolt Virgil L [Mary E], brakeman, h 315 College
Deboo Ernest L [Rosetta], lab, h 214 Heath
Deck George [Viola], tmstr, h 500 Chicago
Deck Lawrence [Mary], lab, h 1329 Spear
Peck Sophia, b 1329 Spear
Decker John, lab, b 204½ 6th
Dederick Walter C [Jessie A], trav agt Bridge City Candy Co, h 909
    Linden av
Dee James plasterer, b 521 High
Deegan Bridget, domestic 213 Eel River av
Deel May, attendant Insane Hospital, b same
DeFord Henry A [Emma], carp h s s Charles, 3 w Standley (S T)
DeFord Joseph [Lilly], lab, h w s Burlington rd, S s Wash tp rd
DeFord Metta, student, b s s Charles, 3 w Standley (S T)
DeGroot Harry H, b 218½ 6th
DeGroot Mary E [wid Wm H H], h 218½ 6th
DeHaven Andrew J [Anna E[, paper hanger Logansport Wall Paper
    Co, h 226 Brown
DeHaven Charles H [Minnie], bartender John Eckert, h 300 Burling-
    ton av
DeHaven Estella, b 2029 North
DeHaven Joseph, attendant Insane Hospital, b same
DeHaven Mary C [wid Samuel], b 1114 Eric av
DeHaven Nancy A [wid Christopher], b 2029 North
DeHaven Samuel [Carrie A], driver C L Woll, h 408½ 3rd

Iaven Wm [Mary], engr, h 1100 Spear
Iaven Wm W, engr, b 1700 Spear
trich Joseph F [Hattie M], mgr Maxinkuckee Lake Ice Co, h 528 Chicago
aplane John [India], lab, h 1605 Spear
ong Allen [Jennie], carp h 1630 North
ong Nelson, student, b 1630 North
zell (*see also Dalzell*)
zell David E [Harriet M], dentist 416½ Market, h 1918 North
nerly Charles [Myrtle A], barber, h 312 Miami
lotte Wm B [Mary E], lab, h 730 15th
npsey Edward [Mary E], tmstr, h 706 Clifton av
npsey Elmer V [Nora], bottler, h 709 Chicago
npsey Frank A, tmstr, b 706 Clifton av
npsey James O, lab, b 706 Clifton av
npsey Joseph [Demaras], car rep, h 2007 North
npsey Thomas J [Matilda], lab, h 404 Clifton av
luth Catherine [wid Edward], chambermaid Island View Hotel, r 418 3rd
bo Alvin [Ada M], letter carrier, h 616 North
bo J Earl, stripper, b 521 Ottawa
bo Eliza [wid Robert], h 521 Ottawa
bo Harry, cigar mnfr 504½ Broadway, b 521 Ottawa
bo Robert, cigarmkr, b 521 Ottawa
nehy Daniel [Margaret], fireman, h 50 Washington
ning Mary, domestic 1726 Broadway
nis Gertrude, b 225 Washington
nis Katharine [wid Marion], b 225 Washington
ton Sadie L, laundress, h 507 North
zler Wm, fireman Panhandle, r 1069 Toledo
Poy Minnie, domestic 418 4th
1 Daisy, domestic 810 Broadway
lin Wm [Margaret], lab, h 426 16th
ees Allen L [Frances M], bartender M J Bligh, h 510 Miami
eese Bertha A, domestic 1515 Broadway
eese Oliver [Evaline], stonemason, b 102 n 6th
eese Thomas J [Elizabeth L], lab, h 15 Cecil
eese Wm II [Sarah], mason, h n s Howard 1 w Frank (S T)
ey Bessie, music teacher 1202 North b same
ey Fannie, b 1202 North
enter Herman J, clk Dewenter & Co, r 303½ 4th
enter John C [Louise] (Dewenter & Co), h 929 High
enter & Co (John C Dewenter), hatters and mens' furnishers, 303 4th (See adv class Hatters)
ertmann Bernard [Nellie], lab, h w s Johnson 1 s Franklin
Tolf Carrie M, stenogr S M Velsey, b 112 Pawnee
Tolf Edward A, fireman Panhandle, b 426 12th

De Wolf Henry W [Caroline P], agt, h 112 Pawnee
Diamond Frances D, b e s Balsam 2 n Pink
Diamond John W, lab, b e s Balsam 2 n Pink
Diamond Wallace [Eliza], lab, h e s Balsam 2 n Pink
Diamondstone Anna, b 117 9th
Diamondstone Benjamin, clk, b 117 9th
Diamondstone Mendal [Mary] dry goods 424 Broadway, b 117 9th
Diamondstone Ray, bkkpr, b 117 9th
Diamondstone Rebecca, b 117 9th
Dickerhoff Emma M, queensware 415 Broadway, b 737 Spencer
Dickerhoff Mary A [wid Matthew M], h 737 Spencer
Dickey Anna, domestic 829 Spear
Dickey Belle, domestic 1614 Market
Dickey Lafayette E, lab, b n w cor Knowlton and 18th
Dickey Miles [Mary], engr Panhandle, h s s Knowlton 1 e 17th
Dickey Oliver, mach, b 1101 Toledo
Dickey Perry H [Mattie J], h 1101 Toledo
Dieckmann Charles [Sophia], ck clk Wabash, h 401 Helm
Dieckmann Louis [Elizabeth], staple and fancy grocer 218 Market, h
204 w Broadway
Diehl Edwin J [Anna], livery stable 1027 Erie av, h 1024 Toledo
Diehl Frank J [Mary E], bartender R Kreuzberger, h 1817 North
Diehl Harvey, r 414 First
Dietl Eva [wid George], b 1920 George
Dietl Joseph J [Dora], lab, h 1920 George
Dietrich Charles F, pres Logansport & Wabash Valley Gas Co, h
New York City
Dietrich Mary, domestic 823 Market
Dietsche Gustave [Mary], bartender Charles Smith, h 521 Helm
Diffenbaugh Bessie, clk John Gray, b 1729 Broadway
Dill Charlotte, attendant Insane Hospital, b same
Dill Walter E, student Hall's Business College, b 1706 Broadway
Dilley Clinton L [Mamie] (C L Dilley & Co), h 322 Eel River av
Dilley C L & Co (Clinton L Dilley), lime, cement, coal, flour and
feed 515 Market (See adv class Lime and Cement)
Dillon Anna, attendant Insane Hospital, b same
Dillon Katharine [wid Patrick], h r 21 315½ 4th
Dilts Harry E, b 121 Osage
Dingman Andrew J, b 1412 High
Dingman Harry L [Adella], foreman Panhandle, h 1412 High
Dinnen Anna, domestic 202 Broadway
Diperd Ellsworth A [Matilda], lab, h s e cor Daisy and Garden
Dipert Elza [Tillie], lab, h 308 Burlington av
Dirton George, carp, b 66 Washington
Dirton Wm, carp, b 66 Washington
Dirton Wm [Mary V], lab, h 66 Washington
Discher John F [Dessie], fireman Panhandle, h 804 17th

$186,000,000 of Life Insurance
WAS WRITTEN BY THE
METROPOLITAN LIFE. of New York. in 1896

W. O. WASHBURN,
Superintendent
Logansport District,
Crawford Block.

| DIV | 98 | DON |

Diver George, b 1303 George
Diver Henry [Minerva], lab, h 1303 George
Diver John, clk, b 1303 George
Dixon Alonzo [Jane], tmstr, h e s Burlington rd, 1 n Wash tp rd
Dixon Daisy S, student, b 1221 High
Dixon Drucilla [wid John], b Biddle's Island
Dixon Elias D, crater I N Cool, b 1420 Toledo
Dixon Monroe, condr Panhandle, h 1221 High
Doan John Wm [Mary E], lab, h 24 Uhl
Doan Marshal [Minnie], h s s Shultz, 2 e Standley (S T)
Dodd Albert B, civil engr, b 1405 High
Dodd Arthur, student, b 502 Melbourne av
Dodd Wilbur [Ida B], carp, h 502 Melbourne av
Dodd Wm J [Margaret E], agt, h 1405 High
Dodds Catharine [wid Samuel], wks Marshall's Steam Laundry, b 1815 North
Dodds Thomas J [Louise], switchman Panhandle, h 1611 North
Dodge Charles G, secy National B L and S Assn, b 2331 Broadway
Dodge J Edward [Catharine], trav agt J T Elliott & Son, h 415 13th
Dodrill George W [E Jane], foreman Logansport & W V Gas Co, h 214 Washington
Doggett Harry [Kate], gas fitter A W Stevens, h 10 State National Bank Bldg
Doggett Susan [wid Lee H] housekeeper 1829 Toledo
Dolan Catharine, b 1301 Spear
Dolan Edward, student, b 1301 Spear
Dolan J Edward [Mary], bkkpr, h 1717 Broadway
Dolan Gertrude M, student, b 622 Market
Dolan John T [Mary], engr Panhandle, h 1214 George
Dolan Katharine M, b 622 Market
Dolan Margaret M, b 622 Market
Dolan Michael P, fireman Panhandle, b 1301 Spear
Dolan Opera House, Wm Dolan, propr, s w cor 3d and Broadway
Dolan Patrick [Ellen], lab, h 1301 Spear
Dolan Robert L, student, b 622 Market
Dolan Sylvester, brakeman Panhandle, r 1224 Wright
Dolan Thomas, lab, b 810 e Wabash av
Dolan Wm (Wm Dolan & Co), propr Dolan Opera House, h 622 Market
Dolan Wm H [Olive M], molder, h 718 11th
Dolan Wm J [Elizabeth], switchman Panhandle, h 1006 Erie av
Dolan Wm & Co (Wm Dolan), mnfrs water wheels, n w cor Canal and Berkley
Donahue (*see also Donoho*)
Donahue Bridget [wid Michael], h n e John 1 w Michael
Donahue Louise, ironer Insane Hospital, b same
Donaldson Albert N [Susan E], photographer 406½ Broadway, h 128 Sycamore

Schuyler Powell

1031-1035 Toledo St.

aldson Clara, student, b 1726 Broadway
aldson Edna, b 1726 Broadway
aldson Mary, ironer Insane Hospital, b same
aldson Nevance R [Ida], frt agt Panhandle, h 1726 Broadway
aldson Wm J [Kate A], saloon 411 Market, h 927 Race
nelly Wm [Catharine T], car rep Wabash, h 125 Washington
oho (*see also Donahue*)
oho James, vet surgeon, 422 4th, r 408½ Market
ovan Edward L, dep county treas, r 9 Barnes Blk
ley Lawrence M [Emma], condr Panhandle, h 103 Helm
ley Lewis [Fannie], blacksmith, h 1703 Knowlton
ley Nicholas W [Dollie], brakeman Panhandle, h 20 Eel River av
little Clarence H [Minnie E], mach Panhandle, h 1726 North
little George E [Harriet], mach Panhandle, h 1406 Market
little Montraville, lab, b 1406 Market
ett Harry R [Minnie B], tailor W D Craig, h 417½ 4th
man Mary [wid Wm], b s s Logan & Western pike, 2 w Burlington av
sch Andrew [Catharine A], stonemason, h 221 Melbourne av
sch August W [Eva], storekpr Insane Hospital, h 200 State
d Rebecca J [wid Eventus], b 210 State
gherty Joseph J, clk John Gray, b w s Standley, 1 n Lincoln (S T)
gherty Michael, cigarmkr, b w s Standley, 1 n Lincoln, (S T)
gherty Margaret [wid Philip], h w s Standley 1 n Lincoln (S T)
glass Albert H [Elizabeth], supt public schools, office n w cor
  7th and Broadway, h 1219 Market
glass Amanda, seamstress, h 212 7th
glass Amor W, waiter, r 1 Burlington av
glass Daisy, b e s Tanguy, 2 n Clay
glass Edward D, student, b 432 Sycamore
glass George R, butcher, b e s Tanguy, 2 n Clay
glass James L, lab, b 914 Linden av
glass James M [Lillian], agr implements 228 5th, h 712 High
glass John R [Helen], gardener, h w s Johnson, 2 n Fulton
glass Marion [Louise], tmstr, h 914 Linden av
glass Robert, waiter, r 1 Burlington av
glass Wm [Sarah R], h 716 North
glass Wm E, lab, b 914 Linden av
glass Zenith [wid James], h e s Tanguy, 2 n Clay
ll Ellen [wid Lewis], b e s Washington, 1 s Biddle (S T)
ley Bridget, domestic, b 523 North
ley Dottie, student, b 106 Front
ley Frank [Julia], saloon 408 Wall, h 1427 Broadway
ley Geneva, student, b 106 Front
ey Jasper A [Julia], physician and surgeon 413½ Broadway,
  106 Front
ey John, lab, b 523 North

Downey Katharine, domestic, b 523 North
Downey Mamie E, student, b 106 Front
'Downey Mary [wid Jeremiah], h 523 North
Downham Daniel [Viola], steward Island View Hotel, h 420½ 3rd
Downham Emma J, student, b 16 Osage
Downing J Frank, condr, r 402½ Market
Downs Chas R, clk Panhandle, b 1727 High
Downs Wm H [Eleanore], condr Panhandle, h 1727 High
Doyle Alice, student, b 116 Wheatland
Doyle Anna, milliner, b 824 Race
Doyle Charles F, student, b 19 Ottawa.
Doyle Charles J, student, b 824 Race
Doyle J Edward, student, b 19 Ottawa
Doyle Harry, student, b 19 Ottawa
Doyle James C [Cecelia], carp Panhandle, h 815 19th
Doyle John E [Rebecca], carp h 824 Race
Doyle Michael [Sarah], sec foreman, h 19 Ottawa
Drake Walter [Jennie], brakeman Panhandle, h 1107 Toledo
Dravenstadt J Bruce [Gwendolin], brakeman, h 419½ Market
Dreyer Gustave, staple and fancy grocer 73 Bates, h 226 Pratt
Dreyer Gustav H, clk G Dreyer, b 226 Pratt
Dreyer Minnie [wid Henry], h 226 Pratt
Drew Anna, attendant Insane Hospital, b same
Driscoll Honora [wid Lawrence], h 10 Washington
Driscoll John W, molder, b 10 Washington
Driscoll K & M (Kate and Mame), dressmkrs 10 Washington
Driscoll Kate (K & M Driscoll), b 10 Washington
Driscoll Lawrence, fireman Vandalia, b 10 Washington
Driscoll Mame (K & M Driscoll), b 10 Washington
Driscoll Michael R, molder Bridge City Construction Co, b 10 Washington
Dritt Edith, student, b 628 Miami
Drompp Frederick G [Lena E], clk G W Seybold & Bros, h 309 Wheatland
Drompp Henry F mach hd Parker & Johnston, h 223 Main
Drompp John F [Sophia], lab, h 300 Humphrey
Drompp Sophia, tailor, b 223 Main
Duckworth Dora E, b 409 North
Duckworth Frank [Anna], law student, b 409 North
Duckworth Housen [Cynthia], h 409 North
Duckworth Wm, clk, r 311½ 3d
Duesner Philip [Alice C], mgr Western Union Tel Co, h 627 North
Dugan Harry, student Hall's Business College, b 1920 High
Dugan John [Catharine], core mkr, h 1920 High
Dugan John P, student, b 1920 High
Dunbaugh John F [Catharine], stonemason, h 1606 Wright
Duncan Archelaus [Ella M], comp, h 100 Helm

Duncan Clarence, coachman 328 w Market
Duncan Joseph [Nellie], carp, h 202 Berkley
Duncan Louise M [wid James], domestic 1112 North
Duncan Nellie domestic 813 Market
Duncan Wm B [Hulda], baggagemaster Panhandle, h 205 Osage
Dunham Ella A, dressmkr 207 3d, h same
Dunham Judson [Mary], lab, h 1302 Spear
Dunham May, b 512 Fitch
Dunham Milton, b 218 Miami
Dunkel (see also Dunkle)
Dunkel Gertrude, b e s Burlington rd 5 s Wash tp rd
Dunkel Johanna, b 2023 Spear
Dunkel John A [Elizabeth], agt, h e s Burlington rd 5 s Wash tp rd
Dunkel John A jr, student, b e s Burlington rd 5 s Wash tp rd
Dunkel Mary, b e s Burlington rd 5 s Wash tp rd
Dunkel Rose, b e s Burlington rd 5 s Wash tp rd
Dunkelberg Charles A [Anna C], h 817 Spear
Dunkin Albert, b 904 Race
Dunkin Alice M, domestic, b 904 Race
Dunkin Frank N [Josephine], lab, h 904 Race
Dunkle (see also Dunkel)
Dunkle Amy [wid Peter], boarding 1124 Broadway
Dunkle Elizabeth, b 1124 Broadway
Dunkle John, painter, b 1124 Broadway
Dunkle Sarah L, supervisor Insane Hospital, b same
Dunkle Wm D, clk McCaffrey Bros, b 913 Race
Dunlap Esther J [wid Edward B], h 224½ Market
Dunlap Lalla O, student, b 224½ Market
Dunn Bros (Edward F and Patrick F), grocers 425 3rd
Dunn Catharine L, dressmkr, b 1716 Smead
Dunn Edward F [Frances] (Dunn Bros), h 425½ 3rd
Dunn John [Bridget], h 214 Canal
Dunn Patrick F [Margaret] (Dunn Bros), h 322 w Broadway
Dunn Terrence [Catharine], h 810 e Wabash av
Dunn Thomas C, bkkpr First National Bank, b 214 Canal
Dunn Sophia, teacher, b 316½ Broadway
Dunn Wm C, cashier Logansport & W V Gas Co, b 214 Canal
Dunn Wm C [Anna M], clk Louis Dieckmann, h n s Market, 1 w C
Dunsey John, hostler 927 North
Dunsey Sarah, domestic 927 North
Dunwoody Allie L [wid John W], h 626 Miami
Durham Daisy, domestic 1 7th
Duschen Christopher, cigarmkr, b 616 12th
Duschen Louise [wid Michael], h 1305 Wright
Duschen Louise E, domestic 926 North
Duschen Michael, painter, b 1305 Wright
Duvall Edward, coachman, b 1520 George

Duvall Matilda, h 1520 George
Dwire George W [Christina], h 1816 North
Dwyer Agnes, domestic 1104 Broadway
Dwyer Martin J, stoker gas wks, b 416 2d
Dwyer Patrick [Maria], stoker gas wks, h 128 State
Dye Mary R [wid Wm S], b 518 Market
Dykeman Charles E [Mary E], restaurant 322 Broadway, h 827 Linden av
Dykeman David D [Mary T], lawyer 204½ 4th, h 127 Broadway
Dykeman Frederick A, baker 317 Market, r 312½ Market
Dykeman Richard [Louise], engr Vandalia, h 1119 Linden av
Dziegielewski Policarp [Anna], lab, h 21 Ottawa

E

Eads Pearl, domestic, b 127 Ash
Eads Wm C, b 629 Sycamore
Earley Anna E, b 909 High
Earley George [Margaret], condr Panhandle, h 917 High
Earley James W, condr Panhandle, h 909 High
Earley Wm F, lab, b 909 High
Earp Ella, dressmkr, b s s L & W rd, 5 w Anthony
Easterday Arthur, student, b 91 Michigan av
Easterday, Jacob [Margaret], h 91 Michigan av
Easty John E, foreman I N Cash, r 322½ Market
Eberle Henry J [Anna E], clk Wm J Parker, h 1804 Toledo
Eberle Wm R, student, b 527 Sycamore
Eberlein C Augustus, stoves, tinware, all kinds of roofing, galvanized iron and copper work 505 12th, r 506 12th (See adv class Furnaces)
Eberts David [Samantha], lab, h n w cor Standley and Biddle (S T)
Eberts Henry, lab, b n w cor Standley and Biddle (S T)
Eberts Stephen, asst janitor court house, b 507 North
Eberts Stephen E, painter, r 203½ 6th
Eckerle Carl [Mary A], butcher, h 119 Barron
Eckert Christian [Aurilla K], blksmth 1 3d, h 119 Osage
Eckert Barbara [wid Ignatius], b 413 2d
Eckert Elizabeth, domestic 1205 High
Eckert Elizabeth [wid Frank], b 513 w Market
Eckert Frederick J, lab, b 411 Bates
Eckert John, imported and domestic wine, beer, liquors and cigars 230 Market, h 224 Eel River av (See adv p 6)
Eckert John D, lab, b 411 Bates
Eckert Lizzie W, domestic, b 411 Bates

.sa J [wid Wm], h 411 Bates
1a [wid John], laundress, h e s Anthony, 1 n Clay
Arthur, lab, b 20 Uhl
1rtha J [wid John] b 20 Uhl
eodore [Hannah L], sec foreman, h 20 Uhl
John C [Lura H], local agt T H & I R R Co (Vandalia
302 Wheatland
Alvin, brakeman Panhandle, r 417½ Market
1rora M, student Hall's Business College, b 107 Hanna
1arles N [Emma B], driver Star Steam Laundry, h 615

Grant [Minnie], engr Vandalia, h 627 Sycamore
1ward J, brakeman, b 415½ 3rd
iza [wid John W], b rear 121 Front
1nnie, b s s Bartlett, 3 e Kloenne (S T)
·auk W [Ella B], draughtsman Panhandle, h 1523 North
2orge W [Aurora M], fire insurance and loans 314½ 4th,
1anna
1rry, brakeman, b 413½ 3rd
hn [Mary], condr Panhandle, h 1222 Toledo
llie M, student, b 412 Pratt
·man B [Mary E], ins agt, h 412 Pratt
1nna, b s s Bartlett 3 e Kloenne (S T)
be [wid Richard E], b 720 Spencer
·ust [Mary], hide dealer, h 11 Columbia
1, student, b 11 Columbia
b 721 Race
· [wid John], h 1503 Spear
)uis D, supervisor music public schools, b 1004 North
·y N [Selinda], h n s Culbertson 2 w Kloenne (S T)
a M, b n s Culbertson 2 w Kloenne (S T)
Alice R, bkkpr T N Quigley & Co, b 1317 North
Florence, student Hall's Business College, b 1317 North
George C [Ellen], bench hd Stevens Bros, h 202 Pratt
Georgiana [wid George W], h 1317 North
Nellie, bkkpr and notary Wm T Wilson 206½ 4th, b
·th
tharine [wid Samuel W], b 1527 Market
muel W [Lizzie], fireman, h 1527 Market
eng hostler Panhandle, h 418 Helm
1, domestic 1501 George
a M, wks Bridge City Candy Co, b 7 Uhl
e, wks Bridge City Candy Ca, b 7 Uhl
[Kate], h 7 Uhl
ne, student, b 7 Uhl
, b Camp Chase 2 n Davis Bridge
) [Sophia] farmer, h Camp Chase 2 n Davis Bridge

gdalen, b 420 16th

id A, bkkpr J T Elliott & Son, h Camp Chase 1 n Davis

Lydia, h 117 Market

Stewart [Charity], watchman Logansport & W \ Gas Co,) Toledo

idolin **Orchestra**, Edgar E Powell mgr, 505 Broadway (See lass Bands, etc)

ank E [Rosanna], marble cutter Schuyler Powell, h 1030 lo

orge D [Elizabeth], carp, h 719 14th

:ethusa M, student, b 927 North

anche, student, b 820 North

lward, trav agt, r 411½ 4th

nma, b 1426 High

:ther, student, b 927 North

arry S, secy The J T Elliott Co, b 927 North

:hu T [Caroline], vice pres and treas The J T Elliott Co, h North

hn W [Olive], bridge carp Panhandle, h 808 Sycamore

seph, fireman Panhandle, r 1224 Wright

T Co, The, Wm N Elliott pres, Jehu T Elliott vice pres and , Harry S Elliott secy, wholesale grocers 309–315 Broadway

ouise E, b 829 Market

Martin [Priscilla], expert horseshoer 318 3d, h 820 North adv back cover)

issouri, dressmkr 101 4th, b same

phronia J [wid De Witt C] h 829 Market

ubal, h 101 4th

illard [Mary], motorman, h 1917 High

m H [Ida M], trav agt J T Elliott & Son, h 1426 High

m M, pres The J T Elliott Co, b 829 Market

rest, attendant Insane Hospital, b same

lerick, brakeman Panhandle, b 624 North

a A, b 117 Market

eorge, lab, b 1417 Broadway

lichael, student, b 1417 Broadway

:ichael H [Margaret F], street contr 1417 Broadway, h same

/m, student, b 1417 Broadway

Jos W, lab, b 928 Erie av

Minnie, b 4 Canal

Wm [Caroline], truckman Panhandle, h 928 Erie av

r Andrew [Elizabeth], lab, h n s Culbertson 2 e Kloenne (S T)

r Frank, clk Schmitt & Heinly, b n s Culbertson 2 e Kloenne)

/m T, trav agt Schuyler Powell, h Remington, Ind

iarles J, insp G W Seybold & Bros, b 715 Linden av

s Frank E, attendant Insane Hospital, b same
s Henry, cigarmkr, b 705 Linden av
s John [Catherine], lab, h 705 Linden av
s Joseph [Annetta], clk, h 222 Pratt
s Josephine, student, b 715 Linden av
s Louisa, b 705 Linden av
s Margaret A [wid Charles], h 715 Linden av
s Wm H, b 715 Linden av
s Wm H [Minnie], butcher, h 931 Linden ar
George S, wks Ash & Hadley, b e s Burlington rd 3 s Wash tp rd
oth R Dale, coachman 2300 Broadway
oth Lulu, domestic 1317 Market
oth Worley E [Mae], fireman, h 501 Fitch
y Charles F [India], painter, h w s Sycamore 1 s Pleasant Hill
y Joseph [Martha], h n e cor Shultz and Frank (S T)
y Robert C, carp, b n e cor Shultz and Frank (S T)
ett Harriet C [wid Wm], dressmkr 1110 Spear, h same
ett Lycurgus [Cora H], marble and granite monuments n e cor
th and High, h 212 Hanna (See adv p 5)
ett Lylie [Cora], marble cutter L Emmett, h 212 Pleasant Hill
ett Percy, marble cutter L Emmett, b 204 Ottawa
ett Wm C, marble cutter, b 1110 Spear
re Mills, D & C H Uhl proprs, cor Front and Melbourne av
h Edward E [Vola V], clk The Otto Shoe and Clothing Co, h
13 North
s Charles W [Belle], del clk, h 2125 Smead
brecht Clara E, bkkpr Louis Dieckmann, b 110 Pawnee
brecht Emilie, clk Wiler & Wise, b 110 Pawnee
brecht Henry W [Mary], teacher, h 110 Pawnee
brecht Louise, tailor, b 110 Pawnee
brecht Mary, dressmkr 110 Pawnee, b same
brecht Wm F, student, b 110 Pawnee
fried Louise [wid Frederick], h 410 Grove
nd Laura, domestic 321 North
Harry, brakeman, b 1211 Toledo
sh Lutheran Church, Rev. B. E. Shaner pastor, s w cor First
id Market
John W [Lina E], artist 310½ Market, h 1425 North
Melvina [wid Harvey], h s s Wab River rd, 5 e Coles
Frederick [Grace G], clk Adams Ex Co, h 103 Osage
ld Elizabeth, b 1400 Wright
ld Lewis [Ella], moulder, b 130 Pawnee
ld John [Mattie], stone mason, h 1400 Wright
ld John W, lab, b 1400 Wright
ld Wm, tinner C A Eberlein, b 1400 Wright
t Carrie B, b s,s Smith, 2 e Morgan
t Charles A [Carrie C], letter carrier, h 316 Michigan av

ASSETS
of Metropolitan Life
AT THE END OF 1896

~OVER~
$30.000.000

NY 106 EVA

Enyart Charles M, lather, b s s Smith, 2 e Morgan
Enyart Frank L, b s s Smith, 2 e Morgan
Enyart Nora E, wks T M Quigley & Co, b s s Smith 2 e Morgan
Enyart Wm B [Kate M] (Enyart & Chambers), h s s Smith 2 e Morgan
Enyart & Chambers (Wm B Enyart, Oliver Chambers), bottlers 214 6th
Epping Elizabeth [wid John B], h 625 Linden av
Epping Frank J, lab, b 625 Linden av
Epping George, tinner H J Crismond, b 625 Linden av
Epping Mary E, b 625 Linden av
Epstine Louis [Mary E], clk, h 123 4th
Epstine Mary E, clairvoyant 123 4th, h same
Erbaugh Charles M [Addie E], tel opr, h 141 Park av
Erdmann August, lab, b 1804 Knowlton
Erdmann Herman [Mary], h 1804 Knowlton
Ertle John H, barber C D Marshall, b 1813 George
Ervin (see also Erwin, Irvin)
Ervin Anna, laundress, h 616 High
Erwin Helen W, student, b 1007 Linden av
Erwin Joseph E [Elizabeth], druggist, h 1007 Linden av
Eskew Anthony [Clarissa], lab, h s w cor Wilkinson and Railroad
Eskew Stella R, b s w cor Wilkinson and Railroad
Estabrook Amelia E [wid John L], h 1314 North
Estabrook David L [Mary E], lab gas wks, h 114 10th
Estabrook Edward J, clk Wabash, b 1314 North
Estabrook George H, del clk Wiler & Wise, b 114 10th
Estabrook May, teacher, b 1314 North
Ettinger Albert, brakeman, r 417½ Market
Ettinger Finley C [Lettie], carp, h w s Park av, 3 n Wabash av
Etnire Charles E [Anna] (Ray & Etnire), h 918 Linden av
Etnire David F [Jennie], tmstr, h 2003 Market
Etnire Elwood, finisher I N Cool, b 2003 Market
Etnire Eugene, student **Hall's Business College,** b 3 m e city
Etnire Frank A, clk Ray & Etnire, b 626 Michigan av
Etnire Isaac [Cynthia], carp h 626 Michigan av
Etnire John M [Lottie], clk Ash & Hadley, h 922 Linden av
Etnire Osmond, upholsterer Ash & Hadley, b 626 Michigan av
Euper Florence, b 12 Canal
Euphrat Charles [Cora E], cigarmkr John Mulcahy, h 200 w Wabash av
Eurit C Norton [Bertha M], clk Adams Ex Co, h 122 State
Evans Belle, clk Wiler & Wise, b 514 Miami
Evans Edward, condr Panhandle, r 1 State National Bank Bldg
Evans Harvey (Rush & Evans), b 2022 Spear
Evans Jesse J [Effie], fireman Panhandle, h 1729 Market
Evans W Otis [Lulu B], clk Panhandle, h 414 13th
Evans Rebecca [wid John M], h 514 Miami

veringham Mary L [wid John S], b 1117 Market
versole Charles D [Anna S], dentist 330½ Market, h 1725 North
vilsizer (*see also Uebelshaeuser*)
vilsizer Charles, student, b 308 Miami
vilsizer Conrad [Sarah], fireman Vandalia, h 308 Miami
vilsizer, Conrad W, cigarmkr, b 308 Miami
vilsizer James T, clk The Otto Shoe and Clothing Co, b 308 Miami
vilsizer John, cigarmkr, b 308 Miami
xcelsior Mfg Co, Isaac Himmelberger pres, Horace J Crismond secy
    and treas, drugs 528 Broadway

F

aber August [Mary], mach Panhandle, h 219 Main
aber Janet S [wid Ruel], h 727 Spencer
aber Mary, clk Wiler & Wise, b 219 Main
aber Rosa C, clk Wiler & Wise, b 219 Main
aber Rudolph [Louise], carp Panhandle, h 821 17th
air Grant [Daisy E], painter I N Cool, h 1224 Toledo
airchild M Jane, h 24 Melbourne av
airchild Jesse, barber, b 24 Melbourne av
airchild John F, tmster, b 24 Melbourne av
airchild Margaret J, b 24 Melbourne av
airman Daisy, student, b 1400 High
airman George [Catharine], engr Panhandle, h 1424 Market
airman Ida, student, b 1400 High
airman James C [Caroline], h 1423 High
airman James W [Mary A], condr Panhandle, h 1400 High
lbush Charles B, del clk J H Foley, b 528 Pratt
lbush Frederick [Mary K], h 528 Pratt
lbush Michael J, painter, b 528 Pratt
ley Anna E, b 127 Smith
ley James [Anna], h 127 Smith
ley Mary, b Asylum rd ½ m w Cicott st bridge
ley Mary C, b 127 Smith
ll Daniel, lab, b 721 Chicago
ll Frank, lab, b 721 Chicago
ll Kate, b 1416 Ohio
ll Martin, plumber, b 1416 Ohio
llon Anna [wid John], cook Tucker House, r 411 Linden av
nsler Austin D [Jessie M], city editor The Pharos, h 513 Miami
nsler Johanna [wid Michael, b 150½ George
ranbaugh Lizzie, domestic 913 Market
rmer Grace, ironer Insane Hospital, b same

Farmer Samuel W, bkkpr, r 419 Market
Farnsworth Flora [wid Walter S], h 1919 High
Farrell Bernard [Nancy], lab, h 609 12th
Farrell Frank, lab, h 2015 Market
Farrell Josephine, dressmkr 128 Canal, h same
Farrell Namie, student, b 609 12th
Farrell Margaret, b 128 Canal
Farrell Margaret [wid Patrick], h 128 Canal
Farrell Michael [Della M], train desp Panhandle, h 2303 North
Farrell Patrick J (Farrell & Ludders), b 128 Canal
Farrell Regina, b 1514 Broadway
Farrell Thomas, b 1422 Broadway
Farrell Thomas J, b 2015 Market
Farrell Wm, flagman, b 19 Ottawa
Farrell Wm [Mary A], car insp Panhandle, h 1514 Broadway
Farrell Wm T, dep county surveyor, b 1514 Broadway
Farrell & Ludders (Patrick J Farrell, John Ludders), saloon 502
    Broadway
Farrer Alice [wid Joseph M], h e s Sherman 2 s Lincoln (S T)
Farrer John [Anna], tmstr, h s s Shultz 3 e Standley (S T)
Farrer Lula, domestic, b e s Burlington rd 1 n Wash tp rd
Faulkner Peter [Ida A], lab, r 316½ Market
Favors Kate, seamstress Insane Hospital, b same
Fegans Pearl, domestic, s s Bates 1 w Panhandle R R
Felker Charles [Eliza], h 224 Colfax
Felker Elizabeth, b 224 Colfax
Felker Frank F, switchman Panhandle, b 224 Colfax
Felker George F, condr Panhandle, b 224 Colfax
Felker Nettie M, b 224 Colfax
Fellers John E [Davy], carp, h s s Bartlett 1 e Standley (S T)
Fender George [Lizzie E], clk G W Seybold & Bros, h 317 w Broadway
Fender George W [Susie A], lawyer and justice of the peace, 11–12
    Baldwin-Thornton Bldg, h 619 Melbourne av
Fennimore Charles H, lab, b 600 e Wabash av
Fennimore Nannie C, domestic 22 State
Fenton Charles O [Carrie B], propr Logansport Times, h 1012 Spear
Fenwick Hannah [wid Henry], h 1119 Toledo
Fenwick Harry [Ella], boilermkr, h 913 12th
Fenwick Thomas [Jean A], plumber, h 619 Ottawa
Fergus Cornelius [Melissa], tmstr, h 1218 Toledo
Fergus Ella, domestic 1124 Broadway
Fergus Frank, clk, b 500 Michigan av
Fergus Georgiana, tobacco stripper, b 1218 Toledo
Fergus James A, lab, b 1218 Toledo
Fergus Rose, domestic, b 112 Ash
Ferguson (*see also Furguson*)
Ferguson Ada [wid Maurice], dressmkr 110 Sycamore, h same

'erguson Andrew J, barber, b 200 Cicott
'erguson Charles S, clk J D Ferguson & Jenks, b 520 w Market
'erguson Catharine, waiter Hotel Johnston, b 110 Sycamore
'erguson Elmer, foreman, b 522 12th
'erguson Frank R, foreman E F Stewart, r 414½ 4th
'erguson Ida I, b 520 w Market
'erguson James, house mover 1320 North, h same
'erguson John D [Ella] (J D Ferguson & Jenks), h 801 Broadway
'erguson J D & Jenks (John D Ferguson, Almon P Jenks), cloth-
　iers, hatters and furnishers, 322 Market
'erguson Mary, b 110 Sycamore
'erguson Sebastian C [E Lucinda], contractor, h 520 w Market
'erguson Warren H, student, b 801 Broadway
'ernald Willmont L [Emma], lumber cor 5th and High, h 1003 North
'erriter Ellen [wid Patrick], b 521 Melbourne av
'errier Sarah M, domestic 231 w Market
'ettig Anthony [Mary], mach hd Panhandle, h 424 Grove
'ettig Benedict, lab, b 1807 Jefferson
'ettig Charles [Mary], blacksmith, h 1404 Smead
'ettig Charles C [Catharine], car rep Panhandle, h 1528 Smead
'ettig Edward [Ella], drayman, h 623 Race
'ettig Frank [Amelia], lab, h 518 13th
'ettig George, mach Panhandle, b 1404 Smead
'ettig George [Sophia], lab, h 1807 Jefferson
'ettig John, del clk J J Rothermel, b 1404 Smead
'ettig John, b 518 13th
'ettig John [Mary], car insp Panhandle, h 1014 19th
ettig Joseph, lab, b 1807 Jefferson
ettig Joseph [Catharine], lab, h 1306 Wright
ettig Joseph A [Anna], cornicemkr, h 423 Grove
ettig Michael [Margaret], lab, h 1803 Jefferson
ettig Sophia, domestic 1530 Broadway
ezler Wilson E, comp The Times, b 217 Broadway
ickle David D [Carrie], lawyer, also receiver Logansport Ry Co,
　214½ 4th, h 1401 Market
idler Ada, b 1814 Market
idler August [Jane], trav agt, h 915 High
idler Frank P [Mary E], clk James Beshoar, h 212 w Wabash av
idler Harry, student, b 915 High
idler Jane E [wid Curtis], h 330 Eel River av
idler Wm F [Martha J], dealer in junk, hides, pelts, furs, tallow,
　and wool 322 5th, h 1814 Market (See adv class Junk Dealers)
ield Adrian A [Nancy], engr Panhandle, h 2009 Broadway
ields Mabel, domestic 1710 High
ife John J [Sarah J], tmstr Stevens Bros, h 215 State
igley Charles, student, b 519 Canal
igley Katharine, h 519 Canal

Fike David [Lavina], tinstr, h 1420 Toledo
Filler Clemence [Sarah], engr, h 710 13th
Fillman Julius, agt, r 224½ Market
Fillmore Ernest [Catharine], car rep Panhandle, h 1312 Indiana
Fillmore Julius, carp, b n e cor Canal and Oak
Filson George, harnessmkr Kreis Bros Mfg Co, b 406 High
Finch Alice, student, b 1430 High
Finch Charles W [Anna J], supt bridges Vandalia, h 1430 High
Finch Juliet, clk C W Graves, b 1430 High
Findlay Cora B, teacher of music, 429 North, h same
Findlay Frank L [Cora B], piano tuner, 429 North, h same
Findling Henry [Elizabeth], lab, h 808 15th
Finegan Arthur, blksmth, h 724 Linden av
Finegan Arthur E, blksmth, b 724 Linden av
Finegan Margaret S, b 724 Linden av
Finegan Patrick, b Logan House
Finegan Robert J, student, b 724 Linden av
Finfrock James W, condr Panhandle, b Hotel Johnston
Fink Cora E, student, b 810 Race
Fink Earl, elevator boy The Barnett, b n s Shaw 1 w Clifton av
Fink Eli W [Sarah C], condr Panhandle, h 810 Race
Fink George, b n s Shaw 1 w Clifton av
Fink Jacob A [Minerva J], lab, h n s Shaw 1 w Clifton av
Fink Olive B, student, b 810 Race
Fink Selig [Tillie], lab, h w s Standley 2 s Biddle (S T)
Fink H Shelby, lab, b n s Shaw 1 w Clifton av
Finlay Brewing Co, Burgman & Bro agts, n e cor 15th and Smead
Finn James [Mary], saloon 6 3d, h same
Finning James [Anna], boilermkr Panhandle, h 1716 Smead
First National Bank, Andrew J Murdock pres, Wm T Wilson vice
    pres, Wm W Ross cashier, John F Brookmeyer asst cashier, 314
    4th   (See adv front cover)
First Presbyterian Church, Rev Douglas P Putnam pastor, s e cor
    7th and Spencer
First Universalist Church, ——— ——— pastor, s s Broadway bet 8th
    and 9th
Fischer (*see also Fisher*)
Fischer Catharine [wid Samuel], h 717 Bringhurst
Fischer Daisy, bkkpr, b 717 Bringhurst
Fischer Wm C [Ida W], trav agt, h 717 Bringhurst
Fishel Harry, brakeman Panhandle, b 522½ Broadway
Fisher (*see also Fischer*)
Fisher Ben [Rose M], drugs, paints, oils and physicians' supplies

H. J. GRISMOND, 312 Market Street,
All Kinds of Metal Roofing.

| FIS | 111 | FLA |

Fisher Jennie [wid Wm], laundress, h 317 17th
Fisher John W H, lab, b 317 17th
Fisher Joseph [Martha], notions, h 226 Osage
Fisher Katie [wid Solomon], h 524 Market
Fisher Mamie, student, b 226 Osage
Fisher Mary, dressmaker 206 Pratt, h same
Fisher Max J [Clara] (Henry Wiler & Co), h 715 Broadway
Fisher Morris, trav agt, b 524 Market
Fisher Nelson D [Vina A], railway mail clk, h 501 Melbourne av
Fisher Oscar B, student **Hall's Business College,** b 108 Hanna
Fisher Pearl R, b 108 Hanna
Fisher Sadie, b 226 Osage
Fisk Helen B [wid Charles W], h 928 North
Fissel Andrew J [Minnie M], carp, h s w cor Treen and Norcross
Fitch Leroy [Anna R], trimmer city electric light wks, h 301 Helm
Fitch Martha G [wid Frederick], boarding, 510 Market
Fitz Charles, caller Panhandle, b 1505 Spear
Fitz Joseph [Dora], fireman Panhandle, h 600 e Wabash av
Fitz Kate, domestic 314 3rd
Fitzer Bertie J, student, b 511 w Market
Fitzer Henry C [M Catharine] (Fitzer & Singer), h 511 w Market
Fitzer Willard C, lawyer 212½ 4th, r 1203 Broadway
Fitzer & Singer (Henry C Fitzer, Harry E Singer), grocers, 431
    Broadway
Fitzgerald Alice, cigarmkr, b 306 Pratt
Fitzgerald John J [Mary A], engr, h 12 Washington
Fitzgerald Josephine, b 17 Uhl
Fitzgerald Kate, dressmkr, b 17 Uhl
Fitzgerald Lizzie A, carpet sewer G W Seybold & Bros, b 17 Uhl
Fitzgerald Mary, stenog, b 17 Uhl
Fitzgerald Mollie, housekeeper The Barnett, b same
Fitzgerald Morris [Bridget], lab, h 17 Uhl
Fitzgerald Morris, jr, fireman Vandalia, b 17 Uhl
Fitzgerald Wm [Mary A], insp Logan & W V Gas Co, h 320 North
Fitzsimmons Bridget [wid Patrick], b 313 7th
Flaherty Roger C [Mary G], engr Vandalia, h 217 Vine
Flanagan (*see also Flanegin*)
Flanagan Frank, granite cutter Schuyler Powell, b 16 Michigan av
Flanagan George W [Eliza], auctioneer 16 Michigan av, h same
Flanagan Henry W, gas fitter, b 16 Michigan av
Flanagan John, brakeman Panhandle, b 922 Erie av
Flanagan John S, lab, b 16 Michigan av
Flanagan J Maud, b 16 Michigan av
Flanagan Owen, lab, b 810 e Wabash av
Flanders Lucius W, lab, Insane Hospital, b same
Flanegin (*see also Flanagan*)
Flanegin Alexander M [Anna J], fireman, h 708 Miami

Flanegin Blanche, b 208 w Market

Flanegin John T [Alice A], hardware, stoves, bicycles and sporting goods, 310 Market, h 208 w Market

Flanegin Mary [wid John], b 708 Miami

Flanegin Mary E, student, b 708 Miami

Flanegin Nellie J, student, b 708 Miami

Flanegin Thomas J, student, b 208 w Market

Fleshman George W [Loretta], lab, h 1723 Knowlton

Flickinger Donald B [Agnes], trav agt, h 900 High

Flood Margaret, domestic 102 10th

Flory Marion [Jennie M], foreman Stevens Bros, h 172 w Wabash av

Floyd Edward J, student, b 629 12th

Floyd Leo, student, b 629 12th

Floyd Nathaniel, lab, b 629 12th

Floyd Richard [Mary], boilermkr Panhandle, h 629 12th

Floyd Wm R, letter carrier, b 629 12th

Flynn Adelbert P, dpty county clerk, b 1 7th

Flynn Andrew P [Nettie B], county clk, h 1 7th

Flynn Ida, teacher, r 914 Broadway

Fogerty Adelia [wid John], b 26 Uhl

Foglesong Daniel S [Etta C], awnings and tents 212 6th, h 703 Ottawa (See adv class Awnings and Tents)

Foglesong John P [Nancy J], real estate 15 State Natl Bank Bldg, h 417½ 4th

Fohrer Charles [Anna], saloon 221 4th, h same

Fohrer Edward, del clk Louis Dieckmann, b 330 w Broadway

Fohrer Elizabeth, b 330 w Broadway

Fohrer Frank, b 330 w Broadway

Fohrer Frederick, stonemason, h 330 w Broadway

Fohrer Jacob, clk Schmitt & Heinly, b 330 w Broadway

Foley James H [Elizabeth J], grocer 228 Market, h 615 Race

Foley James J [Anna], bartender, h 214 Humphrey

Foley James P, captain of police, h 1504 North

Foley James P jr, helper M M Hughes, b 1504 North

Foley Mary, student, b 1504 North

Foley Thomas, engr Panhandle, r 1069 Toledo

Foley Thomas F, stenogr student **Hall's Business College,** b 1504 North

Follen Agnes H, student, b 821 Spear

Follen Anna, seamstress, b 821 Spear

Follen Anna, dressmkr, b 628 12th

Follen John A, student, b 821 Spear

Follen Katharine, opr Logansport M Tel Co, b 821 Spear

Follen Mary, b 821 Spear

Follen Michael, eng hostler Panhandle, b 628 12th

Follen Owen [Bridget], flagman Wabash, h 821 Spear

Follen Owen W, clk H Wiler & Co, b 821 Spear

ollen Patrick F, tel opr Wabash, b 821 Spear
ollen Peter [Bridget], lab, h 628 12th
ollen Peter E, student, b 821 Spear
ord Charles H [Ada], fireman Panhandle, h 1717 North
ord Ephraim, agt, h 7½ Sycamore
ord George M [Ford & Hayworth], h s w cor Shultz and Frank (ST)
ord Husher C [Stella B], chiropodist 413½ Broadway, h same
ord James G, baggagemaster Panhandle, r 403 High
ord Milo A [Jennie], fireman Panhandle, h 417 15th
ord & Hayworth (George M Ford, Wm H Hayworth), wood and iron pumps, sinks etc, well drilling a specialty, 312 5th
orgy George B [Alice O], investment banker 5 Baldwin-Thornton Bldg, h 1228 Market
orgy Glen C, b 1228 Market
orman Mary L, student, b 136 Eel River av
ornoff Anna K, b 416 4th
ornoff Henry J, barber, b 416 4th
ornoff Kate L, dressmkr 416 4th, b same
ornoff Michael F [Catharine], barber 416 4th, h same
ornoff Michael L, barber, b 416 4th
ornoff Savenia, b 520 Canal
orqueran Charles W [Della], tmstr Thompson Lumber Co, h 602 Canal
orqueran J Frank [Ellen], lab gas wks, h 7 Humphrey
orch Emil [Anna], baker, b s s Columbia, 1 e Sycamore
orsyth John L [Nancy], agt, h 1728 Smead
orsyth Ida M, dressmkr, b 1728 Smead
oskett Wesley E [Mattie], engr Panhandle, h 1706 Broadway
oskett Charles W [Belle], fireman Panhandle, h 1617 North
ossler, Adolf [Anna], mach Pan, h s s Charles, 2 e Wab R R (S T)
ossler Anna, b s s Charles, 2 e Wab R R (S T)
ossler Catharine, dressmkr, b 1429 Wright
ossler Charles [Ursula], gardener, h n w cor Shultz and Frank (S T)
ossler Louis [Catharine], lab, h 1429 Wright
ossler Mollie, b 1429 Wright
ossler Wm, attendant Insane Hospital, b same
oster David [Sarah], condr Panhandle, h 2011 Spear
oster Gay H [Edna], trav agt, h 1615 North
oster George W, harnessmkr, b 1214 Spear
oster Harry T, farmer, b n s John, 1 e Creek
oster John [Sarah A], mach Panhandle, h 1416 North
oster John [Sarah E], auctioneer, h n s John, 1 e Creek
oster Margaret, domestic 2115 Broadway
oster Mary A, dressmkr, 1416 North, b same
oster Stella, h 414½ 3rd
oster Wm M, mach hd Panhandle, h 1522 George
oster Wm Reuben, driver J F Grable, b 101 John

Fournier Napoleon L F, trav agt, r 411½ 4th
Foust Arthur W [Alice L], clk G W Seybold & Bros, h 203 Pratt
Foust Myrtle, b 37 Bates
Foust Robert T [Sarah R], carp, h 37 Bates
Fouts Jacob M [Matilda E], drayman, h 229 Montgomery
Fowler Effie, domestic 1315 High
Fowler Hattie, laundress, h n s Miami, 1 e 6th
Fowler Horace F [Niota], brakeman Panhandle, h 722 17th
Fox A Burt [Stella], brakeman, h 1312 George
Fox Charles, lab, b 420 16th
Fox Emanuel, b 420 16th
Fox George W, paper hanger, r 224½ Market
Fox John, painter, b 420 16th
Fox John R, b 1230 North
Fox Joseph [Mary], b 315½ Market
Fox Joseph J [Emma], yd condr Panhandle, h 1719 Spear
Fox Mame B, clk, b 1230 North
Fox Mary A, h 420 16th
Fox Patrick, h 1230 North
Foy Mary, b 1220 Smead
France E James [Sarah A], wks Jas O'Donnell, h 317 Eel River av
Frank Wm, engr, b 418½ 3d
Frankenthal Amelia [wid Siegfried], h 210 8th
Frankenthal Joseph (Berwanger Bros & Co), b 210 8th
Franklin Alvin B [Mollie E], condr Panhandle, b 923 Spear
Franklin Jay A [Anna], fireman Panhandle, h 1700 Smead
Franklin Mary J [wid Jacob A], h 1422 Market
Franklin Kalman [Sarah M], trav agt, b Hotel Johnston
Franklin Meyer E, trav agt, b Hotel Johnston
Frazee Moses R [Mary C], dry goods, carpets, wall paper etc, 418
    Broadway, h 802 Market
Frazee Stuart R, clk M R Frazee, b 802 Market
Frazier Henry, engr Panhandle, r 1069 Toledo
Frazier John, condr Panhandle, b 1224 Wright
Frazier Stephen [Eliza], plasterer, h 217 13th
Freeland Caroline, b 307 n 6th
Freeland Stella A, bindery girl, b 307 n 6th
Freeland Wm B [Hattie J], mach hd Parker & Johnston, h 307 n 6th
Freeman Dora B, b 52 Bates

UP-TO-DATE IN DESIGNS OF MONUMENTS
. We Operate the Only Steam Granite Works in the State.
SCHUYLER POWELL, 1031-1035 TOLEDO STREET.

FRE 115 FUN

Frese Bernard, clk, b 407 Miami
Frese Frederick, shoemkr 325 5th, h 407 Miami
Frese Minnie, b 407 Miami
Frese Minnie [wid Henry], h 407 Miami
Frese Wm, shoemkr, b 407 Miami
Freshour Jennie, domestic 216 3d
Freshour Otta W, lineman Wabash, r 302 North
Friday Susanna [wid George], b 1211 Toledo
Fridiger Wm F [Emma C], clk, h 400 Melbourne av
Frieman Samuel, tailor C W Keller, r 215 Market
Friemel Albert R, bartender, b 520 Canal
Friend Anna, domestic 725 Broadway
Friend Ellen, b 530 Wheatland
Friend George [Mary], blacksmith, h 530 Helm
Friend Mame, bkkpr, b 530 Helm
Friend Margaret M, domestic 724 High
Friend Martin [Mary], h 530 Wheatland
Friend Martin J [Catharine], lab, h 1417 Smead
Friend Thomas, fry cook The Barnett, r Baker's European Hotel
Fries (*see also Frese*)
Fries Andrew, upholsterer Panhandle, b 603 12th
Fries Jacob [Bertha O], boilermkr Panhandle, h 1026 19th
Fries Margaret [wid Jacob], b 1014 19th
Fries Nicholas [Mary], saloon 3 n 6th, h 5 n 6th
Fries Peter, shoemkr 201 5th, h same
Fries Peter [Mary], stone cutter, h 16 Uhl
Friskey John, lab, b e s Washington, 1 s Biddle (S T)
Fritz Wm [Kate], upholsterer J W Henderson & Sons, h 900 Race
Fromeyer Joseph W, mgr Standard Oil Co, h Indianapolis, Ind
Fry M Elizabeth, b 421 w Broadway
Fry Joseph G [Anna M], check clk Panhandle, h 421 w Broadway
Fry Nancy J [wid Martin], b 402 Michigan av
Frye Emma E, trimmer I N Cool, b 1069 Toledo
Fuller Augusta [wid John W], b 720 North
Fuller Clayton E, painter I N Cool, b 1403 Toledo
Fuller Edith R, student, b 719 Miami
Fuller C Frank [Amelia], finisher I N Cool, h 1403 Toledo
Fuller Jethro, student Hall's Business College, b 719 Miami
Fuller John A [Elizabeth M], h 719 Miami
Fuller Milo H, clk, b 719 Miami
Fuller Wm J, b 720 North
Fullgraff Otto C [Amelia], upholsterer Ash & Hadley, h 1109 Linden av
Fultz Otto L [Grace], brakeman Panhandle, h 1507 Smead
Funk George W [Clara A], (Magee & Funk), also U S commissioner, h 500 10th
Funnell Harmon, student, b rear 121 Front

THE BUSY BEE HIVE.
THE PROGRESSIVE DRY GOODS HOUSE.
409-411 Broadway.　　　　　306 Fourth St.

| FUR | 116 | GAL |

Furbec Alpheus L [Ellen G], trav agt, b 128 Eel River av
Furey Alfred, clk, b 708 Bringhurst
Furey Cyrus R, clk, h 708 Bringhurst
Furey Edward, comp The Journal, b 708 Bringhurst
Furey Elizabeth, b 708 Bringhurst
Furguson (*see also Ferguson*)
Furguson Hugh, vice pres Logansport Creamery Co, h Wab River rd, 3 m e city

G

Gagyhan Wm [Elizabeth], condr, h 1016 Toledo
Gaines Mary J [wid Alexander], h n s Bartlett 2 w Anthony (S T)
Galbraith (*see also Gilbreth*)
Galbraith Jefferson, h w s Washington 1 s Biddle (S T)
Gall (*see also Gohl*)
Gall Edward, painter Panhandle, b 2217 Market
Gall John N [Julia], condr Panhandle, h 1406 George
Gall Wm [Laura F], comp The Pharos, h 2217 Market
Gallagan Hannah [wid Thomas], b 1241 Toledo
Gallagan Seth T [Clara], mach hd, h 1241 Toledo
Gallagher Charles, clk, b 516 12th
Gallagher Ella M, dressmkr, b 503 Canal
Gallagher Frank, painter, r 322 3d
Gallagher George S, clk Standard Oil Co, student **Hall's Business College**, b 101 Helm
Gallagher Hugh [Josephine], lab, h 503 Canal
Gallagher John, lab, h 13 Smith
Gallagher John G [Joan], special officer Panhandle sta, h 101 Helm
Gallagher N Josephine, clk G W Seybold & Bros, b 101 Helm

Ask the Clerk
at the Hotel for
the . . . .
Work Done In 5 Hours
WITHOUT EXTRA CHARGE.

 ★ LAUNDRY LISTS.

GEO. OTT, Propr.   405 Market Street.

GAL   117   GAR

Gallion Mary J, h 620 Michigan av
Gallion Wm S, laborer, b w s Oak 2 n Sugar
Galloway Dora, b 304 Clifton av
Galloway George [Emma], lab, h 619 Michigan av
Galloway Henry C, lab, h 304 Clifton av
Galloway Henry W [Delpha], lab, h 13 Nobley
Galloway James, ditcher, b 304 Clifton av
Galloway Orin N, student, b 302 North
Galloway Sarah, b 304 Clifton av
Gallt Joseph W [Mary], foreman J H Lux, h s e cor Bartlett and
    Kloenne (S T)
Gamble George A (Hale & Gamble), b 823 Broadway
Gamble A Wallace [Lucy], teacher, h 1904 North
Gamby Margaret J [wid Casper], grocer, 525 12th, h same
Gammill (*see also Gemmill*)
Gammill Edward F (Schaffer & Gammill), b 601 Helm
Ganger Henry [Maria], mach, h 17 McCarty
Ganger Henry, jr, press feeder Longwell & Cummings, b 17 McCarty
Ganger Mary, b 17 McCarty
Ganger Wm H, pressman, b 17 McCarty
Ganger Wm H [Lizzie O], clk Snider & Alber, h 703 Linden av
Gangloff David, helper, b 124 State
Gangloff Elizabeth, h 308 Burlington av
Gangloff George [Jennie], engr, h 2129 Smead
Gangloff Glenora, student, b 2129 Smead
Gangloff James [Julia], finisher Ash & Hadley, h 126 State
Gangloff John F [Julia E], car rep Panhandle, 124 State
Gangloff Mamie E, student, b 2129 Smead
Gangloff Wm [Ada], car rep Panhandle, h 902 20th
Gannon Patrick [Bridget], h 1416 Ohio
Ganson M Jane, boarding, 528½ Broadway
Ganson John S [M Jane], vet surgeon 306 6th, h 528½ Broadway
Ganter Martin [Mabel], engr Panhandle, h 1815 Market
Ganter Mollie, b 1815 Market
Ganter Susan, b 1815 Market
Gapen Henry C [Harriet W], engr, h 612 Melbourne av
Gapen Walter B, b 612 Melbourne av
Gardner Edwin S [Della], condr Panhandle, h 210 12th
Gardner J Harvey [Sadie], trav agt, h 1319 North
Garnatz Henrietta, dressmkr, 530 Miami, h same
Garnatz John F [Mary], del clk, h 528 Miami
Garrett Austin E [E Florence], baggageman, h 906 Linden av
Garrett Charles W, clk Insane Hospital, b same
Garrett Delmar W, student, b 906 Linden av
Garrett Henry [Christina], clk, h 523 12th
Garrett Lillian, b 523 12th
Garrett Russellus, finisher I N Cool, b 523 12th

PIERCE, The Tailor, CAN MAKE CLOTHES TO FIT YOU.
318 BROADWAY.

| GAR | 118 | GEM |

Garrett Theresa H, student, b 906 Linden av
Garrigan Michael [Catharine J], b 308 North
Garrity John [Mary], h 814 Linden av
Garrity Mary E, milliner 312½ 4th, b 814 Linden av
Garrison Jane, b 81 Washington
Garver Eidson, student, b 1325 North
Garver Margaret [wid Lewis], h 1325 North
Gasaway Armilda, dressmkr, b 728 Linden av
Gaskell J Willis [Rose], fireman Panhandle, h 1822 Spear
Gaskins Wm, attendant Insane Hospital, b same
Gaston Ellis D [Susan M], trav agt, h 631 Sycamore
Gates Edward H, mess W U Telegraph Co, b 13 Ottawa
Gates George [Mary A], lab, h 13 Ottawa
Gates James H [Martha L], clk, h 302½ Market
Gates Jennie B [wid Wm N], boarding 128 Pawnee
Gates Joseph, painter, b 718 12th
Gates W Louis, del clk, b 302½ Market
Gates Nora A, music teacher 128 Pawnee, b same
Gatton Eva, domestic 1218 Market
Geary Robert G [Alice], trav agt, r 809 North
Gee John, lab, b 1405 Wright
Gehring Alpheus M, painter, b 1912 Spear
Gehring Charles [Flora], h 321 12th
Gehring Jennie, h 1912 Spear
Gehring Margaret, teacher, b 1912 Spear
Gehring Sarah A, b 1912 Spear
Gehrking Henry, clk, b 123 Woodland
Gehrking Minnie, seamstress, b 123 Woodland
Gehrking Wm [Lottie], lab, h 123 Woodland
Gehrking Wm jr, lab, b 123 Woodland
Geiger August [Stella], brickmason, h 227 Osage
Geiger Bros (A George, John E and J Henry), cigar mnfrs 422 3d
Geiger Frank, baker, b 26 Front
Geiger George, bartender, b 26 Front
Geiger A George [Pauline M] (Geiger Bros), h 8 Osage
Geiger J Henry (Geiger Bros), b 212 Burlington av
Geiger John E (Geiger Bros), b 212 Burlington av
Geiger Lisette, b 212 Burlington av
Geiger Lisette [wid Jacob], h 212 Burlington av
Geiger Phœbe [wid Frank], domestic 206 6th
Geiselman Jacob, comp, b 206 Canal
Geisey Wm M [Rosa], fireman, h 711 14th
Gemberling Leota, student, b 796 Sycamore
Gemmill (see also Gammill)
Gemmill Elizabeth, h 110 10th
Gemmill Robert, printer, b 110 10th
Gemmill Thomas B, student, b 110 10th

1. J. CRISMOND, 312 Market Street,
Gasoline Stoves, Screen Doors and Windows.

EN   119   GEI

enter Bertha, ironer Insane Hospital, b same

eorge Frederick K, city editor The Journal, b 416 North

eppinger (*see also Gippinger*)

eppinger Jacob E [Rachael] cigarmkr, h 534 Pratt

eppinger John [Lizzie], blksmith, h 131½ 6th

eppinger Judson, lab, b n s Douglass, 1 e 15th

erard August S [E May], janitor court house, h 507 North

erard John [Honora], farmer, h cor Perrysburg and Adamsboro rds

erberding Robert L [N Belle], wks E F Stewart, h 517 Erie av

erhart Anna C, housekpr 609 High

erhart David J [Ellen], blksmth, h 408 Burlington av

etty John A, asst mgr M Rumley Co, b 1109 High

etty John F [R Edwina], mgr M Rumley Co 318 5th, h 1109 High

eyer Gustave A, painter Panhandle, b 1411 Wright

eyer Harry, tinner C A Eberlein, b 1411 Wright

eyer Ida L, dressmkr, b 1411 Wright

eyer John A, student, b 1629 Smead

eyer John E [Albertine], clk Panhandle. h 1629 Smead

eyer Louise [wid Joseph], h 1411 Wright

eyer Mary [wid George], h s s Logan & W pike, 3 w Burlington av

haris Charles H [Margaret], pipeman hose co no 5, h 412 Helm

haris Ida B, dressmkr, h 218½ Market

ibbard Joseph R [Emma], plumber Messinger & Son, h 1725 Broadway

ibbons Edward [Margaret], lab, h n s Shultz, 2 w Frank (S T)

ibbs Charles A, lab, b e s Washington, 1 s Biddle (S T)

ibbs Fannie [wid John], domestic 202 w Broadway

ibbs John, lab, b e s Washington, 1 s Biddle (S T)

ibbs John E [Mary M], poultry dealer 109 Burlington av, h e s Washington, 1 s Biddle (S T)

ibbs Wm [Ida], lab, h 320 15th

ibson Arthur F, clk Melvin Castle, b 114 10th

ibson J Edward (Redmond & Gibson), b 912 North

ibson R Frank [Mary], agt, h 1615 Wright

ibson James M [Julia], fireman Panhandle, h 1810 Spear

ibson Jessie, clk G W Seybold & Bros, b 511 w Market

ibson John A, drayman, b 1220 Linden av

ibson Marie, b 912 North

ibson Marion E, lab, b 1220 Linden av

ibson Milo L [Katharine], wks Parker & Johnston, h 306 Wheatland

ibson Minnie, b 109 Columbia

ibson Oscar P, student **Hall's Business College,** b 1810 Spear

ibson Walter, del clk, b 114 10th

ibson Wm H [Martha], grocer 109 Columbia, h same

isubel John [Dorothy], lab, h n s Bartlett, 5 w Frank (S T)

isubel John H, clk The Wide Awake Grocery, b n s Bartlett, 5 w Frank (S T)

Giesubel Peter, lab, b n s Bartlett, 5 w Frank (S T)

Giffe Wm T [Nannie J], pres The Home Music Co, h 1004 North

Giffin Herbert I [Minnie B], driver Adams Ex Co, h 402 Michigan av

Giffin John [Georgiana], h 1901 Toledo

Gifford Charles W [Ella], condr Panhandle, h 2025 George

Gifford Samuel, railway mail clk, b 415½ 3d

Gifford Wm H, brakeman, b Island View Hotel

Gilbert Emery S [Nettie], barber, h 700 e Wabash av

Gilbert James L [Effie], physician 414½ Market, h same

Gilbreth (see also Galbraith)

Gilbreth John [Ella A], mach Panhandle, h 802 Race

Giles Van D, fireman Vandalia, b 321 Sycamore

Gillam Walter A, barber 431½ Sycamore, b 401 Sycamore

Gillespie Anna (wid James), h 1500 Ohio

Gillespie Daniel A [Florence], grain dealer e s 18th 1 s Wabash river,
    h 1514 Market

Gillespie Ella, domestic 811 Broadway

Gillespie Thomas P [Nannie], sawyer Hillock & Pitman, h 317 15th

Gillespie Wm P, lab, b 1500 Ohio

Gillis Charles H, tel opr, b 803 17th

Gillis Harry E, tel opr, b 803 17th

Gillis Perry A [Sarah E], brakeman Panhandle, h 803 17th

Gillis Viola C, student, b 803 17th

Gillis Wm P, b 803 17th

Gilman Margaret, teacher, r 105 w Broadway

Gilmore Carrie, b rear 115 4th

Gilmore Clara M, b rear 115 4th

Gilmore Harry, hack driver James O'Donnell, b rear 115 4th

Gilmore James P [Catharine], mach Panhandle, h 1705 George

Gilmore Joseph, student, b 1705 George

Gilmore Mame, student, b rear 115 4th

Gilmore Matthew W, book binder, b 1705 George

Gilmore Peter [Mary], hack driver James O'Donnell, h rear 115 4th

Gilsinger Alexander, farmer, b 410 Pratt

Gilsinger Andrew [Mary A], farmer, h 410 Pratt

Gilsinger George, lab, b 410 Pratt

Gilsinger Sophia, b 410 Pratt

Gingrich John F [Jennie A], carp, h 210 w Wabash av

Ginn Myrtle, domestic 1629 Toledo

Gipe Lincoln [Flora B], engr Panhandle, h 2016 Broadway

Gipe I Newton, brakeman Panhandle, b 123 w Broadway

Gippinger (see also Geppinger)

Gippinger Henry G [Dora], cigar mnfr 17 Ottawa, h same

Gippinger Louis L [Anna], packer Logan Milling Co, h 15 Ottawa

Gipson Charles A [Luna E], restaurant 324 3d, h same

Givens Anna [wid Wm], b 930 Linden av

Givens Richard [Susan], cabinet mkr, b 415½ 3d

CRZ, The Tailor

409 MARKET STREET.

Our Reputation for Good Work and Artistic Styles Is Well Established.

121　　　　　　　　　　　　　　GOL

mon John S [Emma], lab, h 11 Biddle av
cy Ambrose, tmstr, b 609 12th
cy Anna, b 609 12th
cy Joseph F, del clk, b 609 12th
cy Wm, tmstr, b 609 12th
co Benjamin, molder, b 509 10th
co Charles, switchman Panhandle, b 509 10th
co Ellen, domestic 715 North
co Mary J [wid Thomas], h 509 10th
er Albert [Mary J], mach Panhandle, h 1431 George
er John [Mary J], engr, h e s 19th, 3 n Stevens
er John jr, lab, b e s 19th, 3 n Stevens
er John R [Bertha], lab h 1421 Ohio
er Susan, student, b e s 19th, 2 n Stevens
sbrenner Peter (Glassbrenner & Bible), r 407½ Market
sbrenner & Bible (Peter Glassbrenner, Wm E Bible), patent gate, 322 Pearl
ford M Catharine, student, b 1816 Spear
ford Wm H [Sarah M], engr Panhandle, h 1816 Spear
on Honora [wid Dennis], h s s Logan & W rd 1 w Standley
on James E [Nora], foreman, h 714 14th
on John J [Josephine], condr, h 1034 Toledo
on Josephine, student, b 1034 Toledo
on Patrick [Etta], brakeman, h 22 Melbourne av
e Anna M, student, b 415 w Market
e August [Christina], contracting mason 415 w Market, h same
e Katherine A, bkkpr Schmitt & Heinly, b 415 w Market
e Mame M, milliner T A Spry, b 415 w Market
en Orrie S [Olive], trav agt, h 1119 High
　Clothing House, Rothschild Bros proprs, cor 4th and Market
ler Christian [Kate], lab, h s s Perrysburg rd, 2 e Michigan av
ler Katharine M, domestic, b s s Perrysburg rd, 2 e Michigan av
ler Mary, b s s Perrysburg rd, 2 e Michigan av
Andrew [Lizzie], saloon 430 Market, h same
Clara, domestic 414 10th
Mary, domestic 420 10th
rd Charles D [Victoria E], engr Vandalia, h 1129 North
ey Thomas J [Emma J], engr electric light wks, h 1106 High
zig Agnes, b 3 Cole
zig Charles [Minnie], bridge carp Panhandle, h 3 Cole
zig Matilda [wid Frederick], b 3 Cole
ig Max, butcher, b 3 Cole
lla, h 207 Elm
see also Gall)
Edward W [Grace], fireman Panhandle, h 418 12th
n Rule, The, Schmitt & Heinly proprs, dry goods and notions, 9-331 Market, s w cor 4th

All Kinds of Life Insurance from $6.00 to $50,000 Written
——BY THE——
Metropolitan Life Insurance Co., of New York.
W. O. WASHBURN. SUPT. LOGANSPORT DISTRICT Office rooms 1, 2 and 3 Crawford Block

GOL . 122 GOS

Goldey Emma [wid Joseph], h 1230 Broadway

Golding Mary, b 1503 Market

Goldsberry Margaret, b 209 n 6th

Goldsberry Rebecca [wid Josiah], h 209 n 6th

Goldsmith Anna [wid Peter], h 215 Grove

Goldsmith Minnie, b 215 Grove

Goldsmith Peter, clk Wiler & Wise, b 215 Grove

Goltz Emil [Otilda P], lab, h 605 Wilkinson

Goltz Mary A, b 221 Wheatland

Goltz Wm C [Minnie G], lab, h 221 Wheatland

Gonser George [Madge C], insurance and real estate 3 Pythian Castle, h 421½ 4th (See adv class Ins Agts)

Good Harry J, mess W U Tel Co, b 300½ Market

Good Helen, tailor, h 300½ Market

Good Ivy N, harnessmkr George Harrison, r 601 Broadway

Good James F, comp, b 6½ Sycamore

Good Samuel O, tailor, r 6½ Sycamore

Good Silas L [Laura M], comp, h 6½ Sycamore

Good Wm A, lab, b 127 Cicott

Goodrich Margaret C [wid John], b 1005 Linden av

Goodridge Henry C, engr Panhandle, b Hotel Johnston

Goodwin Amanda E, music teacher 729 North, b same

Goodwin Lillian P, b 917 North

Goodwin Thomas D, student, b 917 North

Gordon Byron B, draughtsman and patent atty 1–2 Spry Blk, b 1530 Broadway

Gordon Daisy B, student, b 1530 Broadway

Gordon Melville M, comp The Chronicle, b 1530 Broadway

Gordon Moses M [Emma E], real estate and pension claim agt 1–2 Spry Blk, h 1530 Broadway

Gordon Wm [Edith], engr, h 1819 Broadway

Gordon Wm M, tel opr Panhandle, b 1530 Broadway

Gore Luella, h 410½ 3d

Goring James [Ellen], h 618 Miami

Gorman Amanda [wid Silas], b 601 Melbourne av

Gorman Arthur, lab, b n s Bates 3 w Vandalia R R (Dunkirk)

Gorman Daniel V, driver Adams Ex Co, b 1811 George

Gorman Edward, molder, b 601 Melbourne av

Gorman Elizabeth, b 1811 George

Gorman James, lab, b n s Bates 3 w Vandalia R R (Dunkirk)

Gorman James H [Margaret], clk Island View Hotel, h 906 Lytle

Gorman Martha [wid], h n s Bates 3 w Vandalia R R (Dunkirk)

Gorman Riley, carp, b n s Bates 3 w Vandalia R R (Dunkirk)

Gormely Edward, b 1924 Market

Gormely Edward jr [Bridget B], lineman, h 1924 Market

Goss James [Margaret], car insp Panhandle, h 1704 Spear

Goss James, jr, mach Panhandle, b 1704 Spear

HIGHEST GRADES . MONUMENTS
LOWEST PRICES . . MONUMENTS
SCHUYLER POWELL, 1031-1035 Toledo St.

;OS   123   GRA

;oss Joseph H, painter Panhandle, b 1704 Spear
;oss J Thomas, mach Panhandle, b 1704 Spear
;ottselig Rosa [wid John], h 21 Melbourne av
;ottshall Grant, motorman, b 1829 North
;ough Nellie [wid Thomas], b 1923 North
;ould Burt N, pharmacist, b s w cor 12th and Market
;raas Ferdinand H [Elizabeth], clk Wiler & Wise, h 305 Wheatland
;raber Frank J [Anna], painter Panhandle, h 702 Duret
;rable Florence E, student, b 103 6th ·
;rable Jonathan [Esther L], farmer, h 914 Broadway
;rable Jonathan F [Anna E], oil dealer and feed yard 111 6th, h
    103 6th
;race Daisy, b 22 Colfax
;race Edward H, dentist 316½ Market, b 22 Colfax
;race George [Frances A], lab, h 700 Sycamore
;race Joseph G [Cora L], h 610 w Broadway
;race Myndus M, lab, b 700 Sycamore
'race Richard [Ella], mason, h e s Sherman, 3 s Biddle (S T)
race Sadie, b 22 Colfax
race Wm [Sara C] (Wm Grace & Co), h 22 Colfax
race Wm, jr, clk, b 22 Colfax
race Wm & Co (Wm Grace, Tillman W Purkey), "The White House
    Clothiers," 316 Market
rady John, b 1321 Indiana
rady Margaret, b 1321 Indiana
rady Martin, lab, h 1321 Indiana
rady Martin, jr, comp The Pharos, b 1321 Indiana
rady Patrick [Mary], engr Panhandle, h 608 12th
rady Peter [May], switchman Panhandle, b 1321 Indiana
raf Adam (Linton & Graf), r 427½ 5th
raf Henry [Anna], clk Panhandle, h 1430 Smead
raf Jacob, plumber Linton & Graf, r 427½ 5th
raf John H [Minnie], grocer 593 Michigan av, h 595 Michigan av
raf Joseph H [Jeannette], switchman Panhandle, h 210 Berkley
raffis Charles N [Martha J], trav agt, h 610 Linden av
raffis George, student, b 1002 Broadway
raffis Myra, b 612 Linden av
raffis Wm A [Florence V], letter-carrier, h 14 Osage
raffis Wm M [Ella L], shoes 312 4th, h 1002 Broadway
rafflin Henry C [Margaret] (S D Grafflin & Son), h 1115 Market
rafflin S D & Son (Harry C Grafflin, Guy Hensley), brokers,
    415½ 4th
aham Anna H [wid Alexander], b 302 Wheatland
aham Bessie C, domestic 717 High
aham Catharine, b 1217 Market
aham Cyrus J, patrolman, b 1217 Market
aham Dudley C, marble cutter Thos A Peden, b 1217 Market

Established 1867.   Still in the Lead.

DRY GOODS, CLOAKS, FURS,
409-411 Broadway.   WILER & WISE.   306 Fourth Street.

GRA   124   GRA

Graham George H [Josephine], h 1828 North
Graham Harvey W [Eda C], trav agt, h 826 Linden av
Graham Julia A, b 724 Michigan av
Graham Mary A [wid James], h 103 6th
Graham Samuel L [Olive R], tel opr Panhandle, h 105 Osage
Graham Willis G [Catharine,] h 1217 Market
Grainger (see also Granger)
Grainger Emma [wid Samuel C], h 602 Canal
Grainger John I, cook, b 602 Canal
Grainger Minnie E, b 602 Canal
Grainger Wm, porter, b 602 Canal
Graney Dennis, truckman Panhandle, b 1028 Toledo
Graney Dennis P, fireman Panhandle, b 1425 Ohio
Graney Frank [Carrie], switchman Panhandle, h 1427 Erie av
Graney John [Hannah], lab, h 1425 Ohio
Graney Katherine, b 1425 Ohio
Graney Michael [Penelope], lab, h 1028 Toledo
Graney Michael jr, b 1028 Toledo
Graney Patrick, engr Panhandle, r 218 Canal
Graney Wm E, b 1425 Ohio
Granger (see also Grainger)
Granger Albert, brakeman Panhandle, b 213 20th
Granger Catharine E, student, b 122 Canal
Granger Leslie M [Jennie], brakeman Panhandle, h 213 20th
Granger Martin E [Catharine], baker, h 122 Canal
Gransinger Alice R, clk H M Wright, b 203 w Market
Grant Alice M, stenogr Magee & Funk, b 524 Fitch
Grant Angeline [wid Louis C], h 524 Fitch
Grant Charles A [Agnes], wks Kreis Bros, h e s College 1 s Columbia
Grant Charles W [Kate N], bkkpr Stevens Bros, h 112 Canal
Grant Cloyd E, del clk Clover Leaf Dairy, b 155 Park av
Grant George C, comp, b 401 Canal
Grant Gertrude domestic 916 North
Grant Harrison A [Laura E], carp, h 155 Park ave
Grant Harry, student, b 627 Chicago
Grant Jessie, student Hall's Business College, b 155 Park av
Grant Jonas, tmstr, h 626 Chicago
Grant I Louis [S Elizabeth], tmstr, h 1330 Toledo
Grant Mabel, b 308 Wheatland
Grant J Taylor [Emma E], lab, h 121 7th
Grant Wm, tmstr, b 626 Chicago

Graves Ezra B [Julia], carp, s s Shultz, 4 e Standley (S T), h same
Graves Harry, lab, b 606 Canal
Graves Judith N [wid George M], h 701 North
Gray (see also Grey)
Gray Alice, b 518 Miami
Gray Charles [Elizabeth J], baggage master Pan, h 801 w Market
Gray Clark [Catharine], carp, h 66 Bates
Gray Eldon [Anna], brakeman, h 707 Miami
Gray Eli [Mary E], condr Panhandle, h 2227 Broadway
Gray John [Anna], dry goods, notions and hosiery 323-325 4th, h
    1013 North
Gray Millie, b 1013 North
Gray Owen, lab A W Stevens, b 418½ 3rd
Greely Elbert [Lena], brakeman Panhandle, h 1408 George
Green Carl, student, b 1628 Market
Green Carl R, student, b 1203 Broadway
Green Charles R [Minnie L], train desp Panhandle, h 1203 Broadway
Green Charles S [Mary S], painter 1310 Broadway, h 1302 Broadway
Green Elizabeth [wid Benjamin], b 816 Race
Green Emma, dressmkr 816 Race, h same
Green Fannie C, b 520½ Broadway
Green Frank, r 224½ Market
Green Grace, student, b 1921 Spear
Green Harry N [Mabel L], boilermkr Panhandle, h 1520 Spear
Green W Harry [Arena], condr Panhandle, h 1617 Smead
Green W Harvey [Sadie M], engr, h 1921 Spear
Green John O [Myrtle], derrick man Schuyler Powell, h 213 Berkley
Green Lucius C, painter, b 1302 Broadway
Green Marion [Anna], h 1628 Market
Green Marion E, engr Panhandle, b 1914 North
Green Melvina [wid Wm H], h 1914 North
Green Oliver [Jennie], granite cutter Schuyler Powell, h 516 13th
Green Rhoda, student, b 1628 Market
Green Robert B, mach, b 520½ Broadway
Green Robert G [Martha], engr Panhandle, h 520½ Broadway
Green Wm B, painter, b 1302 Broadway
Green Wm N [Eva], foreman, h 517 Clifton av
Greensfelder Aaron, dealer in fine shoes n e cor 3rd and Market, b
    118 10th
Greensfelder Eli [Fannie], clothier 315 Market, h 806 Market
Greenwood Wm, lab, r 315½ 4th
Gregery (see also Gregory)
Gregery Charles, lab, b 509 12th
Gregery Hattie, domestic, b 509 12th
Gregery Johanna, student, b 509 12th
Gregery J Wm [Mary], carp, h 509 12th
Gregg Wm H [Jennie] (Williamson & Gregg), h 406 High

Will Show You a Handsome Line of TROUSERINGS.
PIERCE, the Tailor, 318 Broadway.

| 126 | GRI |

ory (*see also Gregery*)

ory Myrtle, domestic 1928 High

ory Ruth [wid John], h 320 Eel River av

ory Sadie, seamstress, b 320 Eel River av

le Alexander W (Grelle & Reed), h 701 Race

le Byron G, clk, b 701 Race

le Gilbert, clk, b 701 Race

le Zora, b 701 Race

le & Reed (Alexander W Grelle, Wm H Reed), gunsmiths 420½ Broadway

singer Adam [Belle], tailor P J Pierce, h cor Noble tp rd and Clifton av

(*see also Gray*)

Frank, student, b 2010 Market

Patrick [Catharine], fireman Panhandle, h 2010 Market

e Alfred C, Adams Express messenger, r 314½ Market

ley Leona F, student, b 203 w Market

s Frank [Anna], meat market 1526 Market, h 609 Linden av

n Catharine, b w s Sherman 1 s Lincoln (S T)

n Edward [Mary E], h w s Sherman 1 s Lincoln (S T)

n Frank, b 1207 Smead

n Λ Jennie, h 412½ 3d

n John, b w s Sherman 1 s Lincoln (S T)

n John [Julia], lab, h 1207 Smead

n Joseph, wks Wm Heppe & Sons, b w s Sherman 1 s Lincoln (ST)

n Lizzie, b 64 Front

n Λ amie, seamstress, b 1207 Smead

n Mary J, b 64 Front

n Nellie, student, b 1207 Smead

n Robert [Jane], lab, h 64 Front

n Wm, student, b 1207 Smead

n Wm, wks Wm Heppe & Sons, b w s Sherman 1 s Lincoln (S T)

th Benjamin [Emily], tmstr, h 1513 George

th Catharine [wid Griffin], h 1219 Smead

th David [Elizabeth], foreman Panhandle, h 1607 Smead

th John, boilermkr, b 1219 Smead

th Thomas, boilermkr 9 6th, h 1219 Smead

th Wm, boilermkr, b 1219 Smead

th Wm, painter, b 206 6th

by Florence, h 509 12th

es Charles, lab, b 1232 Toledo

es Edith, b 1232 Toledo

le Madge, student Hall's Business College, b 123 Colfax

le Theresa [wid Wm C], h 220 Colfax

r Christina [wid Martin], h 6 Canal

r George, bartender, b 415½ 3d

r George P, lab, b 6 Canal

H. J. GRISMOND, 312 Market Street,
Hardware, Stoves and Tinware.

GRI · 127 GRU

Griner Wm F [Elizabeth], barber, h 517 Miami
Grisley Wilhelmina [wid Wm], housekeeper 321 North
Griswold Marcus L [Lavisa], agent, h 518 Market
Groff Conrad H [Rachael A], sewing mach repr, h 418 w Broadway
Groff Effie, dressmkr, b 418 w Broadway
Grogan Mary [wid James], b 2015 Market
Groh Christine, b s w cor Day and Tipton
Groh Frank M [Emma], baker 431 12th, h 1307 Market
Groh John A [Mary], condr Panhandle, h 414 15th
Gross August [Pauline], lab, h w s Lobelia 2 n Daisy
Gross Elizabeth, student, b 216 Michigan av
Gross Frank E [Anna], engr Vandalia, h 213 7th
Gross Frederick, butcher, b w s Lobelia, 2 n Daisy
Gross John [Kate], sec foreman, h 219 State
Gross Katie, student, b 216 Michigan av
Gross Nettie A, clk H Wiler & Co, b 216 Michigan av
Gross Regina [wid Frederick], h 216 Michigan av
Gross Simon [Elizabeth] (Gross & Ritter), h 510 w Broadway
Gross Wm, tailor, b 215 Market
Gross & Ritter (Simon Gross, Louis H Ritter), grocers 416 3d
Grosvenor Charles, brakeman, b 1209 Toledo
Groth Tillie, b 1529 Niles
Grove (see also Groves)
Grove Charles L, clk, b 704 Chicago
Grove Emma J, h 314½ Market
Grove Ruby, domestic 500 Canal
Grovemeyer Dinah [wid Charles], b 108 4th
Grover Frederick A, wood turner, b 86 Michigan av
Grover Julia A [wid John B], h 318 Eel River av
Groves (see also Grove)
Groves Calvin S [Mary], painter, h 423 Canal
Groves Mary, dressmkr 423 Canal, h same
Groves Rachael E, b 510 10th
Groves Rebecca C, h 510 10th
Groves Wm S [Lydia F], clk I N Crawford, h 116 Osage
Growell (see also Grauel)
Growell Charles A [Ella E], foreman, h 12 Franklin
Growell Charles A jr, painter George Harrison, b 12 Franklin
Groyall Oliver H [Melvina S], cooper, h 115 Franklin
Grubb Harry, student, b 525 12th
Grubb Otto [Isabelle M], drayman, h 525 12th
Grubbs Lewis E [Alice R], tel opr, h 913 Race
Gruber Henry S [Martha C], carp, h 215 Washington
Gruenoch Frederick [Augusta], mason, h e s Sherman 1 n Wash tp rd
Gruenoch Frederick jr, b e s Sherman 1 n Wash tp rd
Gruenoch Lena, b e s Sherman 1 n Wash tp rd
Grusenmeyer Anthony [Elizabeth C], h 96 Eel River av

Grusenmeyer Catharine, domestic, b e s Burlington rd 8 s Wash tp rd

Grusenmeyer Charles X [Theresa], grocer n e cor Burlington and Colfax, h 223 Burlington av

Grusenmeyer Elizabeth, b e s Burlington av 8 s Wash tp rd

Grusenmeyer Frederick M [Susan], blksmth Panhandle, h 317 Montgomery

Grusenmeyer George, gardener, b e s Burlington rd 8 s Wash tp rd

Grusenmeyer Joseph [Mary], gardener, h e s Burlington rd 8 s Wash tp rd

Grusenmeyer Joseph G, clk, b e s Burlington rd 8 s Wash tp rd

Grusenmeyer Lizzie, waiter Island View Hotel, r 405½ Market

Grusenmeyer Lizzie J, b 96 Eel River av

Guard John W, clk, b 2 Osage

Guest Isaac D [Mary W], trav agt, b 206 Canal

Guge Charles, lab, b 232 Toledo

Gugel Catharine, domestic 800 Linden av

Gugel Katharine, pantry woman The Barnett, b same

Guinup Amanda F [wid Wm M], seamstress, h 313½ Market

Guinup George D [Viola C], condr Panhandle, h 627 w Market

Guinup Henry [Mollie], bartender, b 608 Ottawa

Guinup Isaac H, condr Panhandle, b 313½ Market

Guinup Lottie, b 313½ Market

Guinup Merle J, b 627 w Market

Gulick Charles, comp, b 206 Canal

Gundrum Samuel R [Minnie], fireman Panhandle, h 725 17th

Guss Daniel F, lab, b n e cor Wabash av and Lockwood

Guss John [Lena], stone mason, h n e cor Wabash av and Lockwood

Guss John L, lab, b n e cor Wabash av and Lockwood

Guss Ferdinand, lab, b n e cor Wabash av and Lockwood

Gust August [Catharine A], driver, h 14 Johnson

Gust Emma, domestic Insane Hospital

Gust Hugo E, finisher J W Henderson & Sons, b 14 Johnson

Gust Martin G [Minnie C], clk C C Kasch, h 23 Ottawa

Gust Wm, fireman Insane Hospital, b same

Guthrie Frank V [Katharine] (Guthrie & Guthrie), also notary public 428½ Broadway, h 507 Sycamore

Guthrie Joseph [Caroline M], farmer, h 1328 North

Guthrie Margaret J, b 331 w Broadway

Guthrie Mary, h 107 Osage

Guthrie Robert [Laura] (Guthrie & Guthrie), 509 Sycamore

Guthrie Thomas C [Matilda], capitalist, h 331 w Broadway

Guthrie & Guthrie (Robert and Frank V), real estate, loan and rental agents 428½ Broadway

Guy Fama, h 1229 Erie av

Guy Ida, b 515 14th

Guy James D [Emma], lab, h 1014 Toledo

Guy John F [Mary], carp, h 63 Bates

Prices Always Con- | HERZ, The Tailor
. sistent with the |
Times. | 409 MARKET STREET.

GUY   129   HAI

Guy Lavina, b 1229 Erie av
Guy Mary J, domestic 831 High
Guy G Milton [Jennie], horseman, h 1226 Spear

H

Haas Caroline, domestic 1328 Smead
Haas Henry, tmstr, b 1609 Douglass
Haas Louis E, student, b s w cor Anthony and Bartlett (S T)
Haas Magdalen [wid Louis], h s w cor Anthony and Bartlett (S T)
Haberthur Benedict [Delphine] (Haberthur & Knecht), h s e cor 15th
    and Erie av
Haberthur Linus, blksmth, b s e cor 15th and Erie av
Haberthur & Knecht (Benedict Haberthur, Richard Knecht),
    blksmths, s e cor 15th and Erie av
Hackenburg James F [Anna], lab, h 617 17th
Hackett Alice [wid Lincoln], h 2 Logan
Hackett Blanche, domestic 1014 Toledo
Hackett Emma, student, b 830 15th
Hackett Martha A [wid Stephen], b 24 Uhl
Hackett Tillman [Elizabeth], tmstr, h 830 15th
Hackett Walter [Celestia], bartender, h 830 15th
Hackett Wm [Theresa], lab, h 416 16th
Hadley J Chester [Clara M], h 113 11th
Hadley George M, bkkpr Ash & Hadley, b 115 9th
Hadley Joshua C [Margaret C] (Ash & Hadley), h 115 9th
Hadley Mary B, student, b 115 9th
Hadley Rev Oren S [Ida V], pastor Seventh Day Adventist Church,
    h 510 Sycamore
Hagenbuck Earl [Emma], bkkpr H Wiler & Co, h 419 15th
Hagenbuck Edward W [Iona], mach, h 208 n 6th
Hagenbuck Henry [Lucinda], engr, h 208 n 6th
Hagenbuck Nora, clk, b 208 n 6th
Hagenbuck Wm [Mary], h 1527 Broadway
Hager Charles, lab, b 601 w Market
Hager Elizabeth [wid Michael], h 601 w Market
Hager Elizabeth E, domestic 205 Broadway
Hager Joseph [Mary T], tmstr Thompson Lumber Co, h 605 w Market
Hager Matthew, lab, b 601 w Market
Hager Matthew A, carriage trimmer Geo Harrison, b 605 w Market
Hager Michael, lab, b 601 w Market
Hagerty Amos [Sarah], agent, h 409 Wilkinson
Hahn Minnie, domestic 1122 Market
Haigh George W [Inez], h 816 North

$186,000,000 of Life Insurance | W. O. WASHBURN,
WAS WRITTEN BY THE | Superintendent
| Logansport District,
METROPOLITAN LIFE. of New York. in 1896 | Crawford Block.

HAL 130 HAM

Halderman T John [Lillie], brakeman Panhandle, h 1313 Smead
Hale Charles E [Kate A] (Hale & Gamble), h 714 Broadway
Hale & Gamble (Charles E Hale, George A Gamble), lawyers 5-6 Masonic Temple
Haley Daniel E, sec foreman, b n w cor Market and Holland
Hall Byron G, brakeman Panhandle, b 418½ 3d
Hall Charles E, pressman, b 53 Bates
Hall Edward S [Anna], condr Panhandle, h 1427 Spear
Hall Florence B, domestic 713 Helm
Hall Frank [Daisy], clk, h 728 High
Hall James M, bartender, b 2 Wheatland
Hall John R [Mary], saloon The Barnett, h 2 Wheatland
Hall Mary E [wid George W], h 53 Bates
Hall Myrtle C, student, b 53 Bates
Hall Sarah A [wid Francis J], restaurant 311 3d, h same
Hall Walter A, student, b 1427 Spear
Hall's Business College, Charles F Moore pres and genl mgr, Frank S Moore vice-pres, John B Best secy and treas, n w cor 6th and Broadway
Hallam Albert [Dora A], bartender, h s s Stevens 1 w 18th
Hallam Alfred, brakeman Panhandle, b 830 15th
Hallam David [Lavina], saloon and grocery s w cor 18th and Stevens, . h w s 18th 1 n Stevens
Hallam Frank, lab, b w s 18th 1 n Stevens
Hallanan Joseph, physician and surgeon, n w cor 4th and North, h same
Halpin Anastasia, student, b 1420 North
Halpin Josephine, clk Wiler & Wise, b 1420 North
Halpin Margaret, clk Wiler & Wise, b 1420 North
Halpin Nellie, student, b 1420 North
Halpin Wm [Catharine], sec foreman, h 1420 North
Halstead Charles E, lab, b 107 5th
Hamel Barbara [wid Bernard], b s s Shultz 3 e Standley (S T)
Hamilton Frederick G, student **Hall's Business College,** b 717 High
Hamilton George, waiter, r 401 Canal
Hamilton Georgia, h 437 Canal
Hamilton Jackson [Mary], carp, h 1809 Spear
Hamilton James C, mach, b 717 High
Hamilton John W [Mary F], condr Panhandle, h 629 Sycamore
Hamilton Mary, carpet weaver 1809 Spear, h same
Hamm John [Elender], drayman, h 310 Humphrey
Hammerly Eva, grocer, e s 17th, 1 n Stevens, b 1704 Knowlton
Hammerly Harriet [wid Wm], h w s Holland, 2 s State
Hammerly Mary, student, b w s Holland, 2 s State
Hammon George A [Nora E], tmstr Thomas Jones, h 225 State
Hammon Henry [Mary J], lab, h 116 State
Hammon Larkin L [Elizabeth], tmstr Thomas Jones, h 227 State

Iammon Lydia, domestic 415½ 3d
Iammon Francis M [Addie], car insp, h 727 Ottawa
Iammontree Charles F, student, b 2029 George
Iammontree Elizabeth A [wid Henry C], b 2029 George
Iammontree Harry C, student, b 2029 George
Iammontree John, b 2029 George
Iammontree Robert E, student, b 2029 George
Iamptdon Louis, lab, b 1203 Toledo
Ianafy Mary, domestic 218 8th
Ianawalt John C [Ella], carp, b 1504 Water
Ianawalt Valentine C [Emma L], postmaster, h 810 Broadway
Iance Frank C [Hattie B], turner Stevens Bros, h 102 Pawnee
Iance Jane D [wid Joseph D], b 102 Pawnee
Iance Pearl, b 102 Pawnee
Iance Zoe, b 102 Pawnee
Iancock Anna W [wid James N], h 407½ Market
Iancock Deva B, b 407½ Market
Iand Charles L [Sarah], engr Panhandle, h 1729 Spear
Iand C Earl, student, b 1729 Spear
Iand George R [Mary M], carp, h 1210 Linden av
Iand Jeannette, dressmkr, 1210 Linden av, b same
Iand Julia [wid Michael], laundress, h 417 Wheatland
Iand Rosa, h 1415 Erie av
Iandt Joseph, tailor P J Hooley, r 403½ Market
Iandy Wilson T [Edith], condr, h 1809 High
Ianey Carrie E, b 722 Broadway
Ianey Louisana [wid Wm W], h 722 Broadway
Ianey Sarah [wid Wm H], h 225 3d
Ianey Wm E, capitalist 316 Pearl, r same
Iankee (see also Henke)
Iankee Dora C, b 509 w Market
Iankee Edward [Carrie], clk G W Seybold & Bros, h 211 Pratt
Iankee George, wks Hillock & Pitman, b 1701 17th
Iankee James A [Dora B], clk, h 907 14th
Iankee Jesse [Nora], driver, h 512 Fitch
Iankee Joseph [Emma], grocer and carp 1701 17th, h same
Iankee Solomon [Mary J], bridge carp, h 509 w Market
Iankey Louise, h 1891 19th
Ianley Alexander [Margaret] (Hanley & Shanahan), h 1206 Broadway
Ianley Anna, student, b 1206 Broadway
Ianley Anna M, h 422 5th
Ianley Ezekiel, lab, b 521 High
Ianley Frank [Ella], engr Panhandle, h 1418 George
Ianley Margaret, b 1418 George
Ianley Pearl A, student, b 422 5th
Ianley Wm, student, b 1206 Broadway

The Best in the Business. | Wiler & Wise,
DRY GOODS, | 409-411 BROADWAY.
CLOAKS.   FURS. | 306 FOURTH STREET.

HAN   132   HAR

Hanley & Shanahan (Alexander Hanley, John Shanahan), new and second hand furniture and house furnishing goods, 209 6th

Hannah Charles M [Josephine L] (C M Hanna & Co), h 717 North

Hanna C M & Co (Charles M and Josephine L Hanna), picture frames 421 Market

'Hanna Ella R, laundress, h 123 6th

Hanna Frederick H, tmstr, b 123 6th

Hanna Josephine L (C L Hanna & Co), h 717 North

Hanna Lebbeus G [Maud], feed store 315 Linden av, h 333 Linden av

Hanna Nellie, b 717 North

Hannegan Anna, teacher, b 112 Canty

Hannifin Michael [Nora], bkkpr The J T Elliott Co, h 1101 George

Hannon James J [Ella A], foreman Panhandle, h 816 Spear

Hanschen Bertha, b 620 12th

Hanschen Emma, student, b 620 12th

Hanschen Martin [Elizabeth], lab, b 620 12th

Hansen Christian [Hansine], lab, h 1009 19th

Hansen Jacques, lab, b 1500 Toledo

Hansen Neils [Mary], oil and junk dealer, rags, iron and metals, hides, pelts and furs, sink and vault cleaning and contracting teamster 515 Broadway, h 1829 Broadway

Hanson Antwine [Bridget], grocer 424 3d, h 123 Market

Hanson James L [Blanche], pharmacist B F Keesling, h 1821 High

Hanson Mamie, b 123 Market

Hanzel W Robert, tailor C W Keller, b 206 Canal

Harbin John E [Lydia J], huckster, h 18 Nobley

Harbold Maria [wid Wm], b 8 Helm

Harbolt Mary J [wid Jonathan], h 612 Linden av

Harder Carrie M, b 918 Lytle

Harder C Frederick, frt cashr Panhandle, b 918 Lytle

Harder Lizzie A, cashr Wiler & Wise, b 918 Lytle

Harder Mary [wid Andrew], h 918 Lytle

Harding Richard A [Charlotte A], vet surgeon 511 North, h 1805 Broadway

Hardt (see also Hart and Hartz)

Hardt Gertrude [wid John], b 130 Osage

Hardt Sophia M [wid Frederick], h 130 Osage

Hardy Alexander [Evaline], vice-pres The Logansport Journal Co, h 112 Market

Hardy Edward, b 112 Market

Hardy Ellen, student, b 1218 Linden av

Hardy Frank L [Louisa L], clk Dr J W Stewart, h 220 Front

Hardy George D [Mary], h 1218 Linden av

Hare Mary [wid Daniel], seamstress, b 401 ½ Broadway

Harker Jonathan J, railway mail clk, r 114 Canal

Harker Lewis [Nora], lab, h e s Washington 2 s Biddle (S T)

Harlan Orla, mach hd Panhandle, b 512 Barron

rland Edward, brakeman, b 321 Sycamore
rley Elmore [Emma], tinner Panhandle, h 1728 High
rley Melvin G [Rosa M], watch mkr Ben Martin, h 2329 North
rley Milo C [Stella], retoucher A N Donaldson, h 1416 Broadway
rloff Charles [Anna], painter, h 1020 19th
rnasch Anna, domestic, b 2014 Spear
rnasch Elizabeth, b 2014 Spear
rnasch Frederick [Mary], mach hd Panhandle, h 2014 Spear
rnasch Pauline, domestic, b 2014 Spear
rnasch Pearl, domestic 2114 Broadway
rner John A [Mary C], carp Panhandle, h 206 Bates
rp Wm N [Mary M], fruit grower, h 2201 Smead
rper James M [Josephine], engr Panhandle, h 1410 George
rrell Charles E [Ida M], check clk Panhandle, h 1710 North
rrell J Frank, b 216 13th
rrell Minnie D, clk, b 216 13th
rrell Theophilus R [Priscilla], truckman Panhandle, h 216 13th
rrigan Rose, domestic 715 Broadway
rrington Alvah [Pearl], lab, b 213 Heath
rrington Anna [wid John], h 617 Ottawa
rrington Anna E, seamstress, b 617 Ottawa
rrington Dollie, student, b 220 Humphrey
rrington J Edward, hoop coiler, b 1234 Toledo
rrington John J, lab, b 1234 Toledo
rrington Margaret, student, b 1234 Toledo
rrington Mary E, domestic 718 Market
rrington Michael [Bridget], lab, h 220 Humphrey
**rrington Ormus L [Mae] (Anderson & Harrington), h 508½
  Broadway**
rrington Thomas, student, b 220 Humphrey
rris Bert D, solicitor, b 1127 Market
rris Frank, baker, b 412 Vine
rris George [Margaret], brakeman, b 412 Vine
rris George F [Mary M], carp, h 80 Washington
rris Hamilton, bartender A L Anderson, r 318½ Broadway
rris Harry S [Eva], flagman, h s w cor Elm and Marydyke
rris Harvey, harnessmkr Kreis Bros Mfg Co, b 521 High
rris Henry [Lizzie J] (Harris & Jones), h 724 Melbourne av
rris James, b 412 Vine
rris Joseph [Marrimas], carp 412 Vine, h same
rris Laura A, dressmkr, b 412 Vine
rris & Jones (Henry Harris, Cager S Jones), barbers, 313 Market
rrison Caroline, b 408 Canal
rrison Charles, mach hd Ash & Hadley, b 1232 Toledo
rrison Charlotte, b 2000 High
rrison Elizabeth, tailor, b 425 5th
**rrison George [Maria], carriage and harness mnfr and seedsman
  617-623 Broadway, h 2000 High**

Harrison Matilda, cigarmkr, b 425 5th
Harrison Orre, student, b 2000 High
Harrison Robert [Ella], brakeman Panhandle, h 1232 Toledo
Harrison Walter V [Dorothy], clk George Harrison, h 1815 Broadway
Harrison Wm, student, b 2000 High
Hart (see also Hardt and Hartz)
Hart Edward N [Elizabeth], baggageman, h 516 12th
Hart Eliza E, b 615 North
Hart Glenna, student, b 301 Sycamore
Hart Lillie, clk, b 301 Sycamore
Hart Nina, student, b 301 Sycamore
Hart Samuel C [Ellen], painter 204 Sycamore, h same
Hart Wm A [Mary], painter Panhandle, h 301 Sycamore
Hart Wood A [Elizabeth], painter, h 124 Plum
Hartel Frederick H G [Julia], foreman Panhandle, h 1325 Market
Hartel Minnie, b 1325 Market
Harter Stella, h 409½ Market
Hartgrove Robert, carp, b 1806 Spear
Hartley John E [Eva E], brakeman, h 12 Helm
Hartley Richard [Ann], h 216½ Market
Hartman George W [Nellie], blksmth Panhandle, h 1220 Wright
Hartmann Carl A, asst brew master Columbia Brew Co, b 408 High
Hartmann Dorothy, dressmkr 311 Montgomery, b same
Hartmann Emma, b 311 Montgomery
Hartmann Henry [Caroline], wagonmkr, h 311 Montgomery
Hartmann Henry jr, del clk, b 311 Montgomery
Hartmann Joseph F [Kate A], cabinet mkr, h 313 Cummings
Hartmann Louise S, bkkpr S W Ullery & Co, b 311 Montgomery
Hartmann Mary, tailor, b 311 Montgomery
Hartsook Thomas [Lavinia], condr Panhandle, h 1722 High
Hartwick Christopher [Ella], lab, b 1227 Erie av
Hartwick John, lab, b 1821 Toledo
Hartwick Joseph [Kate], switchman Panhandle, h 1402 Ohio
Hartwick Levi, lab, b 1528 George
Hartz (see also Hardt and Hart)
Hartz Andrew [Gertrude], mach, h 1625 Toledo
Hartz John [Mary], blksmth Panhandle, h 211 Osage
Hartz John J [Gertrude], painter, h 20 Ottawa
Hartz Joseph [Mary], bridge carp, h 710 Ottawa
Hartz Mame B, wks Marshall's Steam Laundry, b 211 Osage
Hartz Wm P, b 211 Osage
Harvey Amanda, b 628 Miami
Harvey Edmund W [Flora], trav agt, h 302 North
Harvey John W [Minnie A], lawyer 428½ Broadway, h e s Sycamore
    4 s Pleasant Hill
Harwood Frank M [Margaret], h 116 Eel River av
Hasel (see also Hazle)

H. J. CRISMOND, 312 Market Street,
Stoves and Kitchen Furnishings.

| HAS | 135 | HAY |

Hasel Caroline, domestic, b w s Anthony 1 n Wabash R R
Hasel Louis [Julia], lab, h w s Anthony 1 n Wabash R R
Hasket Addison [Malinda A], pres Logan Heading Co, b 501 Helm
Hasket Frank O, lineman electric light wks, h 501 Helm
Haslet Clara, b 1910 North
Hassett Anna C, b 727 Linden av
Hassett James H, bridge carp, b 727 Linden av
Hassett Leo, student, b 727 Linden av
Hassett Nora [wid John], h 727 Linden av
Hassett Wm, student, b 727 Linden av
Hatch Elmer M [Anna B], physician s w cor 7th and Broadway, h same
Hathaway Arthur E, brakeman, h 824 12th
Hathaway Ella, domestic 1302 High
Hathaway Frederick, cook Insane Hospital, b same
Hattery Hiram D [Isabelle E], physician and surgeon s w cor Miami
　　and Plum, h 712 Miami
Hattery Uba S, b 712 Miami
Haughey Ethel, student, b 216 3d
Haughey Thomas, engr Panhandle, r 1224 Wright
Haughey Wm [Jeannette], trav agt, b 216 3d
Hauk Bessie, student, b 1229 Broadway
Hauk Dio A [Elizabeth], watches, clocks and jewelry 410 Broadway,
　　h 1229 Broadway
Haun Albert E [Sarah E], foreman, h 1816 North
Hawkins Allen J, plasterer, b 503 Clifton av
Hawkins Anderson [Luella], clk, h 1823 North
Hawkins Blanche, student, b 1823 North
Hawkins Charles R, lather, b 503 Clifton av
Hawkins Edward, mach, b 1505 Spear
Hawkins Fayette V, lab, b 503 Clifton av
Hawkins Frank [Anna], lab, h s s Noble tp line rd, 2 w Clifton av
Hawkins Gertrude, stenogr, b 1823 North
Hawkins Harry A, mach, b 1505 Spear
Hawkins John [Rachael], engr, h 503 Clifton av
Hawkins John [Hester], asst r h foreman Panhandle, h 1505 Spear
Hawkins John E, mach Panhandle, b 1505 Spear
Hawkins Laura, student, b 1823 North
Hawkins Wm C [Jennie], plasterer, h 508 Clifton av
Hawley Wm H [Lula], carp 601 Ottawa, h same
Hayden Ethel M, domestic 209 Colfax
Hayden Viola, cook Gipson's restaurant, b 416 Wabash av
Hayes Albert A, lab, b 527 12th
Hayes Arthur D, attendant Insane Hospital, b same
Hayes Edward E, lab, b 527 12th
Hayes George W [Elizabeth], peddler, h 527 12th
Hayes Ida, domestic Insane Hospital
Hayes John E [Grace L], h 419½ Market

Hayes John V, lab, b 527 12th
Hayes Nellie, domestic 910 Lytle
Hayes Rutherford B, lab, b 527 12th
Hayes Rutherford B, cigars 115½ Sycamore, b 306 Sycamore
Hayes Thomas J, lab, b 527 12th
Hayes Wm F, porter, b 527 12th
Hayes Wm H [Eliza], condr Vandalia, h 306 Sycamore
Hayes Wm V, engr, r 312½ Market
Haymer Charles A [Mary E], carp, h 300½ Market
Haynes Albert [Lillie M], plasterer, h s w cor Daisy and Garden
Hayworth Alva H, student, b 1910 Spear
Hayworth Joseph C [Margaret], barber 429 12th, h 1317 Spear
Hayworth Wm H [Josephine] (Ford & Hayworth), h 1910 Spear
Hazeltine Harry, student **Hall's Business College,** b 531 w Broadway
Hazeltine James R [Nannie M], drayman, h 531 w Broadway
Hazeltine John, carrier The Journal, b 531 w Broadway
Hazeltine Mamie, b 531 w Broadway
Hazen George W [Ellen], b n e cor Oak and Canal
Hazle (*see also Hasel*)
Hazle Cecelia, b 608 Ottawa
Hazle John, b 608 Ottawa
Hazle John [Ellen], lab, h w s Tanguy 2 s Wabash R R
Hazle Richard, lab, h 608 Ottawa
Hazle Richard jr, clk Wiler & Wise, b 608 Ottawa
Headlee Belle, b 30 State
Healey Elizabeth, b 1415 Smead
Healey Jennie, b 1415 Smead
Healey Lawrence [Elizabeth], h 1415 Smead
Healey Mary, b 1415 Smead
Healey Sarah A [wid Abner P], b 416 2d
Hearne M Alice, wks Maiben's Laundry, b 227 State
Heater Edith, domestic 1630 High
Heaton Amy, b 1422 Erie av
Heaton Harriet, opr C U Tel Co, b 1422 Erie av
Heaton Henry [Elizabeth], mach Panhandle, h 1422 Erie av
Hebel Agnes R, clk, b 807 Race
Hebel Alice, b 807 Race
Hebel Charles, lab, b 807 Race
Hebel Jacob, h 807 Race
Hebel Lizzie, dressmkr, b 807 Race
Hebel Mame, clk Schmitt & Heinly, b 807 Race
Hecht Jordan [Rebecca], h 724 High
Heck Abraham [Mary], lab, h 1813 North
Heck Calvin [Louisa], agt Metropolitan Life Ins Co, h 513 Ottawa
Heck Charles, lab, b 1813 North
Heck Henry E [Eva J], hostler James O'Donnell, h 1813 North
Heck Phillip, hostler James O'Donnell, b 1813 North

RZ, The Tailor

)9 MARKET STREET.

Our Motto:
FAIR TREATMENT
TO ALL.

137   HEL

N Margaret, student, b 125 State
Nancy S [wid Thomas], h 125 State
Mamie, student, b 400 Miami
Mary, b 1508 North
Mary [wid Patrick], h 1508 North
Michael [Mary], bridge carp, h 400 Miami
Sarah, b 1508 North
Charles O [Mary S], insurance, real estate and loans 14
ldwin-Thornton Bldg, h 831 Spear
Samuel, bartender, b 611 North
Anna, b 325 w Broadway
Elvira, student, b 325 w Broadway
Henry [Louise], saloon 325 Market, h 325 w Broadway
John, b 325 w Broadway
ger John, lab, b 1222 Spear
enry [Mary], h 1222 Spear
an Herbaugh F, student, b 723 Ottawa
an Jacob, cigarmkr, b 616 12th
an Julia, h 723 Ottawa
A W (Schmitt & Heinly), h Danville, Ill
h Oscar, carp, b 116 Ash
h Wm, ins agt, b 116 Ash
aun George F [Margaret], contr 1713 George, h same
aun Lena, bindery girl, b 1713 George
an Sophia, stripper Julius Wagner, b 1713 George
ouis A [Bertha], baker, h 518 Fitch
Christian C [Ada], trav agt T M Quigley, b 1126 Broadway
Abbie A [wid Ivory H], tailor, h 211 3d
Bernard, shoemkr 215 6th, h 1429 Usher
Bernard L, granite cutter Schuyler Powell, b 1429 Usher
Catharine T [wid Thomas B], h 202 Hanna
George J, painter, b 1429 Usher
acob B, blksmth, b 1229 Smead
oseph J [Catharine], car rep Panhandle, h 1229 Smead
Alvin [Julia D], clk Wm Grace & Co, h 406 w Broadway
Grant [Easie C], motorman, h 2201 Market
fohn [Elizabeth], b 2201 Market
Louise, b 2201 Market
Orville E [Della], motorman, h 1626 Spear
Abraham U [Sarah A], restaurant 304 5th, h 131 w Market
Charles [Rose], fireman, h s e cor 17th and Douglass
Charles H, waiter, b 131 w Market
Edwin, tel opr, b 1731 High
Frank O [Florence], carp, h cor Bartlett and Anthony (S T)
George A [Lucy], saloon 309 3d, h 311½ 3d
Gertrude M, dressmkr, b 1731 High
ohn D, waiter, b 131 w Market

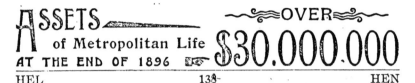
Helvie Leora E, dressmkr 112 Market, h same
Helvie Ora E, b 1731 High
Helvie Richard, lab, b 619 Ottawa
Helvie Samuel S [Elvira] (Helvie & Sellers), h 1731 High
Helvie Samuel L, cook, b 131 w Market
Helvie Walter M, b 1731 High
Helvie & Sellers (Samuel S Helvie, Edward D Sellers), clothiers,
   batters and furnishers, 426 Broadway
Hemphill Edward [Ida], brakeman, h 1718 Market
Hench Belle, b 1922 Market
Hench Belle J [wid Frank P], music teacher, 406 High, h same
Hench Horace G, Painter, b 1922 Market
Hench John H, painter 1922 Market, h same
Hench John Q, painter, b 1922 Market
Hendee Elmer E [Margaret], tmstr, h 123 n 6th
Hendee Jonathan H, b 2206 Broadway
Hendee Sireno H [Lucy E], ins agt 2206 Broadway, h same
Henderson Charles (J W Henderson & Sons), b 1317 Market
Henderson Ellen M, teacher of elocution 1317 Market, b same
Henderson Elmer E [Dessa], freight caller Panhandle, h 1617 George
Henderson Frank E, second hand goods 326 5th, b 310 n 6th
Henderson George W, student Hall's Business College, b 1617 George
Henderson James P (J W Henderson & Sons), also pres Logansport
   Construction Co, b 1317 Market
Henderson James P, lab, b 310 n 6th
Henderson John C (J W Henderson & Sons), b 1317 Market
Henderson Joseph W [Sarah] (J W Henderson & Sons), h 1317
   Market
Henderson J W & Sons (Joseph W, James P, John C and Charles),
   furniture mnfs, retail dept 320 4th, factory s e cor 5th and Erie
   av (See adv p 15)
Henderson Laura D, music teacher, 1317 Market, b same
Henderson Parson [Jane], h 310 n 6th
Henderson Samuel A [Ella], condr Panhandle, h 17 14th
Henderson Wm S [Alice], fireman Panhandle, h 1704 Smead
Hendricks Hattie A, bindery girl, b 1531 George
Hendricks John T [Adelaide], h 1531 George
Hendricks John T, jr, clk, b 1531 George
Hendricks Wallace E, barber, b 1531 George
Hengstler Anna, attendant Insane Hospital, b same
Hengstler Margaret, attendant Insane Hospital, b same
Henke (see also Hankee)
Henke Frank T, patternmaker Panhandle, b 1322 Broadway
Henke Henry, painter, h n s Charles, 4 w Standley (S T)
Henke Wm [Barbara], patternmkr Panhandle, h 1322 Bsoadway
Hennsesy James, b 208 Wheatland
Henry Florence L, b 86 Bates

ꞓnry John Wm, butcher, h 86 Bates

ꞓnry Lee A [Grace], tinner, h 310½ Market

ꞓnry Sadie, h 519 Canal

ꞓnry Wm F, student **Hall's Business College,** b 86 Bates

ꞓnry Wm Ν [Anna E], carp Panhandle, h 145 Park av

ꞓnschen Bertha, b 620 12th

ꞓnschen Martin [Elizabeth], mach hd Panhandle, h 620 12th

ensel Frederick [Winnie G], tailor C W Keller, h 2016 Spear

ꞓnsell John [Emma], car insp, h 220 Colfax

ꞓnsell Levi [Nancy] lab, h 207 Colfax

ꞓnsley Alice E [wid Richard], h 1629 Market

ꞓnsley Guy [Florence A], train desp Panhandle, h 830 North

ꞓnzley Louis, lab, b 705 12th

ꞓpner George L [Hannah A], asst supt Prudential Life Ins Co, h 611 North

ꞓpp Charles F A [Christina], mach Panhandle, h 1127 North

ꞓpp Clara, clk Wiler & Wise, b 1127 North

ꞓpp Theresa, clk Wiler & Wise, b 1127 North

ꞓppe Amelia, student, b s s L & W rd 4 w Standley

ꞓppe Andrew F (Wm Heppe & Sons), b s s L & W rd 4 w Standley

ꞓppe Ferdinand, student **Hall's Business College,** b s s L & W rd 4 w Standley

ꞓppe **Frederick sr,** [Anna C], choice wine, beer, liquors and cigars 517 12th, h 510 12th

ꞓppe Frederick jr [Catharine], electrician Panhandle, h 1931 Market

ꞓppe Gustav C (Wm Heppe & Sons), b s s L & W rd 4 w Standley

ꞓppe Herman, bartender F Heppe, b 510 12th

ꞓppe Ida, b s s L & W rd 4 w Standley

ꞓppe Wm [Amelia] (Wm Heppe & Sons), b s s L & W rd 4 w Standley

ꞓppe Wm H [Amy D] (Wm Heppe & Sons), b s s L & W rd 2 w Standley

ꞓppe Wm & Sons (Wm, Wm H, Andrew F and Gustav C), soap mnfrs s s L & W rd 3 w Standley, office s w cor Erie av and Elm

rbst Bernard [Sarah E], butcher, h n s Wash tp rd 2 w Sherman

rkomer Gottlieb [Catherine], baker, h 15 Plum

rman (*see also Herrmann*)

rman Aloysius [Elizabeth], mach hd Panhandle, h 1508 George

rman Elias, h 430 Humphrey

rman Joseph, letter carrier, b 430 Humphrey

rman Mary, student, b 430 Humphrey

ronemus Adam [Wanda], butcher, h cor Bartlett & Franklin (S T)

ronemus George, b n e cor Bartlett & Franklin (S T)

rrick Carey D [Mary], clk Panhandle, h 1232 High

rrick George [Elizabeth E], h 1228 High

rring Charles A [Eugenia], engr, h 1706 High

rring Ethel, student, b 1706 High

rring Herbert G (Olive), brakeman, h 1901 North

The Busy Bee Hive,
409-411 Broadway.
306 Fourth Street.

Dry Goods, Cloaks, Furs.

HER 140 HIG

Herring Jessie M, stenogr **Hall's Business College**, b 1706 High
Herrmann (*see also Herman*)
Herrmann Arthur J [Frances P], physician and surgeon 421 4th, h same
Herrmann Francis J, physician and surgeon 414 4th, b 114 Pawnee
Herrmann John, physician, h 114 Pawnee
Herrmann Wm A, student, b 114 Pawnee
Herrod Herman D [Alvira A], leader Rescue Mission 124 6th, h same
Herspberger Jacob [Elizabeth], horse dealer, h 118 w Market
Hershey Adah L, student, b 521 High
Hershey Cloyd G, student, b 521 High
Hershey George D, finisher, b 521 High
Hershey John R, lab, b 521 High
Hershey Lottie E [wid Daniel W], boarding 521 High
Hervey David F [Jessie A], fireman h 1425 Erie av
Herz Jacob [Mathilde R], merchant tailor 409 Market, h 1006 Broadway (See adv right top lines)
Herz Matthias J, clk, b 118 10th
Herz Sarah, b 118 10th
Herz Selig, student, b 1006 Broadway
Hessler Mary A, h 419 Pratt
Hesser Robert, asst physician Insane Hospital, b same
Hetherington John P [Mame], asst physician Dr J B Shultz 417 4th h same
Hetzner John [Fredericka], foreman Panhandle, h 702 13th
Hetzner Mamie, stenogr, b 702 13th
Hetzner Otto, student, b 702 13th
Hewlett Leroy, painter, b 700 Michigan av
Hiatt T Sherman, farmer, b 406 Pleasant Hill
Hickey Wm J [Elizabeth], h 1802 Spear
Hickle Etta, domestic 214 8th
Hickman Allen, lab, b 4 Canal
Hickman Duff, cabinetmkr, b 300 Sycamore
Hickman Harry, lab, b 4 Canal
Hickman Harry [Anna], lab, h 710 Miami
Hickman Henry, bridge carp, r 116 Canal
Hickman Lizzie [wid Blueford], h 4 Canal
Hickman Myrtle, wks Bridge City Candy C, b 312 Linden av
Hicks Harriet [wid Jacob H], h 818 Market
Hieber Christian F [Mary], driver, h cor Fulton and Michigan av
Hieber Henry C, clk John Gray, b n w cor Fulton and Michigan av
Hieber Mary D, b n w cor Fulton and Michigan av
Higbee Welford V [Minna], fireman Panhandle, h 1404 High
Higgins Ella F, b 812 Market
Higgins Lizzie A, h 812 Market
Higgins Martin [Mary], lab, h 619 14th
Higgins Martin M, lab, b n e cor College and Columbia

Higgins Patrick, comp, b n e cor College and Columbia
Higgins Wm, b 619 14th
High Levi, helper I N Cool, h 804 15th
High Myrtle, b 804 15th
Hight Frank, mason, h s s Charles, 3 e Wab R R (S T)
Hight George, student, b s s Charles, 3 e Wab R R (S T)
Hight Samuel, student, b s s Charles, 3 e Wab R R (S T)
Higley John [Sarah J], engr Vandalia, h 202 Sycamore
Hildebrandt Anna L, music teacher 408½ 4th, b same
Hildebrandt Catharine [wid August], h 408½ 4th
Hildebrandt Charles J [Anna], cigar mnfr 616 12th, h same
Hildebrandt Charles W, student, b 616 12th
Hildebrandt John [Susan], h 1326 Wright
Hildebrandt John D [Louise], lab, h 726 17th
Hildebrandt John J [Katharine], plumber, pumps and electrical sup-
    plies 408 4th, h 817 High
Hildebrandt Louisa [wid Justice], h 1326 Wright
Hildebrandt Marvin, b 1326 Wright
Hildebrandt Mary K, wks T M Quigley & Co, b 616 12th
Hile John E [Carrie], porter, h s s River rd 5 e Cole
Hiles Andrew, lab, h 89 Michigan av
Hiles Della, b 105 Michigan av
Hiles John, b 105 Michigan av
Hiles Thomas W [Elizabeth], lab, h 81 Michigan av
Hiles Wm [Sarah], clk, h 105 Michigan av
Hill Charles W, barber, b 126 Helm
Hill George C, barber H B Turner, b 312 3d
Hill Gertrude S, milliner, b w s Holland 1 n State
Hill John O [Ida M], fireman Panhandle, h 1704 George
Hill John O [Maggie], fresh and smoked meats and sausage, oysters
    and fish 217 Cicott, h 21 Melbourne av
Hill Joseph J [Sarah A], brick mason, h w s Holland 1 n State
Hill Lillian M, b w s Holland 1 n State
Hill Milton [Mary], fireman Panhandle, h 1616 Spear
Hill Orris [Elizabeth], driver, b 1313 Wright
Hill Roland [Gemilla], trimmer I N Cool, b 519 Fitch
Hillhouse Anna E, dressmkr, h 1202 North
Hillhouse Charles L [Harriet], h 720 e Wabash av
Hillhouse Hugh B [Sarah], carp, h 1231 Market
Hiller Mary, student, b 812 North
Hillis H Frank [Mary E], court bailiff, h 421 High
Hillis Lizzie C, student, b 421 High
Hillis Robert C, student **Hall's Business College**, b 421 High
Hillock Wm G (Hillock & Pitman), h Newcastle, Ind
Hillock & Pitman (Wm G Hillock, Edward E Pitman), mnfrs han-
    dles s e cor 16th and Toledo
Hilton Alfarretta, stenogr, b 2020 Broadway

Hilton Alvin [Julia D], clk, h 406 w Broadway
Hilton James E, del clk J W Henderson & Sons, b 1408 Wright
Hilton Merritt, opr W U Tel Co, b 2020 Broadway
Hilton Wm, b 2020 Broadway
Hilton Wm W [Julia], clk Panhandle, h 2020 Broadway
Himmelberger Isaac [Catharine], pres Excelsior Mfg Co, h 1601 Broadway
Himmelberger Nettie, b 1601 Broadway
Hineman John D [Myrtle], brakeman Panhandle, h 1204 Spear
Hines Wm N [Laura], brakeman, h 2021 Market
Hinkle Howard D, carp, b e s Burlington rd, 2 s Wash tp rd
Hinkle Mary J [wid John], h e s Burlington rd, 2 s Wash tp rd
Hinkle Riley [Martha], h w s Burlington rd, 2 s Wash tp rd
Hipsher Alvin, lab, b 28 Uhl
Hipsher Charles, lab, b 28 Uhl
Hipsher Clara B, b 28 Uhl
Hipsher Isola M, b 28 Uhl
Hipsher James A, lab, b 28 Uhl
Hipsher John A, lab, b 28 Uhl
Hipsher John H [Gertrude], lab, h 605 Michigan av
Hipsher Lulu, mach opr W D Craig, b 706 Helm
Hipsher Matthias [Lucy A], lab, h 28 Uhl
Hipshire Ella J, mach opr W D Craig, b 706 Helm
Hipshire Emma L, seamstress, b 706 Helm
Hipshire Ida, domestic 309½ Market
Hipshire Isaac [Caroline W], lab, h 706 Helm
Hipshire Isaac M, mach hd Stevens Bros, b 706 Helm
Hipshire Jane M, b 706 Helm
Hire John, carp, b 415½ 3d
Hirschauer George [Elizabeth], blksmth, h 215 Tanguy
Hitchens George W [Martha E], constable, h 618 e Wabash av
Hitchens Grace, student, b 1304 Wright
Hitchens Hulda [wid James], seamstress, h 1110 Spear
Hitchens Richard M [Mame], drayman, h 79 Washington
Hitesman Chester E, student, b 507 Melbourne av
Hites Jonathan [Elizabeth A], foreman, h 507 Melbourne av
Hoag Cora L, student Hall's Business College, b 711 Broadway
Hobson Arthur [Matilda], cabinet mkr, h 2029 Spear
Hobson Ellsworth G, cabinet mkr, b 2029 Spear
Hockenbeamer August F, chief clk engr's office Pan, b 26 Market
Hockenbeamer Frederick [Hulda], tailor P J Pierce, h 26 Market
Hockenbeamer Frederick, jr, fireman, b 26 Market
Hockenbeamer Paul, student, b 26 Market
Hodge George M [Eva], chef The Barnett, h 522 Linden av
Hodgins Robert, fireman Panhandle, b 1224 Wright
Hodgson Wm G, draughtsman J E Crain, r 409 North
Hoerner John A [Mary C], carp, h 206 Bates

atrick [Julia], h 6 Taylor
llie M, b 207½ 6th
izabeth A, h 207½ 6th
:nry, porter, r n e cor Duret and Berkley
unie, bindery girl Longwell & Cummings, b 3 Pratt
ohn, student, b 527 Sycamore
Isaac N [Mary E], carp, h 116 Canal
erth J Wm, carpet weaver 502½ Market, h same
n (see also Hoffmann and Huffman)
n Asa, dairyman Insane Hospital, b same
n Andrew E, lab, b 1510 Water
n Bernard V [Henrietta A], clk, h 311½ 3d
n Calvin, fireman Insane Hospital, b same
n Catharine, dressmkr, b 208 Linden av
n Elizabeth, b 407 w Broadway
n Elizabeth M, clk Schmitt & Heinly, b 1 Barnes Blk
n George [Ellen], carp, h 14 Michigan av
n George W [Adelia], trav agt, h w s Lobelia 3 n Daisy
n Isadore C [Edith], trav agt, h 2130 North
n John A, carpet layer H Wiler & Co, b 208 Linden av
n Joseph A [Rose F], drayman, h 1129 High
n Lena, b 208 Linden av
n Mary, b 14 Michigan av
n Mary, clk Schmitt & Heinly, b 208 Linden av
a Mary [wid George], h 208 Linden av
1 Mary F [wid John A], dressmkr 1 Barnes Blk, h same
1 Wm, cook Insane Hospital, b same
1n (see also Hoffman and Huffman)
nn George W [Inez E], prescription druggist 321 4th, h 1515
·ket
1n Matthias, tailor 807 15th, h same
1n Maximilian [Kate], bookbinder, h 1236 Toledo
corge [Mary], h 417½ Market
1 Sarah J, teacher, b 1430 North
1er Charles E [Sarah] (Holbruner & Uhl), h 223 Brown
er John H [Matilda E], carriage trimmer Holbruner & Uhl,
01 Wilkinson
er & Uhl (Charles E Holbruner, Miller Uhl), carriage mufrs
cor Market and Eel River av
Charles E, plumber, b w s Sycamore 2 s Pleasant Hill
Daniel, blksmth Vandalia, h w s Sycamore 2 s Pleasant Hill
Daniel jr, fireman Vandalia, b w s Sycamore 2 s Pleasant Hill
Dora, waiter The Barnett, b same
Elizabeth, b w s Sycamore 2 s Pleasant Hill
James A, gardener, h 328 Bates
James H [Martha], marble cutter, h 228 Pratt
John W, plumber M N Hughes, b w s Sycamore 2 s Pleasant

Holland Josephine, student Hall's Business College, b w s Sycamore
2 s Pleasant Hill
Holland Wm F [Mary], painter Panhandle, h 1916 Smead
Holle (see also Holley)
Holle Louis [Catharine], lab, h 1805 Jefferson
Holler George, stone mason, b 1520 George
Hollerung Emma, b 629 17th
Holley (see also Holle)
Holley Charles [Elizabeth], lab, h s e cor 19th and Jefferson
Holley David T [Mary], h e s Washington, 1 n Lincoln (S T)
Holley Flora, domestic, b e s Washington, 1 n Lincoln (S T)
Holley Jasper N [Cornelia], lab, h w s Washington, 1 s Lincon (S T)
Holley Minnie M, domestic, b w s Washington, 1 s Lincoln (S T)
Holley Rebecca [wid Wm], h 217 13th
Holley Schuyler C, lab Stevens Bros, b 217 13th
Holliday Ida M, trimmer, b 313 7th
Holloway Wm A [Myrtle], physician 407 4th, h 125 Market
Holmes James O [Margaret], engr Panhandle, h 717 17th
Holt Henry, lab, b w s Michigan av, 1 n John
Holt James [Mary], plasterer, h w s Michigan av, 1 n John
Holt James, jr, lab, b w s Michigan av, 1 n John
Holton A Henry, engr Vandalia, r 228 Sycamore
Holy Angel's Academy (for girls) under auspices Sisters of the Holy
Cross, s e cor 9th and Broadway
Holzman Elizabeth, b 1231 Erie av
Holzmann Frank [Ella], agt, h 2 Logan
Homburg Charles W, county sheriff, h 321 North
Homburg Frederick [Sarah], supt Cass County Poor Asylum, h same
Homburg Elizabeth J, stenogr F H Wipperman, b 19 Elm
Home for the Friendless, Margaret A Smith Matron, 630 Race
Home Music Co, The, Wm T Giffe pres, Thomas H Wilson secy,
Robert Humphreys treas, pubs Home Music Journal, 200 4th
Home Music Journal, The Home Music Co pubs, 200 4th
Honecker Carrie, domestic 1821 Market
Honig Anna, b 2201 Broadway
Honig Elizabeth, b 2201 Broadway
Honig Mary, domestic, b 2201 Broadway
Hoogenboom Leonard, lab, b s s Bates, 1 w Vandalia R R (Dunkirk)
Hooke Joseph W [Bertha E], principal commercial dept Hall's Busi-
ness College, h 1423 Market
Hooker J Wm [Jennie], lab, h 803 19th
Hooker Walter C [Marie A], brakeman Panhandle, h 1109 Toledo
Hooley Catharine, b 731 Miami
Hooley James [Ella], foreman, h 314 Burlington av
Hooley Mary, bkkpr The Pharos, b 731 Miami
Hooley Michael [Nora], tailor P J Hooley, h 731 Miami
Hooley Michael, jr, tailor P J Hooley, b 731 Miami

HERZ, The Tailor

a, student **Hall's Business College**, b 731 Miami
rick **J** [Lena G], fashionable tailor 418 Market, h 729

us C, attendant Insane Hospital, b same
rence D [Roxana], bicycle repairer I N Crawford, h 417
and
a, student, b 214 Market
i, student, b 214 Market
ry W [Mary], grocer 301 Market, h 214 Market
y, b 214 Market
lso Horne)
er P, lab, b 716 Race
Elizabeth [wid James], h 1829 High
George F, fireman Panhandle, b 1829 High
Robert [Malinda], engr Panhandle, h 1830 Market
also Horn)
ge C [Martha J], carp Panhandle, h 1123 Broadway
h, tailor, b 1123 Broadway
ssie B, student, b 1108 Broadway
harles [Emma L], boot and shoe mkr 507 Broadway, h
oadway
orence M, student, b 1108 Broadway
nry P, shoemkr Charles Horning, r 314 4th
v C [Lucy C], letter carrier, h 203 Market
Fred [Clara B] (Fred Horstman & Co), h 417 w Broadway
Fred & Co (Fred Horstman), staple and fancy grocers, n
front and Market
John [A Susan], staple and fancy grocer, n w cor Market
wn, h 309 Melbourne av
i, b n w cor 6th and Hanna
le, nurse 1130 Linden av, b same
tha, b 1130 Linden av
ce L, dressmkr 1130 Linden av, b same
ana C [wid Warren E], h 1130 Linden av
e W, b 1130 Linden av
get [wid Patrick], h 403 Wilkinson
bertus B, painter, b Logan House
ton, John D Johnston propr, 314-316 Canal
eorge II [Ida M], patrolman, h 410 Brown
so Hauk)
e H [Sarah], lab, h w s Standley 1 n Biddle (S T)
M [Susan], lab, h 716 Race
n, brakeman Panhandle, b 415½ 3d
les, student, b 529 Sycamore
sley [Hattie S], foreman, h 722 Ottawa
i, b 519 Canal
H, student, b 2230 Spear

Howard Erasmus M [Lizzie S], clk Panhandle, h 2230 Spear
Howard Morey A, fireman Panhandle, r 408½ 3d
Howard Pearl M, domestic, b w s Standley 2 n Shultz (S T)
Howe Abby C, b 704 North
Howe Abby G, clothing clk Insane Hospital, b same
Howe Anna A, student, b 114 State
Howe Frank O [Irma E], h 616 Michigan av
Howe John, lab, h 813 Canal
Howe John C, stock raiser, h 630 High
Howe John C, student, b 704 North
Howe John J, lab, b 114 State
Howe Laura A, student, b 704 North
Howe Mae E, b 704 North
Howe Michael [Anna], lab, h 114 State
Howe Michael jr, lab, b 114 State
Howe Nora, b 114 State
Howe Otis D, student **Hall's Business College,** b 704 North
Howe Samuel E [Catharine A], handle mnfr n e cor 5th and High, h
    704 North
Howe Samuel E jr, student, b 704 North
Howe Sarah [wid Patrick], h 816 Spear
Howe Sophia, dressmkr, b 114 State
Howe Wm, lab, h 813 Canal
Howell Edward J, del clk Campbell's Laundry, b 517½ Broadway
Howell Joseph [Mary], mgr Singer Mfg Co, h 517½ Broadway
Hoyt Anna [wid James], h n s Richardville 1 e Sycamore
Hoyt Edwin M, clk Vandalia, b n s Richardville 1 e Sycamore
Hub Clothing Co, The, Berwanger Bros & Co proprs, 313 4th
Hubbard Sarah E, dressmkr 524 North, b same
Hubbs David C [Viola A], trav agt, h 717 Wilkinson
Hubler Andrew [Tillie], trav agt, h 414 North
Hubler Jerome [Lillie], clk, h w s Horney 1 w Franklin
Huckleberry Rev Francis M [Eugenia A], pastor Second Baptist
    Church, h 218 7th
Huckleberry Frank M, student, b 218 7th
Huckleberry Myrtle, b 218 7th
Huckleberry Wm, clk, b 218 7th
Huck Henry C, tailor C W Keller, b 703 Linden av
Huddleston Isaac [Julia], drayman, h 428 Michigan av
Huddleston Reuben, drayman, b 428 Michigan av
Hudson Anna, b 27 n 6th
Hudson Charles, tmstr, b 27 n 6th
Hudson Joseph [Mary], lab, h 318 Coles
Hudson Wm, tmstr, h 27 n 6th
Huebenthal Charles [Elizabeth], lab, h 2116 Market
Huebenthal Elizabeth [wid Christian], b 2116 Market
Huebenthal Henry, b 2116 Market

Iuff John, carp, b 208 Ottawa
Iuffman (*see also Hoffmann*)
Iuffman Charles, b 216 College
Iuffman Minnie, stenogr Elliott & Co, b 216 College
Iuffman Providence [wid Jacob], h 216 College
Iuffman W Wert, helper Holbruner & Uhl, b 216 College
Iughes Emma, attendant Insane Hospital, b same
Iughes Martin M [Rose C], plumber, gas and steam fitter, iron pumps and electrical supplies 324 5th, h 111 4th (See adv back cover and class Plumbers)
Iughes Richard T, condr Panhandle, r 1 State Natl Bank Bldg
Iughes Sarah E [wid Leroy C], b 516½ Broadway
Iughes Thomas A [Anna T], cornice wkr, h 516½ Broadway
Iumbert I Frank [Ora L], trav agt, h 221 w Market
Iumbert Josiah [Margaret], engr, h 606 Canal
Iumes Anna, agt, b 1919 Market
Iumes James, carp, b 1919 Market
Iummel Lee, painter, b 206 6th
Iumphrey Danforth [Mary A], carp, h 18 Melbourne av
Iumphrey David, second hand goods 221 6th, h 1314 Broadway
Iumphrey Hattie N, mach opr W D Craig, b 18 Melbourne av
Iumphrey John S [Mary], car rep Panhandle, h 616 19th
Iumphrey Maud P, student, b 18 Melbourne av
Iumphreys Dallas R, b 1828 Toledo
Iumphreys Ellen [wid Edward], b 227 w Broadway
Iumphreys Ida M, bindery girl, b 1828 Toledo
Iumphreys John, boilermkr, b 1219 Smead
Iumphreys John C [Nancy C], carp, h 1828 Toledo
Iumphreys Robert [Anna D] (Wilson, Humphreys & Co), h 2400 Broadway
Iunt Charles, fireman Vandalia, b 324 Sycamore
Iunt Edgar S [Mae H], dentist, high grade dental work a specialty, 323½ 4th, h 1119 Broadway
Iunt Elizabeth A [wid John], h 1402 Broadway
Iunt Mae H, physician and surgeon, diseases of women and children a specialty 323½ 4th, h 1119 Broadway
Iunt Ray, route agt, b 1402 Broadway
Iunter Bessie, b 127 Melbourne av
Iunter Edna J, teacher, b 615 Pratt
Iunter Frank L, waiter, r n e cor Cummings and Cecil
Iunter George W [Sidona A], carp rear 521 Broadway, h 127 Melbourne av
Iunter Jairus P [Sarah E], carp, h n e cor Cummings and Cecil
Iunter John [Ella], condr Panhandle, h 213 Burlington av
Iunter John T, baker, b n e cor Cecil and Cummings
Iunter Samuel A, b 700 Bringhurst
Iunter Sarah E, carpet weaver n e cor Cummings and Cecil, h same

Huntley Cora, attendant Insane Hospital, b same
Huntsinger Cora, domestic 410½ 3d
Hupp Adam, lab, b 318 Linden av
Hupp Charles, student, b 318 Linden av
Hupp Emma, b 318 Linden av
Hupp George, lab, b 318 Linden av
Hupp Ida, b 318 Linden av
Hupp Jacob, tmstr, b 76 Bates
Hupp Wm [Augusta], contractor 318 Linden av, h same
Hurd Ella, domestic 2101 Broadway
Hurley Mae E, b 213 Eel River av
Hurley Thomas [Mary A], car insp Panhandle, h 213 Eel River av
Hurst Grace, domestic 328 w Market
Hutchens Luther S, stenogr, r 511 Canal
Hutchison Rebecca [wid John], b 408 Burlington av
Hutchison Arthur W, clk Panhandle, b 418 Grove
Hutchison Irvin, fireman Vandalia, h 204 n 6th
Hutchison Nora [wid Samuel], h 418 Grove
Hutt Frederick C, fireman, b 522½ Broadway
Hutton Edward P [Alta L], clk supt Panhandle, h 119 w Broadway
Hyers Assey, chambermaid Hotel Johnston, b same
Hynes Chloe, student, b 312 w Market
Hynes John [Jennie], county Assessor, h 325 Melbourne av
Hynes Samuel [Jane M], farmer, h 312 w Market
Hyre Alcie, dressmkr, b 524 North

I

Ice Ransom, saloon n s Bates 9 w Vandalia R R (Dunkirk), h same
Ide Bruce B, engr Panhandle, h 2023 North
Ide Harry H, student, b 2023 North
Immel George W, r 318½ Broadway
Immel T Jefferson [Helen M], h n w cor 9th and Spear
Indianapolis **Brewing Co,** Gottlieb Schaefer agt, 207 Cicott (See adv p 3)
Ingalls George B [Minnie], brakeman, h 1000 Toledo
Inman Allen H, attendant Insane Hospital, b same
Insley Bird P [Sayde E], comp The Reporter, h 316 Helm
Iorns Herbert L, comp, r 313½ Pearl
Irelan Charles, student **Hall's Business College,** b 2230 Spear
Irvin (*see also Ervin and Erwin*)
Irvin Jennie, domestic 703 Broadway
Irvin John C [Margaret], engr Panhandle, h 314 North
Irvine Nelson A [Lula E], clk Panhandle, h 420 8th

Ask the Clerk
at the Hotel for
the . . . .

Work Done In 5 Hours
WITHOUT EXTRA CHARGE.

☆ LAUNDRY LISTS.

GEO. OTT, Propr.

405 Market Street.

IRW   149   JAC

Irwin George S, bkkpr, b 411 Burlington av
Irwin John E [Anna], painter, h 411 Burlington av
Irwin Margaret E, b 411 Burlington av
Isaacs James M, clk, b 205 State
Isaacs Wm L [Rosa Z], del clk Montgomery Bros, b n s Monroe 1 e
    Clifton av
Isgrigg Jesse, student, b 713 Miami
Island View Hotel, Harry D Case propr, 322–324 Canal
Ivans Joseph [Jane], carp, h 109 Osage
Ives Burk P, clk Ford & Hayworth, b 418½ 3d
Iula Emil [Bridget], musician, h 15 Oak
Izor Charles E, clk, b 705 Helm
Izor Emmet L, clk, b 705 Helm
Izor John W [Laura V], grocer 705 Helm, h same

J

Jack Lewis L, foreman, h 1508 Toledo
Jackson Alice, chambermaid Hotel Johnston, b same
Jackson Andrew [Emma], shoemkr 600 Canal, h same
Jackson Belle V, bill clk Bridge City Candy Co, b 631 Linden av
Jackson Bertha M, student, b 631 Linden av
Jackson Bessie A, wks Bridge City Candy Co, b 631 Linden av
Jackson Charles W [Lydia M], mason, h 17 Plum
Jackson Cora, student, b 701 Bringhurst
Jackson Ella, b 619 High
Jackson Elza A [Ida], carp Panhandle, h 1715 High
Jackson Emery J, carp, b 204 Park av
Jackson Flora, student, b 1517 High
Jackson Frank P [Lucy], car rep Panhandle, h 631 Linden av
Jackson Frederick H, student, b 619 High
Jackson George R, painter, b 1429 George
Jackson Harry student, b 1317 High
Jackson Ida C, b 619 High
Jackson Ira, student **Hall's Business College,** b 1517 High
Jackson James, b 631 Linden av
Jackson John [Emeline], livery stable 114 6th, h 619 High
Jackson John W [Margaret J], painter I N Cool, h 103 Melbourne av
Jackson Lenora, opr C U Tel Co, b 1317 High
Jackson May E, b 619 High
Jackson Newton [Flora], ins agt, h 1317 High
Jackson Ollie M, domestic, b rear 214 4th
Jackson Samuel D [Mary M], painter, h 1429 George
Jackson Thomas W [Anna], carp, h 204 Park av

Jacobs Daniel [Sarah], mach hd, h 1306 Spear
Jacobs Lizzie G [wid Benjamin E], boarding, 415½ 3d
Jacobus Libbie, dressmkr 1726 North, b same
James Adam [Ida], tmstr, h 5½ Sycamore
James Claude R [Eva], trav agt, b 128 Pawnee
James Samuel [Susan J], lab, h s s Daisy, 2 w Garden
Jameson Charles F, lab, b 814 Race
Jameson Elvira C, b 456 Michigan av
Jameson Emma, attendant Insane Hospital, b same
Jameson George E, street commissioner, b 814 Race
Jameson Harry A, clk, b 814 Race
Jameson Samilla L, student, b 456 Michigan av
Jameson Sarah E [wid Martin], h 814 Race
Jameson Willard N, saw filer, b 814 Race
Jann John [Mary], eng insp Panhandle, h n s Stevens, 3 e 18th
Jann Mamie, student, b n s Stevens, 3 e 18th
Jaretschewitsch Anna, student, b 1900 Knowlton
Jaretschewitsch Emma, domestic, b 1900 Knowlton
Jaretschewitsch Jacob [Emily], lab, h 1900 Knowlton
Jarrett Daniel [Ida], mach hd Parker & Johnston, h 724 Spencer
Jarret Mary [wid Harrison], b 724 Spencer
Jasch Frederick, lab, h 230 Washington
Jasorka Frederick [Elizabeth], mach hd Panhandle, h 2111 Market
Jasorka Otto A, comp, b 2111 Market
Jay Mary [wid Anderson], b n s Culbertson, 2 e Frank (S T)
Jeannerette G Cecil, foreman, b 700 High
Jeannerette Christopher, ice dealer 406 4th, h 700 High
Jeffries George H [Susan], condr Panhandle, h 1701 North
Jenkines Albert G [Catharine] (McConnell & Jenkines), h 2102 Broadway
Jenkins Elmer [Lucy], stock buyer, h n s Shultz 3 w Kloenne (S T)
Jenkins John [Ida], lab, h s s Shultz 3 w Kloenne (S T)
Jenks Ada B, student, b 114 9th
Jenks Almon P [Lizzie A], secy Logansport & Wabash Valley Gas Co (J D Ferguson & Jenks), h 114 9th
Jenks Fannie M, student, b 114 9th
Jenks John W [Helen], mach Panhandle, h 1116 Market
Jenks June, b 1116 Market
Jenks Virgil B, b 114 9th
Jenness Horace, lab, b 1608 Toledo
Jenness Marvin A, b 1822 Market
Jenness Maurice E [Catharine M], train desp Pan, h 831 Linden av
Jenness Oliver P, cornice mkr, b 1822 Market
Jenness Perry [Margaret], condr Panhandle, h 1822 Market
Jenness Walter E, student, b 831 Linden av
Jennings J Harry, clk Fred Horstman & Co, b 224 w Broadway
Jennings Mary L, bkkpr, b 224 w Broadway

H. J. CRISMOND, 312 Market Street,
Gasoline Stoves, Screen Doors and Windows.

| JEN | 151 | JOH |

Jennings Max [Nollie], cornice mnfr 316-318 5th, h 224 w Broadway
Jensen Henry [Johanna] (Marshall & Jensen), h 1814 Broadway
Jerolaman Mary [wid Gearge M], b 136 Eel River av
Jester J Emeric [Elizabeth], clk railway mail service, h 528 12th
Jester Nellie, student, b 528 12th
Jewell Bass [America], lab, h s s Wabash River rd 7 e Coles
Johns Francis M [Henrietta C], brakeman Panhandle, h 627 12th
Johns Jesse, lab, b 718 12th
Johns Louis, tel opr, b 718 12th
Johns Mary [wid Abraham], h 718 12th
Johnson (see also Johnston)
Johnson Agnes, head waiter Hotel Johnston, b same
Johnson Andrew [Margaret], fireman Panhandle, h 1815 North
Johnson, Becker & Co (Wm D and George I Johnson and Harmon V
    Becker), hoop mnfrs 1309 Toledo
Johnson Bertha, domestic, b w s Kloenne 1 n Bartlett (S T)
Johnson Bridget, b 207 Berkley
Johnson Charles [Mary E], h 1224 Spear
Johnson Charles E [Elizabeth F], route agt Pacific Ex Co, h 1710 High
Johnson Charles G, student, b 1710 High
Johnson Charles T [Anna] brakeman Panhandle, h 208 Berkley
Johnson Clarence W, clk Pacific Ex Co, b 1710 High
Johnson Edward [Elizabeth], h s s Bartlett 3 e Kloenne (S T)
Johnson Elizabeth, domestic, 2019 North
Johnson Ella [wid Wm H], h 1418 Market
Johnson Frank, lab, h 706 e Wabash av
Johnson Floretta [wid Spencer], b 219 w Broadway
Johnson George I (Johnson, Becker & Co), b 1314 High
Johnson Harry, student, b 1928 High
Johnson Harvey N [Rebecca], h 1824 Market
Johnson Horace G (Taggart & Johnson), h Indianapolis Ind
Johnson Howard [Elizabeth], fireman Panhandle, h 1408 Wright
Johnson Isabel, dressmkr, b 1224 Spear
Johnson James, attendant Insane Hospital, b same
Johnson James P, condr Panhandle, b 207 Berkley
Johnson Josephine, b 731 Linden av
Johnson Lewis [Martha], janitor, h w s n 4th, 1 s Miami
Johnson Mary [wid James], h 207 Berkley
Johnson Mary E, carpet weaver 1224 Spear, h same
Johnson Mattie P, h 328 w Market
Johnson Minnie, b 1824 Market
Johnson Minnie [wid John W], housekpr, n w cor 4th and North
Johnson Minnie A, bkkpr, b 1314 High
Johnson Otto, brakeman Panhandle, b 1701 Spear
Johnson Richard [Emma], clk Baker's European Hotel, h n s Cul-
    bertson, 2 e Standley (S T)
Johnson Samuel F [Mattie E], asst train master Pan, h 1928 High

LOGANSPORT WALL PAPER CO.
Furnishes the Best Wall Paper Hangers and Decorators,
407 MARKET STREET.

JOH   152   JON

Johnson Sarah [wid Wm H], h 813 Market
Johnson Susan [wid Wm], h w s Kloenne, 1 n Bartlett (S T)
Johnson Wm, driver, b 706 e Wabash av
Johnson Wm [Margaret], lab, h n s Biddle, 2 w Standley (S T)
Johnson Wm D [Clara S] (Johnson, Becker & Co), h 1314 High
Johnson Wm F, floorman James O'Donnell, b 706 e Wabash av
Johnston (*see also Johnson*)
Johnston Anna [wid James D], b Hotel Johnston
Johnston Emma, housekpr Insane Hospital
Johnston Emma, agt, b 1211 Toledo
Johnston **Harry P** [Florence] (Johnston & Lux), h 16 8th
Johnston Isaac S [Mary], cigarmkr John Mulcahy, h 2225 High
Johnston John **D** [Elizabeth], propr Hotel Johnston, h same
Johnston John **M** [Emma], druggist 400 Broadway, h 2328 Broadway
Johnston John McC [Emma] (Parker & Johnston), h 1301 Market
Johnston Robert **F** [Sarah A], township trustee basement Masonic
      Temple, h 2307 Broadway
Johnston R Roy, mach hd Parker & Johnston, b 1301 Market
Johnston & Lux (Harry P Johnston, Frank B Lux), fancy grocers,
      306 5th
Jolley Peter [Katharine], lab, h 1027 21st
Jones Abraham L [Ida J], feed stable 517 North, h 400 Helm
Jones Albert W [Viola], car rep Panhandle, h 1909 George
Jones Alfred W [Olive], mach hd, h 313 n 6th
Jones Archibald E, trimmer I N Cool, b 1226 Spear
Jones Belle, ironer Insane Hospital, b same
Jones Cager S [Mary E] (Harris & Jones), h 81 Washington
Jones Cassius A [Mabel], carp, h 712 e Wabash av
Jones Charles W [Mary], barber H B Turner, h 730 Miami
Jones Claburn S [Margaret K], chief clk supt Panhandle, h 102 10th
Jones Clarence H [Jennie B], bkkpr G W Seybold & Bros, h 621 High
Jones Clement V [Zella Z], artist 600½ Broadway, h same
Jones David W [Margaret S], h 1524 Spear
Jones Edward, b 324 3d
Jones Elbridge G [Hannah C], clk The Wide Awake Grocery, h 1816
      Smead
Jones Elmer E [Ella B], tailor J F Carroll, h 712 13th
Jones Emmet B [Julia E], brakeman Panhandle, h 1125 Erie av
Jones Fanny, domestic, b s s Charles 3 e Wabash R R (S T)
Jones Frank L, bkkpr Thomas Jones, b 420 10th
Jones Frederick, student, b 1524 Spear
Jones George W [Aura B], carp, h 210 State
Jones George W [Florence B], lab, h 117 Oak
Jones Harley A, bkkpr and notary C O Heffley, b 125 Pratt
Jones Harry, b 910 Race
Jones Ida N [wid Frank], h 521½ Broadway
Jones James B [Anna V], tailor W D Craig, h 125 Pratt

Jones John, shoemkr, b 1209 Toledo
Jones Lorena, domestic 128½ 6th
Jones Madison [Anna], drayman, h 401 Bates
Jones Mary J, domestic, b 117 Oak
Jones Percy, porter The Barnett, b 510 Pratt
Jones Rena L, b 910 Race
Jones Roland D [Josephine], trav agt, h 705 North
Jones Samuel (Catharine), fireman Panhandle, h 1718 Spear
Jones Samuel M, student, b 420 10th
Jones Thomas [Hannah M], lumber and coal s w cor 9th and Erie av, h 420 10th
Jones Thomas A, carp, b 128 Sycamore
Jones Wm H [Minnie A], brakeman, h 510 Helm
Jones Winifred E, b 705 North
Jordan Albert G [Martha J], lab, h w s Lobelia 3 n Pink
Jordan Mattie, seamstress, h 409½ Market
Jordan Michael A, physician and surgeon, 410 4th, h same
Jordan Paul W [Urhetta], brakeman Panhandle, h 121 4th
Jordan Pearl, stenogr G W Walters, b 409½ Market
Jost Catharine [wid John], b 6 Humphrey
Joseph Jennie, attendant Insane Hospital, b same
Jox Henry F [Edith], h 1625 Spear
Judson George, blksmth, r Baker's European Hotel
Julian Hattie, domestic 2300 Broadway
Julian Ida N, b 709 Race
Justice Daisy, b 1005 Market
Justice Dewitt C [Margaret], lawyer 218 4th, h 1005 Market
Justice Nina, teacher, b 1005 Market
Justice Parker [Amy J] veterinary surgeon 209 Market, h Biddle Island (See adv back cover)
Justice Zenith A [wid James M], b 1005 Market

K

Kahler Charles R [Loretta], brakeman Panhandle, h 1823 Toledo
Kahler David L [Amanda J], lab, h 215 Burlington av
Kahler Emma [wid John], h s s Wab River rd, 3 w 18th
Kahler Rose, student, b s s Wab River rd, 3 w 18th
Kaiser (*see also Keiser*)
Kaiser Catharine E, student, b 401 Melbourne av
Kaiser George [Mary E], driver Columbia Brew Co, h 401 Melbourne av
Kaiser Lulu M, b 401 Melbourne av
Kale Nathaniel L [Elizabeth], carp, 601 Sycamore, h same

Kallam Luther E, student, b 432 Sycamore
Kammerer Henry, clk Wiler & Wise, b 228 Sycamore
Kammerer Mary [wid Christian], h 228 Sycamore
Kane (see also Cain)
Kane John F, hostler, r 116 6th
Kapp Harry F [Martha M], newsdealer 322 Broadway, h 112 State
Kardes Joseph, clk T P Swigart, b 1712 George
Kardes Vincent [Catharine], grocer, china glass and queensware 314 Market, h 1429 Market
Kart George [Emma], lab, h 1726 Toledo
Kasch (see also Cash)
Kasch Charles C [Mary S], flour, feed and rock salt n e cor 5th and Market, h 303 Cummings
Kasch Ella B, b 303 Cummings
Kasch Emma L, mach opr W D Craig, b 303 Cummings
Kasch Herman, fireman Panhandle, b 500 Canal
Kasner Augusta, domestic 215 3d
Kauder John [Mary], lab, h 514 Linden av
Kauder Louis, porter, b 514 Linden av
Kaufman (see also Coffman)
Kaufman Bertha S, student, b 116 8th
Kaufman Julius [Rose], clk The Otto Shoe & Clothing Co, b 116 8th
Kaufman Sidney V, vice-pres the Otto Shoe & Clothing Co, b 116 8th
Kaufman Wm B, comp The Journal, r 116 Canal
Keane Jeremiah, lab, b 1409 Wright
Kearney (see also Carney)
Kearney Alphonso, painter, b 124 Pawnee
Kearney Anna, b 124 Pawnee
Kearney Belle, nurse, h 212 Helm
Kearney Edward F [Emma], chief clk trainmaster Pan, h 216 Helm
Kearney Eva, student, b 910 Broadway
Kearney Henry, painter, b 124 Pawnee
Kearney James [Anna], brickmason, h 212 Pratt
Kearney John, lab, b 910 Broadway
Kearney Joseph [Johanna], lab, h 910 Broadway
Kearney Katharine, stenogr, b 910 Broadway
Kearney Margaret, dressmkr, h 212 Helm
Kearney Mary, dressmkr 910 Broadway, h same
Kearney Patrick [Anna], painter 124 Pawnee, h same
Keefer Henry [Harriet M], carp, h e s Burlington rd 6 s Wash tp rd
Keeley Michael [Mary], lab, h 202 n Pearl
Keelum Benjamin [Ada], lab, h 73 Bates
Keelum Wm H, b 73 Bates
Keen Chester L [Pearl L], hostler, h 510 Pratt
Keen Joseph, waiter, r 314½ Market
Keener Lewis D [Catharine], tinner, h 317 12th
Keep (see also Keip)

HIGHEST GRADES . MONUMENTS
LOWEST PRICES . .
SCHUYLER POWELL, 1031-1035 Toledo St.

KEE   155   KEL

Keep Wm C [Melissa], h 409 Clifton av
Keeport Ada, b 1302 High
Keeport Amos B [Anna], pres and secy A B Keeport & Co, h 1302 High
Keeport A B & Co, Amos B Keeport pres and secy, Abraham Charles vice president and gen'l foreman, mnfrs Anchor Marblehead Lime, office 515 Market, works Keeport Ind   (See adv opposite back paster)
Keesling (*see also Kieszling*)
Keesling Arthur R, bkkpr B F Keesling, b 907 North
Keesling Benjamin F [Anna B], drugs, paints, oils and varnishes 305 4th, h 907 North
Keever Robert N [Clara], tmstr Hillock & Pitman, h 703 Michigan av
Keever Samuel [Rosa], drayman, h 716 Linden av
Keever Susan [wid George R], b 716 Linden av
Kehoe Julia [wid Michael], b 4 Taylor
Keip (*see also* Keep)
Keip John G [B Henrietta], secy and gen'l mgr Columbia Brewing Co, h 408 High
Keis (*see also* Keys)
Keis Albert [Caroline], condr Panhandle, h 218 Sycamore
Keis Edmund T [Jessie], trav agt L Emmett, h 1726 High
Keis Elias, brakeman, b 210 Sycamore
Keis Frank, b 210 Sycamore
Keis G Frederick [Cynthia], tmstr, h 1505 Broadway
Keis John [Barbara], h 210 Sycamore
Keis Louise, b 210 Sycamore
Keis Quincy, brakeman Panhandle, r 320½ Broadway
Keis Wm F [Katharine], h 419 Helm
Keiser (*see also Kaiser*)
Keiser Charles, dynamo tender electric light wks, b 626 North
Keiser Jesse, student **Hall's Business College,** b 124 Canal
Keiser Willard N, student, b 124 Canal
Keiser Wm H [Harriet B], blksmth 2 Burlington av, h 124 Canal
Kelleher Hugh [Margaret], lab, h 623 Ottawa
Kelleher Jeremiah, lab, b 623 Ottawa
Keller J Augustus, b 405½ Broadway
Keller Carl W, tailor and draper 311 Market, b Barnett Hotel (See adv stencil edge)
Keller Carrie, cashier Schmitt & Heinly, b n w cor Lockwood and Wabash av
Keller Charles A, baker, b 910 Linden av
Keller Emil F [Frances S], mgr The Barnett, h same
Keller Florian L [Mary], h 108 Melbourne av
Keller Frank, b 623 Race
Keller Harry G, clk H Wiler & Co, b 224 Front
Keller Harry I [Barbara], clk, h 224 Front
Keller Henry [Sophia], tailor, h 910 Linden av

Keller Jacob, ship clk A J Bligh, b n w cor Wabash av and Lockwood
Keller Jennie, domestic 1108 Market
Keller John [Sadie], h 405½ Broadway
Keller John F, carp, b 910 Linden av
Keller Louise S, student, b 910 Linden av
Keller Peter [Caroline], carp, h n w cor Wabash av and Lockwood
Keller Wm H, comp The Times, b 910 Linden av
Kelley (see also Kelly)
Kelley Agnes, domestic 2026 Broadway
Kelley Edward W, bkkpr Wiler & Wise, b 1414 Broadway
Kelley Elizabeth, domestic 814 Race
Kelley John F [Mary], mach, h 1414 Market
Kelley Mary, domestic, b 7 Humphrey
Kelley Wm [Johanna], engr, h 1414 Market
Kelly (see also Kelley)
Kelly Andrew, fireman Panhandle, b 1305 Indiana
Kelly Charles E, fireman Panhandle, b 1325 Smead
Kelly Daniel [Mary], agt, h 825 Canal
Kelly Edward, b 1305 Indiana
Kelly Edward S [Alice J], blksmth I N Cool, h 226 13th
Kelly Elizabeth [wid Peter], h 1305 Indiana
Kelly Gertrude, insp Wiler & Wise, b 1329 Smead
Kelly James [Mary C], lab, h 1325 Smead
Kelly John, lab A W Stevens, b 706 Duret
Kelly Mary, b 2 Biddle av
Kelly Patrick F, hostler I N Cash, b 2 Biddle av
Kelly Thomas [Elizabeth], watchman Bridge City Construction Co,
  h 2 Biddle av
Kelly Wm R [Hattie], fireman Panhandle, h 1620 Market
Kelso Anna [wid Samuel], h 1905 High
Kelso Charles G, lab, b 1905 High
Kelso Helen A, b 1905 High
Kelso John C [Eliza], lumber insp, h 1910 North
Kemp David J [M Ella], ship clk The J T Elliott Co, b 1210 Spear
Kempfler Elizabeth [wid Herman], b 1318 George
Kempfler Grace, attendant Insane Hospital, b same
Kendall Charles L [Lenora], barber, h 417 Burlington av
Kendall Mary, dressmkr, b 1410 George
Kendall Minnie, domestic, b 9 Humphrey
Kendall Nora, domestic, b 9 Humphrey
Kendall W Scott [Mary], lab, h 9 Humphrey
Kendall Slaton L [Susan A], engr Parker & Johnston, h 1929 North
Kendall Thomas [Maria], lab, h 416 Burlington av
Kendall Walter [Thurza], foreman Jas O'Donnell, h 512 e Wabash av
Kennedy (see also Canedy)
Kennedy Charles, engr Panhandle, r Baker's European Hotel
Kennedy Daniel, brakeman Panhandle, r 206 Canal

Kennedy George W [Anna L], saloon 7 Sycamore, h 223 Osage
Kennedy Hugh B [Jane], h s w cor Anthony and L & W rd
Kennedy John, engr Panhandle, h 1830 George
Kennedy John R, real est 310½ Market, r same
Kennedy Margaret, b 114 Melbourne av
Kennedy Margaret [wid Dennis], h 114 Melbourne av
Kennedy Nancy E [wid John C], tailor, h 411½ 4th
Kennedy Walter, student, b 1830 George
Kenney (see also Kinney)
Kenney Frank, brakeman Panhandle, r 114 Canal
Kenney Frank R, student Hall's Business College, b 1625 Broadway
Kenney James [Edith], condr Panhandle, h 2224 North
Kenney Joseph [Emma A], condr Panhandle, h 1625 Broadway
Kent Cleo H, tel opr, b 817 Linden av
Kent George W, adv mgr The Journal, b 310½ Broadway
Kenworthy Thomas E [Ella], signalman Panhandle, h 1721 Market
Keough Patrick [Anna], stone mason, h 312 Melbourne av
Keplinger Slayton E [Indiana], paper hanger H Wiler & Co, h 210 18th
Keppler Anna, b 1528 Wright
Keppler Charles [Julia], engr Panhandle, h 1528 Wright
Keppler, Charles J, b 1528 Wright
Keppler John A, mach hd Panhandle, b 1528 Wright
Keppler Joseph, lab, b 1528 Wright
Keppler Matilda, dressmkr, b 1528 Wright
Kerber Wm [Mary], eng insp Panhandle, h 100 State
Kerlin Charles D [Mary], electrician Panhandle, h 1630 Spear
Kerlin Isaac [Mary], lab, h 208 Helm
Kerlin Joseph B [Arethusa L], car insp Pan, h 602 Melbourne av
Kerlin Sylvester B [Emma J], condr Panhandle, h 103 Cicott
Kern (see also Kerns)
Kern Anna, b 235 College
Kern Catharine [wid John S], h 814 Broadway
Kern Henry [Christina], lab, h 14 Columbia
Kern Paul, lab, b 235 College
Kern Sophia [wid Peter], h 235 College
Kern Wm, lab, b 235 College
Kerns (see also Kern)
Kerns Charles [Rebecca], h e s Washington, 1 s Biddle (S T)
Kerns Charles, jr, lab, b e s Washington, 1 s Biddle (S T)
Kerns Charles W [Anna], carp, h 601 Melbourne av
Kerns Elmer, drayman, b 208 Montgomery
Kerns George W [Florence], brakeman Panhandle, h 616 e Wabash av
Kerns James C [Catharine A], carpenter, contractor and builder
    612 12th, h same
Kerns Jeremiah [Lydia], drayman, h 208 Montgomery
Kerns Luther, lab, b e s Washington, 1 s Biddle (S T)
Kerns Matilda, b e s Washington, 1 s Biddle (S T)

Kerns Nathaniel [Florence V], carp 1500 Water, h same
Kerns Theodore S, trav agt, b Hotel Johnston
Kerns Warren D, lab, b 5 Columbia
Kerr Benjamin U, clk, b 519 Canal
Kerr Ella, h 519 Canal
Kesling George E, mach Bridge City Construction Co, b 527 Miami
Kesling Guy, press feeder, b 619 Ottawa
Kesling Myrtle I, b 527 Miami
Kesling Perry [Mary I], agt, h 527 Miami
Kessler Homer [Ella T], gen agt Union Central Life Ins Co 314½ 4th, h 1118 High
Kessler Peter F, b 1118 High
Kestle Luella E, domestic 829 High
Kettenring August [Elizabeth], tailor H G Tucker, h n s Culbertson 3 w Kloenne (S T)
Keys (*see also Keis*)
Keys Charles C [Rhoda], clk McCaffrey Bros, h 921 High
Keys Irvin H, b 57 Johnson
Keys John, condr Panhandle, r 403 High
Keys Marticia R, h 415½ Broadway
Keys Stella, student **Hall's Business College,** b 1721 North
Keys Thomas M, agt, b 57 Johnson
Keys Wm G, h 57 Johnson
Keystone Grocery, Wm J Parker propr, n w cor 6th and Broadway
Keyt John H, engr, b 932 Toledo
Kiehl Mary A [wid Michael], b s s Columbia 1 e Sycamore
Kiehl Michael [Louise], h 514 12th
Kienly Frank G, choice wine, beer, liquors and cigars 2 w Market, b same
Kienly Joseph A [Genevieve], h 2 w Market
Kienly Lena [wid Louis], h 1306 Smead
Kieszling (*see also Keesling*)
Kieszling Christian [Caroline], gardener, h 1 m n w city
Kieszling Margaret, student, b 102 Sycamore
Kieszling Minnie [wid John], dry goods 102 Sycamore, h same
Kihm Wm, lab, b 1329 Smead
Kilborn Albert, stone cutter L Emmett, b 610 Michigan av
Kilborn Florence M, b 610 Michigan av
Kilborn John L [Minnie E], bench hd Stevens Bros, h 610 Michigan av
Kilborn Lyman G J [Lulu], carpenter and builder 324½ 5th, h 300 North
Kilborn Martha J [wid Charles], b 112 Pleasant Hill
Kilborn Sadie H, wks T M Quigley & Co, b 610 Michigan av
Kilp Monroe [Viola], tmstr, h w s Holland 1 n Pink
Kilgore James [Mollie], h 313 Bates
Kimbrough James M, student, b 1702 High
Kimener Agnes, student **Hall's Business College,** b 909 20th

H. J. GRISMOND, 312 Market Street,
Hardware, Stoves and Tinware.

KIM   159   KIS

Kimener Leonore, b 909 20th
Kimener Peter J [Belle], fireman Panhandle, h 812 19th
Kimener Peter J [Honora], insp, h 909 20th
King Catharine, student, b 1619 George
King Charles E [Effie C], trav agt, h 116 11th
King Charles W [Ella], tmstr, h 415 Day
King Drill Co, Elihu S Rice pres, John F Burrow vice-pres, Elwood
    G Wilson secy, Andrew J Murdock treas, s e cor 5th and High
King Emmett, fireman, b 1619 George
King George C [Lula M], janitor city bldg, h 75 Bates
King Grant W, clk J J Rothermel, b 206 6th
King Harry, brakeman Panhandle, b Island View Hotel
King Lewis [Alice], clk Panhandle, h 15 Melbourne av
King Lottie I, student, b 75 Bates
King Peter [Margaret], fireman, h 1619 George
King Sylvester J [Clara], drayman, h 2006 Smead
Kinneman Richard, gardener, h s s Shultz, 4 e Kloenne (S T)
Kinney (*see also Kenney*)
Kinney Alice, student, b 1300 George
Kinney Clinton D [Elizabeth S], mess Adams Ex Co, h 122 Osage
Kinney Emma, dressmkr, b 1300 George
Kinney Frank W, oysters, fish, game and poultry 513 Broadway, b
    1300 George (See adv class Oysters, Fish and Game)
Kinney Joseph E, pharmacist, b 1300 George
Kinney Mamie, b 1300 George
Kinney Patrick J [Frances J], clk G W Seybold & Bros, h 1300 George
Kinsey Alva D [Ida], car rep Panhandle, h 2010 Smead
Kipfer James M [Emma], fireman Vandalia, h 201 College
Kirby Agnes, domestic, b w s Tanguy, 2 s Wab R R
Kirby Edward [Julia E], b 407 Canal
Kirby Michael [Catharine], lab, h w s Tanguy, 2 s Wab R R
Kircher George [Emma], blksmth Panhandle, h 106 Front
Kircher John [Catharine], truck rep Panhandle, h 327 Tipton
Kircher John, jr [Elizabeth], lab, h 327 Tipton
Kirk Charles E [Harriet E], foreman W D Craig, h 526 Chicago
Kirk Frank W [Frances E], bartender, h 615 Ottawa
Kirk Rebecca A, h s w cor Massachusetts and Vermont (Dunkirk)
Kissinger Wm F [Mary], lab, h 606 Canal
Kistler Abby, domestic, h 7 Taylor
Kistler Anna, b 207 State
Kistler Carrie, b 207 State
Kistler Charles, lab, b e s 18th, 1 s Usher
Kistler Burlie, domestic 226 Brown
Kistler Elias, feed stable 205 5th, h 207 State
Kistler Elmore E [Samantha], carp, h 2330 Spear
Kistler Eva, nurse 204 w Market, h same
Kistler Frank M [Emma M], lawyer 7-8 Baldwin-Thornton Bldg, h
    2100 North

at the Logansport Wall Paper Co.,

Kistler George S, lawyer 9 Baldwin-Thornton Bldg, also prosecuting atty Cass County, r 417½ Market
Kistler Gertrude, wks Campbell's laundry, b 207 State
Kistler Harry student Hall's Business College, b 207 State
Kistler James [Sarah], lab, h e s 18th, 1 s Usher
Kistler Jesse, lab, b 315 w Market
Kistler John W [Mary M], clk, h 2 17th
Kistler June, wks Campbell's laundry, b 207 State
Kistler Nancy [wid Henry], b 22 Claude
Kleckner Charles W [Sarah], lab, h 704 Chicago
Kleckner Elias, engr Vandalia, b 628 Miami
Kleckner James T [Margaret], desk sergeant of police, h 606 Chicago
Kleckner Olive M, student, b 606 Chicago
Kleckner C Roy, lather, b 704 Chicago
Klein (*see also Kline and Cline*)
Klein Alvis, lab, b 1002 12th
Klein Angeline, cigars 711 12th, h same
Klein Carrie, dressmkr, b 2104 Market
Klein Charles U [Angeline], barber 711 12th, h same
Klein Edith, b 714 Miami
Klein Etta, dressmkr 1604 Spear, h same
Klein Frank [Anna], lab, h 809 21st
Klein Frank F, horseshoer, b 714 Miami
Klein Jacob, cigarmkr John Mulcahy, r 613 Race
Klein Joseph [Caroline], lab, h 1002 20th
Klein Joseph [Margaret], lab, h 1010 19th
Klein Joseph B, clk G W Seybold & Bros, b 1010 19th
Klein Joseph J, clk F Wm Klein, b 714 Miami
Klein Lizzie, b 714 Miami
Klein Margaret [wid John], h 2104 Market
Klein Margaret K, seamstress, b 1010 19th
Klein Mary, b 2104 Market
Klein Minnie, student, b 2104 Market
Klein Nicholas, tailor 400½ Market, h 714 Miami
Klein Ophelia [wid Edward], h 128½ 6th
Klein F William [Ona], grocer 504 Linden av, h 621 Miami
Kleinhenz Michael J [Emma], baker, h 402 Linden av
Klesel Anna E, wks T M Quigley & Co, b 1216 Smead
Klesel John [Elizabeth], mach hd Panhandle, h 1216 Smead
Klesel Rose M, wks Campbell's Laundry, b 1216 Smead
Klinck Charles E [Carrie E], clk Panhandle, h 1925 Broadway
Klinck Charles J [Sarah A], carp Panhandle, h 2009 North
Klinck Harry W, clk, b 1929 Broadway
Klinck Henry [Christina], car insp Panhandle, h 1924 Broadway
Klinck John [Mary], foreman Panhandle, h 1929 Broadway
Kline (*see also Klein and Cline*)
Kline Catharine [wid Joseph], b 400 Pleasant Hill

·ices Always Con- | HERZ, The Tailor
sistent wlth the | 409 MARKET STREET.
Times.

,I   161   KNI

ıne Isabelle [wid Wm], b 715 North
ıne John S, h 2019 North
ıne Joseph, painter, b 400 Pleasant Hill
ıne Marietta B [wid Jacob], b 621 High
ıne Pauline, b 400 Pleasant Hill
ıne Thomas W [Letitia], carp Panhandle, h 1613 Market
ıne Toler A, comp, b 709 High
ıng Anna, domestic 926 North
ıng John R [Elizabeth], condr Panhandle, h 221 Osage
ınsick Frederick H (Stevenson & Klinsick), b 114 Canal
ınsick Henry [Anna L], h 109 Market
ınsick Minnie [wid Henry], h 114 Canal
ınsick Wm [Jennie], del clk, h 1212 Erie av
ıse Jacob [Arlepha], carp, h 617 12th
ıse Noah [Mary], lab, 2116 Wright
ɔenne Charles F [Lizzie], engr Panhandle, h 1626 Toledo
ɔenne Julius G, driver hose co no 4, b 901 Linden av
ɔtz Joseph, b 1002 20th
ɔtz Michael [Carrie], lab, h 917 20th
ımp Agatha M, student, b s s Charles, 1 e Wab R R (S T)
ımp Anna M, domestic, b s s Charles, 1 e Wab R R (S T)
ımp Anna M [wid John G], h s s Charles, 1 e Wab R R (S T)
ımp Caroline C, domestic, b s s Charles, 1 e Wab R R (S T)
ımp Christian, lab, b s s Charles, 1 e Wab R R (S T)·
ımp Edith R, waiter Tucker House, r 318½ Broadway
app (see also Knepp)
app A Scott [Katharine H], h 1111 George
auss Charles L [Harriett], engr Columbia Brew Co, h 725 Race
auss Charles L, jr, student, b 725 Race
auss Grace, stenogr Winfield & Winfield, b 725 Race
auss James E, comp, b 725 Race
auss Theodore G, student, b 725 Race
ɔcht Richard (Haberthur & Knecht), b s e cor 15th and Erie av
ɔpp (see also Knapp)
ɔpp Harry H, student, b 528 Fitc
ɔpp John H [Margaret], clk, h 528 Fitch
ɔpp Myrtle, student, b 528 Fitch
ɔpper Wilson J [Hattie], trav agt, b 530 Ottawa
ght George, cement contr 1203 Toledo, b same
ght Margaret [wid Thomas], boarding 1230 Toledo
ght Robert [Cora], painter Panhandle, b 1203 Toledo
ght Thomas, engr, b 1203 Toledo
ght Wm J [Julia M], engr Panhandle, h 1530 Market
ll Arthur W [Martha J], agt, h 423½ Market,
ll Cora, b 423½ Market
ll Frederick A [Emma], clk, b 318 Barron
ll Mamie, b 423½ Market

$186,000,000 of Life Insurance
WAS WRITTEN BY THE

METROPOLITAN LIFE. of New York. In 1896

W. O. WASHBURN,
Superintendent
Logansport District,
Crawford Block.

KNI 162 KOO

Knisely Alexander [Mary E], trav agt, h 501 Wheatland

Knoderer Ross F [Addie], fireman Panhandle, h 1305 Spear

Knouff Charles [Ida], janitor, h 1914 Market

Knowles Joseph, teas 127 6th, b 4 m w city

Knowlton Alice E, b 128 Eel River av

Knowlton Charles N [Flora C], engr Logan Milling Co, h 101 Michigan av

Knowlton Ellen G [wid Charles B], h 128 Eel River av

Knowlton Horace H, rodman Panhandle, b 128 Eel River av

Knowlton Lavinia, teacher, b 128 Eel River av

Knowlton Margaret [wid Charles R], b 1605 Market

Knowlton Robert H, packer, b 1605 Market

Knox Mary [wid Robert], b 609 w Broadway

Kobel George W, lab, b 184 w Wabash av

Kobel Jennie E, student, b 184 w Wabash av

Kobel Wm [Susan E], baggageman Panhandle, h 124 w Wabash av

Kochmeyer Elizabeth [wid Bernard], b 212 Montgomery

Koehne Rev Henry, pastor St Joseph's Catholic Church, h n w cor 2d and Market

Koehnlein Anna, b 213 Helm

Koehnlein Martin [Minnie], lab, h 213 Helm

Koenig Frederick Wm [Louise D], lab, h 104 Helm

Koenig Louise W, mach opr W D Craig, b 104 Helm

Koenig Mary E, tobacco stripper, b 104 Helm

Koerner George [Martha], lab, b 219 n Pearl

Koerner Matthias [Barbara], h 219 n Pearl

Kohl (see also Coale and Cole)

Kohl Arthur N [Theresa], physician 9 to 11 Masonic Temple, h 113 Market

Kohtz (see also Coats)

Kohtz Edward, barber 318 Sycamore, b 421 12th

Kohtz Elizabeth [wid Bernard], ice cream 421 12th, h same

Kohtz Frederick, tel opr, b 421 12th

Kohtz Harry A [Emma], barber, 423 12th, h 1116 Spear

Kollman (see also Coleman)

Kollman Charles, lab, b 5 Columbia

Koon (see also Koons, Kuhn, Kuns and Coon)

Koon Bessie, student, b 1422 Usher

Koon Grace, student, b 1422 Usher

Koon Joseph H [Mary E], car rep Panhandle, h 1422 Usher

Koons (see also Koon, Kuhn, Kuns and Coon)

Koons Ella E, trav agt, b 114 Washington

Koons Emma F, bindery girl, b 114 Washington

Koons Nathan [Nancy A], lab, h 114 Washington

Koons Palmer J, student, b 114 Washington

Koopmann Henry, lab, h 531 Pratt

Koopmann Sophia, b 531 Pratt

Koop Daniel [Jennie], bottler Columbia Brew Co, h 515 Sycamore
Kopp George, car rep Panhandle, b 1318 Smead
Koppe (see also Cuppy)
Koppe Christina, h 6 Washington
Koppe George J, ball player, b 6 Washington
Koppe Jacob C, stripper, b 6 Washington
Koppe Lydia A, b 6 Washington
Koppe Wm B [Anna], stone mason, h 210 Pratt
Kops Elizabeth de Bruyn, artist 413½ Broadway, h same
Korner Henry [Eva], mach hd, h n s Pleasant Hill, 2 w McCarty
Kornmann John H [Amanda], foreman The Journal, h 318 Elm
Kortos Emanuel G [Kate], tailor Jacob Herz, h 613 Race
Koski Anna, b 116 n Pearl
Koski August [Mary], car insp, h 116 n Pearl
Koski Augusta [wid Henry], h 124 Woodland
Koski Catharine, student, b 317 15th
Koski Christina, student, b 317 15th
Koski George, del clk, Snider & Alber, b 317 15th
Koski John [Nevada], lab, h 12 Columbia
Koski Minnie, domestic 12 Columbia
Koski Wilhelmina, b 116 n Pearl
Kowalski Frank [Mary], lab, h 116 Garden
Kramer Frederick [Elizabeth], mason, h 217 Montgomery
Kramer Theodore, dairyman Insane Hospital, b same
Kraus Otto A [Bertha W], pres The Otto Shoe and Clothing Co, h 800 North
Krauss Elizabeth A [wid Henry], h 622 North
Krauss Lucy E, milliner 323 Pearl, b 622 North
Kraut Henry A [Elizabeth], wks G W Seybold & Bros, h 1006 Linden av
Kraut John H, pressman The Pharos, b 215 Market
Kraut Katherine E, b 215 Market
Kraut Martha A [wid Henry], h 215 Market
Kraut Wm [Mary], barber 403 Market, h same
Kreider Charles E ['Tillie], h 1210 High
Kreider Edith R, b 1217 High
Kreider Joseph [Catharine], h 1217 High
Kreider Nellie, b 1210 High
Kreider Wm N [Irene], h 1212 North
Kreis Bros Mfg Co (Joseph and Charles Kreis) mnfrs harness, and saddlery and dealers in buggies, wagons, bicycles, seeds and implements 414 Broadway
Kreis Joseph [Effie] (Kreis Bros Mfg Co), b Johnston Hotel
Kreis Charles [Minnie V] (Kreis Bros Mfg Co), h 923 North
Kreuzberger Katharine M, b 86 Eel River av
Kreuzberger John W, student, b 86 Eel River av
Kreuzberger Robert [Mary], importer, wholesale and retail dealer in wines and liquors s w cor 3d and Market and 413-415 3d, h 86 Eel River av (See adv p 4)

Kreuzberger Robert F, bkkpr R Kreuzberger, b 86 Eel River av
Krieg Jacob H [Lena], lab, h 1621 Spear
Krigbaum Bros (Wm S and Albert D), dyers 429½ Market
Krigbaum Albert D (Krigbaum Bros), h 429½ Market
Krigbaum Wm S (Krigbaum Bros), h 429½ Market
Kripp August C, pressman, b 100 Helm
Kroeger (*see also Krueger*)
Kroeger Rev Bernard, pastor St Bridget's Cath Ch, h 400 Wheatland
Kroeger Bernard A [Fronie] (Kroeger & Strain), h 407 w Broadway
Kroeger Elizabeth, housekpr 400 Wheatland
Kroeger & Strain (Bernard A Kroeger, Rodney Strain), undertakers
    and embalmers 613 Broadway
Kroenke John H, b 31 Eel River av
Kroll Anthony [Elizabeth], h 1317 Wright
Kroll Nellie, student, b 1317 Wright
Kruck E Henry, clk T J Minneman, b 117 Osage
Kruck Henry, bartender, b 4 Sycamore
Kruck Henry J [Elizabeth H], h 117 Osage
Kruck Mary, domestic 1006 Broadway
Krueger (*see also Kroeger*)
Krueger Gotlieb [Anna], flagman, h 217 Grove
Krueger Minnie, b 217 Grove
Krueger Wm [Catharine], lab, h 216 Pratt
Krug Elizabeth, b 5 Humphrey
Krug Elizabeth [wid Henry] h 5 Humphrey
Kruse Caroline, domestic 805 Market
Kruse John C [Emily], mach hd Panhandle, h 1917 Broadway
Kuellsen Anna, tailor, b 107 Pratt
Kuellson Christian, wood turner, h 107 Pratt
Kuellsen Henry, lab, b 107 Pratt
Kuellsen Wilhelmina, b 107 Pratt
Kuhn (*see also Kuns, Koon, Koons and Coon*)
Kuhn Frederick G, bartender, b 14 Front
Kuhn Harry, engr Vandalia, h 207 Pratt
Kuhn Nellie, teacher, b 708 Chicago
Kuhn Raino [Mary], saloon 431 Market, h 14 Front
Kuhn Robert R, showman, b 708 Chicago
Kuhn Thomas J [Malinda A], engr, h 708 Chicago
Kujath Gottlieb [Catharine], lab, h 932 Erie av
Kunkle Saunders [Zeak], carp, h n e cor Standley and Shultz (S T)
Kuns (*see also Kuhn, Koons, Koon and Coon*)
Kuns Horace J [Florence E], lab, h 130 Woodland
Kuns John C, bkkpr, r 313½ Pearl
Kuns Mary [wid Jacob], b 717 Linden av
Kuntz Anna, b 1308 Wright
Kuntz Henry [Mary], mach hd Panhandle, h 1308 Wright
Kuntz Wm M [Mary], lab, h 1727 Knowlton
Kyle Charlotte, b 1130 Market

L

Lacey Everett, brakeman, r 403 High

Lackey Ida, nurse 1015 Spear, h same

Ladow John [Margaret], tmstr, h s s Massachusetts, 3 w Vermont (Dunkirk)

Lafever Maude, housekpr 921 Broadway

LaFuse Wm J, clk, r 427 5th

Laing (see also Long)

Laing Charles [Anna], engr Panhandle, h 901 14th

Laing David [Christina], justice of the peace 218½ 4th, h 907 14th

Laing Eva M, student, b 121 4th

Laing George [Mary], lab, h 1409 Usher

Laing Harry, student, b 901 14th

Laing Katharine D, b 121 4th

Laing Stella M, student, b 901 14th

Laird Charles G [Dora], painter, h w s Kewanna rd, 2 n Pleasant Hill

Laird Gwin, painter, b w s Kewanna rd, 2 n Pleasant Hill

Laird Nettie, student, b w s Kewanna rd, 2 n Pleasant Hill

Lairy (see also O'Leary)

Lairy John S, lawyer 9-10 Baldwin-Thornton Bldg, b 406 High

Lairy Moses B [Mazetta] (Lairy & Mahoney), h 430 10th

Lairy & Mahoney (Moses B Lairy, Michael F Mahoney), lawyers 220 4th

Lake James W [Mary], horse trainer, h 215 Heath

Lake Thomas, janitor, h 7 Eel River av

Lamb Hugh, lab, h 7 6th

Lambert Gas and Gasoline Engine Co, Will B Place genl agt, factory Anderson, Ind, local office n e cor 5th and North (See adv p 8)

Lambert Rev George W [Esther E], pastor U B Church, h 628 Michigan av

Lambert Sarah O, student, b 628 Michigan av

Lamborn Charles, tmstr, b s s Wash tp rd, 3 w Burlington rd

Lamborn George T [Harriet], carp Panhandle, h s s Washington tp rd, 3 w Burlington rd

Lamborn Mary, b s s Wash tp rd, 3 w Burlington rd

Lamborn Paul, lab, b s s Wash tp rd, 3 w Burlington rd

Lamborn Wm G, press feeder, b s s Wash tp rd, 3 w Burlington rd

Lamme Benjamin C [Rachael], horseshoer, h 103 9th

Lancaster Ellen [wid Wm], h 608 e Wabash av

Landers Ellen, attendant Insane Hospital, b same

Landis Catharine, b 1706 Market

Landis Frances, teacher, b 1706 Market

Landis Frederick, lawyer 222½ 4th, b 1706 Market

Landis Mary K [wid Abraham H], h 1706 Market

Landry Mary E [wid Simon F], h 1600 Broadway
Landry Otto B (Coyle & Landry), b 1600 Broadway
Landry Staley M, Lieut U S N, b 1600 Broadway
Lane (see also Layne)
Lane Wm G, carp, r 201½ 6th
Langton Mack L [Mary E], cigarmkr, h 56 Bates
Langton Sarah M [wid David W], h 202 Hanna
Lennan Margaret, domestic, b 43 Washington
Lanza Frank, peddler, r 509 Broadway
La Orange Bridget, h 301 Melbourne av
La Orange Charles H [May], truckman Panhandle, b 200 Colfax
La Orange Isaac A, carp, h 428½ Broadway
La Orange Joseph [Rosa], flour and feed 100 Burlington av, h 200 Colfax
La Orange Joseph H, tel opr, b 301 Melbourne av
La Orange May, b 200 Colfax
La Orange Peter [Annie], carp, h 113 Melbourne av
Lape Ollie V, domestic 224 Eel River av
Lapp Henry G V [Augusta], mach A W Stevens, h 1223 Erie av
Larger Frank J B [May], baggagemaster Panhandle, h 601 Wilkinson
Larger Jerome A [Phœbe M], yd master Pan, h 417½ Market
Larimer Alice H, b 1306 High
Larimer Celia A [wid Harvey J], boarding and furnished rooms 206 6th
Larimer Charles, lab, b s s Bartlett 2 w Kloenne (S T)
Larimer Earl, lab, b s s Bartlett 2 w Kloenne (S T)
Larimer Harvey H [Catharine], lab, b s s Bartlett 2 w Kloenne (S T)
Larimer Louise [wid John], h 1306 High
Larimer Myrtle, domestic, b s s Bartlett 2 w Kloenne (S T)
La Rue Alfred N [Ida], hostler, h 1430 Broadway
Larway Emma, b 500 w Market
Larway Hannah B, clk Snider & Alber, b 500 w Market
Larway James B, carp, h 500 w Market
Larway John L, student, b 500 w Market
Lashley S Everett, condr Panhandle, r 403 High
Lasselle Charles B, probate commissioner of circuit court, also lawyer, office court house, r 408½ Broadway
Latham Ollie [wid Charles], b 213 Heath
Latz Edward, r 408½ 3d
Latz Jacob [Elizabeth E], carp, h 610 e Wabash av
Latz Joseph, cook, b 610 e Wabash av
Laughlin Alphonse, student, b 415 Wheatland
Laughlin Anna, teacher, b 1323 Spear
Laughlin Catharine [wid Daniel], h 415 Wheatland
Laughlin Emma E, clk, b 415 Wheatland
Laughlin Florence J, clk T A Spry, b 415 Wheatland
Laughlin Harry D, yd clk Panhandle, b 415 Wheatland

H. J. CRISMOND, 312 Market Street,
Stoves and Kitchen Furnishings.

LAU	167	LEF

Laughlin James, switch tender, b 1323 Spear
Laughlin Margaret [wid Michael], h 1323 Spear
Lauterbach George J [Emma], engr Vandalia, h 116 Pratt
Lautz Lulu, domestic 408 High
Lavelle Kate, attendant Insane Hospital, b same
Lavelle Minnie, domestic Insane Hospital
Lawrence Wm W [Martha], plasterer 127 College, h same
Lawson Christian A, plumber, b 715 Bringhurst
Layman (*see also Lehmann*)
Layman Alfred [Minerva J], lab, h 29 Uhl
Layman Alfred, jr, lab, b 29 Uhl
Layman Anderville [Emma], engr, h 126 Woodland
Layman Edward D [Alice], lab, h 213 Washington
Layman Grace, domestic, b 126 Woodland
Layman Harry A, b 126 Woodland
Layne (*see also Lane*)
Layne Laura, b 524 Fitch
League Stephen D [Hariet E], brakeman Panhandle, h s e cor Pratt
　　and Barron
League Susan E [wid Elijah], h 628 Miami
Leahy Bridget, b 1112 Spear
Leahy John [Alice], h 1112 Spear
Leahy Mary, student, b 1112 Spear
Leahy Wm, b 1112 Spear
Lease (*see also Lees*)
Lease Ella, domestic 919 Broadway
Leasure John H, foreman I N Cool, h 1415 Smead
Leasure Tacy, domestic 823 Broadway
Leavell Pearl, domestic 18 Columbia
Lebo (*see also Liebo*)
Lebo James [Zetta], lab, h 601 Clifton av
Lebo John [Sarah], lab, h e s Clifton av, 3 n Fulton
Lechlitor Jedediah D, comp, b n e cor Canal and Oak
Lee Alice, domestic 1129 High
Lee Charles H [Cora], engr Panhandle, h 1807 High
Lee Clarence D [Bettie], yd clk Panhandle, h 6 17th
Lee Claud J, brakeman, b 1804 North
Lee Cleva, student, b 1804 North
Lee David C [Delina], yardmaster Vandalia, h 1804 North
Lee Frank, lab, b 623 Michigan av
Lee Henry G [Florence], agt, b 1124 Broadway
Lee James W [Anna], feed 511 North, h 1121 High
Lee Wm H [Anna], lab, h 623 Michigan av
Lees (*see also Lease*)
Lees Isaac [Lillie], carp, h 1317 Smead
Leffel Joel [Ida A], clk Hub Clothing Co, also feed yard, 306 6th, h
　　506 Wabash av

Leffert Catharine [wid John P], laundress, b 110 Wheatland
Leffert Edward J, candy mkr Bridge City Candy Co, b 630 Miami
Leffert Elizabeth [wid Joseph], h 719 Ottawa
Leffert George F [Katie C], molder, h 119 Helm
Leffert Ida, domestic 220 w Market
Leffert John F [Caroline], car rep Panhandle, h 1308 Smead
Leffert Joseph H [Mary C], clk McCaffrey Bros, h 630 Miami
Leffert Leo J, foreman The Pharos, b 630 Miami
Leffert Margaret, domestic 405 w Broadway
Leffert Mary A [wid John], h 121 Helm
Leffman Julius, butcher, b 429 3d
Legg Bessie C, student, b 514 w Broadway
Legg Charles M, baker, b 601 Miami
Legg Emily [wid Lyman R], h 601 Miami
Legg Irene M, clk G W Seybold & Bros, b 601 Miami
Legg Thomas J [Elizabeth] trav agt, h 1414 Spear
Legg Wm H [Catharine], clk Panhandle, h 514 w Broadway
Lehmair Jacob R [Ella], boarding 910 Lytle, h same
Lehmann (see also Layman)
Lehmann Anthony, lab, b w s Adamsboro rd, 1 n Perrysburg rd
Lehmann Ferdinand [Edna], gardener, h w s Adamsboro rd, 1 n
    Perrysburg rd
Lehmann Martha, b n s Charles, 3 w Standley (S T)
Lehmann Wm [Mary], lab, h n s Charles, 3 w Standley (S T)
Leisher Charles A [Carrie R], physician 321½ 4th, h 412 w Broadway
Lemon Ella, domestic 212 Broadway
Lemon Ulysses, b 7 Taylor
Lennon Grattan, tmstr, b 437 Sycamore
Lennon Wm, tel opr, r 216½ Market
Leonard Alonzo [Mary E], lab, h n s Norcross, 1 w Horney
Leonard Edward F [Sarah F], trav agt, h 124 Osage
Leonard Elizabeth [wid Zephaniah], h 232 Osage
Leonard John L [Dora], staple and fancy grocer 215 Plum, h 202
    Osage
Leonard Marvin T, b 232 Osage
Lerch Clinton [Lillie], fireman Vandalia, h 309 College
Lerch John S, lab Panhandle, h n s Eel River 2½ m e city
Lester J Evart, b w s Burlington rd 5 s Wash tp rd
Lester Henry C, marble cutter, b w s Burlington rd 5 s Wash tp rd
Lester Rebecca J, h w s Burlington rd 5 s Wash tp rd
Lewis Allen [Edna], contractor and builder 210 Burlington av, h
    same (See adv p 15)
Lewis Barclay Z [Susan A], jeweler 523 Broadway, h 1100 Market
Lewis Clayburn J [Violette], bartender, h 314 Eel River av
Lewis Mary E, nurse 639 12th, h same
Lewis Walter B, bicycles 523 Broadway, b 1100 Market
Lewis Wm, condr, r 402½ Market

HERZ, The Tailor
409 MARKET STREET.

Our Motto:
FAIR TREATMENT
TO ALL.

LID · 169 LIV

Lidgard John [Daisy], tmstr, b 1211 Toledo
Liebo (*see also Lebo*)
Liebo George [Mary], eng hostler Panhandle, h 1228 20th
Liebo Mary, b 2111 Market
Lienemann Albert J, butcher, b 100 8th
Lienemann Edmund, tailor, h 100 8th
Lienemann Gertrude J, student, b 627 Race
Lienemann Henry, engr, b 418½ 3d
Lienemann Julius F [Magdalene], tailor 504 Broadway, h 627 Race
Lienemann Oscar J, student, b 627 Race
Liggett Charles B [Bertie], mess Adams Ex Co, h 120 Osage
Light Bertha, student, b 209 Bates
Lighthiser James P [Pearl E], lab, b 1728 George
Lighthiser George W [Elizabeth J], engr Panhandle, h 1728 George
Lillis John [Bridget], h 408 Day
Lillis Patrick, houseman, s w cor Anthony and L & W rd
Liming Eliza [wid Richard], h 117 5th
Liminj J Edmund [Nettie], patrolman, h 406 Linden av
Lindsey John, cook Hotel Johnston, b same
Lindsey Sarah [wid Paul], b 707 Ottawa
Lingquist Louis, lab, b 120 Garden
Linquist Matilda, b 120 Garden
Linquist Peter J [Catharine], stonemason, h 416 w Market
Linquist Swan, mason, h 120 Garden
Lintner John A [Nettie], clk, h 120 Wheatland
Linton George A [Mary E] (Linton & Graf), h 206 Burlington av
Linton Horace B [Augusta], switchman, h e s Sherman 1 s Biddle (ST)
Linton Wm H, trav agt J C Bridge, b 1114 Broadway
Linton & Graf (George A Linton, Adam Graf), plumbers, gas and
    steam fitters, pumps, steam and hot water heaters, 325 Pearl
Lintz Joseph [Emma], car rep Panhandle, h 1819 Spear
Linvill Emma F, teacher, b 714 North
Linvill Horace C, bkkpr Parker & Johnston, b 714 North
Linvill Joseph L, agt Pacific Ex Co, b 714 North
Linville Rebecca H [wid Wm F], h 714 North
Lipe Henry, engr Panhandle, b Hotel Johnston
Lispenard Mary [wid Charles F], laundress, h s s Shultz 2 w Frank (ST)
Lispenard Samuel J, bicycles 125 6th, b s s Shultz 3 w Frank (S T)
Litle (*see also Lytle*)
Litle Charles A [Lilly M], car rep Panhandle, h 1211 Erie av
Litle David H, broom mkr, b 1301 Indiana
Litle Louis L, lab, b 1301 Indiana
Litle Mary [wid Alfred], h 1301 Indiana
Little Hester, domestic 1301 Market
Little Matthias A [Louisa M], trav agt, h 1316 Linden av
Little C Rollin [Amanda], switchman, h 109 Front
Livengood John W, book binder, b 411½ 4th

ringston Blanche, clk A L Moynihan, b e s Morgan 2 s Smith
ringston Charles E [Mary C], capt hose co 5, h 124 Pratt
ringston Frank, tmstr, b 1600 High
ringston Rufus [Annetta], tmstr Logan Milling Co, h e s Morgan 2 s Smith
vingston Wm [Esther], tmstr, h 714 Clifton av
oyd Frank, baker The Barnett, r 416½ 2d
oyd May, dressmkr, b 2005 George
ckridge Alice, domestic 908 Market
ckwood John Deloss, yd master Wabash, r 216 Broadway
ewer Dorothy [wid August], b 609 Linden av
ftus Anna, b 1400 Ohio
ftus Cecelia, b 1400 Ohio
ftus Charles, plumber J J Hildebrandt, b 1400 Ohio
ftus Daniel W, mach hd Panhandle, b 1400 Ohio
ftus David, clk McCaffrey Bros, b 1400 Ohio
ftus David [Mary], fine wine, beer, liquor and cigars 426 Market, h 103 Market
ftus Ellen, attendant Insane Hospital, b same
ftus Katharine, b 103 Market
ftus Margaret, student Hall's Business College, b 1400 Ohio
ftus Thomas [Margaret], carp Panhandle, h 1400 Ohio
ftus Thomas jr, lab, b 1400 Ohio
ftus Wm F, billiard and pool room 428 Market, b 103 Market
gan Grace [wid David H], b 1213 Toledo
gan Heading Co, Addison Haskett pres, David C Shirk secy, John H Tyner Treas, junction Panhandle and Vandalia Rys
gan House, Lucinda J Pierson propr 316 6th
gan Milling Co, John T Obenchain pres, Stephen B Boyer secy and treas, mnfrs of High Grades of Roller Flour cor Erie av and Elm (See adv front cover)
gan Steam Dye Works, Marshall & Jensen proprs, 608 Broadway
gansport Advance (weekly) J Edmund Sutton propr 218 6th (See adv p 9)
gansport Cement Works, Col Robert Cromer propr, mnfr cement sewer pipe, building block, grave vaults, window caps and sills w Market opp Peoria Junction (See adv p 5)
gansport Chronicle (weekly), Henry J McSheehy propr 324½ Broadway (See adv back fly leaf)
gansport Construction Co, James P Henderson pres, Dennis Uhl secy and treas, Henry F Coleman mgr 322 3d (See adv p 15)
gansport Creamery Co, Abraham Shideler pres, Hugh Furguson vice pres, John Palmer secy, Lewis Ray treas s e cor Vine and Osage
gansport Furniture Co, Ash & Hadley proprs 303–307 Linden av, office 425–427 Market
gansport Hotel Co, Emil F Keller mgr, proprs The Barnett n e cor 2d and Market

Logansport Journal (daily and semi-weekly) The Logansport Journal Co proprs 217-219 4th

Logansport Journal Co, The, Williamson S Wright pres, Alexander Hardy vice pres, Stephen B Boyer secy and treas, pubs The Daily and Weekly Journal 217-219 4th

Logansport Linseed Oil Works, Wm L Norris mgr, s s Wab Riv rd, 4 e Burlington av

Logansport Mutual Telephone Co, Ellsworth B Overshiner mgr 327 4th

Logansport Pharos (daily and semi-weekly), Louthain & Barnes proprs 216 4th (See adv p 10)

Logansport Public Library, S Elizabeth McCullough, librarian, 616 Broadway

Logansport Reporter (daily and Semi-weekly), J Edmund Sutton propr 218 6th (See adv p 9)

Logansport State Bank, The, George W Seybold pres, Victor E Seiter vice pres, Wm C Thomas cashier, s e cor 4th and Market

Logansport Steam Granite Works, Schuyler Powell propr, 1031-1035 Toledo (See adv right top lines)

Logansport Street Railway Co, David D Fickle receiver 214½ 4th

Logansport Times (weekly), Charles O Fenton propr 222 4th (See adv back fly leaf)

Logansport Wall Paper Co, John R Pratt propr, wall paper, room moulding, pictures and frames 407 Market (See ad left top lines)

Logansport and Wabash Valley Gas Co, Charles F Dietrich pres, James Murdock asst to pres, Samuel T Murdock genl mgr, A B Proal treas, Almon P Jenks secy 317-319 Pearl

Loman Joseph, lab, b 7½ Sycamore

Loman Mary [wid Joseph], b 7½ Sycamore

Loman Perry [Lula], lab, h e s Washington, 1 s Lincoln (S T)

Loman Wesley, lab, b 7½ Sycamore

Loner Jacob [Cecelia], boilermkr Panhandle, h 621 14th

Loner Mary J, b 621 14th

Long (see also Laing)

Long Aaron [Anna], grocer 410 3d, h 214 w Market

Long Benjamin F, teacher, r 630 North

Long Charles H, clk, b 16 Pleasant Grove

Long Eliza [wid David] h 16 Pleasant Grove

Long Elizabeth A [wid John H], laundress, h 313½ 3d

Long Ella, b 230 w Market

Long Ellen, b 16 Pleasant Grove

Long Everett, baker, b 508 Broadway

Long Frederick, barber, b 1126 Broadway

Long Harry E, clk Schmitt & Heinly, b 1126 Broadway

Long Harvey L, barber, b 16 Pleasant Grove

Long Helen D, dressmkr 1126 Broadway, h same

Long Henry A [Jennie], clk, h 230 w Market

Long John [Mary], brakeman, h 216 Miami
Long John F [Charlotte A], wagon mkr, h 409 Canal
Long John H [Clara], lab, h 218 Miami
Long Lewis A, carp, b 38 Bates
Long Lillie D, missionary, b 124 6th
Long Lizzie M, dressmkr 327½ Pearl, b same
Long Martin [Caroline B], lab, h 1423 Smead
Long Peter J, finisher, h 327½ Pearl
Long Susan E, mach opr W D Craig, b 327½ Pearl
Long Willard C [Barbara K], lab, h 108 Helm
Longabaugh Harry H [Minnie], engr Panhandle, h 1715 High
Longabaugh Thomas [Amelia], engr Panhandle, h 1814 Spear
Longwell Albert J, medical student, b 410 Bates
Longwell Benjamin F, b 410 Bates
Longwell **Charles B** [Stella] (Longwell & Cummings), h 308 Wheat-
    land
Longwell Harry [Mollie], foreman The Journal, h 306½ Market
Longwell Louisa [wid Joseph], h 410 Bates
Longwell Mayme, b 410 Bates
Longwell & Cummings (Charles B Longwell, Wm G Cummings),
    printers, binders and blank book mnfrs, Masonic Temple, n e cor
    4th and North
Loser Jesse [Emma B], carp, h 107 Cicott
Losey Ulysses A [Myrtle], stonecutter Panhandle, h 614 15th
Loudenback Bessie, b 1224 High
Lough (see also Lowe)
Lough Frank M [Mattie], fireman Panhandle, h 514 15th
Louthain Benjamin F [Matilda M] (Louthain & Barnes), h 906
    Broadway
Louthain & Barnes (Benjamin F Louthain, John W Barnes), proprs
    The Logansport Pharos, 216 4th   (See adv p 10)
Lowe (see also Lough)
Lowe Willard R [Catharine], evangelist, h 1516 North
Lowe Victoria R, student, b 1516 North
Lower John, lumberman, r 820 Sycamore
Lower Robert, lumberman, b 324 Sycamore
Lowman Barbara, domestic 2017 George
Lowry Barbara E, student, b 621 12th
Lowry Daisy G, bkkpr, b 107 5th
Lowry John R [Louisa], asst yd master Panhandle, h 621 12th
Lowry Otto [Minnie], lab, h 1431 Wright
Luce Charles D [Olive], engr Panhandle, h 416 12th
Luce Edward A [Ida], agt P C C & St L R R Kenneth, h 1915 High
Luce Mary C, mach opr W D Craig, b 411 Wilkinson
Luce Maude, b 1915 High
Luce Percia B, dressmkr, b 416 12th
Luce Thomas J [Sarah E], plasterer, h 411 Wilkinson

Luce Vallie, student, b 411 Wilkinson
Luckey Elnora, b n s Culbertson, 2 e Frank (S T)
Luckey Jonas H [Mary A], teacher, h n s Culbertson, 2 e Frank (S T)
Luckey Otto V, student, b n s Culbertson, 2 e Frank (S T)
Lucy Amos, lab, b 521 High
Lucy Charles E [Orvilla], tmstr, h n s Biddle, 4 w Standley (S T)
Lucy Effie, b n s Biddle, 4 w Standley (S T)
Lucy George W [Clara], agt, h 228 w Market
Lucy Myrtle, domestic, b n s Biddle, 4 w Standley (S T)
Lucy Wm, lab, b 214 Washington
Ludders Anna M, b 2 Bates
Ludders August, cooper, b 2 Bates
Ludders John (Farrell & Ludders), b 2 Bates
Ludders Leonard [Mary L], bkkpr, h 219 w Market
Ludders Margaret [wid Henry], h 2 Bates
Ludders Mary [wid Dedrick], h 123 Pratt
Ludders Richard J [Minnie], agr impls 415 3d, h 517 Ottawa
Ludders Richard J [Sophia], engr Panhandle, h 20 Bates
Ludwig Carrie, housekpr 630 High
Ludwig Ernest J [Emma], baker, h 1422 Wright
Ludwig Ida M, b Noble tp line rd, 4 w Clifton av
Ludwig John G [Minnie A], teamstr], h 2209 Market
Ludwig Samuel, lab, b Noble tp line rd, 4 w Clifton av
Ludwig Sarah [wid Martin], h Noble tp line rd, 4 w Clifton av
Ludwig Wm, student, b Noble tp line rd, 4 w Clifton av
Lufcy Tolivar A [Helen], car rep Panhandle, h 915 20th
Luick Frank, clk, b 619 Race
Luick Louis L [Emm A], clk Wm Rowe, h 619 Race
Lunsford Charles T [Katharine M], patrolman, h 6 Morgan
Lunsford John L [Catharine], h 131 Smith
Lunsford Maude M, student, b 6 Morgan
Lusher Alice E, domestic, b 401 Pratt
Lusher Emanuel [Sarah J], garbage contr, h 401 Pratt
Lusher Emma A, domestic 112 Market
Lusher Mary E, student, b 401 Pratt
Lusher Minnie E, b 401 Pratt
Lustig Stella M, b 1326 George
Luther Narcissa C [wid Frank M], dry goods 1431 Spear, b 1515 Market
Lutman David, lab, b 796 Sycamore
Lutman Frederick B [Keziah], mail mess P O, h 796 Sycamore
Lutman George, student, b 796 Sycamore
Lutman Wm H [Elizabeth], stone cutter, h 101 n 6th
Lux Albert J, student, b 214 Barron
Lux Anna M, student, b 120 Eel River av
Lux Antoinette, student, b 120 Eel River av
Lux Charles W, clk The J T Elliott Co, b 120 Eel River av

Lux Edwin H, tinner, b 214 Barron
Lux Frances C, b 120 Eel River av
Lux Frank B [Martha A] (Johnston & Lux), h 1310 North
Lux Harry [Lulu], trav agt The J T Elliott Co, h 310½ Broadway
Lux John [Frances C] (Lux & Talbott), h 120 Eel River av
Lux John H [May], lime mnfr, wholesale lime, cement and hair, real estate and grocer, s s Shultz 3 w Frank, h s s Shultz 4 w Frank (S T)   (See adv)
Lux & Talbott (John Lux, Maurice A Talbott), stone quarry 310 Broadway
Lynas Ethel, asst postmaster and money order clk, b 810 Broadway
Lynas George H [Ethel] (Lynas & Son), h 810 Broadway
Lynas James B [Sarah E] (Lynas & Son), h 1128 Broadway
Lynas Wm T [Viola], Turkish baths 411½ 4th, h same
Lynas & Son (James B and George H), medicine mnfrs 411½ 4th
Lynch Anna [wid Philip], b 1406 Wright
Lynch Bernard E [Nellie], engr Panhandle, h 1816 George
Lynch Charles A J [Mary J], b 601 w Broadway
Lynch John, carp Thompson Lumber Co, b 217 Broadway
Lynch Patrick H [Mary], car rep Panhandle, h 1406 Wright
Lynch Richard, lab, h s s Wabash river rd 8 e Coles
Lynch Thomas [Mary], watchman, h 112 Canty
Lyon Henry [Lima], tmstr, h 1231 Market
Lyons Charles, tailor, b 401 Canal
Lyons Emma, pastry cook Hotel Johnston, b same
Lytle (see also Litle)
Lytle Mary E [wid Thomas], laundress, h 208 Ottawa
Lytle Mary, domestic Orphans Home

Mc

McAllister A U & Sons (Esther, Elmer A and Leon M), boiler mnfrs s e cor Erie av and Elm
McAllister Edward V [Mary], mach, h 1906 Spear
McAllister Elmer A [Mary E] (A U McAllister & Sons), h 210 7th
McAllister Esther [wid Alfred U] (A U McAllister & Sons), h 421 10th
McAllister Leon M (A U McAllister & Sons), b 421 10th
McCabe Charles E, student, b 1719 Market
McCabe Elizabeth, b 1719 Market
McCabe Helena, student, b 1719 Market
McCabe John F, mach Panhandle, h 1719 Market
McCabe John J, clk The Globe Clothing House, b 1719 Market
McCaffrey Anthony F, student, b 117 4th

H. J. GRISMOND, 312 Market Street,
All Kinds of Metal Roofing.

McCaffrey Bros (Charles P and Michael J), grocers 410 Market and 600-602 Broadway

McCaffrey Charles P (McCaffrey Bros) (M McCaffrey & Co), b 117 4th

McCaffrey John J, clk McCaffrey Bros, b 117 4th

McCaffrey Margaret, b 117 4th

McCaffrey Mary, b 117 4th

McCaffrey Michael [Mary] M McCaffrey & Co), h 117 4th

McCaffrey Michael J (McCaffrey Bros) (M McCaffrey & Co), b 117 4th

McCaffrey M & Co (Michael, Charles P and Michael J McCaffrey), wholesale grocers 410 Market

McCain Emma A, b 104 Osage

McCain Martha J [wid Robert L], h 104 Osage

McCandless Jessie, student, b w s Kewanna rd, 4 n Pleasant Hill

McCandless Thomas [Martha A], farmer, h w s Kewanna rd 4 n Pleasant Hill

McCauliss Anna B, tel opr, b 531 Broadway

McCauliss Harriett A [wid Robert L], h 531 Broadway

McCann Elizabeth [wid Thomas], b 314 Eel River av

McCann John J [Ella], carp Panhandle, h 706 14th

McCarter Francis A [Anna], insp Panhandle, h 1203 Smead

McCarter Rachel [wid Samuel], b 1203 Smead

McCarthy (see also McCarty)

McCarthy Ida, b 2 Wheatland

McCarthy Jeremiah E, fireman electric light wks, h 629 Miami

McCarthy John J [Minnie] engr Panhandle, h 705 11th

McCarthy John T [Mary], clk Panhandle, h 1231 Wright

McCarthy Louis F, fireman Panhandle, r 203 Market

McCarthy Margaret [wid Michael], b 2 Wheatland

McCarthy Mary, b 1231 Wright

McCarthy Michael [Nettie], plumber A M Stevens, h 1318 George

McCarthy Nellie A, dressmkr, b 1231 Wright

McCarthy Nora L, dressmkr 407½ Broadway, b 1231 Wright

McCarthy Thomas, helper Linton & Graf, b 1231 Wright

McCarthy Timothy J [Ellen M], sec foreman Vandalia, h 614 Miami

McCartney George A, comp, b 206 Canal

McCarty (see also McCarthy)

McCarty Charles, lab, b 1891 19th

McCarty Charles L, lab, b 3 Stevens

McCarty Dennis F, letter carrier, b 1000 Erie av

McCarty Edward T, student, b 717 Linden av

McCarty Elizabeth [wid Joseph], b 514 Market

McCarty Jeremiah [Elizabeth], h 518 10th

McCarty Jeremiah J, brakeman Panhandle, b 518 10th

McCarty Justin, student, b 1000 Erie av

McCarty Louis, waiter, b 109 Osage

McCarty Margaret [wid Jonn], h 1000 Erie av
McCarty Thomas A, clk John Gray, b 1000 Erie av
McCarty Wm J, mach, b 518 10th
McCauley John, lab, n n s Bates 6 w Vandalia R R (Dunkirk)
McCauley Margaret, b n s Bates 6 w Vandalia R R (Dunkirk)
McCauley Thomas W, lab, b n s Bates 6 w Vandalia R R (Dunkirk)
McClaeb Wm F [Ollie], lab. h n s Biddle 3 w Standley (S T)
McCloskey Charles A [M Gertrude], h and l co no 2, h 97 Bates
McCloskey Edward W, carp, b 306 Wheatland
McCloskey Malinda [wid George], dressmkr, h 415½ Broadway
McCloskey Roland G, clk Kroeger & Strain, r 613 Broadway
McCloskey Viola E, teacher, b 306 Wheatland
McClure Thomas J [Maria C], tmstr, h e s Sherman 2 s Lincoln (S T)
McClurg Scott, lab, b s s Wabash river rd 3 w 18th
McClurg Sylvanus [Stella], lab, h s s Wabash river rd 2 w 18th
McClurg Wm [Nancy G], h w s Standley 2 n Shultz (S T)
McConaha Cap B [Ena], tel opr, b n s Richardville 2 e Sycamore
McConaha Ena (Robinson & McConaha), b n s Richardville 2 e Sycamore
McConnell Dyer B [Harriet] (McConnell & McConnell), h 1127 Broadway
McConnell Edgar B [Minnie M] (McConnell & McConnell), h 2114 Broadway
McConnell Elizabeth, teacher, b 1127 Broadway
McConnell Helen, student, b 1127 Broadway
McConnell May, stenogr McConnell & McConnell, b 1127 Broadway
McConnell Stewart T [Eloise L] (McConnell & Jenkines), h 132 Eel River av
McConnell & Jenkines (Stewart T McConnell, Albert G Jenkines), lawyers 214 4th
McConnell & McConnell (Dyer B and Edgar B), lawyers 1 to 4 Baldwin-Thornton Bldg
McCord Wm H [Florence] (Spraker & McCord), h 713 High
McCorkle Wm, boilermkr, b 707 Miami
McCormick Oliver G [Sarah H], wks Holbruner & Uhl, h 700 Helm
McCormick Ross [Nancy A], clk Vandalia, h 2 Hillside
McCoy Cordelia, domestic, 1117 North
McCracken Oraen, wks Star Steam Laundry, r 717 North
McCracken Otis, trav agt The J T Elliott Co, b 1810 North
McCrary (see also Creery)
McCrary Martin L, hostler E F Stewart, b 324 4d
McCuaig Wm C [Anna], mnfr health foods 203 5th, h 429 North
McCue Sadie, waiter The Barnett, b same
McCullough Belle [wid Thomas C], b 1519 Broadway
McCullough S Elizabeth, librarian public library, b 823 North
McCullough John A [Lillie H], tkt agt P C C & St L R R Co, h 823 North

Don't Carry Anything
ıt Reliable Goods and
atest Novelties.

HERZ, The Tailor
409 MARKET STREET.

177   McG

une Arthur, carp, b 401 Canal
une Jennie, domestic 720 North
une Harriet B, b 112 Eel River av
lermet David B [Allie C], tel opr, h 609 Wilkinson
lermott Elizabeth, b e s Heath 1 n Broadway
lermott Frederick A [Nellie], clk, h 126 Wheatland
lermott Wm, molder, b e s Heath, 1 n Broadway
lonald Abraham [Phoebe], h 1407 Broadway
lonald Archibald H [Lillie], cement contr 1400 Market, h same
lonald Lovie, student, b 624 Sycamore
lonald Margaret, student, b 514 Canal
lonald Martin V [Jennie], lab, h 331 Bates
lonald Mary E, b 514 Canal
lonald Truman C [Rose], tinner, h Noble tp line rd, 3 w Clifton av
lonald Wm [Julia S], ins agt, h 1138 High
lonough Lawrence [Ellen], foreman Vandalia, h 520 Ottawa
onough Verda, b 520 Ottawa
lheny Hallie, b 1003 Broadway
lheny James [Mary], plasterer 1503 Market, h same
lheny Mary E [wid Andrew W], h 4 Uhl
lheny Robert W [Ida M], ship clk The J T Elliott Co, h 1003 Broadway
lheny Thomas, clk The J T Elliott Co, b 1003 Broadway
lheny Wm T, barber, b 4 Uhl
lwain Hattie, h 114 7th
adden Belle, domestic 615 13th
adden Edward, tmstr, b 218 College
adin Samuel L, h 414½ Market
ann Sadie E [wid Frank], laundress, h 59 Bates
arland Willard, painter, b 1514 Smead
etridge Mary E, domestic Insane Hospital
alliard Francis R [Alice], trav agt T M Quigley & Co, h 2101 Market
alliard Tyrone, student, b 2101 Market
alliard Willard C, trav agt T M Quigley & Co, h Marion, Ind
aughey Alice, clk, b 106 Sycamore
aughey Elizabeth, dressmkr 106 Sycamore, b same
aughey Grace A, cashier, b 510 Canal
aughey James [Johanna], hostler E F Stewart, h 510 Canal
aughey James [Laura] (Pomeroy & McGaughey), h 319½ Sycamore
aughey Mary, forelady W D Craig, b 106 Sycamore
aughey Mary, b 1409 North
aughey Mary, domestic 1401 Market
aughey Michael [Bridget], lab, h 703 12th
aughey Michael, wks Ash & Hadley, b 1409 North

SURPLUS of the METROPOLITAN LIFE
at the end of 1896, over $5,000,000
Number of Claims Paid During Year, 63,909

| McG | 178 | McG |

McGaughey Neil [Mary], engr Panhandle, h 1123 Toledo
MbGaughey Owen, lab, h 1409 North
McGaughey Patrick, barber, b 106 Sycamore
McGaughey Sarah [wid Patrick], h 106 Sycamore
McGaughey Thomas F, mach opr W D Craig, b 106 Sycamore
McGee Orlando J [Mary J], clk Melvin Castle, h 34 Washington
McGillen John, lab, b 1318 George
McGinley Anna, b 601 w Broadway
McGinley John, lab, b 1209 Toledo
McGinnis (see also Meginnis)
McGinnis Amber, b 725 Chicago
McGinnis Edward, painter, b 725 Chicago
McGinnis Edward, student, b 1507 Market
McGinnis Elizabeth [wid James], b 725 Chicago
McGinnis Frank W, buggy washer, b 1507 Market
McGinnis Harvey, painter, h 725 Chicago
McGinnis John W [Ann], painter, h 1507 Market
McGinnis Marion, solicitor, r 430 North
McGinnis Mary, seamstress, b 4 Uhl
McGinnis Mollie, domestic 1930 Market
McGinnis Oscar J, hostler, b 1507 Market
McGovern Alice, student Hall's Business College, b 223 Sycamore
McGovern Emma, presser W D Craig, b 516 Linden av
McGovern Esther, student, b 309 7th
McGovern John J, clk Vincent Kardes, b 223 Sycamore
McGovern Terrence A [Elizabeth], real est 214½ 4th, h 309 7th
McGowen Charles S [Alice], baggageman Pan. h 1710 Broadway
McGowen Harry S, student Hall's Business College, b 1710 Broadway
McGrath Frank [Bridget], saloon s w corner Michael and L & W rd, h same
McGraw Catharine A [wid Wm], wks Campbell's Laundry, h 713 Linden av
McGraw Charles, fireman Panhandle, r 1224 Wright
McGraw Eliza [wid Thomas], b 420 Linden av
McGraw Thomas C, studemt, b 713 Linden av
McGreevy Cornelius F, clk Nelson & Myers, b 216 3d
McGreevy John W [Sarah C], lawyer 222½ 4th, h 119 7th
McGreevy Richard J [Mollie], trav agt M J Bligh, h 105 4th
McGreevy Wm, baggageman Panhandle, b 417½ 4th
McGregor Charles J, clk, b 1409 High
McGregor Ella W, b 1409 High
McGregor Elizabeth A, teacher, b 1409 High
McGregor John C [Elizabeth A], lawyer, h 1409 High
McGregor Marie B, milliner, b 1409 High
McGrew Frank M [Alice], mach hd Stevens Bros, h 200 Park av
McGrew John, paper hanger, b 200 Park av
McGrew Mary F, student, b 200 Park av

McGrew Wm P [Rachel), millright, h 403 Melbourne av
McGuire Elias [Julia], lab, h 1514 Smead
McGuire Jeannette F, student, b e s Burlington rd 3 s Wash tp rd
McGuire John, shoemkr Charles Horning, r 524 North
McGuire John J [Eliza B], lab, h e s Burlington rd 3 s Wash tp rd
McGuire Lorinda J, domestic, b e s Burlington rd 3 s Wash tp rd
McGuire Minnie [wid Elisha], domestic, b 306 Sycamore
McGuire Samuel [Martha], insurance 408½ Broadway, h 20 Helm
McHale Genevieve, b 308 North
McHale Martin [Margaret M], saloon 430 3d, **h 1510 Broadway**
McHale Mary J [wid Patrick], h 308 North
McHenry Nyel R [Rebecca S], foreman J F Grable, h 204½ 6th
McIlvain Wm E, cigarmkr; r 100 6th
McIlwain David, motorman, b 1224 Wright
McIntire Charles T, painter, b 228 Osage
McIntire Hattie E, student, b 228 Osage
McIntosh Arthur, student, b e s Lockwood 1 n Wabash av
McIntosh Jennie, teacher, b 1107 Broadway
McIntosh John F [Addie], tmstr, h e s Lockwood 1 n Wabash av
McIntyre Avice F, student, b 437 Michigan av
McIntyre Charles [Orsie], carp, h 416 Day
McIntyre Egbert E [Mary M], carp, h 437 Michigan av
McKague James [May], billiards 326 Broadway, h 421½ Market
McKee Andrew J, fireman Vandalia, b 201 College
McKee Hon George P [Clara J], mayor city of Logansport, h 216 Osage
McKee Lina, student, b 216 Osage
McKee Maud, b 216 Osage
McKee Wm H, rodman city engr, b 216 Osage
McKeever Bridget A [wid John], h 8 Barnes Blk
McKeever Clarence P [Grace], ship clk, h 412½ 4th
McKeever Ella M, student **Hall's Business College,** b 101 Osage
McKeever Thomas [Anna], car rep Wabash, h 101 Osage
McKeever Thomas W, student, b 101 Osage
McKelvey John B [Amanda], carp, h 639 12th
McKinney Socrates S [Mary A], carp, h 214 Burlington av
McKinsey Joseph N [Libbie A], real estate agt, h 700 Bringhurst
McLean John, lab, b 317 Eel River av
McLelland Wm P [Mattie], draughtsman, h 622 Ottawa
McMacken James A, b 302 Wheatland
McMacken John L [Anna], foreman, h 312 Brown
McMahon Josephine F [wid John], h 109 Osage
McManus Charles, engr Panhandle, b Island View Hotel
McManus Eva, b 1824 Toledo
McMaster Jay L, clk, b 1800 North
McMeans Susan [wid Thomas E], b 800 Melbourne av
McMillen Bessie M, student, b s s Bates, 1 w Panhandle R R

McMillen Charles S, gardener, b s s Bates, 1 w Panhandle R R

McMillen David E [Mary A], foreman, h 932 Toledo

McMillen George [Rosa], trav agt Kreis Bros Mfg Co, h Roya Center rd, 1½ m n w city

McMillen Harriet [wid George], b 1413 Market

McMillen James H [Elizabeth], gardener, h s s Bates, 1 w Pan R :

McMillen John E, music teacher 315½ 3d, b s s Bates, 1 w Pan R :

McMillen Lella, milliner, b n e cor Canal and Oak

McMillen Nellie, b 1519 Spear

McMinn Anna [wid John H], h 722 Race

McMinn Sarah, clk John Gray, b 722 Race

McMullen Alice [wid Hugh], b 830 North

McMullen Harry O [Belle V], lab, h 115 Melbourne av

McMullen Miriam, music teacher 830 North, b same

McNamee Rose, waiter Island View Hotel, r same

McNary Joseph T [Belle T], lawyer and real estate 412½ Broadway h 921 Broadway

McMinnie Jesse, baggage Panhandle, b Island View Hotel

McNitt Carrie C, music teacher 100 Melbourne av, b same

McNitt Isabella I [wid Charles M], h 901 Race

McNitt James D [Mary E], farmer and stock dealer, h 100 Melbourne av

McNitt Maud, b 901 Race

McNitt Miriam S, student, b 100 Melbourne av

McNitt Robert J, student, b 100 Melbourne av

McNitt Willard C, student, b 100 Melbourne av

McNitt Wm H [Hattie], tkt clk Panhandle, h 901 Race

McPhee John, attendant Insane Hospital, b same

McPherson (see also *Pherson*)

McPherson Ann E [wid Cyrus], h 320 Eel River av

McQuade Hugh J, comp, b 206 Canal

McQuiston Wm H [Melvina R], bkkpr I N Cool, b 717 High

McReynolds Scott (McReynolds & Shibley), b 530½ Broadway

McReynolds & Shibley (Scott McReynolds, Charles A Shibley) artis 530½ Broadway

McSheehy Harry J, comp The Chronicle, b 1217 North

McSheehy H James [Minnie], propr The Chronicle, h 1217 Nort

McSheehy Lloyd, student, b 1217 North

McTaggart (see also *Taggart*)

McTaggart Alice M, dressmkr 311 w Market, b same

McTaggart Lanta, confectioner 6 Sycamore, b 508 Broadway

McTaggert John J, clk, h 311 w Market

McTaggart Kate C, organist, b 311 w Market

McTaggart Margaret, b 311 w Market

McTaggart Michael, tailor, h 311 w Market

McTaggart Sarah [wid James], h 415 High

McTaggart Rose, b 415 High

M

Maahs Jacob, lab, b 514 12th
Mabbitt Frank B [Rosa L], grain dealer, h 1821 Market
Mabry George W [Mary], barber 515 Broadway, h 602 Ottawa
Mack Grace, b 631 Sycamore
Mack Hannah, domestic 906 Market
Mack James D [Minnie M], tkt clk Vandalia, h 509 Miami
Mack John [Margaret], h 109 Ash
Mack Martin, lab, b 109 Ash
Mackey James H [Effie], brakeman Panhandle, h 617 15th
Mackey Mary [wid Edward], b 1216 Wright
Mackin Rose [wid Peter], h 68 Washington
Mackin Margaret, b 68 Washington
Mackessy John, lab, b 1309 Indiana
Madary (*see also Madory*)
Madary August M, miller C L Dilley & Co, b 113 Osage
Madary Edward J, bkkpr, b 113 Osage
Madary Esther [wid Edward], h 113 Osage
Madary Louise, dressmkr, b 113 Osage
Madden Orrin C, bicycle rep Burgman Cycle Co, b 313½ Broadway
Mader Bird M, b 101 Bates
Mader Daniel [Rachel], merchant tailor 300 Broadway, h 101 Bates
Mader Edith S, student, b 101 Bates
Mader Frank [Laura], condr, h 118 Pratt
Mader Frederick [Etta], fireman Vandalia, h 915 Linden av
Mader Harvey D, cigars, tobacco and smokers articles 406 4th, b 101 Bates
Mader John B, pressman The Journal, b 101 Bates
Madison Charles, barber, b 126 Helm
Madory (*see also Madary*)
Madory Elizabeth [wid Peter], b 622 North
Magee Mamie, b 313 9th
Magee Margaret, b 313 9th
Magee Mary, cook Insane Hospital, b same
Magee Rufus (Magee & Funk), h 313 9th
Magee & Funk (Rufus Magee, George W Funk), lawyers 406½ Broadway
Magnus Johanna, tailor, b 215 w Broadway
Mahoney Daniel [Bridget], sect foreman, h 208 Wheatland
Mahoney Dora [wid Marquis], student **Hall's Business College,** b 909 20th
Mahoney Ella, student, b 208 Wheatland
Mahoney Ella, b 402 Ottawa
Mahoney James P, clk McCaffrey Bros, b 208 Wheatland

Mahoney John, lab, h 402 Ottawa
Mahoney Mary, b 208 Wheatland
Mahoney Mary, b 414 Ottawa
Mahoney Michael F [Catharine](Lairy & Mahoney), h 2101 Broadway
Mahoney Patrick [Nellie], blksmth Panhandle. h 414 Ottawa
Mahoney Thomas F [Anna], foreman, h 300 Sycamore
Maiben Charles H, laundry 115 Melbourne av, h 123 Melbourne av
Maihen John, h 123 Melbourne av
Maiben Walter, clk, r 813 North
Maier (see also Meier and Meyer)
Maier Christina, h 318 3d
Mailhot (see also Malott)
Mailhot Joseph O [Emma R], barber, h 206 Ottawa
Malay John T [Ella], eng Panhandle, h 423½ 4th
Malcom Edward E [May], brakeman Panhandle, h 1032 Toledo
Malone Frederick, agt, b 117 Washington
Malone George, barber, b 117 Washington
Malone James, engr Panhandle, b 1224 Wright
Malone Joseph [Nora], barber 321 Broadway, h 117 Washington
Maloney James S [Catharine], lab, h 905 Linden av
Malott Goldie, student **Hall's Business College,** b 46 Michigan av
Malott George B, b 602 12th
Malott Hattie [wid Stanley], h 46 Michigan av
Malott Samuel F G [Roseltha], baggage master Pan, h 602 12th
Mancourt Charles P, condr Vandalia, r 315 Sycamore
Mandel Charles J, student, b 610 Market
Mandel Joseph [Hannah], clk Wiler & Wise, h 610 Market
Mandel Sarah J, b 610 Market
Manders Emma teacher, b 225 Coles
Manders Eva, student, b 225 Coles
Manders Grace E, student, b 225 Coles
Manders Robert [Mary A], genl del clk post office, h 225 Coles
Manderville Wynett, condr Panhandle, h 1829 Toledo
Manes Edward, lab, b 616 18th
Manes John, engr Panhandle, r 320½ Broadway
Manion Kate, attendant Insane Hospital, b same
Manlove Henry T [Elizabeth F],dentist 401½ Broadway, h 1124 North
Manly Martha M [wid Wm T S], h 613½ Broadway
Manly Mary, student, b 613½ Broadway
Mann Elizabeth, h 1213 Toledo
Mann James H, comp, b 1213 Toledo
Manring Daisy, student, b 2300 North
Manring George E [Ella], condr Panhandle, h 2300 North
Manring Raleigh C, student, b 2300 North
Manuels W Lewis [Anna], lather, h n s Bartlett 3 w Frank (S T)
Manwaring Wm, lab, r 408½ Market
March Eli N [Nellie], del clk The Wide Awake Grocery, h 1824 Toledo

H. J. CRISMOND, 312 Market Street,
Gasoline Stoves, Screen Doors and Windows.

| MAR | 183 | MAR |

Marchand Casper [Kate], celery grower, h s s Bates 1 w Vandalia R R (Dunkirk)

Markert Charles [Catharine], gardener, h s s Pleasant Hill 2 e Sycamore

Markert Christine, b cor Pleasant Hill and Pleasant Grove

Markert Frederick [Frederika], h cor Pleasant Hill and Pleasant Grove

Markert Frederick jr, clk, b cor Pleasant Hill and Pleasant Grove

Markert John D, driver Pacific Ex Co, b cor Pleasant Hill and Pleasant Grove

Market Street M E Church, Rev Wm S Stewart pastor, s s Market bet 14 and 15th

Markle Charles, porter, b 415½ 3d

Markley Frank M [Lavina], cigar mnfr, h 1331 High

Markley Frank W, clk Busjahn & Schneider, b 1833 Clifton av

Markley John W [Jennie], abstractor 214½ 4th, h 1833 Clifton av

Markley Lizzie, b 203 w Market

Marple Emma J, housekeeper 905 Race

Marquis Dessie, domestic 1120 North

Marquis Keziah [wid Spencer, b n w cor Howard and Anthony (S T)

Marquiss David W [Sylvia], h 214 College

Marsden Charles [Lynn], engr Panhandle, h 1709 Spear

Marsh Wm, lab, b 1209 Toledo

Marsh Rev Wm H H [Jane A], h 8 Helm

Marshall Anna, b 123 w Broadway

Marshall Charles D [Stella], barber 804 15th, h 1412 Wright

Marshall Charles E [Jennie], propr Marshall's Steam Laundry (Marshal & Jensen), h 112 11th

Marshall Cora A, teacher, b 123 w Broadway

Marshall George A, clk D E Pryor, b 123 w Broadway

Marshall George D [Stella], horseshoer J M Elliott, h 1425 Smead

Marshall George K [Elizabeth], clk H J Crismond, h 123 w Broadway

Marshall James J, b 512 Fitch

Marshall John, news dealer, h 1605 Market

Marshall Margaret [wid John H], h 512 Fitch

Marshall Millie, domestic, r 7 Eel River av

Marshall & Jensen (Charles E Marshall, Henry Jensen), proprs Logan Steam Dye Works 608 Broadway

Marshall's Steam Laundry, Charles E Marshall propr, 608 Broadway

Marter (see also Morter)

Marter Charles, student, b 1319 Short

Marter John J [Agnes C], carp, h 1319 Short

Marter Joseph [Catharine], lab, h 1510 George

Marter Joseph A, mess G W Seybold & Bros, b 1319 Short

Marter Louis A, lab, b 1319 Short

Martin Albert E, tmstr, b n w cor Howard and Anthony (S T)

Martin Albert J [Julia E], prin Central Bldg, h 421 10th

LOGANSPORT WALL PAPER CO.
Furnishes the Best Wall Paper Hangers and Decorators,
407 MARKET STREET.

| MAR | 184 | MAS |

Martin Alma, housekpr 1508 Toledo
Martin Benjamin [Augusta], jeweler 310 4th, h 1205 High
Martin Bessie, student, b 1214 Broadway
Martin Catharine [wid George O], b 100 8th
Martin Charles H [Emma J], truckman Wabash, h 2104 Spear
Martin Charles L, railway mail clk, b 516 North
Martin Ellen V, teacher, b 1408 North
Martin Elsie J, teacher, b 1408 North
Martin Emerson G, finisher Hillock & Pitman, b 1429 Wright
Martin Francis S [Caroline], h 1408 North
Martin George N [Cora E], lab, h 18 Nobley
Martin Harriet M, b 1408 North
Martin Henry W, roof painter 630 North, r same
Martin Ida B, b 521 High
Martin Isaiah [Mary E], carp, h n w cor Howard and Anthony (S T)
Martin James P [Zeruah A], stoneware and sewer pipe 216 6th, h
    1214 Broadway
Martin Jane [wid John], h 516 North
Martin Jane [wid Joseph], domestic, h cor Howard and Frank (S T)
Martin John H [Frances A], carp Thomas Jones, h 700 Clifton av
Martin John L, student, b 516 North
Martin Joseph [Alice], lab, h e s Washington, 3 s Lincoln (S T)
Martin Martha E, carpet weaver, 718 12th, h same
Martin Michael [Margaret], h 1906 Market
Martin Patrick H [Alice], cigarmkr Julius Wagner, h 363 Sycamore
Martin Stella, student, b 1214 Broadway
Martin Thomas E [Cordelia], brakeman Panhandle, h 819 16th
Martin Willard [Martha E], shoemkr 718 12th, h same
Martindale Rosetta, b 411 Humphrey
Marvin Alpha, domestic, b e s Creek 1 n John
Marvin Belle, domestic 310 North
Marvin Claud, student, b e s Creek, 1 n John
Marvin George, lab, h n s Miami, 1 e n 6th
Marvin Homer, lab, b e s Creek, 1 n John
Marvin Wm [Josephine], lab, h e s Creek, 1 n John
Mason John, student **Hall's Business College**, b e s Royal Center rd,
    1 n Pleasant Hill
Mason Truman [Mary], lab, h 1210 Erie av
Masonic Club, Henry C Cushman pres, Charles E Dykeman first vice
    pres, Victor E Seiter second vice pres, David A Middleton secy,
    Joseph L Linvill treas, Masonic Temple n e cor 4th and North
Massena Charles, tel opr, b w s Kewanna rd, 3 n Pleasant Hill
Massena Etta, teacher, b w s Kewanna rd, 3 n Pleasant Hill
Massena Matthias [Lucinda], foreman, h w s Kewanna rd, 3 n
    Pleasant Hill
Massena Nannie, student, b w s Kewanna rd, 3 n Pleasant Hill
Massick Elizabeth, b 325 Tipton

HERZ, The Tailor
409 MARKET STREET.

Our Reputation for Good Work and Artistic Styles Is Well Established.

MAS   185   MEC

Massick John [Veronica], mach hd Panhandle, h 325 Tipton
Massick John J [Nora], lab, h 216 Humphrey
Masslich Susan [wid Stephen G], b 700 Helm
Masters Alfred W [Margaret A], carp Thompson Lumber Co h 14 17th
Matchett Alonzo [Linnie B], foreman, h 731 Linden av
Matt Crescentia [wid Joseph], h 431 5th
Matt Edith M, sec) Cass County B & L Assn, b 431 5th
Matt Joseph F, saloon 431 5th, b same
Matt Josephine, b 431 5th
Matt Sophia, b 431 5th
Mattes Joseph [Lina], artist, h 115 Ash
Mattes Julius [Anna], gardener Insane Hospital, b same
Mattes Maximilian, musician, b 115 Ash
Matthews Dudle) D, student, b 1600 North
Matthews Edward [Margaret], h 1600 North
Matthews Elmer E, mach Panhandle, b 1600 North
Matthews Judson H, student, b 1600 North
Matthews Robert B, ticket receiver Panhandle, r 112 Market
Matthews Robert E, r 112 Market
Matthews Webster P, student, b 1600 North
Mattoon Caroline, b n s Richardville 1 e Sycamore
Maudlin Irene, mach opr W D Craig, h 2 Hillside
Maurer Isabelle E [wid Elias], h 701 North
Maurice (see also Morris)
Maurice Charles L [Bessie], clk, h 715 Race
Maurice Frances A, h 723 High
Maurice John L [Indiana], meat. market 130 6th, h 703 High
Mavis Clara, b 1208 North
Maxinkuckee Lake Ice Co, Joseph Deitrich mgr, 511 Broadway
Maxwell Albert L [Augusta F], engr Panhandle, h 1721 Broadway
Maxwell John [Anna], baggagemaster Panhandle, h 1900 Market
Maxwell Madge, b 1721 Broadway
Maxwell Wilson H [Jeannette], broom mnfr 415 Canal, h w s Burlington rd 1 n Wash tp rd
Maxwell Wm [Elizabeth], h w s Burlington rd 1 n Wash tp rd
May Alma, student, b 312 Michigan av
May Charles D [Katharine], bkkpr, h 15 Pleasant Grove
May Eva, b n s Shultz 2 e Standley (S T)
May Frank [Mary], carp, h 312 Michigan av
May Harry N [Cora B], train master Panhandle, h 1012 Market
Mayhill Walter E, lab, b 516 Clifton av
Mayhill Wm [Sarah], huckster, h 516 Clifton av
Mayhill Wm jr, lab, b 516 Clifton av
Mealey Edward, agt Mills Bros, b 321 Sycamore
Means Oscar A [Minnie], druggist 1228 Broadway, h 1415 North
Meek John G [Ella G], lawyer 222½ 4th, h 1401 High

Meek Margaret J, b 1401 High
Mcdaris Alta, teacher, r 828 North
Medbourn Benjamin F [Rose O], lab, h 117 5th
Medland Edward F, student, b 98 Eel River av
Medland Frank S (John Medland & Sons), b 98 Eel River av
Medland John [Bridget] (John Medland & Sons) h 98 Eel River av
Medland John G, tel opr, b 98 Eel River av
Medland John & Sons (John, Wm J and Frank S), brick mnfrs and
    contractors 98 Eel River av (See adv p 15)
Medland Mary C, b 98 Eel River av
Medland Wm J (John Medland & Sons), b 98 Eel River av
Medland Sarah J, b 98 Eel River av
Medsker Almeda J, domestic 1418 High
Medsker Gertrude, student, b 722 Race
• Meehan James P, helper M M Hughes, b 1201½ Smead
Meehan John [Catharine], h 1201½ Smead
Meehan John A, clk, b 1201½ Smead
Meek Delmer F, lab, b rear 214 4th
Meek Hattie, h rear 214 4th
Meek Wm T, painter Holbruner & Uhl, b rear 214 4th
Meginnis (*see also McGinnis*)
Meginnis Edward J [Carrie S], brakeman Panhandle, h 209 Helm
Meginnis James H, b 508 Sycamore
Mehaffie George, tinner, b 709 High
Mehaffie Harriet [wid Hugh], h 709 High
Mehaffie Henry C [Elizabeth], mach Panhandle, h 108 Osage
Mehaffie John M [Minnie], tinner 315 5th, h 1518 Market
✓ Mehaffie Margaret E, clk G W Seybold & Bros, b 108 Front
Mehaffie Myron, tinner, b 1315 High
Mehaffie Robert, b 709 High
Mehrle August F, bartender M Zahlbaum, b 518 13th
Mehrle Gustav [Bridget], clk Wide Awake Grocery, h 114 Melbourne av
Meier (*see also Maier and Meyer*)
Meier Dora, boarding 611 North
Meier Herman [Dora], watchman Columbia Brew Co, h 611 North
Meisner Frederick [Mary], mason, h 2201 Broadway
Melton Henry M [Anna I], carp, Insane Hospital, h 180 w Wabash av
Mendenhall Charles I, physician 304 Broadway, b same
Menke Frederick [Ella], tailor H G Tucker, h 600 Chicago
Meranda James [Ada], condr Panhandle, h 820 15th
Merriam Aurora N [wid John C], b 718 Market
Merrick Pauline, b 217 3d
Merrifield Earl, student, b 1728 North
Merrifield Harry E, clk S W Ullery & Co, b 1728 North
Merrifield Hugh D, student, b 1728 North
Merrifield Ormando P [Helen], h 1728 North
Merritt Alfred L [Anna B], plumber 1310 Broadway, h 1526 High

Merritt Elmer W, clk, b 1526 High
Merz Andrew J, student Hall's Business College, b 729 Miami
Merz Anna, domestic, b 729 Miami
Merz Catharine [wid John C], h 729 Miami
Merz John L]Maud], cigarmkr, h 127 Ash
Merz Mary M, tailor, b 729 Miami
Messersmith George, lab, h s s Adamsboro rd, 1 e Perrysburg rd
Messersmith Orael, lab, b s s Adamsboro rd, 1 e Perrysburg rd
Messersmith Urdie, b s s Adamsboro rd, 1 e Perrysburg
Messinger Edward S [Laura] (Messinger & Son), h 121 Wheatland
Messinger Ferdinand [Christina], wks Col Brew Co, h 335 Linden av
Messinger Joseph B [Mary E] (Messinger & Son), h 109 w Market
Messinger Jerusha, h 203 Market
Messinger Wm, lab, b 335 Linden av
Messinger Wm H [Rose], florist 823 Linden av, h same
Messinger & Son (Joseph B and Edward S), plumbers, gas and steam
    fitters 521 Broadway
Metcalf John E, b e s Lockwood 1 n Wabash av
Metropolitan Life Insurance Co, The, Wm O Washburn, supt, rms
    1-2-3 Crawford Blk   (See adv left top lines and class Ins Cos)
Metz John, lab, b 504 Fitch
Metz Martha, b 504 Fitch
Metz Susan, attendant Insane Hospital, b same
Metzger Edgar F, city editor The Reporter, b 416 North
Metzger Floyd B, student Hall's Business College, b 2230 Spear
Metzger Harry C, city circulator The Reporter, b 416 North
Meyer (see also Maier, Meier and Meyers)
Meyer Carrie A, bkkpr, b 2002 Market
Meyer Charles [Anna], carp Panhandle, h 417 Day
Meyer Emma B, student, b 2002 Market
Meyer Hattie M, b 2002 Market
Meyer Jacob, lab, b 4 Sycamore
Meyer John [Emma], blksmth 518 North, h 2002 Market
Meyer Joseph [Elizabeth], h 1811 Jefferson
Meyer Louise [wid Wm], h 215 w Broadway
Meyer Michael, lab, b 1811 Jefferson
Meyer Oliver C [Abby M], lab, h 34 Uhl
Meyer Thomas, salesman Henry Tucker, h 417 North
Meyer Wm H, clk G W Hoffmann, b 215 w Broadway
Meyers Lillian M, stripper John Mulcahy, b e s Horney 1 n Franklin
Meyers Mary E [wid Martin L], h e s Horney 1 n Franklin
Michael Albert J, tmstr, b 712 Clifton av
Michael Charles L, student, b 226 Michigan av
Michael Eva A, wks Campbell's Laundry, b s s Shultz 2 w Kloenne (ST)
Michael George L [Irinda B], del clk, h 120 State
Michael George W [Ada C], pres Michael's Business College, h
    414 10th

Established 1867.   Still in the Lead.

DRY GOODS, CLOAKS, FURS,

409-411 Broadway.   WILER & WISE.   306 Fourth Street.

MIC   188   -   MIL

Michael Hannah M [wid Andrew D], h s s Shultz 2 w Kloenne (S T)
Michael Herbert, student, b 414 10th
Michael James G [Ida M], tinstr, h 226 Michigan av
Michael Jerome T [Cecelia F], carp, h 113 Sycamore
Michael John W [Rosa], mason, h n s Culbertson 2 w Anthony (S T)
Michael Rachel A [wid Thornly], h 712 Clifton av
Michael Samuel A [Margaret R], stock dealer, h 922 North
Michael Susan, dressmkr 712 Clifton av, h same
Michael's Business College, George W Michael pres, Wm H Atha
    secy, Luther H Boyd treas, 310½ to 314½ Broadway
Michelle Bruce E, comp, b 902 North
Michelle Charles N [Fannie], foreman, h 902 North
Michelle Nina V, student, b 902 North
Michelle Zaidee B, b 902 North
Middendorf Clement [Dorothy], tailor 320½ Market, h 107 College
Middendorf Edward H, tailor C W Keller, b 107 College
Middendorf Wm, tailor, b 107 College
Middleton David A, deputy city treasurer, b 1417 George
Middleton Eliza [wid David], h 1417 George
Miles Orlando W [Hattie N], trav agt The J T Elliott Co, h 713 Helm
Miller (*see also Mueller*)
Miller Absolom [Mary E], h 501 Sycamore
Miller Addie, domestic 1801 Broadway
Miller Andrew, engr Panhandle, b Island View Hotel
Miller Anna L, b 1410 High
Miller August, lab, h 118 Washington
Miller August, lab, b 1241 Toledo
Miller August H [Mattie], lab, h 523 Chicago
Miller Caroline, domestic 820 Spear
Miller Caroline [wid Wm], dressmkr, b 530 Miami
Miller Christina, b 72 Bates
Miller Conrad, lab, h n s Eel River R R 1 e Perrysburg rd
Miller David R [Mary A] (D R Miller & Son), h 115 Brown
Miller D R & Son (David R and John K), blksmiths n w cor Erie av
    and Berkley
Miller David W [Inez A], lineman, h 314 w Broadway
Miller Edward, brakeman Vandalia, b 355 Sycamore
Miller Edwin P, brakeman Vandalia, b 501 Sycamore
Miller Eliza A [wid Jonas], h 2 Washington
Miller Elsie N, b 400½ Broadway
Miller Emmeline, h e s Burlington rd 11 s Wash tp rd
Miller Frank M, fireman Panhandle, b Island View Hotel
Miller Hannah [wid John], h 317 Barron
Miller Henry [Olive], lab, h s s Bates 1 w Vandalia R R (Dunkirk)
Miller Henry W, lab, b 1410 High
Miller Huldah, domestic 1913 Market
Miller Ira S [Eliza], ins agt, h 922 Broadway

Miller Jesse F, asst secy Y M C A, b 1410 High
Miller John [Cecelia], saloon 1500 Toledo, h same
Miller John A, tinner Panhandle, b 1409 High
Miller John A. lab, h 7½ Sycamore
Miller John H [Elizabeth], car rep Panhandle, h 72 Bates
Miller John H, carp, b 1130 Toledo
Miller John K [Minnie], (D R Miller & Son), b 115 Brown
Miller Josephine, waiter Island View Hotel, r 72 Bates
Miller Mark P [Catharine], barber 310 Pearl, h 821 Linden av
Miller Mary, domestic 202 Broadway
Miller Mary C, b 723 Ottawa
Miller Minnie, domestic 203 w Broadway
Miller Maud M, bkkpr The Logansport Journal Co, b 400½ Broadway
Miller Mollie [wid Niles W], h 129½ Osage
Miller Oliver M, restaurant 320 Broadway, r 14 State Natl Bank Bldg
Miller Otto, sausage mkr, b 1504 Smead
Miller Samuel R, b 115 Brown
Miller Thaddeus, cigarmkr John Mulcahy, b 2 Washington
Miller Thomas [Lena], lab, h 203 Osage
Miller Wm G [Catharine], stone cutter, h 408 w Broadway
Miller Wm T, clk, b 72 Bates
Milligan Alice W, teacher, b 828 North
Milligan James W, asst physician Insane Hospital, b same
Milligan Luisa F [wid Thomas S], h 828 North
Millikan Mahlon, b 22 State
Millikan Thomas W [Ora], condr Panhandle, h 22 State
Milner Wm W, broker 324½ Market, r 216½ Market
Mills Bros, Edward Mealey agt, who fruits cor Ottawa and Van-
    dalia R R
Mills Hugh, fireman Panhandle, b 1224 Wright
Milstead Francis [May], brakeman Panhandle, h 718 e Wabash av
Minick Anna [wid Valentine], h 523 w Broadway
Minick Charles W, lab, b 315 Melbourne av
Minick Robert H, clk Schmitt & Heinly, b 523 w Broadway
Minick Wm H [Ruth A], cement contr, 315 Melbourne av, h same
Minneman Elizabeth, nurse 215 16th, b same
Minneman Frederick W [Lena], bartender G W Kennedy, h 605
    Ottawa
Minneman Jacob G [Katie], propr Clover Leaf Dairy, h Asylum rd,
    ½ m w Cicott st bridge (See adv class Dairies)
Minneman John B [Delia], drayman, h 229 Montgomery
Minneman John H [Margaret], drayman, h 407 Helm
Minneman Joseph M [Elsie], fireman Panhandle, h 215 16th
Minneman Katharine T, clk G W Seybold & Bros, b 407 Helm
Minneman Rosa C, b 217 Osage
Minneman Theodore F [Lucinda L], condr Panhandle, h 217 Osage
Minneman Theodore J [Julia A], feed store and wood yard 8 Syca-
    more, h 16 Osage

Minter George H [Cora I], dyer, h 55 Bates
Minx Gustav, florist Insane Hospital, b same
Misner Wm B [Ella], condr Wabash, h 1621 Broadway
Mitchell Bert, lab, b e s Tanguy, 2 n Main
Mitchell Fannie, opr C U Tel Co, b 705 High
Mitchell George, lab, b e s Tanguy, 2 n Main
Mitchell John, lab, b e s Tanguy, 2 n Main
Mitchell John [Anna], h 324 Melbourne av
Mitchell John W [Mary J], mach hd Parker & Johnston, h e s
    Tanguy, 2 n Main
Mittchel Wm, lab, b 421 Coles
Mize Nancy [wid Edward], b 1414 George
Moak Jacob T [Rebecca], engr Panhandle, h 1612 Spear
Moesta Louise, b 1217 Smead
Moesta F Wm [Fredericka], teacher, h 1217 Smead
Moesta Wm C, clk, Wm Peters, b 1217 Smead
Mohler Nelson J [Mary L], lab, h 320 Melbourne av
Molique John, lab, b 1426 Usher
Molique Joseph [Nettie], blksmith Panhandle, h 813 17th
Molique Lena [wid George], h 1426 Usher
Monahan (*see also Moynihan*)
Monahan James [Bridget], lab, h 1409 Wright
Monahan Margaret [wid Martin], b 1409 Wright
Monahan Maria A, domestic 604 Market
Monahan Mary, teacher, b 411 Burlington av
Monahan Michael [Ann], lab, h 1523 George
Monigan Henry [May] drayman, h 1830 Market
Monroe Edward, attendant Insane Hospital, b same
Montague Anna, domestic s e cor Perrysburg and Adamsboro rd
Montfort Catharine M, clk John Gray, b 1318 High
Montfort Frederick J, b 1318 High
Montfort Henry H, supt water wks, b 1318 High
Montfort Rebecca [wid Wm B], h 1318 High
Montgomery Bros (Robert and George S), carpet cleaners, 117 Bur-
    lington av
Montgomery Emma A, student, b 604 Linden av
Montgomery **George S** (Montgomery Bros), h Rockfield, Ind
Montgomery Harry, lab, b 3 Spring
Montgomery Horace L, student, b 308 Burlington av
Montgomery Margaret J, h 210½ 6th
Montgomery Mary, student **Hall's Business College**, b 308 Burling-
    ton av
Montgomery Robert [Linda E] (Montgomery Bros), h 308 Burling-
    ton av
Montgomery Robert [Eliza], lab, h 604 Linden av
Montgomery Sarah, waiter Hotel Johnston, r 604 Linden av
Montgomery Susan [wid John], h 3 Spring

H. J. CRISMOND, 312 Market Street,
Hardware, Stoves and Tinware.

| MON | 191 | MOO |

Montgomery Tilman M [Emma], h 600 Sycamore
Moody Caroline, laundress, h n s Hanna 3 w 6th
Moody Clinton, agt, b 708 Chicago
Moon Bessie, b 1717 George
Moon Clara, b 205 Montgomery
Moon Edward, condr Panhandle, r 12 State Nat'l Bank Bldg
Moon Helen E, student **Hall's Business College,** b 1717 George
Moon Irad S, carp Panhandle, r 506 12th
Moon Lillie M, comp, b 205 Montgomery
Moon Lloyd C, student, b 1717 George
Moon Percy [Lilly], painter, h 205 Montgomery
Moon Silas B [Margaret E], switch tender Panhandle, h 1717 George
Mooney David [Jennie], lab, h 815 Canal
Mooney Elizabeth, b 49 Washington
Mooney Ellen [wid Anthony], h 49 Washington
Mooney John A [Agnes], drayman, b 49 Washington
Moore Ada, student, b 1517 North
Moore Allen [Mary], painter, h 60 Bates
Moore Andrew J [Elizabeth], carp, h rear 121 Front
Moore Arley R [Cora], switchman Panhandle, h 528 10th
Moore Bartholomew, cigarmkr John Mulcahy, r 5 Barnes Blk
Moore Bert, brakeman Panhandle, r 1 State Natl Bank Bldg
Moore Carrie Z, bkkpr, b 1514 High
Moore Charles F [Nellie], pres Hall's Business College, h 704 Bring-
  hurst
Moore Charles J [Clara], mach hd Panhandle, h 728 15th
Moore Charles O, painter, b 60 Bates
Moore Charles P, b 1219 Toledo
Moore Charles P, clk Hotel Johnston, b same
Moore Cornelia, teacher, b 1717 North
Moore Dora E, stenogr, b 1514 High
Moore Elizabeth [wid Hamilton, h 119 Franklin
Moore Elizabeth, b e s Burlington rd, 7 s Wash tp rd
Moore Flora, h 421½ Market
Moore Frank S, vice pres Hall's Business College, h Lafayette, Ind
Moore Harry, lab, b e s Burlington rd, 7 s Wash tp rd
Moore Harry L, lab, b 519 Fitch
Moore Henry H B [Mary E] foreman Panhandle, h 1514 High
Moore Herbert C, press feeder, b 728 15th
Moore James A, b 220 Burlington av
Moore James F [Lucinda], tmstr, h 1219 Toledo
Moore John R [Christina E], comp, h 222 w Broadway
Moore John S [Flora E], agt, h 508 13th
Moore John W, lab, b 1017 Linden av
Moore Lamb, music teacher 414 North, r same
Moore Margaret, b 1017 Linden av
Moore Margaret [wid Daniel E], h 1517 North

Moore Mary, b 1017 Linden av
Moore Patrick [Sarah], tmstr, h 1017 Linden av
Moore Peter W [Margaret], h 2018 North
Moore Samuel [Amanda C], brakeman, h 19 Plum
Moore Thomas [Elizabeth], lab, h e s Burlington rd, 7 s Wash tp rd
Moore Thomas J, carp, b 119 Franklin
Moore Willis [Rosetta J], h 231 Osage
Moore Wm E, student, b 60 Bates
Moorman Emanuel W, carp, b 418½ 3d
Moorman Ida M, trimmer I N Cool, b 639 12th
Moorman Wm lab Insane Hospital, b same
Moran Frank, lab, b 1408 Smead
Moran James [Bridget], lab, h 1408 Smead
Moran Mary, domestic 812 Market
Morehart Alonzo [Emerilla], hackman Jas O'Donnell, h 511 Pratt
Morehart Burrell G, st car condr, b 1315 High
Morehart Charles B, stenogr Vandalia, b 511 Pratt
Morehart David H, fireman Panhandle, b 1315 High
Morehart Edgar L, del clk Logansport Wall Paper Co, b 1315 High
Morehart Jacob W [Mary A], farmer, h 1315 High
Morehead Andrew M, lather, h 12 Bartlett (Dunkirk)
Morehead Charles E [Alice], plasterer, h s s Bartlett, 3 w Frank (S T)
Morgan Annna, stenogr Hall's Business College, b 1123 North
Morgan Bridget [wid John], h 1123 North
Morgan Curdie A, lab, b s w cor Massachusetts and Vermont (Dunkirk)
Morgan Felix S (Cummings & Morgan), b 1123 North
Morgan Henry [Missouri], farmer, h n s Stoney Pike, 1 e Hamilton
Morgan James, cigars 427 12th, b 1123 North
Morgan John N, mach hd, b 938 Erie av
Morgan Lucius [Emma], timber buyer, h 1431 Spear
Morgan Mollie, comp, b 1423 High
Morgan Nathaniel B [Mary E], tmstr, h s w cor Massachusetts and Vermont (Dunkirk)
Morgan Ola, student, b 1431 Spear
Morgan Silas [Caroline[, detective, h 938 Erie av
Morgan Thomas [Bridget], h 602 Canal
Moriarty Blanche, b 107 n 6th
Moriarty George E, grocer 101 n 6th, b 107 n 6th
Moriarty Michael G [Eliza], carp Panhandle, h 107 n 6th
Morris (see also Maurice)
Morris Anna, b 213 Market
Morris Charles, lab, b 1410 George
Morris Charles W [Anna D], condr Panhandle, h 316½ Broadway
Morris Daisy P, student Hall's Business College, b 213 Market
Morris Fannie V, domestic 624 North
Morris Florence D, b 23 McCarty
Morris Henry, lab, b n s Michigan av, 1 s E R Ry

Morris Henry, lab, b s s Adamsboro rd, 1 w Perrysburg rd
Morris Isaac [Ella], lab, h n s Michigan av, 1 s E R Ry
Morris John, lab, b 1409 Wright
Morris John C [Nellie], agt, h 23 McCarty
Morris Mark B [Anna], h 213 Market .
Morris Mark C [Uba G], lab, h 513 Sycamore
Morris Martin, lab, b 110 e Wabash av
Morris Thomas [Katie], police sargent, h 211 Berkley
Morris Warner H, agt Metropolitan Life Ins Co, b 316½ Broadway
Morris Wm, [Rosetta B], lab, h 117 Franklin
Morris Wm L [Lulu A], mgr Logansport Linseed Oil Works, h 435 Sycamore
Morrisey Martin [Katharine], watchman, h 826 Race
Morisey Michael, b 213 Eel River av
Morrison George W, wks Ind Pipe Line Co, h 1 e Spencer pk
Morrison Jane A [wid ———], dressmkr, h 213 Cole
Morrow Ellen F [wid John S], b 216 3d
Morrow Emmett, b 216 3d
Morrow George B [Sarah S], carp, h 2021 George
Morrow Huldah J, dressmkr 1905 Market, b same
Morrow Wm F [Anna E], carp, h 1905 Market
Morse Stella F, student Hall's Business College, b 925 High
Morter (see also Marter)
Morter Jacob [Amanda], car rep, h s s Howard, 2 w Anthony (S T)
Morter Joseph [Mary], lab, h n w cor Bartlett and Frank (S T)
Morter Joseph, jr, lab, b n w cor Bartlett and Frank (S T)
Mote Oliver E, waiter, r 523½ Broadway
Mote Ora [Fledie], lab, h 313 Bates
Mowrey John A [Margaret E] engr J W Henderson & Sons, h 18 Pleasant Hill
Moynihan (see also Monahan)
Moynihan Arthur L, wall paper, decorations and room mouldings 210 6th, h same
Muckenfuss Anna, b 323 Tipton
Muckenfuss John S [Barbara], car rep Panhandle, h 323 Tipton
Muckenfuss Lawrence, cabinet mkr, b 323 Tipton
Muckenfuss Wm E, clk, b 323 Tipton
Mucker Henry B [Elizabeth], painter 329 Wheatland, h same
Mucker Jennie, b 329 Wheatland
Mueller (see also Miller)
Mueller George [Catharine], lab, h 1026 20th
Mueller Ursula [wid John], h n s Shultz 2 e Frank (S T)
Mulcahy Daniel [Mary], flagman, h 511 Ottawa
Mulcahy George [Mary], cigarmkr John Mulcahy, h 1417 Spear
Mulcahy James, h 1501 George
Mulcahy John [Mary], cigar mnfr 324 Broadway; h 2220 Broadway
Mulcahy Mary, clk Wiler & Wise, b 1501 George

$186,000,000 of Life Insurance

WAS WRITTEN BY THE

METROPOLITAN LIFE. of New York. In 1896

W. O. WASHBURN,
Superintendent
Logansport District,

Crawford Block.

MUL   194   MUR

Mulford Jesse A [Angeline], engr, h 54 Bates
Mulford Mary S, b 54 Bates
Mulholland Samuel E [Flora], bkkpr Logansport & W V Gas Co, h 318 9th
Mull Daniel H [Sarah S], clk, h 801 North
Mull Fannie, clk Schmitt & Heinly, b 801 North
Mullen Daniel, baggagemaster Panhandle, r 1 State Natl Bank Bldg
Mullen James, lab, b 603 12th
Mullendore Oliver [Ida], lab, h 318 Coles
Mullett Benjamin, driver, b 317½ Sycamore
Mullert George W, b 808 Spear
Mullett Jacob [Margaret], lab, h 808 Spear
Mummert John H [Minnie A], clk Dr J B Shultz, h 419½ 4th
Mummey Louise, dressmkr 324½ 4th, h same
Muntz Gillis J, lab, b 223 13th
Muntz Mary J [wid Alexander], h 223 13th
Murdock Andrew J [Margaret], pres First National Bank, also treas King Drill Co, h 906 Market
Murdock J Frederick, clk W O Murdock, b 920 Market
Murdock Gertrude C, b 906 Market
Murdock Henry S [Theodosia], boots and shoes 408 Market, h 920 Market
Murdock James, asst to pres Logansport & Wabash Valley Gas Co, h Lafayette Ind
Murdock Carl F, messenger First Natl Bank, b 920 Market
Murdock Samuel T, genl mgr Logansport & Wabash Valley Gas Co, h Lafayette, Ind
Murdock Will O, exclusive men's furnisher s e cor 4th and Broadway, b 920 Market
Murphey Elizabeth T [wid Cyrus], b 403½ Broadway
Murphey Frank E [Netta], bkkpr The J T Elliott Co, h 218 8th
Murphy Anna L, student, b 724 North
Murphy Augustus F [Catharine], farmer, h s w cor Standley and Wash tp rd
Murphy Crawford C [Ida], b 1826 Market
Murphy Daniel [Christine], mach Panhandle, h 1810 George
Murphy Forrest C, student, b 1911 Market
Murphy Francis M [Luella], clk Island View Hotel, h 1911 Market
Murphy Frank B, clk, b s w cor Standley and Wash tp rd
Murphy Frank C [Jessie], condr Panhandle, h 1630 High
Murphy George C [Addie], brakeman Panhandle, h 203 Sycamore
Murphy George W [Alice B], brakeman Panhandle, h 405½ Market
Murphy Gertrude, b s w cor Standley and Wash tp rd
Murphy Hannah, b 215 Elm
Murphy Henry, student, b s w cor Standley and Wash tp rd
Murphy James, lab, h 600 Miami
Murphy James C [Margaret], baggage agt Pan, h 2003 w Market

hy James D, letter carrier, b 215 Elm
hy James T, lawyer 309½ 4th, r same
hy Jeremiah, lab, h 630 Ottawa
hy John, fireman Panhandle, b 1227 Erie av
hy John, lab, b 630 Ottawa
hy John [Kate F], mach Panhandle, h 515 Erie av
hy John A [Elizabeth], cook, h 419 Grove
hy John B, dpty county surveyor, b 220 College
hy John H [Margaret C], lab, h 215 Elm
hy Lulu, dressmkr, b 1810 George
hy Lydia [wid James], h 1227 Erie av
hy Magdalen, b 1613 Douglass
hy Margaret, b 630 Ottawa
hy Martin [Elizabeth], grocer 1201 Erie av, h same
hy Mary, b 600 Miami
hy Mary, tailor, b 1810 George
hy Mary [wid Patrick], h e s Washington, 3 s Biddle (S T)
hy Mary, b e s Washington 3 s Biddle (S T)
hy Mary J, student, b 1201 Erie av
hy Michael [Johanna], bartender, h 416½ Market
hy Michael, condr Panhandle, b 1224 Wright
phy Michael W [Maudella G], teacher stenography, Hall's Business College, h 628 Bringhurst
hy Norris, clk, b 1201 Erie av
hy Nathan H [Rena], painter, h 203 College
hy Nellie, wks Bridge City Candy Co, b 215 Elm
hy Owen [Lulu], baggage agt Panhandle, h e s Burlington rd, 10 s Wash tp rd
hy Patrick, farmer, b 630 Ottawa
hy Paul, clk Jacob Herz, b s w cor Standley and Wash tp rd
hy Sadie, clk, b 1810 George
hy Thomas F, conductor Panhandle, r 403 High
hy Thomas F [Anna], carp, h 722 Miami
hy Wm [Catharine], blksmth Panhandle, h 409 Humphrey
hy Wm [Johanna], painter, h 1012 Toledo
hy Wm W, b 818 Race
ay Bud M, trav agt, r 425½ 5th
ay Edward [Eva], carriage trimmer, b 1320 North
ay George [Margaret], stone mason, h 652 12th
ay Wm A, trav agt, b 327 Bates
elman David [Eliza], buggy washer I N Cash, h 509 Canal
elman Harvey M, attendant Insane Hospital, b same
elman Jacob, b 203 w Market
elman Jessie, b 509 Canal
elman Lulu, b 509 Canal
elman Maude, b 509 Canal
elman Michael, tmstr C L Dilley & Co, b 1220 Smead

Musser Timothy L, carp, b 717 North
Mutschler Catharine [wid John], h 310 Helm
Mutschler Frederica A, b 310 Helm
Mutschler Wm L, b 310 Helm
Myers (*see also Meyer, Maier and Meier*)
Myers Alva L [Lydia], baggageman Vandalia, h 311 Sycamore
Myers Charles [Mary], lab, h s s Wabash river rd 3 e Coles
Myers Charles A, b n w cor Market and Holland
Myers Courtney D [Carrie], switchman Vandalia, h 529 Sycamore
Myers Elizabeth, seamstress, h 607 12th
Myers Frank, carp, b 355 Sycamore
Myers John J, switch tender Panhandle, b 128½ 6th
Myers Madge, student, b 1830 George
Myers Prudence [wid Wm], housekeeper 1830 George
Myers Quincy A [Jessie C] (Nelson & Myers), h 1004 Market
Myers Rollin H. janitor, b 229 Pratt
Myers Samuel D [Harriet E], lab, h n w cor Market and Holland
Myers Sarah [wid John], h rear 312 Eel River av
Myers Schuyler, r 216½ Market
Myers Wm T [Emma M], brakeman Panhandle, h 725 Linden av

N

Nading Wm A [Pauline], patrolman, h 108 Marydyke
Nagle Amanda, domestic 1527 Broadway
Nagle Anna, b 1510 Market
Nagle Harriet R [wid Jacob], h 1510 Market
Nagle Joseph, brakeman Panhandle, b 1510 Market
Nagle Matilda A, agt, r 316½ Market
Narzinski Agnes, domestic 920 Market
Narzinski August, lab, h 229 Washington
Narzinski Hattie, b 229 Washington
Narzinski John [Johanna], gardener, h Michigan rd 1½ m n city
Narzinski Minnie, b 229 Washington
Narzinski Paul, clk, b Michigan rd 1½ m n city
Narzinski Robert, lab, b 229 Washington
Nash Belle [wid Marcellus H], h 106 9th
Nash F Mae, student, b 106 9th
Nash Otis L, b 106 9th
National Express Co, Herbert A Brown agt, 318 4th
National Loan & Savings Association of Indiana, Alexander Hardy
    pres, John B Winters vice-pres, Charles B Stevenson treas, Charles
    G Dodge secy, 323 Broadway
Naughton Anna, seamstress Insane Hospital, b same

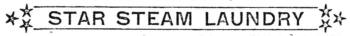
Nave Charles, mach hd, b 1300 e Wabash av
Nave Oliver, lab, b 1211 Toledo
Nave Tete [Elizabeth], grocer 600 Sycamore, h 602 Sycamore
Nave Wm [Anna], lab John H Lux, h 1300 E Wabash av
Navin Edward, student, b 1319 Indiana
Navin James, brakeman Panhandle, b 1319 Indiana
Navin John, switchman Panhandle, b 2024 Market
Navin John [Margaret J], engr Panhandle, h 1416 George
Navin Martin [Hannah], car insp Panhandle, h 1319 Indiana
Navin Michael [Catharine], lab, h 2024 Market
Navin Thomas, brakeman, b 2024 Market
Navin Thomas, b 1319 Indiana
Navin Wm, lab, b 2024 Market
Naylor Alvyron C [Lillie V], cashier Wabash frt depot, h 1823 Market
Neal (see also Neill and O'Neal)
Neal Charles A [Jennie], condr Panhandle, h 1605 High
Neal Harry, b 609 High
Neal James E [Josephine], painter, h 424 5th
Neal Mary A [wid Israel], h 609 High
Needham Harvey A, clk, b 625 Sycamore
Needham Joseph A [Phoebe A], painter, h 625 Sycamore
Neely Edward, agt, r 315 Sycamore
Neff Carl B [Lydia], car rep Vandalia, h 1 Pratt
Neff Charles W, clk, h 814 Race
Neff Clara, domestic s s Shultz 4 w Klqenne
Neff Hattie, student,, b 716 North
Neff Jasper N [Flora], physician 2000 Broadway, h same
Neff Katharine E [wid Franklin], dressmkr 311½ Market, h same
Neff Margaret, domestic Island View Hotel, h 217 3d
Neff Marion [Laura], oil pressman, h 2 m s city
Neff May, student, b 421 Day
Neff Minnie, b 421 Day
Neff Rose, domestic, b 531 Ottawa
Neff Walter S [June M], carp Thompson Lumber Co, h 610 Miami
Neff Wm H [Anice], brakeman Panhandle, h 1321 Smead
Neher Byron G [Della], trav agt, h 603 Wilkinson
Neill (see also Neal and O'Neal)
Neill Floyd, student, b 304 Burlington av
Neill Jessie, student, b 304 Burlington av
Neill Joseph, lab, b 304 Burlington av
Nelson Alice C, b 627 Market
Nelson Allen E, student, b 627 Market
Nelson Anna, teacher, b 1307 High
Nelson Anna, domestic 2224 North
Nelson Charles, lab, b 1307 High
Nelson Charles, b 2029 Market
Nelson Charlotte, domestic, b 2029 Market

Nelson Elizabeth, Ironer Insane Hospital, b same
Nelson Frank, barber, b 1307 High
Nelson George W, trav agt N Rumley & Co, h Nonon, Ind
Nelson Ida [wid Peter], h 1701 Spear
Nelson Irene, b 412½ 3d
Nelson Helen C, b 627 Market
Nelson James V, student, b 627 Market
Nelson John A [Nellie], h 2029 Market
Nelson John C [Mary C] (Nelson & Myers), h 627 Market
Nelson Mary [wid Gustav], h 1307 High
Nelson Minnie, student, b 1307 High
Nelson Minnie, b 2029 Market
Nelson & Myers (John C Nelson, Quincy A Myers), lawyers 212 4th
Nethercutt Melvin E [Emma], clk Ray & Etnire, h 604 Miami
Nethercutt Milda, b 1716 Broadway
Nethercutt Moses F [Louise], h 1716 Broadway
Neusbaum Wm H [Mary], brakeman Panhandle, h 1720 Toledo
Neville Frederick J [Emma G], clk Wm Grace & Co, h 214 w Broadway
Neville James P, car rep Panhandle, b 316 Eel River av
Neville John, lab, b 316 Eel River av
Neville Mary [wid John], b 214 w Broadway
Nevitt Daniel, butcher Insane Hospital, b same
Newark Mary, b 109 Market
Newby Harry, student **Hall's Business College,** b 609 w Broadway
Newby James H [Gertrude S], florist J A Newby, h 525 w Broadway
Newby John A [Elizabeth], florist 609 w Broadway, h same
Newby John A, jr, b 609 w Broadway
Mewcomet Horace E, draughtsman Panhandle, r 314 North
Newell Charles G [Martha E], local agt Wabash Railroad Co, h 820 Spear
Newell Helen M, student, b 820 Spear
Newer Charles M, carp, b 430 Burlington av
Newer George W, farmer, b 430 Burlington av
Newer James C [Phœbe A] (Newer & Reeder), h 430 Burlington av
Newer Lillie, b 43 Burlington av
Newer & Reeder (James C Newer, Thomas B Reeder) lawyers 220½ 4th
Newkirk Wm, b 603 12th
Newman Charles, butcher, b 400 High
Newman John, clk, b 300 Linden av
Newman Joseph W, candy mkr Bridge City Candy Co, b 300 Linden av
Newman Josephine, laundress, h 300 Linden av
Newman Mary F, b 300 Linden av
Newmyer (see also Niemeyer
Newmyer Catharine, b 1319 George
Newmyer Catharine, domestic 1506 Broadway
Newmyer Joseph [Elizabeth], car rep Panhandle, h 1319 George

Newmyer Rose, domestic 1229 North
Newport Abraham G, photographer 510 Broadway, b 421 High
Newport James H [Stella], photographer, h 227 13th
Niblick C Elmer [Aura B], truckman Panhandle, h 825 Race
Niblick D Franklin, lab, b 108 n 6th
Niblick Jesse A, clk, b 108 n 6th
Nice Edgar O, lab, b 1233 Toledo
Nice Henry C [Susan], lab, h 1434 Ohio
Nice Philander F [Eliza], carp, h 1233 Toledo
Nichols Alice J, boarding 624 North
Nichols Anna, seamstress, h n e cor 19th and Stevens
Nichols, Emma, h n e cor 19th and Stevens
Nichols Frank, condr Panhandle, b 206 6th
Nichols Geneva Mary, prin free kindergarten, b 214 8th
Nichols Harry L, student, b 308 3d
Nichols Susan [wid David], b 1626 High
Nichols Thomas W [Charity], agt, h 703 Michigan av
Nichols Thomas W [Lottie A], trav agt, h 308 3d
Nicholson Harry E [Elizabeth], brakeman Panhandle, h 1428 Toledo
Nickel John [Mary], carp Panhandle, h 811 Linden
Nickum Albert, b 230½ Market
Nickum Minnie, b 230½ Market
Nickum Robert W [Elizabeth], h w s Burlington rd 7 s Wash tp rd
Nickum Sylvanus B, model mkr 230½ Market, h same
Niemeyer (*see also Newmeyer*)
Niemeyer Andrew, lab, b s s L & W rd 4 W Standley
Noel Emma, stenogr N J Bligh, b 319 n 6th
Noel Lillian, clk, b 319 n 6th
Noel Marcellus E [Bridget], carp, h 319 n 6th
Noel Nellie, clk, b 319 n 6th
Nolan George C [Ellen], lab, h 8 Franklin
Nolan Hannah, b 629 12th
Nolan Timothy J, cigarmkr, r 116 Canal
Norman Alexander J [Ida], peddler, h 427½ 5th
Norris Alma B, clk Panhandle, b 214 Osage
Norris Thomas W [Hattie J], ticket receiver Panhandle, h 214 Osage
North Logan United Brethren Church, Rev George W Lambert, pastor, n e cor Sugar and Oak
Northern Indiana Hospital for Insane, Dr Joseph G Rogers medical supt, 2 m w city
Northwestern Loan & Investment Co, Charles L Wool pres, Joseph L Linvill vice-pres, James T Cockburn secy, Wm H Porter treas, 8 Masonic Temple
Norton Cornelia A, teacher, b 723 Bringhurst
Norton Jane M [wid Leroy], h 723 Bringhurst
Nuhfer Wm, engr Panhandle, b 1916 Broadway
Nulf Leroy, lab, b s e cor Howard and Frank (S T)

Nulf Robert [Lydia J], lab, h s e cor Howard and Frank (S T)
Nulf Wm D, tmstr Stevens Bros, b s e cor Howard and Frank (S T)
Nutt Joseph [Rose], carp, h 318 15th
Nye Albert F, physician 410 4th, r same

O

Oates Charles, asst undertaker Kroeger & Strain, r 613 Broadway
Oates Martin H, drayman, b 208 Montgomery
Obenchain E Frank [Mary A], riding bailiff, h 1429 High
Obenchain John T [Orilla F], pres Logan Milling Co, h 814 Spear
Obenchain Matthew W [Tacy C], miller Logan Milling Co, h 802 Spear
Obenchain Nellie, student, b 111 Hanna
Obenchain Thomas J [Carrie], draughtsman, h 111 Hanna
Obenchain Wm [Elizabeth], carp, h 10 Ottawa
O'Connell Agnes, student, b 112 Chicago
O'Connell Anna, b 112 Chicago
O'Connell Austin A, mailing clk postoffice, b 1316 Spear
O'Connell Daniel, brakeman, b 321 Sycamore
O'Connell Emma, domestic 420 10th
O'Connell James [Clotilda], blksmth Panhandle, h 1316 Spear
O'Connell John, attendant Insane Hospital, b same
O'Connell Kate, b 112 Chicago
O'Connell Loretta, teacher, b 1316 Spear
O'Connell Mame, b 112 Chicago
O'Connell Nellie, b 112 Chicago
O'Connell Pauline, student, b 112 Chicago
O'Connell Urban F, bkkpr Campbell's Laundry, b 1316 Spear
O'Connell Wm [Mary], lab, h 112 Chicago
O'Connor (*see also Connors*)
O'Connor Josephine, b 600 e Wabash av
O'Connor Mary, h 600 e Wabash av
O'Day, Joseph, b 13 Biddle av
Oddon Constance, housekpr s w cor 9th and Spencer
Odom John, lab, b s s Wab River rd 7 w 18th
Odom Henry [Sarah], lab, h s s Wab River rd 7 w 18th
O'Donnell James [Ella], livery and sale stables, passenger and baggage transfer line 419–425 3d, h 218 Canal
O'Donnell John F, student, b 218 Canal
Offutt Minnie, b 1509 George
Ogborn Wm M, mach hd Panhandle, b 1514 High
O'Hara Edward [Lola], lab Insane Hospital, h 400 Pratt
O'Hara Ellen J [wid Thomas], h 12 Bates
O'Hara Thomas, plumber, b 12 Bates

O'Hearn Elizabeth [wid Michael], b 109 Osage
O'Herren Joseph J [Sophia] brakeman Panhandle, h 301 w Broadway
Oldham Charles C, switchman, b e s Horney 2 n Franklin
Oldham Eugene, student, b e s Horney 2 n Franklin
Oldham Jesse D [Alice E], h e s Horney 2 n Franklin
O'Leary (see also Lairy)
O'Leary John [Johanna], watchman Panhandle, h 1101 George
O'Leary Katharine, b 1101 George
O'Leary Mary, clk G W Seybold & Bros, b 1101 George
Oliver Charlotte, domestic 1601 Broadway
Oliver Frank [Josephine], del clk G W Seybold & Bros, h 1415 North
Oliver Joseph S [Emma], sawyer, h 705 12th
Oliver Roy, porter Hotel Johnston, b same
Ollinger George [Sophia,] lab, h 806 15th
Olsen Henry J, clk Neils Hansen, b 2001 Broadway
Olsen Jens, air brake insp Panhandle, b 2001 Broadway
Olsen John [Eva], carp Panhandle, h 2001 Broadway
Olsen Susanna, b 2001 Broadway
O'Mara Catharine, b 1410 Ohio
O'Mara D Edward, mach Panhandle, b 407 Wilkinson
O'Mara Ellen, bkkpr, b 326 Humphrey
O'Mara Johanna, waiter Island View Hotel, b 326 Humphrey
O'Mara John J, switchman, b 1410 Ohio
O'Mara John T, carp, b 326 Humphrey
O'Mara Lizzie, domestic 906 Lytle
O'Mara Mary [wid Thomas], h 407 Wilkinson
O'Mara Mary [wid Patrick], h 326 Humphrey
O'Mara Minnie, waiter The Barnett, b same
O'Mara Nellie I, student Hall's Business College, b 326 Humphrey
O'Mara Philip [Mary A], lab, h 1410 Ohio
O'Mara Rose, waiter The Barnett, b 326 Humphrey
O'Mara Sadie J, dressmkr 407 Wilkinson, b same
O'Morrow John B [Anna M], clk, h 517 Helm
O'Neal (see also Neal and Neill)
O'Neal Dennis, brakeman Vandalia, r 212 Sycamore
O'Neal Margaret, domestic 417 North
Oppenheimer Isaac Mgr [Cora], queensware 322 4th, h 1211 North
Orr Charlotte, b 2000 High
Orr Harry K [Rosa], brakeman Panhandle, h 413 Day
Orr James K [Margaret J], constable, h 410 Burlington av
Orr John [Dora], lineman, h 6 Front
Orr Lillie, waiter, b 206 6th
Orwin James B [Anna], carp, h s s Shultz, 2 e Kloenne (S T)
Osborn Andrew J [Mary], condr Panhandle, h 1414 North
Osborn Clayton R [Harriet O], miller C L Dilley & Co, h 228 Osage
Osborn Enos L [Emma], blksmth, h 929 Race
Osborn Ethel C, student, b 1414 North

Osborn Harry A, student, b 1414 North
Osgood Charles V, agt, h 129 College
Osmer Frederick L, student, b 1823 Broadway
Osmer Walter A [Anna V], civ engr, h 1823 Broadway
Osmer Wm L, student, b 1823 Broadway
Ott George [Della], propr Star Steam Laundry 405 Market, r 717
    North   (See adv right top lines)
Otto Frederick B, roofer, b 1510 Market
Otto Shoe and Clothing Co, The, Otto A Kraus pres, Sidney V
    Kaufman vice pres, Harry N Ward secy and treas, clothiers, hat-
    ters, furnishers, boots and shoes, 317–319 4th
Overfield Christina, domestic Insane Hospital
Overholser Bertha M, student, b 321 Pleasant Hill
Overholser Daniel L [Catharine], dentist 415½ Broadway, h 321
    Pleasant Hill
Overholser Wiley L, asst Dr D L Overholser, b 321 Pleasant Hill
Overpeck Edward [Louisa], farmer, h s s Stanley, 2 e Clifton av
Overpeck Francis M [Mary E], farmer, h e s Hamilton 1 s Stoney Pike
Overpeck Harriet E E, domestic se cor Stoney Pike and Hamilton
Overpeck Rosa E, b 113 Franklin
Overpeck Thomas J [Isabelle], lab, h 113 Franklin
Overshiner Ellsworth B [Lorena], mgr Logansport Mutual Tele-
    phone Co, h 1530 North
Owen Wm D, Secy of State, b Barnett Hotel
Owens Frank, clk Panhandle, b 119 w Broadway
Owens Wm, fireman Vandalia, r 315 Sycamore
Oyler Anna, h 204 Ottawa
Oyler Charles J, painter I N Cool, b 204 Ottawa
Oyler Frank, marble cutter, b 204 Ottawa
Oyler Roxie L, mach opr W D Craig, b 204 Ottawa
Oyler Simon, mason, b 217 Montgomery

P

Pacific Express Co, Joseph L Linvill agt, 320 Pearl
Packard Edgar [Hattie], teacher, h 1325 North
Paden Wm S (Dora), restaurant 321 Sycamore, h 530 Ottawa
Painter August H, student, b 631 Race
Painter John H, clk, b 631 Race
Painter Wm H, cigarmkr F J Pixler, b 631 Race
Painton Ethel M, student, b 227 w Broadway
Painton Everett W, student, b 227 w Broadway
Painton Joseph M, shoemkr 121 Front, h same
Painton Wm W [Luna], carp rear 121 Front, h 227 w Broadway

Palmer Amos, student, b 416 Montgomery
Palmer Dudley, student, b 416 Montgomery
Palmer Fennetta [wid Amos], h s w cor Clay and Humphrey
Palmer Florence, domestic 500 10th
Palmer George W [Catharine], planing mill 111 Burlington av, h 416 Montgomery
Palmer John, secy Logansport Creamery Co, h Kokomo rd 2½ m s city
Palmer Joseph P [Josephine], turner Hillock & Pitman, h 2129 Market
Palmer Loring E, wks Hillock & Pitman, b 2129 Market
Palmer Nettie, student, b 416 Montgomery
Panabaker Samuel [Mary J], h 1419 North
Panton Allen, mess G W Seybold & Bros, b 717 Miami
Panton Christian J [Caroline], cutter C W Keller, h 717 Miami
Parish George, cigarmkr, b 523 Fitch
Parish Isaac M [Eliza J], engr Panhandle, h 900 Erie av
Parish Harriet [wid Richard T], h 523 Fitch
Parish John, condr Panhandle, b Island View Hotel
Parish Kate M, dressmkr, b 523 Fitch
Parish Mary, clk, b 523 Fitch
Parish Richard, brick mason, b 523 Fitch
Park Bertha, bkkpr Maxinkuckee Lake Ice Co, b n s Richardville 1 e Sycamore
Park Harlow [Martha L], baggage agt Vandalia, h n s Richardville 1 e Sycamore
Park James [Bertha M], clk Vandalia, h 504 Sycamore
Park Oliver L, mach, b n s Richardville 1 e Sycamore
Parker Arthur W [Maud M], switchman Panhandle, h 229 State
Parker Benjamin H, switchman, b 1200 Linden av
Parker Catharine, b 1200 Linden av
Parker Charles H [Cecelia A] (Parker & Rea), h 311 Miami
Parker Dennis A, lab, b 1200 Linden av
Parker Elmer F [Ida], butcher, h 1310 Wright
Parker Emma [wid James E], h 1117 Market
Parker Emma, h 1200 Linden av
Parker Ezra T [Laura M] (Parker & Johnston) h 312 w Broadway
Parker Frank H, student, b 312 w Broadway
Parker George C, clk H Closson & Co, b 311 Miami
Parker John H, lab, b 1200 Linden av
Parker John W [Allie D], letter carrier, h 718 Miami
Parker Lilly M, student, b 312 w Broadway
Parker Mabel L, student, b 718 Miami
Parker Oscar J [Maud M] (Parker & Son) h 416 11th
Parker Samuel, switchman Panhandle, b 400 Linden av
Parker Stephen [Alzina] (Parker & Son), h 1103 Market
Parker Ulysses S, switchman, h 1200 Linden av
Parker Wm J [Della], propr Keystone Grocery n w cor 6th and Broadway, h 1623 Market

The Busy Bee Hive, 409-411 Broadway. 306 Fourth Street.
Dry Goods, Cloaks, Furs.

PAR   204   PAU

Parker & Johnston (Ezra T Parker, John McC Johnston), lumber, lath, shingles, sash, doors and blinds, s e cor Berkley and Spencer (See adv front paster)

Parker & Rea (Charles H Parker, Wm G Rea), barbers 223 6th

Parker & Son (Stephen and Oscar J). grocers 501 12th

Parkhurst Alinus N [Sarah E], pumps 129 6th, h 709 Linden av

Parks Frances [wid John], b 2015 Spear

Parks Wilber S, condr Panhandle, r 408 Canal

Parks Wm, brakeman Panhandle, b 1920 Spear

Parks Wm M [Lillian], condr Panhandle, h 2015 Spear

Parmeter John [Matilda], lab, h 600 w Market

Parmeter Wm, b 819 Canal

Patchell John C [Anna], lab, h 103 Michigan av

Patrick Daniel K, mach, b n e cor Canal and Oak

Patrick Rev David A [Louise J]. Universalist minister, h 2022 Market

Patrick George, lab Insane Hospital, b same

Patrick Jessie, b 2022 Market

Patrick John H, car rep Vandalia, b 220 Broadway

Patrick Maud, music teacher 2022 Market, b same

Pattengale Blanche, b 19 Pleasant Grove

Pattengale Harvey W, lab, b 19 Pleasant Grove

Pattengale James, b 218 College

Pattengale Lewis [Henrietta], lab, h 19 Pleasant Grove

Pattengale Stephen D [Elizabeth], tmstr, h 218 College

Patterson Brough, student, b 1601 North

Patterson Burt J, r 112 Canal

Patterson Ezra T [Alice], fireman Panhandle, h 610 18th

Patterson Frank W [Rose L], fireman Panhandle, 616 10th

Patterson James M [Sarah E], foreman Panhandle, h 1728 Spear

Patterson John M [Nettie], carp Panhandle, h 1601 Spear

Patterson Joseph [Anna B], h 1601 North

Patterson Lemuel G [Malinda], insurance and loans 410½ Broadway, h 917 North

Patterson Robert, lab Stevens Bros, r 112 Canal

Patterson Simon E, b 316 15th

Patterson Wm E [Rose M], car rep Panhandle, h 1801 George

Patton Ezra [Dorothy A], truckman Panhandle, h n w cor Culbertson and Kloenne (S T)

Patton Flora, dressmkr 820 Sycamore, b same

Patton Isaac [Isabella], clk John Horstman, h 704 Helm

Patton Mary A [wid John], b 2204 Market

Pauffenberg Addie, agt, r 523½ Broadway

Paugh Frederick A student, b 900 Linden av

Paugh Junius O, b 900 Linden av

Paugh Martha J [wid Jasper A], h 900 Linden av

Paul Ferdinand [Mary], blksmth Panhandle, h 1529 Spear

Paul Henry [Louise], mach hd Panhandle, h 622 12th

Paulson Henry J, engr, b 126 Woodland
Pavey John B, brakeman Panhandle, b 415½ 3d
Peak Catharine [wid Moses], laundress, h n s Miami 1 e n 6th
Peak Elizabeth, domestic, b n s Miami 1 e n 6th
Peak Moses, lab, b n s Miami 1 e n 6th
Pearson Hannah [wid Wm], b n w cor Culbertson and Kleonne (S T)
Pearson Olive I, wks Campbell's Laundry, b 107 Hanna
Peck D Wesley [Jennie], well driller Ford & Hayworth, h 1930 Spear
Peckham Charles S [Jennie] trav agt, h 1220 High
Peden Ella, b 1525 High
Peden Lizzie, student, b 1525 High
Peden Martha, student, b 1525 High
Peden Thomas A [Sarah J], marble and granite works 1529 High, h 1525 High
Pelton Anna, milliner, b 206 w Market
Pelton James H [Emma], h 206 w Market
Pelton Marguerite, milliner, b 206 w Market
Pelton Nettie, milliner 327½ Market, b 206 w Market
Peirce (*see also Pierce*)
Peirce Jessie E, b s s Perrysburg rd 3 e Michigan av
Peirce Matilda S [wid Lucius], h s s Perrysburg rd 3 e Michigan av
Peirce Sarah S, b s s Perrysburg rd 3 e Michigan av
Penn B Oscar, student **Hall's Business College,** b 114 7th
Pennel Riley H, clk Fred Horstman & Co, b 415½ 3d
Pennock Daisy, domestic 805 North
Pennock Wm [Mary], carp, h 1318 Smead
Pennock Wm C, master mech Panhandle, r 730 Broadway
Penny Mildred, student, b e s Sherman 1 s Lincoln (S T)
Penny Samuel B, stripper, b e s Sherman 1 s Lincoln (S T)
Penny Susan E, milliner T A Spry, b e s Sherman 1 s Lincoln (S T)
Penny Wesley [Mary], tmstr, h e s Sherman 1 s Lincoln (S T)
Penny Willard, hostler, b e s Sherman 1 s Lincoln (S T)
Penrose Edward R [Mary], lab, h 1104 Spear
Penrose Jessie, student, b 1427 High
Penrose Joseph H [Laura M], agt Gaar, Scott & Co 126 6th, h 1427 High
Penrose Harry W, barber 305 Broadway, b 1104 Spear
Penrose Mabel, student **Hall's Business College,** b 1427 High
Penrose Maud [wid Joseph E], h 626 Linden av
Penrose Wilsie, student, b 1427 High
Penzel Adam [Anna], butcher, h n s Miles, 1 e 15th
Penzel Charles [Bertha], lab, h 1431 Smead
Penzel Charles A, clk C W Graves, b 416 2d
Penzel Christian, b 416 2d
Penzel Lena, b 1431 Smead
Penzel Louise M, boarding 416 2d
Penzel Minnie, domestic 1729 North

Percival Rev H Atwood [Catharine], pastor Broadway Presbyterian Church, h 823 Broadway
Perkins Francis M, lab, b 1416 Toledo
Perkins Olive M, b 1416 Toledo
Perkins Sarah [wid Samuel], h 1416 Toledo
Perkins Thomas, brakeman Vandalia, b 321 Sycamore
Perkins Wm [Johanna], tmstr, h 1509 Erie av
Perry Hattie, seamstress, r 927 Market
Personett Benjamin F, clk, b 217 6th
Personett Charles M [Melissa], grocer 217 6th, h same
Peru Brewery, J O Cole propr, Alexander Appel local agt 1100 Toledo
Peters Anna [wid John W], h 207 n 6th
Peters Elizabeth, dressmkr 1220 Broadway, h same
Peters George B, embalmer C L Woll, r 417 Market
Peters Henry W [Anna], foreman The Reporter, h 205 n 6th
Peters Horace B [Mary A], h 215 3d
Peters Mary, b 207 n 6th
Peters Rosa, domestic 1118 High
Peters Wm, grocer 1430 Wright, h same
Peterson Anna, student, b e s 18th, 1 n Usher
Peterson Hilda, domestic 129 College
Peterson James P [Emma], tailor, h 99 Bates
Peterson Oscar [Anna], tmstr, h e s 18th, 1 n Usher
Peterson Samuel [Eva], car insp Panhandle, h 1212 High
Petrie Elizabeth, b 2116 Wright
Petrie Frank, hostler St Joseph's Hospital, b same
Petrie John [Mary], h 1225 Smead
Petrie Louise [wid John], h 1516 George
Petrie Mary, b 1225 Smead
Petrie Rosina [wid Jacob], h 100 Canal
Petrie Peter F [Ella J], brick mason, h 615 Linden av
Petrie Wm, del clk Schmitt & Heinly, b 1516 George
Petrich Frederick J [Minnie F], lab, h 121 Washington
Petrich Johanna [wid John], b 331 Ottawa
Petrig John F [Anna], lab, h 33 Bates
Pettiford Lillian, student, b 216 Cicott
Pettiford Rev Louis [Laura A], pastor A M E Church, h 216 Cicott
Peyton Abraham L, carp, h 709 Spencer
Peyton Harry, carp Insane Hospital, b same
Peyton Mahala, domestic 1115 Market
Peyton Rebecca A, h 709 Spencer
Pfaff Anna, b 1506 Toledo
Pfaff Carrie M, wks Star Steam Laundry, b 1506 Toledo
Pfaff Wm [Caroline], lab, h 1506 Toledo
Pfeiffer Henry H [Mary J], farmer, h 509 Clifton av
Pfeiffer Oscar, gunsmith, b 509 Clifton av
Pfiffer Jacob [Arvilla], lab, h 615 Michigan av

iffer Robert, lab, b 615 Michigan av

ieister Iva, student **Hall's Business College,** b 1902 George

ieister Nancy [wid Samuel], nurse 1902 George, h same

ieister Zelda M, domestic, b 1902 George

ierson (*see also McPherson*)

ierson Elizabeth, clk Wiler & Wise, b 1907 North

ierson George W [Mary J], switch tender Panhandle, h 1907 North

ierson John F, student, b 1907 North

ierson Lloyd C, mach Panhandle, h 1907 North

ilbrick Chester O [Anna], engr Vandalia, h 624 Sycamore

iillips Albert [Ada], fireman Panhandle, h 1506 Toledo

iillips Frank T [Clara], lab, h 213 Heath

iillips Robert E [Bertha], brakeman, h 1227 High

iipps Hubert J, student, b 310 Michigan av

iipps Nathaniel W [Jane A], carp, h 310 Michigan av

ckard Wm M [Emma], painter 2017 George, h same

ickell Josephine [wid Alonzo], boarding 426 12th

ickell Rollo, student **Hall's Business College,** b 426th 12th

ickett Margaret, stenogr, b 213 Burlington av

ickett Mary [wid Patrick], h 128 Woodland

ickett Wm, clk, b 128 Woodland

ckford Charles, attendant Insane Hospital, b same

erce (*see also Pcirce*)

erce Effie, domestic, b 335 Burlington av

erce Elizabeth, b 928 Broadway

erce Florence J, boarding 519 Fitch

erce James [Emma], condr Panhandle, h 1622 Toledo

erce James S [Amanda], mason, h 335 Burlington av

erce John C [Josephine], cook Baker's European Hotel, h 700 e
Wabash av

erce John H [Sarah M], drayman, h 1241 Toledo

erce Mary J, b 928 Broadway

erce Michael [Mary A], lab, h 523 North

erce Minnie, b 335 Burlington av

erce Nina, b 335 Burlington av

erce Patrick, b 416½ Market

erce Patrick J, merchant tailor 318 Broadway, b 928 Broadway
(See adv left top lines)

erce Peter M, tel opr Panhandle, b 928 Broadway

erce Thomas [Mary A], h 928 Broadway

erce Thomas E, b 928 Broadway

erce Wm H, lab, b 122 Pratt

erce Wm W, clk P J Pierce, b 928 Broadway

erson Lucinda J, propr Logan House 316 6th, h same

lcher George M, mason, b 200 Canal

lling Lincoln [Albertha], h 1101 High

tman Benjamin V [Hattie C], engr Panhandle, h 1322 High

иаи Edward E [Nina L] (Hillock & Pitman), h 1104 Broadway

иаи Mabel, b 2305 High

иаи Mildred A, student, b 1322 High

иаи Webster C [Lusetta V], engr, h 2305 High

man Alice L, b 231 w Market

man Bessie M, b 231 w Market

man George C, carp Hanbandle, h 231 w Market

sburg, Cincinnati, Chicago and St Louis Ry Co, division offices and passenger station cor 4th and Canal, freight depot s s Duret, bet Scott and Taylor

er Joseph D [Margaret], brick paver, h 429 3d

er Margaret, boarding 429 3d

ler Frank J [Anna V], cigar mnfr also billiard and pool room 302 Market, h 921 Spear

ce Will B [Dora E], genl agt Lambert Gas and Gasoline Engine Co, n e cor 5th and North, h 900 Broadway (See adv p 8)

ce Willard [Eliza J], agr implements, cor 5 and North, h 1200 High

ick Sarah J [wid Wm H], h 1725 North

ick Walter W, finisher George Harrison, b 1725 North

ik A Chalmer [Ella M], del clk Standard Oil Co, h 1426 North

ik David C [Matilda], gardener, h n s Bates, 10 w Vandalia R R (Dunkirk)

ik Emma A, dressmkr, b n s Bates, 10 w Vandalia R R (Dunkirk)

ik Henry O, gardener, b n s Bates, 10 w Vandalia R R (Dunkirk)

ik Howard D [Lydia], h 500 w Broadway

ik Minnie, b 500 w Broadway

singer George [Ada], tmstr, h 2101 Usher

ner Charles A, b 4 Biddle av

ner Daniel M, brakeman Panhandle, b 4 Biddle av

ner George W, lab, b 4 Biddle av

ner James [Ann M], h 4 Biddle av

ner James F, clk, b 4 Biddle av

ner John D [Louise], lab, h 1528 George

ler Charles, student, b 308 Linden av

ler Frederick [Mary], packer, h 308 Linden av

ler Sophia, b 308 Linden av

ter Harvey [Barbara A], lab, h n s Bates, 2 w Vandalia R R (Dunkirk)

Henry, cemetery sexton, h n w cor Broadway and Front

Henry, jr, clk W H Porter, b n w cor Broadway and Front

Louise, b n w cor Broadway and Front

iseck August II [Mary], wks Jas O'Donnell, h 129 Woodland

iseck, Michael [Augusta], lab, h 226 Washington

iseck Paul, lab, b 226 Washington

Anna [wid Henry H], h 90 Bates

Caleb C, piano tuner J C Bridge, h 714 Spencer

Frank M [Edith], ship clk Kreis Bros Mfg Co, h 818 Race

We Don't Carry Anything but Reliable Goods and Latest Novelties. | HERZ, The Tailor
409 MARKET STREET.

POL 209 POT

Polk Joseph, lab, h 5½ Sycamore
Polk Lottie F, clk A R Frazee, b 732 Linden av
Polk Minnie, b 90 Bates
Polk Thomas, student, b 714 Spencer
Polk Wm F [Augusta], lab, h 732 Linden av
Pollock George N [Henrietta], lab, h 1616 Toledo
Pomeroy (see also *Pumroy*)
Pomeroy Catharine [wid Frank], h 54 Johnson
Pomeroy Edward L [Mary E] (Pomeroy & McGaughey], h 110 Sycamore
Pomeroy Frank F, lather, b 54 Johnson
Pomeroy George W, lather, b 54 Johnson
Pomeroy & McGaughey (Edward L Pomeroy and James McGaughey), saloon 319 Sycamore
Pontius Adelia [wid ———], h 1826 Broadway
Pontius Belle, clk, b 1826 Broadway
Popowski Frederick H G [Albertine], kettleman Columbia Brew Co, h 331 Ottawa
Porter Acie, drayman Bridge City Candy Co, b 217 College
Porter Albert, lab, b s s Wash tp rd 2 w Burlington rd
Porter Daniel [Bertha], condr Panhandle, h 531 12th
Porter Eleanor M, tailor, b 1523 High
Porter Frank R [Emma E], poultry 431 Sycamore, h 437 Sycamore
Porter Harry, painter, b 204 Ottawa
Porter Homer, b 217 College
Porter James D, clk G W Seybold & Bros, b 104 Osage
Porter Justus [Emeline], lab, h s s Wash tp rd 2 w Burlington rd
Porter Lewis E [Orie E], car rep Panhandle, h 66 Bates
Porter Margaret B, h 1523 High
Porter Martha J [wid Wm A], b 1125 Erie av
Porter Martin I, engr Panhandle, b 1523 High
Porter Oliver [Emma] drayman, h 217 College
Porter Thomas G, carp, r 412½ Market
Porter Wm H, drugs, paints, oils and varnishes n w cor 4th and Market, r 96 Eel River av
Posey Stephen S [Mary], lab, h 386 Clifton av
Post Office, Valentine C Hanawalt postmaster, 216 Market
Potter Frank L [Edith L], painter, h 517 Broadway
Potter Frank W [Nina], painter 1318 Spear, h same
Potter Sarah, milliner 517 Broadway, h same
Potthoff Amelia, b 1445 Ohio
Potthoff Casper H [Margaret], lab, h 1445 Ohio
Potthoff Charles W, book binder, b 1445 Ohio
Potthoff George A, engr Parker & Johnson, b 1445 Ohio
Potthoff John H [Frederica], h 1403 Wright
Potthoff Catharine L, clk, b 1403 Wright
Potthoff Minnie, b 1403 Wright

Pottmyer Edward, tmstr, b 1600 High
Pottmyer Frank W, saloon 119 Front, h 419 Front
Pottmyer John F [Anna], bench hd J W Henderson & Sons, h 522 Pratt
Pottmyer Lucy, b 419 Front
Pottmyer Mary, h 712 11th
Pottmyer Theresa [wid Edward], h 228 w Market
Pottmyer Wm, lab, b 228 w Market
Pottowattomie Club, John C Nelson pres, Zachary Taylor vice-pres, John F Brookmeyer, treas, Charles B Stevenson secy, s w cor Broadway and Pearl
Potts Harry [Nannie], carp, h 714 11th
Potts John O [Kate E], storekeeper Panhandle, h 710 North
Potts Peter H [Prudence J] tmstr, h 406 Clifton av
Potts Wm E, lab, b 406 Clifton av
Powell Anna, student, b Noble tp line rd, 1 w Clifton av
Powell Anna L, photo printer A N Donaldson, b 530 Linden av
Powell Dwight C, student, b 220 6th
Powell Edgar E [Hattie E], music and musical mdse, also mgr Elite Mandolin Orchestra 505 Broadway, h 612 e Wabash av (See adv class Bands, etc)
Powell Elizabeth F [wid Joseph C], h 530 Linden av
Powell Frederick, brakeman, b 717 High
Powell James [Anna], lab, h 1723 Knowlton
Powell R Jay [Mary F], clk E E Powell, h 612 e Wabash av
Powell Jehu Z [Louise F], physician and surgeon 220 6th, h same
Powell John A [Frances E], carp, h 518 Clifton av
Powell John A [Kate], lab, h rear 1434 Ohio
Powell John W, granite cutter Schuyler Powell, b 1829 North
Powell Jonah, lab, b 1723 Knowlton
Powell Josiah G [Ada C], county auditor, h 1729 North
Powell Levi E [Jennie], mach hd Panhandle, h 802 17th
Powell Mabel, stenogr Schuyler Powell, b 1034 Toledo
Powell Maude, boarding 500 Canal
Powell Roger G, student, b 1729 North
Powell Sarah A [wid John T], b 1416 Broadway
Powell Schuyler [Viola E], propr Logansport Steam Granite Works 1031-1035 Toledo, h 1034 Toledo (See adv right top lines)
Powell Thomas, store porter Insane Hospital, b same
Powell Wm [Catharine], lawyer 220½ 4th, h 455 Michigan av
Powell Wm E [Emily M], supt gas works, h 614 Melbourne av
Powell Wm P, b n s Noble tp line rd, 1 w Clifton av
Powers Edward G [Mary E], h 121 Woodland
Powers Henry J, student, b 213 Eel River av
Powers James N, molder, b 206 Berkley
Powers John W [Nettie], well driller, h 3 Pratt
Powers John W [Hannah], lab, h 3 Pratt
Powers Mary, h 1423 Ohio

UP-TO-DATE IN DESIGNS OF MONUMENTS
We Operate the Only Steam Granite Works in the State.
SCHUYLER POWELL,   1031-1035 TOLEDO STREET.

POW   211   ·   PRO

Powers Matthew, lab, b 1423 Ohio
Powers Michael, lab, b 1423 Ohio
Powers Thomas [Anna], stone cutter, h 206 Berkley
Powers Wm G, b 121 Woodland
Powers Wm G, carp, b 1617 Smead
Powlen David W [Florence V], grocery and Meat Market 201-203
    Sycamore, h 518 Miami
Powlen George [Lizzie], clk McCaffrey Bros, h 701 Miami
Powlen James [Sarah], engr Panhandle, h 1824 George
Powlen Jesse [Augusta], watchman, h 213 Sycamore ·
Pownell Ambrose J [Belle], lab, h 1611 Market
Pownell Ella, domestic 206 n 6th
Pownell Mary, domestic 108 Hanna
Pranke Frederick H, clk J H Foley, b 516 e Wabash av
Pratt Dudley H, clk D E Pryor, b 113 11th
Pratt Fern A, student, b 1904 High
Pratt John R [Alice B C], propr Logansport Wall Paper Co 407
    Market, h 1904 High (See adv left top lines)
Pratt Myrtle C, student, b 1904 High
Prescott Andrew J [Elizabeth], foreman engs Pan, h 1617 Broadway
Prescott George H [Cornelia M], engr Vandalia, h 216 Bates
Prescott Grace, b 1617 Broadway
Price Anna, domestic 210 8th
Price Christopher, condr Vandalia, r 212 Sycamore
Price Eva B, student, b cor D and State
Price Francis M, mason, b cor D and State
Price Frank, condr Vandalia, b 321 Sycamore
Price Frank tmstr, b 1509 Erie av
Price George W, mason, b cor D and State
Price John H [Minnie], brakeman Panhandle, h 934 Erie av
Price Margaret, dressmkr 705 Miami, b same
Price Sadie A, student, b cor D and State
Price Scott E [Mary] contractor and builder of stone and brick
    masonry, also special agt Red Men's Insurance dept cor D and
    State, h same
Pricer Lewis C [Hattie M], trav agt, h 1826 Broadway
Pritchett Alonzo [Utica L], tmstr, h 1428 Water
Pritchett Willard P [Catharine L], tmstr, h 415 Pratt
Proal A B, treas Logansport & Wabash Valley Gas Co, h N Y City
Prophet Alvin [Mary], lab, h w s Washington 2 s Lincoln (S T)
Prophet Charles, lab, b w s Washington 2 s Lincoln (S T)
Prophet Wm, lab, b w s Washington 2 s Lincoln (S T)
Propst Anna, waiter Hotel Johnston, b s s Bartlett 2 w Anthony (ST)
Propst Augusta, domestic 206 Canal
Propst Christina, domestic, b s s Bartlett 2 w Anthony (S T)
Propst George [Bertha], lab, h s s Bartlett 2 w Anthony (S T)
Propst John, bartender, b s s Bartlett 2 w Anthony (S T)

Prosch Anna, student, b 332 Linden av
Prosch Anna, b 1917 Spear
Prosch August C [Minnie], shp clk The J T Elliott Co, h 319 Pratt
Prosch Clara, b 332 Linden av
Prosch Daniel [Mary], shoemkr 427 12th, h 1917 Spear
Prosch Henry [Sophia], pump rep Linton & Graf, h 332 Linden av
Prosch Otto, b 1917 Spear
Prosch Theodore G, clk Aaron Greensfelder, b 1917 Spear
Prudential Insurance Co, George L Hepner asst supt, 326½ Market
Pruitt Ota, lab, b 429 3d
Pryor Daniel E [Esther A], drugs, paints, oils and varnishes, also storage warehouse 516 Broadway, h 710 Broadway
Pryor Ethel F, b 710 Broadway
Pryor Lincoln, foreman, b 1524 Spear
Pryor L Mabelle, student, b 710 Broadway
Pryor Walter [Daisy], porter Adams Ex Co, h 303 Sycamore
Pumroy (*see also Pomeroy*)
Pumroy James V [Libby], condr Panhandle, h 22 Front
Puntency James N [Julia], lab, h e s McCarty 1 n Pleasant Hill
Purcell Charles B [Celestia], clk G W Seybold & Bros, h 330 Eel R av
Purcell Harry C, b 1506 Broadway
Purcell John H [E Ellen], lab, h 316½ Broadway
Purcell Josiah [Margaret], driver J F Grable, h 229 Osage
Purcell Lemuel S [Sarah S], claim agt Pan, h 1506 Broadway
Purcell Mary E [wid Hannibal], h 334 Eel River av
Purcell Michael J [Johanna], janitor Vandalia pass station, h 6 Columbia
Purcell Wm W [Nina R], baggageman Pan, h 300 w Broadway
Purdy Charles W [Cora], dr'vr Columbia Brew Co, h 314 Michigan av
Purkey Tillman W [Lila] (Wm Grace & Co), h 1436 High
Pursch Alfred [Ida], eng insp Panhandle, h 1326 Ohio
Puterbaugh Charles E [Emma J], stock dealer, h 709 North
Puterbaugh Gertrude E, dressmkr 413½ Broadway, h same
Puterbaugh Hannah I, h 413½ Broadway
Puterbaugh Harry B [Della], clk, h 200 w Market
Puterbaugh Jacob J, b 216 Brown
Putnam Rev Douglas P [Jeannie W], pastor First Presbyterian Church, h 913 Market
Putnam Edna E, student, b 913 Market
Putnam Jeannie D, student, b 913 Market
Putnam John W, del clk, b 913 Market
Putnam Lydia H, b 913 Market
Putnam Mary A, teacher, b 913 Market
Pyle Maud, usher Insane Hospital, b same

Q

Quade Anna, domestic 1112 Market
Quade Emma, domestic, 1209 Market
Quaintance Zoe, stenogr McConnell & McConnell, b 710 Race
Quealy J Albert [Catharine], h 2021 Broadway
Quealy Louise, student, b 2021 Broadway
Quigley Elizabeth, b 1728 Broadway
Quigley George, student, b 1728 Broadway
Quigley Thomas M [Margaret] (T M Quigley & Co), h 1728 Broadway
Quigley T M & Co (Thomas M and Wm F Quigley), mnfrs and
    wholesale confectioners 217–219 5th (See adv class Confectioners)
Quigley Wm, wks T M Quigley & Co, b 1728 Broadway
Quigley Wm F (T M Quigley & Co), h Indianapolis, Ind
Quillen Edward, student, b e s Park 2 n Wabash av
Quillen T Edward [Elizabeth], quarryman, h e s Park 2 n Wabash av
Quinlan John, tailor P J Pierce, r 314½ Market
Quinn Alice, student, b 625 Ottawa
Quinn Anastasia, seamstress, b 625 Ottawa
Quinn Bridget, h 412½ 3d
Quinn John A [Mary], tinner, h 625 Ottawa
Quinn John H [Emma], pianos 420 Broadway, h 717 Race
Quinn Joseph E, mach, b 625 Ottawa
Quinn Stella M, student, b 717 Race
Quirk Michael [Louise], bartender, h 19 Melbourne av
Quirk Wm W, bartender James Finn, b 1429 Wright

R

Rabung Jacob, granite cutter Schuyler Powell, b 1414 Smead
Rabung John, butcher, b 1414 Smead
Rabus Magdalen [wid Matthias], b 322 Linden av
Radcliff Wm R [Phoebe A], lab, h 604 w Market
Radebaugh Carrie W [wid Charles], stenogr, b 106 8th
Radebaugh Daniel [Mary M], agt, h 17 Plum
Radebaugh Ida M, teacher, b 17 Plum
Radebaugh Robert [Mollie], h 7 Biddle's Island
Rader James H [Sarah A], lab, h 1901 North
Radkey Andrew [Catharine], lab, h 825 21st
Radkey Anna [wid Lawrence], b 825 21st
Radkey Henry [Catharine], lab, h 825 21st
Radkey Henry [Mary], lab, h 1022 19th
Radkey John L, lab, b 1022 19th

PIERCE, The Tailor, CAN MAKE CLOTHES TO FIT YOU.
318 BROADWAY.

RAD   214   RAV

Radkey Lawrence B, tel opr, b 1022 19th
Radkey Lena, b 1022 19th
Radkey Robert R, lab, b 1022 19th
Rady Dennis, fireman Panhandle, r 1224 Wright
Rady Timothy, brakeman Panhandle, r 1224 Wright
Rages George W, porter H Closson & Co, r 506 Broadway
Raichel Philip [Emily], lab, h 1429 Ohio
Railsback John H [Catharine], condr Panhandle, h 2008 Broadway
Railsback Richard, brakeman Panhandle, r 421½ Market
Rambo Victor, b 415½ 3d
Ramer Catharine [wid Henry], h s w cor Day and Tipton
Ramer Louis [Minnie], meat market 800 15th, h 822 15th
Ramsey Charles A [Laura], driver J F Grable, h 716 e Wabash av
Ramsey George D [Florence] condr Panhandle, h 1229 Market
Randall Charles A draughtsman J H Rhodes, b 910 Race
Randall Daniel W [Gertrude], brakeman Panhandle, h 1244 Toledo
Randall Grant [Ella], brakeman Panhandle, h 1330 Smead
Randall India M, teacher free kindergarten, b 1107 North
Randall Samuel A, lab, r 1110 Spear
Randall Wm D [Matilda], painter 1107 North, h same
Randall Wm S [Belle A], gear mkr I N Cool, h 1328 Smead
Raney Martin [Mary J], lab, h rear 80 Washington
Rank Charles J [Lucy L], foreman, h 923 Race
Rankin Adam M [Lina A], clk Stevenson & Klinsick, h 1313 North
Rankin Lillie, b 1313 North
Rankin Robert F [Margaret], sign painter H Wiler & Co, h 520 13th
Rans Sadie, domestic 913 North
Rapsh Mary C [wid Edward], h 715 Bringhurst
Rasher Margaret, b 524 12th
Rasher Michael, baggageman Panhandle, h 524 12th
Rasher Wm J, clk Panhandle, b 524 12th
Rathfon Catharine [wid Joseph], h 922 Broadway
Rathfon Clara L, teacher, b 922 Broadway
Rau (see also Rauch and Rowe)
Rau Emma, b 1408 Spear
Rau John [Lena], mach Panhandle, h 1408 Spear
Rau Minnnie, dressmkr, b 1408 Spear
Rau Peter, fireman Panhandle, b 1408 Spear
Rauch (see also Rau and Rowe)
Rauch Charles F [Louise M] (Walker & Rauch), h 903 Market
Rauch Frederick B, student, b 903 Market
Rauch John D [Minnie M] civil engineer (J D Rauch & Co), 3 Pythian
    Castle, b 407 High
Rauch J D & Co (John D Rauch, Oliver J Stouffer), proprs the
    Stouffer Self Supporting Roof, 3 Pythian Castle
Raver Edward M [Agnes], motorman, h 1816 George
Raver Wm, motorman, b 1829 North

H. J. CRISMOND, 312 Market Street,
Gasoline Stoves, Screen Doors and Windows.

| RAY | 215 | REA |

Ray (*see also Rea and Wray*)
Ray Andrew [Isabelle], meat market 413 Market (Ray Bros), h 108 Front
Ray Bert A, clk, b 108 Front
Ray Bros (Lewis and Andrew), grocers 303 Market
Ray Charles H [Mary H], bartender, h 531 Ottawa
Ray Charles M, clk, b 905 Race
Ray Clare M, lineman, b 905 Race
Ray Frederick, wks Bridge City Construction Co, b 905 Race
Ray Gertrude E, b 108 Front
Ray Jane, b 2 Osage
Ray John F, b 905 Race
Ray John R [Catharine A], h 713 Chicago
Ray Lewis [Susan J] (Ray & Etnire) (Ray Bros), treas Logansport Creamery Co, h 2 Osage
Ray Marie I, student, b 108 Front
Ray Mary A, stripper John Mulcahy, b 520 Miami
Ray Maud, student, b 905 Race
Ray Menta, domestic 416 2d
Ray Metta P, student, b 2 Osage
Ray Minnie, domestic 616 Linden av
Ray Robert [Harriet], saloon 404 Market, h 520 Miami
Ray Walter C, clk, b 531 Ottawa
Ray Webb B, city engineer, h 905 Race
Ray Wm B, b 520 Miami
Ray Wm D, bartender, b 520 Miami
Ray & Etnire (Lewis Ray, Charles E Etnire), staple and fancy grocers 412 3d
Rea (*see also Ray and Wray*)
Rea Edwin F, eng insp Panhandle, b 705 Race
Rea Frank [Elizabeth N], car rep Panhandle, h 904 20th
Rea John C [Anna F], tmstr, h 316 15th
Rea John C [Mary H], engr, h 705 Race
Rea Lulu M, dressmkr, b 705 Race
Rea Terrence [Etta] (Bundy & Rea), h 222 Michigan av
Rea Wm G [Lorraine] (Parker & Rea), h 705 Race
Read (*see also Reed and Reid*)
Read Burleigh C D [Ida], ins agt, h 1617 High
Read Clara I, mgr Ladies Exchange, b 1617 High
Read Lois, student, b 1617 High
Ream (*see also Reem and Rehm*)
Ream Anna, b 305 Sycamore
Ream Annie E [wid Littleton], restaurant 226 Market, h same
Ream Idona, waiter, b 226 Market
Reames Lena, domestic Insane Hospital
Reardon James J [Ella M], blksmth Panhandle, h 620 Sycamore
Reardon Mary A, b 128 Woodland

Rebhorn John, plumber Messinger & Son, b n s Shultz 2 e Frank (ST)

Recht Lena, domestic 427 10th

Record George W, lab, b 111 Melbourne av

Rector Robert [Rosette], lab, h 321 Bates

Redd Elizabeth [wid Daniel], h 614 North

Redd Ida, teacher, b 626 Linden av

Reder (*see also Reeder*)

Reder Bertha G, mach opr W D Craig, b 322 Cummings

Reder Claud C, clk Johnston & Lux, b 322 Cummings

Reder Emma [wid James N], h 322 Cummings

Reder Lucy, h 315½ 4th

Reder Orlando B, clk Island View Hotel, b 322 Cummings

Reder Samuel F [Mary], baggageman, h 206 n Pearl

Reder Truda E, mach opr W D Craig, b 322 Cummings

Redmond Harriet, b 912 North

Redmond John E [Ida] (Redmond & Gibson), h 912 North

Redmond Lawrence [Ellen], sexton St Vincent de Paul cemetery, h 415 Pleasant Hill

Redmond Patrick, clk McCaffrey Bros, b 415 Pleasant Hill

Redmond & Gibson (John E Redmond, J Edward Gibson), contrs 912 North

Redwood John I [Delia], mason, h 723 High

Redwood Mabel, student, b 723 High

Reed (*see also Read and Reid*)

Reed Andrew J, book agt, b 30 State

Reed Rev Alexander [Susanna], h 30 State

Reed Bertha F, teacher, b 202 w Broadway

Reed Blanche, b 924 Erie av

Reed Charles, r 511 Canal

Reed Clara M, h 316 w Market

Reed Della L, mach opr W D Craig, b 924 Erie av

Reed Elsie, student, b s w cor Burlington rd and Wash tp rd

Reed Frank H [Florence], condr Panhandle, 1510 Spear

Reed Harrison [M Catharine], flagman, h 924 Erie av

Reed Harry A [Anna M], comp, h 1515 High

Reed Harry G student Hall's Business College, b Burlington rd, 3 m s city

Reed Isaac R [Anna], tmstr, h 605 Chicago

Reed Jacob [Ida], barber 110 Burlington av, h 14 Main

Reed James H, carver J W Henderson & Son, b 317 Humphrey

Reed May, b s w cor Burlington rd, and Wash tp rd

Reed May, domestic 524½ Broadway

Reed Mary A [wid Benjamin], h 317 Humphrey

Reed Minnie M, dressmkr, b 317 Humphrey

Reed Nellie, mach opr W D Craig, b 317 Humphrey

Reed Robert R, h 817 North

Reed Sadie O B, laundress, h rear 4 Canal

HERZ, The Tailor

409 MARKET STREET.

Our Reputation for Good Work and Artistic Styles Is Well Established.

REE   217   REH

Reed Sarah [wid Michael], h 316 w Market
Reed Sylvester, marble wks s w cor Burlington rd and Wash tp rd, h
   same
Reed Thomas L, h 202 w Broadway
Reed Wm H (Grelle & Reed), h 317 Humphrey
Reed Wm T [Anna], clk G W Seybold & Bros, h 517 Wilkinson
Reeder (*see also Reder*)
Reeder Alonzo, clk, r 523½ Broadway
Reeder Clyde, coachman Insane Hospital, b same
Reeder Lillie D, domestic, b rear 164 Smith
Reeder Nancy C, h rear 164 Smith
Reeder Pearl, domestic, b rear 164 Smith
Reeder Thomas B [Minnie B] (Newer & Reeder), h 10 Cicott
Reeder Wm J [Sophia], brakeman, h 1722 Market
Reeder Wm W, lab, b rear 164 Smith
Reem (*see also Rehm and Ream*)
Reem Jacob, h 315½ Market
Rees Carl [Mary], trav agt R Kreuzberger, h 616 Linden av
Rees Sarah W [wid Maxwell], h 710 Linden av
Reeser Susan [wid David], b 419 13th
Reeves Edith, student, b 311 3d
Reeves Jeannett, student, b 1628 George
Reeves Jennie, domestic 422 North
Reeves John [Mary L], engr Panhandle, h 1628 George
Reeves John B [Anna], student Hall's Business College, h 1612
   Broadway
Regan John E [Johanna T], horseshoer 205 6th, h 709 Miami
Regan John J, horseshoer, b 709 Miami
Regan Julia T, student, b 709 Miami
Regan Nellie A, b 709 Miami
Regan Thomas E, del clk Marshall's Steam Laundry, b 709 Miami
Rehm (*see also Reem and Ream*)
Rehm Amelia, domestic Insane Hospital
Rehm Frederick [Gertrude], trimmer I N Cool, h 1301 Toledo
Rehm John, porter Charles Smith, b 418½ 3d
Rehm John L [Rose], painter 308 W Market, h same
Rehm Mary, b 414 Day
Rehm Matthilda, h 308 w Market
Rehm Philip [Mary], mach Panhandle, h 414 Day
Rehwald Adam, b 24 Bates
Rehwald Bros (Wm and John C),, meats 105 Sycamore
Rehwald Elizabeth M, b 24 Bates
Rehwald Frederick W (Rehwald & Schrimp), b 24 Bates
Rehwald John C (Rehwald Bros), b 24 Bates
Rehwald Sophia A, student, b 24 Bates
Rehwald Wm [Elizabeth C] (Rehwald Bros), h 29 Washington
Rehwald & **Schrimp** (Frederick W Rehwald, Henry Schrimp), meat
   market 71 Bates

All Kinds of Life Insurance from $6.00 to $50,000 Written
———BY THE———
Metropolitan Life Insurance Co., of New York.
W. O. WASHBURN. SUPT. LOGANSPORT DISTRICT Office rooms 1, 2 and 3 Crawford Block

REI   218   REY

Reichardt (*see also Richhart*)
Reichardt Frank J [Ida], tailor Jacob Herz, h 154 Park av
Reid (*see also Read and Reed*)
Reid Charles R, student, b 413 Wilkinson
Reid Elliott S [Anna], painter Parker & Johnston, h 106 19th
Reid James [Sarah J], gardener, h s s Stoney Pike 1 e Hamilton
Reid John H [Emma F], butcher, h 413 Wilkinson
Reid Loretta F [wid Henry C], h 632 Sycamore
Reid May, tailor, h 632 Sycamore
Reid Ralph, carp, b 632 Sycamore
Reigle Lena, domestic 220 6th
Reimbolt Adam [Sophronia], engr Panhandle, h 2019 Broadway
Reinhart (*see also Rhinehart and Rinehart*)
Reinhart Wm [Minnie], agt, h 409 Wilkinson
Reinhart Stella, student, r 112 Market
Reinheimer Adam, painter, b 931 19th
Reinheimer Albert, carp, h 611 12th
Reinheimer, Christina [wid Jacob], h 1121 Market
Reinheimer Edward [Myrtle], carp, b 611 12th
Reinheimer Emma, b 611 12th
Reinheimer, John, b 1121 Market
Reiser Louis, baker, b 1307 Market
Reist (*see also Reitz and Ries*)
Reist Cyrus P. [Mary E], blksmth, h s s Shultz, 2 w Anthony (S T)
Reist Florence M, b s s Shultz, 2 w Anthony (S T)
Reist Glenn A, adv mgr Hall's Business College, b s s Shultz, 2 w Anthony (S T)
Reist Kirby S, comp The Reporter, b s s Shultz, 2 w Anthony (S T)
Reist Sadie O, student, b s s Shultz, 2 w Anthony (S T)
Reitemeier Joseph H [Mary B], pres Bridge City Candy Co, h 316 North
Reitz (*see also Refst and Ries*)
Reitz Andrew, brakeman Panhandle, r 111 4th
Reitz Carrie L. domestic 800 North
Reitz Eugene, lab, b 214 Berkley
Reitz Godfrey [Frederica], lab, h 1427 Ohio
Reneau Charles [Anna], mach hd Panhandle, h 2019 Broadway
Renn Carl, b 318 Barron
Renn Cora B, b s s Shultz, 4 e Standley (S T)
Renn Ernest L, clk S W Ullery & Co, b 318 Barron
Renn Henry [Catharine], shoemkr 17 6th, h 318 Barron
Renn J Henry [Mary] tailor C W Keller, h s s Wab River rd, 4 e Coles
Renn Mary, b 318 Barron
Rephorn Dora [wid Joseph], b 1302 Spear
Revington Florence, h 513 North
Reynolds Bertha, domestic St Joseph Hospital
Reynolds Charles J [Eva P], secy and treas Bridge City Construction Co, h 215 3d

Reynolds David A [Della M], fireman Vandalia, h 612 Miami
Reynolds Wm W [Ellen L], h 424 10th
Rhinehart (see also Reinhart and Rinehart)
Rhinehart Wesley A [Sarah], barber, h s s Shultz, 3 w Anthony (S T)
Rhoads Daniel W [Laura], hostler, h 415 Ottawa
Rhodes Frank [Neda V], cigarmkr, h 624 Chicago
Rhodes James H [Mattie], architect and superintendent 427½ Broadway, h 910 Race
Rhodes John E, student Hall's Business College, b 407 High
Rhorer Claude, brakeman, b 804 Sycamore
Rhorer Frederick, mess W U Tel Co, b 804 Sycamore
Rhorer Garrett J [Ida], agent, h 804 Sycamore
Rice Christian, b 1226 Toledo
Rice Elihu S (E S Rice & Son), pres King Drill Co, h 729 Market
Rice E S & Son (Elihu S and Frank M) hardware 415 Market
Rice Frank M [Lottie F] (E S Rice & Son), h 615 Market
Rice John, tmstr, b 1226 Toledo
Rich Frank [Julia], quarryman, h w s Lockwood, 1 n Wab av
Richards Robert, newsboy, b 317 19th
Richards Samuel [Louise], lab, h 317 19th
Richards Zula, milliner, b 317 19th
Richardson (see also Richason and Richeson)
Richardson Allen [Sarah A], real est 315 5th, h 431½ Broadway
Richardson Frank [Sarah], carp, b 216 11th
Richardson George L [Emma S], clk, h 1509 Broadway
Richardson John [May], barber, h 227 Barron
Richardson John B [Matilda], lab, h e s 18th 2 s Usher
Richardson Lavinia E [wid Thomas], h 1101 North
Richardson Mary A [wid Wm], b s w cor Standley & Wash tp rd
Richardson Oliver P, brakeman, b 306 Sycamore
Richardson Richard, b 511 Canal
Richardson Samuel B [Rebecca S], h 207 7th
Richardson Wm S [Susan F], carp 1010 North, h same
Richason (see also Richardson and Richeson)
Richason Floyd [Josephine], engr Panhandle, h 1916 Market
Richason Frank M [Elizabeth], engr Panhandle, h 1809 Broadway
Richason F Pierce [Jennie], engr Panhandle, h 1913 Market
Richeson (see also Richardson and Richason)
Richeson Wm H [Jennie] (Richeson & Stough), h 1425 Broadway
Richeson & Stough [Wm H Richeson, D Alfred Stough), barbers 1224 Broadway
Richey Myrtle I, student, b 100 Bates
Richey Walter F, student, b 100 Bates
Richey Wm E [Annetta M], mnfr ice cream 100 Bates, h same
Richhart (see also Reichardt)
Richhart Alfred [Margaret], bartender, h 401 w Broadway
Richhart Alfred jr, lab, b 401 w Broadway

Established 1867.   Still in the Lead.

DRY GOODS, CLOAKS, FURS,
409-411 Broadway.   WILER & WISE.   306 Fourth Street.

RIC   220   ROB

Richhart Mary, student, b 401 w Broadway
Riddell B Earle, yd clk Panhandle, b 403 High
Riddell George J, b 403 High
Riddell Mary C [wid Benjamin], h 403 High
Riddle John E [Mattie], switchman Panhandle, h 2025 Broadway
Ridenour Charles N [Dora B], barber, h 609 Ottawa
Ridenour James [Mary], wks Hillock & Pitman, 1510 Toledo
Ridinger Effie, clks G W Seybold & Bros, b 1117 George
Ridinger Nathan [Lavina J], h 1117 George
Riebling Herman, porter Insane Hospital, b same
Riegel David H [Olive], lab, h n s Maple 3 e Michigan av
Riemenschneider George, lab, b 215 Market
Riepsen Andrew [Elizabeth], porter, h 226 Montgomery
Ries (*see also Reist and Reitz*)
Ries Frederick, clk, b 122 Melbourne av
Ries George E, b 122 Melbourne av
Ries Louise [wid J Thomas], h 122 Melbourne av
Ries Wesley F, b 122 Melbourne av
Rife Ida, b 1127 North
Riggle Araminta, seamstress Insane Hospital, b same
Riggle M Elizabeth [wid Ebenezer], h rear 312 Eel River av
Riley Bernard, brakeman, b 512 e Wabash av
Riley James [Mary], lab, h 601 w Broadway
Riley Theresa, student, b e s 18th 1 s Usher
Riley Thomas [Mary], h 4 Taylor
Riley Wm, plasterer, b 500 Canal
Riley Wm A [Augusta], comp, h 218 13th
Rinehart (*see also Reinhart and Rhinehart*)
Rinehart John, drayman The J T Elliott Co, b 521 High
Rinehart Ella, h 108 n 6th
Ringleben Charles [Kate], h 106 Wheatland
Ringleben Dudley D, clk Twells & Behmer, b 106 Wheatland
Ringleben Frank L, b 106 Wheatland
Risberger Walburga [wid Jacob], b 819 Broadway
Riser Lillie, waiter, r 5 State Natl Bank Bldg
Ritter Gertrude, student, b 813 Linden av
Ritter Irvin [Anna], h 621 College
Ritter Louis H [Catharine] (Gross & Ritter), h 813 Linden av
Ritter Wm [Jennie], h 621 Chicago
Rizor Lillie, waiter The Barnett, b same
Roach Andrew J [Mary E] sawyer, h 1417 Erie av
Roach Henry [Dollie], plumber A W Stevens, h 826 12th
Roach Henry J [Martha A], drayman, h 1614 North
Roach May, student Hall's Business College, b 1417 Erie av
Roach Richard, drayman, b 1614 North
Robb George [Jane], stone mason, h 613 Ottawa
Robb Nellie M, trimmer I N Cool, b 1614 Spear

Robbins Charles D, b Tucker House
Robbins Sidney, r 216½ Market
Roberts Alva S [Cora M], editor The Journal, h 128 Osage
Roberts Edward, baggage master Pan, r 1 State Natl Bank Bldg
Roberts Lydia [wid John], h 313 Miami
Robinson Aaron F [Hattie], trav agt, h 506 Helm
Robinson Andrew J [Rachael J], real est, h 1100 North
Robinson Anna, b 1100 North
Robinson Charles, barber, b 1521 George
Robinson Eleanore, student, b 1100 North
Robinson Henrietta A (Robinson & McConaha), h 433 Sycamore
Robinson James, brakeman, b 321 Sycamore
Robinson Lawrence A, photo retoucher, b 1521 George
Robinson Louise, b 1100 North
Robinson Marie, milliner, b 1100 North
Robinson Nellie, b 1000 Erie av
Robinson Riley W [Henrietta A], grocer 433 Sycamore, h same
Robinson Robert [Ellen], lab, h 1521 George
Robinson Susan, b 1100 North
Robinson Wm [Catharine], fireman Panhandle, h 1228 Wright
Robinson & McConaha (Henrietta A Robinson, Ena McConaha),
    milliners 433 Sycamore
Robison Margaret, wks Marshall's Steam Laundry, b 409½ Market
Rock Gustav [Lena], meat mrkt 102 Burlington av, h 214 Tanguy
Rodefer Blanche, milliner, b 31 Eel River av
Rodefer Eusebia [wid James], h 831 High
Rodefer George W [Marie], real estate and loans 410½ Broadway, h
    31 Eel River av
Rodefer James K, brick mason, b 831 High
Rodefer Lillie, student, b 31 Eel River av
Rodgers (*see also Rogers*)
Rodgers John C [Janet], carp Thompson Lumber Co, h 4 Maple
Rodgers Martin, porter The Barnett, r 123 Cicott
Rodius Mame C, domestic 320 Broadway
Rodrick John [Alice], hostler, h 218 13th
Rodrick Hulda, student, b 218 13th
Roe Lillian, dressmkr, b 719 Bringhurst
Rogan Anthony, lab, b 1408 Smead
Rogan Charles J, lab, b 1408 Smead
Rogan Michael, lab, b 1408 Smead
Rogers (*see also Rodgers*)
Rogers Clark, student, b Long Cliff
Rogers Edwin C [Jennie M], carp, h 1501 Douglass
Rogers Frank P [Nettie A], clk city electric light, h 104 15th
Rogers Harry A, clk county auditor, b 1805 High
Rogers Hester A [wid Joseph P], h 1805 High
Rogers Dr Joseph G [Margaret], medical supt Northern Indiana
    Hospital for Insane, h same

Rogers Lynn, student, b Long Cliff
Rogers Margaret, student, b Long Cliff
Rogers Marie, student, b Long Cliff
Rogers Sadie J [wid Stephen], laundress, h 523½ Broadway
Rogers Thomas B, merchant policeman, r 430 North
Robe Mary, domestic 719 Market
Rohr Albert [Louise], lab, h 1622 Smead
Roles Josephine [wid Wm], h 12 Canal
Roles Matthew F, condr Panhandle, b 12 Canal
Roles Wm, brakeman Panhandle, b 12 Canal
Rollins Jonathan K [Mary E], h 327 Bates
Rollings Lee, student **Hall's Business College,** b 214 18th
Rollings Thomas [Louise], motorman, h 214 18th
Rollings Wm, lab, b 214 18th
Rolsten Fay E, clk, b 1124 Broadway
Rombold Edward, clk J L Leonard, b 106 Osage
Rombold John [Anna M], eng hostler Panhandle, h 106 Osage
Rombold W Joseph, student, b 106 Osage
Romich Clara [wid Oscar P J], h 212 Sycamore
Roodhouse James, baggageman Panhandle, r 6 Canal
Roop Alfred M, editor The Advance, r 213 7th
Roop Florence (Roop Sisters), h 719 Broadway
Roop Sisters (Susan and Florence), dressmkrs 719 Broadway
Roop Susan (Roop Sisters), b 719 Broadway
Root Frank D, fireman Panhandle, b Island View Hotel
Rose David W, attendant Insane Hospital, b same
Rose Elizabeth, milliner, b 1427 Wright
Rose Frank, b 1427 Wright
Rose John [Elizabeth], lab, h 523 Pratt
Rose John [Theresa], mach Panhandle, h 1427 Wright
Rose John jr, mach, b 1427 Wright
Rose Joseph, molder, b 706 Duret
Rose Joseph P, lab, b 1427 Wright
Rose Samuel A [Anna B], local agt Standard Oil Co, h 120 Canal
Rose Tillie [wid Wm], h 13 16th
Rosenthal Gertrude, stenogr, b 118 9th
Rosenthal Sarah E, h 118 9th
Rosier Loulena, student **Hall's Business College,** b 1825 North
Rosier Wm S [Lulu I], foreman The Times, h 1825 North
Roskuski Agnes, attendant Insane Hospital, b same
Roskuski Peter, attendant Insane Hospital, b same
Roskuski Peter [Emily], gardener, h n s Bates 7 w Van R R (Dunkirk)
Ross Alice M, clk H Wiler & Co, b 901 North
Ross August [Adelia], cornice mkr, h 415 Wilkinson
Ross David S, attendant Insane Hospital, b same
Ross Eliza [wid Hewitt], b 601 Chicago
Ross Emma, b 901 North

H. J. GRISMOND, 312 Market Street,
Hardware, Stoves and Tinware.

| ROS | 223 | ROU |

Ross Frederick, brakeman Vandalia, r 315 Sycamore
Ross George E [Isabelle] (N O & G E Ross), h 908 Market
Ross George E jr, student, b 908 Market
Ross Joseph, lab, b e s Dakota, 1 n Bates (Dunkirk)
Ross Nathan O, student, b 908 Market
Ross Nathan O [N O & G E Ross), r 216½ Market
Ross N O & G E (Nathan O and George E), lawyers 220½ 4th
Ross Philip E [Frances L], lab, h 1418 Water
Ross Wm E [May], sec hand, h 609 Helm
Ross Wm W [Elizabeth S], cashier First Natl Bank, h 901 North
Roth Thomas, del clk, r 508 Broadway
Rothermel Albert J, clk J J Rothermel, b 1414 Smead
Rothermel Charles E [ary], lab, h 129 Wilkinson
Rothermel Charles J, clk John Gray, b 1414 Smead
Rothermel Elizabeth, b 1414 Smead
Rothermel Emma, bkkpr J J Rothermel, b 1410 Smead
Rothermel Jacob J, grocer and meat market 520 Broadway, r 737
   Spencer
Rothermel John [Catharine], meat mkt 1226 Broadway, h 1414 Smead
Rothermel Joseph [Anna], mach Panhandle, h 1410 Smead
Rothermel Joseph C, clk G W Seybold & Bros, b 1410 Smead
Rothermel Joseph C [Augusta], carp, h 1612 Toledo
Rothermel Laura T, bindery girl, b 1410 Smead
Rothermel Mary, clk, b 1410 Smead
Rothermel Peter J [Emma], bench hd Parker & Johnston, h 416 Grove
Rothhaas James, baggageman Panhandle, r 6 Canal
Rothschild Bertha, b 1201 High
Rothschild Bros (Louis H and Julius), proprs The Globe Clothing
   House, clothiers, hatters and furnishers, n e cor 4th and Market
Rothschild Hattie, b 1201 High
Rothschild Isaac [Eva], h 1201 High
Rothschild Julius (Rothschild Bros), b 1201 High
Rothschild Louis H (Rothschild Bros), b 1201 High
Rothschild Louise J, b 1201 High
Rotroff David N, student, b 617 Melbourne av
Rotroff David P [Mary E], miller D & C H Uhl, h 617 Melbourne av
Rotroff Edith M, teacher, b 617 Melbourne av
Rotroff Mary A, student, b 617 Melbourne av
Roush Albert, agent, b 210½ 6th
Roushkoulp Emanuel [Catharine], lab, h 407 Melbourne av
Roushkoulp Henry E, sec hand, b 407 Melbourne av
Roushkoulp Wm J, del clk John Horstman, b 407 Melbourne av
Routh Anna, domestic 814 Broadway
Routh Etta, student, b 1218 Market
Routh Wallace, bkkpr, b 1218 Market
Routh Wm C [Sarah], meat market 512 Broadway and 503 12th, h
   1218 Market

ROW	224	RUS

Rowe (*see also Rau and Rauch*)
Rowe George W, clk Wm Rowe, b 1418 High
Rowe John [Helen M], engr Panhandle, h 1629 Broadway
Rowe John M, student, b 1418 High
Rowe Wm [Cora E], meat market 503 Broadway, also engr Panhandle, h 1418 High
Rubsam Andrew [Lizzie], wks R Kreuzberger, h 226 Montgomery
Ruch Anna, b s e cor Shultz and Frank (S T)
Ruch Julius [Louisa], lab, h 811 Ottawa
Ruch Theodore C [Mary A], engr Hotel Johnston, h s e cor Shultz and Frank [S T]
Rudolph Catharine, domestic 2026 Broadway
Rue Joseph, mach hd, b 204 6th
Rue Stanley, waiter C A Gipson, r 204 6th
Ruff Belle, asst housekpr The Barnett, b same
Ruff Christian F [Nancy], carp, h 117 Cicott
Ruff Christian F, jr [Daisy A], car insp Panhandle, h 28 Main
Ruff Daniel F [Minnie], clk, h 417 Barron
Ruff John P [Maude], car rep Panhandle, h 1323 George
Ruhl Charles A [June], saloon 414 3d, h 304 Wheatland
Ruhl Josephine, b 304 Wheatland
Rumble Frank W, turner Parker & Johnston, r 630 North
Rumell Charles N [Esther], engr Panhandle, h 1309 High
Rumell Ferry C, fireman Panhandle, b 1309 High
Rumell Harold J, wks Logansport Wall Paper Co, b 1309 High
Rumell Wiler A, clk, b 1309 High
Rumely M Co, John F Getty mgr, engines and threshers, 316 5th
Rupp Jacob, baker, b s e cor 6th and Ottawa
Rush Albert, b n e cor Canal and Oak
Rush Charles F, del clk McCaffrey Bros, r 117 5th
Rush Charles M, b e s Canty, 1 s Water
Rush David L [Myrtle V], comp the Reporter, b 931 19th
Rush Elizabeth [wid Jacob], b e s Canty, 1 s Water
Rush Frank, lab, h 229 George
Rush Frederick, engr, r 507 North
Rush George W [Sarah], motorman, h 1524½ Market
Rush Jacob L [Christina B], car rep, h 201 Washington
Rush John A [Emma J], lab, h e s Cantey, 1 s Water
Rush Mary E, student, b 201 Washington
Rush Willard [Anna], barber, h 2022 Spear
Rush & Evans (Willard Rush, Harvey Evans), barbers 113 6th
Russell Belle, dressmkr, b 120 Pratt
Russell Edward L [May], barber, h 120 Pratt
Russell Elvira, student, b w s Lobelia, 1 n Daisy
Russell Harrison W [Delilah], cook, h w s Lobelia, 1 n Daisy
Russell Ithamer, cook, b w s Lobelia, 1 n Daisy
Russell Jesse H, trav agt, b 218 Front

Russell John W, cook, b w s Lobelia, 1 n Daisy
Ryan Ann [wid Thomas], h 201 Montgomery
Ryan Ellen J, b 529 Fitch
Ryan Hannah, domestic 421 4th
Ryan John engr Vandalia, r 315 Sycamore
Ryan Martin, fireman Vandalia, b 324 Sycamore
Ryan Michael [Mary], h 529 Fitch
Ryan Michael D [Anna E], train desp Panhandle, h 213 w Market

S

Safford Charles P, clk Panhandle, b 828 Broadway
Safford Jennie P [wid James M], h 828 Broadway
St Bridget's Catholic Church Rev Bernard Krœger pastor, n e cor
    Wheatland and Wilkinson
St Clair Harry [Wilhelmina], engr Panhandle, h 415 18th
St Clair James, lab, b 20 Pleasant Grove
St Clair James B [Nellie], lab, h 54 Washington
St Clair Mattie M, b 54 Washington
St Clair Wilhelmina, Grand Secy G I A to the B of L E 415 18th, h
    same
St Jacob's Lutheran Church, Rev Martin Tiremenstein, pastor, n
    e cor 9th and Spear
St Joseph's Catholic Church, Rev Henry Kœhne rector, n w cor 2d
    and Market
St Joseph's Hospital, conducted b Sisters of St Francis, s s L & W
    rd, 1 e Anthony
St Luke's English Lutheran Church, Rev E B Shauer pastor, s w cor
    First and Market
St Vincent De Paul Catholic Church, Very Rev Matthew E Campion
    rector, s w Cor 9th and Spencer
St Vincent De Paul School (for boys), under auspices Sisters of the
    Holy Cross, s e cor 8th and Spear
Sala Margaret M [wid Wm G], h 1202 Market
Sala Ora, student, b 1202 Market
Sales Samuel [Charlotte A], carp 1414 George, h same
Salsbury Bridget, laundress, h 316 Eel River av
Salsbury Mary [wid Jay], h 409 Grove
Sample Ila H [Gertrude L], claim agt Panhandle, h 828 Broadway
Sample May, student, b 1502 Spear
Sample Theodore [Nellie], condr Panhandle, h 1502 Spear
Sample Tilden, caller Panhandle, b 1502 Spear
Samsel George W [Susan], carp Panhandle, h 701 Ottawa
Samsel James E [Louise], carriage trimmer, b 706 13th

$186,000,000 of Life Insurance
WAS WRITTEN BY THE
METROPOLITAN LIFE. of New York. In 1896

W. O. WASHBURN,
Superintendent
Logansport District,
Crawford Block.

SAM   226   SCH

Samsel Tilman [Nancy], carp Panhandle, h 706 13th
Sanderson Frank W [Emma], lab, h 1726 Market
Sanderson Harley, houseman, b 1726 Market
Sanderson John L, lineman Vandalia, b 321 Sycamore
Sands Edgar P [California], tel opr Vandalia, h 27 Ottawa
Sands Lizzie, domestic, 218 w Market
Sargent Oliver B, land agt Chicago P L Co, r 1928 North
Satterthwaite Benjamin C [Elizabeth], truckman Pan, h 408½ 3d
Sauer Charles [Dora A], tmstr Parker & Johnston, h n s Melbourne av 1 e Western av
Sauer Frederick [Laura M], quarryman, h w s Lockwood 2 n Wab av
Sauer Isaac [Mary], bartender M J Bligh, h 26 Front
Sauer John H [Sophia], h n w cor Main and Tanguy
Sauer Louis, lab D & C H Uhl, b 117 Osage
Sauer Theodore [Ada], bartender, h 5½ Sycamore
Saxon Birch [Florence M], condr Panhandle, h 1216 High
Saxon Leah A [wid Gillespie], b 1216 High
Saxon Mame, waiter The Barnett, b same
Scarff James C, cook Insane Hospital, b same
Schaefer (*see also Schafer, Schaffer, Shafer and Shaver*)
Schaefer Andrew [Anna M], car insp Panhandle, h 1207 Broadway
Schaefer Caroline, student, b 1207 Broadway
Schaefer Charles F, wks Marshall's Laundry, b n e cor n 6th and Henry
Schaefer Christian [Lena], h 1416 Wright
Schaefer Elizabeth, clk Wiler & Wise, b 1207 Broadway
Schaefer Emanuel F [Catharine E], bkkpr, h 720 High
Schaefer Frank [Gertrude], dairyman, h s s Columbia 1 e Sycamore
Schaefer George A, horseshoer 506 North, b 1207 Broadway
Schaefer George G, bkkpr Indianapolis Brewing Co, b n e cor n 6th and Henry
Schaefer Gertrude, b s s Columbia 1 e Sycamore
Schaefer Gottlieb [Frederika], h 14 Columbia
Schaefer Gottlieb A [Rachel N], agt Indianapolis Brewing Co 207 Cicott, h n e cor n 6th and Henry (See adv p 3)
Schaefer Henry, mess Adams Express Co, b 14 Columbia
Schaefer Henry, clk Wm Peters, b 1416 Wright
Schaefer John C, lab, b 1416 Wright
Schaefer Mary, student **Hall's Business College,** b s s Columbia 1 e Sycamore
Schaefer Walter O, student, b n e cor n 6th and Henry
Schaefer Wm L, lab, b 1416 Wright
Schafer (*see also Schaefer, Schaffer, Shafer, Shaffer and Shaver*)
Schafer Charles H [Cordelia], secy and treas Bridge City Candy Co, h 2028 Broadway
Schaffer Edward [Louise] (Schaffer & Gammill) h 601 Helm
Schaffer & Gammill (Edward Schaffer, Edward F Gammill), cigar mnfrs and wholesale and retail dealers in cigars, tobacco and smokers supplies·2 w Market (See adv class cigar mnfrs)

We use Steam—others work by hand. By doing so we can do you Better Work and Save you Money. TRY US. ♪ ♪ ♪ ♪

Schuyler Powell

1031-1035 Toledo St.

SCH   227   SCH

Scharff George P [Rebecca M], blksmth Holbruner & Uhl, h 430 North
Schaninger Leo, b 1403 George
Schauinger Margaret, student, b 1403 George
Schauinger Mary, student, b 1403 George
Schaninger Theresa [wid Leo], h 1403 George
Schaumloeffel Conrad, b 2008 Broadway
Schell Carl [Caroline], cellerman Columbia Brew Co, h 316 Linden av
Schell Charles F pkge boy Wiler & Wise, b 316 Linden av
Scherer Albert R [Lizzie F], tailor C W Keller, h 143 Park av
Scherer Charles [Ida], lab. h 1003 19th
Scheu John [Martha E] (Zimmerman & Scheu), h 631 Race
Scheu Katharine, domestic 411 Market
Scheu Mary A, housekpr 224 Eel River av
Scheumann (see also Shewmon)
Scheumann Etta, b 120 Helm
Scheumann Ferdinand [Mary], mach Panhandle, h 120 Helm
Scheumann Frederick H, clk J D Ferguson & Jenks, b 120 Helm
Scheumann Lulu D, clk G W Seybold & Bros, b 120 Helm
Scheumann Wm, mach, b 120 Helm
Schiele Charles, tailor Henry Weber, b 1420 Indiana
Schiele Christian [Margaret], lab, h 1420 Indiana
Schiele Frederick, lab, b 1420 Indiana
Schillinger Louise, domestic 320 Broadway
Schlademan Anna, b 104 6th
Schlademan August [Christina], h 104 6th
Schlademan Jessie, b 104 6th
Schlater Maria L, b 918 Broadway
Schleiger Charles E [Lucy A], locksmth 215 6th, h 619 Linden av
Schleiger Frank L, del clk Marshall's Laundry, b 621 Linden av
Schleiger Mary E [wid Louis], wks Campbell's Laundry, h 621 Linden av
Schloss Alfred F, student, b 125 w Broadway
Schloss Clement [Sophia], shoemkr 55 Front, h 125 w Broadway
Schlosser Catharine [wid George], h 1429 Usher
Schlosser Josephine, b 1429 Usher
Schludecker Louis C, tinner J T Flanegin, b 4 Sycamore
Schmaltz John, watchman Panhandle, b 514 12th
Schmerber Elizabeth, laundress, h 4 Humphrey
Schmerber Mary, laundress, b 4 Humphrey
Schmerber Wm, porter Hotel Johnston, b 4 Humphrey
Schmidt (see also Schmitt and Smith)
Schmidt Charles, lab, h e s Humphrey, 1 n Clay
Schmidt Frederica [wid Ferdinand], h 2204 Market
Schmidt Frederick, lab, b 15 Plum
Schmidt Frederick C, carp Insane Hospital, b same
Schmidt Sophia [wid John], laundress, h 120 n Pearl
Schmidt Wm [Ida], hostler, b 120 n Pearl

Schmitt (see also Schmidt and Smith)
Schmitt Eginhard [Susan C], mgr The Golden Rule, h 218 w Market
Schmitt Herman (Schmitt & Heinly), h Danville, Ill
Schmitt Lula, student, b 218 w Market
Schmitt Minnie, b 230 Washington
Schmitt & Heinly (Herman Schmitt, A W Heinly), proprs The Golden Rule 329–331 Market s w cor 4th
Schnabel Anna, chambermaid The Barnett, b same
Schnabel Mary A, domestic 306 North
Schneeberger Clara A, student **Hall's Business College**, b 228 Eel River av
Schneeberger Frederick W, student, b 228 Eel River av
Schneeberger Matthias [Mary], agt Columbia Brew Co, also livery stable n w cor 3d and Eel River av, h 228 Eel River av
Schneider (see also Snider and Snyder)
Schneider Agnes M, student, b 323 w Market
Schneider Catharine, b 110 Burlington av
Schneider Edward, bkkpr R Kreuzberger, b 110 Burlington av
Schneider Florence T, cashier The Wide Awake Grocery, b 323 w Market
Schneider George M [Catharine], saloon 817 15th, h 1314 Smead
Schneider John W [Carrie] (Busjahn & Schneider), h 925 Linden av
Schneider Joseph, clk Wiler & Wise, b 110 Burlington av
Schneider Joseph G [Lizzie], mach hd Panhandle, h 319 w Market
Schneider Peter [Maline], engr, h 323 w Market
Schneider Wm, musician, b n e cor Oak and Canal
Schnitz Anna, student, b 407 Burlington av
Schnitz Frances, domestic, b 407 Burlington av
Schnitz John V [Lena], lab, h 407 Burlington av
Schnitz Vincent [Mary], cooper, h 213 Osage
Schoenradt Adolph, bottler Columbia Brew Co, b 33 Bates
Schoenradt Anna, b 601 Wheatland
Schoenradt August L, lab, b 601 Wheatland
Schoenradt Charles [Hulda], kettleman Columbia Brew Co, h 33 Bates
Schoenradt John [Amelia], car rep Panhandle, h 601 Wheatland
Schockome Anthony [Mary], blksmth, h 6 Humphrey
School City of Logansport, James D McNitt pres, Jehu T Elliott treas, Quincy A Myers secy, 212 4th
Schork Andrew [Mary], lab 1118 Spear
Schork Andrew F, bkkpr Columbia Brew Co, b 1118 Spear
Schork Henry J, messenger Panhandle, b 1118 Spear
Schork Mary, b 1118 Spear
Schott Gottlieb [Christina], lab, h 2028 George
Schrader (see also Schroeder)
Schrader Fenie, b 305 w Broadway
Schrader Frank, del clk, b 305 w Broadway
Schrader John [Lottie] lab, h 328 Bates

chrader Louis C, cigar mkr Julius Wagner, b 8 Biddle Island
chrader Mary [wid Charles], h 8 Biddle Island
chrader Nellie, b 8 Biddle Island
chrader Peter J [Elizabeth], car rep Wabash, h 305 w Broadway
chrader Wm H, cigar mkr Julius Wagner, b 8 Biddle Island
chreyer (see also Schroyer)
chreyer Catharine [wid Josiah], h 599 Michigan av
chreyer Henry [Ella], carp, h e s Morgan 3 s Smith
chreyer Wm [Ella], patrolman, h 599 Michigan av
chrier (see also Schryer)
chrier Charles E [Alice], engr Vandalia, h 605 Linden av
chrier Willard B, mach, h 720 Spencer
chrimp Henry [Sarah] (Rehwald & Schrimp), h 211 Wilkinson
chrock Elmer E, fireman Panhandle, b 1807 Toledo
chrock George E, clk D M Watts, b 1807 Toledo
chrock Henry [Phoebe], carp, h 1807 Toledo
chrock John L [Alice], carp, h 1017 19th
chrock Wm H [Ida M], carp, h 17 Biddle av
chroeder (see also Schrader)
chroeder August [Louise], lab, h n s Bartlett 2 w Frank (S T)
chroeder Wm H, clk, b 308 Linden av
chryer (see also Schrier)
chryer Frank R [Isabel], eng insp Vandalia, h 517 Sycamore
chubach Charles [Edna], clk b 217 Heath
chubach Charles W, watchmkr J D Taylor, b 520 Canal
chubach Frank [Carrie], blksmth 51 Front, h 513 w Market
chubach George P, cigar mkr Julius Wagner, b 520 Canal
chubach Kate [wid George], saloon 520 Canal, h same
chuldecker Louis, tinner, b 4 Sycamore
chultz (see also Shultz)
chultz Hester [wid Frederick], h 1711 North
chultz Wm, engr Panhandle, b 1711 North
chutter Christian [Catharine], gardener Insane Hospital, h 211
    Humphrey
chutter Johanna, b 211 Humphrey
chutter Martha A, b 507 North
chuttrumpf Henry, student, b 15 Biddle av
chuttrumpf John [Christina], shoemkr 15 Biddle av, h same
chwantes Alta, b 1429 Indiana
chwartz Charles W [Margaret M], clk Panhandle, h 401 Wheatland
chwartz Frank [Emma], blksmth Panhandle, h 1504 Toledo
chwartzmann George, lab, b u s Shultz, 2 w Anthony (S T)
chwartzmann Lena, b n s Shultz, 2 w Anthony (S T)
chwartzmann Mary, b n s Shultz, 2 w Anthony, (S T)
chwartzmann Martin [Barbara], lab, h n s Shultz, 2 w Anthony
    (S T)
chweinzger Walter [Mary], cigar mkr, h s s Charles, 2 w Standley

Schweistall Anna, dressmkr 8 Uhl, h same
Schwerdman Conrad [Semme], h 607 Miami
Schwerdman Harry, clk J L Leonard, b 224 Osage
Schwerdman John H [Josephine V], clk McConnell & Jenkines, h 224 Osage
Schwerdman John R, student, b 224 Osage
Schwier Anna [wid Christian], h 203 Market
Schwier Henry, clk The Otto Shoe and Clothing Co, b 410 First
Schwier John, clk, b 410 First
Schwier Louise [wid Christian], h 410 First
Schwiering Ada, b 1314 Wright
Schwiering Caroline [wid Frederick], h 1916 Broadway
Schwiering Frederick W, driver James O'Donnell, b 1916 Broadway
Schwiering Henry [Della], brakeman Panhandle, h 116 Barron
Schwiering Wm [Elizabeth], engr Panhandle, h 1314 Wright
Scidmore Charles J, student Hall's Business College, b 1817 George
Scott Albert, coachman 813 North
Scott Andrew J [Minnie B], sawyer Hillock & Pitman, h 1824 Toledo
Scott Craig, carp, b 206 6th
Scott Edward, fireman Panhandle, b 1224 Wright
Scott Eleanor M [wid Daniel], b 200 Bates
Scott Elias W [Laura E], carp, h 726 Michigan av
Scott Gottlieb [Christina], lab, h 2021 George
Scott John R [Lydia], contractor 629 Chicago, h same
Scott Nancy E [wid Wm], dressmkr 2101 Market, b same
Scott Newton E, carp, b 730 Miami
Scott Richard R [Mattie A], watchman Panhandle, h 919 Race
Scott Samuel T, lab, b 726 Michigan av
Scott Sarah A [wid Isaiah], h 302 North
Scott Wm, fireman Panhandle, r 1224 Wright
Scott Wm A, truckman Panhandle, b 919 Race
Scott Wm H [Odessa], train desp Panhandle, h 1515 Broadway
Scribner Edwin S, clk Panhandle, b 1714 Spear
Scribner Lettie A [wid Charles H], h 1714 Spear
Scribner Walter S [Marie H], city electrician, h 700 Bringhurst
Seagraves Elizabeth [wid Milton B], laundress, h 11 Ottawa
Seagraves James B [Jennie E], carp, h e s Western av 1 n Wabash av
Searight Harry A [Disa G], railway mail clk, h 1101 Linden av
Sears Anna, domestic Logan House
Sears Elizabeth, b 825 Canal
Sears John, carp, b 321 Sycamore
Sears Martha E [wid Alfred N], h 825 Canal
Sebastian Jacob P [Della J], saloon 225 4th (D A Youngker & Co), h 326½ Broadway
Second Baptist Church, Rev Francis M Huckleberry pastor, n e cor 7th and Broadway
Sedam Marshel, student, b 1215 Market

Sedam Wm P [Martha A], del clk J D Ferguson & Jenks, h 1215 Market

See Charles F [N Viola], lab, h 727 Spencer

See D Frank [Lodoska], fireman Panhandle, h 1418 Toledo

See Wm B, clk, b 1233 Toledo

Seeger Nettie W, student Hall's Business College, b 1423 Market

Segner Mary L, b n s Bates 1 w Vandalia R R (Dunkirk)

Segner Rebecca [wid George], b n s Bates 1 w Van R R (Dunkirk)

Sehrt Henry [Mary G], foreman Bridge City Construction Co, h s s L & W rd 2 w Charles

Sehrt Wm, mach, b 521 High

Sein Margaret, domestic 817 Market

Seiter Katharine [wid Joseph], h 223½ 4th

Seiter Victor E, vice-pres The Logansport State Bank, b 223½ 4th

Selby Alonzo, lab, b 1211 Toledo

Selby David [Julia], lab, h 1211 Toledo

Selby Julia, boarding 1211 Toledo

Selby Margaret, b 1211 Toledo

Selby Susanna, b 1211 Toledo

Se Legue Charles W [Sarah L], watchmaker and engraver n e cor 4th and Broadway, h 201 n 6th   (See adv front cover)

Sell Flora [wid Benjamin], dressmkr 511 14th, h same

Sellers Andrew J [Wilda], condr Panhandle, h 510 Oak

Sellers Charles, comp, b 1631 George

Sellers Charles D, chief fire dept, headquarters 608 North, r same

Sellers Edward D (Helvie & Sellers), b 1631 George

Sellers Frank, b 1631 George

Sellers Harry I, b 1616 Market

Sellers Harvey, lab, b 1616 Market

Sellers Jacob [Frederica], h 1631 George

Sellers Joseph [Rebecca] (J & M Sellers), h 1514 Spear

Sellers Joseph H [Adah J], brakeman Panhandle, h 26 Melbourne av

Sellers J & M (Joseph and Morris), grocers 1201 Market

Sellers Lydia [wid Warren W], h 1616 Market

Sellers Mame B, bindery girl, b 1631 George

Sellers Morris [Cynthia] (J & M Sellers), h 1215 North

Sellers M Frank [Cora A], liv stable 217 12th, h 421 15th

Sellers Nettie, b 1514 Spear

Sellers Samuel H, lab, b 220 13th

Sellers Sarah J [wid Robert], h n s Monroe, 1 e Clifton av

Sellers Walter, hostler, b 1514 Spear

Semans Clara E, student, b 806 Broadway

Semans Rev Ephraim L [Amelia G], pastor Broadway M E church, h 806 Broadway

Semans Raymond L, student, b 806 Broadway

Sence Audie, student, b 606 w Broadway

Sence Frank [Caroline], lab, 606 w Broadway

Sence Lena, student, b 606 w Broadway

Settels Jennie, student **Hall's Business College,** b 29 Washington

Seventh Day Adventist Church, Rev Oren S Hadley pastor, 510 Sycamore

Seward Mark [Jane L], engr, h 501 Miami

Sewell Theodore R [Isabelle], clk Panhandle, h 214 8th

Seybold J Abner [Jennie S] (George W Seybold & Bros), h 220 w Market

Seybold George W [Alice R] (George W Seybold & Bros), also pres The Logansport State Bank, h 715 Market

Seybold George W & Bros (George W, J Abner and Oscar M), proprs Seybold's Trade Palace 319–321 Market

Seybold John G [Ursula], h w s Burlington rd, 3 w Wash tp rd

Seybold Nettie, student, b 1101 High

Seybold Oscar M [Mamie J] (George W Seybold & Bros), h 111 11th

Seybold Sylvester H [Nellie G], floor walker G W Seybold & Bros, h 300 Wheatland

Seybold Wm H [Anna], lab, h 124 Washington

Seybold's Trade Palace George W Seybold & Bros props, dry goods, carpets and queensware 319–321 Market

Shade Anna M [wid Nelson], h 1215 High

Shade Julia, b 1215 High

Shadock John [Catharine], lab, h 821 21st

Shafer (*see also Shaffer, Schafer, Schaffer, Schaefer and Shaver*)

Shafer Arthur E [Sarah E], fireman Panhandle, h 1702 George

Shafer Bertha, b 1127 Market

Shafer Clyde J, finisher I N Cool, b 1415 Smead

Shafer Edward [Adelaide], excavation contr 2211 High, h same

Shafer Erwin H [Blanche], brakeman Panhandle, h 1121 Market

Shafer James A [Mabel], brakeman Panhandle, h 117 Barron

Shafer Margaret, milliner, b 1127 Market

Shafer Nancy [wid Abram], h 1127 Market

Shaffer Andrew J [Martha J], carp 18 Claude, h same

Shaffer Oliver B, brakeman Panhandle, r 216½ Market

Shaffer Thomas [Lulu], clk, 1206 George

Shaffer Samuel H [Emma J], brakeman Panhandle, h 1825 George

Shaffer Willard, wks laundry, b 226 Market

Shaffrey Charles S, clk, b 416 10th

Shaffrey Clarence, student, b 416 10th

Shaffrey Cornelia, clk G W Seybold & Bros, b 416 10th

Shaffrey Thomas, student **Hall's Business College,** b 528 12th

Shaffrey Thomas S, mailing clk post office, b 1112 Spear

Shanahan Anna, b 102 Hanna

Shanahan Charles, tailor, b 102 Hanna

Shanahan Hugh, clk Wiler & Wise, b 102 Hanna

Shanahan John (Hanley & Shanahan), r 408½ Broadway

Shanahan May, clk Wiler & Wise, b 1521 Market

HERZ, The Tailor

409 MARKET STREET.

Our Motto:

FAIR TREATMENT
TO ALL.

SHA   233   SHE

Shanahan Thomas H [Josephine], carp Pan, h 1521 Market
Shanahan Wm [Mary], real est agt 408½ Broadway, h 102 Hanna
Shaner Rev E B, pastor St Luke's English Lutheran Church after
　　August 1st, h ——
Shank Phillip M [Lillie C], harness mkr Henry Tucker, h 1127 High
Shanks Ernest [Mary A], meat market 5 6th, h same
Shanks Lucinda, laundress Island View Hotel, h 11 Biddle av
Shanks Marvy [Lucinda], lab, h 11 Biddle av
Shanks Taylor B, brakeman, b 324 Sycamore
Shannon Ida, h 1305 e Wabash av
Sharp Ann Eliza [wid James S], b 531 w Broadway
Sharp Charles N [Geneva], lab, b 18 Pleasant Grove
Sharp Margaret A [wid David B], h 1504 High
Sharp Walter, lab, b 1504 High
Sharts Benjamin F, bkkpr The Logansport State Bank, r 401 Market
Sharts Wm A, student Hall's Business College, h Anoka, Ind
Shaver (see also Shafer, Shaffer, Schafer, Schaffer and Schaefer)
Shaver Albert, b 1926 Spear
Shaver George H [Addie], engr Panhandle, h 1706 North
Shaver Grace, b 1926 Spear
Shaver Harry, b 621 North
Shaver John B [Mary A], blksmith 12 6th, h 621 North
Shaver John B jr, plumber, b 621 North
Shaver Mamie, b 1706 North
Shaver Samuel W [Mary], engr Panhandle, h 1926 Spear
Shaver Wm [Bertha], plumber J J Hildebrandt, h 214 Berkley
Shaw George W [Emma I], watchman Insane Hospital, h 224 State
Shaw John L, lab, b 221 w Market
Shaw Opediah T [Laura L], harness mkr Kreis Bros Mnfg Co, h 300
　　Michigan av
Shearer James C, attendant Insane Hospital, b same
Shearer Wm I [Ida I], mnfr and wholesale dealer in ice cream s e
　　cor 13th and Erie av, h 1315 Market (See adv p 8)
Shecklin Otto, wagon mkr, b s e cor 15th and Erie av
Shedell Margaret L, b 625 w Market
Shedell Milton [Mary E], scroll sawyer Parker & Johnston, h 625 w
　　Market
Shedell Minnie G, student, b 625 w Market
Shedron Oliver P [Mary A], condr Vandalia, h 231 Pratt
Sheerin John J [Mary], foreman Panhandle, h 416 10th
Sheerin Margaret J, clk Logansport & W V Gas Co, b 416 10th
Sheerin Marie, student, b 416 10th
Sheerin Simon P [Mary A] (S P Sheerin & Co), h 1125 Market
Sheerin S P & Co (Simon P Sheerin), investment brokers 204 4th
Sheets Franklin A [Laura], tmstr, h 617 Chicago
Sheets Lewis [Roxanna], brick mason, h w s Royal Center pike 3 n
　　Pleasant Hill

Shelly Edward, painter, b 531 w Broadway

Shepard Mary L [wid Samuel], h 100 6th

Shephard Bruce E, stenogr Panhandle, b 413 Burlington av

Shephard Joseph H [Kay], baggageman Pan, h 413 Burlington av

Shephard Otis L [Rose M], switchtender Pan, h 429 Burlington av

Shepherd Anna L, teacher, b Biddle Island

Shepherd Caroline L [wid Benjamin F], h Biddle Island

Shepherd Frederick, painter Insane Hospital, b same

Sherrard Isaac [Anna], bridge carp Panhandle, h s w cor Shultz and Anthony (S T)

Shewmon (see also Scheumann)

Shewmon Jessie, clk, b 409 Melbourne av

Shewmon Joseph L, lab, b 409 Melbourne av

Shewmon Mary, dressmkr, b 409 Melbourne av

Shewmon Walter, painter, b 409 Melbourne av

Shewmon Wm R [Jennie], painter, h 409 Melbourne av

Shibley Charles A (McReynolds & Shibley), b 530½ Broadway

Shick Lester A [Lillie B], engr Panhandle, h 1715 Spear

Shideler Abraham [Elizabeth], pres county commissioners, also pres Logansport Creamery Co, h Clinton tp, 2½ mi w city

Shideler Alma, teacher, b 1426 North

Shideler Harry M, bkkpr, b 816 Broadway

Shideler Issac [Madeline], h 816 Broadway

Shideler Isaac N [Sarah E], lab, h 1510 Water

Shideler Mary [wid George], h 1426 North

Shideler Martha C, stenogr Kreis Bros Mfg Co, b 1426 North

Shideler Nora, teacher, b 1426 North

Shideler Wm D, dentist, bridge work a specialty 402½ Market, b 1426 North

Shields Franklin, lab, b 509 Clifton av

Shields Hattie, dressmkr 1407 North, h same

Shields Joshua P [Alice M], h 509 Clifton av

Shields Lilly, domestic, b 1407 North

Shields Mabel, domestic, b 1407 North

Shields Thomas [Hattie], tmstr, h 1407 North

Shields Wm T, fresh and smoked meats and fish 217 Plum, b s e cor Plum and Osage

Shilling Belle [wid Newton], h 721 Ottawa

Shilling Elmer E [Abbie E], ice cream mkr W I Shearer, h 730 Race

Shilling Orva A, student Hall's Business College, b 721 Ottawa

Shilling Samuel, porter, b 1236 Toledo

Shinn Margaret, dressmkr 327 4th, h same

Shinn Peter B [Emma], prin Southside school, h 209 7th

Shipley George W [Cecelia L], boarding 730 North

Shipley Thornberry, lab, h 7 Taylor

Shires Mary C, domestic, h 410 Railroad

Shirk David C, secy Logan Heading Co, h 100 Helm

Shirk Edward [Lida], cook, b 100 Helm
Shirrick Ralph, lab, b 628 Sycamore
Shively Jacob, engr Panhandle, r 529 Market
Shoemaker Daniel W, fireman Panhandle, h 1430 Spear
Shorb Clarence, b 208 Canal
Shorb Edward F, baggageman Wabash pass station, b 208 Canal
Shorb Lillie, b 208 Canal
Shorten John A [Mary], engr Panhandle, h 1923 North
Shortridge Altha, domestic, b 414 13th
Shortridge Sardinia [wid Thurston], h 414 13th
Shott Mary E, b 819 Canal
Shriver Frank M, carriage mkr, b 102 n 6th
Shriver George [Minnie], mach hd, h 102 n 6th
Shriver Henry N, mach hd, b 102 n 6th
Shroyer (*see also Schreyer*)
Shroyer Alexander R [Helen E], h 913 North
Shroyer & Uhl Co (Dennis Uhl pres, Wm C Uhl vice pres, Walter J
    secy and treas), wholesale notions 409-415 4th
Shuey Curtis G, fireman, r 213 State
Shuey Edward [Lena], lab, b e s Burlington rd, 7 s Wash tp rd
Shuey Willard H [Mattie M], bridge carp Pandandle, h 213 State
Shull Wm J [Lizzie], carp, h 215 5th
Shultz (*see also Schultz*)
Shultz Flora, teacher, b 617 Market
Shultz Harry M, student, b 617 Market
Shultz John B [Anna L], physician and surgeon 417 4th, h 919
    Broadway
Shultz John H [Clara P], physician and surgeon 412 4th, h 617
    Market
Shurte Hannah [wid Isaac], b 322 Eel River av
Shurte S Lewis, clk H J Crismond, b 1706 North
Sieber Carrie E, b Camp Chase, 1 n Davis bridge
Sieber Wm D [Elizabeth], dairy Camp Chase, 1 n Davis bridge, h same
Siegmund Charles [Melinda], foreman Panhandle, h 1410 High
Siegmund Charles, jr [Minnie], trav agt, h 405½ Broadway
Siegmund Edward [Henrietta], coppersmith Panhandle, h 708 12th
Siegmund Frederick K [Josephine], condr Panhandle, h 1122 Market
Siegmund Herman W [Amanda E], lab, h 126 n Pearl
Siegmund Wm B, b 1410 High
Sigerfoose Charles M [Martha M], barber, h 103 Osage
Silliman J Arthur, carriage trimmer George Harrison, b Logan House
Simms John, blksmith, b w s Kewanna rd, 1 n Pleasant Hill
Simms Wm, lab, b w s Kewanna, 1 n Pleasant Hill
Simms Wm A [Diana], h w s Kewanna rd, 1 n Pleasant Hill
Simon Calvin B [Adelia F], lab, h 9 Columbia
Simon Dessie A, mach opr W D Craig, b 9 Columbia
Simon Jane, domestic 1128 Broadway

Simon Matthew [Susan], lab, h 823 21st
Simon Michael [Jennie H], lab, h 901 19th
Simon Myrtle D, mach opr W D Craig, b 9 Columbia
Simonds Anna [wid Charles W], housekpr 700 High
Simons George [Isabelle], tmstr D & C H Uhl, h 50 Front
Simons Harley R, b 2 State
Simons James R [Nancy H], lab, h 2 State
Simons John [Erexie J], lab D & C H Uhl, h 14 State
Simons Mary [wid Benjamin], b 1200 Linden av
Simons Oatie, milliner, b 50 Front
Simpson Edward railway mail clk, b 416 2d
Simpson John H [Elizabeth], b 103 6th
Simpson Theodore H [Neenah], condr Pullman, h 916 Broadway
Sine Horace F, student **Hall's Business College,** b 1901 Toledo
Sine Wm J, b 1901 Toledo
Singer Harry E [Clara], h 112 Pratt
Singer Ida M, b 317 Eel River av
Singer Mfg Co, Joseph Howell mgr 231 3d
Singer Wm H [Ada], carp, h 215 Pratt
Sites Katharine H [wid John] h 400½ Broadway
Sitz Anna, b 334 Burlington av
Sitz August [Augusta], wagonmkr 518 North, h 334 Burlington av
Sitz Christina [wid Gottlieb], b 334 Burlington av
Sitz Emil, tmstr, b 224 Colfax
Sitz Henry, b 334 Burlington av
Sitz Julius [Augusta], flagman Panhandle, h 224 Colfax
Six Frederick G [Jessie M], circulator The Pharos, h e s Clifton av 1
    n Fulton
Six Mary, opr C U Tel Co, b e s Clifton av 1 n Fulton
Skeller John, stonemason, b 500 Canal
Skelly James [Alice], stone cutter, h 813 21st
Skelly Thomas, marble cutter, b 500 Canal
Skelton Charles, lab, b 121 7th
Skelton J Ross, carriage trimmer, b 709 Race
Skelton Vincent A, patrolman, h 709 Race
Skinner Blanche [wid Arthur T], h 705 High
Skinner Crete, student, b 2314 Broadway
Skinner Edith V, b 705 High
Skinner Edna B, b 705 High
Skinner Eva, student, b 2314 North
Skinner John B [Sarah L], mgr Central Union Telephone Co, h 2314
    Broadway
Skinner Leroy [Isabelle], plumber, b 609 w Broadway
Skinner Melinda F [wid John C], b 1516 High
Skinner Wm S [Tillie], motorman, h 2314 North
Skowronski Frank [Pauline], lab, h 218 Washington
Skyes Katharine, domestic 132 Eel River av

Skyes Margaret, domestic 1220 Market
Slaceman John [Ellen], painter 421 Grove, h same
Sligard John, fireman Panhandle, r 1224 Wright
Sloan Ella, b 1815 Broadway
Slaybaugh Bertha, student, b 1810 Market
Slaybaugh John P [Elizabeth], shoemkr 417 12th, h 1810 Market
Small Albert G [Olive M], h 220½ Market
Small Alexander [Catharine], farmer, h 219 Humphrey
Small Frank [Lettie], brakeman Panhandle, h 1307 Spear
Small John E [Susan E], baggagemaster Pan, h 109 Eel River av
Small Mable G, student, b 109 Eel River av
Small Lucinda [wid John P], h 217 Coles
Small Stella E, clk, b 219 Humphrey
Smart Louis E [Margaret E], stenogr Pan, h 310 Montgomery
Smith (see also *Schmidt and Schmitt*)
Smith Albert E, attendant Insane Hospital, b same
Smith Albert H [Jennie], switchman Vandalia, h 3 Columbia
Smith Albert L [Emma], lab, h 411 Linden av
Smith Amy L, student, b 103 6th
Smith Andrew J [L Belle], brakeman Panhandle, h 920 Erie av
Smith Anna, b 8 Illinois
Smith Anna, laundress, h 306 Sycamore
Smith Anna R [wid Willis H], h 1503 Broadway
Smith August [Mary], car rep Panhandle, h 1415 Indiana
Smith Augusta [wid George], laundress, h 108 4th
Smith Benjamin M [Elizabeth], lab, h e s Horney 3 n Franklin
Smith Brothers (Demarest and Stelloel), stationers 318½ 4th
Smith Carl [Hannah], mess Adams Ex Co, h 216 Brown
Smith Catharine [wid Leopold A], h 1220 Broadway
Smith Catharine A P [wid Nicholas], b 829 Spear
Smith Charles, b 15 6th
Smith Charles A [Minnie], dep county auditor, h 210 n Pearl
Smith Charles F, saloon 420 3d, b 521 Helm
Smith Curtis [Ida], h 218 n Pearl
Smith David, lab, b 411 Linden av
Smith David J, b 402 w Wabash av
Smith David V [Mary], switchman Vandalia, h s w cor Bartlett and
　　Kloenne (S T)
Smith Demarest (Smith Bros), b 1815 Broadway
Smith Dollie L, student **Hall's Business College,** b 313 Clifton av
Smith Dosi E, b 309 Melbourne av
Smith Edna, b 1113 George
Smith Edward A [Gertrude], warehouseman Standard Oil Co, h 1029
　　Toledo
Smith Edward L [Clara M], carp, h 157 Park av
Smith Emanuel [Elizabeth], h s w cor Shultz and Kloenne (S T)
Smith Emma E, b 108 4th

Smith Eva [wid James], h 1113 George
Smith Fannie [wid Anthony], h 1214 Spear
Smith Frank, foreman, r 224½ Market
Smith Frank A [Mary E], tinner, h 2123 High
Smith Frank M, caller Vandalia, b s w cor Shultz and Kloenne (S T)
Smith Frank M [Pearl], motorman, h 1911 North
Smith Frank W [Mary J], cooper, h 313 Clifton av
Smith Frederick [Mary], cabinet mkr 15 6th, h same
Smith George [Nancy J], lab, h n s Shultz 3 w Frank (S T)
Smith George L, lab, b s s L & W rd 2 w Anthony
Smith George R [Martha], mach Panhandle, h 608 14th
Smith George W [Catharine], cooper, h 130 Smith
Smith Grace A, b 1602 Douglass
Smith Grace L, domestic, b n s Bartlett 3 w Anthony (S T)
Smith Hal B, watchmkr J D Taylor, b 206 n 6th
Smith Hannah J, b 421 High
Smith Harry E, student, b e s Horney 3 n Franklin
Smith Henry, student, b 100 Ash
Smith Herbert [Bridget], switch tender, h 414 Linden av
Smith Hettie, b s s L & W rd 2 w Anthony
Smith Hugh [Laura], druggist 115 Sycamore, h 105 Bates
Smith H Leroy, clk D A Hauk, b 1113 George
Smith Irvin K [Viola M], lab, h 631 Ottawa
Smith Isabelle [wid George], b 517 Sycamore
Smith Israel S [Maria E], shoemkr 216 6th, h 206 n 6th
Smith James, lab, b 1328 Ohio
Smith James W [Margaret A], farmer, h 630 Race
Smith Jessie A, dressmkr n e cor Linden av and n 4th, h same
Smith John, h s s L & W rd 2 w Anthony
Smith John, cooper, b 130 Smith
Smith John, student, b 15 6th
Smith John, student Hall's Business College, b 1415 Indiana
Smith John A, cooper, b 128 Smith
Smith John B [Susan], lawyer 212½ 4th, h 514 e Wabash av
Smith John F [Icey], switchman Vandalia, h s s Shultz, 3 e Kloenne
    (S T)
Smith John H, dep sheriff, b 321 North
Smith Jordan R [Kate A], lab, h n s Fulton, 2 e Clifton av
Smith Joseph, tmstr, b w s Burlington rd, 7 s Wash tp rd
Smith Joseph A [Elizabeth], switchman Vandalia, h 100 Ash
Smith Joseph H, truckman Panhandle, b 1602 Douglass
Smith Josephine, b 209 Wheatland
Smith Lena, domestic 218 Canal
Smith Lincoln, lab, b s s L & W rd, 2 w Anthony
Smith Lizzie, b 108 4th
Smith Lydia, dressmkr 318½ Pearl, h same
Smith Lyman O [Jessie E], carp, h 402 w Wabash av

I. J. GRISMOND, 312 Market Street,
All Kinds of Metal Roofing.

nith Narania C [wid Edwin L], b 317½ 3d
nith Margaret A, matron Home for the Friendless, h same
nith Martha E, domestic 418 Helm
nith Martha J [wid David W], h S Illinois
nith Mary, domestic 525 Market
nith Mary A [wid Peter], h 105 w Broadway
nith Marvin [Anna], lab, h 1803 Toledo
nith Mattie, domestic 206 6th
nith Melvin C, lather, b 313 Clifton av
nith Morgan, lab, b s s L & W rd, 2 w Anthony
nith Nettie, domestic s s Stevens, 1 w 18th
nith Peter D, lawyer 222½ 4th, b 105 w Broadway
nith Philip [Jane], lab h 402 w Wabash av
nith Robert E, lather, b 313 Clifton av
nith Samuel E, musician, b 405 Miami
nith Sarah E, dressmkr 318½ 4th, h 1815 Broadway
nith Solomon [Mandilla J], h 405 Miami
nith Stelloel [Sarah E] (Smith Bros), h 1815 Broadway
nith Susan, b 1415 Indiana
nith Terrence P [Margaret], lab, h 1328 Ohio
nith Thomas [Anna], engr Panhandle, h 1429 Indiana
nith Thomas P, confectioner 323 Market, b 418½ 3d
nith Wm, lab, b 509 Canal
nith Wm B, student Hall's Business College, h Anoka, Ind
nith Wm B [Alice A], harness mkr 308 5th, h 1817 High
nith Wm D [Sarah W], h 106 n 6th
nith Wm H [Laura M], fireman Vandalia, h 403 Miami
nith Wm N [Margaret E], clk D W Powlen, h 103 Bates
nith Wm W [Sarah J], ins agt, h 1602 Douglass
nith Xen Z, student, b 1400 North
nyser Albert, engr Panhandle, r 1224 Wright
eberger Millard, student Hall's Business College, b 628 Bringhurst
ell Charles, clk, r 225 3d
ethen Ezekial, porter Insane Hospital, b same
ider (see also Snyder and Schneider)
ider Adam [Margaret V], engr Stevens Bros, h 10 Canal
ider Ida L, b 10 Canal
ider James, lineman Wabash, r 302 North
ider James E, foreman Campbell's Laundry, b 522½ Broadway
ider Matilda, domestic 2214 Broadway
ider Wm H [Mary J] (Snider & Alber), h 136 Eel River av
ider & Alber (Wm H Snider, John Alber), china, glass and queens-
    ware 414 Market
oke Cleopatra, domestic 514 Market
iffen Oliver, truckman Pan, b n s Norcross 1 w Horney
rder (see also Snider and Schneider)
rder Charles [Amanda], lab, h 1328 George

yder Charles A, clk, b 209 3d
yder Eldora [Ida] (Snyder & Stout), h 209 3d
yder Frances B [wid Andrew J], b 318 First
nder George E [Delia J], brakeman, h 514 16th
yder George J [Christina], mach Panhandle, h 1601 Spear
yder Harry R [Margaret], engr Panhandle, h 112 Canal
yder Joseph F [Jennie], lab, h 1414 Toledo
yder Laura, b 214 w Market
yder Nathan [Bessie], lab, b 719 14th
yder Ollie, domestic 1109 High
yder Richard, clk Island View Hotel, b same
yder Rev Wm E [Lotta], pastor Evangelical Church, h 231 Osage
yder Wm H [Ida], lab, h 1416 Toledo
yder & Stout (Eldora Snyder, John Stout), meat market 313 3d
limano Charles, student, b 416½ Broadway
limano Laurence [Mary], importer and dealer in fruits, confec-
    tionery, ice cream, cigars and tobacco s w cor Broadway and
    Pearl, h 416½ Broadway
limano Matilda, student, b 416½ Broadway
ughton Ellen [wid James], b 1801 George
urbrine Amos J [Susanna], switchman Panhandle, h 613 15th
uthern Express Co, Herbert A Brown agt, 318 4th
uth Side U B Church, Rev George W Lambert, pastor, n w cor
    Washington and Lincoln (S T)
wers John L, railway mail clk, b 416 2d
acy Amanda, boarding 1224 Wright
ader Elizabeth [wid Benjamin], b 112 Pawnee
aid Richard L, student, b 432 Sycamore
alding George B [Minnie], road supervisor Pan, h 218 w Broadway
arrow Hattie, boarding 310½ Broadway
arrow James P [Hattie], comp The Pharos, h 310½ Broadway
arrow Mary [wid John], h 115 5th
arrow Mary A, b 115 5th
arrow Patrick F [Emma], clk Wiler & Wise, h 1900 North
ecie Samuel B [May], lab, h s s Howard 2 w Frank (S T)
eitel Claude, student, b n s Shultz 2 e Standley (S T)
eitel Frank, carp, b n s Shultz 2 e Standley (S T)
eitel Harrison [Mary E], carp, h n s Shultz 2 e Standley (S T)
encer Samuel [Catharine], lab, h 326 15th
encer W Samuel [Alice], fireman Panhandle, h 1215 Smead
ergeon Emma, b 1506 Toledo
icer Mary, domestic 1000 Market
itznagle John W [Nancy], hostler James O'Donnell, h 4½ w Market
leen Ida, attendant Insane Hospital, b same
ohn Frank H, real est 214½ 4th, r 316½ Broadway
rague Daisy F, stenogr, b 432 Sycamore
rague Isolina D [wid Wm S], domestic 432 Sycamore

Spraker Francis M, teacher, (Spraker & McCord), b 713 High

Spraker & McCord (Francis M Spraker, Wm H McCord), grocers 211-213 6th

Springer Joseph M, pattern mkr, h 712 High

Springer Laura L, b 712 High

Spry Charles A, clk T A Spry, b s s Perrysburg rd, 1 e Michigan av

Spry Emma L, clk T A Spry, b s s Perrysburg rd, 1 e Michigan av

Spry Frances A, b s s Perrysburg rd, 1 e Michigan av

Spry Frances M [wid Thomas], h s s Perrysburg rd, 1 e Michigan av

Spry Thomas A, dry goods, notions and millinery 427-429 Broadway, s e cor Pearl r same

Spurlock Stella, bkkpr, b e Burlington rd, 6 s Wash tp rd

Stadtler Barbara, b 9 Biddle Island

Stadtler Frederick [Margaret], mach hd J W Henderson & Sons, h 9 Biddle Island

Stafford George W, carp Panhandle, b 1427 Spear

Stafford Peter A, brakeman, b 700 e Wabash av

Stalnaker H Guy, student, b College Hill, cor Frederick av and Royal Center pike

Stalnaker Winfield S [Alice], contractor and builder College Hill, cor Frederick av and Royal Center pike, h same (See adv class Carp and Builders)

Stamats Aura, teacher, h 104 Front

Stamats D Victor [Aura], brakeman Panhandle, h 104 Front

Stamback Ora, fireman Panhandle, b Island View Hotel

Standard Oil Co, Joseph W Fromeyer mgr, Samuel A Rose local agt 1017 to 1029 Toledo (See adv class Oils)

Standley (*see also Stanley*)

Standley Wm H [Marilla K], h 203 w Market

Stanford Sarah [wid John], b 1611 North

Stanhiser Letitia [wid George], b 629 Chicago

Stanley (*see also Standley*)

Stanley Charles, attendant Insane Hospital, b same

Stanley Ella N, b 610 Linden av

Stanley Horace P, trav agt, b 727 Bringhurst

Stanley James B [Mary A], evangelist, h 727 Bringhurst

Stanley James W, student, b s s Stanley, 1 e Clifton av

Stanley John W [Nora], lab, h s s Stanley, 1 e Clifton av

Stanley Lulu P, student, b 727 Bringhurst

Stanley Mamie B, b 727 Bringhurst

Stanton Anderson B [Priscilla], farmer, h 703 Broadway

Stanton James J, student, b 703 Broadway

Stanton Nellie, student, b 703 Broadway

Star Steam Laundry, George Ott propr, 405 Market (See adv right top lines)

Starr Charles H [Mary E], clk Panhandle, h 100 Front

Starr Minnie R, student, b 100 Front

SUPRPLUS of the METROPOLITAN LIFE
———————— at the end of 1896, over ☞ **$5,000,000**
Number of Claims Paid During Year, 63,909

Stauffer (*see also Stofer and Stouffer*)

Stauffer Benjamin W [Jane], solicitor Metropolitan Life Ins Co, h 719 Broadway

Stauffer Frederick P [Minnie], trav agt, h 801 Linden av

Steckel Mary J [wid Eli], h 615 North

Steel Charles, porter, b n s Miami, 1 e n 6th

Steel Samuel, lab, b n s Miami, 1 e n 6th

Steel Wilmot L, railway mail clk, b 206 Canal

Steele Benjamin F [Jane], h 355 Sycamore

Steele James L, agt Eel River Branch Wabash Railroad Co, h 355 Sycamore

Steele Minnie, ironer Insane Hospital, b same

Steele Retta E, b 355 Sycamore

Stegner Lydia, dressmkr, b 129 w Broadway

Steiner John C [Elvina], lab, h 413 Linden av

Steinhart Wm C [Matilda], piano tuner 624 Race, h same

Steinman Carl, student, b n s Fulton 1 e Clifton av

Steinman Henry C [Salina], lab, h n s Fulton 1 e Clifton av

Steinmets Cora, b 10 Canal

Steinmets Sarah A, h 10 Canal

Stelzer Edward P, b 108 Front

Stelzer Otto [Clara], h 108 Front

Stelzer Otto C, clk, b 108 Front

Stemler Caroline [wid George], h 1503 Smead

Stemler Charlotte, b Biddle Island

Stemler Frederick [Nettie], lab, h 1 Burlington av

Stemler George A [Louise], boilermkr Panhandle, h 1522 Wright

Stemler Jacob, b Biddle Island

Stemler John, carp, b Biddle Island

Stemler Philip [Philippine], tailor, h Biddle Island

Stephenson (*see also Stevenson*)

Stephenson Jonathan J, b 1516 High

Sterling Lewis H, saw filer, h 5½ Sycamore

Stern Abraham, meat market 309 Market, b 525 Market

Stern Bertha, b 525 Market

Stern Caroline [wid Herman], h 525 Market

Stern Isaac, b 525 Market

Stern Solomon, b 525 Market

Sternenbanner, The, Peter Wallrath propr 205 Market (See adv)

Sterrett Anna V, b 1409 Market

Sterrett Elsie I, student, b 1409 Market

Sterrett Joseph E [Amanda S], physician 308½ Market, h 1409 Market

Stetler Addie M, student Hall's Business College, b e s Royal Center rd 1 n Pleasant Hill

Stetler Tilman H [Elva], trav agt M Rumley Co, h e s Royal Center rd 1 n Pleasant Hill

Stevens Albert [Mary R], shoemkr 1432 Market, h same

Stevens Andrew W [Susanna], plumber, gas and steam fitter, machinist and electrical supplies 423 Market, h 824 Broadway (See adv back fly leaf)

Stevens Benjamin C [Luella E], physician and surgeon 418 4th, h same

Stevens Bros (Roderick D and L Benton), lumber and planing mill n w cor First and Canal

Stevens Clinton H, photographer 414½ Market, h 2210 Broadway

Stevens Edna K, b 112 Eel River av

Stevens Elizabeth [wid Elijah T], h 203 w Broadway

Stevens John C [Augusta], switchman Panhandle, h 223 Plum

Stevens Kirk, engr, b 203 w Broadway

Stevens Lulu, student, b 824 Broadway

Stevens L Benton [Anna G] (Stevens Bros), h 108 Eel River av

Stevens Mary A [wid Douglass B], asst lib public library, h same ·

Stevens P Herbert, student, b 112 Eel River av

Stevens Roderick D [Clarissa D] (Stevens Bros), h 112 Eel River av

Stevens Rose, laundress The Barnett, h 219½ 6th

Stevens Sarah A [wid David] b 2023 North

Stevens Sybil G, student, b 418 4th

Stevenson (*see also Stephenson*)

Stevenson Charles B [Elizabeth] (Stevenson & Klinsick), h 2318 Broadway

Stevenson Mary J [wid Thomas W], h 1202 Broadway

Stevenson & Klinsick (Charles B Stevenson, Frederick H Klinsick), shoes "We are the Foot Fitters" 403 Broadway

Stewart (*see also Stuart*)

Stewart Amanda, b 49 Bates

Stewart Charles [Laura], carp, b 1801 Spear

Stewart Cullah C [Margaret], asst supt Metropolitan Life Ins Co, h 2110 Market

Stewart Dorothy, milliner, b 2300 Spear

Stewart Earl, student Hall's Business College, b 312 w Market

Stewart Earl F [Mary C], livery and boarding stable 420-422 4th, h 408 Canal

Stewart Emery H [Martha], fireman Panhandle, h 522 12th

Stewart James W [Amanda], physician and surgeon, 9-10-11 Masonic Temple, h 711 Broadway

Stewart Mary J [wid King], laundress, h 317 Eel River av

Stewart Milton B, physician, 314½ 4th, b 1519 Spear

Stewart Myra, music teacher 1519 Spear, b same

Stewart Olive E, student, b 408 Canal

Stewart Robert E [Nancy], h 1325 High

Stewart Sarah, attendant Insane Hospital, b same

Stewart Wm [Mary], trav agt, h 2300 Spear

Stewart Rev Wm S [Margaret], pastor Market Street M E Church, h 1519 Spear

Stine Wm [Jennie], packer D & C H Uhl, h 819 Canal
Stith Richard [Anna], fireman, h 225 n Pearl
Stitt J Howard, pressman The Journal, b 326½ Broadway
Stitt John B [Eliza J], clk, h 326½ Broadway
Stiver Bertram, student, b 2322 High
Stiver Henry [Sadie], stair builder Stevens Bros, h 2322 High
Stiver Noble, student, b 2322 High
Stocks Carrie, b 1710 Smead
Stocks Cora D, student, b 1818 Stevens
Stocks Charles E eng hostler Panhandle, b 1818 Stevens
Stocks Harvey, clk. b 1710 Smead
Stocks James, mach hd Hillock & Pitman, b 813 21st
Stocks Joseph [Armilda], watchman Panhandle, h 1818 Stevens
Stocks May, b 1710 Smead
Stocks Nancy [wid Wesley], h 1710 Smead
Stocks Nora, b 813 21st
Stofer (see also *Stauffer and Stouffer*)
Stofer George, engr Panhandle, r 111 4th
Stoll Anna K [wid Andrew], h 1629 North
Stoll Anna, b 1629 North
Stoll Anna, b 607 Ottawa
Stoll August F, fireman Panhandle, b 1301 Wright
Stoll Bertha W, coach cleaner Panhandle, b 1301 Wright
Stoll Catharine [wid Leonard], h 1601 High
Stoll Charles, butcher, b 408½ 3d
Stoll Charles, jr [Amelia], h 218 Montgomery
Stoll Elizabeth [wid Jacob], h 1301 Wright
Stoll George A, lab, b 1301 Wright
Stoll Henry A, grocer 1522-1524 Market, b 1629 North
Stoll Jacob H, clk, b 1629 North
Stoll John J [Mary], agt, b 1629 North
Stoll Mollie, h 607 Ottawa
Stoll Otto H, clk H Closson & Co, b 1629 North
Stoltz Bernard [Margaret], watchman Panhandle, h 2021 21st
Stoltz Joseph [Etta], engr Panhandle, h 1426 Smead
Stoltz Mary, domestic 1500 North
Stoltz Wm E, stone mason, b 1411 George
Stolzenburg Lewis C [May], farmer, h w s Michigan av 3 n John
Stone James C [Josephine], clk J J Rothermel, h 719 Bringhurst
Stossmeister Fred [Pauline], business mgr Hall's Business College,
    h 1901 Market
Stouffer (see also *Stauffer and Stofer*)
Stouffer Bessie E, student, b 407 High
Stouffer Oliver J [Anna J], carp 18 6th (J D Rauch & Co), h 407 High
Stough Daniel A [Anna] (Richeson & Stough), h 1115 North
Stough Eli K [Florence], clk Panhandle, h 2017 High
Stough Esther, dressmkr 1109 North, h same

Ask the Clerk
at the Hotel for
the . . . .

**Work Done In 5 Hours
WITHOUT EXTRA CHARGE.**

☆ LAUNDRY LISTS.

GEO. OTT, Propr.   405 Market Street.

STO   245   STU

Stough Maria [wid Samuel], h 1109 North
Stough Nelson B [Lillian], condr Panhandle, h 1829 Spear
Stough Sarah C [wid Henry], h 2017 High
Stout Adam [Matilda], lab, h 709 12th
Stout John (Snyder & Stout) h Royal Center Ind
Stout Rilda, domestic 1211 North
Stout Volney B [Harriet E], tool dresser Schuyler Powell, h 1130
    Toledo
Stout Willis, lab, b 508 Sycamore
Stover James T [Elizabeth A] lab, h s s Bartlett 2 e Frank (S T)
Stover Maud, b s s Bartlett 2 e Frank (S T)
Stover Myrtle, dressmkr, b s s Bartlett 2 e Frank (S T)
Strahle Anna, wks Campbell's Laundry, b 1401 Indiana
Strahle George [Mary], lab, h 1401 Indiana
Strahle Gottlieb [Lena], painter Panhandle, h 920 16th
Strahle Josephine, domestic 1429 Erie av
Strahle Wm, upholsterer J W Henderson & Sons, b 1401 Indiana
Strahlem Harvey, del clk, b 1921 Market
Strahlem Louis [Mary A], driver W J Wemple, h 1921 Market
Strain Geneva, b 1413 Market
Strain Rodney [Susan] (Kroeger & Strain), h 1413 Market
Straw Andrew J [Anna E], genl supervisor Insane Hospital, h 228
    State
Strawbridge Jennie, h 324½ Market
Strebel Joseph [Mary], lab, h 1913 George
Strebel Valentine, bartender R Kreuzberger, b 215 Market
Strecker Amelia, b 316 w Market
Strecker Catharine, student, b 316 w Market
Strecker Charles J, baker, r 508 Broadway
Strecker Daisy, student, b 316 w Market
Strecker George [Rosina], h 316 w Market
Strecker George jr, baker 508 Broadway, b 316 w Market
Street W Scott [Hannah], lab, h 118 Washington
Stretch Blanche, dressmkr, b 1701 North
Stringer Joseph L [Ruth A], agt, h n s Vandalia R R, 1 w Garden
Strock John H [Maria], carp 417½ 12th, h 1203 North
Strouse Catharine A, teacher, b 114 Wheatland
Strouse J Henry [Clara M], engr Vandalia, h 114 Wheatland
Strueve Albert F [Ida S], engr Panhandle, h 926 Toledo
Strugula Catharine, b 43 Balsam
Strugula John, lab, b 43 Balsam
Strugula Michael [Mary], lab, h 43 Balsam
Stuart (*see also Stewart*)
Stuart Arthur C [Anna], clk The Barnett, r 117 Market
Stuart Blanche, teacher, b 914 Broadway
Stuart Charles H, student, b 132 Eel River av
Stuart James J [Minnie A], clks Louis Dieckmann, h 301 Wheatland

PIERCE, The Tailor, CAN MAKE CLOTHES TO FIT YOU.
318 BROADWAY.

| STU | 246 | SUL |

Stuart Joseph H [Mattie J], clk, h 630 Sycamore
Stuart Maud, student, b 914 Broadway
Stuart Nathaniel, trav agt, h 914 Broadway
Stuart Wm B [Sarah E], tailor W D Craig, h 16 Michigan av
Stuart Wm R, clk Marshall's Steam Laundry, b 16 Michigan av
Studebaker Edwin W [Carrie], agt, h w s Burlington rd, 6 s Wash tp rd
Stukey Albert F [Carrie], dep county clk, h 805 North
Stukey Jesse M, trav agt, h 1112 North
Stunkard Jennie, b 24 Montgomery
Stunkard Wm T [Mary], cooper, h 315 Coles
Sturgeon Abraham [Rebecca A], timber dealer, b 2 Helm
Sturgeon J Arthur [Margaret], tel opr Panhandle, h 2 Helm
Sturgeon Warner, horse trainer, r 422½ Market
Sturken Herman [Elizabeth], wagon mkr, h 309 w Broadway
Sturken John A, foreman Parker & Johnston, b 309 w Broadway
Sturken Mary, b 309 w Broadway
Sturken Wm H, [Caroline], drayman, h 311 w Broadway
Stuter Lida J, boarding 206 Canal
Stutesman Frank, fireman Panhandle, b 600 e Wabash av
Stutz Frank A, b 1806 Stevens
Stutz Leonard, lab, b 1806 Stevens
—Sullivan Charles, b 6 Taylor
Sullivan Dennis F, b 906 Lytle
Sullivan Effie A, b w s Sherman, 1 n Lincoln (S T)
Sullivan Elizabeth E, bkkpr McCaffrey Bros, b 1402 Broadway
Sullivan Ellen [wid Michael], b 825 Canal
Sullivan Frank, student Hall's Business College, b 906 Lytle
Sullivan Franklin, lab, b w s Sherman, 1 n Lincoln (S T)
Sullivan Henry, lab, b w s Sherman, 1 n Lincoln (S T)
Sullivan James, b 906 Lytle
Sullivan James, b 825 Canal
Sullivan James [Maud F], condr Panhandle, h s e cor State and
    Wilkinson
Sullivan Jeremiah, saloon 906 Lytle, h same
Sullivan John student, b 1402 Broadway
Sullivan John [Mary], cooper, h 504 Fitch
Sullivan John [Mary J], lab, h w s Sherman, 1 n Lincoln (S T)
Sullivan John C, brakeman Panhandle, h 25 Uhl
Sullivan Josephine, attendant Insane Hospital, b same
Sullivan Josephine [wid Michael], h 1402 Broadway
Sullivan Katharine, wks Bridge City Candy Co, b 1402 Broadway
Sullivan Katharine A, b 25 Uhl
Sullivan Margaret, b w s Sherman 1 n Lincoln (S T).
Sullivan Michael F, bkkpr, b 906 Lytle
Sullivan Patrick, lab, b 328 Bates
Sullivan Timothy, b 825 Canal
Sullivan Timothy [Kate], yd master Panhandle, h 922 Erie av

CRISMOND, 312 Market Street,
asoline Stoves, Screen Doors and Windows.

247	SWI

mothy H, pump rep Panhandle, r 310½ Market

m, b 906 Lytle

m R, lab, b w s Sherman 1 n Lincoln (S T)

thur A, plasterer, b 628 Chicago

arles W, student, b 628 Chicago

loe E, b 628 Chicago

rius M [Ella], h 628 Chicago

Earl, student, b 628 Chicago

1 [Bessie], lab, h 1431 Wright

is [Anna], lab, h 826 15th

lrew J [Barbara], real estate 218 6th, h 610 Broadway

dmund [Inez S], propr Logansport Reporter and Logans-

lvance 218 6th, h 811 Broadway (See adv p 9)

Anna, teacher, h 230 Osage

Carrie E, milliner, b 230 Osage

Ella B [wid Albert] (Ella B Swadener & Co), h 1626 High

Ella B & Co (Ella B and Josephine Swadener), milliners

Emma, b 230 Osage

Frank C, student, b 1626 High

Ieury C [Carrie E], engr Vandalia, 1005 Linden av

ohn, del clk N R Frazee, b 1005 Linden av

osephine (Ella B Swadener & Co), b 230 Osage

Iarion [Etta E], deputy city clk, h 6 Osage

·lington, tel opr, b s s L & W rd 5 w Anthony

hn A [Susan M], carp b s s L & W rd 5 w Anthony, h same

san M, dressmkr, b s s L & W rd 5 w Anthony

L, student, b 520½ Broadway

llis C [Elizabeth], finisher Hillock & Pitman, h 1918 George

ames P [Margaret], plumber Linton & Graf, h 421 2d

hn A [Mary E], carp, h 210 Bates

hn O, shoes 328 Market, r 1 Crawford Blk

Laura E, mach opr W D Craig, b 2 Hillside

Lillian, student, b 2 Hillside

Vm [Emma], plasterer, h 2 Hillside

ink [Margaret I], lawyer 222½ 4th, h 715 North

u F, clk W H Bringhurst, b 715 North

rgaret G, b 729 Bringhurst

er D, student, b 715 North

eodore P [Phoebe A], grocer n w cor 6th and North, h 729

irst

1 M, clk Panhandle, b 715 North

hur O, brakeman, b 717 High

nelius T, [Mary A], lab h 21 Daisy

ebe A, dressmkr 709 High, h same

Vm J, clk G W Seybold & Bros, b 330 Eel River av

n [Emma], lab, h s s Stevens, 1 w 19th

Sylvester Madge, dressmkr 1114 Erie av, h same
Sylvester Sherman H [Madge M], harnessmkr Kreis Bros Mfg Co, h 1114 Erie av

T

Taber Charles E, lawyer 400½ Broadway, b 205 Broadway
Taber George C [Anna], lawyer 204½ 4th, also city attorney, h 729 Market
Taber Jesse, court reporter, b 427 10th
Taber Julia, b 427 10th
Taber Paul [Rose A], h 427 10th
Taber Stephen C, h 205 Broadway
Taggart (*see also McTaggart*)
Taggart Ann [wid Patrick], b 706 Duret
Taggart Daniel, mgr Taggart & Johnson, h 524½ Broadway
Taggart Elizabeth, clk, b 524½ Broadway
Taggart John J [Louise], comp The Pharos, h 706 Duret
Taggart & Johnson (Hannah J Taggart estate and Horace G Johnson), bakers 524–526 Broadway
Talbott (*see also Talburt*)
Talbott Carrie, b 1100 Broadway
Talbott Edward N [Fannie M], real est, h 1100 Broadway
Talbott Helen, student, b 1100 Broadway
Talbott James, b 1100 Broadway
Talbott James [Mary], lab, h 2130 Broadway
Talbott James W [Laura P], physician 223 3d, h same
Talbott Josephine, b 1100 Broadway
Talbott McKee, b 1100 Broadway
Talbott Margaret M, waiter, b 324 Sycamore
Talbott Maurice A (Lux & Talbott), r 411½ 4th
Talburt Charles G [Belle], comp, b n e cor Canal & Oak
Tam Arthur O, lineman Logansport M Tel Co, b 112 Ash
Tam Belle, laundress, h 417 13th
Tam D Frank [Lucy], lineman Logansport M Tel Co, b 112 Ash
Tam John H [Susanna], carp, h 112 Ash
Tam Milo [Elizabeth], drayman, h 1220 Linden av
Tam Robert S [Ella C], plasterer 408 Clifton av, h same
Tanguy George B [Fannie], clk Panhandle, h 2115 Broadway
Tanguy Samuel L [Sarah B], dry goods 407 Broadway, h 2229 Broadway
Tanguy Wm E, pressfeeder The Journal, b 601 w Market
Tapp Frank, shoemkr 1420 Wright, h same
Tarver Daniel [Elizabeth], mach Pan, h s w cor Smith and Morgan

The Tailor

Our Reputation for Good -Work ᴬᴺᴰ Artistic Styles Is Well Established.

RKET STREET.

249 THO

tta B, b s w cor Smith and Morgan
· E, clk, b s w cor Smith and Morgan
', student, b 320½ Market
n, student Hall's Business College, b 320½ Market
cook Island View Hotel, r 320½ Market
la, nurse 618 e Wabash av, h same
ie, physician 215 8th, h same
s, civil engr, b 316 12th
[Lottie], trav agt J Taylor & Sons, h 203 w Broadway
(Joseph Taylor & Sons), h 823 Market
cook, r 25 Elm
d R [Clara E], dentist 401½ Market, h 1500 North
N [Emma], detective Panhandle, h 927 Market
e, b 823 Market
b 614 Broadway
823 Market
Ellen], lab, h n s Maple 2 e Michigan av
[Lorraine], jeweler and optician 309 4th, h 422 North
back cover)
Anna M], saloon 316 Canal, h 6 Biddle Island
V, barber The Barnett, r 123 Cicott
, trav agt J Taylor & Sons, b 823 Market
L [Mattie], physician 1420 Broadway, h same
& Sons (Zachary and Dawes Taylor), wholesale har-
lery, leather and findings 412 Market
W, student, b 1420 Broadway
domestic 2318 Broadway
ll H, brakeman Panhandle, b Island View Hotel
h 823 Market
J, milliner T A Spry, b 1218 Market
nd C [Florilla], h 614 Broadway
[Rose], butcher, h 218 Burlington av
y (Joseph Taylor & Sons), h 823 Market
, b 334 Eel River av
Rebecca A], lab, h n s Bates 1 w Van R R (Dunkirk)
mes G [Martha], h 220 13th
W [Anna B], carp 511 Broadway, h 441 Michigan av
rewing Co, Tandy S Brockman agt, north end Vine
: Indianapolis Railroad Co (Vandalia Line), John C
local agt, passenger station, freight depot and divis-
s e cor Sycamore and Godfrey
[Mattie], fireman Panhandle, h 1520 Toledo
V [Elizabeth], switchman Panhandle, h 820 12th
student, b 321 Pleasant Hill
aroline, laundress, h 209½ 6th
e H, music teacher 818 Market, b same
ter [Elizabeth], ship clk T M Quigley & Co, h 2029

All Kinds of Life Insurance from $6.00 to $50,000 Written
——BY THE——
Metropolitan Life Insurance Co., of New York.
W. O. WASHBURN. SUPT. LOGANSPORT DISTRICT   Office rooms 1, 2 and 3 Crawford Block

THO   , 250   THO

Thomas Cary E [Bertha], lab, h 315 College

Thomas Charles L [Mary E], physician—practice confined to diseases of the eye and ear—Masonic Temple, h 625 High

Thomas Fannie, b 10 17th

Thomas Harry, clk, r 314 North

Thomas Henry A [Laura E], grocer 500 Michigan av, h s e cor Sugar and Oak

Thomas John, tmstr, b 900 17th

Thomas Sarah, nurse 10 17th, h same

Thomas Scott, baggagemaster Panhandle, r 529 Market

Thomas Walter, lab, b s e cor Perrysburg and Adamsboro rds

Thomas Willard, student, b 625 High

Thomas Wm C [Nettie M], cashier The Logansport State Bank, h 1211 High

Thomason (*see also Thompson and Thomson*)

Thomason Gola, student, b 421 Burlington av

Thomason Harriet [wid Levi], b 215 Burlington av

Thomason Peter C [Emma], foreman, h 421 Burlington av

Thompson Abel R, b 102 Bates

Thompson Blanche, clk Logansport & W V Gas Co, b 1124 Market

Thompson Catharine [wid Wm P], h 1124 Market

Thompson Charles F [Elizabeth H] (Thompson Lumber Co), h 1218 Broadway

Thompson Elizabeth [wid Alfred W], domestic 1318 High

Thompson Frederick E, clk Ben Fisher, b 1218 North

Thompson Harry M [Dessie], brakeman, h 802 Spear

Thompson Harry S [Minnie L] (Thompson Lumber Co), h 2322 Broadway

Thompson Isaac W [Mary E], h 14 Mobley

Thompson Isaac W jr, grocer 700 Clifton av, b 14 Mobley

Thompson James L [Clementine], mess Adams Ex Co, h 597 Michigan av

Thompson John M [Martha A], blksmith 120 6th, h 1218 North

Thompson Lulu, student, b s w cor Elm and Marydyke

Thompson Lumber Co (Charles F and Harry S Thompson), contractors and builders, lumber, lath, shingles, etc, n e cor 6th and High

Thompson Robert, lab, b 724 11th

Thompson Rosella M, b 14 Mobley

Thompson Wm H [Harriet F], check clk, h 1715 North

Thompson Wm O B [Emma J], ck clk Vandalia, h 102 Bates

Thomson Amy C, seamstress H Wiler & Co, b 129½ 6th

Thomson Clara, domestic 629 High

Thomson George W, student Hall's Business College, b 114 7th

Thomson Harriet [wid James C], h 129½ 6th

Thomson James W [Belle], plasterer, h 617 North

Thomson Lillian, opr C U Tel Co, b 710 North

Thomson Raymond T [Lillian], tel opr W U Tel Co, h 1218 North

;HEST GRADES . MONUMENTS
WEST PRICES . .
SCHUYLER POWELL, 1031-1035 Toledo St.

251   TOL

ison Walter, clk, b 617 North
n Charles L [Jane], carp Panhandle, h 1116 Broadway
n Willis W [Laura B], tel opr, b 1116 Broadway
iiburg John [Ruth], meat market 209 College, h same
nton Ethel A, student, b 914 Race
nton Horatio [Jennie], h 1202 North
nton Jeremiah E [Lucy M], house mover 914 Race, h same
nton Mary J [wid Wm], b 414 First
n John [Minnie], lab, h 903 19th
n Mary L F, student, b 903 19th
ckmorton Bert, painter, b 10 Biddle Island
ckmorton Edward, painter, b 10 Biddle Island
ckmorton John, lab, h 10 Biddle Island
er Laura, domestic, 1420 Broadway
y Wm F [Mary], lab, h 16 Pleasant Hill
erman George L [Eliza J], farmer, h 622 Sycamore
erman Lulu J, b 622 Sycamore
on Wm J [Lucy M], carp, h 617 Helm
ley Alfred, trav agt, b 619 Linden av
ham Michael D C [Mary G], trav agt, h 101 Helm
ett Elmer E [Anna], mach, h 110 Elm
ett Homer L [Mary A], brakeman Pan, h 722 Melbourne av
ett Samuel L, b 722 Melbourne av
on Frank M, painter, b 1729 Broadway
on John [Nellie V], painter, h 1928 North
on Tillie, h 1729 Broadway
nenstein Adolf F, b 424 9th
neustein Louis C, student Hall's Business College, b 424 9th
nenstein Rev Martin [Amalie], pastor St Jacob's Lutheran
 Church, h 424 9th
nenstein Walter, student, b 424 9th
ck Andrew, mason, b 21 Daisy
ck Anthony [Josephine], blksmth, h 21 Daisy
ck George C. mason, b 21 Daisy
ck John M, lab, b 21 Daisy
ck Viola, b 21 Daisy
ck Wm, b 21 Daisy
 Anna, waiter The Barnett, b same
 Mary H [wid Samuel], h 312½ 3d
 Peter B [Lillie M], billiards 315 Sycamore, h same
 Roy, clk, b 315 Sycamore
 Albert J, student Hall's Business College, b 1500 High
 Cora, student, b 1500 High
 Harry B, comp, b 1500 High
 James B [Etta], plasterer 1500 High, h same
 John F [Oral A], motorman, h 1517 Douglass
 d Blanche E, b 620 Linden av

TOL   252   TRO

Toland Charles [Ida], lab, h rear 1819 Toledo
Toland Naude A, student, b 620 Linden av
Toland Owen N [Jennie A], baggagemaster Pan, h 620 Linden av
Tolley Theodore [Phoebe], condr Panhandle, h 1930 Market
Tolon James [Nancy], carp, h n s Biddle 1 w Washington (S T)
Tolon Mary J, b s w cor Howard and Anthony (S T)
Tomlinson Daniel W [Harriet E], real est 400½ Broadway, h 118 7th
Tomlinson Elizabeth, b 1425 Erie av
Tomlinson Frederick, student, b 118 7th
Tomlinson Harry T, student, b 118 7th
Tomlinson Joseph T, lawyer 400½ Broadway, b 118 7th
Tomlinson Katharine, seamstress, h 704 Bringhurst
Toney Albert R, tailor J F Carroll, b 2228 North
Toney Caroline [wid Samuel], h 2228 North
Toney Ulysses G, student, b 2228 North
Torr Charles C, clk Wabash, b 1115 Broadway
Torr Emma A [wid Harry], cooperage cor 8th and Erie av, h 1115
    Broadway
Torr Mary D, student, b 1115 Broadway
Torr Thomas W, b 1115 Broadway
Tousley Fannie, b 1910 High
Tousley Gertrude, b 1910 High
Tousley Harry D, student, b 1910 High
Tousley Henry S [Laura A], div opr Panhandle, h 1910 High
Township Trustee's Office, Robert F Johnston trustee, basement
    Masonic Temple
Tracy Charles W, b 208 Pleasant Hill
Tracy Edward L, condr, b 208 Pleasant Hill
Tracy James N [Mary E], h 208 Pleasant Hill
Tracy James W, painter, b 208 Pleasant Hill
Traut Charles W [Mary], propr The Wide Awake Grocery 420 Mar-
    ket, h 1108 North (See adv front cover)
Traut Robert, student, b 1108 North
Tremp Frank [Alice], condr Panhandle, h 1423 Spear
Trick Henry F [Emma D], trav agt, h 306 w Market
Trick Samuel W, trav agt, b 306 w Market
Trickle C Edward [Lillian], clk, h 1811 High
Triesback Winfield S [Jennie], laundry foreman Insane Hospital, h
    519 Helm
Trinity Episcopal Church, Rev Frank C Coolbaugh rector, n w cor
    7th and Market
Tritt Harry C, pharmacist Ben Fisher, b 700 Race
Tritt Samuel B [Adarine], h 700 Race
Troester Anna, dressmkr 203 Osage, b same
Troester Elizabeth, b 203 Osage
Troester Frederick [Elizabeth], lab, h 203 Osage
Troester Frederick B, student Hall's Business College, b 203 Osage

Troll Nettie, domestic 216 8th
Trotter John, tmstr N J Bligh, b 4 Sycamore
Troutman Charles [Elizabeth], carp, h n s Barclay, 3 e Clifton av
Troutman Elizabeth W, student, b 207 Osage
Troutman Harry W [Maude], county surveyor, h 220 College
Troutman John F [Elizabeth A], carp, h 1730 North
Troutman Joseph N [Harriet], floorwalker Schmitt & Heinly, h 207 Osage
Troutman Rodney E, student, b 1730 North
Troutman Stanley W, student, b 1730 North
Truax John Edward, riding bailiff, h 203 College
Truette Nettie, domestic 412½ 3d
Truman Charles H [Nellie M], engr Panhandle, h 1705 High
Truman John [Abbie A], engr Panhandle, h 1312 Spear
Truman John B, student, b 1920 Broadway
Truman Laura L, b 1312 Spear
Truman Lawrence L [Ada M], asst rd foreman engines Panhandle, h 1920 Broadway
Tucker Alice, b 165 Smith
Tucker Arthur W [Emma A], physician 321½ 4th, h 110 9th
Tucker Charles [Bertha], mach hd, h 407 Linden av
Tucker Charlotte [wid Elisha], milliner 406 Market, h same
Tucker Cora, domestic Hotel Johnston, h 812 e Wabash av
Tucker Elisha A [Miriam], lab, h 165 Smith
Tucker Firmen [Rosanna], watchman, h 812 e Wabash av
Tucker Florence I, student, b 718 Market
Tucker Harry G [Sybil], merchant tailor s e cor 4th and Broadway, h 2105 Broadway (See adv back bone)
Tucker Henry [Julia L M], carriages, harness and agricultural implements 519–521 Market, h 718 Market (See adv back paster)
Tucker House, Mrs J H Tucker propr, 304 Broadway
Tucker James B [Catharine], fireman Panhandle, h 1816 Market
Tucker John, lab, b 812 e Wabash av
Tucker Mrs J H [wid John H], propr Tucker House, h same
Tucker Lizzie, domestic 801 Broadway
Tucker Ninnie A, student, b 718 Market
Tucker Sherman L [Sarah A], lab, h 412 Clifton av
Tucker Wm D, attendant Insane Hospital, b same
Tudor John, b 800 Helm
Tudor John H [Emma C], solicitor E D Closson, h 800 Helm
Tudor Philomena, student, b 800 Helm
Tuley Thomas J, lawyer and notary 222½ 4th, r Keystone Blk, n w cor 6th and Broadway
Turley John D [Nancy], letter carrier, h 728 High
Turley Thomas E, brakeman, r 421½ Market
Turner Bartley [Mary], lab, h 1321 Smead
Turner George W, lab, r 404½ Broadway

:r Harry [Nettie], boilermkr, h 728 17th

:r Horace B [Anna May], barber also cigars and tobacco 404 roadway, h 49 Bates

:r James, r 318½ Broadway

:r John H, barber, b 49 Bates

:r Kate [wid Matthias], hairdresser 322½ Market, h same

:r Thomas [Emma], boilermkr Panhandle, h 1800 Stevens

)augh Melissa, domestic w s Michigan av 3 n John

ng Harry, student, b 1429 Erie av

ng Jacob [Louise], saloon 1429 Erie av, h same

ɔ John S [Elizabeth E], clk Stevenson & Klinsick, h 102 15th

ɔ Minnie, r 409½ Market

s Edward C, clk Panhandle, b 608 Linden av

s Godfrey [Anna H] (Twells & Behmer), b 608 Linden av

s Godfrey jr, clk Twells & Behmer, h 608 Linden av

s Jessie H, b 608 Linden av

s Mary, student, b 1800 North

s Richard [Martha B], cigars 417 Broadway, h 1800 North

s Richard S, student, b 608 Linden av

s Sarah, baker, b 406 w Broadway

s Wyndham S [Catharine L], freight transfer and drayage con- actor 1309 Market, h same

s & Behmer (Godfrey Twells, Walter J Behmer), grocers 113 ɔcamore

ɪey Edward J [Catharine], railway mail clerk, h 1825 Market

ɪey Margaret, laundress Hotel Johnston, b same

ɪey Michael [Margaret], lab, h 533 Pratt

ɪey Thomas, lab, b 533 Pratt

David [Nancy], lab, h n w cor Frank and Culbertson (S T)

Melvin, lab, b 602 Canal

Rosa, domestic, b n w cor Frank and Culbertson (S T)

Sarah [wid Lafayette], b s s Wabash River rd 7 w 18th

Caroline E, dressmkr 925 Spear, h same

Edward E, clk, b 522½ Broadway

Grace G, b 112 Helm

John (Walsh & Tyner), b 925 Spear

John H [Louise], treas Logan Heading Co, h 114 Helm

Jordan R [Caroline E], car insp Panhandle, h 925 Spear

Otto, clk J M Johnston, b 310½ Broadway

Vera U, student, b 925 Spear

Paris [Jane], lab, h s s Wabash River rd 6 w 18th

Wm, clk Ray & Etnire, b s s Wabash River rd 6 w 18th

Morton N [Rebecca S], h 500 Helm

H. J. GRISMOND, 312 Market Street,
Hardware, Stoves and Tinware.

| UEB | 255 | UND |

U

Uebelshaeuser (*see also Evilsiser*)
Uebelshaeuser Wm [Elizabeth], mach hd Panhandle, h 410 Miami
Uhl Caroline [wid Joseph], h 13 Melbourne av
Uhl **Charles H** [Evaline] (D & C H Uhl), h 14 Melbourne av
Uhl Clara E, b 2 Melbourne av
Uhl **Dennis** [Sophia J] (D & C H Uhl), pres Shroyer & Uhl Co, sec y and treas Logansport Construction Co, h 2 Melbourne av
Uhl **D & C H** (Dennis and Charles H), proprs Empire Mills, cor Front and Melbourne av
Uhl **Elmore** [Louise], contractor cement work and iron fences 113 Wheatland, h same
Uhl Florence A, b 2 Melbourne av
Uhl Genevera, student, b 2 Melbourne av
Uhl C Harry, bkkpr D & C H Uhl, b 2 Melbourne av
Uhl Jessie L, b 14 Melbourne av
Uhl Leonora, student, b 2 Melbourne av
Uhl Lydia E, b 13 Melbourne av
Uhl **Miller** [Jessie M] (Holbruner & Uhl), h 922 Market
Uhl Walter J [Carrie M], secy and treas Shroyer & Uhl Co, h 919 Market
Uhl Wm C [Sarah L], vice pres Shroyer & Uhl Co, h 813 Market
Ulerick (*see also Ulerich*)
Ulerick Frank [Emma], farmer, h s s High 1 e 25th
Ulery Anna, domestic, b 1529 George
Ulery Harry V [Mary], switchman Panhandle, h 1529 George
Ulery Henry [M Ellen], drayman I N Cool, h 1625 George
Ulery John F, clk, r 306½ Market
Ullery Ada F, domestic 625 High
Ullery Grace, domestic 1310 North
Ullery **G Lincoln** (S W Ullery & Son), b 916 Market
Ullery **Samuel W** (S W Ullery & Son), h 916 Market
Ullery **S W & Son** (Samuel W and G Lincoln), hardware, carriage and wagon stock 318 Market
Ulmer Arthur G [Alice], asst supt Metropolitan Life Ins Co, h 201 State
Ulrich (*see also Ulerick*)
Ulrich Anna, domestic, b 1826 Spear
Ulrich Christopher [Magdalen], lab, h 1028 20th
Ulrich Elizabeth [wid Frederick], laundress, h 1826 Spear
Ulrich Margaret, domestic s w cor Michael and L & W rd
Umbarger George F [Jessie A], painter, h 629 Linden av
Umbarger John B, tmstr, h n s Howard 2 w Anthony (S T)
Underhay Elizabeth, b 2213 Broadway

Underhay John [Mary], painter 225 6th, h 2213 Broadway
Underhay Newton, student, b 2213 Broadway
Unger Henry [Minnie], farmer, h s s L & W rd 5 w Standley
Unger Joseph, farmer, h s s L & W rd 5 w Standley
Unkefer Raymond C, bridge carp Panhandle, b 116 Canal
United Brethren Church, Rev George W Lambert pastor, n e cor Oak
and Sugar
United States Express Co, Joseph L Linvill agt, 320 Pearl
Universalist Church, —— pastor, s s Broadway bet 8th and 9th
Updegraff Charles [Hattie], nurse 1115 George, h same
Updegraff Frank, engr Insane Hospital, b same
Updegraff James H [Ella R] (Updegraff & Son), h 314 Helm
Updegraff John P B [Amanda J] (Updegraff & Son), h 205 State
Updegraff Wm [Elizabeth], broom mkr, h 509 Melbourne av
Updegraff Wm jr [Mary], car insp Panhandle, h 509 Melbourne av
Updegraff & Son (John P B and James H), grocers, 314 Helm

V

Vaas Anna M [wid Emil T], h 1609 Douglass
Vaas Clara, domestic, b 1609 Douglass
Vaas Grace, b 1609 Douglass
Vaile George R [Flora], clk Panhandle, h 1205 North
Vall Robert bartender, r 224½ Market
Vanbel Henry R, student Hall's Business College, b 519 Fitch
Van Buskirk James [Josephine M], saw mill n s Pink 1 e Balsam, h
615 Pratt
Van Buskirk Joseph D [Emma], trav agt b 128 Pawnee
Van Buskirk Winifred, student b 615 Pratt
Van Camp Benjamin F, b 1916 Market
Vance Carl [Carrie], condr h 724 Ottawa
Vance Elmer J [Martha E], clk Louis Dieckmann h 6 State
Vance Emanuel [Martha J], boiler insp Panhandle h 1212 Market
Vance Frank E [Lillian], boiler insp Panhandle h 2020 Spear
Vance Frederick, lab b 1212 Market
Vance Harriet, b 1212 Market
Vance Harry, painter b 1212 Market
Vandalia Line see Terre Haute & Indianapolis Railroad Co
Van Dyke Garrett, lab b w s Perrysburg rd 1 n Adamsboro rd
Van Dyne Charles, tmstr b 202 Burlington av
Van Dyne Susan [wid David], h 202 Burlington av
Van Dyne Wm, tmstr b 202 Burlington av
Van Loon Jacob W [Clarissa], condr Panhandle h 1509 Spear
Van Meter Samuel, clk b 1825 Broadway

Van Meter Susan E, student Hall's Business College, b 1825 Broadway

Van Meter Wm R [Elizabeth], h 1825 Broadway

Vannice David M [Mary E], car rep Panhandle h 1501 Marydyke

Vannice Eva, b 1501 Marydyke

Van Steenberg Alfred W, lab, b 1717 Spear

Van Steenberg Edith, b 1717 Spear

Van Steenberg Ella, b 1717 Spear

Van Steenberg George [Mamie], carp 1826 George h same

Van Steenberg Wm [Anna], engr Panhandle h 1717 Spear

Van Winkle Austin T, carp b 1411 George

Van Winkle Robert M, lawyer, b 1411 George

Van Vinkle Sarah C [wid Austin T], h 1411 George

Vauble Henry, student, b 519 Fitch

Vaughn Eleanore H [wid Artemus], b 1128 North

Vaughn Sidney A [Lilly], lumber dealer, h 1128 North

Vayette Rebecca J, laundress, h 5 Columbia

Veal A Edward [Millie L], oil 314 5th, h 720 11th

Veal Wm, car sealer Panhandle, b 720 11th

Velsey Levi C [Betsy M] b 1420 Broadway

Velsey Seth M [Katherine], abstracts and loans 204 4th, h 2530 Broadway

Vernon Alexander, tmstr, b s w cor Shultz and Frank (S T)

Vernon Dennis, lab, b s e cor Shultz and Standley (S T)

Vernon Edward [Florence D], drayman, h 728 Linden av

Vernon Isaiah [Margaret E], trav agt, h 429 Pratt

Vernon James M [Catherine L], trav agt, h 624 Miami

Vernon Lyman [Mary], carp, h s e cor Shultz and Standley (S T)

Vernon Maud, b s e cor Shultz and Standley (S T)

Vernon Mollie, domestic 1706 Broadway

Vernon Samuel [Anna], lab, h s w cor Shultz and Frank (S T)

Vernon Sanford [Hattie], tmstr, h s s Charles 4 w Standley (S T)

Vernon Thomas H [Mary A], wks Wm Heppe & Sons, h w s Standley 1 n Shultz (S T)

Victor Byron K, switchman Panhandle, r 316½ Market

Victor Byron K jr, tel opr Panhandle, r 316½ Market

Vigus Colin S [Caroline], h 1507 High

Vigus Cyrus B [Mary A] cigarmkr Julius Wagner, h s w cor Main and Grove

Vigus Mary E [wid John H], dressmkr s w cor Main and Grove, h same

Vigus Wm, hostler, r 116 6th

Viney Bert W, b 1305 North

Viney Earl R [Nellie M], wks laundry, h 316 Helm

Viney Harold T, clk O A Means, b 1305 North

Viney James F, candy mkr T M Quigley & Co, b 1305 North

Viney James W [Dora], capt h and l co no 2, h 1305 North

Viney John A [Iona E], upholsterer H Wiler & Co, h 816 Linden av

$186,000,000 of Life Insurance

WAS WRITTEN BY THE

METROPOLITAN LIFE. of New York. In 1896

W. O. WASHBURN,
Superintendent
Logansport District,
Crawford Block.

VIN | 258 | WAG

Vincy Nellie, student, b 1305 North
Vinson Mary, h 519 Canal
Vinson Sadie, b 519 Canal
Virts George, brakeman, b 415½ 3d
Voelkle Christian, tailor, h 237 College
Volk Otto, cabinet mkr, b 706 Duret
Voorhees Andrew, cook, r 408½ 3d
Voorhees Philip [Flora], lumber, lath, shingles, sash doors, blinds
    and builders' material 500 Sycamore, h 434 Sycamore (See adv p 7)
Voss Henry [Catharine], sexton Mt Hope Cemetery, h 456 Pleasant
    Hill
Voss Johanna, student, b 456 Pleasant Hill
Voss John, student, b 456 Pleasant Hill
Voss Otto J, clk John Mulcahy, b 456 Pleasant Hill
Vurpillat Constant [Barbara], carp 409 Linden av, h same
Vurpillat Edward, carp, b 409 Linden av
Vurpillat Malinda, domestic, b 409 Linden av
Vurpillat Otto, carp Panhandle, b 1318 George
Vurpillat Tillie, b 409 Linden av
Vyquesney Edward, engr Vandalia, r 315 Sycamore

W

Wabash Railroad Co, Charles G Newell local agt, passenger station
    cor 9th and Lytle, freight depot cor Ewing and Lytle Eel River
    Branch, passenger station and freight depot e s Vine n Mary-
    dyke, James L Steele agt (See adv p 13)
Wade Luther, millwright, b 626 Miami
Wade Michael C [Susanna], mnfr trunks, traveling bags, etc 327
    Market, h same
Wagner (see also Wagoner and Wanger)
Wagner Anna M, dressmkr, b 4 Sycamore
Wagner Catharine, b 4 Sycamore
Wagner Emma, laundry clk Insane Hospital, b same
Wagner Frank M [Elizabeth], saloon 4 Sycamore, h same
Wagner Frederick, fireman Insane Hospital, b same
Wagner Ida, dressmkr 428 Burlington av, b same
Wagner Jacob P [Josephine], brakeman Pan, h 212 Montgomery
Wagner John H, truckman Panhandle, h 428 Burlington av
Wagner John J [Mary E], horseshoer J M Elliott, h 310 Miami
Wagner Josephine, b 4 Sycamore
Wagner Julius [Gertrude], cigar manufacturer 423 4th, h 1008 Lin-
    den av
Wagner Matilda [wid Wm A], b 428 Burlington av

Wagner Pearl, student, b 428 Burlington av
Wagner Peter, lab, Insane Hospital, b same
Wagner Victor, student, b 4 Sycamore
Wagoner (*see also Wagner and Wanger*)
Wagoner Blanche, domestic, b n s Bartlett 3 w Anthony (S T)
Wagoner Charles, lineman electric light wks, b s s cor Treen and Norcross
Wagoner Charles E [Nettie], trav agt, h 1714 High
Wagoner Daisy, domestic, b n s Bartlett 3 w Anthony (S T)
Wagoner Edward, lab, b n s Bartlett 3 w Anthony (S T)
Wagoner Elmer L [Maud], pipeman hose co no 5, h 507 Michigan av
Wagoner Laura F, mach opr W D Craig, b s e cor Treen and Norcross
Wagoner Margaret E [wid Elias], h n s Bartlett 3 w Anthony (S T)
Wagoner Walter E, shipping clk, b 1714 High
Wagoner Warren L [Sarah], engr, h s e cor Treen and Norcross
Wagoner Wm H, b s e cor Treen and Norcross
Wakeland James [Sarah], foreman Panhandle, h 1523 Spear
Walden Adelaide M [wid Wm B], h 1202 Broadway
Walden Edwin M [Minnie G], shoes 315 4th, h 830 High
Walden Irving H, trav agt, b 1202 Broadway
Waldsmith Frederick, lab, b n e cor Burlington av and Main
Waldsmith Oma, b 300½ Market
Walker Ella L, b 1119 Broadway
Walker Norey B, clk Walker & Ranch, b 1119 Broadway
Walker Myrtle, domestic Insane Hospital
Walker Wm M [Anna L] (Walker & Rauch), h 1119 Broadway
Walker & Ranch (Wm M Walker, Charles F Ranch), boots and shoes 420 Broadway
Walklin Hiram B, lab, b 220 Broadway
Walklin James [Mary A], check clk Panhandle, h 220 Broadway
Wall (*see also Walls*)
Wall Elizabeth [wid Samuel], b n e cor Culbertson and Frank (S T)
Wall Isaac, lab, b n e cor Culbertson and Frank (S T)
Wall John H [Emma], barber 2 Sycamore, h 408 Ottawa
Wall Wm [Edna E], lab, h n e cor Culbertson and Frank (S T)
Wallace Anna, b 1422 Broadway
Wallace Charles O [Rebecca], carp, h 21 Washington
Wallace Edward F, porter The Barnett r 202 Canal
Wallace Eliza M [wid Benjamin F], dressmkr 626 Linden av, h same
Wallace Frank R, comp, b 626 Linden av
Wallace John E, clk Panhandle, b 1422 Broadway
Wallace Mark [Mary], engr Panhandle, h 1422 Broadway
Wallace Rebecca, dressmkr 21 Washington, h same
Wallace Wm, student, b 1422 Broadway
Walling John H [Nona], carp, h w s Lobelia 1 n Pink
Walling Sarah J [wid Jacob], h w s Lobelia 2 n Pink
Walling Thomas [Jennie], lab, h 1704 Knowlton

Wallrath Anna, b 207 Market
Wallrath Henry J, comp The Sternenbanner, b 207 Market
Wallrath Lizzie, b 207 Market
Wallrath Margaret, student, b 207 Market
Wallrath Peter [Katherine], propr The Sternenbanner h 207 Market
  (See adv)
Walls (see also Wall)
Walls Wesley L [Catherine], comp, h n e cor College and Columbia
Walsh (see also Welch, Welsch and Welsh)
Walsh John [Ellen], lab, h 710 14th
Walsh Michael, tailor H G Tucker, b 522½ Broadway
Walsh Patrick [Louisa R], engr water works, h 819 Broadway
Walsh Robert, porter Holy Angels Academy, b same
Walsh Thomas (Walsh & Tyner), h Detroit Mich
Walsh & Tyner (Thomas Walsh, John Tyner), proprs The Barnett
  News and Cigar Stand, n e cor 2d and Market
Walter Albert B, actor, b 1303 North
Walter Cora M, teacher, b 1303 North
Walter Ford C, helper I N Cool, b 1415 Smead
Walter James H [Anna M], carp, h 1303 North
Walter Jessie, stenogr E D Crossley, b 1303 North
Walter John, cigar mkr, b 400 Pleasant Hill
Walters Alice N, b 824 Race
Walters Alva C [Emma], painter, n w cor Standley and Charles (S T)
  h same
Walters Edward E [Etta], carp, h 1601 Toledo
Walters Elizabeth [wid Eli], h 406 Pleasant Hill
Walters Eugene, lab, b 1601 Toledo
Walters George W [Lillie], lawyer and notary 206 4th, h 916 North
Walters Gertrude, student, b n w cor Standley and Charles (S T)
Walters Hannah [wid John], h 1608 Toledo
Walters Jacob H, Justice of the Peace 218½ 4th, b 916 North
Walters James, carp, b 1608 Toledo
Walters Jesse W, r 524 North
Walters John R [Sophia], mgr J R Walters Photo & Enlarging Co
  h 121 5th
Walters Julius M, photo printer J R Walters Photo & Enlarging Co, b
  121 5th
Walters J R Photo and Enlarging Co, John R Walters mgr 121 5th
Walters Myrtle, b n w cor Standley and Charles (S T)
Walters Sheldon, painter, b n w cor Standley and Charles (S T)
Walton Clinton H, supt P C C & St L Ry Co, r 818 Market
Walts Elizabeth B, b 512 Barron
Walts Frank M, student, b 512 Barron
Walts Rev Jacob K [Jennie B], pastor Wheatland Street M E Church,
  h 512 Barron
Wandrei August [Louise], bartender, h 109 Colfax

Wandrei Ewald H [Daisy G], saloon n e cor Duret and Berkley, h 202 Berkley

Wandrei Gustav, lab, b s s Bartlett 1 e Frank (S T)

Wandrei Gustav A [Cora], finisher J W Henderson & Sons, h 318 Burlington av

Wandrei Julius [Emily], carp Panhandle, h s s Bartlett 1 e Frank (S T)

Wandrei Louis, painter, b s s Bartlett 1 e Frank (S T)

Wandrei Louis [Henrietta], bartender, h 22 Main

Wandrei Michael [Clara], car rep Panhandle, h 1327 George

Wandrei Michael [Henrietta], lab Panhandle, h n w cor Anthony and Shultz (S T)

Wanger (see also *Wagner and Wagoner*

Wanger Julius [Louise C], blksmith, h 1806 Market

Wanger Frank W, clk Ira G Wilson, b 1806 Market

Wanmer John [Augusta], huckster, h w s Michigan av 1 s John

Ward Agnes M, opr C U Tel Co, b 613 High

Ward Charles E, mach hd, b 530 Michigan av

Ward Clifton J, student, b 613 High

Ward Harry A, b 530 Michigan av

Ward Harry N [Maude M], secy and treas The Otto Shoe & Clothing Co, h 307 7th

Ward Henry C [Ruth], carp, h n s Biddle 1 e Washington (S T)

Ward James [Frances], switchman Panhandle, h 1517 George

Ward John C [Alice], molder, h 613 High

Ward John W, lab, b n s Biddle 1 e Washington (S T)

Ward Lillian K, opr C U Tel Co, b 613 High

Ward Maude L, b 613 High

Ward May, b n s Biddle 1 e Washington (S T)

Ward Ollie C, clk, b 613 High

Ward Paul R, student, b 613 High

Ward Samuel H [Maude E], physician 17 State Natl Bank Bldg, h same

Ward Wm F, molder, b 613 High

Ward Wm H H [Elizabeth,] lab, h 530 Michigan av

Warden Blanche, b 1228 Spear

Warden Minnie, laundress, h 1228 Spear

Warne Charles B [Anna], painter Panhandle, h 206 Wheatland

Warner (see also *Werner*)

Warner Edward, porter The Barnett, r 202 Canal

Warner Ernest, lab, b 625 17th

Warner George B [Alice], electrician, h 1429 North

Warner Herman [Minnie], mason, h 625 17th

Warner James D [Elizabeth], lab, h 209 Colfax

Warner May, student, b 625 17th

Warnke Henry [Louise], lab, h 2019 Spear

Warnke Henry J, student Hall's Business College, b 2019 Spear

Warnke Minnie, domestic Insane Hospital

Warnke Wm C, lab, b 2019 Spear
Warnock Edward, boilermkr Panhandle, b 321 Tipton
Warnock James, steam fitter N N Hughes, b 321 Tipton
Warnock Mary [wid James], h 321 Tipton
Warnock Mary, clk G W Seybold & Bros. b 321 Tipton
Warnock Wm [Angeline], tmstr, h w s Sherman 2 n Wash tp rd
Warwicker John, harness mkr Henry Tucker, b 521 High
Washburn Bertha A, b 38 Bates
Washburn Catharine A [wid Louis H], h 38 Bates
Washburn Catharine S, waiter, b 38 Bates
Washburn Charles A, b 38 Bates
Washburn E Edna, student, b 164 Smith
Washburn Edward [Mary J], finisher, h 164 Smith
Washburn Effie, domestic 309 College
Washburn Elliott, tmstr, b 1211 Toledo
Washburn George P [Margaret], trav agt, h 1015 Spear
Washburn Harriet, domestic 203 College
Washburn Jennie S, stenogr Hale & Gamble, b 164 Smith
Washburn Mary I, b 38 Bates
Washburn Wm O, supt The Metropolitan Life Ins Co, r 823 Broadway (See adv left top lines and class Ins Co's)
Waterman Claudina, b n s Barclay 1 e Clifton av
Waterman Henry W [Lavinia], barber H B Turner, h n s Barclay 1 e Clifton av
Waters John N [Clara C], clk John Gray, h 800 High
Watkins Emery, student, b 421 Day
Watkins Isaac N [Mary], carp, h 1806 Spear
Watkins Samuel N [Cecelia], foreman, h 421 Day
Watson Cleminda [wid John], b 429 North
Watson Ernest, student, b 1625 George
Watson Sylvester [Ella], fireman Panhandle, h 1100 George
Watts Bertram, lab, b 227 Pratt
Watts Clarence A, b 227 Pratt
Watts Daniel M [Emma C], agricultural implements, threshers, carriages, wagons and harness 126 6th, h 701 Helm (See adv class Agricultural Implements)
Watts Ernest E, plumber Messinger & Son, b 701 Helm
Watts Hannah [wid James], b 230 Osage
Watts Harvey N [Cordelia], lab, h n s Bartlett 5 w Anthony (S T)
Watts Maria M [wid Ezra], h 227 Pratt
Watts Nora, b n s Bartlett 5 w Anthony (S T)
Watts Piny, dressmkr 227 Pratt, b same
Watts Walter, lab, b n s Bartlett 5 w Anthony (S T)
Watts Wm H, clk D M Watts, b 701 Helm
Watts Winfield S, attendant Insane Hospital, b same
Wean J Henry, lab, b 1326 Wright
Wear Bloom [Nancy], pump insp Panhandle, h 231 Bates

H. J. CRISMOND, 312 Market Street,
Stoves and Kitchen Furnishings.

| WEA | 263 | WEE |

Wear Robert W, stenogr Panhandle, b 231 Bates
Weasner Ada F, domestic 521 High
Weaver Ada, domestic 1400 Market
Weaver Angeline, h 1807 Market
Weaver Anna C, b s s Daisy 2 e Garden
Weaver Anna F, student, b 1807 Market
Weaver Barbara [wid George], h s s Daisy 2 e Garden
Weaver Ella J, teacher, b 1807 Market
Weaver George W [Anna D], condr Panhandle, h 714 e Wabash av
Weaver Isaac [Elmira], lab, h 1231 Erie av
Weaver John [Hannah], lab, h 1526 George
Weaver Mary A, b 1807 Market
Weaver Robert B, mach Panhandle, b 1807 Market
Weaver Wm B [Ida M], fireman Panhandle, h 403 Helm
Webb Albert E, student, b n s Howard 3 w Anthony (S T)
Webb Cinthelia [wid Charles], b n s Howard 3 w Anthony (S T)
Webb Mary J [wid Nathaniel], b 1116 Market
Webb Mollie E, bkkpr J H Foley, b 1128 High
Webb Nelson, truckman Vandalia, b n s Howard 3 w Anthony (S T)
Webb Wiley, lab, b n s Howard 3 w Anthony (S T)
Weber Henry [Frances] The Leading Tailor. Best goods at lowest prices. 324 Pearl, h 1 State
Weber Lorena, b 1 State
Weber Otto F, clk Panhandle, b 1 State
Weber Wm G, fireman Panhandle, r 111 4th
Webster Charles M [Alice], patrolman, h 2106 Spear
Webster George N [Rose M], drayman H J Crismond, h 212 Brown
Webster John P, jeweler 307 Market, h same
Webster Weldon, b 307 Market
Wecht Adam [Elizabeth], clk, h 414 First
Wecht Anna, domestic 514 Market
Wecht Charles L [Elizabeth R], merchant policeman, h 413 2d
Wecht Edward A, lab, b 414 First
Wecht Elizabeth [wid Jacob], domestic 614 North
Wecth George, lab, b 430 North
Wecht George J [Mary], bartender Peter Castle, h 516 Linden av
Wecht Leonard [Alice], clk Panhandle, h 1725 Spear
Wecht Lizzie M, b 414 First
Wecht Martha, b 1725 Spear
Weckfus Conrad [Lena], lab, h 630 Chicago
Weckfus Emma, domestic 1004 Market
Weckfus Mary, wks Marshall's Steam Laundry, b 630 Chicago
Weckfus Peter [May], lab, h 54 College
Wedekind Charles, tmstr, r 103 6th
Wedekind Eugene [Angeline], boiler mkr h 300 Cummings
Weeden Bert, b 606 Michigan av
Weeden Seth [Frances], carp, h 606 Michigan av

Wefel Emma C, bkkpr N R Frazee, b 129 w Broadway
Wefel John W [Eliza W], carp 129 w Broadway. h same
Wehling Wm C [Ada L], mach Panhandle, h 1727 George
Weible Frederick, switchtender, r 407½ Market
Weidmeier (see also Witmeyer and Witemyre
Weidmeier Frank, truckman Panhandle, b 210 College
Weidmeier Lena, domestic, b 210 College
Weidmeier Margaret, domestic, b 210 College
Weidmeier Mary, domestic, b 210 College
Weidmeier Wm, student, b 210 College
Weidmeier Wm T [Mary], car sealer Panhandle, h 210 College
Weigand Carrie, b 613 Miami
Weigand George, baker r 508 Broadway
Weigand Henry, mason, h 613 Miami
Weigand Lizzie, seamstress, b 613 Miami
Weigand Mary, b 613 Miami
Weimer Paul E, student, b 527 Sycamore
Weirick (see also Wirick)
Weirick Eliza [wid Henry], h 1 Wheatland
Weise (see also Wiese and Wise)
Weise Carl [Theresa], tailor, h e s Park av 5 s Helm
Weise Mary [wid Theodore], h 1513 Smead
Weise Peter E [Minnie], condr Panhandle, h 1128 High
Weise Wm E, engr, b 1513 Smead
Weisenburger Elizabeth [wid Daniel], h 628 13th
Weisenburger John [Mary], lab, h 1331 Wright
Weisenburger Peter [Elizabeth], engr Panhandle, 822 17th
Weisenstein Leonard, sol Metropolitan Life Ins Co, b 511 Canal
Weiss Charles L [Anna M], lab, h 706 Melbourne av
Welch (see also Walsh Welsch and Welsh)
Welch Adeline [wid John], h 1604 Douglass
Welch Andrew [Bridget], grocer 522 Broadway, h 1007 High
Welch Catherine G, teacher, b 1414 Broadway
Welch Dora, student, b 1519 Broadway
Welch Edward R [Anna], drayman, h 1423 Broadway
Welch George W, switchman Panhandle, h 1519 Broadway
Welch George W, b 522½ Broadway
Welch Hannah, b 1309 Indiana
Welch Henry, drayman, b 417 13th
Welch James, lab, b 1309 Indiana
Welch John [Ellen], lab, h 710 14th
Welch John [Emma C], saloon 425 12th, h same
Welch John F [Hannah M], brakeman Panhandle, h 1827 Spear
Welch Margaret, domestic 313 9th
Welch Mary, b 1309 Indiana
Welch Mary A, bkkpr J D Ferguson & Jenks, b 1414 Broadway
Welch Michael F, pressman, b 1414 Broadway

IERZ, The Tailor

409 MARKET STREET.

Our Motto:

FAIR TREATMENT
TO ALL.

ʹEL   265   WES

ʹelch Patrick [Johanna], lab, h 1309 Indiana
ʹelch Sarah, student, b 1414 Broadway
ʹelch Thomas H [Johanna], mach Panhandle, h 525 11th
ʹelch Thomas J [Elizabeth], blksmth Panhandle, h 1414 Broadway
ʹelch Walter F, caller Panhandle, b 1309 Indiana
ʹellborn Meek, attendant Insane Hospital, b same
ʹelling Wm, fireman Insane Hospital, b same
ʹells, Fargo & Co's Express, Joseph L Linvill agt, 320 Pearl
ʹells James K [Martha E], lab, h e s Treen 3 s Norcross
ʹells John W, student, b e s Treen 3 s Norcross
ʹells Nellie J, seamstress, b e s Treen 3 s Norcross
ʹells Richard [Elizabeth], engr Vandalia, h 223 Sycamore
ʹelsch (see also *Walsh, Welch and Welsh*)
ʹelsch Charles, painter, b 406 Railroad
ʹelsch Frank [Lizzie], painter, h 406 Railroad
ʹelsch Julia, domestic 412 Melbourne av
ʹelsch Lizzie A, domestic 521 Helm
ʹelsh (see also *Walsh, Welch and Welsch*)
ʹelsh Marion, lineman Wabash, r 302 North
ʹelsh Mary A, wks Marshall's Steam Laundry, b 1209 Toledo
ʹelsh Thomas F [M Anna], clk H Wiler & Co, h 112 w Wabash av
ʹelsh Timothy [Bridget], h 518 Canal
ʹemple Wm J [Tillie M], flour and feed 204 6th, h 2302 High
ʹentz Louis E, fireman Panhandle, b Island View Hotel
ʹenzel Amil, porter Baker's European Hotel, b same
ʹenzel Anna, b 216 Pratt
ʹenzel Wm, car rep Panhandle, b 514 12th
ʹermess Frank A, painter, b 600 w Broadway
ʹermess Helen L, domestic 606 Market
ʹermess Margaret [wid John B], h 600 w Broadway
ʹermess Mary A, domestic, 1202 Market
ʹermess Theresa, domestic 627 Market
ʹerner (see also *Warner*)
ʹerner Ada, b s s Bartlett 2 e Kloenne (S T)
ʹerner Amy, b s s Bartlett 2 e Kloenne (S T)
ʹerner Orlando M [Sarah], plasterer, h s s Bartlett 2 e Kloenne (S T)
ʹertheim Julius [Fannie], cigar mkr, h 116 Canal
ʹertz Peter, lab, h e s Dakota 2 n Bates (Dunkirk)
ʹesley Watson, carp, r 203½ 6th
ʹest Abner J, comp, The Reporter b 131 Wheatland
ʹest Rev Abraham L [Emma], h 525 Chicago
ʹest Elizabeth A [wid Dewitt], h 1010 Broadway
ʹest Elizabeth B [wid Thomas], h 131 Wheatland
ʹest George F [Eliza E], meat cutter McCaffrey Bros, h 209½ 6th
ʹest Harry G, waiter, b 131 Wheatland
ʹest James A, lawyer 212½ 4th, b 514 e Wabash av
ʹest John [Emma], bicycle rep, h 1708 Spear

West Miner, bkkpr, b 1010 Broadway
West Sadie, b 131 Wheatland
West Shirley, b 131 Wheatland
Westergreen Axtel, lineman Wabash, r 302 North
Westerman Bessie C, student, b 1405 Broadway
Westerman Claude H, student, b 1405 Broadway
Westerman George [Addie M], grocer, 1401 Broadway, h 1405 same
Western Union Telegraph Co, Philip Duesner mgr 419 4th
Westeweller George [Mary], mach hd J W Henderson & Sons, h 317 Ottawa
Westeweller Jacob, pipeman hose co no 3, b 611 north
Wetherow Homer, student, b 515 14th
Wetherow Irene, b 515 14th
Wetherow Olive [wid George], h 515 14th
Weymer George H [Dollie], lab D & C Uhl, h 52 Front
Weymer Eliza [wid Charles], b 52 Front
Whalen John, barber, b 715 Bringhurst
Whalen Michael [Ida], switchman, h 1014 Toledo
Wharfield George A, mattress mkr rear 314 Pearl, r 425½ 5th
Wharfield Wm H [Marietta], furniture 419 Market, h 619 North
Wharfield Wm M, student Hall's Business College, b 619 North
Wheatland Street M E Church, Rev Jacob K Walts pastor n e cor Wheatland and Barron
Wheaton Albert L, lab, b 20 Melbourne av
Wheaton Hattie [wid Charles], h 20 Melbourne av
Wheeldon Ada L, b 311 Bates
Wheeldon Everley [Louisa], huckster, h 311 Bates
Whinnery Joseph [Nettie], engr Panhandle, h 830 12th
Whipple Hattie, domestic w s Berkley 1 s Spencer
Whipple Wm, lab, b s w cor Howard and Frank (S T)
Whipple Wm, condr Vandalia, b 321 Sycamore
White Abbie, domestic 412½ 3d
White Catherine [wid James] laundress, h 600 Ottawa
White Dessie D, b 117 Melbourne av
White Edward [Belle], carp, h 216 Colfax
White Edward C [Rose], carp, h Biddle Island
White Ellen [wid John], h 407 Canal
White Frank H, stripper, b Biddle Island
White George, baggageman Panhandle, r 111 4th
White Harry S, student Hall's Business College, b 209 w Broadway
White Henry [Barbara], h 209 w Broadway
White Hiram, train desp Panhandle, b 209 w Broadway
White House Clothiers, The, Wm Grace & Co, 316 Market
White Jennie V, wks Naiben's Laundry, h Burlington rd 2 mi s city
White John Z [Ellen L], foreman Panhandle, h Gebhart 5 m n w city
White Kate, teacher, b 209 w Broadway
White C Robert, insp Logansport M Tel Co, b Island View Hotel

White Wm A [Catharine], car insp Panhandle, h 729 17th
Whitehead Herbert, porter Hotel Johnston, b same
Whitehead James E, cook Hotel Johnston, b same
Whitehead Wm C [Mary], plumber A W Stevens, h 1801 Market
Whitesell O Clinton [Sarah], pipeman hose co no 4, h 1608 North
Whitfield Richard [Anna], sawyer, h 1827 Toledo
Whitmore Stephen [Mary] (S Whitmore & Son), h 1516 Spear
Whitmore S & Son (Stephen and William), carpenters 1516 Spear
Whitmore Wm H (S Whitmore & Son), h 1516 Spear
Whitney Charles E, agt Metropolitan Life Ins Co, b Logan House
Whitsett Robert B [Anna C], sewing machines 529 Broadway, h same
Whittaker Elizabeth J, b w Standley 3 s Biddle (S T)
Whittaker Fannie, domestic, b w s Standley 3 s Biddle (S T)
Whittaker Nellie M, teacher, b 420 10th
Whittaker Richard, road supervisor, h w s Standley 3 s Biddle (S T)
Wide Awake Grocery, The, Charles W Traut propr, "Always up to
    Date," 420 Market (See adv front cover)
Widgeon Charles L, b 815 Linden av
Widgeon Edith M, b 815 Linden av
Widgeon Wm E [Jessie M], foreman Vandalia shops, h 815 Linden av
Wiese (*see also Weise and Wise*)
Wiese August [Elizabeth], tailor P J Hooley, h s s Charles 4 w
    Wabash R R (S T)
Wiese Mary, b 1429 Indiana
Wikle Charles W, trav agt, b Hotel Johnston
Wilch Arvilla M, mach opr W D Craig, b 201 College
Wild John H, finisher J W Henderson & Sons, b 19 16th
Wild Robert [Elizabeth], carp Panhandle, h 19 16th
Wilder Ozine, b 301 Melbourne av
Wilder Thomas E, distributing clerk post office, r 114 4th
Wiler Carl, student, b 606 Market
Wiler Clara, b 604 Market
Wiler Henry [Rosetta] (Henry Wiler & Co), h 604 Market
Wiler H & Co (Henry Wiler, Max J Fisher), carpets, oil cloths, wall
    paper and window shades 328-330 Broadway (See adv p 15)
Wiler Joseph [Clara] (Wiler & Wise), h 606 Market
Wiler & Wise (Joseph Wiler, Solomon Wise), proprs The Busy Bee
    Hive Dry Goods Store 409-411 Broadway and 306 4th (See adv
    left top lines)
Wiley Hiram C [Mary], h 20 Front
Wilken John B [Julia A], trav agt, h 310 3d
Wilken Wm L, student Hall's Business College, b 310 3d
Wilkin George A [Caroline E], carp, h 112 Franklin
Wilkin Ira A, lab, b 112 Franklin
Wilkin Mary F, b 112 Franklin
Wilkins Louis G, student, b 306 4th
Wilkins Zola [wid Lee], dressmkr 306 4th, h same

Wilkinson Frank P [Catharine], mach, h 417 17th
Wilkinson Hannah, domestic n s Howard 1 w Anthony (S T)
Wilkinson James [Mary], janitor, h 1825 North
Wilkinson Mary, b 1329 North
Wilkinson Miles, student, b 1825 North
Wilkinson Nellie, clk, b 1329 North
Wilkinson Wm H [Susan L] engr, h 1329 North
Willcuts Nellie, dressmkr 408½ Market, h same
Willette Rae, student, b 813 North
Willey Henry C [Carrie], trav agt, h 510 Melbourne av
Williams Addie, boarding 400 High
Williams Albert [Sarah], lab, h 1305 e Wabash av
Williams Albert S [Jennie], contractor 505 Sycamore, h same
Williams Andrew J [Josephine], lab, h 906 Race
Williams Anna, domestic 817 Linden av
Williams Arthur, plasterer, b 221 Montgomery
Williams Bert, lab, b 221 Montgomery
Williams Bird, lather, b 1413 George
Williams Catharine P [wid Wesley], dressmkr, h n e cor 6th and Hanna
Williams Charles, student, b 906 Race
Williams Charles F, student, b 313½ 4th
Williams David E, lab, b 25 Washington
Williams Eden E [Ione], plasterer 1408 Market, h same
Williams Florence C [wid Addison], b 106 9th
Williams Frank, clk, b 906 Race
Williams Frank [Addie], bartender, h 400 High
Williams Frank [Antonia], driver Maxinkuckee Ice Co, h 52 College
Williams George, b 1413 George
Williams Harvey [Eva], engr Panhandle, h 1601 Market
Williams Ida, b 906 Race
Williams Isaac [Elmira A], lab, h 25 Washington
Williams James E, lab, h w s Sycamore 1 s Pleasant Hill
Williams Jerome M [Alvira], plasterer, h 1413 George
Williams Jesse, lab, b 510 13th
Williams John, clk, b 510 13th
Williams John E [Helen C], junk dealer, h 221 Montgomery
Williams John W [Emma], barber, h 2 Canal
Williams Lizzie, attendant Insane Hospital, b same
Williams Margaret, domestic, b 510 13th
Williams Myrtle, domestic, b 221 Montgomery
Williams Richard [Mary], carp, h s s Bartlett 3 e Frank (S T)
Williams Susan F [wid James F], dressmkr 313½ 4th, h same
Williams Wm S, student Hall's Business College, b 104 Osage
Williams Wm W [Mary A], clk F W Kinney, h 510 13th
Williamson Amanda [wid John A], b 913 Market
Williamson Clara, artist 1429 Broadway, b same
Williamson Frank M [Flora], engr Panhandle, h 1413 High

Williamson George [Lydia A], carp, h 705 Miami
Williamson Horatio G [Alice], (Williamson & Gregg), h 408 Nort
Williamson Jane M [wid David M], h 1429 Broadway
Williamson John [Margaret], engr Panhandle, h 2011 Market
Williamson Joseph S [Rachael], farmer, h 1701 High
Williamson Martha, teacher, b 1429 Broadway
Williamson Mary, teacher, b 1429 Broadway
Williamson Mary A, artist, 913 Market, b same
Williamson Mary J [wid Moses T], b 1730 North
Williamson May, dressmkr, 410 North, h same
· Williamson Mollie, wks Marshall's Steam Laundry, b 313 n 6th
Williamson Nellie, student, b 1429 Broadway
Williamson Rebecca [wid Horatio], h 410 North
Williamson Stuart, student Hall's Business College, b 1429 Broa‹
way
Williamson & Gregg, (Horatio G Williamson, Wm H Gregg) saloc
201 6th
Willis Adrian D, student, b 921 High
Willis Lucy R, b 921 High
Willis Nancy [wid Samuel C], b 921 High
Willis Wm [Nancy], lab, h 1515 George
Wilson Albert H [Adelia F], lab, h 700 Chicago
Wilson Arthur V, attendant Insane Hospital, b same
Wilson A Belle, dressmkr, b 120 Pratt
Wilson Byron [Gracia E], painter, 401½ Broadway h same
Wilson Calvin, condr Vandalia, b 321 Sycamore ·
Wilson Charles A, student Hall's Business College, b 414 North
Wilson J Charles, b 202 Broadway
Wilson Cyrus [Ella], engr Panhandle, h 1730 Market
Wilson Elizabeth, h 529 Market
Wilson Elizabeth E [wid Thomas H], h 202 Broadway
Wilson Ella, domestic 1417 Spear
Wilson Ellwood G [Mary F], lawyer 206½ 4th also secy King Dri
Co, h 212 Broadway
Wilson Everet, brakeman Panhandle, b 1400 Spear
Wilson Frank [Addie], switchman Panhandle, h 1415 Broadway
Wilson Frank N, agt, b 416 18th
Wilson S Freeman, student, b 212 Broadway
Wilson Harrison H [Mary A], cabinet mkr, h 106 Bates
Wilson W Harvey [Lois J], clk Panhandle, h 416 18th
Wilson Henry H [Mary A], cabinet mkr, h 106 Bates
Wilson Hiram [Laura], lab, h 1608 Toledo
Wilson Ida, b 627 Miami
Wilson Ira G [Julia A], grocer 423 15th, h 1426 Spear
Wilson James F [Elizabeth], truckman Panhandle, h 1304 Wright
Wilson John [Jennie], engr Panhandle, h 1400 Spear
Wilson Maria [wid Samuel M], b 1426 Spear

lson Martha A [wid Wm W], h 416 North
lson Myrtle, b 529 Market
lson Myrtle, b 715 Race
lson Nancy A [wid Wm M], b 123 7th
lson Newton, houseman, h 120 Pratt
lson Perry W [Jane], plasterer 508 Sycamore, h same
lson Raymond, comp Longwell & Cummings, b 1400 Spear
lson Rose, laundress The Barnett, b 327½ Pearl
lson Thomas H [Orpha M] (Wilson, Humphreys & Co), secy The
  Home Music Co, h 200 Eel River av
lson Thurzah [wid Leonard], b 508 Sycamore
lson Walter F [Maude M], house painter, sign writer, paper
  hanger and decorator 212 6th, h 706 Race
lson Wendell, student, b 1730 Market
lson Wm, carp, b 616 Michigan av
lson Wm T [Martha L], lawyer 206½ 4th, also vice pres First National Bank, h 514 Market
lson Wm W [Ella P], trav agt, h 1209 Market
lson, Humphreys & Co (Thomas H Wilson, Robert Humphreys),
  printers 200 4th
ndisch Frank G [Mary], condr Panhandle, h 1924 George
negardner Earl S, clk, b 121 State
negardner Rev Wm Y [Esther], evangelist, h 121 State
nemiller Robert A [Flora], engr Panhandle, h 1722 Spear
nfield Maurice [Jennie M] (Winfield & Winfield), h 719 Market
nfield Maurice J [Abbie] (Winfield & Winfield), also pres The
  Bridge City Construction Co, b 719 Market
nfield & Winfield (Maurice and Maurice J), lawyers 400½ Broadway
nger John M [Samantha], rd supervisor Panhandle, h 305 Helm
nklebleck Amanda, h 313½ Pearl
nklebleck Bessie, bkkpr The Reporter, b 313½ Pearl
nklebleck Grace, opr Logansport M Tel Co, b 313½ Pearl
nklebleck Nancy [wid Samuel], b 1815 Broadway
nn Mattie, h 1801 Spear
nnie Wm P [Minnie], switchman, h 730 Miami
nquist Adolph, clk, b 1507 Spear
nquist Leontina, student, b 1507 Spear
nquist Leopold, lab, b 1507 Spear
nquist Marie [wid John], h 1507 Spear
nsch John [Mary A], shoemkr 326 Pearl, h 712 Race
nsell George [Eliza], carp Panhandle, h 1705 Spear
nsell Martha, b 1705 Spear
nslow Arthur G, cook, b 200 Cicott
nslow Elwood T [Sarah L], barber, h 200 Cicott
nslow Guerney F, barber H B Turner, b 200 Cicott
nslow Jessie E, student, b 200 Cicott

H. J. GRISMOND, 312 Market Street
All Kinds of Metal Roofing.

Winslow Maude E, b 200 Cicott
Winslow Wm P [Josephine], barber 103½ Sycamore, h 930 Linden av
Winter J Burt, clk Elias Winter, b 720 Linden av
Winter Cora C, teacher, b 720 Linden av
Winter Elias [Mary E], boots, shoes and slippers 510 Broadway, h 720 Linden av
Winters Albert lab, b 400 High
Winters Andrew [Mary], lab, h 106½ n 6th
Winters Gertrude, b 106 8th
Winters John B [Ruth A], shoes 324 Market also city clerk, h 106 8th
Winters John R, tailor W D Craig, b 218 Brown
Winters Wilbur D, student, b 106 8th
Winters Wm R [Mary], lab, h 1819 Toledo
Wipperman Charles [Elizabeth], h s w cor Howard and Anthony (S T)
Wipperman Frank H [Clara B], abstracts and loans 206 4th, h 160 North
Wipperman Henry [Maria], h 222 13th
Wirebaugh Dora E, dressmkr, 922 North, h same
Wirick (*see also Weirick*)
Wirick Guy, student, b 128 w Market
Wirick N Maude, b 501 w Broadway
Wirick Washington L, staple and fancy grocer 217 Cicott, h 501 w Broadway
Wirick Winfield S [Lizzie], fireman, h 128 w Market
Wirth August [Magdalene] lab, h 316 w Broadway
Wirwahn Andrew [S Belle], patrolman, h 56 College
Wise (*see also Weise and Wiese*)
Wise Adam, b 415 Miami
Wise Carl S, supt Wiler & Wise, b 805 Market
Wise Claude O [Lotta B], clk Dewenter & Co, h 913 North
Wise Edward H, shoemkr Elias Winter, b 415 Miami
Wise George, painter, b 1509 George
Wise Ida C, student Hall's Business College, b 1721 High
Wise Ira A, b 206 Washington
Wise John H [Agnes], shoemkr 4 Front, h 415 Miami
Wise James H [Margaret], carp 206 Washington, h same
Wise L Maud, teacher, b 206 Washington
Wise Mollie, b 805 Market
Wise Philippine [wid Aaron], h 1721 High
Wise Solomon [Caroline], (Wiler & Wise,) h 805 Market
Wisner Abraham, lab, b s s Wab river rd 7 w 18th
Witmeyer (*see also Witemyre and Weidmeier*)
Witmeyer Joseph, coachman 906 Broadway
Witemyre John H [Winona], pianos 118 4th, h same
Wolf Adam A [Frances], mason, h s s Shultz 1 e Kloenne (S T)
Wolf Albert B, attendant Insane Hospital, b same
Wolf Arthur J, b 76 Bates

Wolf Bessie, dressmkr 116 Osage, b same
Wolf Catharine [wid Henry], h 1313 Wright
Wolf Charles, stone mason, b 1313 Wright
Wolf Daniel, student Hall's Business College, b 308 w Market
Wolf Edward, driver, b 1313 Wright
Wolf Harry, lab, b 712 13th
Wolf Henry J [Lena M], contractor 76 Bates, h same
Wolf Jesse [Myrtle] lab, h 1704 Knowlton
Wolf John [Mary], stone mason, h 712 13th
Wolf John A, supervisor Insane Hospital, b same
Wolf Joseph [Elizabeth], stone mason, h 827 17th
Wolf Kate J, b 76 Bates
Wolf Leonard J [Mary], saloon 317 Sycamore, h 16 Columbia
Wolf Rebecca [wid Jacob], h 701 Clifton av
Wolf Sadie, b 712 13th
Wolf Samuel J H [Lanche], clk, h 1203 High
Wolfe Albert, harnessmkr Kreis Bros, b 521 High
Wolfe Elizabeth J [wid Wm L], b 630 North
Wolfe Sarah E, h 116 Osage
Woll Charles L [Mary A], undertaker and embalmer 417 Market, h 1400 North, (See adv p 7)
Woll Lottie, b 128 Sycamore
Woll John F [Rilla], upholsterer Panhandle, h 519 Ottawa
Wolpert Alonzo, lab, h 828 Linden av
Wolter S August, tailor, P J Pierce, b 828 Linden av
Wood Charles A, trav agt Schuyler Powell, h Kentland Ind
Wood George A, molder, b 622 Ottawa
Wood Harry A, student, b 821 High
Wood John B [Jane], baker 4 w Market, h 1330 High
Wood John R, clk, b 1330 High
Wood John Y [Louise B], chief clk Panhandle frt office, h 821 High
Wood Thomas [Margaret], tinner H J Crismond, h 19 Horney
Wood Zilla, b 1630 High
Woodhouse Daniel [Siner], county commissioner, h Adams Township (Twelve Mile P O)
Woodhouse George, bridge carp, b n e cor Canal and Oak
Woodling Frank E [Clara], tel opr Panhandle, h 1418 Spear
Woodling George, carp, b 700 Bringhurst
Woodruff Harriet [wid John], h 222 State
Woodruff Lawrence G [Emma], engr Panhandle, h 1323 George
Woodruff Nannie B, dressmkr, b 222 State
Woodside Jonathan A [Susan], h 305 Montgomery
Woodward James [Mary], h 1817 George
Woolman Lewis, brakeman Vandalia, b 321 Sycamore
Wooster Elizabeth, waiter, b 7 Biddle's Island
Wooster Jacob, waiter, b 7 Biddle's Island
Wooster John [Caroline], lab, h 121 Cicott

Worley Levi A [May E], carp, h w s Lobelia 2 n Pink
Wormer Jacob H, lab, b 1517 Wright
Worstell M Benjamin [L Belle], granite letterer S Powell, h 1916 Spear
Worstell Charles W, comp, b 1829 North
Worstell Dora, attendant Insane Hospital b same
Worstell Elmer E, photographer, b 1829 North
Worstell Ida, b 1829 North
Worstell Sarah S [wid Otis P], h 1829 North
Wray (see also *Ray* and *Rea*)
Wray Anna, domestic, 1119 Broadway
Wright Amos, brakeman Panhandle, r 614 Market
Wright Arthur W [Alice], ship clk Bridge City Candy Co, h 225 w Broadway
Wright Bertram L [Pearl R], fireman Vandalia, h 1115 Linden av
Wright Bessie G, student, b 202 Bates
Wright Blanche, cigarmkr, b w s Anthony 1 n Wabash R R (S T)
Wright Charles b w s Anthony 1 n Wabash R R (S T)
Wright Edna, b 2025 North
Wright Ernest [Mary], switchman Panhandle, h 212 Berkley
Wright Etta B, b 1215 Broadway
Wright Fannie [wid Charles P], h 1425 Market
Wright Fay, student, b 2025 North
Wright Frank D [Anna M], tinner, h 433 Michigan av
Wright Harry L, clk T A Spry, b w s Anthony 1 n Wabash R R (S T)
Wright Harry T, deputy county recorder, b 2025 North
Wright Harvey W [Etta M], fireman Panhandle, h 212 7th
Wright Herbert M, confectioner, also ice cream parlors 315 Pearl, b 719 Bringhurst (See adv p 6)
Wright Jacob W, county recorder, h 2025 North
Wright John J [Emma E], foreman, h 202 Bates
Wright Julia [wid Reuben], b 225 w Broadway
Wright, Lora, cigarmkr, b w s Anthony 1 n Wabash R R (S T)
Wright Mary A [wid Wm H], boarding 522½ Broadway
Wright Mary E, domestic s w cor State and Wilkinson
Wright Minerva J [wid Jackson P], b 1418 Market
Wright Nancy A [wid Wm], h w s Anthony 1 n Wabash R R [S T]
Wright Robert [Barbara], carp, h 1516 Wright
Wright Wiley [Christine], lab, h 421 Coles
Wright Wm, lab, b n w cor Market and Holland
Wright Wm A, student, b 202 Bates
Wright Wm T, engr Columbia Brew Co, h 1418 Market
Wright Williamson S, pres Logansport Journal Co, r 400½ Broadway
Wunderlay Christena, mach opr W D Craig, b 122 Pawnee
Wunderlay Emma, h 122 Pawnee
Wunderlay John L, bookbinder Longwell & Cummings, b 122 Pawnee
Wunderlay Margaret, dressmkr 122 Pawnee, b same

SUPRPLUS of the METROPOLITAN LIFE
at the end of 1896, over ☞ $5,000,000
Number of Claims Paid During Year, 63,909

WUN	274	YOU

Wunderlich James [Angeline], sawyer, h 1306 Spear
Wunderlich Mary, student, b 1306 Spear
Wusham Joseph, condr Vandalia, r 315 Sycamore
Wyatt Wm H [Alice M], carp, h 201 Wheatland
Wynkoop Wm [Margaret], lab, h s s Standley 3 e Clifton av

Y

Yager Joseph [Mary], stone mason, h 219 Osage
Yager Martha, domestic 720 15th
Yarbro Florence, waiter, b 324 Sycamore
Yarbro Francis B [Sarah E], restaurant 324 Sycamore, bicycles 128
    6th, h 324 Sycamore
Yarbro Lloyd O, clk, b 324 Sycamore
Yarbro Roy F, student Hall's Business College, b 324 Sycamore
Yarlott Charles E, bkkpr The J T Elliott Co, r 630 North
Yates Angeline [wid Thomas], h 1100 Spear
York Arthur M [Hattie], painter 213 College
York George, engr Insane Hospital, b same
York Howard H [Mary], chief engr Insane Hospital, b same
York Phoebe [wid Lewis], b 213 College
Yost see Jost
Young Albert T, tailor 304½ Market, b 614 Market
Young Alta R, dressmkr, b 614 Market
Young Arthur B, truckman Panhandle, b 24 Montgomery
Young Augustus L, truckman Panhandle, b 24 Montgomery
Young California [wid Augustus], h 24 Montgomery
Young Carrie E, dressmkr 614 Market, b same
Young Charles B [Sadie F], harness 306 Market, h 629 High
Young Charles H. clk Hotel Johnston, b same
Young Clarence H, bkkpr, b 1911 George
Young Dell W, r 96 Eel River av
Young Dora, b 1717 High
Young Edith A, student, b 200 Bates
Young George W [Elva], drayman, h 1708 Spear
Young John A [Vesta A], carp, h 509 Ottawa
Young John W [Ida], h 1911 George
Young Joseph W, carp, b 509 Ottawa
Young Julia A [wid John J] b 509 Ottawa
Young Mamie, b 1911 George
Young Mens' Christian Association, A Clinton Davisson genl secy,
    410 Canal
Young Orbie, porter Insane Hospital, b same
Young Susan E [wid Alexander], h 614 Market
Young Wendelin, clk Vincent Kardes, b 314 3d

Youngker David A [W Name] (D A Youngker & Co), h 44 Front
Youngker D A & Co (David A Youngker, Jacob P Sebastian), cigar mnfrs 225 4th
Youngker John [Minnie], trimmer I N Cool, h 525 Fitch
Youngker John, engr Panhandle, r 1069 Toledo

Z

Zahlbaum Michael [Emma], fine wine, beer, liquors and cigars 224 Market, h 403½ Market
Zahrt Walter G [Alice], steward Insane Hospital, h 214 14th
Zanger Louise, domestic 715 Market
Zartman Daniel K [Naomi], painter 930 High, h same
Zech August [Olga], car rep Panhandle, h 1721 George
Zech Rudolph [Augusta], clk I N Crawford, h 200 Wheatland
Zellers Joseph, boot black Sol H Cohn, r 529 Market
Zider George F [Mary A], tmstr, h e s Liberty 1 n Water
Zider Murl, student, b e s Liberty 1 n Water
Zider Stella M, b e s Liberty 1 n Water
Zimmerman Adolph [Otilda], lab, h 1503 Smead
Zimmerman Bernard [Louise], (Zimmerman & Scheu), h 1318 Wright
Zimmerman Jacob [Barbara], h 202 Colfax
Zimmerman Joseph [Catherine], mach hd Pan, h 1721 Knowlton
Zimmerman Mary [wid Frank], laundress, h n s Miami 1 e n 6th
Zimmerman Mary [wid Valentine], h 1425 Usher
Zimmerman Oliver A [Catharine], truckman Vandalia, h 601 Michigan av
Zimmerman & Scheu, (Bernard Zimmerman, John Scheu) meat mrkt 702 12th
Zinn J Halleck [Mildred], bkkpr A B Keeport & Co, b 1302 High
Zinn Orlando M [Ella], ins agt, h 415 Wilkinson
Zolt Anthony [Margaret], saloon, 312 Pearl h 701 Melbourne av
Zolt Anthony B, student, b 701 Melbourne av
Zolt Lena, b 701 Melbourne av
Zook Charles, painter, b 521 High
Zook Charles [Lizzie E], h 500 Michigan av
Zook Claude M, teacher, b 320 Michigan av
Zook Daniel [Euphemia], miller Logan Milling Co, h 320 Michigan av
Zorger Jacob F, condr Panhandle, b Island View Hotel
Zubler John [Agnes], lab, h 116 Ash

LONGWELL & CUMMINGS'
LOGANSPORT CITY DIRECTORY.

1897-98.

CLASSIFIED BUSINESS DIRECTORY.

Headings marked thus (*) are special, and are inserted only when specially contracted for.

Abstracts of Title

Markley John W, 214½ 4th
Velsey Seth M, 204 4th
Wipperman Frank H, 206 4th

Agricultural Implement Dealers

Barnett Benjamin F, 507 Broadway
Crawford Isaac N, 432 Broadway
Douglass James M, 228 5th
Kreis Bros Mfg Co, 414 Broadway
Ludders Richard, 415 3d
Penrose Joseph H, 126 6th
Place Willard, 500 North
Rumely M Co, John F Getty mgr,318 5th
Tucker Henry, 519-521 Market (*See adv back paster*)
Watts Daniel M, 126 6th (*See adv*)

*Agricultural Implement Mnfrs

Rumely M Co, John F Getty mgr,318 5th

. the Clerk
he Hotel for
• • • • • •

☆ **LAUNDRY LISTS.**

Work Done In 5 Hours
ITHOUT EXTRA CHARGE.

GEO. OTT, Propr.   405 Market Street.

BUSINESS DIRECTORY.   277

OSEPH E. CRAIN

PRACTICAL

RCHITECT

5 MASONIC TEMPLE

Is fully prepared to draw
Plans and Specifications of
Public Buildings and
Private Residences

Architects

n **Joseph E**, 4–5 Masonic Tem-
 (*See adv*)
les James H, 427½ Broadway

Architectural Iron Work

ansport Construction Co, 322
 (*See adv p 15*)

Artists

· Wils, 828 Sycamore
s John W, 310½ Market
s Clement V, 600½ Broadway
 Elizabeth de Bruyn, 413½ Broad-
 y
amson Clara, 1429 Broadway
amson Mary A, 913 Market

Artists' Materials

rhurst W H, 308 Market
ahn & Schneider, 308 4th (*See
 front cover*)
r Ben, 311 4th

Johnston John M, 400 Broadway
Keesling Benjamin F, 305 4th
Means Oscar A, 1228 Broadway
Porter Wm H, 330 Market
Pryor Daniel E, 516 Broadway

Attorneys at Law

(*See Lawyers*)

Auctioneers

Flanagan George W, 16 Michigan av
Foster John, n s John 1 e Creek

Awnings and Tents

Foglesong Daniel S, 212 6th (*see adv*)

Bakers—Retail

Bauer Frank, 10 Front
Dykeman Frederick A, 317 Market
Groh Frank M, 431 12th
Strecker George jr, 508 Broadway
Taggart & Johnson, 524–526 Broadway
Wood John B, 4 w Market

Bakers--Wholesale

Taggart & Johnson, 524-526 Broadway

*Bands and Orchestras

(*See also Miscellaneous Directory*)

Elite Mandolin Orchestra, Edgar E Powell mgr 505 Broadway (*See adv*)

Banks and Bankers

City National Bank, s w cor 4th and and Broadway

First National Bank, 314 4th (*See adv front cover*)

Forgy George B (Investment), 5 Baldwin-Thornton Bldg

Logansport State Bank, 401 Market

Miller Mark B, 310 Pearl

Parker & Rea, 223 6th

Penrose Harry, 305 Broadway

Reed Jacob, 110 Burlington av

Richeson & Stough, 1224 Broadway

Rush & Evans, 113 6th

Turner Horace B, 404 Broadway

Wall John H, 2 Sycamore

Winslow Wm 1, 103½ Sycamore

Baths

Brooks Lindsey G, 302 5th

Kraut Wm, 403 Market

Baths—Turkish

Lynas Wm T, 411½ 4th

Barbers

Anheier Jacob A, 418 3d

Brooks Lindsey G, 302 5th

Carter Frank J, 312 3d

Carter James A, 1 w Market

Culp Joseph M, 219 6th

Day Nicholas, 501 12th

Fornoff Michael F, 416 4th

Gillam Walter A, 431½ Sycamore

Harris & Jones, 313 Market

Hayworth Joseph C, 429 12th

Klein Charles U, 711 12th

Kohtz Edward, 318 Sycamore

Kohtz Harry A, 423 12th

Kraut Wm, 403 Market

Mabry George W, 515 Broadway

Malone Joseph, 321 Broadway

Marshall Charles D, 804 15th

Bicycle Dealers

Bringhurst Alfred T, 308 Market

Burgman Cycle Co, s e cor 5th and Market

Crawford Isaac N, 432 Broadway

Crismond Horace J, 312 Market (*See adv right top lines*)

Flanegin John T, 310 Market

Kreis Bros Mfg Co, 414 Broadway

Lewis Walter B, 523 Broadway

Lispenard Samuel J, 125 6th

Yarbro Francis B, 128 6th

Bicycle Repairers

Burgman Cycle Co, s e cor 5th and Market

Crawford Isaac N, 432 Broadway

Kreis Bros Mfg Co, 414 Broadway

Bill Poster

leiger Charles E, 215 6th

Billiard and Pool Rooms

rns James, 203 6th
sson W L & Co, 316 Broadway
tus Wm F, 428 Market
Kague James, 326 Broadway
ler Frank J, 302 Market
us Peter B, 315 Sycamore

acksmiths and Horseshoers

also Horseshoers)
derson Roland W, n w cor 18th and
tevens
cert Christian, 1 3d
liott J Martin, 318 3d (*See adv back
over*)
megan Arthur, rear 312 5th
bertbur & Knecht, s e cor 15th and
Erie av
iser Wm H, 2 Burlington av
yer John, 518 North
ler D R & Son, n w cor Erie av and
Berkley
gan John E, 205 6th
aefer George A, 506 North
ubach Frank, 51 Front
iver John B, 12 6th
ompson John M, 120 6th

Blank Book Mnfrs

ngwell & Cummings, Masonic
Temple

Boarding Houses.

ee Elizabeth, 418½ 3d
nett Susan M, 527 Broadway
ifield Asel O, n e cor Canal and Oak
riger Mary A 603 12th
mors Sarah, 1209 Toledo
Armand Sarah, 511 Canal
nkle Amy, 1124 Broadway
ch Martha G, 510 Market
ason M Jane, 528½ Broadway
tes Jennie B, 128 Pawnee
rshey Lottie E, 521 High
obs Lizzie G, 415½ 3d
ight Margaret, 1203 Toledo
rimer Cecelia A, 206 6th
mair Jacob R, 910 Lytle
ier Dora, 611 North
rrow Ellen F 216 3d
hols Alice J, 624 North
zel Louise M, 416 2d
kell Josephine, 426 12th

Pierce Florence J, 519 Fitch
Pitzer Margaret, 429 3d
Powell Maude, 500 Canal
Selby Julia, 1211 Toledo
Shipley George W, 730 North
Spacy Amanda, 1224 Wright
Sparrow Hattie, 310½ Broadway
Stuter Lydia J, 206 Canal
Williams Addie, 400 High
Wright Mary A, 522½ Broadway

Boiler Mnfrs

Grffith Thomas, 9 6th
McAllister A U & Sons, s e cor Elm and
Erie av

Book Binders

Longwell & Cummings, Masonic
Temple

Books and Stationery

(*See also Newsdealers*)
Bevan Carrie D, 406 Broadway
Cohn Sol H, 326 Market
Graves Charles W, 413 Broadway
Logansport Wall Paper Co, 407
Market (*See adv left top lines*)
Smith Bros, 318½ 4th

Boots and Shoes

Graflis Wm M, 312 4th
Greensfelder Aaron, n e cor 3d and
Market
Murdock Henry S, 408 Market
Otto Shoe and Clothing Co, The, 317-319
4th
Stevenson & Klinsick, 403 Broadway
Sweetser John Q, 328 Market
Walden Edwin M, 315 4th
Walker & Rauch, 420 Broadway
Winter Elias, 510 Broadway
Winters John B, 324 Market

Boot and Shoemakers

Berry Samuel H, 331 Sycamore
Burnett John, 104 Sycamore
Frese Frederick, 325 5th
Fries Peter, 201 5th
Helms Barnhard, 215 6th
Horning Charles, 507 Broadway
Jackson Andrew, 600 Canal
Martin Willard, 718 12th
Painton Joseph M, 121 Front
Prosch J Daniel, 427 12th
Renu Henry, 17 6th
Schloss Clemens, 53 Front

Boot and Shoemakers—Continued

Schuttrumpf John, 15 Biddle av
Slaybaugh John P, 417 12th
Smith Israel S, 216 6th
Stevens P Albert, 1432 Market
Tapp Frank, 1420 Wright
Winsch John, 326 Pearl
Winter Elias, 510 Broadway
Wise John H, 4 Front

Bottlers—Beer

Burgman & Bro, n e cor 15th and Smead
Columbia Brewing Co, n w cor 5th and High

Bottlers—Imported Wines

Kreuzberger Robert, s w cor 3d and Market and 413-415 3d (See adv p 4)

Bottlers—Mineral Water

Enyart & Chambers, 214 6th

Brewers

Columbia Brewing Co, n w cor 5th and High

Brewers' Agents

Appel Alexander, (Agt Peru Brewery) 1100 Toledo
Brockman Tandy S, (Agt Terre Haute Brewing Co) n end Vine
Burgman & Bro, (Agts Finlay Brewing Co) n e cor 15th and Smead
Schaefer Gottlieb, (Agt Indianapolis Brewing Co, 207 Cicott (see adv p 3)

*Brick Dealers

Dilley C L & Co, 515 Market (See adv) class Lime and Cement)

Brick Mnfrs

Barnes John E & Son, yards w s Clifton av s Noble tp line
Medland John & Sons, yards n Franklin bet Horney and Clifton av, office 98 Eel River av

Brokers—Grain and Provisions

Grafflin S D & Son, 415½ 4th
Milner Wm W, 324½ Market

Brokers—Investment

Sheerin S P & Co, 201 4th

Broom Mnfrs

Maxwell Wilson H, 415 Canal

*Builders' Hardware

Parker & Johnston, s e cor Berkley and Spencer (See adv front paster)

*Builders' Material

Dilley C L & Co, 515 Market (See adv class Lime and Cement)
Parker & Johnston, s e cor Berkley and Spencer (See adv front paster)
Voorhees Philip, 500 Sycamore (See adv p 7)

Building & Loan Associations

(See Miscellaneous Directory)

Business Colleges

Hall's Business College, n w cor 6th and Broadway
Michael's Business College, 310½ to 314½ Broadway

*Butterick's Patterns

Wiler & Wise, 409-411 Broadway and 306 4th (See adv left top lines)

Cabinet Makers

Smith Frederick, 15 6th

Carpenters, Contractors and Builders

(See also Contractors)
Benson John A, 2200 Broadway
Cook James A, 609 Chicago
Ferguson Sebastian C, 520 w Market
Graves Ezra B, s s Shultz 4 e Standley (S T)
Harris Joseph, 412 Vine
Hawley Wm H, 601 Ottawa
Hunter George W, rear 521 Broadway
Kale Nathaniel L 601 Sycamore
Kerns James C, 612 12th
Kerns Nathaniel, 1500 Water
Kilborn Lyman G J, 324½ 5th
Lewis Allen, 210 Burlington av (See adv p 15)
McIntyre Egbert E, 437 Michigan av
Miller John H, 1130 Toledo
Painton Wm W, rear 121 Front
Richardson Wm S, 1010 North
Sales Samuel, 1414 George

Carpenters, Contractors and Builders—Continued

Shaffer Andrew J, 18 Claude
Stalnaker Winfield S, College Hill, cor Frederick av and Royal Center Pike (See adv)
Stouffer Oliver J, 18 20 6th
Strock John H, 417½ 12th
Swallow John A, s s L & W rd 5 w Anthony
Teeple Samuel W, 511 Broadway
Thompson Lumber Co, n e cor 6th and High
Troutman & Cramer, 1730 North
Van Steenberg George, 1826 George
Vurpillat Constant, 409 Linden av
Wefel John W, 129 w Broadway
Whitmore S & Son, 1316 Spear
Williams Albert S, 505 Sycamore
Wise James H, 206 Washington
Woodling George, 700 Bringhurst

Carpet Cleaners

Montgomery Bros, 117 Burlington av

Carpet Weavers

Barron Jacob M, 429 5th
Binney Eva, 10 Columbia
Hamilton Mary, 1809 Spear
Hofferberth J Wm, 502½ Market
Hunter Sarah E, n e cor Cummings and Cecil
Johnson Mary E, 1224 Spear
Martin Martha E, 718 12th

Carpets, Oil Cloths, Etc

Frazee Moses R, 418 Broadway
Seybold George W & Bros, 319-321 Market
Wiler H & Co, 328-330 Broadway

Carriage Repositories

Kreis Bros Mfg Co, 414 Broadway
Smith Wm B, 308 5th
Tucker Henry, 519-521 Market (See adv back paster)
Watts Daniel M. 126 6th (See adv Agricultural Implements)

Carriage and Wagon Mnfrs

Aman Joseph A, 101 Burlington av
Boerger Frederick, s s Logan and Western Pike 1 w Burlington av
Cool Isaac N, s e cor 14th and Toledo
Harrison George, 617-623 Broadway
Holbruner & Uhl, n w cor Market and Eel River av
Sitz J August, 518 North

*Carriage and Wagonmakers' Supplies

Ullery S W & Co, 318 Market

*Ceilings—Steel

Eberlein C Augustus, 505 1 (See adv class Furnaces)

---

*Cement Contractors

(See also Contractors)
Barnes George, 219 Plum *(See adv)*

*Cement Works
Logansport Cement Works, w
Market opp Peoria Junction *(See adv. p 5)*

China Glass and Queensware
Dickerhoff Emma, 415 Broadway
Kardes Vincent, 314 Market
McCaffrey Bros, 410 Market and 600 Broadway
Oppenheimer Isaac mgr, 322 4th
Seybold George W & Bros, 319-321 Market
Snider & Alber, 414 Market
Traut Charles W, 420 Market *(See adv front cover)*

Chiropodists
Bailey Ranaldo A, 414 North
Ford Husber C, 413½ Broadway

Cigar Manufacturers
Alford L A & Son, 425 5th
Carter Charles E, 416 w Market
Closson W L & Co, 402½ Broadway
Denbo Harry, 504½ Broadway
Geiger Bros, 422 3d
Gippinger Henry G, 17 Ottawa
Hildebrandt Charles J, 616 12th
Mulcahy John, 324 Broadway
Pixler Frank J, 302 Market
Schaffer & Gammill, 2 w Market
(See adv)
Wagner Julius, 423 4th
Youngker D A & Co, 225 4th

*Cigars—Wholesale
Bridge City Candy Co, 303-305-307
3d *(See adv class Confectioners)*
Quigley T M & Co, 217 219 5th *(See adv class Confectioners)*

Cigars and Tobacco—Retail

(See also Druggists and Grocers)
Alcazar Cigar Co, 321 Broadway
Bush Wade H, 307 Broadway
Cohn Sol H. 326 Market
Geiger Bros, 422 3d
Klein Angeline 711 12th
Mader Harvey D, 406 4th
Morgan James. 427 12th
Mulcahy John, 324 Broadway
Pixler Frank J, 302 Market
Solimano Laurence. 421 Broadway
Schaffer & Gammill, 2 w Market
   (See adv Cigar Mnfrs)
Turner Horace B, 404 Broadway
Twells Richard, 417 Broadway
Wagner Julius, 423 4th
Walsh & Tyner, n e cor 2d and Market

Civil Engineers

Bridge City Construction Co,
   Biddle Island *(See adv p 4)*
Coleman Henry F, 322 3d
Rauch John D, 3 Pythian Castle

Clairvoyants

Epstine Mary E, 123 4th

*Cloaks and Shawls

Wiler & Wise, 409-411 Broadway and
   306 4th *(See adv left top lines)*

Clothiers

(See also Merchant Tailors)
Ferguson J D & Jenks 322 Market
Globe Clothing House n e cor 4th and
   Market
Grace Wm & Co, 316 Market
Greenstelder Eli. 315 Market
Helvie & Sellers, 426 Broadway
Hub Clothing Co, The 313 4th
Otto Shoe and Clothing Co, The 317-319
   4th

Clothing Manufacturers

Craig Wm D, 416 Broadway *(See adv
back cover)*

Coal and Wood

Dilley C L & Co, 515 Market *(See
adv class Lime and Cement)*
Jones Thomas, s w cor 9th and Erie av

Commission Merchants

Beatty DeWitt C, 417 5th
Kasch Charles C, 330 5th

Confectioners — Manufacturing

Bridge City Candy Co, 303-305-307
   3d *(See adv)*

Picnic Supplies a Specialty   303-305-307 THIRD ST.

284   BUSINESS DIRECTORY.

Confectioners — Manufacturing
—Continued

Quigley T M & Co, 218-219 5th (*See adv*)

Confectioners—Retail

(*See also Bakers*)
Binney B Frank, 121 6th
Burgman Wm, 3 Burlington av
McTaggart Lanta, 6 Sycamore

Rush & Evans, 113 6th
Solimano Laurence, 421 Broadway
Smith Thomas P, 323 Market
Wright Herbert M, 315 Pearl (*See adv p 6*)

Contractors

(*See also Carpenters, Contractors and Builders*)
Barnes George (cement), 219 Plum (*See adv Cement Contrs*)
Barnes Harry A (brick and stone), 1016 Linden av

Barnes John E & Son (brick), 228 Front
Bunker Herman (teamster), 101 Pratt
Bush David L (store), 117 7th
Butterworth Thomas (street), 1327 High
Cavin Thomas (brick and stone), 1628 Toledo
Corden Daniel (street) 900 17th
Ellison Michael H (street), 1417 Broadway
Ford & Hayworth (wells), 312 5th
Gallion Bros (cement), 724 Michigan av
Gleitze August (brick and stone), 415 w Market
Hausen Neils (teamster), 515 Broadway
Heitzmann George F (brick and stone), 1713 George
Hight Frank (stone), s s Charles 3 e Wab R R (S T)
Hupp Wm (excavation), 318 Linden av
Knight George (cement), 1203 Toledo
Logansport Construction Co (general), 322 3d (*See adv p 15*)
McDonald Archibald H (cement), 1400 Market
Medland John & Sons (brick), 98 Eel River av (*See adv p 15*)
Murray George (stone), 662 12th
Price Scott E (brick and stone), cor D and State
Redmond & Gibson (brick and stone), 912 North
Scott John R (ditch), 629 Chicago
Shafer Edward (excavation), 311 High
Twells Wyndham S (drayage), 309 Market
Uhl Elmore (cement), 113 Wheatland
Wolf Henry J (stone), 76 Bates
Wolf Leonard J (stone), 16 Columbia

Coopers

Torr Emily, cor 8th and Erie av

Cornice Manufacturers

Jennings Max, 316-318 5th

Coupon Manufacturers

Longwell & Cummings, Masonic Temple

Creameries

Logansport Creamery Co, s e cor Vine and Osage

Clover Leaf
Dairy

❋

JACOB G. MINNEMAN, Prop'r

Pure Milk and Cream

Our Milk is Strictly Pure, and can be fed to Infants and Children.

CITY ADDRESS:

Care General Delivery, Postoffice

DAIRY:

Asylum Road, one-half mile west of Cicott Street Bridge

Dairymen

Clover Leaf Dairy, Jacob G Minneman propr, Asylum rd ½ mi w Cicott st bridge (*See adv*)

Schaefer Frank, s s Columbia 1 e Sycamore

Sieber Wm D, Camp Chase, 1 n Davis bridge

*Dancing Teachers

Culp Joseph M, 219 6th

Dentists

Bozer Francis M, State Natl Bank Blk, s w cor 4th and Broadway

Cushman Henry C, 418½ Broadway

Delzell David E, 116½ Market

Eversole Charles D, 330½ Market

Grace Edward H, 316½ Market

Hunt Edgar S, 323½ 4th

Manlove Henry T, 401½ Broadway

Overholser Daniel L, 415½ Broadway

Shideler Wm D, 402½ Market

Taylor Edward R, 401½ Market

Directory Publishers

Longwell & Cummings, Masonic Temple

Dressmakers

Baldwin Lizzie, 117 Melbourne av

Barry Margaret, 1113 Toledo

Bazin Mary, 1523 North

Beach Dora, 1220 Smead

Beatty Emma, 1314 Linden av

Bischoff Emma A, 809 Race

Booker Callie E, 309½ 4th

Bowles Susan M, 1302 Broadway

Breckenridge Charlotte, 1105 Market

Brogan Susan, 227 College

Brownewell Della E, 403½ Broadway

Bryant Anna B, 514 Canal

Bryer Jennie, 830 Race

Burns Mary E, 310½ Market

Cooke Clemmie, 16 n 6th

Corden Mamie M, 900 17th

Dailey Mary E, 1314 Broadway

Driscoll K & M, 10 Washington

Dunham Ella A, 207 3d

Elliott Missouri, 101 4th

Emmett Harriet C, 1110 Spear

Englebrecht Mary 110 Pawnee

Farrell Josephine, 128 Canal

Ferguson Ada, 110 Sycamore

Fisher Mary, 206 Pratt

Fornoff Kate L, 416 4th

Foster Mary A, 1416 North

Garnatz Henrietta, 530 Miami

Green Emma, 816 Race

Grover Mary, 423 Canal

Hand Jeannette, 1210 Linden av

Hartman Dorothy, 311 Montgomery

Helvey Leora E, 112 Market

Hoffman Mary F, r 1 Barnes Blk

Hosmer Grace L, 1130 Linden av

Hubbard Sarah E, 524 North

Jacobus Libbie, 1726 North

Kearney Mary, 910 Broadway

Klein Etta, 1604 Spear

Long Helen D, 1126 Broadway

Long Lizzie M,   Pearl

McCarthy No: ·7¼ Broadway

McGaughey F,   h, 106 Sycamore

McTaggart A?   311 w Market

Michael Susan.   ifton av

Morrow Huld.   5 Market

Mummey Loui~   '1½ 4th

Nett Catherine 1, 911 Market

O'Mara Sadie J, 4 7 Wilkinson

Patton Flora, 820 Sycamore

Peters Elizabeth, 1220 Broadway

Price Margaret, 705 Miami

Puterbaugh Gertrude E, 413½ Broadway

Dressmakers—Continued

Roop Sisters, 719 Broadway
Schweistall Anna, 8 Uhl
Scott Nancy E, 2101 Market
Sell Flora, 511 14th
Shields Hattie, 1407 North
Shinn Margaret, 327 4th
Smith Jessie A. n e cor Linden av and n 4th
Smith Sarah, 318½ 4th
Smith S Lydia, 318½ Pearl
Stough Esther, 1109 North
Stover Myrtle, s s Bartlett 2 e Frank (S T)
Swallow Susan M, s s L & W rd 5 w Anthony
Swihart Phoebe A, 709 High
Sylvester Madge, 1114 Erie av
Troester Anna, 203 Osage
Tyner Caroline E, 925 Spear
Vigus Mary E, s w cor Main and Grove
Wagner Ida, 428 Burlington av
Wagoner Laura E, s e cor Treen and Norcross
Wallace Eliza M, 626 Linden av
Wallace Rebecca, 21 Washington
Watts Piny, 227 Pratt
Wilkins Zola, 306 4th
Willcuts Nellie, 408½ Market
Williamson May, 410 North
Wirebaugh Dora E, 922 North
Wolf Bessie, 116 Osage
Wunderlay Margaret, 122 Pawnee
Young Carrie E, 614 Market

*Driven Wells

Ford & Hayworth, 312 5th

Druggists

Bean Louis B, 409 12th
Bringhurst W H, 308 Market
Busjahn & Schneider, 308 4th (See adv front cover)
Closson Homer & Co, 506 Broadway
Coulson John F, 301 Market
Excelsior Mfg Co, 528 Broadway
Fishe Ben, 311 4th
Hoffmann George Wm, 321 4th
Johnston John M, 400 Broadway
Keesling Benjamin F, 305 4th
Means Oscar A, 1228 Broadway
Porter Wm H, 330 Market
Pryor Daniel E, 516 Broadway
Smith Hugh, 115 Sycamore

Dry Goods

Diamondstone Mendal, 424 Broadway
Frazee Moses R, 418 Broadway

Gray John, 323-325 4th
Kieszling Minnie, 102 Sycamore
Luther Narcissa C, 1431 Spear
Schmitt & Heinly, 329-331 Market
Seybold George W & Bros, 319-321 Market
Spry Thomas A, 427 429 Broadway, s e cor Pearl
Tanguy Samuel L, 407 Broadway
Wiler & Wise, 409-411 Broadway and 306 4th (See adv left top lines)

Dyers and Scourers

Krigbaum Bros, 429½ 4th
Logan Steam Dye Works, 608 Broadway
Middendorf Clemens, 520½ Market

Electrical Supplies

Blackford John W, 314 Pearl (See adv p 15)
Hildebrandt John J, 408 4th
Hughes Martin M, 324 5th (See adv back cover and class Plumbers)
Stevens Andrew W, 423 Market (See adv back fly leaf)

Elevators—Grain

Logan Milling Co. cor Erie av and Elm (See adv front cover)
Uhl D & C H, corner Front and Melbourne av

Engine Builders—Gas and Gasoline

Lambert Gas & Gasoline Engine Co, Will B Place agt, n e cor 5th and North (See adv p 8)

Engravers—Wood and Metal

Longwell & Cummings, Masonic Temple

*Etchings and Engravings

Logansport Wall Paper Co, 407 Market (See adv left top lines)

Express Companies

Adams Express Co, 318 4th
American Express Co, 318 4th
National Express Co, 318 4th
Pacific Express Co, 320 Pearl
Southern Express Co, 318 4th
United States Express Co, 320 Pearl
Wells, Fargo & Co's Express, 320 Pearl

act Manufacturers

on, 407½ 4th

Feed Yards

ivery, Feed and Sale Stables)
, H, 508 North
George, 507 and 512 North
Broadway
athan F, 111 6th
aham L, 517-521 North
as, 205 5th
L, 306 6th

rtilizers—Dealers

L & Co, 515 Market (*See adv*
me and Cement)

Fish and Game

rs, Fish and Game)

Florists

k Mrs O G & Co, 700 Helm
Wm H, 823 Linden av
m A, 609 w Broadway

Flour Mills

illing Co, cor Erie av and
adv front cover)
H, cor Front and Melbourne

r and Feed—Retail

[W, 415 12th
L & Co, 515 Market (*See*
Lime and Cement)
beus G, 315 Linden av
rles C, n e cor 5th and Mar-

Joseph, 100 Burlington av
W, 511 North
Theodore J, 8 Sycamore
m J, 204 6th

nd Feed—Wholesale

L & Co, 515 Market (*See*
Lime and Cement)
illing Co, cor Erie av and
adv front cover)
H, cor Melbourne av and

nders—General

achinists)
lty Construction Co,
land (*See adv p 4)*

Fruits—Retail

(*See also Confectioners*)
Cambish C & Co, 509 Broadway
Solimano Laurence, 421 Broadway

Fruits—Wholesale

Beatty DeWitt C, 206 6th
Mills Bros, cor Ottawa and Vandalia
R R

Funeral Directors

(*See Undertakers*)

*Furnaces—Hot Air

Eberlein C Augustus, 505 12th (*See*
adv)

Furniture Dealers

Ash & Hadley, 425-427 Market
Cummings & Morgan, 229 3d (*See*
adv p 7)
Hanley & Shanahan, 209 6th
Henderson J W & Sons 320 4th
Wharfield Wm H, 419 Market

Furniture Manufacturers

Cummings & Morgan, 229 3d (*See adv p 7*)

Henderson J W & Sons, factory s e cor 5th and Erie av office and salesroom 320 4th

Logansport Furniture Co, Ash & Hadley proprs, factory 303-307 Linden av office and salesroom 425-427 Market

*Furs

Wiler & Wise, 409-411 Broadway and 306 4th (*See adv left top lines*)

Galvanized Iron Work

Crismond Horace J, 312 Market (*See adv right top lines*)

Eberlein C Augustus, 505 12th (*See adv class Furnaces*)

Flanegin John T, 310 Market

Jennings Max, 316-318 5th

Gas Companies

Logansport and Wabash Valley Gas Co, 317 319 Pearl

Gas and Steam Fitters

(*See Plumbers, Gas and Steam Fitters*)

*Gasoline Stoves

Crismond Horace J, 312 Market (*See adv right top lines*)

Gas and Gasoline Engines

Bridge City Construction Co, Biddle Island (*See adv p 4*)

Lambert Gas and Gasoline Engine Co, Will B Place gen agt n e cor 5th and North (*See adv p 8*)

Gents' Furnishing Goods

(*See Mens' Furnishing Goods*)

*Gloves—Foster's Kid

Wiler & Wise, 409-411 Broadway and 306 4th (*See adv left top lines*)

Grain Dealers

Gillespie Daniel, e s 18th 1 s Wabash River

Logan Milling Co, cor Erie av and Elm (*See adv front cover*)

Uhl D & C H, cor Front and Melbourne av

Grain Drill Mnfrs

King Drill Co, s e cor 5th and High

Grain Elevators

(*See Elevators—Grain*)

Grocers—Retail

Ahern John R, 1201 Smead

Beatty Wm H, e s Heath 2 n Wheatland

Bieg Louis J, 1830 Broadway

Boerger Bros, 419 Broadway

Burgman & Bro, n e cor 15th and Smead

Castle Melvin, 101-103 Sycamore

Conrad Virgil, 427 5th

Cooper Mary E, 1701 George

Dieckmann Louis, 218 Market

Dreyer Gustave, 73 Bates

Dunn Bros, 425 3d

Fisher Cornelius, 5 Sycamore

Fitzer & Singer, 421 Broadway

Foley James H, 228 Market

Gallagher Michael J, 115 Cicott

Gamby Margaret J, 525 12th

Gibson Wm H, 109 Columbia

Graf John H, 593 Michigan av

Gross & Ritter, 416 3d

Grusenmeyer Charles X, n e cor Burlington av and Colfax

Hallam David, s w cor 18th and Stevens

Hammerly Eva, e s 17th 1 n Stevens

Hankee Joseph, 1701 17th

Hansen Antwine, 424 3d

Hoppe Henry W, 301 Market

Horstman Fred & Co, n w cor Front and Market

Horstman John, n w cor Market and Brown

Izor John W, 705 Helm

Johnston & Lux, 306 5th

Kardes Vincent, 314 Market

Klein F William, 504 Linden av

Leonard John L, 215 Plum

Long Aaron, 410 3d

Lux John H, s s Shultz 3 w Frank (S T) (*See adv*)

McCaffrey Bros, 410 Market and 600-602 Broadway

Moriarty George E, 101 n 6th

Murphy Martin, 1201 Erie av

Nave Tete, 600 Sycamore

Parker Wm J, 530 Broadway

Parker & Son, 501 12th

Personett Charles M, 217 6th

Peters Wm, 1430 Wright

Powlen David W, 201 Sycamore

Ray Bros, 402 Market

Ray & Etnire, 412 3d

Grocers—Retail—Continued

Robinson Riley W, 433 Sycamore
Rothermel Jacob J, 520 Broadway
Sellers J & M, 1201 Market
Spraker & McCord, 211-213 6th
Stoll Henry A, 1522-1524 Market
Swigart Theodore P, 131 6th
Thomas Henry A, 500 Michigan av
Thompson Isaac, 700 Clifton av
Traut Charles W, 420 Market, cor Pearl *(See adv front cover)*
Twells & Behmer, 113 Sycamore
Updegraff & Son, 314 Helm
Welch Andrew, 522 Broadway
Wes'erman George, 1401 Broadway
Wilson Ira G, 423 15th
Wirick Washington L, 219 Cicott

Grocers—Wholesale

Elliott J T Co The 309-315 Broadway
McCaffrey M & Co, 410 Market

Guns and Ammunition

Crawford Isaac N, n w cor 5th and Broadway
Crismond Horace J, 312 Market *(See adv right top lines)*
Flanegin John T, 310 Market

Gunsmiths

Grelle & Reed, 420½ Broadway

Hair Goods and Dressers

Turner Kate, 322½ Market

Handle Mnfrs—General

Hillock & Pitman, s e cor 16th and Toledo

Handle Mnfrs—Plow

Howe Samuel E, n e cor 5th and High

Hardware

Crawford Isaac N, 432 Broadway
Crismond Horace J, 312 Market *(See adv right top lines)*
Flanegin John T, 310 Market
Rice E S & Son, 415 Market
Ullery S W & Son, 318 Market

Harness and Saddlery—Retail

Harrison George, 617-623 Broadway
Kreis Bros Mfg Co, 414 Broadway
Smith Wm B, 308 5th

Tucker Henry, 519-521 Market *(See adv back paster)*
Watts Daniel M, 126 6th *(See adv Agr Impls)*
Young Charles, 306 Market

Harness and Saddlery—Wholesale

(See also Saddlery Hardware)
Kreis Bros Mfg Co, 414 Broadway
Taylor, Joseph & Sons, 412 Market

Hatters

Dewenter & Co, 303 4th *(See adv)*
Ferguson J D & Jenks, 322 Market
Globe Clothing House, n e cor 4th and Market
Grace Wm & Co, 316 Market
Helvie & Sellers, 426 Broadway
Hub Clothing Co, The, 313 4th
Otto Shoe & Clothing Co, The, 317-319 4th

Heading Manufacturers

Logan Heading Co, junction Panhandle and Vandalia Rys

Health Food Mnfrs

McCuaig Wm C, 203 5th

*Heaters—Steam and Hot Water

Linton & Graf, 325 Pearl

Hides, Furs, Pelts and Tallow

Barnard Moses, 1 w cor 6th and High
Fidler Wm F, 322 5th (*See adv class Junk Dealers*)
Hansen Neils, 515 Broadway

*Hollow Ware—Stransky Steel Ware

Crismond Horace J, 312 Market (*See adv right top lines*)

Hoop Manufacturers

Johnson, Becker & Co, 1309 Toledo

Horseshoers

(*See also Blacksmiths*)
Elliott J Martin, 318 3d (*See adv back Cover*)

Hotels

Baker's European Hotel, 318-320 Canal
Barnett The, 1 e cor 2d and Market
Hotel Johnston, 314-316 Canal
Island View Hotel, 322-324 Canal
Logan House, 316 6th
Tucker House, 304 Broadway

House Movers and Raisers

Ferguson James, 1320 North
Thornton Jeremiah E, 914 Race

Ice Cream—Retail

(*See also Confectioners*)
Kohtz Elizabeth, 421 12th
Solimano Laurence, 421 Broadway
Wright, Herbert M, 315 Pearl (*See adv p 6*)

Ice Cream—Wholesale

Richey Wm E, 100 Bates
Shearer Wm I, s e cor 13th and Erie av (*See adv p 8*)
Wright Herbert M, 315 Pearl (*See adv p 6*)

Ice Dealers

Baker There a, 1600 High
Jeannerette Christopher, 466 4th
Maxinkuckee Lake Ice Co, 511 Broadway

Ice Manufacturers

Columbia Brewing Co, n w cor 5th and High

Insurance Agents

Briggs Frederick J, 218½ 4th
Closson Edgar D, 222 4th
Closson Seymour M, 319½ Pearl
Cockburn Bros, 8 Masonic Temple (*See adv p 8*)
Edwards George W, 314½ 4th
Gonser George, 3 Pythian Castle (*See adv*)
Heffley Charles O, 14 Baldwin-Thornton Bldg
Hendee Sireno H, 2206 Broadway
Hepner George L, 326½ Market
Kessler Homer, 314½ 4th
McGuire Samuel, 408½ Broadway
McKinsey Joseph M, 412½ Broadway
Patterson Lemuel G, 410½ Broadway
Washburn Wm O, Supt Metropolitan Life Ins Co 1-3 Crawford Blk (*See adv left top lines and class Ins Co's*)

*Insurance Companies—Life

Metropolitan Life Insurance Co, Wm O Washburn supt, 1-2 3 Crawford Blk (See adv also left top lines)

*Iron Fences

Uhl Elmore, 113 Wheatland

Junk Dealers

Barnard Moses, 1 w cor 6th and High
Fidler Wm F, 322 5th (See adv)
Hanson Neils, 515 Broadway

Justices of the Peace

Fender George W, 11-12 Baldwin-Thornton Bldg
Laing David, 218½ 4th
Walters Jacob H, 218½ 4th

Label Printers

Longwell & Cummings, Masonic Temple

*Ladies' Furnishing Goods

Wiler & Wise, 409-411 Broadway and 306 4th (See adv left top lines)

*Ladies Suits

Wiler & Wise, 409 411 Broadway and 306 4th (See adv left top lines)

Laundries

Campbell's Steam Laundry, 429 Market
Maiben Charles H. 115 Melbourne av
Marshall's Steam Laundry 608 Broadway
Star Steam Laundry, 405 Market (See adv right top lines)

Lawyers

Briggs Frederick J, 218½ 4th
Chappelow John A, 222½ 4th
Chase George P, 220 4th
Cotner James A, 222½ 4th
Dykeman David D, 204½ 4th
Fender George W, 11-12 Baldwin-Thornton Bldg

Lawyers – Continued

Fickle David D, 211½ 4th
Fitzer Willard C, 212 4th
Hale & Gamble, 5-6 Masonic Temple
Harvey John W, 428½ Broadway
Justice DeWitt C. 218 4th
Kistler George S, 9 Baldwin-Thornton Bldg
Kistler Frank M, 7-8 Baldwin-Thornton Bldg
Lairy John S, 9-10 Baldwin-Thornton Bldg
Lairy & Mahoney, 220 4th
Landis Frederick, 222½ 4th
Lasselle Charles B, Court House
McConnell & McConnell, 1-4 Baldwin-Thornton Bldg
McConnell & Jenkines, 214 4th
McGreevy John W, 222½ 4th
McNary Joseph T, 412½ Broadway
Magee & Funk, 406½ Broadway
Meck John G, 222½ 4th
Murphy James T, 309½ 4th
Nelson & Myers, 212 4th
Newer & Reeder, 220½ 4th
Powell Wm, 220¼ 4th
Ross N O & G E, 220 4th
Smith John B, 212½ 4th
Smith Peter D, 222½ 4th
Swigart Frank, 222½ 4th
Taber Charles E, 400½ 4th
Taber George C, 204½ 4th
Tomlinson Joseph T, 400½ Broadway
Tuley Thomas J, 222½ 4th
Walters George W, 206 4th
West James A, 212½ 4th
Wilson Wm T, 206½ 4th
Winfield & Winfield, 400½ Broadway

Leather and Findings

Taylor Joseph & Sons, 412 Market

Lime Manufacturers

Keeport A B & Co, 515 Market (See adv opp back paster)
Lux John H, s s Shultz 3 w Frank (S T) (See adv)

Lime and Cement—Retail

Dilley C L & Co, 515 Market (see adv)

Lime and Cement—Wholesale

Keeport A B & Co, 515 Market (See adv opp back paster)
Lux John H, s s Shultz 3 w Frank (S T (See adv)

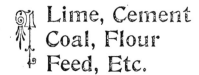
Linseed Oil Mnfrs

(See Oils)

Lithographers

Longwell & Cummings, Masonic Temple

Livery, Feed and Sale Stables

(See Feed Yards)
Cash Isaac N, 209 Market
Clem Emanuel A, 315 8th
Diehl Edwin J, 1024 Erie av
Jackson John, 111 6th
O'Donnell James, 419-425 3d
Schneeberger Matthias, n w cor 3d and Eel River av
Sellers M Frank, 217 12th
Stewart Earl F, 420-422 4th

Loan Agents

Clevenger Bros, 7 Masonic Temple
Closson Edgar D, 222 4th
Closson Seymour M, 319½ 1 earl
Cockburn Bros, 8 Masonic Temple
(See adv p 8)

:nts—Continued

W, 314½ 4th
5 Baldwin-Thornton

e, 428½ Broadway
14 Baldwin-Thornton

!onnell, 1-4 Baldwin-

l G, 410½ Broadway
V, 410½ Broadway
4 4th
rank H, 206 4th

:smiths

E, 215 6th

—Hardwood

t L, n e cor 5th and

:h and Shingles

'ls)
.v cor 9th and Erie av
iston, s e cor Berkley
ce adv front paster)
cor First and Canal
:r Co, n e : or 6th and

p, 500 Sycamore (*See*

hinists

:)
:struction Co, Bid-
adv p 4)
v W, 123 Market (*See*
')

and Grates

nce J, 312 Market
:p lines)

Granite Works

:us, n e cor 6th and
5)
1520 High
:r, 1031-1035 Toledo
p lines)
.v cor Burlington rd

anufacturers

:rgan, 229 3d (*See*

Meat Markets

Beshoar James, 204 w Market
Bundy & Rea, 222 Michigan av
Burgman Harry C, 618 15th
Carter Wm H H, 220 Market
Gries Frank, 1526 Market
Hill John O 217 Cicott
McCaffrey Bros, 410 Market and 600-602
Broadway
Maurice John L, 130 6th
Powlen David W, 203 Sycamore
Ramer Louis, 800 15th
Ray Andrew, 413 Market
Rehwald Bros, 105 Sycamore
Rehwald & Schrimp, 71 Bates
Rock Gustave, 102 Burlington av
Rothermel Jacob J, 520 Broadway
Rothermel John, 1226 Broadway
Routh Wm C, 512 Broadway and 503 12th
Rowe Wm, 503 Broadway
-Shanks Ernest, 5 6th
Shields Wm T, 217 Plum
Snyder & Stout, 313 3d
Stern Abraham, 309 Market
Thornburg John, 209 College
Zimmerman & Scheu, 702 12th

Medicine Manufacturers

Excelsior Mfg Co, 528 Broadway
Lynas & Son, 407½ 4th

Mens' Furnishing Goods

Dewenter & Co, 303 4th (*See adv
class Hatters*)
Ferguson J D & Jenks, 322 Market
Globe Clothing House, n e cor 4th and
Market
Grace Wm & Co, 316 Market
Helvie & Sellers, 426 Broadway
Hub Clothing Co, The, 313 4th
Murdock Will O, s e cor 4th and Broad-
way
Otto Shoe and Clothing Co, 317-319 4th
Wiler & Wise, 409-411 Broadway
and 306 4th (*See adv left top lines*)

Merchant Tailors

(*See also Tailors*)
Booth Burrel W, 313½ 4th
Carroll John F, 1222 Broadway (*See
adv p 6*)
Craig Wm D, 416 Broadway (*See adv
back cover*)
Herz Jacob, 409 Market (*See adv
right top lines*)
Hooley Patrick J, 418 Market
Keller Carl W, 311 Market (*See adv
stencil edge*)

294   BUSINESS DIRECTORY.

Merchant Tailors—Continued

Lienemann Julius F, 504 Broadway
Mader Daniel, 300 Broadway
Pierce Patrick J, 318 Broadway
(See adv left top lines)
Tucker Harry G, s e cor 4th and
Broadway (See adv backbone)
Weber Henry, 324 Pearl
Young Albert T, 304½ Market

Millinery and Fancy Goods

Bruggeman Rose A, 416 Market
Cummings Jessie, 405 Broadway
Garrity Mary E, 312½ 4th
Krauss Lucy E. 323 Pearl
Pelton Nettie, 327½ Market
Potter Sarah, 517 Broadway
Robius n & McConaha, 433 Sycamore
Spry Thomas A, 427-429 Broadway s e
cor Pearl
Swadener Ella B & Co, 324 4th
Tucker Charlotte, 406 Market

Mineral Water Mnfrs

Enyart & Chambers, 214 6th

Music Publishers

Home Music Co, The, 200 4th

Music Teachers

Booth Alice E, 1107 Broadway
Cockburn Maria, 1316 North
Cornell Ruby L, 611 Race
Dewey Bessie, 1202 North
Gates Nora A, 128 Pawnee
Goodwin Amanda E 922 Broadway
Hench Belle J, 406 High
Findlay Cora B, 429 North
Henderson Laura D, 1317 Market
Hildebrandt, Anna L, 408½ 4th
McMillen John E, 315½ 3d
McMullen Marian 830 North
McNitt Carrie C, 100 Melbourne av
Moor A Lamb, 414 North
Patrick Maud, 2022 Market
Stewart Myra, 1519 Spear
Thayer Clarence H, 818 Market

Music and Musical Merchandise

(See also Pianos and Organs)
Graves Charles W, 413 Broadway
Powell Edgar E, 505 Broadway

Newspapers

Logansport Advance (weekly), 218
6th (See adv p 9)
Logansport Chronicle (weekly),
324½ Broadway (See adv back fly leaf)
Logansport Journal, (daily and
semi-weekly) 217-219 4th
Logansport Pharos (daily and semi-
weekly) 216 4th (See adv p 10)
Logansport Reporter (daily and
semi-weekly) 218 6th (See adv p 9)
Logansport Times (weeky), 222 4th
(See adv back fly leaf)
Sternenbanner The (weekly), 205
Market (See adv)

News and Periodical Dealers

(See also Books and Stationery)
Beall Albert A, 510½ Broadway
Bevan Carrie D, 406 Broadway
Cohn Sol H, 326 Market
Graves Charles W, 413 Broadway
Kapp Harry F 322 Broadway

Notaries Public

Blasingham Gertrude, 212 4th
Cornwell Emma, 220 4th
Eikelburner Nellie, 206½ 4th
Gordon Moses M, 1-2 Spry Blk
Guthrie Frank V, 428½ Broadway
Jones Harley A, 14 Baldwin-Thornton
Bldg
Mahoney Michael F. 220 4th
Tuley Thomas J, 222½ 4th
Velsey Seth M, 204 4th
Walters George W, 206 4th
Wipperman Frank H, 206 4th

Notary Public Seals

Longwell & Cummings, Masonic
Temple

Notions and Fancy Goods—Retail

Craig Joseph S, 428 Broadway
Fisher Joseph, 314 Brown
Frazee Moses R, 418 Broadway
Gray John, 323-325 4th
Schmitt & Heinly, 329-331 Market, s w
cor 4th
Seybold George W & Bros, 319-321 Mar-
ket
Spry Thomas A, 427-429 Broadway, s e
cor Pearl
Wiler & Wise, 409-411 Broadway and
306 4th (See adv left top lines)

Notions and Fancy Goods—Wholesale

Shroyer & Uhl Co, 409-415 4th

I. J. CRISMOND, 312 Market Street,
Stoves and Kitchen Furnishings.

BUSINESS DIRECTORY.   295

tandard Oil Company

DEALERS IN
ALL KINDS OF

OILS

ɛASOLINES, ETC.

Ask your Dealer for

n-Explosive Perfection Headlight Oil

OFFICE, TOLEDO ST.
REAR WABASH FREIGHT DEPOT

Nurses

chanan Mary A S, 319½ Pearl
tts Josephine, 304 Burlington av
mer Elizabeth J, 208 Canal
e Lillie, 216 Broadway
smer M Belle, 1130 Linden av
tler Eva, 204 w Market
·key Ida, 1015 Spear
ris Mary E, 639 12th
meman Elizabeth, 215 16th
·ister Nancy, 1902 George
·lor Amanda, 618 e Wabash av
›mas Sarah, 10 17th
degraff Charles, 1115 George

Oculists and Aurists

· also *Physicians*)
›mas Charles L, 1 Masonic Temple

Oil Mnfrs—Linseed

ansport Linseed Oil Works, Wab.
v rd 4 e Burlington av

Oils—Illuminating—Retail

Grable Jonathan F, 111 6th
Hansen Neils, 515 Broadway
Veal A Edward, 311 5th

Oils—Illuminating and Lubricating—Wholesale

Standard Oil Co, 1017 to 1029 Toledo
(*See adv*)

Opera Houses

Dolan Opera House, s w cor 3d and
Broadway

Opticians

Baker Arthur N, 310 4th
Canfield Sarah A, n e cor Canal and Oak
Taylor Jay D, 309 4th (*See adv back
cover*)

Overall Manufacturers

Craig Wm D, 416 Broadway (*See
adv back cover*)

Longwell & Cummings

_

PRINTERS

BLANK BOOK MAKERS

STATIONERS

_

Masonic Temple, Fourth and North

Oysters, Fish and Game

Beshoar James, 204 w Market
Cory Isaac N, 311 5th
Hill John O, 217 Cicott
Kinney Frank W, 513 Broadway
(See adv)
Shields Wm T, 217 Plum

Packers—Beef and Pork

Routh Wm C, office 512 Broadway

Painters—House and Sign

(See also Paper Hangers)
Baker Jesse W, 820 Sycamore
Beatty John C, 628 Linden av (See adv)
Burns Leonidas H, 7 Horney
Green Charles S, 1310 Broadway
Hart Samuel C, 201 Sycamore
Hench John H, 1922 Market
Jackson Samuel D, 1429 George
Kearney Patrick, 121 Pawnee
Mucker Henry B, 401 Wheatland
Pickard Wm M, 2017 George

Potter Frank W, 1318 Spear
Randall Wm D, 1107 North
Rehm John L, 308 w Market
Shewmon Wm R, 409 Melbourne av
Slaceman John, 421 Grove
Underhay John, 225 6th
Walters Alva C, n w cor Standley and Charles (S T)
Wi'er H & Co, cor 4th and Broadway
Wilson Byron, 401½ Broadway
Wilson Walter F, 212 6th
Zartman Daniel K, 930 High

Paints and Oils

Bringhurst W H, 308 Market
Busjahn & Schneider, 308 4th (See adv front cover)
Closson Homer & Co, 500 Broadway
Crawford Isaac N, 432 Broadway
Excelsior Mfg Co, 528 Broadway
Fisher Ben, 311 4th
Keesling Benjamin F, 305 4th
Porter Wm H, 330 Market
Pryor Daniel E, 516 Broadway

ngers and Decorators

inters)
)hn C, 628 Linden, av *(See
painters)*
'r: Wall Paper Co, 407
'ee adv left top lines)
trthur L, 210 6th
,o, 328-330 Broadway
ter F, 212 6th

tent Solicitors

on B, 1-2 Spry Blk
D, 3 Pythian Castle

and Model Makers

vanius B, 230} Market

on Claim Agents

:s M, 1-2 Spry Blk

ie Manufacturers

, 407} 4th

Photographers

Anderson & Harrington, 421 5th
(*See adv*)
Donaldson Albert X, 406½ Broadway
Newport Abraham G, 510 Broadway
Stevens Clinton H, 414½ Market
Walters J R Photo & Enlarging Co, 121
5th

Physicians and Surgeons

(*See also Oculists and Aurists*)
Allen J Henry, 314½ 4th
Baker Ira J, (rectal and rupture)
415½ Broadway (*See adv front cover*)
Ballard John W, 400½ Market
Banta Henry J, 431 Wheatland
Barnfield John H, 311½ 4th
Bell Wm H, 313 Pearl
Bradfield Benjamin D, 318 3d
Busjahn Frederick A 407 4th
Cady Nelson W, 600½ Broadway
Coleman Asa, 322 3d
Cowgill Nathan C, 203 Sycamore
Crismond John W, 528 Broadway
Downey Jasper A, 413½ Broadway
Gilbert James L, 414½ Market
Hallanan Joseph, n w cor 4th and North
Hatch Elmer M, s w cor 7th and Broad-
way
Hattery Hiram D, s w cor Miami and
Plum
Herrmann Arthur J, 421 4th
Herrmann Francis J, 414 4th
Hetherington John P, 417 4th
Holloway Wm A, 407 4th
. unt Mae H, (women and children)
323½ 4th
Jordan Michael A, 410 4th
Kohl Arthur M, 9 to 11 Masonic Temple
Leisher Charles A, 321½ 4th
Lynas James B 407½ 4th
Neff Jasper N, 2000 Broadway
Nye Albert F, 410 4th
Powell Jehu Z, 220 6th
Shultz John B, 417 4th
Shultz John H, 412 4th
Sterrett Joseph E, 308½ Market
Stevens Benjamin C, 418 4th
Stewart James W, 9-10-11 Masonic
Temple
Stewart Milton B, 314 4th
Talbott James W, 223 3d
Taylor Caroline, 215 8th
Taylor Joseph L, 1420 Broadway
Thomas Charles L (eye and ear), 1 Ma-
sonic Temple
Tucker Arthur W, 321½ 4th
Ward Samuel H, 17 to 20 State Natl
. Bank Bldg

Piano Tuners

Capron Wells D, 219 Sycamore
Findlay Frank L, 429 North
Polk Caleb C, 410 Broadway
Steinhart Wm C, 624 Race

Pianos and Organs

(See also *Music and Musical Mdse*)
Bridge James C, 410 Broadway
Graves Charles W, 413 Broadway
Quinn John H, 420 Broadway
Witemyre John H, 118 4th

Pictures and Frames

Graves Charles W, 413 Broadway
Hanna C M & Co, 421 Market
Logansport Wall Paper Co, 407
   Market (*See adv left top lines*)

*Picture Frames and Mouldings

Logansport Wall Paper Co, 407
   Market (*See adv left top lines*)

Planing Mills

Palmer George W, 111 Burlington av
Parker & Johnston, s e cor Berkley
   and Spencer (*See adv front paster*)
Stevens Bros, 1 w cor First and Canal
Stouffer Oliver J, 18-20 6th

Plasterers

Conway James, 77 Washington
Lawrence Wm W, 127 College
McElheny James, 1503 Market
Tam Robert S, 408 Clifton av
Toby James B, 1500 High
Williams Eden E, 1408 Market
Williams Jerome M, 1413 George
Wilson Perry A, 508 Sycamore

Plumbers, Gas and Steam Fitters

Hildebrandt John J, 408 4th
Hughes Martin M, 324 5th (*See adv
   also back cover*)
Linton & Graf, 325 Pearl
Merritt Albert L, 1310 Broadway
Messinger & Son, 521 Broadway
Stevens Andrew W, 423 Market
   (*See adv back fly leaf*)

Poultry Dealers—Retail

Kinney Frank W, 513 Broadway
   (*See adv Oysters, Etc*)

Poultry Dealers—Wholesale

Brooks James A, s e cor Canal and Elm
Gibbs John E, 109 Burlington av
Porter Frank R, 431 Sycamore

Printers—Book and Job

Fenton Charles O, 222 4th (*See adv
   back fly leaf*)
Logansport Journal Co, 217 4th
Longwell & Cummings, Masonic
   Temple, n e cor 4th and North
McSheehy Henry J, 324½ Broadway
   (*See adv back fly leaf*)
Sutton J Edmund, 218 6th (*See adv
   p 9*)
Wilson, Humphreys & Co, 200 4th

Publishers

Bowen A W & Co, 626 Erie av
Longwell & Cummings, Masonic
   Temple

Pumps—Wood and Iron

Ford & Hayworth, 312 5th

Pumps—Wood and Iron—Continued

Hildebrandt John J, 408 4th
Hughes Martin M, 324 5th (*See adv back cover and class Plumbers*)
Linton & Graf, 325 Pearl
Messinger & Son, 521 Broadway
Parkhurst Alinus N, 129 6th

*Pump Repairers

Ford & Hayworth, 312 5th

Railroad Tickets—Brokers

John Sol H, 326 Market

Real Estate Agents

Beaulieu Ida B, 1902 North
Bebee Eda F, 113 4th
Clevenger Bros, 7 Masonic Temple
Closson Symour M, 319½ Pearl
Cockburn Bros, 8 Masonic Temple (*See adv p 8*)
ordell Charles M, 218½ 4th
Conser George, 3 Pythian Castle (*See adv class Ins Agts*)
ordon Moses M, 1-2 Spry Blk
uthrie & Guthrie, 428½ Broadway
leffley Charles O, 14 Baldwin-Thornton Bldg
ennedy John R, 310½ Market
IcGovern Terrence A, 214½ 4th
IcNary Joseph T, 412½ Broadway
.ichardson Allen, 315 5th
.odefer George W, 410½ Broadway
hanahan Wm, 408½ Broadway
pohn Frank H, 214½ 4th
utton Andrew J, 218 6th
'omlinson Daniel W, 400½ Broadway

*Real Estate Dealers

.ux **John H**, s s Shultz 3 w Frank (S T) (*See adv*)

*Refrigerators

Crismond Horace J, 312 Market (*See adv right top lines*)

Restaurants

Baker's European Hotel, 318-320 Canal
Bryant R Frank, 355 Sycamore
unningham Patrick F, 401 Canal
Dykeman Charles E, 322 Broadway
ipson Charles A, 324 3d
fall Sarah A, 311 3d
lelvie Abraham U, 304 5th
'land View Hotel, 322-324 Canal

Miller Oliver M, 320 Broadway
Paden Wm S, 321 Sycamore
Ream Annie E, 226 Market
Solimano Laurence, 421 Broadway
Yarbro Francis B, 324 Sycamore

*Roofers—Tar and Gravel

Dilley C L & Co, 515 Market (*See adv class Lime and Cement*)

Roofers—Tin, Iron and Slate

Crismond Horace J, 312 Market (*See adv right top lines*)
Eberlein C Augustus, 505 12th (*See adv class Furnaces*)
Flanegin John T, 310 Market

Rubber Stamps

Longwell & Cummings, Masonic Temple

Saddlery Hardware

Taylor Joseph & Sons, 412 Market

Safety Deposit Vaults

City National Bank, s w cor 4th and Broadway

Saloons

Ahern John R, 633 12th
Anderson Alfred L, 300 3d
Barnett Atwater C, 309 Broadway
Baker & Anbeier, 318-320 Canal
Bauer John J, 223 4th
Bligh Martin J, 305 Market
Bopp Wm F, 13 6th
Brown Daniel, 314 3d
Burgman Wm, 1 Burlington av
Burgman & Bro, n e cor 15th and Smead
Burns Bros, 511 Broadway
Castle Peter, 311 Pearl
Coyle & Landry, 317 3d
Downey Frank, 408 Wall
Eckert John, 230 Market (*See adv p 6*)
Farrell & Ludders, 502 Broadway
Finn James, 6 3d
Fohrer Charles, 221 4th
Fries Nichola , 3 n 6th
Gloss Andrew, 430 Market
Hall John R, The Barnett
Hallam David, s w cor 18th and Stevens
Helvie George A, 309 3d
Heiden Henry, 325 Market
Heppe Frederick, 517 12th
Ice Ransom, n s Bates 9 w Vandalia R R (Dunkirk)

BUSINESS DIRECTORY.   299

Pumps—Wood and Iron—Continued

Hildebrandt John J, 408 4th
Hughes Martin M, 324 5th (*See adv back cover and class Plumbers*)
Linton & Graf, 325 Pearl
Messinger & Son, 521 Broadway
Parkhurst Alinus N, 129 6th

*Pump Repairers

Ford & Hayworth, 312 5th

Railroad Tickets—Brokers

Cohn Sol H, 326 Market

Real Estate Agents

Beaulieu Ida B, 1902 North
Bebee Eda F, 113 4th
Clevenger Bros, 7 Masonic Temple
Closson Seymour M, 319½ Pearl
Cockburn Bros, 8 Masonic Temple (*See adv p 8*)
Cordell Charles M, 218½ 4th
Gonser George, 3 Pythian Castle (*See adv class Ins Agts*)
Gordon Moses M, 1-2 Spry Blk
Guthrie & Guthrie, 428½ Broadway
Heffley Charles O, 14 Baldwin-Thornton Bldg
Kennedy John R, 310½ Market
McGovern Terrence A, 214½ 4th
McNary Joseph T, 412½ Broadway
Richardson Allen, 315 5th
Rodefer George W, 410½ Broadway
Shanahan Wm, 408½ Broadway
Spohn Frank H, 214½ 4th
Sutton Andrew J, 218 6th
Tomlinson Daniel W, 400½ Broadway

*Real Estate Dealers

Lux John H, s s Shultz 3 w Frank (S T) (*See adv*)

*Refrigerators

Crismond Horace J, 312 Market (*See adv right top lines*)

Restaurants

Baker's European Hotel, 318-320 Canal
Bryant R Frank, 355 Sycamore
Cunningham Patrick F, 401 Canal
Dykeman Charles E, 322 Broadway
Gipson Charles A, 321 3d
Hall Sarah A, 311 3d
Helvie Abraham U, 304 5th
Island View Hotel, 322-324 Canal

Miller Oliver M, 320 Broadway
Paden Wm S, 321 Sycamore
Ream Annie E, 226 Market
Solimano Laurence, 421 Broadway
Yarbro Francis B, 324 Sycamore

*Roofers—Tar and Gravel

Dilley C L & Co, 515 Market (*See adv class Lime and Cement*)

Roofers—Tin, Iron and Slate

Crismond Horace J, 312 Market (*See adv right top lines*)
Eberlein C Augustus, 505 12th (*See adv class Furnaces*)
Flanegin John T, 310 Market

Rubber Stamps

Longwell & Cummings, Masonic Temple

Saddlery Hardware

Taylor Joseph & Sons, 412 Market

Safety Deposit Vaults

City National Bank, s w cor 4th and Broadway

Saloons

Ahern John R, 633 12th
Anderson Alfred L, 300 3d
Barnett Atwater C, 309 Broadway
Baker & Anbeier, 318-320 Canal
Bauer John J, 223 4th
Bligh Martin J, 305 Market
Bopp Wm F, 13 6th
Brown Daniel, 314 3d
Burgman Wm, 1 Burlington av
Burgman & Bro, n e cor 15th and Smead
Burns Bros, 511 Broadway
Castle Peter, 311 Pearl
Coyle & Landry, 317 3d
Downey Frank, 408 Wall
Eckert John, 230 Market (*See adv p 6*)
Farrell & Ludders, 502 Broadway.
Finn James, 6 3d
Fohrer Charles, 221 4th
Fries Nichola, 3 n 6th
Gloss Andrew, 430 Market
Hall John R, The Barnett
Hallam David, s w cor 18th and Stevens
Helvie George A, 309 3d
Heiden Henry, 325 Market
Heppe Frederick, 517 12th
Icr Ransom, n s Bates 9 w Vandalia R R (Dunkirk)

Saloons—Continued

Kennedy George W, 7 Sycamore
Kienly Frank G, 2 w Market
Kreuzberger Robert, s w cor 3d and Market and 413-415 3d *(See adv p 4)*
Kuhn Raino, 431 Market
Loftus David, 426 Market
McGrath Frank, s w cor Michael and L & W road
McHale Martin, 430 3d
Matt Joseph F, 431 5th
Miller John, 1500 Toledo
Pomeroy & McGaughey, 319 Sycamore
Pottmyer Frank W, 119 Front
Ray Robert, 404 Market
Ruhl Charles, 414 3d
Schneider George M, 817 15th
Schubeck Kate, 520 Canal
Sebastian Jacob P, 225 4th
Smith Charles, 422 3d
Sullivan Jeremiah, 906 Lytle
Taylor John, 316 Canal
Tussing Jacob, 1429 Erie av
Wagner Frank M, 4 Sycamore
Wandrei Ewald H, n e cor Duret and Berkley
Welch John, 425 12th
Williamson & Gregg, 201 6th
Wolf Leonard N, 317 Sycamore
Zahlbaum Michael, 221 Market
Zolt Anthony, 312 Pearl

Sash, Doors and Blinds

Crawford Isaac N, 432 Broadway
Jones Thomas, s w cor 9th and Erie av
Parker & Johnson, s e cor Berkley and Spencer *(See adv front paster)*
Stevens Bros, n w cor First and Canal
Thompson Lumber Co, n e cor 6th and High
Voorhees Philip, 500 Sycamore *(See adv p 7)*

Saw Mills

(See also Lumber etc)
Bennett G W, 1308 Toledo
Closson Edgar D, s e cor 15 and Toledo
Van Buskirk James, n s Pink 1 e Balsam

School Books

(See Books and Stationery)

Second Hand Household Goods

Campbell George W, 518 Broadway
Cornell Wm, 12 6th
Hanley & Shanahan, 209 6th
Henderson Frank E, 326 5th

Seedsmen

Crawford Isaac N, 432 Broadway
Harrison George, 617-623 Broadway
Kreis Bros Mfg Co, 414 Broadway

*Sewer Pipe—Cement

Logansport Cement Works, w Market opp Peoria junction *(See adv p 5)*

Sewer Pipe Dealers

Dilley C L & Co, 515 Market *(See adv class Lime and Cement)*
Logansport Cement Works, w Market opp Peoria junction *(See adv p 5)*
Martin James P, 216 6th

Sewing Machines

Singer Mfg Co, 231 3d
Whitsett Robert B, 529 Broadway

*Shorthand and Typewriting Schools

Halls's Business College, n w cor 6th and Broadway

Soap Manufacturers

Heppe Wm & Sons, s s L & W rd 3 w Standley office s w cor Erie av and Elm

Sporting Goods

Burgman Cycle Co, s e cor 5th and Market
Crawford Isaac N, n w cor 5th and Broadway
Crismond Hornce J, 312 Market *(See adv right top lines)*
Flanegin John T, 310 Market

Stationers

ngwell & Cummings, Masonic
'emple

Steamship Agents

Sheehy H James, 324½ Broadway
llrath Peter 207 Market

*Stenographers

.ll's Business College, n w cor
th and Broadway

Stone Quarries

x & Talbott, office 310 Broadway

Stoneware

rtin James P, 216 6th

Storage

yor Daniel E, 516 Broadway

Stoves and Tinware

e also Hardware)
.rnhart John & Son, 422 Broadway
·ismond Horace J, 312 Market
See adv right top lines)
·erlein C Augustus, 505 12th (*See
1dv class Furnaces*)
anegin John T, 310 Market

*Stransky Steel Ware

·ismond Horace J, 312 Market
See adv right top lines)

Street Railways

·gansport Street Railway Co, 214½ 4th

Tailors

e also Merchant Tailors)
·ffmann Matthias, 807 15th
ein Nicholas, 400½ Market

Telegraph Companies

estern Union Telegraph Co, 419 4th

Telephone Companies

·ntral Union Telephone Co, 315½ 4th
·gansport Mutual Telephone Co, 327
4th

Ticket Brokers

e Railroad Tickets)

Tinners

(*See also Stoves and Tinware*)
Cline Bros, 500 Broadway
Crismond Horace J, 312 Market
(*See adv right top lines*)
Eberlein C Augustus, 505 12th (*See
adv class Furnaces*)
Flanegin John T, 310 Market
Mebaffie John M, 314 5th

Transfer Line—Passenger and Baggage

O'Donnell James, 419-425 3d

Transfer Line—Freight

Twells Wyndham S, 1309 Market

Trunks and Valises

Ferguson J D & Jenks, 322 Market
Grace Wm & Co, 316 Market
Helvie & Sellers, 426 Broadway
Otto Shoe & Clothing Co, The, 317-319
4th
Wade Michael C, 327 Market

*Typewriters

Hall's Business College (Sole agts
Smith-Premier Typewriter), n w cor
6th and Broadway

*Typewriter Supplies

Hall's Business College, n w cor
6th and Broadway

Undertakers

Kroeger & Strain, 613 Broadway
Woll Charles L, 417 Market (*See
adv p 7*)

Upholsterers

Ash & Hadley, 425-427 Market
Cummings & Morgan, 229 3d (*See
adv p 7*)
Henderson J W & Sons, 320 4th

Vault and Sink Cleaners

Hansen Neils, 515 Broadway

Veterinary Surgeons

Corbett Wm C, 116 Canal
Donoho James, 422 4th
Ganson John S, 306 6th
Harding Richard A, 511 North
Justice Parker, 200 Market (*See
adv back cover*)

Wall Paper and Window Shades

Frazee Moses R, 418 Broadway
Logansport Wall Paper Co, 407 Market (*See adv left top lines*)
Moynihan Arthur L, 210 6th
Wiler II & Co, 328-330 Broadway

Watches, Clocks and Jewelry

Church Carl H, 519 Broadway
Hauk Dio A, 410 Broadway
Lewis Barclay Z, 523 Broadway
Martin De ', 310 4th
Se Legue Charles W, 400 Broadway (*See adv front cover*)
Taylor Jay D, 309 4th (*See adv back cover*)
Webster John P, 307 Market

Water Wheel Manufacturers

Dolan Wm & Co, n w cor Canal and Berkley

Wines and Liquors—Retail

Foley James H, 228 Market
Kreuzberger Robert, s w cor 3d and Market and 413-415 3d (*see adv p 4*)
McCaffrey Bros, 410 Market

Wines and Liquors—Wholesale

Bligh Martin J, 408 3d
Kreuzberger Robert, 229-231 Market and 413-415 3d (*See adv p 4*)

*Wool Dealers

Fidler Wm F, 322 5th (*See adv class Junk Dealers*)

H. J. GRISMOND, 312 Market Street,
All Kinds of Metal Roofing.

GAZETTEER. 335

LONGWELL & CUMMINGS'

GAZETTEER

OF

CASS COUNTY, INDIANA

1897-98.

BEING A COMPLETE LIST OF BUSINESS MEN
AND LAND OWNERS.

OFFICIAL DIRECTORY.

Congressman from 11th District—Hon George W Steele, Marion
State Senator—Hon Martin W Collett, Metea
State Representative, Hon Frank Sence, Logansport
Joint Representative—Hon Peter Wallrath, Logansport

COUNTY OFFICERS

Judge of Cass Circuit Court—Dudley H Chase
Prosecuting Attorney—George S Kistler
Clerk—Andrew P Flynn
Auditor—Josiah G Powell
Treasurer—Isaac N Cash
Recorder—Jacob W Wright
Sheriff—Isaiah A Adams
Sheriff-elect—Charles W Homburg
Surveyor—Harry W Troutman
Coroner—Dr Frederick A Busjahn
County Assessor—John Hines
County School Superintendent—J Frank Cornell
County Attorneys (to Board of Commissioners)—Nelson & Myers
Board of County Commissioners—Abraham Shideler pres, Joseph
E Crain, Daniel Woodhouse
Superintendent of County Poor Asylum—Frederick Homburg

TIMES OF HOLDING COURT IN CASS COUNTY

Cass Circuit Court, first Monday in January, April, September and November

COMMISSIONERS' COURT

First Monday in March, June, September and December

TREASURERS OF CORPORATE TOWNS AND CITIES

Logansport—George E Barnett
Royal Center—G A Rea
Walton—Frank Fair

SCHOOL TRUSTEES OF TOWNS AND CITIES

Logansport—J D McNitt pres, Quincy A Myers secy, Jehu T Elliott treas

Royal Center—O M McCombs pres, J J Schmidt secy, W G Sweet treas

Walton—Owen Engler pres, James Davis secy, Samuel Betz treas

JUSTICES OF THE PEACE

Township	Name	P O Address
Adams	Samuel M McCoy	Adamsboro
"	John Hoover	Hoover
Bethlehem	Samuel N Grable	Fletchers
Boone	James F Fry	Royal Center
Clay		
Clinton	Joseph S St Clair	Clymers
Deer Creek	Levi A Price	Young America
"	James W Cree	Deacon
Eel	David Laing	Logansport
"	George W Fender	Logansport
"	Jacob H Walters	Logansport
Harrison	Edward Whitfield	Lucerne
"	Daniel J Remley	Lucerne
Jackson	John Q Symons	Galveston
Jefferson	A J Wilson	Lake Cicott
Miami		
Noble	John Tam	Logansport
Tipton	Obediah M Barnard	Walton
"	Fahn Haas	Walton
Washington	Stephen A Guthrie	Logansport

TOWNSHIP TRUSTEES.

Township	Name	P O Address
Adams	Wm Carson	Hoover
Bethlehem	Alonzo Cover	Pine
Boone	Wm S Kistler	Royal Center

GAZETTEER. 337

TOWNSHIP TRUSTEES—CONTINUED.

Township	Name	P O Address
Clay	Robert Barnett	Logansport
Clinton	N V Martin	Logansport
Deer Creek	Thomas Flynn	Deer Creek
Eel	Robert F Johnston	Logansport
Harrison	Philip Wolford	Lucerne
Jackson	John N Wilson	Lincoln
Jefferson	George Calloway	Lake Cicott
Miami	D J Forgy	New Waverly
Noble	Wm Noss	Logansport
Tipton	Wm Shafer	Anoka
Washington	Silas Storer	Logansport

TOWNSHIP ASSESSORS.

Township	Name	P O Addrees
Adams	Enoch Jones	Twelve Mile
Bethlehem	Oliver P Leffel	Pine
Boone	B Vaughn	Royal Center
Clay	E C Netsker	Logansport
Clinton	W H Tyner	Gordon
Deer Creek	Marvin Babb	Deacon
Eel	Allen Richardson	Logansport
Harrison	Frank Threewits	Lucerne
Jackson	J A Radabaugh	Galveston
Jefferson	D F Wilson	Lake Cicott
Miami	John Kidd	Adamsboro
Noble	Wm Livingston	Logansport
Tipton	Frank Taggart	Onward
Washington	H K White	Logansport

VILLAGES IN THE COUNTY.

ADAMSBORO

Ackerly C D, blacksmith
DeMoss J A, blacksmith
Gingrich S I, saw mill
Herring T J, grocer
Morgan M J, postmaster also general store
Myers David, feed-mill
Oliver M T, grocer

ANOKA

Berry Meshack, postmaster
Dykeman George P, general store
Helvie S S, flour mill

Jackson & Zimmerman, music dealers
Like Wm, flour mill
Puterbaugh J W, general store
Tousley Wm R, railroad and express agent
Turnbaugh S, blacksmith

CLYMERS

Dickerson F, barber
Gillispie W H, grocer
Creen Mrs M, dressmaker
Hinkle Mrs Fannie, postmaster
Landry H M, grocer
Parish H D, physician

SUPRPLUS of the METROPOLITAN LIFE
at the end of 1896, over ☞ $5,000,000
Number of Claims Paid During Year, 63,909

338 GAZETTEER.

CRITTENDEN

Harness G W & Son, live stock
Murphy & Douglass, saw mill
Simon L A, physician
Simon L A & Sons, live stock

CURVETON

Miller Abraham, postmaster

DEACON

Armstrong Albert, carpenter
Cree Watt, carpenter
Deacon W R, painter
Ervin Albert, saw mill
Friend Edward, blacksmith
Martin H B painter
Shanks J T, postmaster also general store
Shanks Mrs J T, dressmaker
Turner Mrs Annie, dressmaker

DEGO

Endicott Mrs A O, dressmaker
Odell Price, postmaster, grocer and druggist

FORD

Cotner James, postmaster

GALVESTON

Beall F H, druggist
Bell Alson, barber
Bell N O, grocer
Bevington S P, hardware
Cole B H M, shoemaker
Conwell G W, grocer and grain dealer
Davis Alban C, postmaster
Davis G W, general store
Eisenbrey J H Sons, harness and carriages
Herbert S C, blacksmith
Lawrence Willard, barber
Loop Z U, physician and druggist
Lytle H W, barber
Lytle Mrs M A, milliner
McMahon Mrs M J, milliner
Miller H H, physician
Miller & Doran, meat market
Faulus Fred baker
Platt Walter, barber
Richards B B, lawyer
Rule A B, blacksmith
Shiveley W H, hardware
Smith J S, physician
Spradling V M, meat market
Stanley Maggie, grocer also restaurant

Thomas F H & Bro, general store
Thomas John, furniture dealer
Tweley D M, grain dealer
Williams G W, grocer
Wood H W, livery stable

GORDON

Cohee John W, miller
Haseltine John, blacksmith
Miller Abraham, saw mill
Nethercutt Charles, blacksmith
Nethercutt George W, wagon maker
Reish & Ieck, saw mill
Reish, Peck & Gordon, flour mill
Wiley John T, postmaster and general store
Wilson John, barber

HOOVER

Clouse J L, postmaster
Clouse J R, wood dealer
Enyart Peter, carpenter
Richardson Samuel, poultry dealer
Robison John, grocer
Schneider F L, saw mill
Tyson J R, hardware
Working D, grain dealer

KENNETH

Becker M J, bookkeeper
Binns O H, superintendent
Breen Hugh, foreman
Byers N B, foreman
Casparis Stone Co (S Casparis pres and gen mgr, T S Brooks secy and treas)
Davis D C, driller
Flemming James, teamster
Gibson J E, powder man
Higgins Stephen, foreman
Jordan Wm, laborer
McCanley John, driller
McCarthy T J, foreman
Martin Charles, farmer
Midener Peter, blacksmith
Nighman G W, postmaster, also assistant superintendent
Strothers M E, driller
Summerville S, driller
Webster Wm, fireman

LAKE CICOTT

Lontz S P, postmaster and genl store

LINCOLN

Bell Mahlon, hardware and lumber
Burrows & Thomas, grocers

LINCOLN—Continued

Dye H, blacksmith
Graff Louise, dressmaker
Howard Mrs Vesta, dressmaker
Parrett H M, physician
Ullery George E, postmaster and
telegraph operator
Watkins A P, grain dealer and ry agt

LUCERNE

Frushour G M, postmaster
Hefferman & Dalzell, grocers
Hilkert Bros, grocers
Kane F C, physician
Larose N J, physician
Mellinger J S, blacksmith
Turner James, grocer
Whitfield Mrs Ed, dressmaker
Whitfield & Frushour, hardware, grain
and drain tile dealers
Winn & Winn, grain dealers
Zinninger Ella, grocer and dry goods

METEA

Reder Daniel C, postmaster and
general store

NEW WAVERLY

Castle P W & Son, blacksmiths
Fernald W L, lumber dealer
Forgy C P & Bro, general store
Graves A E, physician and surgeon
Hogentogler I F, blacksmith
McCoy S M, grocer
Mercer & Neal, flour and feed
Patton G M, postmaster, also cigar
dealer and barber
Fennel S N, grocer
Quick I L and R H, physicians
Quick W L, printer
Runnels Emanuel, broom mnfr

ONWARD

Conn T P, postmaster
Phillips Edgar E, grocer and druggist
Rice Z W, saw mill
Smith Peter, blacksmith
Snyder E D, physician and surgeon
Snyder W H, grocer and druggist

PINE

Kirtland James, dealer in tobacco
cigars and stationery

ROYAL CENTER

Anderson C M, general store
Bingaman, W H, hardware
Carroll S J, furniture and carriages

Clovis & Wyand, undertakers
Conn A J, saloon
Conn G W, livery stable
Day L R, grocer
Fouts D N, physician
Fox Valentine, shoemaker
Ginther & Sloan, jewelers
Gould E P, physician
Grant Henry, blacksmith
Gundrenn & Robbins, real estate
Hamilton C O, barber
Hand O M, editor The Record
Hendee George, taxidermist
Hopkinson S S restaurant
Humes James, drayman
Kennell Jacob, photographer
Kistler & Beckley, grocery and meat
mrkt
Kistler F M, physician
Kistler M W, justice of the peace
Laemle M, restaurant
Layne & Winslow, real estate
Lee & Kistler, hardware and harness
Leydit Charles E, mason
Long & Gangwier, novelty works
Long & McCombs, lumber and tile
Lutz Wm H, shoemaker
Lux Bros, general store
McCabe J C, shoemaker
Million D, physician
Potter Frank, blacksmith
Rea E J & Son, druggist
Rhodes Bros, flour mill
Robbins C S, hotel
Robbins & Kistler, livery barn
Royal Center Bank
Runkle Ellie, milliner
Runkle & Carroll, grain dealers
Schmidt J J, jr, general store
Shell J W, pastor M E Church
Skinner G M, R R agent
Sullivan J F, barber
Sweet T P, general store and live stock
Thomas E B, insurance agent
Thomas J L, druggist
Ubelhauser John, saloon
Watson Emma, milliner
Wildermuth John, hotel
Wirwahn C C, blacksmith
Wiseley E H, postmaster
Wiseley J M, drayman

TWELVE MILE

Bash F M, blacksmith
Beamer Michael, blacksmith
Black W C, barber
Black & Deniston, general store,
Carson Wm, trustee Adams township
Decker Mrs J B, dressmaker

TWELVE MILE—Continued

Egman J W, postmaster also general store
Hoover John, Justice of the Peace
Hoover T J & Co, saw mill
Miller Lewis C, physician and surgeon
Rogers W C, painter
Sarver Frank, general store,

WALTON

Baker James, railroad agent
Betz S, grocer
Bingamer Isaac, saw mill
Bishop George W, wagon maker
Bishop G W, excelsior manufacturer
Bishop W W, undertaker
Bishop G W Sons, general store
Branaman W W, restaurant
Brasket Julia, dressmaker
Bumgarner Isaac, saw mill
Deatrick B A, barber
Dutchess C O, physician and druggist
Engler Owen, general store
Erney J O, blacksmith
Green L B, blacksmith
Guy W A, painter
Hearrell A W, postmaster
Kelley & Shedron, live stock dealers
Kennedy R J, hardware
Lindersmith C A, barber
Neff J L, physician
Hurd Owen & Son, grain dealers
Ruth E F, saloon
Shaffer John, tile
Small John, painter
Small & Davis, undertakers

Snyder W H, restaurant
Stagg Mrs A, milliner
Stagg John, general store
Walton Canning Co
Wazerman D, meat market

YOUNG AMERICA

Beck E L, wagon maker and plasterer
Beck S J, notary public and collection agent
Cost John W, druggist
Cost & Barnett, agricultural impls
Dreseen Theodore, blacksmith
Forgy Frank, undertaker and furniture dealer
Gard O C & Co, druggists, also general store
Gray A I, physician
Hendrix J O, hotel
Henry Charles, lawyer
Howser G C, tinner
Hubler H H, meat market
Hunter Nancy, dressmaker
Hunter Robert H, harness maker
Hunter Wm, boots and shoes
Jacobson S, flour mill
Johnson A, saw and planing mill
Johnson James G, hardware and grocer
Lybrook Wm E, physician
Martindale J I, milliner
Nolan Wm E, blacksmith
Peter A & Son, groceries
Price Levi A, livery barn
Simmons & Tadhunter, tile mnfrs
Spencer A J, milliner
Staley David A, postmaster, also general store

LAND OWNERS.

NOTE.—20 a, after the name, means that the party owns 20 acres.

Aaron Joseph, 42 a Galveston
Abshire Lorenda, 89 a Twelve Mile
Adair John N estate, 80 a
Adams Carbin, 45 a Walton
Adams James, 160 a Clymers
Adams James jr, 124 a Clymers
Adams Jane, 17 a Clymers
Adams John, 18 a Clymers
Alber Eben, 40 a Metea
Alber John and Bettie, 63 a City
Alber Lucinda, 18 a Metea
Albert Mary A, 80 a Burnettsville
Albertson Edward F. 25 a Walton
Albertson Sarah B, 50 a Walton
Albright F T, 100 a Ford
Allen Joseph M.40 a Ford
Allman George C, 97 a Pipe Creek
Allread James I, 80 a Young America
Allread Lucinda, 40 a Young America
Alspaugh L, 20 a Walton
Alspaugh Sarah A, 1 a Lincoln
Aman Anthony, 100 a City
Aman David, 80 a Walton
Amos Harry E, 36 a, Clymers
Amos Sarah E, 2 a, Twelve Mile
Amos Wm R, 20 a, Clymers
Amthaner Conrad, 120 a, Deacon
Anderson A W, 80 a, New Waverly
Anderson Eliza J, 110 a, Pine
Anderson Emma, 160 a, New Waverly
Anderson E P, 162 a, New Waverly
Anderson Francis, 40 a, Anoka
Anderson George W, 145 a, Pine
Anderson James M, 160 a, New Waverly
Anderson James M and Willard S, 47 a,
   New Waverly
Anderson John D, 2 a, City
Antrim D B, 95 a, Royal Center
Applegate Edwin E and Sidney A, 80 a,
   Royal Center
Armstrong F G, 320 a, Lincoln
Armstrong Isaac, 80 a, Dego
Armstrong Wm, 110 a, Galveston
Armstrong Wm M, 160 a, City
Army Bernard, 78 a
Army Margaret J, 40 a, Onward
Arnold Wm F, 122 a, Lucerne
Athow Thomas, 116 a, Twelve Mile
Arthurhultz Samuel, 42 a, Twelve Mile
Ault Adam, 160 a, Hoover
Ault Albert, 10 a, Hoover
Ault Eliza E, 90 a, Hoover,

Ault Willard, 80 a, Twelve Mile
Austin Thomas, 1 a, City
Babb James N, 34 a, Deacon
Babb James N, and Ira Campbell,100 a
Babb John A, 100 a, Deacon
Babb Marvin, 40 a, Deacon
Babb R B and J M, 200 a, Deacon
Baber Christopher, 234 a,
Bachman Henry W, 30 a, Ford
Backus George, 75 a, Lucerne,
Backus John W, 80 a, Lucerne
Backus Nancy, 45 a, Lucerne
Backus Wm, 171 a, Lucerne
Badde Conrad, 93 a, Gordon
Bair Isaac J, 25 a, Royal Center
Baker Celestia, 8 a
Baker Emanuel, 26 a, Lincoln
Baker Henry, 87 a, Gordon
Baker John, 153 a, City
Baker John D, 80 a, Lincoln
Baldwin D P, 225 a, City
Baldwin Thornburg, 2 a, Galveston
Ball David, 80 a City
Ball Eleanor, 22 a, City
Ball Lafayette, 49 a, City
Ball Wm B, 100 a, City
Ball Winfield S, (dead) (wife Laura), 80
   a, City
Banks Lorenda, 42 a, Walton,
Banta Benjamin, 160 a, Curveton
Banta Caleb B, 61 a, Curveton
Banta Catharine, 80 a, Curveton
Banta Everett, 50 a, Curveton
Banta John, 171 a, City
Banta Mary M, 14 a, City
Banta Wm, 235 a Curveton
Barker Owen W, 60 a, Walton
Barnes John E, 32 a, City
Barnett Anna L, 75 a, City
Barnett David D, 19 a, City
Barnett Harrison, 40 a, Lucerne
Barnett Robert H, 134 a, City
Barnhart Caroline, 100 a, City
Barnhart George W, 110 a, Twelve Mile
Barnhart John sr, 14 a
Barnhart Wm D & Eliza, 49 a, Galveston
Barr Joseph W, 160 a, Lake Cicott
Barr Mary B, 80 a, Walton
Barr Rebecca R (dead), 40 a
Barr Thomas, 349 a, Ford
Barr Thomas, estate 738 a
Barr Thomas L, estate 40 a

Barr Wm A, 70 a, Lake Cicott
Barrett John sr, 140 a, Lucerne
Barron Mary A (dead), 97 a
Bartlett Elizabeth, 2 a, City
Bassler Christina, 50 a, Metea
Bassler Frederick C, 44 a, Metea
Bassler Henry, 80 a, Metea
Bassler John, 90 a, Metea
Bassler Sarah I, 24 a, Metea
Batty Fanny 20 a, Lucerne
Batty Richard, 57 a, Lucerne
Bauchman O E, 240 a, City
Bauman Michael, 160 a
Baxter John W, 40 a, Metea
Bayless George W, 40 a
Bayless H H 40 a, Twelve Mile
Beall S Z & F H, 8 a, Galveston
Bear Wm H, 80 a, Lake Cicott
Beard Elizabeth, 14 a, Metea
Beattie Ada R, 6 a, Metea
Beattie John H, 20 a
Beattie Mary J, 24 a, Metea
Beauchamp W S & H A, 33 a, Royal Center
Bechdol Alice et al, 3 a, Walton
Bechdol John, 40 a, Anoka
Bechdol Joshua, 96 a, Walton
Bechdol Samuel P, 80 a, Walton
Bechtelheimer David, estate 74 a
Beck George E, 80 a, Young America
Beck Jacob E, 80 a, Deer Creek
Beck Samuel J, 106 a, Young America
Beckley Albert R, 80 a, Royal Center
Beckley Ann R, 140 a, Royal Center
Beckley Catharine E, 30 a, Royal Center
Beckley Edward L, 120 a, Royal Center
Beckley Frances J, 40 a, Royal Center
Beckley George W, 234 a, Royal Center
Beckley Ira B, 65 a, Royal Center
Beckley Thomas J, 80 a, Royal Center
Beebe Samuel T, 100 a, Walton
Beecher Sarah C, 80 a
Beighler Kate G, 78 a, Galveston
Bell George M D & Lottie E, 80 a, Lucerne
Bell James, 120 a, Lincoln
Bell Mahlon, 158 a, Lincoln
Bell Michael, 80 a
Bell Nathaniel, 232 a, City
Bell Perry M, 40 a, Lincoln
Bell Wm, 70 a, Walton
Bell Wm H, 33 a, City
Bender Peter, 80 a
Benn Eva J, 1 a, Young America
Benn Louisa J, 1 a, Deacon
Benner Andrew J, 40 a, Onward
Benner Henry, 256 a, Gordon
Benner John, 194 a, Gordon
Benner Samuel, 202 a, Gordon

Bennett John N, 45 a, Metea
Bennett Joseph, 53 a
Bennett Sandy, 40 a, Metea
Bennett Wm and Annetta, 10 a
Benson Alwilda, 43 a, Onward
Benson Emma, 10 a, Onward
Benson John A and Mary, 80 a, Lake Cicott
Benson Robert, 79 a, Anoka
Berkshire Charles, 122 a, Royal Center
Berkshire Martin V, 140 a, Royal Center
Berkshire S M, 40 a, Royal Center
Berkshire Wm H, 193 a, Royal Center
Bernard Anna M, 40 a, Twelve Mile
Bernard Ella A, 30 a, City
Berry Israel, 1 a, Adamsboro
Berry Margaret, 40 a, Lake Cicott
Berry Rebecca, 6 a, Pipe Creek
Berry Sarah et al, 54 a, Adamsboro
Best Charles, 80 a, City
Best Christian, 80 a, Gordon
Best Mattie E and Charles W, 40 a, Royal Center
Bettcher Martin, 15 a, New Waverly
Betz Samuel, 12 a, Walton
Bevington Hyrcanus, 39 a
Bevington John W, 39 a
Bickell Margaret J, 53 a, Lincoln
Bigger John D, 80 a, Dego
Bigger Martha A, 98 a, Dego
Bingaman C C, 20 a
Bingaman Charles E, 40 a, Oak
Binney B F, 40 a, City
Binney George W, 40 a, Ford
Bird Benjamin F, 424 a, Deacon
Bish Cinderilla, 60 a, Walton
Bishop George W, 345 a, Walton
Bixler Christina, 1 a, Twelve Mile
Black Andrew, 88 a, Metea
Black Elizabeth, 20 a, Twelve Mile
Black Ellen, 200 a, Twelve Mile
Blackburn G W, 112 a, Lucerne
Blackburn Mary, 10 a, Lucerne
Blackburn R S, 54 a, Lucerne
Blacketter, J W F, 80 a, Twelve Mile
Blackford Wesley, 49 a, Royal Center
Blackwell Wm F, 40 a, City
Blatt Levi, 57 a, Pipe Creek
Bliss Lucinda, 127 a, Royal Center
Bliss John M, 390 a, Royal Center
Bliss Wm O, 95 a, Royal Center
Blue Uriah, 80 a, Deer Creek
Bockovor Eliza J, 87 a, Twelve Mile
Boehne Morris, 148 a, Lake Cicott
Boerger Fred, 2 a, City
Bohman Elizabeth et al, 40 a, Crittenden
Bohn Daniel, 40 a, Walton
Born Frank, 80 a, Lincoln
Booher Wm, 8 a, Walton

H. J. CRISMOND, 312 Market Street,
Gasoline Stoves, Screen Doors and Windows.

GAZETTEER. 343

Booker John, 8 a, Walton
Bookholtz Henry, 20 a
Bookwalter Elias, 60 a, Metea
Bookwalter Martha, 52 a, Twelve Mile
Bookwalter Olive B, 40 a, Twelve Mile
Bookwalter Wm J, 65 a, Metea
Boose Margaret, 24 a, Royal Center
Boose Valentine & Lucinda, 70 a, Royal Center
Booth DeHart, 80 a, City
Booth E J, 17 a, City
Booth Jasper N, 13 a, City
Booth Lucy N, 3 a, City
Booth Martha M, 25 a, City
Bosh Frank M, 5 a, Twelve Mile
Bosh Matilda, 20 a, Twelve Mile
Bowen A H, 160 a
Bowen Rebecca S, 180 a, Gordon
Bowlin Lucius H, 60 a
Bowman Jacob P, 80 a, New Waverly
Bowman John P, 131 a, New Waverly
Bowman J P, 156 a, Twelve Mile
Bowyer Adelbert C and Mary C, 80 a, Walton
Bowyer Allen W, 85 a, Pipe Creek
Bowyer Daniel sr, 40 a, Walton
Bowyer Elizabeth, 27 a
Bowyer George W, 4 a, Walton
Bowyer Henry, 13 a, Onward
Bowyer J M, 224 a, Pipe Creek
Bowyer Lewis F, 30 a, Walton
Bowyer Lavina A, 13 a, Onward
Bowyer Susanna, 40 a, Walton
Bowyer Sylvester C, 103 a, Pipe Creek
Bowyer S C, 145 a, New Waverly
Bowyer W L, 19 a, Walton
Boys Nathan H, 132 a, Pipe Creek
Braden Elizabeth, 40 a, Twelve Mile
Bradfield Benjamin D, 72 a, City
Bradfield Marietta, 40 a, City
Bradfield Mary E, 39 a, City
Bradfield Richard D, 32 a, City
Bradfield Thomas D, 30 a, City
Bradly Bennett B, 97 a, Walton
Bradley Catharine, 25 a, Walton
Braithwaite Jane, 120 a, City
Braithwaite Peggy 111 a, City
Brandt Charles A & Albert O, 196 a, City
Brandt Elizabeth J, 35 a, City
Brandt Nelson S, 80 a, City
Brandt O P, 80 a, City
Brannan Mary E, 27 a, Pine
Brenkle Jacob et ux, 40 a, Lucerne
Brennan John, 75 a, City
Bridge Ida, 32 a, City
Bridge Margaret A, 40 a, Young Amer
Briggs Duncan L, 57 a, Clymers
Briggs Loran A, 76 a
Bright Francis V, 175 a, Ind'pls

Bright Margaret J, 58 a, Gordon
Brill John I, 8 a
Bringhurst W H, 50 a, City
Britton C M, 72 a, Deacon
Britton Walter I, 58 a
Brobaker W H & Sarah C, 74 a, Twelve Mile
Brookmyer Henry, 241 a, City
Brophy John C, 210 a, City
Brough Mary A, 80 a, Walton
Brower Daniel, 160 a, Hoover
Brown Benjamin F, 20 a,
Brown Catherine, 52 a, Twelve Mile
Brown Elizabeth, 70 a, Metea
Brown Elizabeth J, 10 a, Adamsboro
Brown Emma, 35 a, Adamsboro
Brown George C, 26 a, City
Brown Ira T, 150 a, Lucerne
Brown John M, 80 a, Lucerne
Brown Levi H, 48 a, City
Brown Lewis, 195 a, Metea
Brown Mark A, 115 a, Royal Center
Brown Mary E, 100 a, Ford
Brown Mary E, 10 a, City
Brown Matthias, 1 a, Walton
Brown Perina, 3 a, Anoka
Brown Richard M, 120 a, Lucerne
Brown Samuel S, 120 a, Metea
Brown Sarah A, 100 a, City
Brown Willard 90 a, Lucerne
Brown W H, 22 a, Lake Cicott
Brolyer Martin, 40 a, Young America
Brolyer Sarah E & Martin, 30 a, Young America
Bruner Daniel, 130 a, Deacon
Bruner Henry, 100 a, Lucerne
Buchanan A M, 3 a, Metea
Buchanan E B, 112 a, Metea
Buchanan George W, 176 a, Metea
Buchanan Harriet H, 21 a, Metea
Buchanan James, 204 a, Metea
Buchanan James E, 204 a, Lake Cicott
Buchanan John G, 87 a, City
Buchanan J M and Daniel Reeder, 77 a, Metea
Buchanan Mary A, 110 a,
Buchanan Mary E, 60 a,
Buchanan R A, 153 a, Lake Cicott
Buchanan Sarah A 91 a, Curveton
Budlington W R, 60 a, Walton
Buhrmeister H C, 10 a, City
Buller Emma, 40 a, Twelve Mile
Bumgarner Isaac, 479 a, Walton
Bundy Benjamin, 100 a, Lucerne
Bundy George W, 80 a, Lucerne
Bundy Levi B, 80 a, Lucerne
Bunn Ida J, 21 a, Lake Cicott
Buntain John L, 60 a, Clymers
Burch Martha A, 100 a, City

Burdge Laura B, 80 a, Hoover
Buren Wm C, and Anna B, 10 a, City
Burge Catherine, 66 a, Adamsboro
Burge Eli, 67 a, Adamsboro
Burge Washington, 80 a, Gordon
Burges Mary, 20 a, Anoka
Burgman Frederick, 18 a, New Waverly
Burgman John, 57 a, New Waverly
Burke John, 40 a, Lucerne
Burke Mary M, 88 a, Gordon
Burket Daniel sr, 100 a, Curveton
Burket Dorotha A, 14 a, Lake Cicott
Burket Frank, 1 a, Lake Cicott
Burket George jr, 59 a, Lake Cicott
Burket George sr, 115 a, Lake Cicott
Burket G W, 120 a, Deacon
Burket Laura A, 40 a, Lake Cicott
Burket John M and Jane A, 40 a, City
Burket Wm H, 40 a,
Burkit Alvin, 380 a, Deacon
Burkit Daniel jr, 19 a, Lake Cicott
Burkhart George, 211 a, City
Burkhart Millie, 68 a, City
Burley Willard, 41 a, City
Burnett James 29 a, Adamsboro
Burnett John H, 158 a, City
Burnett Levi, 60 a, Adamsboro
Burnett Mary J, 48 a, City
Burrows Amelia, 7 a
Burrows John E, 95 a, Young America
Burrows Joseph R, 40 a, Dego
Burrows J B, 56 a, Deacon
Burrows Martha, 30 a, Deacon
Burrows Mary 65 a, Dego
Burrows Mary E, 60 a, Dego
Burrows M V, 71 a,
Burrows Warren L, 90 a, Dego
Burrows Wm est, 46 a,
Burrows Wm H, 194 a, Deacon
Burrows Wm J, 43 a, Galveston
Burton Catherine, 95 a, Royal Center
Burton Elmer, 40 a, Lucerne
Burton Francis A, 120 a, Royal C
Burton Leonard, 497 a, Lucerne
Burton Levi, 160 a, Lucerne
Burton Richard, 175 a, Lucerne
Burton Wm L, 113 a, Lucerne
Busard Philip A, 105 a, City
Button Albert F, 30 a, Royal Center
Button Clarissa, 50 a, Royal Center
Button Jesse, 80 a, Royal Center
Butz Charles H, 10 a
Butz Jennie C, 30 a
Byers Sarah, 80 a, Ford
Cage J E and Anna, 80 a, Lincoln
Caldwell Andrew, 80 a, Deacon
Caldwell John H, 57 a
Callahan James et al, 12 a
Callahan James T, 136 a, Fletchers

Callahan Sarah M and Rebecca, 5 a, Lucerne
Calloway Elizabeth, 40 a
Calloway Emma, 38 a, Lake Cicott
Calloway George, 140 a, Lake Cicott
Calloway Izora, 140 a, Lake Cicott
Calloway J W, 120 a, Lake Cicott
Calloway Wm, 23 a, Lake Cicott
Calvert D J, 40 a, City
Campbell B F, 188 a, City
Campbell Ira, 40 a, Deacon
Campbell James H, 80 a, Walton
Campbell John, 420 a, Lincoln
Campbell John C, 80 a, Lake Cicott
Campbell J M & J H, 150 a, Deacon
Campbell Levi, 80 a
Campbell Lewis J, 40 a
Campbell Louisa, 21 a, Ford
Campbell Robert, 35 a, Walton
Campbell Robert, 80 a, Deacon
Campbell Robert A, 16 a, City
Campbell W H, 40 a, Walton
Campbell W H & L J, 40 a
Canine Addie A, 177 a, Lincoln
Cantley J M & A, 33 a, City
Cantley Sarah J, 19 a, City
Caple Anna & Otto, 80 a, Twelve Mile
Cappel Charles, 51 a, City
Carson Wm, 83 a, Hoover
Casebeer Geo W, 110 a, New Waverly
Casebeer Marion, 110 a, New Waverly
Carey Arthur P, 25 a, Walton
Carey Frank, 25 a, Walton
Carey Joseph, 60 a, Walton
Carmion Joseph B, 120 a, Anoka
Carney Amelia A, 13 a, City
Carney Bridget A, 46 a, Lake Cicott
Carney H B, 66 a, City
Carney John R, 43 a, Lake Cicott
Carney Martin V, 1 a, City
Carney Robert M, 80 a, City
Carney Samuel J, 60 a, City
Carney Solomon, 170 a, Lake Cicott
Carr Sarah E, 25 a, City
Carroll Eli J & Maria T, 80 a, City
Carroll Lillie B, 20 a
Carroll Thomas, 18 a
Cart Adam, 128 a, New Waverly
Carter Egbert, 66 a, Adamsboro
Carter Donna, 1 a
Carter Lizzie, 80 a, City
Carson Thos & Mary A, 1 a, City
Casey Patrick B, 31 a, Clymers
Castle Mary, 80 a, City
Castle Thos P, 111 a, City
Caw John W, 24 a, Metea
Caw Mariba, 40 a, City
Caw Samuel and Harriet Williams, 1 a, City

HERZ, The Tailor
409 MARKET STREET.

Our Reputation for Good Work and Artistic Styles Is Well Established.

GAZETTEER. 345

Caw Sarah A, 8 a, Metea
Chambers Christina 80 a, City
Chambers Jemima, 5 a, City
Champ Melvin S, 35 a, Twelve Mile
Charles Abraham & Amos Keeport, 60 a, City
Charles Henry M & Maggie, 36 a, Adamsboro
Chase D H, 20 a, City
Chase Wm (dead), 3 a
Chestnut Joseph M, 328 a, Adamsboro
Chick Wm P, 160 a, Walton
Chidester Josephine, 11 a, City
Chilcott Benjamin B, 1 a, City
Chilcott Elizabeth, 15 a, Lake Cicott
Chilcott Henry, 52 a, City
Choen Jasper, 156 a, Clymers
Choen J and C G, 2 a, Clymers
Christman Charles and Arabella 106 a, Hoover
Clary Isaac N, 571 a, Lucerne
Clary Isaac N, jr, 110 a, Lucerne
Clary Jacob W, 200 a, Lucerne
Clary John W, 140 a Lucerne
Clary Nellie, 40 a, Lucerne
Clelland Leander J, 40 a,
Clevenger George W, 60 a, City
Clevenger Lafayette R 80 a, City
Cline John W and Laura A, 80 a, Oak
Clinginpeel Samuel P, 91 a, Anoka
Close Sarah A, 85 a, Lake Cicott
Closson E D, 92 a City
Clouse John L, 1 a, Hoover
Clymer D H, 3 a, City
Coble Richard, 2 a, Gordon
Coblentz A est, 155 a,
Coblentz D A G, 50 a, Onward
Coblentz Jesse, 134 a Onward
Coblentz Joseph est, 76 a
Coblentz Joshua, 110 a, Onward
Coblentz Wm, 80 a, Onward
Cochran Lucinda, 100 a, Gordon
Cochran Phoebe 20 a
Cogley S M, 110 a, Ford
Cohee Rebecca, 40 a, Deer Creek
Coin Anna E, 80 a, City
Coin Samuel R, 118 a Young America
Coleman Anzonetta, 100 a,
Coleman Asa, 80 a, City
Coleman Lafayette 60 a
Collett Marcus W, 320 a, Metea
Collett Sarah A, 70 a, Metea
Collins Mary P, 40 a, Anoka
Condon E B, 40 a, Hoover
Condon E B and E C, 40 a Hoover
Condon Mary 271 a, City
Condon Wm, 179 a City
Conk Michael, 80 a, Lincoln
Conkling Walter, 132 a, Tine

Conn George est, 120 a
Conn George W, 40 a, Royal Center
Conn Hanna T, 42 a, Royal Center
Conn Jesse, 280 a, Royal Center
Conrad George W, 102 a, Metea
Conrad Isaac, 80 a, Twelve Mile
Conrad John H, 62 a, Pine
Conrad John Q, 5 a, City
Conrad John S (est), 40 a
Conrad Llewellyn A, 1 a, Twelve Mile
Conrad Otto, et al, 160 a, City
Conrad R G, 10 a, Metea
Conrad S G, 494 a, Metea
Conrad Thomas F, 90 a, Pine
Conroy Martin, 120 a, Clymers
Conroy Thomas, 3 a, Adamsboro
Conwell George W, 80 a, Galveston
Cook Chas N, 40 a, City
Cook Mary M, 40 a,
Cook Nancy J, 40 a, Lincoln
Cook Perry B, 80 a, Twelve Mile
Coons Dugal F, 20 a, Adamsboro
Coons George W, 80 a, Adamsboro
Cooper Mary L, 30 a, Twelve Mile
Cornell Benjamin D, 40 a, Dego
Cornell Jeremiah (heirs), 40 a
Cornell Joseph H, 40 a, Twelve Mile
Cornell J Frank, 20 a, Dego
Cornell Nancy, 57 a, Deacon
Cornwell Cornelius, 60 a, Twelve Mile
Cost Elizabeth, 120 a, Metea
Cost James T, 80 a,
Cost John W, 81 a, Young America
Cost Leonard H, 80 a
Costenborder W F, 23 a, Pipe Creek
Costner David, 80 a, Ford
Cotner Easton, 120 a, Ford
Cotner Ellen et al, 40 a Lake Cicott
Cotner Grace I, 40 a
Cotner Henry, 137 a, Fletchers
Cotner Henry, 40 a, Lake Cicott
Cotner Ira, 166 a, Royal Center
Cotner Isabella, 35 a, City
Cotner John est, 140 a
Cotner Jonathan, 40 a
Cotner Levi M, 35 a, City
Cotner Mary, 150 a, City
Cotner Mary D, 80 a, Lake Cicott
Cotner Richard A, 190 a, City
Cotner S A & Lucy, 57 a, Ford
Cotterman Harmon, 81 a, Dego
Countryman Isaiah, 114 a, Lincoln
Countryman James N, 100 a, Dego
Countryman John A, 120 a, Lincoln
Countryman Nancy E, 40 a, Lincoln
Countryman Wm E, 120 a, Lincoln
Coves Alonzo A, 200 a, Pine
Cowell Alice C (dead), 40 a
Cox Andrew J, 48 a, Twelve Mile

All Kinds of Life Insurance from $6.00 to $50,000 Written
BY THE
Metropolitan Life Insurance Co., of New York.
W. O. WASHBURN. SUPT. LOGANSPORT DISTRICT   Office rooms 1, 2 and 3 Crawford Block

346   GAZETTEER.

Cox Jonathan, 80 a, New Waverly
Cox Joseph, 239 a, Metea or City
Cox Wm, 80 a, Hoover
Coyle Jesse, 1 a, Walton
Crabb Benjamin F et al, 50 a
Cragan Harry W, 1 a, Lucerne
Cragan Sylvester S, 137 a, City
Cragan Zachariah, 94 a, City
Craig Joseph, 40 a
Crane Elizabeth, 80 a
Crane James H, 71 a, City
Crawford James H, 117 a, Dego
Crawford John A, 80 a, Twelve Mile
Cree James M, 1 a
Cree James W, 39 a
Cree Melissa J, 14 a, Deer Creek
Cree Thomas M, 59 a, Deacon
Creekmore John, 35 a, Deacon
Creswell Anna E, 79 a
Crites George, 12 a, Lucerne
Crim W H, 40 a, Walton
Crimmins John P, 110 a, Lucerne
Crimmins Maria, 86 a, Lucerne
Cripe Jacob, 160 a, Deacon
Cripe Sarah, 80 a, Dego
Cripe Wm, 50 a, Dego
Crippen Wm T, 60 a, Pine
Crisler Charles A & Nancy, 80 a, Galveston
Crisler Elizabeth, 8 a, Galveston
Crist Callista, 42 a
Crockett Frank H, 65 a
Crockett Henry A, 80 a, Deacon
Crockett John S, 119 a, Deacon
Crockett Mattie A, 40 a
Cromer Mary & Robert, 8 a, City
Cromwell Blanche M, 26 a, Lake Cicott
Cronder John F & Wm F, 100 a, Crittenden
Crooks Alva C, 20 a, Metea
Crooks Maria et al, 56 a, Metea
Crooks Patrick H, 160 a, Hoover
Crooks Wm H, 80 a, Pine
Crowell John N & A B Irelan, 136 a
Cummings Joseph, 22 a
Cummings Zelphonzo, 76 a
Cunningham Sarah, 21 a
Curtis A F, 80 a, Walton
Custer Chauncey M, 40 a, City
Custer Grace P, 25 a, City
Custer Hannah S, 1 a, City
Custer L B, 91 a, City
Custer Mary E, 57 a, City
Daggett Charles, 80 a, Galveston
Daggett Daniel, 160 a, Galveston
Daggett Freeman, 200 a, Galveston
Dague David N, 28 a, Twelve Mile
Dague George W, 80 a
Dahill Dennis, 40 a

Dale Anna M, 1 a, New Waverly
Dalzell Charles W, 40 a, Metea
Dalzell Isabelle, 72 a, Twelve Mile
Dalzell John A, 80 a, Lucerne
Dalzell Robert, 315 a, Metea
Dalzell Robert (heirs), 125 a
Dalzell Wm, 215 a, Pine
Damm Adam, 51 a, Hoover
Darland Albert, 32 a
Darland David A, 36 a, Walton
Darland Elizabeth, 40 a, Walton
Darland Wm R, 36 a, Walton
Davenport Sarah C, 80 a, Anoka
Davidson David, 120 a, Lincoln
Davidson Joseph, 34 a, City
Davidson Nancy J, 119 a, Lincoln
Davidson Rosetta, 5 a, Lucerne
Davis Frank, 84 a, Burnettsville
Davis John, 165 a, City
Davis John, 52 a, Walton
Davis Nancy A, 40 a, Walton
Davis N M, 286 a, Deacon
Davis Richard P, 137 a
Davis Sarah L, 45 a, Burnettsville
Davis Thomas W, 132 a, Deer Creek
Davis Vashti A, 128 a, Walton
Davis Vina, 40 a
Davis Wm M, et al 22 a, Burnettsville
Dawson Isaac T, 20 a, Fletchers
Day Nicholas and Catherine, 168 a, Galveston
Deacon Wm C, 9 a, Deacon
Dean Benjamin, 80 a, City
Dean John A, 120 a, Ford
Dean Robert E, 169 a, New Waverly
DeBoo John A, 83 a, City
DeBoo Samuel, 96 a, Ford
Deboo Samuel A, 14 a, City
Deck George W, 40 a
Deck Mollie C, 40 a
Decker A J, 20 a, Twelve Mile
Decker Samuel, 1 a, Twelve Mile
DeHaven Abner B, 160 a, Deacon
DeHaven Cyrus O, 160 a, Deacon
DeHaven Jane and Ambrose, 40 a, Deacon
DeHaven John D, 239 a, Deacon
DeHaven Joseph W, 101 a, Galveston
DeHaven Wesley 120 a, Deacon
DeHaven Wm L, 80 a, Galveston
Deisch Aaron O, 34 a Walton
Deisch Matthias 120 a
Deitrich Rachel, 9 a City
Deitz Mary, 95 a
Deleplane James, 72 a, Deer Creek
Delawter Jacob W, 80 a, Pipe Creek
Deleplane Sarah, 112 a, City
Deleplane Wm (dead) 112 a
DeMoss Wm R & wife, 10 a, Galveston

Deniston James M, 18 a, Hoover
Dennin James F, 40 a, Lucerne
Dewenter John C, 130 a, City
DeWolf Caroline, 68 a, City
Dice James, 100 a, Royal Center
Dickerson Nancy & John, 3 a, Clymers
Dickey Martha J, 23 a, City
Dickinson Noble, 21 a, Lake Cicott
Dickinson Rachel, 3 a
Diffenbaugh Florence, 108 a
Diffenbaugh Ida M, 112 a
Diffenbaugh J A, 28 a City
Dill Alfred M, 180 a, Royal Center
Dillard Thomas, 90 a, City
Dillman Eva, 16 a, City
Dillman Samuel S. 16 a, City
Dillman Soloman F, 95 a, Hoover
Dillman Wm H, 100 a, Hoover
Diltz George, 60 a, Oak
Diver Sarah, 20 a, City
Divinney John, 20 a
Divinney Mary J, 20 a
Dixon Elizabeth, 32 a, City
Dodds Andrew, 120 a, City
Dodds Elizabeth, 77 a, City
Dodds Matthew, 118 a, City
Dodt Henry, 160 a, Lucerne
Dodt Henry jr, 50 a, Royal Center
Dodt Wm and Mary, 50 a, Lucerne
Dohle Susan, 30 a, City
Donaldson A N, 10 a, City
Donaldson Margaret, 1 a, Clymers
Donily John & Martha P, 20 a Twelve
Mile
Donovan James 124 a, Lucerne
Donovan Wm J, 120 a, Lucerne
Doolittle I N, 84 a, Ford
Dorsey Martha E & Rosa M, 40 a, Deacon
Douglass George S, 15 a, City
Douglass George W, 40 a, Crittenden
Douglass Harriet, 34 a, City
Douglass Tyre 100 a Lucerne
Douglass Wm 264 a, City
Drake Ella, 20 a, Walton
Drake David C 20 a, Walton
Dritt Henry est, 320 a,
Dritt Wm H, 176 a, City
Dritt Zach W, 56 a, City
Drummond John R, 64 a, City
Duncan Geo W and Laura B, 80 a, City
Duncizer John, 15 a, Lake Cicott
Duncizer Frank, 67 a, Lake Cicott
Duncizer Sarah, Mary and Lewey, 40
a, Lake Cicott
unham John, 20 a, City
unkin B F, 80 a, Young America
unkin Peter, 63 a, Young America
unkin Wm, 80 a, Young America

Dunkle Benjamin, 20 a, City
Dunkle Jacob, 40 a, Walton
Dunn John, 16 a, City
Dunn Edward A. 1580 a (non-resident)
Dupler Mary E, 10 a, Galveston
Dutchess Charles P, 81 a, Walton
Dykeman Charles E, 77 a, City
Dykeman D D, 365 a, City
Dykeman Fred A, 80 a, City
Dykeman George P, 240 a, Anoka
Earl Harper M, 34 a, Clymers
Early David, 120 a, Metea
Eckerlee Leopold, 80 a
Eckley John, 20 a, Walton
Eckert John, 204 a, City
Eckert Mary A, 2 a
Edgerton Franklin, 50 a, Twelve Mile
Edgeworth Lura M, 20 a, City
Edwards Mary E, 40 a
Eglyn John, 319 a, Lucerne
Egman Isaac W, 152 a, Twelve Mile
Eidson Ira B, 2 a
Eisenbry J F & Geo W, 21 a, Galveston
Eisert John C, 15 a, City
Eisert Sophia & John, 140 a, City
Eldridge Franklin, 20 a
Eldridge Franklin J et al, 40 a
Elkins Anna E, 82 a, City
Elkins John, 40 a, Walton
Elliott Alfred, 53 a. Lucerne
Elliott Alice M, 40 a, City
Elliott Ambrose, 222 a, Lucerne
Elliott Eleanor G, 65 a, City
Elliott James T, 100 a, Crittenden
Elliott John P, 69 a, Crittenden
Elliott Margaret A, 40 a, Crittenden
Ellis Abraham, 80 a, Metea
Ellis Sarah J, 7 a, City
Emerick Anderson, 120 a, Galveston
Emerick David H, 140 a, Galveston
Emery Isaac, 51 a, City
Engel John H, 45 a, Onward
Engel Margaret, 46 a, Onward
Engler Owen, 60 a, Walton
English Charles, 60 a, City
Ensley Prior W, 40 a
Enyart David B, 343 a, Onward
Enyart Israel, 50 a, City
Enyart Lewis, 80 a, City
Enyart Susannah, 53 a, Pine
Enyart Temperance, 19 a, City
Enyart Wm B, 16 a, City
Erbaugh John C, 80 a, Twelve Mile
Erbaugh Oliver P, 80 a, Walton
Eschker Wm, 160 a, Young America
Eshleman Mary J, 80 a
Estabrook C H, 40 a
Estabrook James W, 25 a, City
Estabrook Robert, 120 a, Lucerne

348   GAZETTEER.

Erny Joseph F et ux, 48 a, Walton
Erwin Malinda & A A, 80 a, Deacon
Etnire James M, 82 a, City
Etnire Peter L, 158 a, City
Eurit Stephen, 207 a, Twelve Mile
Evans Mary E, 143 a, Twelve Mile
Ewell Thomas H, 50 a, Adamsboro
Ewing Mary, 63 a, Young America
Eyman Jacob, 140 a, Gordon
Fahl Edward, 180 a, Twelve Mile
Fair Martha J, 40 a, City
Fair Parker A, 10 a, Adamsboro
Fairchild Thomas, 40 a, Lake Cicott
Fall Rachel, 1 a, Lucerne
Farley James M, 80 a, Walton
Fawber Nathaniel, 80 a, Anoka
Fawber Nathaniel (trustee), 70 a, Anoka
Fawcett Alex D & Charles E, 7 a, Galveston
Fawcett Ellen, 70 a, Deacon
Fennell Richard M, 40 a, Lake Cicott
Fenton Alonzo and Emma, 1 a, Lucerne
Fergus Geo F, 44 a, Metea
Ferguson Harry P, 80 a, Ford
Ferguson John D, 147 a, City
Ferguson J W et al, 152 a, New Waverly
Ferguson Mary E, 80 a, Fletcher
Ferguson Nancy J, 130 a, Ford
Ferguson Oscar B, 46 a, New Waverly
Ferguson R W, 41 a, Hoover
Ferguson S O, 40 a, Hoover
Ferguson Winfield S, 80 a, Hoover
Ferguson W S & Emma M, 80 a, Hoover
Fern John & Mary A, 10 a, Deacon
Fernald W E, 1184 a, City
Fetrow Daniel, 95 a, Twelve Mile
Fickle Henderson, 80 a, Galveston
Fickle Rebecca, 124 a, Galveston
Fickle Wilson T, 136 a, Galveston
Fiddler August, 34 a, City
Fiddler Catherine, 37 a
Fiddler Charles, 4 a, Lucerne
Fiddler Charles M, 80 a, Adamsboro
Fiddler Christian 20 a, Lucerne
Fiddler Daniel, 50 a, Metea
Fiddler Emma E, 8 a, Metea
Fiddler George, 61 a, Metea
Fiddler John H, 26 a, New Waverly
Fiddler Malinda, 75 a, New Waverly
Fiddler Michael, 72 a, Deer Creek
Fiddler Wm H, 101 a, New Waverly
Field Martin 60 a
Field Mary and H F, 160 a, Pipe Creek
Fife Josephine, 2 a, Young America
Fife Laura B, 2 a, Young America
Fiscel Henry and Emma, 60 a, City
Fisher Asa A and Minnie J, 90 a, Lake Cicott
Fisher Cornelius, 80 a, City

Fisher David and Sarah, 75 a, Royal Center
Fisher Halleck A, 27 a, Lake Cicott
Fisher Minnie J, 10 a, Lake Cicott
Fisher Myrtle B, 103 a, New Waverly
Fisher Sarah E, 40 a, Curveton
Fisk Helen B, 80 a, City
Fisk Julia C, 30 a, New Waverly
Fitzer Alfred B, 60 a, Gordon
Fitzer Hugh, 618 a, Clymers
Filzer Rachel, 220 a, Gordon
Flanagan Eliza A, 3 a, Clymers
Flanagan Charles, 80 a, Walton
Flannegan Eliza, 100 a, Lake Cicott
Flinn Thomas, 80 a Deer Creek
Flock John, 25 a, Lucerne
Flomerfelt Virgil, 84 a, Walton
Flook Martha A, 19 a, Walton
Flory David, 165 a, City
Flory Jennie, 22 a, City
Flynn, P O est, 85 a
Flynn Susan, 40 a, Twelve Mile
Foglesong Daniel & Sarah, 76 a, Metea
Foglesong Mary J, 95 a, Lucerne
Foote Charles H, 382 a, (non-resident) (Kenneth Quarries)
Ford Armilda A, 72 a, Ford
Ford F C, 40 a, Ford
Ford Joseph, 40 a, Lincoln
Ford Mary E, 22 a, Metea
Fording Mary J, 88 a, Galveston
Forgy Charles E, 88 a, Marion, Ind
Forgy C P & Bro, 86 a, New Waverly
Forgy D J, 76 a, New Waverly
Forgy George B, 583 a, City
Forgy Emma J, 78 a, New Waverly
Forlow James, 52 a, City
Forlow James and Kate, 60 a, City
Forlow Samuel, 119 a, City
Forlow Simon, 136 a, City
Fossion Martin, 4 a, Clymers
Fossion Martin & Maria, 63 a, Clymers
Fouts Finis E, 80 a, Deer Creek
Fouts Henry, 86 a, Young America
Fouts Solomon, 57 a Deer Creek
Foutz Maggie, 40 a
Fowler Anna A, 40 a
Fox Hezekiah, 100 a
Fox Mary J, 5 a, New Waverly
Frahm Henry and Wm, 80 a
Frank Mary, 31 a, City
Frankam Wm, 40 a, Twelve Mile
Frederick Thomas, 160 a, Lucerne
French Joseph W, 38 a, City
Freshour Edward estate, 71 a
Freshour George, 701 a, City
Freshour Jerome, 80 a, Lucerne
Freshour John W, 180 a, Lucerne
Freshour Loren C, 120 a, Lucerne

reshour Lucy J, 40 a, City
reshour Michael, 69 a, Royal Center
reshour W A & Alice C, 41 a, Lucerne
reshour Wm V, 80 a, City
riemel Frank, 37 a, Royal Center
riend Edward, 1 a, Deacon
riend John P, 40 a, Gordon
rush Hezekiah, 80 a, Lincoln
rush Sarah, 80 a, Lincoln
ry Alex, 80 a, Royal Center
ry Frank, 122 a, Lake Cicott
ry James F & Malinda, 34 a, Royal Center
ry James M, 26 Metea
ry Jerome and Adaline, 127 a, Royal Center
ry John, 40 a, Royal Center
ry Martin est, 40 a
ry Samuel, 159 a, Royal Center
ry Solomon, 40 a, Ford
ry Wm M, 80 a, Royal Center
uller Elizabeth, 40 a
uller John A, 220 a, City
ultz Andrew J & Julia, 80 a, City
ultz Cyrus, 60 a, Royal Center
ultz Daniel, 3 a, Royal Center
ultz Lavina, 31 a, Royal Center
ultz Melanchton, 187 a, Royal Center
ultz Otto L, 9 a, Royal Center
ultz Warren, 9 a, Royal Center
unk Andrew D, 130 a, Royal Center
unk Elizabeth, 137 a, Royal Center
unk Jra, 6 a, Royal Center
unk Joseph G, 156 a, City
unk Rudolph, 40 a, Royal Center
unk Rudolph jr, 136 a, Royal Center
unk Wm A, 41 a, City
inston Wm, 185 a, City
irrow Mathias, 160 a, Clymers
ilbraith John C, 40 a, Walton
ilbraith Samuel, 160 a, Lake Cicott
illahan George W, 160 a, Adamsboro
illahan, Ida M, 174 a
ird Canada, estate, 96 a
ird Mary, estate, 56 a
irrett Joshua, 33 a, Lincoln
irrish Frank, 80 a, Royal Center
irritson Rachel E, 18 a, Galveston
rver Henry E, 120 a, Deer Creek
rver Lewis F & Margaret, 80 a, City
rver Samuel, 70 a, Deer Creek
rver Sarah E, 40 a, Deacon
rver Wm, 80 a, Deer Creek
saway Nancy, 35 a, Gordon
tes James, 92 a, Royal Center
tes James W, 240 a, Royal Center
tes J Warren, 140 a, Ford
ir Benjamin F, 45 a, City
ir Elizabeth A, 80 a, City

Gearhard Arthur A, 4 a, Galveston
Gearhard Daisy B, 4 a, Galveston
Geer Sarah A, 34 a, Lake Cicott
Gehman Joseph, 240 a, Twelve Mile
Gerhart Hannah, 96 a, Adamsboro
Getty John F, 140 a, City
Gibson Frederick, 40 a
Gibson Kate, 133 a, Curveton
Gibson Joseph H & Viola L, 1 a, City
Gibson Robert M, 80 a, Curveton
Gibson S C, 78 a, Curveton
Gibson, Wm, 40 a, Deacon
Gibson Wm J, 65 a, Gordon
Giffin Georgiana, 27 a, City
Gillin Herbert I, 53 a, City
Gilliam Mary, 79 a
Gillsinger Andrew and Mary, 51 a, City
Girton B M, estate, 23 a
Girton Henderson T, 120 a, Gordon
Gish Elizabeth, 208 a, Deer Creek
Gish James G, 80 a
Giveler Samuel A, 33 a, Onward
Gleason Dennis, 1 a, City
Gleitze August, 6 a, City
Goldsberry Leona J, 28 a, Crittenden
Goldsberry Wm C, 92 a, City
Glodsberry Wm R, 29 a, Crittenden
Goldsberry Simon M, 45 a, Crittenden
Good Samuel H, 80 a, Lake Cicott
Goodbaster Mary E, 10 a, Walton
Goodrich H E, 140 a, Royal Center
Goodwin Richard, 80 a, City
Gorman Edward, 2 a, Fletcher
Gorman John, 2 a, City
Goss James, 4 a, City
Gottshall Alva C, estate, 153 a
Gottshall Ann, 7 a, City
Gottshall Henry, 254 a, Anoka
Gottshall Horace and Susie, 80 a, City
Gottshall Sarah J, 80 a, City
Gottshall Susan, 80 a, City
Gould Nancy E, 75 a, Pine
Grable Edith and Joram, 75 a, Twelve Mile
Grable John C, 80 a
Grable Jonathan, 208 a, City
Grable Samuel McM, 210 a, Fletcher
Graham Daniel, 74 a, Deer Creek
Graham Ed L, 40 a, Lincoln
Graham Israel, estate, 18 a
Graham Lavina, 141 a, City
Graham Walter M, 160 a, Lincoln
Gransinger Joseph, 160 a, Hoover
Gransinger Peter, 80 a, Deer Creek
Grant Emma E, 30 a, Royal center
Grant Isaac, 307 a, Royal Center
Grant Wm H, 80 a, Royal Center
Grant Wm J, 47 a, Gordon
Grauel Francis M, 40 a, Ford

Grauel Mary E. 6 a, Clymers
Grauel Sylvester, 54 a, Ford
Graves Ada B, 20 a, Lincoln
Graves G W, 140 a, Galveston
Graves Newberry W, 281 a, Galveston
Graves Phiny, 113 a, Lincoln
Graves Warren W, 100 a, Galveston
Gray Alex, 47 a, Lake Cicott
Gray Barzilla, 140 a, Lucerne
Gray Blair B, 28 a, Gordon
Gray Ellie C, 25 a, Gordon
Gray Eva, 120 a, Galveston
Gray Francis, 40 a, Lucerne
Gray Harriet A, 46 a, Gordon
Gray Harrison, 46 a, Lake Cicott
Gray James W, 20 a, Lake Cicott
Gray John, 89 a, Lake Cicott
Gray John (heirs), 40 a
Gray John A, 50 a, Lucerne
Gray Joseph, 929 a, Dego
Gray Joseph jr, 1 a
Gray Joseph and Samuel, 116 a
Gray Martha J, 12 a, Lake Cicott
Gray Mary C, 46 a, Gordon
Gray Matthew H, 160 a, Clymers
Gray Rebecca, 121 a, Lake Cicott
Gray Samuel, 870 a, Galveston
Gray Samuel P and Andrew, 159 a
Gray W Albert, 50 a
Greasley estate, 80 a
Green Charles R, 192 a, City
Green Cornelius, 60 a, Twelve Mile
Green Elizabeth, 40 a, New Waverly
Green Levi, 71 a, Curveton
Green Margaret J, 150 a, City
Green Sydney F, 60 a, Lake Cicott
Greenbank Thomas, 140 a
Greisser, Constantine, 40 a, City
Gremelspacher Marvin, 80 a, Deacon
Gremelspacher R, 160 a, Deacon
Grenert Conrad & Catharine, 35 a, Lucerne
Gribben Wm, 162 a, Pipe Creek
Gribben Wm P, 155 a, New Waverly
Griffin Joseph W & wife 160 a, Dego
Griffith Rufus, 173 a, Galveston
Grimes John, 80 a, New Waverly
Grimes Joseph, 92 a, New Waverly
Grimes Samuel, 40 a, New Waverly
Groninger Charles W, 40 a, Deer Creek
Grow James, 103 a, Fletcher
Gruner E H, 40 a, Cordon
Grusenmyer Anthony, 20 a, City
Grusenmyer John F, 60 a, City
Guard Americus 191 a, New Waverly
Guard Emma J, 54 a
Guard Rufus M, 46 a, New Waverly
Gugle Christian, 80 a, Royal Center
Gugle John, 76 a

Gundrum Paul, 80 a, City
Gundrum Wm 430 a, Royal Center
Guthrie Emily J, 48 a, Gordon
Guthrie Joseph, 188 a, City
Guthrie Matilda, 9 a, Deacon
Guthrie Stephen A, 40 a, City
Guy Andrew R, 12 a, Walton
Guy Granville & Ida E, 40 a, Walton
Guy Hiram est, 40 a
Guy James, 200 a
Guy Jefferson, 4 a, Anoka
Guy Martha C, 69 a, Lake Cicott
Guy Martha J, 40 a, Walton
Guy Wm A, 24 a, Walton
Haas Anna P, 66 a, Onward
Haas Faber, 20 a, Onward
Haas Mary E, 20 a, Onward
Haas Wm H, 20 a
Hagenbuck Wm, 19 a, City
Hager Melvina, 50 a, Metea
Hager Philip, 62 a, Metea
Hahn James D, 48 a, Onward
Hahn Phoebe A, 70 a, Onward
Hahn Wm, 70 a, Anoka
Hahn Wm W, 40 a, Anoka
Hahn W H, 50 a, Anoka
Hahnert Adam, 200 a, Anoka
Hahnert John H and Mary, 47 a, Adamsboro
Hahnert Wm, 40 a, Anoka
Haigh George & Mart Elliott, 40 a, City
Haigh Sarah I, 58 a, City
Hale Charles E, 651 a, City
Hall Gabriel S, 150 a, Metea
Hall John W, 205 a, Lucerne
Hall Kinney N, 20 a, City
Halterman Adam, 20 a, Twelve Mile
Hamilton A H, 1210 a
Hamilton Ellen, 200 a
Hamilton Fremont et al, 66 a
Hampshire Jno, 200 a, Young America
Hammon Joseph L, 55 a, City
Hamilton Margaret V, 527 a
Hamilton Montgomery, 388 a
Hamilton Phoebe A, 786 a
Hauer Jay, 94 a, City
Haney Carrie E, 48 a, City
Haney Louisana, 824 a, City
Haney Wm E, 948 a, City
Hankee Henry, 78 a, City
Hankee Mary E, 90 a, City
Hankee Nancy, 58 a, City
Hankee Richard A, 30 a, Clymers
Hanna D W, 40 a, Ford
Hanna Elihu, 98 a, City
Hanna James W, 80 a, City
Hanna Jas W & Elihu, 80 a, City
Hannah James W, 40 a, Ford
Hanna Rebecca, estate, 4 a, City

H. J. GRISMOND, 312 Market Street,
Hardware, Stoves and Tinware.

GAZETTEER. 351

Harder Andrew, 165 a, Pipe Creek
Hardy George C, 77 a, City
Hardy Wm and Mary E, 45 a, City
Harley Rose M, 82 a, City
Harmon Viola, 60 a, Twelve Mile
Harness Addison, 80 a, Dego
Harness Anneta et al, 95 a
Harness Calvin & Queen V, 160 a, Lake Cicott
Harness George W, 300 a, Crittenden
Harness George W jr, 160 a, Crittenden
Harness Louisa, 60 a, Crittenden
Harness Maggie D, 25 a, Dego
Harness Solomon J, 111 a, Young America
Harness Wm, 120 a, Dego
Harness Wm, 840 a, Lake Cicott
Harper Braden F, 80 a, Clymer
Harrington John M, 120 a, Ford
Harris Henry, 44 a
Harrison John T, 42 a, Anoka
Harrison Mary E, 16 a, Anoka
Harrison Rebecca E, 30 a, Royal Center
Harrison Sarah J, 1 a, Adamsboro
Hartley Ann, 62 a, Ford
Harvey Dora M, 7 a, New Waverly
Harvey John W, 133 a, City
Harvey Lydia A, 167 a
Hattery Esias M, 20 a, Metea
Hawk Cora D, 7 a, Young America
Hayden Ethel M, 21 a, City
Hayes Stephen, 85 a, City
Hays Wm N, 1 a. City
Healey Bernard W, 63 a, City
Healey Bessie et al, 26 a
Hedley Catharine, 40 a, City
Healey Lawrence, 386 a, Lake Cicott
Hearne Margaret, 40 a. City
Heckard David, 15 a, City
Hedde Andrew, 93 a, City
Hedde John, 43 a, City
Hedges James H & Clara, 1 a, Royal Center
Hedrick James G, 80 a, Ford
Hedrick Nancy S, 153 a, Ford
Heffley S P, 88 a
Heiney Henry M & Eva J, 40 a, Gordon
Heinmiller Jno, 160 a, Young America
Helm Fred, 168 a, Walton
Helvie Abram, 11 a, Pipe Creek
Helvie John, 35 a, Walton
Helvie Mary, 80 a, Pipe Creek
Helvie Viola B, 40 a
Helvie Wm M, 285 a, Anoka
Hemmersbaugh Wm A, 432 a, Hoover
Hendee George, 14 a, Royal Center
Hendee Oliver, 40 a, Royal Center
Henderson James P, 80 a, Lake Cicott
Henderson J W, 90 a, Ford

Hendrickson David, 80 a, Deacon
Hendrix Geo W, 80 a, Young America
Hendrixson John, 126 a
Henry Jacob, estate, 64 a
Henry Mary C, 1 a, Lake Cicott
Henry Rebecca, 40 a, City
Henry Thomas, 370 a, Young America
Henry Wm, 80 a, Young America
Henry W H, 16 a, City
Hensley Richard, 20 a, City
Hepler Elias, 44 a
Heppe Wm, 19 a, City
Herbert Lizzie, 6 a, Royal Center
Herd George, 1 a
Herd John, 280 a, Lucerne
Herd Thomas, 22 a, Royal Center
Herd Thomas, 140 a, Royal Center
Herd Wm, 118 a, Lucerne
Herrick George, 80 a, City
Hertsel Matilda J, 50 a, New Waverly
Heslin John P, 20 a, Lucerne
Heslin Thomas, 165 a, Lucerne
Heslin Thomas, 120 a, Lake Cicott
Hetton Wilhemina, 71 a, City
Hetzner Peter, 30 a, City
Heward Benjamin, 79 a, Walton
Hickermann James C, 117 a
Hickey John, 60 a, Lucerne
Hickey John jr, 25 a
Hicks Isaac H, 40 a, Lincoln
Hicks John, 92 a, Royal Center
Hicks Robert W, 24 a, Royal Center
Higgins James A, 80 a, Ford
Hildebrand Abram, 34 a, Gordon
Hilderbran Wm, 20 a, Deacon
Hilderbrand Samuel, 120 a, Gordon
Hilderbrand A W, 157 a, Gordon
Hilderbrand Jay I & Alice B, 69 a, Gordon
Hilderbrant Louisa 90 a, Anoka
Hile Daniel, 15 a Lucerne
Hile Daniel, 313 a, Royal Center
Hile Peter, 183 a, Royal Center
Hill Israel J, 189 a
Hill Joseph 104 a, Fletchers
Hill Mary E, 50 a, City
Hill Thomas, 40 a Twelve Mile
Hiller James R, 160 a, Dego
Hiller Mary 80 a, New Waverly
Himmelberger Isaac, 133 a, City
Hiner James F, 60 a, New Waverly
Hitchens John, 110 a, Lake Cicott
Hitchens Thomas W, 48 a, Lake Cicott
Hoehne August G jr, 73 a, Metea
Hoehne John G jr, 70 a, Metea
Hoehne Martin 5 a, Metea
Hoffman Frederick, 102 a, Lucerne
Hoffman George est, 32 a
Hoffman Isaac, 154 a, Royal Center

offman Isaiah 16 a, Clymers
Hoffman Isaiah & Emanuel, 32 a, Clymers
Hoffman Jacob F, 41 a, Lucerne
Hoffman Jacob F, 66 a, Royal Center
Hoffman Samuel P & Alice 40 a, Royal Center
Hogle Mary (wife of George), 16 a, City
Holcome Cathauine, 65 a, Pine
Holland James, 1 a, City
Holland James A est, 5 a
Holland Wm H, 400 a, Dego
Hollenback G W, 67 a, Fletchers
Hollenback George W & Margaret, 39 a, Metea
Hollenbeck Simon P, 80 a
Hollis Elizabeth, 242 a, Royal Center
Hollis Robert G, 80 a, Royal Center
Holman James W, 20 a Galveston
Holmes Jackson, 92 a, Royal Center
Holsey Mary E, 2 a, Metea
Homburg Adam C est, 40 a
Homburg Christiana, 121 a, City
Homburg Elizabeth, 139 a
Homburg H H & A L, 110 a, Clymer
Hoover Anthony, 55 a, Twelve Mile
Hoover Eliza J, 44 a, Twelve Mile
Hoover Isaac, 85 a, Walton
Hoover J M, 27 a Royal Center
Hoover Rachel, 326 a, Hoover
Hoover Sarah E, 80 a, Twelve Mile
Hoover Susannah 1 a, Metea
Hoover Theodore J & Samuel E, 47 a, Twelve Mile
Hoover Thomas S, 15 a, City
Hoover Wm S, 98 a, Royal Center
Hopkins John E, 40 a, Crittenden
Hopkins Joseph P, 34 a, Hoover
Hopkins Webster W, 40 a
Hopper Franklin, 360 a, Onward
Hopper Henry, 40 a
Hopper John M, 40 a. Onward
Hopper Wm, 160 a, Onward
Hopper Wm A, 80 a, Pipe Creek
Horn Charity, 120 a, City
Horn Francis, 79 a, Metea
Horn George and Ciba, 100 a, City
Horn Levi B, 64 a, Metea
Hornbeck Joseph J, 40 a, Royal Center
Horney George, 94 a, City
Horney Hattie, 39 a, City
Horney Matilda, 84 a, City
Horney Nancy J, 37 a, City
Horton Priscilla, 124 a, Pine
House John W, 66 a
House Melvin E, 40 a, Royal Center
House Simeon A, 260 a, Lincoln
House Wm, 202 a, Royal Center
Howard Andrew C, 80 a, Lincoln

Howard Charles P, 6 a, Onward
Howard George F, 20 a, Walton
Howard John C, 80 a, Lincoln
Howard Nancy A, 20 a, Walton
Howe Samuel E & J C, 242 a, City
Howell Maria, 100 a
Hower Josephine & Absolom, 40 a, City
Hubenthal Charles T, 80 a, City
Hubenthal Christina, 80 a, Metea
Hubler Geo W, 160 a, Young America
Hubler Henry, 75 a
Hubler H H, 8 a, Young America
Hubler Lydia, 5 a
Hubler Wm, 94 a
Huffman Ferdinand, 80 a, City
Hughes Mary E, 57 a, Lake Cicott
Hummel George A, 80 a
Hume James A, 115 a, Lake Cicott
Hume Margaret, 44 a, Lake Cicott
Hunter Andrew J, 112 a, Anoka
Hunter J H, 80 a, Pipe Creek
Hunter Mary, 40 a, Onward
Hunter Robert, 118 a, Young America
Huntsinger Samuel, 60 a, Ford
Hurd Charles A, 4 a, City
Hurd D I & Sarah E, 40 a, Walton
Hursh Mary A, 100 a, Young America
Husted D M estate, 80 a
Hutton Samuel W, 128 a, Lake Cicott
Hyatt Harmon, 38 a
Hyatt W R & Mary, 80 a, Lincoln
Hyman Lewis, 225 a
Hyman Mary E, 40 a, Deer Creek
Hyman Wm M, 40 a, Young America
Hynes John jr, 301 a, Gordon
Hynes Samuel, 160 a, City
Hyre Abram, 149 a, New Waverly
Hyre Arthur, 109 a, New Waverly
Hyre Diantha, 35 a, Adamsboro
Ijams Anna E, 40 a, Walton
Immel Thomas J, 80 a, City
Incleton Alfred sr, 2 a, City
Inclinrock A J, 2 a, Royal Center
Insley John F, 75 a, Royal Center
Irwin John C, 10 a, City
Irwin Lewis T, 74 a, Twelve Mile
Irwin Mary A, 24 a, Twelve Mile
Isaacs Enos W, 30 a, City
Isler Jonathan, 50 a
Jack Eliza A, 56 a, Anoka
Jackson Andrew, 89 a, Ford
Jackson Frank P, 94 a, City
Jackson John H, 20 a, Galveston
Jackson Marion, 32 a, Clymers
Jackson Wm B, 80 a, Galveston
Jackson Wright, 8 a, Clymers
James Nancy J, 80 a, City
James Maurice, 80 a, Anoka
Jamison D N, 85 a, City

Jamison Harry A, 40 a, City
Jamison Thomas, 45 a, City
Jeffe Morris J, 322 a, Royal Center
Jenkins Elizabeth, 80 a
Jenkins M F, 10 a, Royal Center
Jenkins Wiley, 21 a
Jenks Catharine, 21 a, Galveston
Johnson Thomas and Rachel, 112 a,
    Metea
Johnson Wm A & Martha L, 40 a, Deacon
Johnson Wm H, 62 a, City
Joice James, 22 a, Metea
Joice Patrick jr, 22 a, Metea
Joice Patrick sr, 60 a, Metea
Jones Albert W, 50 a
Jones Andrew J, 80 a, Twelve Mile
Jones Caroline W, 6 a, Twelve Mile
Jones Evaline L, 3 a, City
Jones Harry C, 120 a, City
Jones James C, 8 a, Anoka
Jones Jerome B, 75 a, Twelve Mile
Jones John W, 120 a, Twelve Mile
Jones Roney V, 22 a, Royal Center
Jones Sarah L, 80 a, Twelve Mile
Jones Willard 32 a, City
Jones Wm A, 38 a, Metea
Jones W H, 45 a, Metea
Jordan M A, 159 a, City
Josarka Martin and Mary, 80 a, Metea
Joy Maria A, 100 a
Julian George W, 84 a, City
Julian John H, 2 a, New Waverly
Julian John J, 57 a, City
Julian Marietta, 21 a, City
Julian Reed 25 a, City
Jump Nearcy 80 a, Lincoln
Jump Wm H, 150 a, Lincoln
Justice Chas R, 18 a,
Justice Frank, 120 a, Burrows
Justice Frank L, 325 a, City
Justice Jerome, 88 a, Gordon
Jus ice Milroy, 40 a, Burrows
Justice Parker, 40 a, City
Justice Rebecca, 48 a, Burrows
Justice Susan 2 a, Royal Center
Kahl Ezra, 55 a, Young America
Kauffman George, 40 a
Kauffman Henry, 55 a, Anoka
Kay Caroline, 55 a
Keating Sarah J, 54 a, Young America
Keeport Benjamin B, 78 a
Keeport Susannah, 56 a, City
Keiser Eckard, 35 a
Keiser Wm, 26 a, Walton
Keiser Wm & Lucinda, 5 a, Walton
Keiser Wm H, 66 a, City
Keiszling Christian 22 a, City
Keller Julia, 120 a,
Kelly Clara A, 40 a, City

Kelsey Robert A 40 a
Kemp Ada A, 5 a, Galveston
Kennedy Isaac A, 10 a
Kennedy John R, 20 a, City
Kennell Andrew E, 95 a, Royal Center
Kennell George P, 120 a, Royal Center
Kennell Samuel M, 10 a
Kentner Joseph W, 1 a, Lincoln
Kepner Isaac H, 80 a, Galveston
Kepner Samuel 70 a, Galveston
Kerchner Rignal R, 140 a, Twelve Mile
Kerlin S B, 111 a, City
Kerns Carey, 117 a, Ford
Kesling Granville, 240 a, Pipe Creek
Kesling Katharine, 83 a, Onward
Kesling Joel 171 a, Pipe Creek
Kesling Martin, 269 a, Pipe Creek
Kesling Oliver, 212 a, Walton
Kesling Perry jr, 131 a, Pipe Creek
Kessler Daniel, 120 a
Kessler S R, 40 a, Twelve Mile
Kessler Stephen A, 39 a
Ketchem Wm E, 160 a, Royal Center
Kidd John E, 50 a, Adamsboro
Killion Bernard, 3 a, Metea
Kimberlin John W, 80 a
Kime Henry, 160 a, Twelve Mile
King Barnabas L, 2 a Galveston
King Freemont G, 22 a, New Waverly
King I M, 80 a, Lucerne
King Richard B, 220 a, Royal Center
King Peter, 18 a, City
King P C, estate, 74 a
Kingrey Charles, 40 a, Twelve Mile
Kingrey D M, 135 a, Metea
Kinneman F E, 6 a, Walton
Kinneman Mary A, 20 a, City
Kinneman Mollie, 80 a, Hoover
Kinneman N, 132 a, Pine
Kinneman Thomas A, 120 a, Fletchers
Kinneman W B, 134 a, Twelve Mile
Kinsey Mary S, 51 a, Adamsboro
Kinsey Minerva, 80 a, City
Kinsinger David, 5 a, City
Kinzie A T, 136 a
Kinzie Benjamin A, 40 a, Adamsboro
Kinzie B F, 40 a, Twelve Mile
Kinzie Charlotte F, 80 a, Hoover
Kinzie Cornelius T, 175 a, Hoover
Kinzie Emma R, 19 a
Kinzie Isaac, 19 a
Kinzie Jacob F, 80 a, New Waverly
Kinzie James E, 90 a, Pine
Kinzie Mary E, 200 a, Adamsboro
Kinzie Samuel F, 19 a
Kirkman Conrad H, 80 a, Deacon
Kirtland Eliza M, 101 a, Pine
Kirtland James, 46 a, Pine
Kistler Amos, 240 a, Royal Center

$186,000,000 of Life Insurance | W. O. WASHBURN,
Superintendent
WAS WRITTEN BY THE | Logansport District,
METROPOLITAN LIFE. of New York. in 1896 | Crawford Block.

354   GAZETTEER.

Kistler Annette J, 85 a, Lake Cice···
Kistler Benjamin F, 6 a, Royal Ce··r
Kistler Carrie E, 40 a, Royal Cente
Kistler Clara, 12 a, Royal Center
Kistler Elias, 60 a, Royal Center
Kistler Felix, 22 a, Royal Center
Kistler George jr, 120 a, Royal Center
Kistler George W, 253 a, Royal Center
Kistler Henry A, 48 a, Royal Center
Kistler Huldah, 6 a, Ford
Kistler John H, 15 a, Royal Center
Kistler John W, 49 a, Royal Center
Kistler Jonas jr, 38 a, Royal Center
Kistler Joshua C, 147 a, Royal Center
Kistler Madison W, 25 a, Royal Center
Kistler Susan E, 1 a, Gordon
Kistler Wm H, 62 a, Ford
Kistler Wm S, 170 a, Royal Center
Kitchell Daniel C, 256 a, Deacon
Kittinger Elizabeth, 79 a, Lincoln
Klapp Jos & Lizzie, 80 a, Royal Center
Klepinger James, 73 a, Gordon
Klepinger Minnie J, 70 a, Clymers
Klepinger M P, 80 a
Kline Alice, 13 a, Twelve Mile
Kline John S, 161 a, City
Kline Joseph, 80 a, Onward
Kline Joseph S, 20 a, New Waverly
Kline Letitia V, 20 a, City
Kling Frederick, 122 a, Royal Center
Kling Martin, 40 a, Lucerne
Kling Martin, estate, 80 a
Klise Byron M, 20 a, Twelve Mile
Klise Jacob, 20 a, Twelve Mile
Knickerbocker H L, 70 a, Clymers
Knickerbocker J H, 54 a, Clymers
Knight Dehlia F, 40 a, Deacon
Koons Elizabeth E, 10 a, Anoka
Koon M L, 154 a, Lucerne
Koons Joseph, 20 a, Lucerne
Kramer Clement L, 40 a, Royal Center
Kramer Douglass and Laura, 4 a, Royal Center
Kramer Hannah, 18 a, Royal Center
Kramer Wm H, 118 a, Royal Center
Kramer Wm J, 73 a, Royal Center
Krauss Ambrose & M, 60 a, Walton
Kreider Leroy M, 32 a, Pine
Kreider Marion, 25 a, Pine
Kreider Marion P, 22 a, Pine
Kreider Martha T, 97 a, Pine
Kreis Charles & Joseph, 15 a, City
Kreis Philip, estate, 100 a
Kroeger John, 40 a, City
Kulb Andrew J, 75 a, Onward
Kulb Penniah, 80 a, Onward
Kulb Solomon, 80 a, Onward
Kuns Francis O, 40 a, City
Kuns H J & Flora M, 83 a, City

Kuns W A, John C & Wm W, 40 a
Kunse Wm H & Amanda, 60 a, City
Kurtz Isaac W, et al 80 a
Kurtz John, 50 a, Walton
Lafever Hezekiah, 80 a
Lafever Wilson, 40 a
Lairy Moses B & John, 61 a, City
Lake Wm B, 40 a, Lincoln
Lambert George, 80 a
Lamb Matilda 2 a, Lincoln
Landis Abraham H (dead), 13 a
Landis Jeremiah, 115 a, Twelve Mile
Larimer Susan and Wm Puterbaugh and wife, 78 a, Onward
LaRose John M, 210 a, City
LaRose John S, 57 a, City
LaRose Joshua S, 200 a City
Latourette Henry, 106 a New Waverly
Latourette Joseph 80 a, City
Laycock Matilda 1 a, Adamsboro
Layton Harrison, 15 a, City
Layton Henry, 32 a, Walton
Layton Henry, 56 a, City
Leach Elijah, 86 a, City
Leazenbry Henry B, 30 a, Clymers
Leazenbry John W, 40 a
Leedy Daniel est, 102 a
Leedy Matilda J, 40 a, Twelve Mile
Leedy Wm H, 52 a, Anoka
Leffel Arthur, 164 a, Pine
Leffel Arthur P, 72 a, Pine
Leffel Edwin A, 160 a, Pine
Leffel Jacob, 80 a, Pine
Leffel John C, 80 a, Pine
Leffel John C and Dora M, 82 a, Pine
Leffel Lorinda, 17 a, Twelve Mile
Leffel Mary E, 1 a, Pine
Leffel Oliver P, 2 a Pine
Leffel Sarah C, 75 a, Twelve Mile
Leffel Wm B, 9 a, Pine
Leffel Wm T, 135 a, Pine
Leffert Harmon 82 a, City
Lemon Henry, 68 a, Fletcher
Lemon Mary E, 80 a, Fletcher
Lemon Wm, 80 a, Fletcher
Lennon David D, 120 a, Deacon
Lennon George W, 80 a, Deacon
Lennon James M, 80 a
Leonard Wm C, 40 a, Walton
Lesh B B, 94 a, Burrows
Lesly George P, 20 a, Twelve Mile
Lester Rebecca J, 103 a, City
Lewis James A, 653 a, Galveston
Lewis Wm R, 180 a, Pipe Creek
Lidgard Mary E, 60 a, Royal Center
Light Wm A, 191 a, City
Like Wm, 46 a, Anoka
List Wm N, 80 a, Lincoln
Little James W, 278 a, Gordon

Little Lewis 349 a, Pipe Creek
Little Thomas, 324 a, Onward
Livingston Esther 24 a, City
Logan Andrew J, 80 a, Lincoln
Logan Charles L, 80 a, Dego
Logan George W, jr, 80 a, Lincoln
Logan George W sr, 109 a, Lincoln
Logan Heading Co, 3 a, City
Logan James S, 120 a, Lincoln
Logan John T, 80 a, Dego
Logan Samuel & Margaret 80 a, Pipe Creek
Logan Thomas W, 85 a, Lincoln
Logan Wm G, 120 a, Anoka
Long Abbie A, 54 a, Pipe Creek
Long James M, 92 a, Walton
Long John M, 117 a
Long Mary E, 120 a, Royal Center
Long Mary & Olive 80 a, City
Long Samuel 45 a, Anoka
Long Simon, 80 a, Anoka
Long Wm, 79 a, Anoka
Longman J M, 1 a, Lucerne
Lontz Affie, 11 a, Lake Cicott
Loop James C, 90 a, Galveston
Loser Amanda, 1 a, Adamsboro
Loser Frank, 55 a, Lake Cicott
Lott Charles W, 80 a, Galveston
Louthain B F, 160 a, City
Louthain G W, 80 a
Louthain Vinson D, 49 a, Walton
Louthain W P, 96 a, Walton
Lowe Willard R, 21 a, City
Lucas G W and Nancy, 42 a, Walton
Lucas W H and S B, 36 a, Walton
Lusher Emanuel, 60 a, Lake Cicott
Lusher Wm, 40 a, Royal Center
Lusher Wm W, 78 a, Ford
Lutz Almana, 40 a, Lincoln
Lutz Joseph, 80 a, Lincoln
Lux John H, 50 a, City
Lybrook Daniel, 116 a, Deacon
Lybrook David, 48 a, Deacon
Lybrook Harvey D, 4 a, Deacon
Lybrook Vallorous, 35 a, Deer Creek
Lybrook Wm E, 162 a, Young America
Lydet Charles E, 8 a, Royal Center
Lynas Cornelius R, 50 a, Lincoln
Lynas Lucas G, 30 a, Lincoln
Lynas Wm W, 86 a, Galveston
Lynch Alfred, 50 a, Walton
Lynch Bernard & Patrick, 86 a, City
Lyon America J, 158 a, City
Lyon H G, 40 a, City
Lyons Stephen, 43 a, City
Lytle Wm, 157 a, Royal Center
McAhron Sarah, 40 a
McAllister A U estate, 15 a
McBain Elizabeth, 9 a, Anoka

McBride Dow F, 40 a, Dego
McBride Thomas, 120 a, Dego
McCaffrey Michael, 31 a, City
McCandless Martha A, 18 a, City
McCauley A L, 159 a, Royal Center
McCauley Wm E, 83 a, City
McCauley W H, 69 a, Lucerne
McClain Alfred, 40 a, Twelve Mile
McClain David T, 10 a, Pine
McClain Granville M, 10 a, Anoka
McClain Hannah, 20 a, Pine
McClain James, 40 a, Deer Creek
McClain Jerome, 70 a, City
McClain Joseph, 100 a, Young America
McClain Maggie E, 40 a, Deacon
McClain Samuel, 90 a, Pine
McClain Sarah, 10 a, Pine
McClelland Mary J, 3 a, Lake Cicott
McCloskey Carrie M, 11 a
McCloskey Edith, 11 a
McCloskey, John, 67 a, Deer Creek
McCloskey Jos, 69 a, Young America
McCloskey Malinda, 19 a
McCloskey Roland, 11 a, Curveton
McCombs Albert, 56 a, Royal Center
McConnell D B, 146 a, City
McConnell Edward B, 120 a, City
McConnell John W, 100 a, Galveston
McConnell Samuel, 2 a, Galveston
McCormick J T et al, 80 a, Burrows
McCracken Ida, 5 a, Young America
McCrea Walter, 100 a, City
McDonald Abraham, 90 a, City
McDonald Abraham jr, 1 a, Pine
McDonald James, 80 a, Curveton
McDonald John E, 80 a, Ford
McDonald Rebecca, 238 a, City
McDougal Edwin H, 50 a, Fulton
McDougal Joshua, 10 a
McDougal Joshua and Lillie M, 34 a
McDowell Catharine, 34 a, City
McDowell David, 80 a, Onward
McDowell Harry & Charles, 160 a, City
McDowell Horace B, 124 a, Pine
McDowell Margaret, 92 a, Gordon
McDowell Willard N, 79 a, City
McGaughey David, 157 a, Lucerne
McGaughey Michael, 100 a, Lake Cicott
McGinnis John, 80 a, City
McGriff Thomas 60 a, Dego,
McGriff Wm T, 20 a, Dego
McGuire Catharine, 1 a, Galveston
McGuire Louis, 120 a, Crittenden
McKaig Elliott E, 80 a, City
McKaig Levi H, 213 a, City
McKaig Wm est, 80 a
McKee Adaline, 60 a Pine
McKee Lillian M, 160 a, Walton
McKee Robert F, 60 a, Pine

McKinney Ida D, 114 a, Lincoln
McKinsey Joseph, 85 a, Lincoln
McLaughlin Clementine, 40 a, Burrows
Mc Lean Ardel, 10 a, Twelve Mile
McManama George 15 a, Y'ng America
McManus Barney, 40 a, Anoka
McMath James M, 120 a, Deacon
McMillen D Z & Cyndessa, 80 a Curve-
   ton
McMillen Elizab th, 29 a, City
McMillen Franklin, 10 a City
McMillen George 21 a, City
McMillen James H, 66 a, City
McMillen Lewis, 246 a, City
McMillen Mary, 20 a, City
McMillen Nellie, 38 a, City
McMillen R M & Jane 38 a, City
McMillen Wm H, 24 a, City
McMullan C F, 78 a
McMullen Mary A, 20 a, City
McNamee James, 43 a, Lake Cicott
McNamer Margaret, 4 a, Pine
McNitt James D, 474 a, City
McNitt Margaret, 50 a
McWhinney Frank 2 a
McWilliams James S, 235 a, Lincoln
Mackassy Thomas 85 a
Mackey Arthur, 40 a, Onward
Madden Dudley, 131 a, Walton
Magee Rufus and George W Funk, 20 a,
   City
Maguire James H, 40 a, Twelve Mile
Mahoney Daniel J, 50 a
Mahoney John 5 a City
Mahoney M F, 1 a, City
Mahoney Patrick, 120 a, Clymers
Manley Mary J, 80 a, City
Manley Wm H est, 178 a
Manthak Mary, 20 a, Royal Center
Marker J B, 100 a, Royal Center
Markert Catherine, 20 a, City
Markert Fred, 6 a, City
Market Catharine, 40 a, Royal Center
Markle Angeline, 24 a, City
Maroney James, 70 a, Lucerne
Maroney John, 89 a, Lucerne
Maroney Margaret, 40 a, Lucerne
Maroney Matthew, 40 a, Lucerne
Marquis Isaac B 80 a, Twelve Mile
Marsh Enos L, 12 a, City
Marshall Amy H and Frank, 20 a, Gal-
   veston
Marshall Ann E, 80 a, Anoka
Marshall Elizabeth, 30 a, City
Marshall George K, 18 a, City
Marshall James H, 20 a, Galveston
Martin Abram E, 139 a, Deacon
Martin Edwin F, 85 a, City
Martin Francis S, 195 a, City

Martin Herman E, 180 a, Anoka
Martin James P, 17 a, City
Martin Jesse, 274 a, City
Martin John 85 a, Walton
Martin John, 80 a, Dego
Martin John P, 2 a
Martin John W, 28 a
Martin Malinda J, 18 a, Lake Cicott
Martin Manassa M, 60 a, Walton
Martin Mary A, 68 a, Dego
Martin Newton J, 160 a,
Martin Nicholas V, 107 a, Clymer
Martin Perry L, 20 a, Dego
Martin Rebecca, 10 a, Twelve Mile
Martin Rollin T, 80 a, Walton
Martin Simon, 160 a, City
Martin Theodore P, 80 a, Dego
Martin Wm, 100 a, Lake Cicott
Martin Wm P, 80 a
Mason Mary, 40 a, Deacon
Masters James W, 10 a, Onward
Matkins W D, 10 a, Galveston
Matthew Edward, 106 a, City
Maudlin Amos J, 79 a, Fletchers
Maudlin Benjamin, 80 a, Fletchers
Maudlin Cyrene, 23 a, Fletchers
Maudlin F A, 20 a, Fletchers
Maudlin Ira B, 75 a, Metea
Maurice John L, 132 a, City
Maus Barbara B, 80, Twelve Mile
Maus Levi, 80 a, Twelve Mile
Maus Wm H, 160 a, Twelve Mile
Mawk Jacob D, 32 a, Cordon
Maxon Simon, 50 a, Royal Center
Mays Edward L, 33 a, Onward
Mays John S, 160 a, Onward
Mays Rebecca J, 53 a, City
Mays Wm L, 40 a, Pipe Creek
Mead Edmund C, 93 a
Means John, 40 a, Pipe Creek
Meck Ella G, 62 a, City
Meck Wm R, 106 a, Young America
Meeks Alice, 55 a, Galveston
Meeks Millie A, 28 a, Crittenden
Mehaffie A A, 1 a, Lucerne
Mehaffie Albert, 40 a, Lucerne
Mehaffie Andrew H, 92 a, Lucerne
Mehaffie Elizabeth, 1 a, Lucerne
Mehaffie Elizabeth M, 20 a, City
Mehaffie Joseph B, 75 a, Lucerne
Mehaffie Joseph J, 20 a, City
Mehaffie Joseph J and Elizabeth M, 40 a,
   City
Mehaffie Mary A, 1 a, Lucerne
Mendenhall Jane, 26 a, Walton
Merriam & Rice, 1 a, City
Merritt John B, 68 a
Merryman Alice A, 80 a, City
Mertz Peter H, 179 a, Burnettsville

Metsker Samuel S, 538 a, City
Meyer Henry, 180 a, Ford
Michaels A P, 20 a, Lucerne
Michaels A P & M A, 96 a, Lucerne
Michaels Charles, 75 a, City
Michaels F L, 155 a, Metea
Michaels George A, 40 a, Lucerne
Michaels George W, 240 a, City
Michaels George W, 65 a, Royal Center
Michaels John A, 78 a, City
Michaels Rebecca J, 42 a, City
Michaels Samuel A, 80 a, City
Michaels Sarah, 54 a, Curveton
Michaels Wm U, 30 a, Lucerne
Miller Cyrus T, 179 a, New Waverly
Miller Daniel, 138 a, Pipe Creek
Miller Caroline, 40 a, Anoka
Miller Christian H, 99 a, Pipe Creek
Miller George 100 a, City
Miller Henry N, 156 a, Deacon
Miller Henry N & James N Campbell,
   80 a, Deacon
Miller James, 150 a, Lake Cicott
Miller Mary A, 67 a, Walton
Miller Matthew, 80 a, Dego
Miller Wendall, 40 a, Anoka
Miller Wm A and wife, 49 a, City
Miller & Simons, 3 a, Young America
Millhouse Margaret, 80 a
Millhouse Martin, 80 a, Royal Center
Millikan F M, 80 a
Million Anderson, 116 a, Ford
Million David, 69 a, Royal Center
Million Francis M, 86 a, Lake Cicott
Million Wm, 177 a, Ford
Millman Orville, 160 a, City
Minglin Eliza J, 90 a, Royal Center
Minneman Christian jr, 45 a, City
Minneman Christian sr, 80 a, City
Minneman Jacob and Catharine, 54 a,
   City
Misner Wm B, 80 a, City
Mitchell Sarah C, 112 a, Adamsboro
Mock Martin sr, 306 a, City
Moenich Elias, 78 a, Walton
Moenich Henry, 80 a, Walton
Moenich John H, 90 a, Anoka
Moenich Susan, 40 a, Walton
Mohn Daniel, 12 a, Lake Cicott
Mohn Jonathan, 42 a, Anoka
Montgomery Andrew, 112 a
Montgomery Anna, 24 a, Lucerne
Montgomery A E, 37 a, Lucerne
Montgomery David, 55 a, Lucerne
Montgomery Edw, 81 a, Young America
Montgomery Emma N, 60 a, Lucerne
Montgomery James jr, 40 a
Montgomery John, 73 a
Montgomery Joseph, 69 a, Lucerne

Montgomery Laura E, 100 a, Lucerne
Montgomery Peter, 37 a, Lucerne
Moon Benjamin, 78 a, Deer Creek
Monyhan John, 11 a, City
Moon Wm, S, 80 a, Twelve Mile
Moore Daniel E, 25 a, Walton
Moore Elizabeth B, 2 a, Adamsboro
Moore Frank R, 5 a
Moore Maggie R, 4 a, Walton
Moore Mary, 4 a, City
Moore Mary 1 a, Royal Center
Moore Thomas L, 80 a, Clymer
Moore Thomas L, 140 a, Metea
Moore Wm R, 259 a, Adamsboro
Morgan J Morgan 1 a, Adamsboro
Morehart Jacob, 60 a, City
Morphet John, 221 a, Lucerne
Morphet John R, 75 a
Morphet Richard L, 1 a
Morphet Sarah J, 54 a, Lucerne
Morris Florence M, 24 a, Twelve Mile
Morrisey Michael, 33 a, City
Morrison Constance, 100 a, City
Morrison Edward & Agnes, 63 a, Lucerne
Morrison Sarah J & George W, 40 a,
   Lake Cicott
Morrison Wm, 106 a
Morrow Abner J, 347 a, Hoover
Mortgage Trust Co of Penn The, 75 a
Moss Abraham, 80 a, Twelve Mile
Moss Alfred N, 59 a, Pine
Moss David, 221 a, Hoover
Moss John H, 124 a, City
Moss Nancy, 5 a, Royal Center
Moss Phoebe E, 100 a, City
Moss Robert F, 5 a, Royal Center
Moss Samuel A, 176 a, City
Moss Wm, 160 a, Twelve Mile
Moss W W and Ellen, 108 a, City
Mulholland Mary A, 151 a, City
Mullendore Mary A, 4 a, Onward
Mummert Henry C, 160 a, Young
   America
Mummert John H, 80 a, Dego
Mummey James E, 80 a, City
Munson George S, 35 a
Munson Horace G, 25 a, Walton
Munson H G and E R, 110 a, Walton
Munson Isaac N, 80 a, Dego
Munson W S, 40 a, Walton
Murden Henry 2 a, Galveston
Murden Wm, 143 a,
Murdock A J, 327 a, City
Murphy Alexander, 80 a, Crittenden
Murphy Catherine, 73 a, City
Murphy Daniel, 143 a, Lucerne
Murphy Francis est, 12 a,
Murphy Francis M, 24 a, Crittenden

Murphy George W, 120 a
Murphy John, 40 a, Lucerne
Murphy Owen J, 5 a, Onty
Murphy Patrick J, 16 a, City
Murphy Timothy, 20 a, Lucerne
Murphy Wm, 70 a, Lucerne
Murray Robert, 126 a
Mussleman Jas S, 114 a, Twelve Mile
Myers Frank R, 60 a, Twelve Mile
Myers Henry C, 459 a, Gordon
Myers Isaac N, 65 a, Lake Cicott
Myers John F, 365 a, Hoover
Myers Mary E, 110 a, Ford
Myers Q A, 679 a, City
Myers Samuel, 200 a, Twelve Mile
Nanna John est, 5 a
Nead Daniel P, 41 a, Onward
Needham David 45 a, Lucerne
Needham Rebecca, 10 a, Lucerne
Neff C P, J M & S, 80 a, City
Neff Daniel D, 158 a, City
Neff Daniel K, 82 a, City
Neff Frank S, Floyd & Orwin, 40 a, City
Neff Jacob jr, 60 a, City
Neff Jacob L, 40 a, Onward
Neff Jasper N, 186 a, Onward
Neff Karen A, 127 a, Metea
Neff Washington, 80 a, City
Nelson Dow G, 20 a,
Nelson James A, 207 a, Deacon
Nelson John A, 80 a, Deacon
Nelson Shadrack and Elcena, 49 a
Nelson Wm H, 120 a, Deacon
Nethercutt Charles, 89 a, Lake Cicott
Nethercutt Emma, 90 a, Ford
Nethercutt Melvin E, 40 a
Nethercutt Moses F, 478 a, City
Nethercutt Rachael, 88 a, Lake Cicott
Neusbaum Minerva & M L, 2 a, City
Newbacher Nellie, 10 a, Ford
Newby Elizabeth, 10 a, City
Newman Elias, 70 a, Lucerne
Newman James P, 160 a, Twelve Mile
Newman Levi, 70 a, Lucerne
Newman Samuel K, 967 a, Hoover
Newman Thomas I, 165 a, Hoover
Newport Anna, 80 a, Deacon
Newport O P, 60 a, Dego
Nickels John M, 108 a, Fletchers
Nickey Samuel N, 300 a, Hoover
Nicodemus Jacob, 110 a, City
Nicodemus Laurietta, 10 a, City
Noel Ephraim, 105 a, Walton
Noel Frank A, 100 a, City
Noel Isaiah jr, 60 a, Walton
Noel Philip, 160 a, Walton
Noel Philip & S R, 20 a, Walton
Noland Israel, 21 a, Royal Center
Noland Wm R, 110 a, Royal Center

Oakley Rosina, 28 a, Twelve Mile
Obarla Nancy V, 18 a
Obenchain Allen, 160 a, Twelve Mile
O'Connor Timothy, 80 a, Lucerne
Odell Price, 80 a, Dego
Oden George W, 110 a, Dego
O'Donnell Celia M, 20 a, Metea
O'Hara Michael H, 89 a, Lincoln
Oliver James, 80 a
Oram Mary E, 160 a, Pipe Creek
Orwin Elizabeth, 90 a, City
Orwin Hannah, 43 a, City
Orwin Henry, 97 a, City
Osmer Anna V, 44 a, City
Oswald James, 60 a, Royal Center
Overholser Catharine, 10 a, City
Overholser D L, 10 a, City
Owens Mary O, 22 a, Clymer
Oyler Joseph, 271 a, Walton
Packard Frank P, 2 a, Onward
Packard Marietta, 87 a, Deacon
Palmer George W, 314 a, City
Palmer John, 200 a, City
Panabaker Minerva, 40 a, Onward
Panabaker Samuel jr, 205 a, Onward
Parker Hannah, 17 a, Twelve Mile
Parks Charles D, 3 a, Young America
Parks David, est, 40 a
Parmeter Mary, 16 a, City
Pasley Robert G, 79 a, Walton
Patterson James E, 80 a, Gordon
Patterson Junietta, 73 a, Lincoln
Patterson Simon E, 50 a, City
Patterson Wm A, 200 a, Lincoln
Patton A V (heirs), 142 a
Patton Eliza A, 40 a, Adamsboro
Patton Stephen C, 22 a, City
Pattongale Elizabeth J & Stephen, 1 a, City
Patty Nathan, 10 a, Galveston
Paul Levi, 170 a, City
Pearcy John, 40 a, Lincoln
Pearson Mary, 80 a, Hoover
Pearson Matthew H, 80 a, Walton
Peck James F, 39 a, Walton
Peden Thomas A, 120 a, City
Pefferman Susan, 221 a, City
Pelton James H, 13 a, City
Penn Benjamin A, 111 a, Gordon
Penzel David, est, 120 a
Perrine Garrett, 1 a, New Waverly
Personett Clinton, 43 a, Lake Cicott
Personett Marshall, 20 a
Peter Adam S, 163 a, Young America
Petrie John, 120 a, City
Petrie John F, 20 a, City
Pfiel Catharine, 65 a, Walton
Phelps Isabelle J, 300 a, Royal Center
Pherson Wm F, 20 a

Phillips Adaline, 30 a, Walton
Phillips Cyrus B, 20 a, Walton
Phillips David, 112 a, Walton
Phillips Helen M, 80 a, Clymers
Phillips, Jabish, 25 a, Anoka
Phillips Mary, 40 a, Walton
Phillips Wm H, 45 a, Anoka
Phillips Wm T, 30 a, Walton
Phoenix Mutual Life Ins Co, 395 a
Pierce Franklin, 169 a, Lake Cicott
Pierce John A, 5 a, Galveston
Pierson Oliver J, 40 a, Walton
Pierson Peter & Sarah, 219 a, Dego
Pinder Frank, 62 a, Metea
Pinder John, 90 a
Pinkerton Virgil H, 5 a, Lucerne
Place James U. 240 a, City
Place Jas U & L J Haynes, 160 a, City
Plank Aaron J. 80 a, Twelve Mile
Plank George C, 120 a, Deacon
Plank Henry A, 80 a, City
Plank Luella F, 80 a, Deacon
Ploss John W, 8 a, Royal Center
Plotner George, 60 a, Royal Center
Plotner Lucinda, 1 a, Royal Center
Plotner Rosa, 53 a, Ford
Plummer Caroline, 114 a, Pipe Creek
Plummer Catharine, 156 a, Onward
Plummer Elihu 3 a, Onward
Plummer Nancy L, 59 a, City
Plummer Stephen et al, 47 a, City
Plummer Thomas, 54 a, City
Porter Albert M, 14 a, Clymers
Porter Alpheus, 77 a, City
Porter Benjamin, 160 a, Clymers
Porter James M, 27 a, Clymers
Porter John F 80 a, City
Porter John W, 20 a, Burnettsville
Porter Maria, 40 a
Porter Martha, 60 a, Clymer
Porter Oliver, 20 a, City
Porter Oliver H, 48 a, City
Porter Rosanna, 20 a, City
Porter Wm R, 22 a, Clymer
Potthoff Henry J, 60 a, City
Poundstone George W. 80 a, Deacon
Poundstone John M, 47 a, Young America
Powell Ada C, 80 a, City
Powell Anson B. 40 a, Metea
Powell Byron, 151 a, Metea
Powell Choral G, 80 a, Lucerne
Powell David J, 1 a, Ford
Powell George, 24 a, Lucerne
Powell George, 10 a, Metea
Powell John, 5 a, Lucerne
Powell J Z, 40 a, City
Powell Lemuel, 251 a, Metea
Powell Orlando, 160 a, Metea

Powell Virgil, 94 a, Metea
Powell Wm, 406 a, City
Powell Wm P, trustee, 80 a, City
Powers John T & Mary A, 80 a, Young America
Powland Jacob, 140 a, Royal Center
Powlen David W, 2 a, City
Powlen D W and wife, 58 a, City
Powlen Michael, 58 a, Ford
Powlen Samuel A, 80 a, Lucerne
Pownell Harriet, 40 a
Pownell Joseph S, 20 a
Pownell Nancy 20 a
Pownell Thomas 40 a
Payne James B, 80 a
Pratt Jane D, 80 a, Gordon
Pressinger J R, 80 a
Price Allen & Sarah, 223 a, Lake Cicott
Price B W, 60 a, Anoka
Price Horatio S, 15 a, Walton
Price Wm J, 20 a, Onward
Prieser Charles H, 40 a, Onward
Pritchett Joshua and wife, 1 a, City
Pryor Horace, 131 a, Curveton
Puterbaugh Aaron, 237 a, Walton
Puterbaugh George M, 60 a, Pipe Creek
Puterbaugh Horace, 110 a, Onward
Puterbaugh John, 114 a, Pipe Creek
Puterbaugh Mary, 54 a, Onward
Puterbaugh Samuel D, 1 a, Onward
Puterbaugh Wm E, 39 a, Onward
Quade Ludwig, 80 a, Anoka
Quick C R, 1 a, New Waverly
Quick Loury L, 7 a, New Waverly
Quick Villa, 17 a, City
Raber Benjamin F, 80 a, Twelve Mile
Raber Wm C, 40 a, Twelve Mile
Railsback Catharine, 32 a, Walton
Rainey Sarah, 71 a, City
Ramer Georgiana, 200 a, City
Ramer John, 154 a, Walton
Ramer Wm, 213 a, Walton
Ray Daniel, 40 a, City
Rayl Frances E, 40 a, Galveston
Red Alma F, 60 a, Adamsboro
Rea Benjamin R, 160 a, Clymers
Rea Eliza J, 47 a, Royal Center
Ream Emanuel, 40 a, City
Reaves John, 77 a, Onward
Reck Anna M, 80 a, Anoka
Redd John W, 218 a, Metea
Reder Charles D, 1 a, City
Reder John W, 100 a, Metea
Redmond John E & Ida, 103 a, City
Reed Abraham, 32 a, City
Reed Clarence B 120 a, City
Reed Charles W, 80 a, Hoover
Reed Emma G, 40 a, City
Reed Frances J, 150 a, Lucerne

Reed Frank F, 80 a, Hoover
Reed George M, 80 a, Onward
Reed Henry C & Addie E, 64 a, Pine
Reed Jacob A, 80 a, City
Reed Madison, 16 a, City
Reed Martha J, 80 a, Onward
Reed Michael, 118 a, City
Reed Nancy, 40 a, Walton
Reed Oliver, 80 a, City
Reed Robert R jr, 106 a, City
Reed Ross & Julia A, 61 a, City
Reed Thomas L, 134 a, City
Reed Wm, 22 a, Lucerne
Reed Wm sr, 35 a, Lucerne
Reed Wm D, 80 a, City
Reed Winfield S, 40 a, Onward
Reese Charles, 1 a, New Waverly
Reese Joseph F & Mary E, 40 a, Pine
Reese Scott, 19 a, Twelve Mile
Rehwald Wm & John, 33 a, City
Reidenback Wm F, 20 a, Walton
Reider Martin, 40 a, Lincoln
Reighter Harry T, & Cassie, 80 a, City
Reish Sallie, 5 a, Gordon
Reitzell Wm H, 60 a, Twelve Mile
Remley Alice, 100 a, Lucerne
Remley James C, 160 a, Deer Creek
Remley John L, 80 a, Lucerne
Remley Wm O, 127 a, Lucerne
Rempler Barbara 120 a, Twelve Mile
Renbarger George, 280 a, Lake Cicott
Rentgers Rachel, 2 a, Lake Cicott
Rhodes John, 162 a, Metea
Rhodes Sarah, 80 a, Metea
Rhorer Caroline, 23 a, Burrows
Rhorer Jane, 63 a, Burrows
Rhorer Joseph, 238 a, City
Rhorer Rosabelle, 24 a, Burrows
Rice Emma G, 54 a
Rice Jared B, 80 a, Clymers
Rice Hannah A, 72 a, Clymers
Rice Solomon S, 80 a Clymers
Richards Rebecca, 1 a, Galveston
Richards Wm F, 79 a, Ford
Richardson H W, 60 a, Twelve Mile
Richardson James M, 43 a, Lake Cicott
Richardson J B, 40 a, Hoover
Richardson Melinda, 40 a
Richason A J, 40 a, Walton
Richason George W, 240 a, City
Richason John A, 40 a, Walton
Richason Joseph M & Lydia, 20 a, Walton
Richason N B, 158 a, Anoka
Richason Peter G, 72 a, New Waverly
Rickett Ida M, 60 a, New Waverly
Ridenour Asbury, 80 a, Deacon
Ridenour Bettie, 10 a, City
Rife Abraham, 6 a, Onward

Rife George, 40 a, Onward
Rife John, 94 a, City
Rinehart Charles B, 5 a, Onward
Rinehart Elizabeth, 62 a, Onward
Risley Henry A, 200 a, Royal Center
Ritter John D, 159 a, Anoka
Roach George M, 84 a, Walton
Robbins Ebenezer H, 40 a
Robbins Ruth M, 70 a, Knox
Robertson Ell' 94 a, New Waverly
Robertson George W, 60 a, Galveston
Robinson John M, 160 a
Robinson Margaret, 80 City
Robinson Robert, 80 a, Ford
Robinson Wm D, 53 a, Lincoln
Rockafield A S, 87 a, City
Rodabaugh Jeff O, 110 a, Galveston
Rodabaugh John, 40 a, City
Rodabaugh Pauline M, 27 a, Gordon
Rodabaugh Phoebe P, 42 a, City
Rodabaugh Willis A, 25 a, City
Roderick Martin G, 82 a, Anoka
Rogers Albert, 120 a, City
Rogers Clara A, 36 a, Peru
Rogers Harry A, 130 a, City
Rogers Wm C & Julia A, 1 a, Twelve Mile
Rolshausen E F, 60 a, City
Rolshausen John F, 40 a, Royal Center
Roudebush Aaron, 6 a, Metea
Roudebush John, 20 a, Metea
Rouk James M, 60 a, Galveston
Ronk Samuel T, 60 a, Galveston
Roop Minnie and Anna, 40 a
Ross Abraham A, 36 a, City
Ross Barbara C, 80 a, City
Ross George E, 20 a, City
Ross James B 78 a
Ross Jas H, 24 a, City
Ross Philip est, 100 a
Ross Samuel 109 a, City
Rowe John and Helen M, 80 a, City
Rudolph Harriet 12 a, New Waverly
Rudolph John W, 94 a, New Waverly
Runnels Elizabeth, 1 a, New Waverly
Runkle G R, 113 a, Royal Center
Runkle J B, 119 a, Royal Center
Rupe Sarah J, 30 a, Royal Center
Rush James W, 40 a, Walton
Rush John B, 20 a
Ruth Samuel, 75 a, Walton
Ryan Andrew J, 72 a, Clymers
Ryan Lillie, 1 a, New Waverly
Ryan Michael 3 a, Clymers
Ryker James P, 40 a, Walton
Sager Wm est, 114 a
Sagesser Columbus A, 80 a, Ford
Sailors Samuel, 120 a, City
St Clair Elizabeth, 33 a, Clymers

Sampson Robert H, 160 a, Pipe Creek
Samsell C F, 33 a, City
Sargent Frances L, 9 a, Lake Cicott
Sargent Tyler, 40 a, Lake Cicott
Sarig Charles S, 80 a, Walton
Sauer Gusta, 5 a
Sarver I N, 160 a, Twelve Mile
Sarver Mary E, 80 a, Twelve Mile
Sarver W K, 419 a, Twelve Mile
Schaefer N F, 160 a, City
Schaen Mary H, 80 a, City
Scherer Jacob, 74 a, New Waverly
Schleigelmich Wm H, 114 a, Royal Cntr
Schneeberger M, 13 a, City
Schneider Fred L, 4 a, Hoover
Schneider George H & Clara, 94 a, City
Schreckenhaust Mary E, 80 a, Ford
Schrier Willard B, 70 a, City
Schwalm Eckard A, 100 a, Walton
Schwalm George H, 100 a, Anoka
Schwalm Henry, 180 a, Walton
Scott Benjamin D, est. 102 a
Scott Enos E, 175 a, Galveston
Scott Nelson B, 103 a, City
Scott Susannah, 4 a, Deacon
Scott W H & Marla L. 60 a, Pine
Seagraves Alphonso, 80 a, Deer Creek
Searight Lewis and Harry, 290 a, City
Searight Wilson, 377 a, Curveton
Searle Mary, 44 a, City
Sedam John, 80 a, City
See Daniel W, 40 a, Twelve Mile
See John E, 80 a, Twelve Mile
Seiter Joseph est, 20 a
Serice Addison 2 a, Young America
Sence Frank, 20 a, City
Sence Isaac, 63 Young America
Sence Samuel estate, 80 a
Sensbaugh Joshua 80 a, Onward
Servis Stephen S, 26 a, Lincoln
Seward Hiram, 160 a
Seward Marquis M, 135 a, Deer Creek
Seybold Frederick, 417 a, City
Seybold George W, 53 a, City
Seybold Henry 323 a, City
Seybold John G, 287 a, City
Shackleford Wm A, 8 a, Adamsboro
Shadd Nancy, 19 a, Ford
Shadinger Wm, 80 a, City
Shaefer Jacob H, 80 a, Walton
Shaff Jacob, 42 a, Pipe Creek
Shaff John H, 80 a, Pipe Creek
Shaff Samuel, 189 a, Anoka
Shaff Sarah J, 80 a, Pipe Creek
Shafer Daniel R, 47 a, Clymers
Shafer Elizabeth, 25 a, Walton
Shafer Gottlieb A, 50 a, City
Shafer Henry, 40 a
Shafer Lorenzo A, 40 a, Royal Center

Shafer John, 19 a, Walton
Shafer Wm, 75 a, Anoka
Shafer Wm T, 160 a, Onward
Shafer William and Laurinda, 20 a
Shaner David and Martha J, 40 a, Lincoln
Shankland J P, 160 a, Young America
Shanks John T, 1 a Deacon
Shanks Joseph, 120 a, Deacon
Shanks Mary E & A F, 11 a, Deacon
Shanks Mary J, 40 a, Onward
Shauteau Willard E, 40 a
Sharp Caleb E, 160 a, Royal Center
Sharp Cora L, 40 a, Lucerne
Sharp Elizabeth J, 20 a, City
Sharp Theodore E, 112 a, Ford
Sharp Wm H, 90 a, City
Shartz A J, 80 a, Anoka
Shartz George P, 60 a, Pipe Creek
Shartz Wm O, 90 a, Anoka
Shaw Mary, 80 a, Lake Cicott
Shedron Sarah, 24 a, Walton
Sheets Charles F, 28 a, Ford
Sheets John E & Martha J, 38 a, Lake Cicott
Shelly G W, 100 a, Dego
Shelly Lucy A, 16 a, Crittenden
Shideler Abraham, 157 a, City
Shideler Asa J, 72 a, City
Shideler Burrows, 40 a, Ford
Shideler Enoch B, 1 a, Lucerne
Shideler Montgomery, 40 a, Lucerne
Shideler Susan J, 15 a, Ford
Shields Joshua P, 1 a, City
Shields Robert, 48 a, City
Shilling Henry B, 100 a, City
Shilling Parmitha, 15 a, City
Shilling Samuel D, 80 a, City
Shirk E H et al, 207 a, Peru
Shope James, 159 a, Walton
Shott Jane, 30 a, Clymers
Shroyer Helen E, 2 a, City
Shuey Danl and Mary, 32 a, Gordon
Shuey Maria, 15 a, City
Shuey John E, 23 a, City
Shultice John, 80 a City
Shultz Clara P & J H, 52 a, City
Shultz J B et ux, 78 a, City
Shuman Minnie, 40 a, Pipe Creek
Shuman Rachel, 40 a, Walton
Shutt John H, 40 a, Anoka
Siddall Jane, 1 a, Gordon
Simons E J, 60 a, City
Simons Mary, 24 a, City
Simons Milroy & Mary F, 40 a, City
Simons Noah, 80 a, Metea
Simpson Jay and Anna L, 58 a, City
Simpson John H, 243 a, City
Simpson Orwin, 70 a, Walton

Singer Thomas J & Harry, 23 a, City
Sizor P C, 5 a, City
Skelton Maria, Ross, Pierce and Osman, 70 a, City
Skillen Benjamin R, 43 a, Royal Center
Skillen Peter, 73 a, Royal Center
Skinner A D, est, 80 a
Skinner R C, 80 a, Twelve Mile
Skinner Thomas H, 70 a, Twelve Mile
Skinner Walter M, 106 a, Twelve Mile
Slater Robert, 20 a, City
Small Alexander, 47 a, Deacon
Small Andrew J, 61 a, Deacon
Small Edward F, 44 a
Small Harriet A, 40 a, Onward
Small W L, 40 a
Smith Abraham, 389 a, Dego
Smith Adam A, 58 a, Walton
Smith Amos, 100 a, Dego
Smith Andrew, 60 a, Metea
Smith Artemas, 220 a, Dego
Smith Charles E, 40 a, Dego
Smith Franklin M, 40 a, Lucerne
Smith Harriet E, 55 a, City
Smith Henry L, 70 a, City
Smith Herman, 32 a, New Waverly
Smith Horace G, 80 a, Metea
Smith Isabella, 3 a, City
Smith James D, 15 a, Royal Center
Smith James H, 80 a, Onward
Smith James W, 12 a, City
Smith James W, 67 a, New Waverly
Smith Jerome, 70 a, Metea
Smith Job E, 168 a, Pine
Smith John H jr, 110 a, Clymers
Smith John J, jr, 150 a, Royal Center
Smith John M, 20 a, Galveston
Smith John P, 122 a, Metea
Smith Josiah, 17 a, Royal Center
Smith Leah, 50 a, Onward
Smith Lydia J, 10 a, Pine
Smith Mahlon H 100 a, Onward
Smith Marion S, 80 a, Onward
Smith Martha, 87 a, Pipe Creek
Smith Mary A, 4 a, City
Smith Mary E, 80 a, City
Smith Rhoda A, 20 a, Royal Center
Smith Samuel 100 a, Lake Cicott
Smith Samuel H, 31 a, City
Smith Sarah A, 6 a, Metea
Smith Wm, 80 a, Anoka
Smoyer Samuel, 80 a, City
Snell George W, 1 a, Pipe Creek
Snell Henry R, 179 a, Pipe Creek
Snell John W, 57 a, Pipe Creek
Snell Samuel H, 115 a, Pipe Creek
Snyder Allen, 59 a, Dego
Snyder Catharine, 99 a, Dego
Snyder Charles, 75 a, Dego
Snyder Daniel K, & Mary, 87 a, Deacon
Snyder David, 80 a, Onward
Snyder Fred A, 40 a, Walton
Snyder Henry 174 a, Onward
Snyder John, 120 a, Deacon
Snyder Levi, 80 a, Onward
Snyder Samuel, 133 a, Deacon
Snyder Sarah, 20 a, Onward
Snyder Wm, 77 a, Deer Creek
Somsel Jacob, 81 a, Lincoln
Somsel J & Isabelle, 72 a, Lincoln
Souder G L, 42 a, City
Souder John H, 117 a, City
Souder Susan D, 22 a, City
Spacy Amanda, 80 a, Anoka
Spence Franklin, 42 a, Lincoln
Spencer Harriet E, 40 a
Spencer James A, 24 a, Lake Cicott
Spencer Joseph A & Mary J, 1 a, Hoover
Spencer Mary 40 a, Adamsboro
Spencer Mary, 231 Royal Center
Spencer Samuel, 18 a, City
Spencer Wm est, 20 a
Spencer Wm M, 120 a, Pine
Sperry James, 40 a, Walton
Sperry Samuel, 40 a, Walton
Spitznagle Conrad, 80 a, City
Spitznagle James & Caroline, 55 a, City
Spitznagle Martha J, 40 a, City
Spitznagle Michael 40 a, City
Spohn Caroline, 40 a, Deacon
Spohn Elizabeth, 65 a, Deacon
Sprinkle George M, 9 a, Lincoln
Sprinkle James L, 40 a, Deacon
Sprinkle John, 320 a, Deacon
Sprinkle J W, 181 a, Lincoln
Sprinkle S B, 90 a, Dego
Sprinkle Wilson E, 155 a, Deer Creek
Spry Thomas A, 40 a, City
Stackhouse Nathan, 160 a, Walton
Staller George W, 100 a, Twelve Mile
Staley John F, 40 a, Twelve Mile
Stanley George, 24 a, Galveston
Stanley James, 12 a, City
Stanley Wm F, 196 a, Lincoln
Stansbury John, 55 a
Stansbury John H, 27 a
Stanton Addison J, 87 a, Royal Center
Stanton A B, 111 a, City
Stanton Priscilla 160 a, City
Starry Uriah 72 a, Walton
State National Bank, 37 a, City
Stauffer John W, 86 Lincoln
Steckle Henrietta, 160 a, City
Steese Lewis, 25 a, City
Steinhart & Voss, 3 a, City
Steinman Henry, 167 a, City
Stephens Caroline, 70 a, City
Stephens Moses, 80 a, City

Stephenson Jens, 40 a
Stern Caroline, 23 a, City
Stern Herman, 80 a, City
Sterrett Jos E & Amanda S, 12 a, City
Stevens D B, 16 a, Gordon
Stevens George W, 160 a, Lucerne
Stevens James, 80 a, Lucerne
Stevens John P and Sarah, 1 a, Adams-
    boro
Stevens Mary E and James M, 40 a, Lu-
    cerne
Stevens Nancy, 79 a, City
Stewart George T, 32 a
Stewart Benjamin F, 35 a, Lake Cicott
Stewart Luther M, 1 a, Metea
Stewart Margaret & Wm S, 38 a, City
Stine Isabelle J, 20 a
Stiver Sadie, 1 a, City
Stiver Wm, 74 a, Ford
Stoll Elizabeth, 120 a, City
Stoll John L and Mary, 82 a, City
Stoner Mary, 51 a, Onward
Storer Henry, 70 a, City
Storer Samuel B, 71 a, City
Stough J H, 34 a, Walton
Stoughton George E, 123 a, City
Stoughton Ira J, 80 a, City
Stoughton Joseph S, 80 a, City
Stout Sarah E, 67 a, Royal Center
Stover Sarah, 2 a, Anoka
Stranch Albert, 80 a
Stroahm Michael, 40 a, Twelve Mile
Strong Rebecca et al, 60 a, Hoover
Stuart Robert F, 192 a, Lake Cicott
Stuart W E & R A, 90 a
Studebaker Amos, 40 a, Deacon
Studebaker David, 89 a, Metea
Studebaker Emma B, 20 a, Deacon
Studebaker Joseph, 79 a, Dego
Studebaker Mary, 39 a
Studebaker Thomas F, 60 a, Metea
Stumbaugh Adam, 1 a, New Waverly
Stutesman Mary J, 117 a
Sullivan Ettie et al, 34 a
Sullivan Frank M, 80 a, Hoover
Sullivan John, 100 a, Twelve Mile
Surface Eliza, 12 a, Anoka
Surface Sarah, 140 a, Onward
Suter Henry D, 27 a, Curveton
Suttles Newman H, 80 a, City
Swalford B B, 220 a, Deacon
Swanson S A, 100 a, Royal Center
Swaringen Chas E, 90 a, Royal Center
Swayze Elizabeth J, 59 a, Royal Center
Sweet T P, 80 a, Royal Center
Sweet W G, 1 a, Royal Center
Swigart Jessie M, 105 a, Adamsboro
Swoveland Wesley, 67 a, Pipe Creek
Taber Jesse, 527 a, City

Taber Rose A, 927 a
Taber Stephen C, 1224 a, City
Talbott A C, 1 a, City
Talbott Isaac W, 142 a, Twelve Mile
Taylor Abagail, 133 a, Pipe Creek
Taylor Lydia E, 20 a, Walton
Taylor Mary E, 25 a
Taylor R C, 104 a, City
Teal Sarah, 36 a, Metea
Teems John H, 40 a, Twelve Mile
Terflinger Diana and Lydia, 74 a, Gal-
    veston
Terrell David, 40 a, Royal Center
Terrell James A, 38 a, Royal Center
Terrell Sarah M, 42 a, Royal Center
Thatcher David A, 20 a
Thomas Cora J, 40 a, Galveston
Thomas Elijah W, 50 a, Lucerne
Thomas John, 1 a, Galveston
Thomas John W, 158 a, Adamsboro
Thomas J Z, 50 a, Lucerne
Thomas Lauretta, 116 a, Walton
Thomas M H, 210 a, Galveston
Thomas Samuel G, 8 a, Onward
Thomas Sarah, 150 a, Onward
Thomas Sarah A, 1 a, Galveston
Thomas Sarah E, 180 a, Galveston
Thomas Wm, 53 a, Anoka
Thomas Wm O, 77 a, Onward
Thomas Wm P, 172 a, Pipe Creek
Thompson Alice B, 120 a, Royal Center
Thompson Andrew, 80 a, Royal Center
Thompson George W, 40 a, City
Thompson James B, 10 a, Royal Center
Thompson Maria, 80 a, City
Thompson Wm N, 1 a, Royal Center
Thornton Horatio, 50 a, City
Thornton Wm C, 12 a, City
Threewits Frank, 2 a, Lucerne
Thrush James, 32 a, Fletcher
Tillett Elizabeth, 40 a, New Waverly
Tillett Wm, 105 a
Tillett Wm F, 42 a, Onward
Tilley B F & Jennie E, 73 a, City
Tilley Charles E, 160 a, Walton
Tilley Susannah, 80 a, Walton
Tilton John, est, 27 a
Tilton Nathaniel, 107 a, City
Tilton Simeon E, est, 152 a
Tilton W I & Nathaniel, 26 a, City
Timmons Silas E, 80 a, Idaville
Tinkle Anna M, 55 a, Royal Center
Tippett Grant S, 24 a, City
Todhunter F M, 2 a, Young America
Tolan Peter, 120 a, Deacon
Toney Amanda J, 40 a, Lincoln
Toney Samuel, 100 a, Deacon
Toney Wm S, 316 a, Walton
Tousley Rachel C, 10 a

Tousley Willis R, 60 a, Anoka
Townsley Margaret, 160 a, Gordon
Tracy Arthur W, 120 a, Twelve Mile
Travelers Ins Co, 272 a
Tresh Michael A, 70 a, Clymers
Tritt Andrew J, 180 a, Walton
Tritt George A, 20 a, Walton
Tritt Lettie E, 2 a, Walton
Troutman Wm, 71 a, Metea
Trowbridge Elizabeth, 3 a, Lake Cicott
Tucker Abraham, 162 a, Lucerne
Tucker Anna, 34 a, Lucerne
Tucker John P, est, 78 a
Tucker Joshua, 92 a, Lucerne
Tucker Mary E, 21 a, Anoka
Tucker Melvin, 42 a, Lucerne
Tudor John H, 88 a, Pipe Creek
Turflinger D W, 88 a
Turley E N, 19 a, Galveston
Turley Henry N, 80 a
Turley Maggie A, 80 a, Young America
Turner Hezekiah, 1 a, Deacon
Turnpaugh Oliver and Julia, 40 a, Walton
Twells James S, 30 a, City
Tyner John O, 100 a, City
Tyner Merideth, 100 a, City
Tyner Sarah E, 40 a, City
Tyner Wm H, 295 a, Gordon
Tyre Louisa, 80 a
Tyson Thornton, 304 a, Hoover
Uhl Charles H, 125 a, City
Uhl Jesse M, 80 a, Lincoln
Uhl Joseph E, 87 a, City
Ullerick Caroline, 40 a, Twelve Mile
Ullerick Henry T, 26 a, Twelve Mile
Ullerick John D, 15 a, City
Ullerick Martha M, 12 a, Twelve Mile
Ullery Mary, 2 a, New Waverly
Ullery Preston W, 1 a, New Waverly
Umbarger B F, 40 a, Deacon
Umbarger Margaret, 55 a, Walton
Umbarger Wm G, 40 a, Deacon
Unger Magdalena, 307 a, Lake Cicott
Unger Minerva J, 63 a, Lake Cicott
Union Central Life Ins Co, 70 a
Universalist Convention of Ind, 184 a
Vanaman Daniel, 80 a, Royal Center
Vanatta Emaline, 37 a, Lake Cicott
Vanatta Sarah J, 15 a, Lake Cicott
Van Emman James D, est, 120 a
Vanskiver Joseph A, 80 a, Walton
Vernon David T, 86 a, Royal Center
Vernon Enslie, 65 a, Deacon
Vernon George, 70 a, Lake Cicott
Vernon Isaiah, 60 a, Lake Cicott
Vernon James, 40 a, Walton
Vernon John C, 40 a, City
Vernon Lydia, 51 a, Royal Center

Vernon Milton W, 120 a
Vernon Robert H, 22 a, Royal Center
Vernon Thomas P, 60 a, City
Vernon Wm H, 100 a, City
Vickers Sophronia, 15 a, Royal Center
Voorhis H M, 158 a, New Waverly
Wagenhols Ellen H, 294 a, Ft Wayne Ind
Wagner F M, 2 a, City
Wagner Wm A, 78 a, City
Wagner Elizabeth J, 100 a, Lucerne
Walker Albert M, 59 a, Adamsboro
Walker Eugene A, 110 a, Adamsboro
Walker Frank, 50 a, Adamsboro
Walker John F, 40 a, Lucerne
Walker John R, 80 a, Dego
Walker Robert W & Emma E, 52 a, Walton
Walker Warren 22 a, Dego
Walker, Rauch & Co, 80 a, City
Wallace Samuel B, 160 a, Galveston
Wallace Samuel B and Maria, 160 a, Galveston
Wallace Wm F, 1 a, Hoover
Walters George W, 15 a, City
Walton Canning Co, 1 a, Walton
Wampler John L, 80 a, Lincoln
Wampler Wm M, 80 a, Lincoln
Ward Enoch, 160 a, Deacon
Ward George, 40 a, Royal Center
Ward Oliver P & Joseph A, 80 a
Warden Albert et ux, 40 a, Royal Center
Warfield S H, 80 a, Lucerne
Warner Fielding G, 145 a, City
Warner John L, 110 a, Pine
Warrenburg George, 80 a, Ford
Warrick Harry G, 45 a, Anoka
Washburn Charlotte 40 a, Lucerne
Washburn George W, 60 a, Anoka
Watson Elias R, 10 a, Clymers
Watson George W, 89 a, Clymers
Watts Eli, 146 a, Lake Cicott
Watts Israel, 281 a, City
Watts James A, 129 a, City
Watts John W, 80 a, Lucerne
Watts John, Wm & Daniel, 179 a, City
Wattsbaugh Louisa, 80 a
Wean Lewis jr, 40 a
Wean Matilda, 40 a, Anoka
Weaver Christian H, 80 a, Onward
Weaver Henry S, 80 a, Lake Cicott
Weaver Isaac, 57 a, New Waverly
Weaver Jerome, 80 a, Ford
Weaver John J, 150 a, Pipe Creek
Weaver Levi, 120 a
Weaver Maria, 56 a, New Waverly
Webb Christina, 10 a, Royal Center
Webster George L, 80 a, Lake Cicott
Webster Laura V, 80 a, Walton

GAZETTEER.   365

'ebster Matthew W, 80 a, Lucerne
'eimer John W, 200 a, Lake Cicott
'eirwahn Anna, 13 a, Royal Center
'eirwant Andrew est, 30 a
'elling Herman est, 73 a
'ells Dudley H, 80 a, City
'emple Matilda, 40 a, City
'endling C F, 80 a, Walton
'enoling John H, 80 a, Walton
'endling Linnie C 17 a, Deacon
'endling Michael, 180 a, Walton
'endling Wm D, 46 a, Walton
'ertz Peter, 3 a, City
'est Mary A, 20 a, City
'estler Joseph, 1 a, Adamsboro
'eyand George W, 188 a, Royal Center
'eyand John H, 260 a, Lucerne
'eyand Granville N, 79 a, Lucerne
'halen Mary, 20 a, Lucerne
'halen Thomas 24 a, Lucerne
'heatley John U, 91 a, Twelve Mile
'hipperman Charles, 120 a, City
'hipperman Henry, 80 a, City
'histler Ephraim, 140 a, Pipe Creek
'histler Henry M, 121 Pipe Creek
'histler Robert A, 142 a, Pipe Creek
'hite Barbara, 160 a, City
'hite Elizabeth 33 a, City
'hite Henry K, 25 a, City
'hite John H, 150 a, City
'hite John W, 56 a, Walton
'hite John Z, 80 a, City
'hite Willard H, 40 a, City
'hitesides Eliza C, 40 a, Crittenden
'hitfield Edward, 80 a, Lucerne
'idan Bernard, 10 a, City
'idner Mary A, 20 a, Walton
'idner Jacob, 20 a, Walton
'ikle Philip, 40 a, Young America
'ild John, 80 a
'ildermuth Caroline, 1 a, Royal Center
'ildermuth John R, 57 a, Royal Center
'ildermuth O P, 189 a, Royal Center
'ildermuth Thos F, 5 a, Royal Center
'ilds John W, 48 a, City
'iley Alice M, 48 a, Lake Cicott
'iley Anna, 22 a, City
'iley Henry, 10 a, Gordon
'iley Rebecca, 52 a, Gordon
'ilhelm Isabelle, 27 a, City
'ilkinson Arabelle, 80 a, Royal Center
'ilkinson James B, 30 a, Royal Center
'illiams Addis L, 79 a
'illiams George W, 1 a, Galveston
'illiams James F, 84 a, Galveston
'illiams John, 171 a, New Waverly
'illiams Martha, 40 a, Deacon
'illiams Mary, 414 a, Fort Wayne, Ind
'illiams Mary H, 363 a, Ft Wayne, Ind

Williams S C, 147 a, New Waverly
Williams Thomas J, 12 a, Royal Center
Williamson Agnes, 82 a, Metea
Williamson D M, 60 a, Metea
Williamson Harriet, 20 a, Metea
Williamson Isaac T, 120 a, Royal Center
Williamson Jane, 80 a, City
Williamson Joshua W, 80 a
Williamson J J, 83 a, Metea
Williamson Mary I, 40 a, Royal Center
Williamson Nancy, 70 a, Royal Center
Williamson Rachel, 80 a, City
Williamson Samuel, 170 a, City
Williamson S A, 360 a, Royal Center
Williamson W A, 104 a, Royal Center
Wills Charles H, 3 a, Young America
Wills Juliet M, 40 a
Wills Wm R, 40 a
Wilson Alforetta, 40 a, Lincoln
Wilson Andrew, 174 a, Anoka
Wilson Catharine, 77 a, Twelve Mile
Wilson Elwood G, 80 a, City
Wilson Emma, 39 a, City
Wilson Florence M, 40 a, Twelve Mile
Wilson George, 73 a, Lake Cicott
Wilson George D, 48 a, Twelve Mile
Wilson Geo W, 238 a, Young America
Wilson Harrison, 78 a, Anoka
Wilson Henry and Mattie, 80 a, Young
    America
Wilson Isaac, 120 a
Wilson James, est, 70 a
Wilson John M, 160 a, Lincoln
Wilson John R, 83 a, Young America
Wilson Marcellus T, 80 a, Onward
Wilson Martha A, 135 a, City
Wilson Mary, 79 a, Lincoln
Wilson Oscar, 94 a, Pipe Creek
Wilson Rebecca, 55 a
Wilson Samuel, 38 a, City
Wilson Sarah, 10 a, Twelve Mile
Wilson Sarah C, 15 a, Young America
Wilson Wm T, 283 a, City
Wilson W T, 80 a, Gordon
Wilt Jacob, 98 a, City
Wimer John W, 118 a, City
Winegardner Jacob, 74 a, Royal Center
Winegardner Maud M, 80 a, Twelve
    Mile
Winehold Joseph, 40 a, Walton
Wingrave Fred, 76 a, Onward
Winn Isaac, 31 a, Lincoln
Winn James W, 50 a, Lucerne
Winn John W, 160 a, Lucerne
Winn Richard jr, 540 a, Lucerne
Winn Willard, 160 a, Lucerne
Winn Wm, 120 a, Lucerne
Winters Jno W, & James A, 50 a, Deacon
Wipperman Frank H, 40 a, City

Wiseley Amos 310 a, Royal Center
Wiseley George 15 a, Royal Center
Wiseley J M, 15 a, Royal Center
Wiseley Thomas J, 55 a, Royal Center
Wiseley Wm E, 30 a, Royal Center
Wissinger Wm, 94 a, Onward
Witmyer Elizabeth, 4 a Twelve Mile
Witters Elizabeth, 20 a, Lucerne
Wlissman Andrew, 80 a, Galveston
Wolf Adam, 70 a, Royal Center
Wolf Christopher & Alice, 41 a, Royal Center
Wolf David, 80 a, Dego
Wolf George, 83 a, Dego
Wolf Herman, 60 a, City
Wolf John, 1 a, City
Wolf Sarah E, 10 a, Deacon
Wolfe Josiah, 80 a, Burrows
Wolford George W, 40 a, Twelve Mile
Wolford Philip, 160 a, Lucerne
Wolnick Martin, 80 a, Adamsboro
Wood Jonathan J 60 a, City
Woodhouse Alfred, 80 a, Twelve Mile
Woodhouse Bonaparte, 40 a, Twelve Mile
Woodhouse Daniel, 91 a, Twelve Mile
Woodhouse Esau 80 a, Twelve mile
Woodhouse Henry, 80 a, Twelve Mile
Woodling Charles E. 40 a, Dego
Woodling George J, 50 a, City
Woodling James, 20 a, City
Woodling James H, 40 a, Pipe Creek
Woodling R J & Francis A. 80 a, City
Woodling Samuel P, 30 a, City
Woodling Virginia. 360 a, Pipe Creek
Woods Hezekiah, 47 a, Royal Center
Woods Isaac U & Elizabeth A, 40 a, Royal Center
Wooley H A, 80 a, Galveston
Wooten Patrick & Lewis J, 1 a, Clymer
Wright George & Albert, 71 a, Onward
Wright Mary, 31 a, City
Wright Williamson est, 1200 a
Yakeley Jesse, 40 a, City
Yakeley Mary, 35 a, City
Yakley Lydia M, 45 a, Deacon

Yantis Benjamin F, 280 a, Metea
Yantis Benjamin F (guard) 40 a, Metea
Yantis Emma, 28 a, Metea
Yantis Esther, Emma, Alice, Ella, and Charlotta, 159 a, Metea
Yantis Harvey C (dead), 160 a
Yantis Jacob, 290 a, Lucerne
Yantis Monroe, 118 a, Metea
Yerkes James L, 40 a, Deacon
Yoder Elizabeth, 110 a, Twelve Mile
Yoder Gabriel, 50 a, Twelve Mile
York Aaron B, 18 a. Pipe Creek.
York Henry, 290 a, Lake Cicott
York James A, 120 a, Lake Cicott
York Nancy I & J. 12 a. Lake Cicott
Yost Abraham jr, 50 a, Clymers
Yost Isaac 50 a, Clymers
Yoxcum Robert F, 5 a, Twelve Mile
Young Andrew J, 263, City
Young Cornelius, 60 a, Twelve Mile
Young David, 80 a, Twelve Mile
Young Tunis & George W Songer 80 a, Royal Center
Younglove A D. 40 a, Onward
Younglove S P, 80 a, Onward
Yund John H, 70 a, Metea
Yund Mary E, 40 a, Metea
Yund Phoebe, 21 a, Metea
Yund Samuel J, 47 a, Metea
Yund Sarah A, 71 a, Metea
Zech August, 40 a, Pine
Zeck Caroline, 40 a, Deacon
Zehring Wm J, 110 a, Galveston
Zeigler Wm A & Sarah, 58 a, Fletchers
Zelner Elias, 45 a, Onward
Zelner James M, 13 a, Onward
Zelner Solomon, 15 a, Onward
Zimmerman Alex, 120 a, Anoka
Zimmerman John, 241 a, City
Zimmerman Phebe, 10 a, Anoka
Zimmerman Sarah A, 20 a, Lincoln
Zinn Daniel K, 40 a, Royal Center
Zinn George, 160 a, City
Zirgenhagen Susan A, 120 a, Deacon
Zollman Charles B, 180 a, Deacon
Zollman Wm A, 140 a, Deacon

Lightning Source UK Ltd.
Milton Keynes UK
UKHW022210140219
337291UK00006B/521/P